WORKING with words

YEAR 4

Paula Goodridge

Contents

Chapter 1:	**Verb tenses**	4
Chapter 2:	**Double consonants**	10
Chapter 3:	**Dictionary skills**	16
Chapter 4:	**Homophones**	22
Chapter 5:	**Using alternative words**	28
Chapter 6:	**Prefixes**	34
Chapter 7:	**Common endings**	40
Chapter 8:	**Common letter strings**	46
Chapter 9:	**Suffixes**	52
Chapter 10:	**Compound words**	58

Published by
Hopscotch Educational Publishing Ltd,
29 Waterloo Place,
Leamington Spa CV32 5LA
Tel: 01926 744227

© 2001 Hopscotch Educational Publishing

Written by Paula Goodridge
Series design by Blade Communications
Illustrated by The Drawing Room
Printed by Clintplan, Southam

ISBN 1-902239-72-5

Paula Goodridge hereby asserts her moral right to be identified as the author of this work in accordance with the Copyright, Designs and Patents Act, 1988.

All rights reserved.
This book is sold subject to the condition that it shall not, by way of trade or otherwise, be lent, hired out or otherwise circulated without the publisher's prior consent in any form of binding or cover other than that in which it is published and without a similar condition, including this condition, being imposed upon the subsequent purchaser.

No part of this publication may be reproduced, stored in a retrieval system, or transmitted, in any form or by any means, electronic, mechanical, photocopying, recording or otherwise, without the prior permission of the publisher, except where photocopying for educational purposes within the school or other educational establishment that has purchased this book is expressly permitted in the text.

Every effort has been made to trace the owners of copyright of poems in this book and the publisher apologises for any inadvertent omissions. Any persons claiming copyright for any material should contact the publisher who will be happy to pay the permission fees agreed between them and who will amend the information in this book on any subsequent reprint.

Introduction

About the series

Working with Words is a series of books aimed at developing word skills using story, poetry and non-fiction texts. There is one book for each year group at Key Stage 2.

The series offers a structured approach which provides detailed lesson plans to teach specific word-level skills. Each lesson also contains follow-up ideas to develop sentence- and text-level skills. A unique feature of the series is the provision of differentiated photocopiable activity sheets, where the same activity is presented at three different levels of ability. This helps to reduce teacher preparation time.

About this book

This book is for teachers of children at Key Stage 2 Year 4 (Scottish level 5). It aims to:
- develop children's word-level skills through sharing and discussion of whole-class texts
- reinforce the skills and concepts learned in the whole-class session through the use of independent group activities
- develop children's sentence- and text-level skills through the provision of a bank of follow-up ideas and activities
- support teachers by providing them with stimulating, interesting texts that can be readily copied or enlarged for whole-class use
- encourage enjoyment and curiosity as well as develop skills of interpretation and response.

Chapter content

Intended learning

This outlines the word-level learning objectives for the lesson which are matched to the National Literacy Strategy's *Framework for Teaching*.

Starting point: whole class

This section contains two headings: 'Working with the text' and 'Working with words'. 'Working with the text' provides the teacher with suggestions for introducing and using the whole-class text. 'Working with words' contains ideas for developing word-level activities from the text.

Both sections provide the teacher with samples of questions to ask the children and ideas for developing the skills and concepts being addressed.

Group work

This explains how the three differentiated activity sheets can be used. Guidance is provided for the type of child who will most benefit from each sheet.

Plenary session

This suggests ideas for the whole-class session to discuss the learning outcomes and responses to the activities.

Class text

This is a photocopiable page that can be given to the children or enlarged for whole-class discussion and interpretation.

Sentence-level activities

This contains lots of additional ideas and suggestions for activities to follow up the word-level lesson. The ideas aim to develop sentence-level skills.

Text-level activities

This contains lots of additional ideas and suggestions for activities to follow up the word-level lesson. The ideas aim to develop text-level skills.

Verb tenses

Intended learning
- To look at verb tenses, recognising present and past.
- To recognise regular past tense verbs ending in 'ed'.
- To spell irregular tense changes, such as go/went.

Starting point: whole class
Working with the text
Photocopy the text 'The hospital' or enlarge it on an overhead projector. Read the text with the children and discuss the following points:

- Where is the text set?
- Who are the characters?
- What does the child think of the hospital?
- What does Gran think of it?
- Find the evidence in the text which supports both viewpoints.
- Why can the same setting make two characters feel differently? (Perhaps Gran is lonely and likes being looked after, cooked for and so on.)
- What do the children think of hospital? Do they have previous experiences themselves and do they have different feelings?

Come to the conclusion with the class that some people like hospitals and some people do not, and that settings can affect characters in different ways.

Working with words
- Ask the children to tell you whether they think the story is set in the past or the present. Look at the verbs to find out. What effect does writing a narrative in the present have?
- Ask the children to underline the verbs in the first paragraph. Write them on the board. Put them into the past tense. Which ones have regular/irregular endings? Form two lists, one for 'ed' endings and one for irregular endings.
- Go through the rest of the text putting the verbs into the past tense. Add the spellings to your two lists. What other verbs can the children think of to add to each list?
- Introduce the group work, telling the children that they will be looking at the verbs in a similar text – a narrative extract – reminding them that some verbs have an 'ed' ending in the past tense but others do not.

Group work
Activity sheet 1
This is aimed at the less-able reader/writer. It uses simple language and encourages children to understand that there are regular and irregular forms in the past tense. It incorporates the practice of forming common words and the challenge of forming new words in the past tense.

Activity sheet 2
This sheet is aimed at independent readers/writers who can be encouraged to write more descriptively. It is intended that they explore new verbs, apply their knowledge of irregular and regular past tense verb formations and use them in context.

Activity sheet 3
This activity is for more able readers/writers who already have a fair understanding of verb tenses. They will be challenged to change more complex phrases into the past tense and to use more complicated vocabulary in context.

Plenary session
Bring the class together again. Go through examples from each activity sheet and compare answers. For example, make lists of regular/irregular past tense verbs on the board and discuss common spelling rules, such as for words ending in 'e' we just add 'd' (hobbled, troubled).

Sentence-level activities

- Discuss the adverbs used in the text. Can the children substitute other adverbs so that the text still makes sense? Can they change the meaning of the text by altering the adverbs? Use flash cards for the children to build sentences, adding adverbs, for example 'The man went home …'

- Look at the punctuation in the text. How many different 'marks' can the children find? Go over the use of question and/or exclamation marks. Can they make up their own questions or exclamations that could be added to the text? For example, a nurse asking Gran a question and Gran's reply.

- Study the dialogue in the text. Remind the children how to use speech marks and give them more examples on the board. Let some of them come and put speech marks in themselves. Prepare texts which have speech marks missing. Ask the children to put them in. Ask them to make up their own dialogue of the conversation between the family members when Gran gets home.

Text-level activities

- Ask the children to study the text and discuss the idea of settings. What does the text say about the hospital? Do they think it is a good description? Is the reader able to imagine what the hospital looked like? Explore setting further by asking the children to suggest some settings they could use to introduce a story and/or share settings from well-known stories. What do the children like or dislike about these descriptions? Ask them to write a description for the beginning of a story.

- Give the children places to write about to encourage descriptive writing on settings. Limit them to just the opening of a narrative so that they focus on the setting, not the storyline; for example 'The Mysterious Planet', 'The Deep, Dark Jungle' and 'The Fantasy Rainforest'.

- Discuss the viewpoint shown by the author in the text. He or she has a negative view. Ask the children to write about the hospital from Gran's point of view. Ask them to use lots of adjectives to make it sound positive.

- Look at the openings of stories, articles or reports – are the settings detailed and descriptive or are they brief and simple?

- Choose three openings from different narrative forms, such as a fairytale, a modern picture book and a novel. Which is the most inviting for the reader and why?

- Ask the children to write a short and simple setting using a sentence each for where, when, who and what.

- Read a description of a famous book character, such as Willy Wonka, Mr Twit, the Big Bad Wolf or Goldilocks. Ask the children to write a description of the character's house or bedroom.

The hospital

When I walk cautiously into the long corridor the hospital smell hits my nostrils, that disinfectant smell, that horribly clean smell. The floor is shiny and looks slippery even though it is not. The bare walls are painted white and one plant sits alone in its pot, the only plant in the long stretch of corridor.

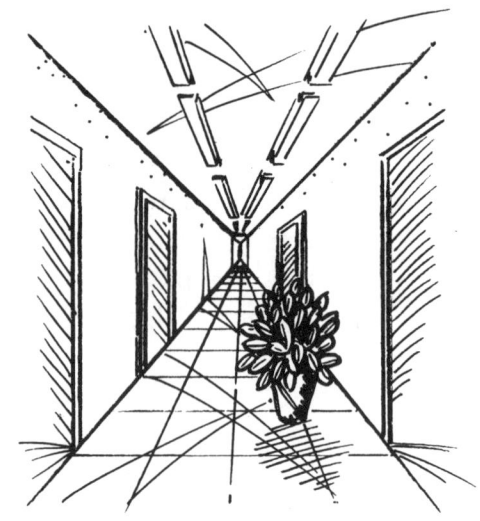

At reception the floor changes rapidly into prickly green floor tiles. Nurses and doctors whisk around swiftly with their paperwork. There we have to wait solemnly until someone is free to see us.

'Which ward is Gran in?' we ask finally. We head promptly to her bedside. Gran is sitting up in her metal bed with its crisp white sheets and that nasty flowery pull-around curtain. She is smiling away very cheerfully.

'We've come to pick you up today, Gran!' we say happily.

'Oh that is a shame,' says Gran sadly, 'I like it here and I'd love to stay!'

It's quite strange that Gran loves this place; I really cannot understand it. Me, I'd rather be at home with my chips and my telly.

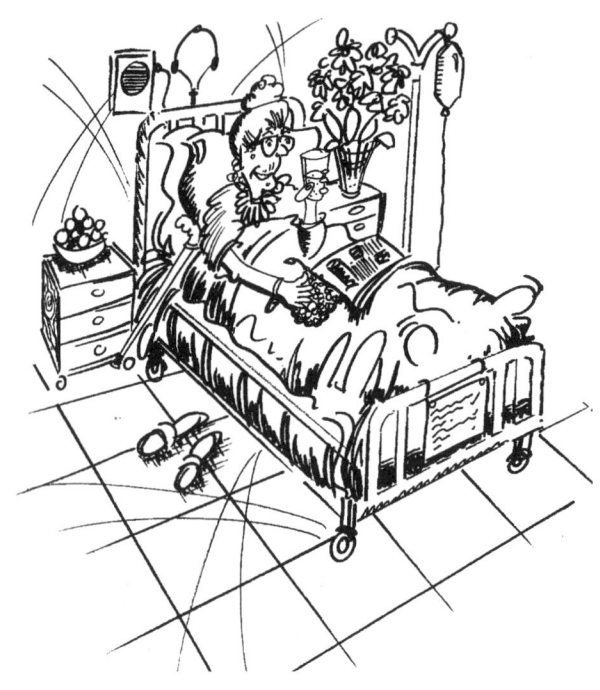

ACTIVITY SHEET ONE

The depths of the sea

> The diver dives down to the bottom of the sea. Brightly-coloured fish of all sizes swim all around her. The water is very clear and she can see really well. She looks at the rocks but does not touch them. Perhaps it is not a rock but a creature hiding there! She floats gently along for an hour or so before she decides to return to the surface.

1. Put these verbs (doing words) into the past tense. The first one has been done for you.

   dives   dived
   swim   _____
   is   _____
   looks   _____
   floats _____

2. Think of two words to replace each of the verbs underlined in these sentences.

   'The diver <u>dives</u> down to the bottom of the sea. Brightly-coloured fish of all sizes <u>swim</u> all around her.'

   _____   _____
   _____   _____

3. 'She looks at the rocks but does not touch them.'
   Use a thesaurus or dictionary to make a list of five other words that mean the same as 'look'. Write them here.

   _____
   _____

4. Find three verbs that will have an 'ed' ending when changed into the past tense. Write them on the back of this sheet.

WORKING WITH WORDS **PHOTOCOPIABLE**

ACTIVITY SHEET TWO

The depths of the sea

> The diver dives down to the bottom of the sea. Brightly-coloured fish of all sizes dart this way and that. The water is very clear and she can see really well.
>
> She continues to move slowly along. She looks at the rocks but does not touch them. Perhaps it is not a rock but a dangerous creature hiding there!
>
> The diver watches her bubbles floating to the surface. She is aware that she must finish her dive soon so she slowly floats back to the surface.

1. Put these verbs from the text into the past tense. The first one has been done for you.

   dive   dived   continues   _____
   dart   _____   looks   _____
   is   _____   hide   _____

2. 'She continues to move slowly along.'
   Think of four verbs that could replace the word 'move'.

   _____

3. Use a dictionary to find four verbs that will not have an 'ed' ending when they are put into the past tense.

   _____

4. Rewrite the second paragraph of the text at the top of the page so that it is in the past tense.

   _____

   _____

   _____

   _____

   _____

   _____

WORKING WITH WORDS PHOTOCOPIABLE

ACTIVITY SHEET THREE

The depths of the sea

> The diver dives down to the bottom of the coral reef. Amazing creatures are swimming all around her. Brightly-coloured fish of all sizes dart this way and that as plants sway in the motion of the water. The water is clear and she can see really well.
>
> The diver continues to move slowly along the reef. She studies the rocks but she does not touch them. Perhaps it is not a rock but a poisonous creature hiding, camouflaged in its surroundings.
>
> The diver is aware of her breathing and the bubbles floating up to the surface. She must not stay below much longer. Sadly, her journey to the depths of the sea is coming to an end … until the next time.

1. Put these phrases from the text into the past tense.

   The diver continues to move slowly along the reef.

   _____

   She studies the rocks _____

   Her journey is coming to an end _____

2. Find all the verbs that involve movement. Then put them into the past tense. (For example, dives – dived.)

   _____

   _____

3. Put these verbs into the past tense. Do they have 'ed' or irregular endings?

   debate _____   oversleep _____

   materialise _____   neglect _____

   multiply _____   will not _____

4. On the back of this sheet, make up another paragraph that would fit into this text. Then underline all the verbs you have used that would have 'ed' when put into the past tense.

WORKING WITH WORDS **PHOTOCOPIABLE**

Double consonants

Intended learning
- To spell two-syllable words containing double consonants.
- To use a rhyming dictionary.
- To scan newspaper reports and notices for specific words or phrases.

Starting point: whole class

Working with the text
- Share the text 'LOCAL BOY IS HERO' with the class. What is the report about? Why is the boy called a hero? What actions did Jamie do that were helpful to the kitten?
- Discuss the layout (headings, paragraphs, columns and so on) and the simple, non complex language that is used in a newspaper report.

Working with words
- Tell the children that this report contains many words with double consonants. Ask them to remind you what consonants are. Write the name Jamie Hopper on the board and ask the children to tell you which the double consonants are. Can they find any other double consonants in the first paragraph?
- Go through the rest of the text, picking out words with double consonants and checking for meaning. Reinforce the meanings of the words by asking the children to put each word into another sentence (verbally).
- Explain that the consonants 'f', 'l', 's' and 'z' are usually doubled at the end of a short vowel, for example cuff, well, mess, buzz, staff, pull, loss and fuzz. Can they find an example of these kinds of words in the text?
- Do the children know of another spelling rule that involves doubling the consonant? Explain the rule about adding 'ed' and 'ing' to verbs (for example, when a word ends in a short vowel followed by a single consonant, the last consonant is doubled before adding 'ed' and 'ing'). Give some examples: hop – hopped, hopping; stop – stopped, stopping; skip – skipped, skipping. Can the children find examples in the text?
- Have fun making lists of double consonant words that rhyme with some of the words in the text, for example: 'Cuddles' rhymes with muddles, huddles, befuddles and puddles. 'Hopper' rhymes with popper, copper, shopper, chopper, whopper, stopper and clodhopper. Demonstrate how to use a rhyming dictionary to find more. Say that knowing a spelling pattern like this can help them to remember how to spell the words.

Group work

Activity sheet 1
This sheet uses the concept of double consonant words but gives the less-able reader/writer less text to focus on. They will need to scan the text for key words.

Activity sheet 2
This sheet is for the able reader/writer who will be able to scan more text and explore more challenging words containing a double consonant.

Activity sheet 3
This sheet is for the most-able readers/writers who will look at more complex words and be able to scan a longer text. They will use double consonant words in the context of their own writing.

Plenary session
- Read the texts together, picking out words with double consonants. Go over the meaning of the more difficult words.
- Write two or three words on the board and ask the children to try to find words that rhyme and have a similar spelling pattern. ('middle', 'riddle' or 'mutter', 'clutter').
- Groups or individuals could choose three words from the list and put them into their own sentences. More able children could create a short story or report using as many words with double consonants as possible.

Sentence-level activities

- Read the text together. Look at how the sentences begin. They do not all start with 'Jamie...', but often use sub-clauses. Ask the children to use some of the sentence beginnings to make up their own sentences. For example, 'After calling the fire brigade...' More-able children could make up their own adjectival sub-clauses. Less-able children could connect two sentences with connective words such as 'and then' and 'while'.

- Study the sentences in other newspaper articles. Are there any adjectives or adverbs? Why are there fewer than in a narrative, for example? The children could rewrite the report to make it more descriptive by adding more adjectives.

- Study the verbs in a newspaper report. Are they exciting? Which words are used instead of 'went' or 'said'? Discuss the children's answers. Use thesauruses to find more powerful verbs to replace those used, such as 'staggered' instead of 'swayed'.

- Discuss the tenses of the verbs used in newspaper reports. Are they usually in the past tense? Why? Challenge the children to rewrite a newspaper report in the present tense.

Text-level activities

- Provide the children with a selection of newspapers and ask them to list the features common to them all. Agree a common list.

- Ask the children to write their own newspaper report. This could be fictional or based on school news. Use computers to design page layouts and create a class newspaper.

- Read a report that describes a local event, such as a fete, a fun day or a visit from a famous person. Ask the children to write a report on a similar event.

- Link literacy to other curricular areas. For example, ask the children to write a report about a historical event. Pretend they are a reporter eye-witnessing a visit by Queen Victoria or Julius Caesar or making a report after an historic battle or a trip down a coalmine.

LOCAL BOY IS HERO – KITTEN SAVED!

Schoolboy saves kitten from drowning

Nine-year-old Jamie Hopper became a local hero yesterday when he saved a kitten from drowning. Jamie, a pupil from Hammer Common Primary School, was strolling to school yesterday morning when he noticed a kitten stuck up a tree. The kitten, later known to be Cuddles, could not get down, so Jamie whizzed back home to call the fire brigade.

After calling the fire brigade Jamie returned to the tree just in time to witness the kitten trying to climb down a branch that overhung the lake. The kitten suddenly slipped into the icy lake. Jamie was quick-thinking enough to grab a branch and hook Cuddles out of the water by her collar. Jamie then took off his duffle coat and wrapped the kitten in it to keep her warm. The kitten was still warmly snuggled up when the fire brigade arrived. Fire-fighter Geoff Spanner was very impressed with Jamie's quick-thinking actions.

Cuddles was safely returned to her owner, Mrs Sally Tilling, who later rewarded Jamie with the toy of his choice. Mrs Tilling was very grateful to Jamie because without him her kitten might have drowned.

Jamie chose a CD Rom as his reward and then returned home to a hero's welcome.

ACTIVITY SHEET ONE

Loving pet needs a home

Our cat this week, Bubbles, is a long-haired white female. She is shy but loving and needs lots of cuddles. The smallest of a litter of six, she is the last kitten left at the animal shelter. An ideal home would be quiet with a single person and no other pets.

If you can give Bubbles a good home ring 0672 523467.

1. Find two words in the report that have double consonants. Underline them.

2. Find words in the text that rhyme with the following words.

   mitten _____

   muddles _____

   bitter _____

3. Make up your own sentences for each of these words from the text.

   a) kitten   b) litter   c) bubble

   a) _____

   b) _____

   c) _____

4. Use a dictionary to find more words with double consonants in them. Write them on the back of this sheet.

WORKING WITH WORDS **PHOTOCOPIABLE**

ACTIVITY SHEET TWO

Loving pets need homes

Our cat this week, Bubbles, is a long-haired white female. She is shy but loving and needs lots of cuddles. The smallest of a litter of six, she is the last kitten left at the animal shelter. An ideal home would be a quiet home with a single person, without other pets.

The dogs of the week are two brilliant friends, Whizzer and Fizzer. As they have made friends at the kennels we are hoping to find a family who will home both dogs. Whizzer is a five-year-old cocker spaniel with a loving temperament. Fizzer is a two-year-old terrier who adores children. We are hoping it will not be necessary to split these two.

If you can give Bubbles, Whizzer or Fizzer a good home ring 0672 523467.

1. Underline all the words in the text above that have double consonants.

2. Make up your own sentence for each of these words from the second paragraph.

   a) kennel _____

   b) brilliant _____

   c) necessary _____

3. Use a rhyming dictionary to find a word that rhymes with:

   kitten _____   litter _____   cuddle _____

4. Use a dictionary to find words with double consonants. List them here.

   _____   _____

   _____   _____

   _____   _____

   _____   _____

   _____   _____

WORKING WITH WORDS PHOTOCOPIABLE

ACTIVITY SHEET THREE

Loving pets need homes

Our cat this week, Bubbles, is a long-haired white female. She is shy but loving and needs lots of cuddles. The smallest of a litter of six, she is the last kitten left at the animal shelter. An ideal home would be a quiet home with a single person, without other pets.

The dogs of the week are two brilliant friends, Whizzer and Fizzer. As they have made friends at the kennels we are hoping to find a family who will home both dogs. Whizzer is a five-year-old cocker spaniel with a loving temperament. Fizzer is a two-year-old terrier who adores children. We are hoping it will not be necessary to split these two.

If you can give Bubbles, Whizzer or Fizzer a good home ring 0672 523467.

1. Underline all the words in the text that contain double consonants.

2. Use a rhyming dictionary to find two words that rhyme with each of these.

   cuddle _____   _____

   litter _____   _____

   kitten _____   _____

3. Use a thesaurus to find two words that have a similar meaning to the word 'necessary'. _____   _____

4. Look at the names used in the text. Make up three other names for the animals, using words with double consonants.

   _____   _____   _____

5. Find ten more words with double consonants in a dictionary. Make a list.

6. Using some of the words from above write a paragraph about a lost animal. Make up names with double consonants. Underline the words with double consonants. How many did you use?

WORKING WITH WORDS **PHOTOCOPIABLE**

Dictionary skills

Intended learning
- To be able to scan an instructional text for specific words.
- To use 3rd and 4th place letters to locate and sequence words in alphabetical order.

Starting point: whole class

Working with the text
- Share the text 'How to make a funny face dessert' with the class. Ask the children to tell you what type of text it is – is it a story, a report, instructions? How can they tell? (Layout, list of what you need, steps, sub-headings and so on.) What are the instructions telling us to make?

Working with words
- Explain that the recipe is to go into a cookery book and the author wants to put key words from the recipe into the index. Discuss how words in an index are listed alphabetically. Which words in the text do they think might go in the index? Underline them (dessert, icecream, chocolate, strawberry, banana). Ask the children to list these words in alphabetical order. Remind them how they need to look at the first letter of each word to see which one comes first in the alphabet.
- Next, ask the children to consider the following words found in the index of the cookery book: berry, banana, biscuits. How will these words be arranged alphabetically? Discuss the need to look at the first AND second letters.
- Repeat this with words that require the children to look at the 3rd and 4th place letters. Examples of 3rd place order: chocolate, chip, cherry, Christmas pudding. Examples of 4th place order: strawberry, stroganoff, strudel.

Group work

Activity sheet 1
This sheet introduces 1st and 2nd place ordering for the less-able children using an instructional text.

Activity sheet 2
This sheet starts with 1st and 2nd place ordering and then extends the concept of alphabetical order to 3rd and 4th place. A similar instructional text is used.

Activity sheet 3
This sheet is for the most-able children. It will extend their experience of alphabetical order to 7th place, and gives them a greater quantity of words to order.

Plenary session
Bring the class together again. Go through examples from each activity sheet of putting words in alphabetical order. Does everyone agree? What have they learned about alphabetical ordering?

Sentence-level activities

- Explore adverbs by making up funny sentences about people and food. For example, 'The bearded man ate the sloppy spaghetti hungrily.'

- Work on verb tenses or words to start sentences (next, then, finally). The children can change the instructions to 'What I made yesterday.' For example 'Yesterday I made a funny face dessert. I put some icecream into a bowl, then put two chocolate buttons on for eyes,' and so on.

- Explore the use of commas for lists. For example, 'For my funny face dessert, I need icecream, raspberries, a bowl, a spoon and a serviette,' or 'To make my favourite sandwich, I need bread, butter, ham, cheese, a knife and a plate.'

- Find a set of instructions or directions, such as in a recipe. Cut them into strips. Challenge the children to put them back together in the correct order so that the instructions make sense.

- Give the children a set of instructions with some vocabulary missing. Ask them to choose appropriate language to fill in the blanks.

- Give the children a set of illustrations for a recipe. Ask them to write sentences or directions for each picture.

Text-level activities

- Use the instructional layout (title, 'You will need' list, bullet points, numbered steps and so on) to write more instructions for preparing food. For example, 'How to make a quick snack' or 'How to boil an egg'.

- Link literacy to other curricular areas. The children could:
  ❖ write a set of instructions for an art activity they have done, such as how to make a collage
  ❖ write a set of instructions for a science experiment, for example how to grow seeds
  ❖ invent a game in PE and write instructions to teach the game to others
  ❖ write a recipe for food from another culture to link to RE or history
  ❖ write directions on how to get from home to school, using a series of numbered steps, for geography.

- Make a book for an infant class and then write instructions to explain to others how to make a book. Put the best work on display as part of a book or reading week.

How to make a funny face dessert

Have fabulous fun making a delicious funny face dessert for your family or friends. Brighten up your bowl! But REMEMBER – always get an adult to help you with any cutting!

You will need (for each dessert):
* one scoop of icecream
* chocolate buttons
* chocolate sprinkles
* one strawberry
* a slice of banana
* a dessert bowl and spoon.

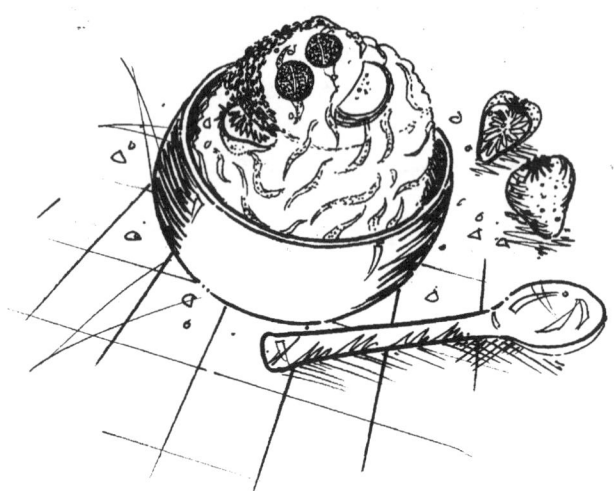

Steps:
1. First, put one scoop of icecream into a bowl and squash it into a round flat shape for the face. (Try using different flavours to make even more colourful faces.)
2. Then put on two chocolate buttons for eyes.
3. Next, get a slice of banana. Chop it into a semicircle and use it as a mouth.
4. Cut your strawberry in half and give your funny face two ears.
5. Finally, use your chocolate sprinkles to make hair.

ENJOY EATING YOUR DELICIOUS FUNNY FACE DESSERT!

More ideas:

* Try making animal faces, such as a cat or a rabbit.
* Use different foods to make other funny faces, such as ice-cream toppings, fruits, sweets or liquorice strings for really loopy hair!

ACTIVITY SHEET ONE

How to make a pancake

You will need: 100g flour, 1 egg, 300ml milk, cooking oil, lemon juice, sugar, a frying-pan and a bowl.

1. Mix the egg, flour and milk together in the bowl.
2. Ask an adult to heat the oil in the pan.
3. Pour the batter mix into the frying-pan.
4. When the bottom of the pancake is cooked, toss it so that it turns over.
5. When the pancakes are cooked, sprinkle with sugar and lemon juice.

a b c d e f g h i j k l m n o p q r s t u v w x y z

1. Find these two words in the title – 'pancake' and 'make'. Underline them.

2. Which word comes first in the dictionary – 'pancake' or 'make'?
   _____

3. Arrange these words from the text in alphabetical order.
   egg, bowl, pancake _____
   sugar, lemon, juice _____
   flour, pan, bowl _____

4. Use a dictionary to find out which of these words comes first.
   bowl or batter?   _____
   ask or adult?   _____
   the or together?   _____

5. List three things you would use for pancake toppings.
   _____   _____   _____

6. On the back of this sheet, write the words you have written on this page in alphabetical order.

WORKING WITH WORDS **PHOTOCOPIABLE**

ACTIVITY SHEET TWO

How to make a pizza face

You will need: a bread roll, tomato puree, grated cheese, ham, a courgette and peas.

1. Cut the bread roll in half and spread tomato puree on each piece.
2. Put two peas close together on each half for eyes.
3. Make a mouth out of ham and a nose and ears from a slice of courgette. (Or other vegetables, if you prefer.)
4. Arrange the grated cheese to form hair.
5. Ask an adult to put the pizza faces under a hot grill until the cheese has melted.

a b c d e f g h i j k l m n o p q r s t u v w x y z

1. Put these words from the title in alphabetical order – 'pizza', 'face', 'make'.
   _____

2. Use a dictionary to put these words from the text into alphabetical order – 'cut', 'courgette', 'cheese'.
   _____

3. Now try to order these words alphabetically.

   ask, adult, arrange _____

   how, hot, hair _____

   pizza, peas, put _____

4. Which word comes first in the dictionary?

   piece or pizza? _____ together or tomato? _____

5. Scan the text. Choose three words beginning with 't' and write them in alphabetical order.
   _____

6. Use a dictionary to find as many words as you can that begin with 'spr'. Write them on the back of this sheet in alphabetical order.

WORKING WITH WORDS **PHOTOCOPIABLE**

ACTIVITY SHEET THREE

How to make hamburgers

You will need: 450g beef mince, 50g bacon, 2 pinches chilli powder, 1 teaspoon sugar, salt and oil.

i. Put the beef, chilli powder, sugar and bacon into a bowl and mix together. Add the salt.

ii. Divide the mixture into three or four burger shapes.

iii. Brush them with oil, and grill for about two minutes on each side.

iv. Place your burgers in bread rolls and add salad or hamburger relish if required. For vegetarians use vegetarian mince cooked in vegetable stock.

1. Put the words below into alphabetical order.

    how, beef, sugar, bacon _____

    beef, bacon, bread, burger _____

    sugar, salt, shapes, side, salad, stock _____

    _____

2. Which word comes first alphabetically?

    mince, mixture or minutes? _____

    vegetarian or vegetable? _____

3. Put these words into alphabetical order, looking at the fifth letter of each word.

    divide, division _____

4. Scan the text for all the words beginning with 't'. Write them in alphabetical order.

    _____

    _____

5. Find six verbs in the text and write them alphabetically on the back of this sheet.

WORKING WITH WORDS **PHOTOCOPIABLE**

Homophones

Intended learning
▸ To distinguish between the spelling and meanings of common homophones.
▸ To scan two poems, based on a similar theme, for specific words and phrases.

Starting point: whole class
Working with the text
▸ Share the poems with the children. What do they think of them? Which one do they prefer? Can they suggest why?

▸ Ask the children to compare the two poems – how are they similar? Make a list on the board. (They have a similar theme, they both use alliteration and both incorporate homophones, rhyme and so on.) How are they different? (One has two verses, the other has four; one has sentences of similar length, the other has sentences of differing lengths; one uses questions, the other does not; in one the poet is known, in the other the poet is not.)

Working with words
▸ Explain that today the children are going to consider one of the things on the list in more detail – the use of homophones. Explain the meaning of the term – words that sound the same but have a different spelling and meaning. Can the children spot the homophones in the title of the first poem? (Whales, meaning the mammal, and Wales, meaning the place.) Can they think of other words that sound the same but are written differently? (To/too/two, for example.) List them on the board.
▸ Reread both poems, asking the children to point out all the homophones they can find (their/there, wear/where, tail/tale, sea/see, high/hi, soar/saw/sore and hear/here). Add these homophones to the list.
▸ Ask the children to make up their own sentences for some of these words to demonstrate their different meanings.

Group work
Activity sheet 1
This sheet is for less-able readers and writers. They are to concentrate on simple, common homophones. They will need to scan the poem, 'The octopus', for some homophones and make up sentences of their own to show understanding of both meanings.

Activity sheet 2
This sheet is for more-able readers/writers who will be challenged to look at more homophones within their text, 'The dolphin', and to use dictionaries for their own research.

Activity sheet 3
This sheet is for the most-able readers and writers who will scan their text, 'A mermaid', for more complex homophones. They will find homophones in a dictionary and use them in the context of their own writing.

Plenary session
Bring the class together again. Share the poems from the activity sheets and then go through the texts picking out words which are homophones. Add them to your class list. Share some of the children's sentences. Do others agree that they have demonstrated the meanings of the words used? What should we do if we are unsure of the exact meanings of words?

Sentence-level activities

- Look at the punctuation in both poems. What can the children find? Do all poems have full stops or commas? Ask the children to write a short poem about a whale, using commas for sub-clauses, or ask them to write in prose putting in the appropriate full stops.

- Brainstorm all the adjectives you can find to describe the sea. Ask the children to write a description of the sea in just five sentences.

- Look at the verb tenses in both poems – are they written in the past or present? Ask the children to write a sea poem using as many verbs ending in 'ing' as possible. A cloze procedure of a poem may be easier for the less able, whereby they can add in appropriate verbs.

- Introduce the concept of similes and metaphors. For example, 'They move like melting mountains' in the first poem is a simile. Can the children think of similes for the sea or for the animals mentioned in the texts?

Text-level activities

- Share the poems again. Focus on the alliterations used. Why does X J Kennedy use 'w' in his poem, for example? Why is 's' often used for sea or water poems?

- Ask the children to write a sea poem using alliteration. Less-able writers could use 's'; more-able writers could try two or three letter sounds.

- Look at the format of the two poems. How many verses are there in each? Ask the children to write a two/three verse poem about a sea creature.

- Give the children examples of haiku/cinquain poems. Ask them to write a short poem in this style about the sea.

- Investigate shape or thin poems. Can the children use a sea shape in which to present their poetry?

- Ask a visitor to come to school to give a poetry workshop. Your local college of higher education or a local bookshop might be good places to contact. Alternatively, you might try the Poetry Society (22 Betterton Street, London WC2H 9BU Tel: 0207 420 9880). After the workshop, review with the children the poems that were used and ask them to write their own poems on similar themes or styles.

- Read some narrative poems, such as 'Jabberwocky' by Lewis Carroll and 'What happened to Miss Frugle?' by Brian Patten from *The Oxford Book of Story Poems* (Oxford University Press, 1990). Link literacy to a drama session and ask groups to perform their favourite poems to an audience.

Two poems

The Whales Off Wales

With walloping tails, the whales off Wales
Whack waves to wicked whitecaps.
And while they snore on their watery floor,
They wear wet woollen nightcaps.

The whales! the whales! the whales off Wales,
They're always spouting fountains.
And as they glide through the tilting tide,
They move like melting mountains.

X J Kennedy

Who can see the sea?

Who can see a seal in the sea?
Dim and dull,
Splashing free.

Who can hear a gull up high?
Squawking, soaring,
Diving down nearby.

Who can touch the sand with their toes?
Slippery, soft,
Down to the sea it goes.

Who can taste the watery spray?
Who can smell the salty sea?
Who can hear and touch and smell?
Who can taste and see?
Who is lucky to do all these things?
I think it must be me!

Anon

ACTIVITY SHEET ONE

The octopus

The octopus has eight legs
It swims at the bottom of the sea
There it hides in a hole
Pretending to be a stone
Staying quiet until danger has gone.

1. Find the following words in the poem and underline them.

    eight   hole   there

2. Make up a sentence for each of these homophones.

    a) eight _____

    b) ate   _____

    c) hole   _____

    d) whole _____

    e) there _____

    f) their _____

3. 'It swims at the bottom of the sea.' 'Sea' and 'see' are homophones. Put the correct word into each sentence below.

    a) He can _____ a cow in the field.
    b) A dolphin swims in the _____

4. Use a dictionary to find more homophones. Write the words in pairs below. (For example, piece/peace.)

The dolphin

A dolphin glides peacefully along
Swimming gracefully in the sea
There it dips and dives through waves
As elegant as can be

A dolphin makes lovely sounds
It talks softly to its mate
It plays and dances and feeds
No one can the dolphin hate.

1. Underline the words in the text that sound the same as:

    see   bee   two

2. 'It talks softly **to** its mate'. Which word – to, two or too?
   Put the correct ones into the sentences below.

    a) I am going _____ the cinema.

    b) It's much _____ hot for me out here.

    c) He'll be here at _____ o'clock.

3. Make up your own sentences for these homophones.

    a) peace _____

    b) piece _____

4. Put the correct words into the sentences below – 'there' or 'their'.

    a) The children made _____ beds.

    b) _____ is my pencil case.

5. Use a dictionary to find other homophones. Write them in pairs.
   (For example, ate/eight and knight/night.)

A mermaid

She is the magical queen of the sea
A woman's body, a fish's tail
Sitting regally on her throne
She reigns with intelligence
Keeping peace at the depths of the ocean
The mermaid is never seen
But she is there
Looking after the creatures of the deep.

1. Find the words in the poem which sound the same as:

   see _____   tale _____

   thrown _____   piece _____

   their _____   made _____

2. Find the meaning of these words in your dictionary.

   a) rein _____

   b) rain _____

   c) reign _____

3. Write your own sentence for each homophone.

   a) made _____

   b) maid _____

   c) throne _____

   d) thrown _____

4. Use a dictionary to find more homophones. List them on the back of this sheet. (For example, sew/so/sow and sum/some.)

5. Add some more lines to the mermaid poem. Use some homophones in your writing.

Using alternative words

Intended learning

▶ To use alternative words and expressions which are more accurate or interesting than the common choices, for example 'got', 'nice', 'good' and 'then'.
▶ To understand that texts can be made more interesting and complex by replacing common words.

Starting point: whole class
Working with the text
Share the extract from 'The hedgehog's race' with the whole class. Discuss the following:
▶ Where have you heard a tale similar to this one? How is it similar to or different from the fable 'The Hare and the Tortoise'?
▶ Who is this story intended for? Young children/adults? How do we know this? Look at the use of simple language, animal characters and so on.
▶ Point out that there is both dialogue and narrative in the story. Does this make the story more interesting/exciting/good to read aloud?

Working with words
▶ Focus on the simple nature of the text. Can the children spot any words that have been repeated? Underline 'nice', 'very', 'old' and 'short'. Are they adjectives, nouns or verbs? Explain that writers of stories for young children often use simple and repetitive language. Why do they think they do this?
▶ Ask the children what might happen to the text if we changed some of these repetitions for other more interesting words that have a similar meaning. Use a thesaurus to look up different words for 'nice'. Agree which of the alternative words listed is the most accurate/appropriate to replace 'nice' in the sentences: 'Am I not a nice person?' and 'Wouldn't it be nice if your legs were like mine...?' Repeat this activity for the words 'old', 'very' and 'short'. You may wish to do this on an OHP as it will give the children a chance to see editing/redrafting more easily.

▶ Read the text again with the synonyms. Is the text more exciting or interesting now? Has it altered the audience for the text? Is it now more suitable for older children/adults?
▶ Have fun with the text by changing the words to make the narrator sound posh or disdainful. For example, 'Now hedgehogs are awfully sensitive about their inadequate legs. And they don't like it jolly much when somebody talks about them because their legs are really exceedingly short!' Has the text now become more humorous/interesting? Discuss how changing just one or two words can totally change the meaning of the text.

Introduce the group work. Explain that you would like them to change the repetitive words in the same way in order to make the text more suitable for an older audience.

Group work
Activity sheet 1
This sheet is for the less-able reader and writer. It focuses on the word 'nice'. The children are asked to change the words to more interesting words of a similar meaning.

Activity sheet 2
This sheet is for able readers and writers. They look at the word 'old' as well as 'nice'.

Activity sheet 3
This sheet is for more-able readers and writers and asks the children to replace the words 'nice', 'very' and 'old'. They will also use synonyms in the context of their own writing.

Plenary session
Bring the class together again. Compare the synonyms that they have found for three or four of the common words. List these on the board. Go through the texts together and change all the words for 'nice' and 'old'. Decide which replacement words have made the text more interesting. You could make a display of synonyms for the wall.

Sentence-level activities

- Look at the word 'said' in the text. Brainstorm all the synonyms for 'said'. Go through the text to replace 'said' with more complex vocabulary, such as 'explained', 'replied', 'cried' and 'answered'. Make up conversations using some of these words.

- Highlight the speech marks in the text. Ask the children to write another paragraph for the tale, continuing the dialogue between Mr Hare and Mr Hedgehog. What happens in the end?

- Use this text as an example for writing descriptive adjectives. Instead of 'short legs', the children could write 'little, brown, hairy legs', for example.

- Add adverbs to the speech verbs. For example, 'said old Mr Hare,' becomes 'asked old Mr Hare curiously.'

- Print out a dialogue from a narrative text without any punctuation. Ask the children to put in the missing punctuation.

- Ask the children to work together in pairs to make up some simple conversations and write them down using the correct punctuation, including speech marks. The conversation could be between:
  – a child and a parent
  – a child and a neighbour
  – a child and a teacher
  – two teachers in the classroom.
  The children could perform their dialogues to the class.

Text-level activities

- Explore further the similarities and differences between this extract and the well-known tale 'The Hare and the Tortoise'. Why are the two similar/different? The children could write an ending to this tale which is similar to or different from the other tale.

- The children could read other traditional tales and change them to create their own version, such as 'Goldilocks and the Three Crocodiles'.

- Share story settings from a variety of stories. Ask the children to write a descriptive setting to set the scene for the hedgehog's meeting with the hare.

- Explore imaginary worlds. Ask the children to invent a science fiction version of the story, such as 'The Spacehopper's Race'.

- Using the same characters, the children could write a narrative with a different setting. For example, 'Mr Hare and Mr Hedgehog go on holiday,' or 'Mr Hare and Mr Hedgehog go mountaineering.'

- Ask the children to imagine the dialogue between two robbers who are planning a job. They could use this dialogue as a starting point for a narrative. What do the robbers do? What happens? Does all go according to plan? Do they get caught?

CLASS TEXT

The hedgehog's race

Now hedgehogs are very sensitive about their short legs. And they don't like it very much when somebody talks about them, because their legs are really very short! Mr Hedgehog said, 'You know, my friend Mr Hare, you are really not a very nice person.'

'And why,' said old Mr Hare, 'am I not a nice person?'

'Well,' he said, 'every time we meet you're always talking about my legs. I can't help it that I've got short legs, because I was born like this.'

Mr Hare said, 'Wouldn't you like to have long legs like me? You know I've got beautiful legs. I can run faster than anyone! Dogs can't even catch me. Wouldn't it be nice if your legs were like mine and you could run as fast as the wind across the fields?'

And old Mr Hedgehog said, 'Well, of course it would be nice to have long legs like you. But you see, Mr Hare, you don't need long legs to run fast, you know.'

'You don't need long legs to run fast?' said old Mr Hare. 'Nonsense! How in the world could you run fast with those short little legs you've got? No way could you run out of the way of a dog or a fox like me. As for me, I can run swifter than the wind!'

'Well,' said old Mr Hedgehog, 'you see, my friend, I'll tell you what I'll do with you. I'll make a bargain with you. I'll challenge you to a race!'

And old Mr Hare cocked up his ears and said, 'Am I hearing you right? You mean you're challenging me to a race?'

'Of course!' said old Mr Hedgehog. 'Are you getting deaf in your old age? I said a race!'

EXTRACT FROM 'THE HEDGEHOG'S RACE' – A SCOTTISH TRAVELLER'S TALE - BY DUNCAN WILLIAMSON
From 'The Big-Wide-Mouthed Toad-Frog and Other Stories' – Kingfisher

ACTIVITY SHEET ONE

Using different words

1. Look in a thesaurus and write down all the words that mean 'nice'.

2. Read the text below and underline all the 'nice' words. Then, using words from your list above, replace all the 'nice' words with more interesting words.

Brown Curls

A nice little girl was walking in a wood one day when she saw a nice cottage. She went in and found some nice soup in the kitchen. She ate the soup and then found a nice chair to sit in. The chair looked nice, but was not very comfortable so she went upstairs and found a nice bed to lie in.

After a nice sleep she woke up and decided to tidy up the cottage. When she finished she had a nice cup of tea and then went home. When the owner of the cottage, a little hedgehog, came home for tea, he was very surprised to see a nice tidy home. 'How nice!' he said to himself.

---

3. Read the text again. Do you prefer it now or as it was in the beginning? On the back of this sheet explain why.

ACTIVITY SHEET TWO

Using different words

1. Using a thesaurus make lists of alternative words for 'nice' and 'old' below.

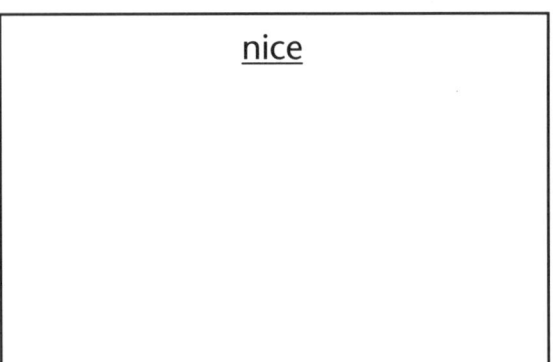

| nice | old |

2. Now read through the text below. Underline the words 'old' and 'nice'. Then, using your lists of words, replace each 'nice' and 'old' with a more interesting word.

Brown Curls

A nice little girl was walking in an old wood one day when she saw a nice cottage. She went in and found some nice soup in the kitchen. She ate the soup and then found a nice old chair to sit in. The chair looked nice, but was not actually very comfortable so she went upstairs and found a nice bed to lie in.

After a nice sleep she woke up and decided to tidy up the old cottage. When she finished she had a nice cup of tea and then went home. When the owner of the cottage, a little old hedgehog, came home for tea, he was very surprised to see a nice tidy home. 'How nice!' he said to himself.

3. Explain how you think this has changed the original text.

_____

_____

_____

WORKING WITH WORDS **PHOTOCOPIABLE**

ACTIVITY SHEET THREE

Using different words

1. Read the text below and underline the words 'old', 'nice' and 'very'.

Brown Curls

A nice little girl was walking in an old wood one day when she saw a very nice cottage. She went in and found some very nice soup in the kitchen. She ate the soup and then found a nice old chair to sit in. The chair looked very nice, but was not actually very comfortable so she went upstairs and found a nice bed to lie in.

After a very nice sleep she woke up and decided to tidy up the old cottage. When she finished she had a nice cup of tea and then went home. When the owner of the cottage, a little old hedgehog, came home for tea, he was very surprised to see a nice tidy home. 'How nice!' he said to himself.

---

2. Use a thesaurus to help you find replacement words for each word underlined in the text. Write the new words above the underlined ones.

3. How do you think this has changed the original text? _____

_____

4. Now find other words for these words. Write them underneath.

nasty	new	fast

5. Use the words from your 'nasty' list to write a short description of a monster on the back of this sheet.

WORKING WITH WORDS **PHOTOCOPIABLE**

Prefixes

Intended learning
- To recognise and spell prefixes, such as 're' and 'un'.
- To use prefixes in the context of own writing.
- To understand that recognising a prefix may help to work out the meaning of an unknown word.

Starting point: whole class
Working with the text
- Share the text extract 'Don't Bin It!' with the whole class. What is the text about? What kind of text is it? Discuss that the passage is an information text. How do we know? (Layout, headings, sub-headings, factual language.)

Working with words
- Ask the children what the words 'reuse' and 'recycle' mean. Write the words on the board. Point out the idea of doing something again. Which part of the word do they think means 'again'? Underline this part of each word. Explain about prefixes and how they go at the beginning of some words. Tell the children that prefixes change the meaning of the original (base) word. Explore this idea with some examples, such as 'true' and 'untrue'.
- Ask why it might be useful to understand the meaning of a prefix. Explain that it can help us to understand the meaning of unknown words. For example, knowing the meaning of 'cent' will help them to understand the meaning of 'century' and 'centenary'.
- Ask the children to tell you any other prefixes they know. List them on the board. Explain that you want to make a word bank of words that have prefixes and that you are going to use the text on recycling to begin the word bank. Go through the text with them and highlight or underline the prefixed words as you go along. Use dictionaries to find out the meanings of the prefixes. For example, 'un' is often added to give an opposite meaning. Can the children think of any more words prefixed with 'un'? Add these to the list.
- Introduce the group work and explain that they will be exploring more words using prefixes.

Group work
Activity sheet 1
This activity is for the less able reader and writer. It focuses on the common prefixes, 'un' and 'dis'. The reader will need to scan the text for specific words and add correct prefixes for a word. They will also use words with prefixes in the context of their own writing.

Activity sheet 2
This sheet is for the able reader, who will need to fill in blanks with correct prefixes. They will also use some words in the context of their own writing.

Activity sheet 3
This sheet for the more able readers challenges them to explore more prefixes, and to complete a cloze procedure. They will also use prefixes in their own writing.

Plenary session
Bring the class together again. Share the texts and ask the children to mark their own additions. Pick out all the words beginning with prefixes, and write them on a paper flip-chart to make up a word bank. Reiterate the fact that prefixes are useful in working out the meaning of an unknown word. For example, if the children know what 'reuse' means they could guess at the meaning of 'reworking' or 'rewriting'. As a follow-on activity you could give each ability group some words and ask them to guess the meaning from the prefix. If they do not know they could check using a dictionary. Words could include rewrite, unfortunate, impossible and untimely.

Sentence-level activities

- The children could work on shortening paragraphs into one sentence. Get them to write a sentence using the key concepts from each paragraph in the text to form a précis.

- Look at verb tenses in the text – are they past or present? Do they give orders? Why are information texts usually written in the present tense? Find another information text and pick out the verbs used. Are there any verbs used that are the same as the ones in this text?

- Use adverbs of intensity (such as very, quite, more, most and rather) to add to the text. Does this have the effect of making the text more powerful or persuasive?

- Look at the adjectives used in a text about litter or pollution. Brainstorm more adjectives that could be used to describe these two themes. Are the words negative or positive? Are there any prefixes used in these words? Ask the children to write some sentences of their own using the adjectives.

- Look at the punctuation or layout in a text about an environmental issue. What is the purpose of using, for example, bullet points, headings, upper/lower case, fonts, exclamation marks, questions and orders? Ask the children to make up an article about the litter in their school, using some of these layout/punctuation concepts.

Text-level activities

- Ask the children to find out more about recycling. They could write a newspaper article or an informational text about what their school/family recycles or needs to recycle but doesn't.

- Organise a group to go and interview the head teacher to find out what he/she thinks about recycling. Ask them to prepare questions and then write up the interview or record it on a tape recorder.

- Ask the children to write an information text in a similar layout to this text on a different subject, such as planets, stars, endangered animals or sea pollution. They should use headings, sub-headings, illustrations, captions and so on.

- Make up posters to put up around the school reminding people not to drop their litter and the effects it will have if they do.

CLASS TEXT

DON'T BIN IT!
REUSE AND RECYCLE IT!

Every day we throw away lots of rubbish that could be reused or recycled. Most rubbish is incinerated (burnt) or buried in the ground (landfilled), but recycling some of these things could reduce the rubbish mountain, and save energy and raw materials.

LITTER

Litter is unsightly, unpleasant and can be harmful. Animals choke on plastic bags, birds and sea creatures get caught on nets, and people cut themselves on bits of broken glass.

WHAT CAN WE DO?

- Instead of throwing your plastic carrier bags into the bin, use them for your next shopping trip, or buy a shopping bag so you don't need to use plastic.
- Take your recyclable cans and bottles to the local bottle and can bank.
- Reduce the amount of packaging you throw away. Take your paper to the recycling plant, or reuse paper and cardboard for artwork.
- Write letters to companies or factories, asking them to be more aware of recycling.
- Ask your head teacher if you can start a paper collection.
- Encourage people to pick up their litter instead of throwing it on the ground.

BE KIND TO THE ENVIRONMENT!
RECYCLE AND REUSE!

Prefixes

1. Add 'un' or 'dis' to the beginning of these words. Use a dictionary to help you.

   kind   appear   lucky

2. Now read the text below.

   RIVER POLLUTION

   Some people are very disappointing and unhelpful. They throw all sorts of unpleasant rubbish into rivers and streams. This makes the water smelly and unclean. Then they wonder why the fish get unhealthy and die.

   People can also get ill if they drink dirty water as it is unsafe.

   Stop this disgusting behaviour! Stop throwing rubbish into our rivers and streams!

   a) Underline all the words in the text that begin with 'un'.
   b) Put a circle around the words that begin with 'dis'.

3. Make up your own sentences using these words.

   unclean
   _____

   unsafe
   _____

   disgusting
   _____

Prefixes

1. Read the passage below and then fill in the blanks with either 'un' or 'dis'. Use a dictionary to help you.

   RIVER POLLUTION

   Some people are very ___appointing and ___helpful. They throw all sorts of ___pleasant rubbish into rivers and streams. This makes the water smelly and ___clean. Then they wonder why the fish get ___healthy and die.

   People can also get ill if they drink dirty water as it can be ___safe.

   Stop this ___gusting behaviour! Stop throwing rubbish into our rivers and streams!

2. Now write the words in two lists below.

   'dis'   'un'

3. Use a thesaurus or dictionary to find words that mean the same as:

   unclean   disgusting   unsafe   disappointing

4. Now think of three words that begin with:

   a) 'al' _____
   b) 'in' _____
   c) 'en' _____

ACTIVITY SHEET THREE

Prefixes

1. Read the article below. Fill in the blanks with appropriate words that begin with 'dis' or 'un'. Use a dictionary to help you.

   RIVER POLLUTION

   Some people are very dis_____ and un_____. They throw all sorts of un_____ rubbish into rivers and streams. This makes the water dis_____ and un_____. Then they wonder why the fish get un_____ and die.

   People can also get ill if they drink dirty water as it can be un_____.

   Stop this dis_____ behaviour! Stop throwing rubbish into our rivers and streams!

2. 'In' is another prefix. Use a dictionary to find six more words starting with 'in'. Write them here.

3. Make a list of words and their opposites (that begin with 'un') below. Use a dictionary to help you. (For example, pleasant – unpleasant, kind – unkind.)

4. On the back of this sheet, write a short paragraph about 'litter in rivers' that could be added to the article above. Use as many words as you can that have prefixes (such as 'al', 'un', 'dis', 'in', 'out', 'pre', 'im' and 'de').

Common endings

Intended learning
- To spell words with common endings, such as 'ight'.
- To use independent spelling strategies, such as spelling by analogy with other known words, for example 'light' and 'fright'.

Starting point: whole class
Working with the text
- Share the text 'How an electric circuit works' with the children. Discuss that this is an explanation text because it tells us how something works. Explain that an explanation text usually includes a description of the subject followed by an explanatory sequence. In this text, the first paragraph gives us a definition and the remaining paragraphs outline how an electric circuit works.
- Ask questions about the text to evaluate the children's understanding. For example, 'What is needed to make a circuit?' and 'What are circuits used for?'

Working with words
- Say that explanation texts often use words that can be difficult to spell. Write the word 'light' on the board. Explain that this word can be difficult to spell but once we learn the spelling pattern it contains (underline 'ight'), it can help us to spell other words with the same ending. Ask 'How might we spell "tight" or "fright", for example?' Write 'ight' on the board and ask the children to think of other words that end in 'ight'. List them on the board.
- Give more examples, using words from the text. For example, 'ow', 'ough', 'ain', 'ment' and 'ance'. What other words do they know that have the same endings?
- Tell the children that they will now be using another explanation text in their group work to find other words with common word endings. Introduce the group work and the three activity sheets.

Group work
Activity sheet 1
This sheet is for less-able readers/writers and concentrates on two common endings, 'ing' and 'our'.

Activity sheet 2
This sheet is for more-able readers/writers who will look at the word endings 'ing', 'our', 'or', 'ant' and 'ure'.

Activity sheet 3
The most-able children will be challenged to explore a greater number of word endings.

Plenary session
Share the answers to the activity sheets. How many different words for each ending could be found? Discuss the fact that although words can have the same spelling in their word endings, they can sometimes be pronounced differently, for example 'through' and 'though'.

Sentence-level activities

▶ Look at the verbs in the text. Things are explained in the present tense. Look at other explanation texts to see if they are also in the present tense. Why do the children think this might be?

▶ Ask the children to rewrite the explanation in the past tense, as if they had set up a circuit yesterday.

▶ Focus on underlining key words and phrases to write a shortened form of the explanation, in just three or four sentences.

▶ Look at other explanations that use diagrams or pictures. How are the captions written? Ask the children to explain a process in pictorial form, making up appropriate sentences for captions. This could be done as a shared writing exercise or individually.

Text-level activities

▶ Look at the layout of the explanation. Give the children a writing frame to plan their own explanation about how something works. A good framework guide is: title, definition of object or process, details of parts, cause and effect, uses and special features. Encourage the children to use paragraphs for each element.

▶ Explanations can be used for processes linked to other curricular areas, for example:
   - The life-cycle of a flowering plant
   - The life of a frog/butterfly
   - How erosion/weathering occurs
   - How valleys are made
   - How the solar system works.

Or – explanations can be used for a more specific purpose, explaining how an object works, for example:
   - How a calculator works
   - How a model works
   - How to load a computer program.

Ask the children to write their own explanation text for one of the above.

▶ Compare instructional texts with explanation texts. Ask the children to comment on the differences and similarities between the two.

How an electric circuit works

An electric circuit is a complete path made up from conductors through which an electric current can flow. Electricity can flow or move. It moves in one direction only. It will only keep moving if the circuit or pathway remains unbroken.

A simple electric circuit can be made using a 1.5v battery, a 1.5v light bulb, a bulb holder and two pieces of insulated wire. (See the diagram below.) Wires are used in circuits because electricity flows easily along metals.

The electricity flows from one end of the battery along the wire to the bulb. When the electricity reaches the bulb, it meets a thinner wire in the filament and has to 'work harder' to get through, because of the wire's resistance. As the wire is thin and coiled and the electricity is 'working harder', the electrical energy is changed to heat and light energy so the filament lights up. An inert gas in the bulb prevents the filament from bursting into flames. The electricity then continues to flow along the other wire into the other end of the battery.

ACTIVITY SHEET ONE

How a refrigerator works

A refrigerator is used for keeping things cool. It works by using the warmth of the food placed inside the fridge to help turn a special liquid into a vapour (gas). As the vapour is formed, the food cools down.

At the back of the fridge is a large curved pipe. The vapour is pumped into this pipe and turns into a liquid again.

The refrigerator has a small electric motor which sends the cooling liquid along all the pipes in the fridge.

The outside of the fridge has a special casing to stop warmth reaching the food inside, helping the food to stay cool.

1. Underline all the words in the text that end in 'ing'. Write them here.

   _____

   _____

2. Choose ONE of these words and write it in a sentence.

   _____

   _____

3. Use a dictionary to find four more words that end in 'ing'.

   _____

4. Inside the fridge a vapour forms. Put a circle around all the words below that have the same word ending as vapour.

   motor   hour   shower   tour   pour   tore   score   more   scour

5. Write your own sentences for these words.

   hour _____

   tour _____

WORKING WITH WORDS **PHOTOCOPIABLE**

ACTIVITY SHEET TWO

How a refrigerator works

A refrigerator is used for keeping things cool. It works by using the warmth of the food placed inside the fridge to help turn a special liquid, called a coolant, into a vapour. As the vapour is formed, the food cools down.

At the back of the fridge is a large curved pipe. The vapour is pumped into this pipe where it condenses and turns into a liquid again.

The refrigerator has a small electric motor which sends the coolant along the pipes inside the fridge. The motor is controlled by a thermostat. When the temperature inside the fridge rises (when warm food is put inside it or when the fridge door is opened), the thermostat comes on and this in turn turns the motor on. Once the fridge has cooled down again, the motor switches off.

The fridge has a special casing on the outside to stop warmth reaching the food inside.

1. Find words in the text that have the same word endings as these words.

   rotor _____   string _____   tour _____

2. Use a dictionary to help you find four more words that have the same word endings as each of these words.

   coolant _____

   temperature _____

3. Put a circle around all the words listed below that have the same word ending as vapour.

   motor   hour   shower   tour   pour   tore   score   more   scour

4. On the back of this sheet, write a sentence for each of these words from the text.

   motor   refrigerator

ACTIVITY SHEET THREE

How a refrigerator works

A refrigerator is an appliance for keeping things cool. It works by using the warmth of the food placed inside the fridge to help turn a special liquid, called a coolant, into a vapour. As the vapour is formed, the food cools down.

At the back of the fridge is a large curved pipe, called the condenser. The vapour is pumped into the condenser where it condenses and turns into a liquid again.

The refrigerator has a small electric motor, called a compressor, which circulates the coolant along pipes inside the fridge. The compressor is controlled by a thermostat. When the temperature inside the fridge rises (when warm food is put inside it or when the fridge door is opened), the thermostat comes on and this in turn turns the compressor on. Once the fridge has cooled down again, the compressor switches off.

The fridge has a special casing on the outside to prevent warmth reaching the food inside. The outside of the fridge is made of metal, while the inside is made of hard plastic. Between the metal and the plastic is a thick layer of insulation. This prevents any warmth getting inside the fridge.

1. Underline words in the text that have the same word endings as these words.

   dance   pour   plant   sting   pain   pure   information

2. Use a dictionary to help you find five more words that have the same word endings as these words. Write them on the back of this sheet.

   coolant   temperature   vapour   motor   insulation

3. Put a circle around all the words listed below that have the same word ending as vapour.

   temperature scour tambour deplore flower manoeuvre flour

4. Find out what all these words mean and write sentences for them.

Common letter strings

Intended learning
- To spell words with common letter strings but different pronunciations; for example tough, through, trough, plough, hour, journey, could, route and four.
- To read a range of poetry in different forms.

Starting point: whole class
Working with the text
- Share the poems with the whole class. Which poem do they like best? Can they say why?
- Compare the poems in terms of content and layout. Explain what a haiku is and look at the syllable pattern of 5, 7 and 5 syllables in each line. Why do they think 'Noise' is called a thin poem? What kind of layout do the other poems have? Do the poems rhyme?

Working with words
- Ask the children to tell you what they think the poems have in common. They should notice that all the poems contain words with 'ou' in them.
- Explain that you are going to look carefully at these 'ou' words. Ask the children to tell you all the words in the poems that have 'ou' in them – list them on the board.
- Explain that many words can have the same spelling pattern and yet are pronounced differently. Ask the children to sort the listed words into groups of words that are pronounced the same, for example 'rough', 'tough' and 'enough'. Talk about the sound 'ou' makes in each group.
- Can the children think of other words to add to each of these groups?
- Explain that they will be looking at more poems in their group work and that they will be scanning these texts for 'ou' words.

Group work
Activity sheet 1
This sheet is for the less-able reader/writer who will concentrate on two poems containing 'ou' words. They will scan the texts for specific words and pick out words that have the same spelling pattern and are pronounced the same.

Activity sheet 2
This sheet is for more-able readers/writers who will look at a larger sample of poems.

Activity sheet 3
This sheet is for the most-able readers/writers who will look at poems with a more complex vocabulary. They will also write their own short poem as an extension.

Plenary session
- Bring the whole class together again. Go through the poems for each group for understanding.
- Pick out the 'ou' words and agree which groups they should be added to in the lists prepared at the beginning of the lesson.
- What have they learned from the activity?

Sentence-level activities

- The children could choose five of the words from the board lists and put them into sentences or try to write a short story with as many 'ou' words as they can find.

- For dictionary work they could find some unknown words containing 'ou' and write their own definitions for these words.

- Choose one or two poems and rewrite them making every singular into a plural word. You may have to spend some time giving examples if the children are not familiar with rules of pluralisation.

- Investigate other common letter strings, such as 'ow'. Make lists of words that have 'ow' and split them into two lists: the 'ow' sound and the 'oh' sound.

    | how | know |
    | owl | blow |
    | now | show |
    | cow | slow |

- Make up sentences or short stories that contain some of the above words.

- Ask the children to make up a thin poem using rhyming words, perhaps using the 'ight' or 'ite' letter strings. For example,

    One night
    A fright
    Moonlight
    A fight
    Daylight.

Text-level activities

- Study the layout/punctuation of the poems and then:
    ❖ Hold a haiku workshop, looking at more published examples and then ask the children to write their own.
    ❖ Ask the children to write a thin poem on a certain theme, such as food, the sea, science or maths.
    ❖ Look at examples of shape poems and ask the children to write a summer poem inside an icecream picture, for example.
    ❖ Link poetry to other subjects. Could the children write a prayer in poetic form or write a poem about a historical figure/event?

- To practise writing poetic forms the children could write more lines for each poem.

- Challenge the children to write a poem about a real event, such as sports day or a school fair.

- Ask them to write a poem of thanks to someone, such as a relative for a birthday present or to someone they know who does a lot for other people.

- Read poems that make the children laugh. Ask them which is their favourite and why. How does the poet make the audience laugh? What language is used? Ask the children to write a funny poem of their own.

Poems

The bully (Haiku)

The bully is rough
The bully is rough and tough
We have had enough!

Tidy that room!
(An angry poem)

What's the noise about?
There's no need to shout.
Yes, I'll tidy my room.
I suppose I could.
Maybe I should.
I'll do it at four.
Just shut the door.

The Jungle

(An adventure poem)

Going on a journey
Through a big jungle
Planning my route
Ploughing through the trees
Only takes an hour
For my jungle is really –
My garden!

Noise (A thin poem)

Shout
Out
Shout
About
Shout
Lout
Clout

Working with poems

1. Put a circle around the words that have the same 'ou' pronunciation as in:

   out   –   shout   bought   mount   about   would

   could –   doubt   would   sour   should

   bought –   ought   about   brought though

2. a) Read the poem below.

   The Plough

   I sit on a bough
   Watching the farmer's big plough
   Then it disappears!

   b) The two words below are from the poem. Find them in a dictionary and write down what they mean.

   bough _____

   plough _____

3. a) Read the poem below.

   THE SNAIL
   I found a snail
   I looked at his round shell
   He was very quiet
   He didn't make a sound.

   b) Colour three words in the snail poem where the 'ou' is pronounced the same as in 'mound'.

ACTIVITY SHEET TWO

Working with poems

1. Read the poems below and underline all the words with 'ou' in them.

THE COUGH

There's no doubt – he's got a cough
Ring the doctor! He feels rough.
So the doctor came round in the hour
And gave me some YUCKY MEDICINE!

THE SNAIL
I found a snail
I looked at his round shell
He was very quiet
He didn't make a sound.

The Plough

I sit on a bough
Watching the farmer's big plough
Then it disappears!

2. Use three different colours to circle words in the poems with 'ou' that are pronounced the same as:

   out   tough   off

3. Use a dictionary to find the meanings of these words from the poem 'The Plough'.

   bough _____
   plough _____

4. Circle the words that have the same 'ou' sound as in:

   hour   –   flour   floor   sour   four

   could   –   ought   should   would   mould

   bought –   ought   about   brought   rough

   tough   –   through   rough   hound   enough

ACTIVITY SHEET THREE

Working with poems

1. Read the poems below and underline all the words with 'ou' in them.

Dreaming

I could, I should, I would
If only I could.
But I couldn't
I shouldn't

THE COUGH

There's no doubt – he's got a cough
Ring the doctor! He feels rough.
So the doctor came round in the hour
And gave me some YUCKY MEDICINE!

The Plough

I sit on a bough
Watching the farmer's big plough
Then it disappears!

THE SNAIL
I found a snail
I looked at his round shell
He was very quiet
He didn't make a sound.

2. a) What does the word 'bough' mean?

_____

 b) Find another word in the same poem that is pronounced the same as bough. Circle it.

3. Fill in the grid below using words from the poems and a dictionary.

Word	Words with 'ou' in them that are pronounced the same
should	could
out	
rough	
through	
cough	

4. On the back of this sheet, write your own poem using 'ou' words.

Suffixes

Intended learning
- To recognise and spell words with common suffixes, focusing on 'able', 'ible', 'ive', 'tion' and 'sion'.
- To use words with suffixes in context.

Starting point: whole class
Working with the text
- Share the advertisement 'Apple Tree Cottage' with the whole class. Discuss the meaning of some of the unknown words, such as 'idyllic' or 'rural'.
- Ask the children to tell you what kind of text it is. What is it trying to persuade us to do? What vocabulary is used to help persuade us? Note the use of positive language, especially in the adjectives used, for example 'good', 'pretty' and 'comfortable'.

Working with words
- Underline the following adjectives: 'wonderful', 'comfortable' and 'hospitable'. What do the children notice about the endings of all these words? What other words do they know that end in 'able'? List them on the board.
- Explain what a suffix is and how the addition of a suffix to a word doesn't necessarily change the meaning of the word but makes the base word fit the way we want to use it in a sentence. Talk about how sometimes the spelling of a word changes when a suffix is added, for example 'beauty' + 'ful' = 'beautiful' and 'shop' + 'ed' = 'shopped'.
- Ask the children to look through the text to find other words with suffixes.
- Write lists of the words on the board so that the children can add to them later. Look for words ending in 'ed', 'al', 'ic', 'ful', 'able', 'ing', 'ly' and so on.
- You may wish to extend the more-able readers/writers and explain that some nouns or verbs, for example, change to adjectives when a suffix is added, for example 'glory' – 'glorify' – 'glorious'. Likewise, verbs can be changed to nouns, for example 'convert' – 'conversion'. As an extension activity this group could find words from the text and explore their ability to make new words by adding a suffix.
- Explain to the children that they will now be looking at another text for words with suffixes in their group work.

Group work
Activity sheet 1
This activity will familiarise the less-able readers and writers with the concept of suffixes, specifically 'tion', 'sion', 'able', 'ible' and 'ive'. They will need to scan the text, think of their own words with suffixes and use a dictionary to find more words.

Activity sheet 2
This sheet is intended to extend the more-able readers' and writers' knowledge of suffixes. They will need to scan a longer text and use a dictionary to find the meaning of new words with suffixes.

Activity sheet 3
This sheet is for the most-able readers and writers. They will need to scan a longer text, use a dictionary to define new words and use adjectives with suffixes in their own writing.

Plenary session
Bring the class together again. Go through the group texts picking out words with suffixes. Check the meaning of more difficult vocabulary. Add the selected words to the lists drawn up at the beginning of the lesson. Revise how words can be changed, for example a noun into an adjective: 'comfort' – 'comfortable'.

Sentence-level activities

- Ask the children to find adjectives or adverbs in the text which give a positive view of a holiday in Apple Tree Cottage. Ask them to use a thesaurus to replace these words with words that have a similar meaning, for example 'fabulous' – 'magnificent'.

- Use the text for a study of comparatives and superlatives, such as 'good', 'better', 'best' and 'pretty', 'prettier' and 'prettiest'. What effect do these have in an advertising text? Pick out words like 'most' and ask the children to add most or more and change the adjectives to superlatives. For example, 'They are most hospitable…'

- Study the use of commas in the text. Some are used to break up sub-clauses while others are used for listings:
  ❖ Ask the children to write about what is in their own rooms at home, using commas for listings, for example 'In my bedroom there is a wardrobe, a bed, a lamp, a bookshelf and a rug.' The more-able children could then add in adjectives as an extension.
  ❖ Ask the children to write about what they can do on holiday, using commas to list their activities, for example 'At the campsite you can swim, play tennis, ride horses or go to the disco'.
  ❖ To introduce children to sub-clauses you could look at the first sentence of the text and ask them to add different endings, for example 'Situated just five miles from Cheltenham, the idyllic Apple Tree Cottage…' Can they find any other sub-clauses? Can they add other endings to these?

Text-level activities

- Share the text and focus on how the writer is persuading you to spend money by using language.

- Ask the children to write their own persuasive text based on the idea of a holiday advertisement, such as a cottage, a caravan or camping site.

- Cut out some advertisements from magazines. Study the methods of persuasion used by the writer/illustrator, for example the adjectives, superlatives and comparatives. Look at the photographs or illustrations – how do these encourage you to buy the product? Does the writer use any facts, such as 'Biologically tested' or '100% Fat Free'? How does this persuade us to buy? Are there any gimmicks used? For example, 'Buy One – Get One Free!' or 'Collect 10 Tokens to Get a FREE Toy'. Does the writer use upper/lower case, bold print or different fonts? What effect does this have?

- Finally, ask the children to design their own advertisements for a product, using some of these persuasive methods, for example a new fizzy drink, or a super new dessert.

YOURS TO RENT!

APPLE TREE COTTAGE –
THE BEST HOLIDAY COTTAGE IN THE COTSWOLDS

Situated just five miles from Cheltenham, the idyllic Apple Tree Cottage stands in the middle of picturesque countryside. It is a beautifully converted rural farm cottage, set in its own enclosed garden, with an orchard to the rear. There are wonderful views in every direction.

The house has three pretty bedrooms and a large, modern bathroom upstairs. Downstairs there is a lounge with comfortable furniture, a good TV and stereo system, a dining room with a six-seater table, and a very well-equipped kitchen.

Nearby, there is a pretty farm where you can buy fresh milk and delicious eggs. The farmer and his wife are most hospitable and welcome children to their farm, where they are encouraged to help out at feeding times.

There is a lot to do in the surrounding area. You can walk across the countryside, ride at the local riding school or drive around glorious Cotswold villages. The historic towns of Cheltenham and Cirencester have much to offer. More details can be obtained from the Tourist Office.

A fabulous holiday at Apple Tree Cottage will offer you fun, relaxation and value for money. Book your best holiday ever with us now!

Ring: 01232 820299 for bookings.

Only £250 per week!

BOOK NOW TO SAVE DISAPPOINTMENT!!

La Colline

La Colline is an attractive campsite, in Brittany, northern France. Set in desirable countryside, the campsite is in an ideal position and there are incredible views all around. There is a playground for the children and an outdoor swimming pool for all the family. Lots to do! Loads of fun! Unbeatable prices! Perfect location! For more details ring 081 67584.

1. a) Read the first line of the text. Write the word that has 'ive' at the end of it. _____

   b) Make up your own sentence using this word.

   _____

2. Find a word that ends in 'ible'. Look up the meaning in a dictionary and write the word and its meaning below.

   _____

3. 'The campsite is in an ideal position.' Use a dictionary to find two more words ending in 'tion'.

   _____   _____

4. Use a dictionary to find other words that end in 'able', such as 'desirable'. Write them here.

5. Conversion ends in 'sion'. On the back of this sheet make a list of other words ending in 'sion'.

ACTIVITY SHEET TWO

La Colline

La Colline is an attractive campsite, situated in Brittany, northern France. Set in desirable countryside, the campsite is in an ideal position and there are incredible views all around. Beaches are easily accessible.

There is an indestructible playground for the children and an outdoor swimming pool for all the family. Due to the conversion of an old barn, there is now a clubhouse with a bar and playroom for evening relaxation.

You may wish to choose a more creative option and take part in one of La Colline's imaginative painting courses – the choice is yours!

Close to the incredible city of Brest you can taste the edible delights of French cuisine in the restaurants or browse around the impressive shops.

Lots to do! Loads of fun! Unbeatable prices! Perfect location!
For more details ring 081 67584.

1. Scan the text for words ending in 'able' and 'ible'. Write them below.

2. What do these words mean? Use a dictionary to help you.

   attractive _____

   impressive _____

   imaginative _____

3. Find a word in the text which ends in 'sion'. Circle it.
   What does it mean? _____
   On the back of this sheet, make a list of more words ending in 'sion'.

4. Underline any other words in the advertisement which you think have a suffix. Use two of them in sentences of your own.

   _____

   _____

WORKING WITH WORDS **PHOTOCOPIABLE**

La Colline

La Colline is an attractive campsite, situated in Brittany, northern France. Set in desirable countryside, the campsite is in an ideal and unbelievable position and there are incredible views all around. Beaches are easily accessible.

There is an indestructible playground for the children and an outdoor swimming pool for all the family. Due to the conversion of an old barn, there is now a clubhouse with a bar, television and playroom for evening relaxation. You may wish to choose a more creative option and take part in one of La Colline's extensive painting courses – the choice is yours!

Close to the incredible city of Brest you can taste the edible delights of French cuisine in the restaurants or browse around the exclusive shops. Or if you prefer staying near your own habitation you can pop to the campsite's café for ample portions of delicious food.
Lots to do! Loads of fun! Unbeatable prices! Perfect location! Be sensible – book now!
For more details ring 081 67584.

1. Scan the text for words with suffixes and sort them into lists below.

   –able   –ible   –ive   –tion   –sion

2. Add the suffix 'ive', 'ible' or 'able' to these words to make adjectives.

   express _____   destruct _____

   laugh _____   collect _____

3. On the back of this sheet, write the meanings of these words.
   habitation, extensive, exclusive, indestructible, conversion, unbeatable

4. Make up your own paragraph to describe a holiday cottage. Use as many adjectives as you can which have the suffixes 'ible', 'able', 'tion', 'sion' and 'ive'. Use your dictionary and words from the text to help.

Compound words

Intended learning
- To discuss a point of view in letter form.
- To investigate compound words and recognise that they can aid spelling.

Starting point: whole class
Working with the text
- Share the text with the children. Discuss that this text is a letter (revise the letter format – address, salutation and so on). What type of letter is it – formal or to a friend? Ask the children to tell you what the letter is about. Discuss how the letter sets out a personal point of view. Underline persuasive phrases used such as 'Anyone can see that…' and 'I believe you have…'

Working with words
- Tell the children that you are going to use the letter to look at a special type of word – compound words. Explain what compound words are and underline all the compound words in the address at the top of the page. What two words is each word made up of? Point out that there is no gap or hyphen with compound words (children often leave one, for example in football).
- Explain that knowing how to spell the little words in a bigger word helps us to remember how to spell the whole word. Tell them that splitting up the word into smaller parts is also a useful reading strategy.
- Ask the children to look for more compound words in the text (bypass, playground, somewhere, countryside). List them on the board. Ask the children to take turns to come out and underline the two parts of each word in a different colour. Explain that compound words can sometimes be made up of more than two words, for example seamanship = sea + man + ship.
- Ask the children to make up some of their own sentences using compound words from the text.
- Tell the children that they will be looking for compound words in another text similar to this one. It will also be a letter of complaint.

Group work
Activity sheet 1
The text for this group is a letter of complaint to a shop manager about a handbag and necklace which break shortly after the buyer gets them. This sheet, for the less-able reader/writer, looks at simple compound words. The children will need to scan the text for specific words and use a dictionary.

Activity sheet 2
The text for this group is a letter of complaint about a football that fails to arrive. The able reader/writer will investigate a greater number of compound words and will need to pick out more from the text. They will use compound words in the context of their own writing and need to use a dictionary.

Activity sheet 3
This letter is a complaint to a plumber about recent work carried out. The most-able readers/writers will be challenged to investigate more complex compound words and to use them in the context of their own writing. They will need to use dictionaries.

Plenary session
Share the texts with the children. Agree the compound words as you go through, checking for meaning. List other examples that the children have found. Challenge the children to write their own letter of complaint using as many compound words as they can.

Sentence-level activities

- Give the children a letter that has some or all of the punctuation missing. Revise letter punctuation with them. Ask them to complete the letter.

- Give the children some letters with some of the words missing, such as 'Dear', 'Yours faithfully' and the date. Challenge them to complete the letters.

- Look at the phrases that the writer of the whole-class text uses. How can we tell she is cross by the sentences she uses? Does the punctuation emphasise her point? (Focus on the exclamation marks, and the words written in upper case letters.) The children could write some sentences on an issue about which they feel strongly (for example, bullying, smoking and litter) and use these elements of language in their own writing.

- Look at real letters or emails. Try to sort them into groups, for example letters of complaint, letters asking for information, letters of thanks and letters of persuasion. Discuss with the children what made each of them put each letter into its group.

Text-level activities

- Share the text again. Ask the children to write a letter to the Prime Minister or the head teacher, complaining about something that makes them cross, for example hunting animals or improvements that could be made to the outside of the school. Use the correct letter format. In the letter they should tell the person what is wrong and suggest ways of improving the situation. More able children could use paragraphs as an extension.

- Tell the children to pretend that they have bought something that breaks as soon as they get it home. They must write a letter of complaint to the shop manager.

- Tell the children to imagine that they have just been on a school trip to a theme park. There was litter everywhere, the food was too expensive, the cafe was dirty and the picnic benches were too old to sit on. Some of the rides were closed for repair and the day was a great disappointment. Ask them to write a letter to the manager of the theme park. They must say what was wrong and how they would like to be compensated.

Cherry Cottage
Whitetown
Near Hopbridge
Hopshire
H2P 6FG

10 January 2001

Dear Councillor Digman,

I am writing to complain about the new bypass which you are planning to build near Whitetown village. I live in this village and the new road will go right through the playground and field next to my house. Can't you build the bypass SOMEWHERE ELSE?

Anyone can see that you are going to SPOIL the countryside. The view from my bedroom window will be RUINED by the sight and sound of traffic. My grandchildren won't be able to play football any more, and just think of all the animals who will lose their homes if YOU cut down the hedgerows. And where will the toddlers play WITHOUT their swings and seesaw???

I believe you have underestimated the strength of feeling of the villagers over this bypass. Even the policemen at the local station are against your plans!

Stop this bypass! You have overstayed your welcome already! Go and build it somewhere else!!!

Yours very crossly,

[signature]

Mrs Ima Grump

Letter of complaint

> 22 Football Road
> Newtown
> Newtownshire
> N16 3B2
>
> 20 January 2001
>
> Dear Manager,
>
> Yesterday morning I bought a handbag and a necklace from your shop in Newtown. As I was coming home on the bus, the handle on the handbag broke. In the afternoon, I was putting on the necklace ready to go outside when the string snapped and left me with beads all over my bedroom floor. I am not very happy, so I am sending you the receipt. Please can you send me my money back straight away.
>
> Yours faithfully,
>
>

1. Underline all the compound words in the letter above.

2. Make up a sentence for each of these compound words.
   a) bedroom
   b) afternoon

3. Join two words to make a compound word and then list the compound words. One has been done for you.

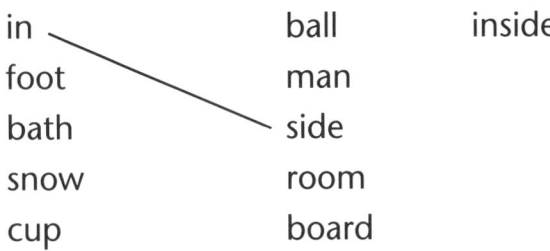

   in   ball   inside
   foot   man
   bath   side
   snow   room
   cup   board

4. Now write a sentence using three of those compound words.

   _____

   _____

5. Use a dictionary to make a list of more compound words.

Letter of complaint

> 3 Cupboard Avenue
> Greentown
> Greentownshire
> GR3 4YJ
>
> 23 January 2001
>
> Dear Customer Services,
>
> Two months ago I ordered a pair of football boots and a football for my granddaughter's birthday present. The boots arrived (without laces!!), but the football still has not come. She will be ten next week and all she wants is a football. Why has it not been delivered? Your catalogue states that it will only take ten days.
>
> Please will you check this order and send me the ball within the next two days, otherwise I will be forced to speak to your manager. I hate to see my grandchild disappointed and this whole thing has made me very cross with your company.
>
> Yours truly,
>
>
>
> Miss V Cross

1. Scan the text to complete these compound words.

   foot   other   grand   cup

2. Make up two sentences of your own using the word 'otherwise'.

   a) _____

   b) _____

3. Use a dictionary to find other compound words beginning with 'foot' or 'hand', for example 'handwriting'. Write them here.

4. How many other compound words can you find in the dictionary? List them on the back of this sheet.

ACTIVITY SHEET THREE

Letter of complaint

> 35 Redrose Street
> Tentown
> Tentownshire
> TW3 65Y
>
> 25 January 2001
>
> Dear Mr Pipe,
>
> I am writing to complain about the work your apprentice did for me on Sunday. I called him out when my bathroom floor was flooded due to a leaking pipe. He came but I think he underestimated the job. He mended the overflow on the toilet but failed to see other holes in the pipework. Shortly after he left, the bathroom cupboard started to get wet and the tiles began to fall off the wall because of the damp.
>
> I have put tape around my pipes but I would be grateful if you could come and put things right as soon as you get back from your holiday. I know you are overworked but I am a loyal customer who does not deserve this kind of repair work!
>
> Yours gratefully,
>
>
>
> Mr Soggy

1. Underline all the compound words you can find in the text.

2. Find the meaning of these words in a dictionary.

    a) overflow _____

    b) underestimate _____

3. Find more compound words that begin with 'over' or 'under'.

    over <u>overstay</u> _____

    _____

    under <u>undersized</u> _____

    _____

4. On the back of this sheet, make a list of compound words that begin with 'in' (for example, income).

5. Pretend you are Mr Pipe. Write a letter back to Mr Soggy, using as many compound words as you can in your letter.

Let It Be:
Living Light in a World
That Still Hurts

By S. M. Keyte

Table of Contents

Introduction

How to Use This Book

Chapter 1.
    What Comes After the Letting Go
    After release, you're left with space — and learning to live in it takes courage

Chapter 2.
    The Art of Enough
    Enoughness isn't something you earn — it's something you decide to believe.

Chapter 3.
    Being Okay When You Don't Know Uncertainty doesn't mean failure; it means you're still alive and unfolding.

Chapter 4.
    You're Allowed to Feel Good Now
    Joy is not betrayal — it's a reclamation of your right to feel whole again.

Chapter 5.
    Letting Life Happen
    Control isn't safety — sometimes the bravest thing is letting life move without you gripping it.

Chapter 6.
 Relating Without Attachment
 Loving fully doesn't require clinging tightly — it asks for trust, not possession.

Chapter 7.
 Creating Space for Something New
 To welcome newness, you must be willing to leave room for what hasn't arrived yet.

Chapter 8.
 Stillness Isn't Laziness
 Rest is not a weakness — it's a radical practice of self-trust and presence.

Chapter 9.
 The Ongoing Practice of Lightness
 Lightness isn't about perfection; it's about softening your grip, again and again.

Chapter 10.
 Let It Be: Becoming Your Own Peace
 Peace isn't found — it's made, moment by moment, by how you choose to live.

Chapter 11.
 Bonus Tools & Reflection Pages

Introduction

Let It Be: Living Light in a World That Still Hurts

There is a moment, after the letting go, that no one prepares you for.

Not the collapse. Not the heartbreak. Not the burnout or the grief or the unravelling.
But what comes next.

The quiet.

The strange spaciousness that follows the shedding.
The awkward breath where there used to be fight.
The question:
Now what?

This book is for that moment.

For the people who have already survived the hard part.
Who walked through the fire. Who let go of something—someone—a version of themselves they thought they had to be. And now find themselves in the wake of it all, asking:

How do I live from here?

Letting go is brave. But *being* after the letting go is a practice.
That's what this book is about.

Not healing as a finish line.
Not peace as perfection.
But the slow, daily, grounded becoming of someone who knows how to be light.
Even in a world that still hurts.

If you've read the first two books in *The Art of Letting Go* series—*Let It Hurt* and *Let It Go*—you've already met the pain. You've made space for it, sat with it, maybe even screamed into your pillow or whispered forgiveness to your younger self.

You've released. You've loosened your grip.
You've done some *really* hard emotional work.

Now we shift.

From tending wounds to tending presence.
From gripping to softening.
From fixing to flowing.

What This Book Will (and Won't) Do

This book won't tell you to ignore the world's pain.
It won't give you a 5-step morning routine to erase your anxiety.

What it *will* do is invite you back into your body.
Into the practice of living with openness, even when you're afraid.
Into a life where peace isn't something you earn—but something you return to.

You'll find:

- Narrative stories that help you feel seen

- Tools that meet you in the everyday

- Journal prompts that ask the *real* questions

- Breath and silence practices to soften your nervous system

- Gentle reminders that you're allowed to feel good, even now

Each chapter is a doorway—not to escape life, but to meet it differently.
To live without clinging.
To love without losing yourself.
To be your own anchor.

How to Use This Book

There's no right pace.
Some readers go chapter by chapter, reflecting weekly. Others keep it by their bed, reading when life nudges. You can move through it linearly or return to a chapter when you need it most.

A Gentle Guide for the Journey Ahead

This book isn't meant to be rushed.
It's not a checklist. It's not homework. It's a companion.
You don't need to be "in crisis" to read it. You just need to be human.

You can move through it in any way that feels supportive:

- Front to back, like a course in peaceful living
- One chapter a week, with space to reflect
- Or intuitively — choosing the page your heart lands on

What You'll Find in Every Chapter:

⏳ A Core Theme
Each chapter centres on one essential idea — from enoughness, to stillness, to surrender. These aren't answers. They're invitations.

📖 Illustrative Stories
Real, resonant moments drawn from life. Not to solve you — but to remind you that you're not alone in how you feel.

Tools and Practices
Grounded, gentle actions. Some are breath-based. Others are written. All are designed to bring you back to yourself.

Reflection Pages
At the end of each chapter, you'll find:

- *Pause Here*: A question that doesn't need to be solved

- *Try This*: A practice to meet the chapter in your body or day

- *Quote to Hold On To*: A piece of wisdom from around the world

A Few Invitations Before You Begin:

You don't have to agree with everything. Take what resonates and leave the rest.

If your mind wanders, let it. This isn't about focus — it's about softening.

Keep a journal close. Let it be messy. Scribbled. Full of half-thoughts and big truths.

It's okay if you stop. Come back when you're ready.

🕯 You're Already Doing It

The fact that you're holding this book means something.
You're showing up — for your peace, for your body, for your life.
And that, in itself, is a kind of freedom.

You don't have to fix or figure it all out.
You just have to be willing to meet yourself here.

Let this book be a conversation.
Let it be a breath.
Let it be enough.

A Note from the Author

I wrote this book because I needed it too.

Because after my own unravelling—after the release, the grief, the fire—I expected peace to just *arrive*. But instead, I met a kind of stillness that felt unfamiliar and unsteady. I had to learn to live in it.
To stop fighting myself.
To trust that lightness didn't mean I was careless or naive.
It meant I was finally free.

So if you've made it here, I want to say this:
You don't have to earn your peace anymore.
You just have to return to it, over and over again.

Let's begin.

— *With softness,*

S. M. Keyte

CHAPTER 1
WHAT COMES AFTER THE LETTING GO

1. What Comes After the Letting Go

Core Focus: Honoring the in-between, meeting the aftermath, softening into uncertainty

There's something strange about waking up after a long stretch of survival.
Not the kind where you're fighting off an obvious threat or navigating a catastrophe.
But the quiet kind.
The kind where you've been bracing for years — clenching through the days, shrinking around pain, keeping everything in motion just enough to avoid falling apart.
And then, one day, it stops.

The pain isn't louder.
It's gone.

Or mostly gone.
Or at least quieter than it used to be.

And that silence?
That's when the disorientation begins.

We don't talk enough about this moment — the one that comes after the big letting go.
After the heartbreak.
After the career burnout.
After the family fallout, the diagnosis, the move, the unravelling.

You survived.
You did the work.
You made the brave decision to let go of something that no longer fit — a version of yourself, a relationship, a dream that had calcified into something too tight.

And now... what?

There's no ticker-tape parade.
No glorious sunrise over your freshly-cleared life.
Just quiet.
And maybe a little loneliness.
Maybe a lot.

It can feel like standing barefoot in a house you just finished cleaning after a fire — walls scrubbed, air cleared — and realizing you don't know what furniture to bring back in.
Or if you even want furniture at all.
Or who you are without the smoke.

In the early months after I left a life I thought I'd be living forever, I remember waking up to this exact quiet.
Not a peaceful one.
A blank one.

I'd spent years learning how to let go — of perfectionism, of people-pleasing, of an entire identity built around being needed more than I was known.
I got good at releasing.

At grieving.
At rewriting what I believed about strength.

But what caught me off guard was what came after: the stillness.

I thought peace would feel like warmth, like freedom, like a homecoming.
And sometimes, it did.
But mostly?
It felt awkward.
Like trying to relax your shoulders after decades of hunching.
Like breathing deeper than your body is used to.

The stillness wasn't just unfamiliar.
It was suspicious.
Was I missing something?
Was I doing it wrong?
Was this it?

There's a quiet kind of fear that follows healing.
Not the fear that something bad will happen again — although that can linger too.
But the fear that nothing *will* happen.
That maybe you cleared all that space for nothing.
That maybe emptiness is your new normal.

But here's what I want you to hear, before we go any further:

The emptiness you feel is not failure.
It's not a sign you let go of the wrong thing.
It's not a void to be filled.

It's space.
Space for something honest to grow.

I once read that after a wildfire, the soil becomes more fertile.
The fire burns away the hard outer layers of seeds that otherwise never would've opened.
That something fierce and destructive can create the exact conditions required for new life to take root.

I think of that often, especially when working with people in the in-between — the after-but-not-yet.

Like Jordan, who walked away from a job that was slowly erasing her health.
She had no backup plan, no next step, just a deep knowing that staying would cost her more than leaving ever could.

The first few weeks were empowering. She felt brave. Bold. Alive.

But then?

"I don't know who I am without being constantly needed," she said, eyes welling up. "I feel useless. Like I don't know how to exist without urgency."

I nodded.
Because of course she felt that way.
We build identities around our pain sometimes.
Not because we want to be martyrs, but because it gives us shape.
It tells us what to do when we wake up.
It gives us a story to live inside.

And when we let go of that pain — even when we *choose* to — we don't just lose the wound.
We lose the narrative.

And without a narrative?
We're just here.
Breathing.
Waiting.
Noticing the quiet.
Trying not to panic.

That's why I say the letting go isn't the hard part.
The being after the letting go is.

It's where the deeper work begins.
The work of not rushing to rebuild.
Of not clinging to the first new story that makes you feel useful again.
Of allowing the stillness to stretch a little longer than your ego wants it to.

Because eventually — quietly, almost imperceptibly — new things begin to emerge.

Not grand plans.
Not perfect clarity.

But flickers.

An idea that excites you.
A song you forgot you loved.
A craving for something your body hasn't asked for in years — rest, creativity, cinnamon toast at midnight.

Tiny signs that you are, indeed, still alive.
And not just alive — *becoming*.

"Ruin is the road to transformation."
— *Elizabeth Gilbert*

Softening Instead of Starting Over

This chapter isn't about setting goals or becoming your "best self."
It's about not rushing into becoming anyone at all.

When life gives you this wide, strange space, don't fill it right away.
Don't stuff it with busyness or self-improvement.
Let it stay open.

Let it breathe.

This is the part of healing where softness matters more than strategy.

Try This: The Space Scan

Sit somewhere quiet.
Place one hand on your belly, the other on your chest.
Close your eyes.
Breathe deeply.

Now ask yourself gently:
What is no longer here?
Don't force answers. Just notice.

Then ask:
What do I feel in its place?
It might be fear. Or freedom. Or a kind of humming unknown.

Breathe into it.
That is your new ground.

Pause Here

- What *used to be* part of your life that now feels like smoke?
- Where do you feel space opening up in your body or day?
- Can you let yourself feel the awkwardness of freedom without fixing it?

There's a moment — and you might already be in it — where even the smallest decision feels strange.

What do I do with this afternoon?
What does it mean that I don't *have* to do anything?
Why does freedom feel... hollow?

This isn't regression. It's recalibration.

Your nervous system is still adjusting to a world without that old, familiar pressure. Without the noise. Without the constant grip of urgency that used to define your day before you even opened your eyes.

And if you've spent years in survival mode — years of pushing through, managing chaos, reacting instead of choosing — then stillness isn't just foreign. It can feel unsafe.

That's okay.

We don't need to rush this part.
We just need to name it.
And be gentle with it.

Let me tell you about my friend Sam.

Sam spent most of her life tending to others — emotionally, financially, logistically — until she hit a wall. It wasn't dramatic. There was no spectacular breakdown. It was more like she woke up one Tuesday and realized that every single thing she did was for someone else. And none of it was asked for anymore.

Her kids were grown. Her parents were gone. The people who once depended on her no longer called, or needed, or expected anything. And she sat there in a house full of items that didn't reflect who she was, just who she'd *had* to be.

When she finally decided to let go — of the volunteer roles, the old furniture, the schedule she'd been operating from for years — she expected to feel weightless.

Instead, she felt like she was floating away. Unanchored. Unfamiliar even to herself.

"I don't know what I want," she told me one afternoon, her tea going cold between sips. "And worse… I don't know if I even know *how* to want anymore."

That sentence stuck with me.
Not because it was rare, but because it was universal. Because after we let go of what we never really wanted — the shoulds, the burdens, the false identities — we sometimes find ourselves face to face with an even harder question:

What do I want now that I finally have room?

And the truth is… it takes time to answer that.
It takes time to remember who you are when you're no longer performing who you were.

This space you're in — this fertile, fragile, uncomfortable space — isn't a mistake.

It's a reintroduction.

It's the echo of your body asking: *Are we safe enough to rest yet?*

It's your heart whispering: *Are we allowed to want something more beautiful now?*

And it's your nervous system slowly — so slowly — learning that tension doesn't have to be your baseline.

But none of that happens instantly.
None of that arrives in a tidy epiphany.
It happens in the small, unremarkable moments.

The first time you leave a day blank on purpose.
The morning you realize you didn't wake up clenched.
The night you stop apologizing for not replying to every message right away.

That's the real healing.
It's not a glow-up.
It's a gentle shedding.

A choosing of quiet over chaos.
Peace over proving.
Being over performing.

And sometimes that choosing will feel awkward. Even wrong.

Because if no one is watching — if there's no one to impress or convince — then why are you doing any of it at all?

That question, uncomfortable as it may be, is sacred.
It's the doorway to a new kind of freedom.
One not built on escaping pain, but on staying with peace.

But here's something I want you to remember: You don't have to fill the space right away.

You're allowed to let it be empty for a while.
To let your days feel unstructured.
To feel the edges of your life without immediately patching them with productivity or noise.

If it feels like you're doing nothing, you're not.
You're re-patterning.
You're learning how to live without the friction.
You're making peace with the stillness.

That's the most important work of all.

Try This: The Soft Schedule

Instead of planning your day around tasks or goals, try creating a soft rhythm.

Write down 3 words that you want your day to *feel* like — maybe grounded, open, kind.
Then ask: What could I do today that supports those feelings?

You might still have a to-do list.
But now it's filtered through a deeper lens.
Now it's not about productivity — it's about presence.

Reflection Questions

- Who am I when no one is needing something from me?
- What feels strange about having space in my life?
- Can I trust that stillness is not stagnation — but something tender and alive?

There's something you may not have expected to grieve: the clarity that pain once gave you.

When you were hurting, you knew what the problem was.
You had a direction, even if it was just away from what burned.
Pain can be a sharp compass. Survival gives you a kind of purpose — not a joyful one, but a defined one.

Now that you're no longer in that crisis, you're faced with something much more nebulous: possibility.

And while possibility sounds like freedom, it can also feel like drowning.
So many open paths.
So many maybes.
So many chances to get it wrong.

That fear is real.
It's not a flaw in your mindset.
It's not a failure of confidence.
It's the echo of living for too long in a world where your choices were shaped by necessity, not desire.

When everything was on fire, you didn't have time to ask, *What would I love?*
You asked, *What will keep me from breaking?*

Now, for the first time in a long while, you get to ask something different.
And that question can feel enormous.

A woman I worked once said, "I spent so long trying to leave my old life that I never considered what kind of life I was heading toward."

She'd left a toxic job, an emotionally draining marriage, and a community that subtly policed who she was allowed to be. And when the dust settled, she stood in the center of her new freedom and realized she didn't recognize herself.

Not because she was lost.

But because she'd never had the space to meet the version of her that wasn't in response to everyone else's expectations.

"I thought I'd be happy," she told me, looking down at her open journal. "But all I feel is… undefined."

That word struck me.

Not broken.
Not empty.
Just — *undefined*.

Like she was still clay, unshaped.
Like her identity was no longer bound to defence, or to performance, or to being needed.

For the first time, she could sculpt something new.
But she didn't know what it was yet.

This is where so many people get stuck — in the in-between.

You're no longer who you were.
But you're not quite sure who you are now.

And because the world loves clear answers and fast turnarounds, it's easy to feel like this space is failure.

It's not.

It's sacred.
It's tender.
And it asks something countercultural:

Patience.

Not passivity.
Not resignation.
But a kind of soft holding.
A trust in the process of emergence.

It's like the season between winter and spring.
Everything beneath the surface is stirring — roots pushing into thawed ground, seeds absorbing warmth — but nothing is visible yet.
And that invisibility can feel like nothing is happening.

But it is.
You are.

Just because it doesn't look like growth doesn't mean it isn't becoming something beautiful.

This chapter exists for *this exact moment*.
To help you stay present in the softness, instead of scrambling to rebuild a version of you that fits some imagined expectation of "healed."

You don't have to be impressive now.
You don't have to be sure.
You don't even have to be ready.

You just have to keep breathing in the quiet you've earned.

Letting it show you things you couldn't see when your life was full of noise.

Like how deeply tired you are.
Like how sweet it feels to eat slowly again.
Like how your shoulders drop two inches when you realize no one is watching.

You don't have to fill the silence.
You can learn to *trust* it.

Because peace doesn't always arrive like a symphony.
Sometimes, it arrives like a room you forgot you had, empty and echoing.
And at first, it's too much.
But soon, you realize it's yours.
And you get to decide what — or who — ever comes inside again.

Try This: The Permission Letter

Take out a piece of paper. Write at the top:

"I give myself permission to not know."

Now, finish the sentence as many ways as you need to:

- I give myself permission to not know what I want next.
- I give myself permission to not have a plan.
- I give myself permission to rest without guilt.

Don't worry about making it eloquent.
Let it be raw.
Let it be honest.
Let it be enough.

Then fold the paper, and place it somewhere safe. Return to it when you forget that this middle place — this undefined season — is part of the path.

"The day you plant the seed is not the day you eat the fruit."
— *Fabienne Fredrickson*

There is a subtle grief that lives in the quiet.
Not for what was lost — you've already mourned that.
But for the version of yourself that no longer knows what to reach for.

That part of you — the doer, the fixer, the overachiever, the caretaker — doesn't disappear just because you've stopped feeding it.
It lingers.
It whispers.
It wants to be useful.

And in this new space, where the frantic pace has slowed, it starts to panic.
What am I supposed to *do* now?
Who am I if I'm not working toward something, proving something, being something for someone else?

You may feel tempted to start filling that space with activity.
To create new goals.
To chase a new version of healing that looks better on paper.
To force meaning back into your day so the silence won't feel so vast.

But this chapter is about resisting that pull — not forever, but just long enough to learn something different.

How to be with yourself.

Not your curated self.
Not your healed self.
Just your real self, right now, in the raw and unedited aftermath.

Here's something I've learned after sitting with dozens of people in this phase of life:

We underestimate how much energy it takes to hold still.

We think stillness is laziness.
Or a pause between better moments.
Or worse — we think it means we've lost momentum.

But true stillness is not passive.
It's radically active.

It's choosing not to self-abandon.
It's listening to your body when it says, *Not yet.*
It's holding the line when your inner critic tells you, *This isn't enough.*

Because here's the truth: You are still detoxing from a culture that worships hustle and applauds exhaustion.

You are learning how to exist in a rhythm that doesn't revolve around proving your worth through productivity.

And that will feel deeply uncomfortable.
Not because you're doing something wrong.
But because you're doing something *new*.

I remember a man named Daniel who came to me after leaving a high-paying role that had nearly destroyed his health.

He had done "all the right things": quit with grace, gone to therapy, read the books, moved into a slower lifestyle. But a few months in, he was restless.

Not because he wanted his old life back — he didn't. But because he didn't know who he was in this new one.

"No one's emailing me at midnight anymore," he said. "I don't have to triple-check flights or memorize numbers or sprint through my mornings."

He paused.

"But I also don't know how to enjoy any of this. I feel like I'm failing at resting."

That sentence — *failing at resting* — broke something open for both of us.

Because that's how many of us feel.
We equate rest with reward.
With permission.
With something earned only after visible output.

So when we finally find ourselves in the stillness we claimed to want, we panic.
We don't know how to metabolize it.

It doesn't look like productivity.
It doesn't validate us externally.
It doesn't make for good social media updates.

But it is *healing*.
It's the deepest kind.

The kind you can't rush.
The kind you can't prove.
The kind that changes who you are — not what you've done.

There's a reason you feel tender right now.

You're in the moulting phase.

The old skin is gone. The new skin is still forming.
Everything is soft.
Everything is exposed.

And it can be tempting, in that state, to Armor up.
To rush into clarity.
To force an identity so you don't feel so undefined.

But I promise: if you can stay here a little longer — in the softness, in the not-yet — you'll start to feel something else rise.

Not certainty.
But *trust*.

Trust that you are being reshaped by this quiet.
Trust that the next version of your life doesn't need to be decided from a place of panic.
Trust that you don't have to *earn* your softness. You can simply *be* in it.

Try This: The Gentle Inventory

Take 10-15 minutes and sit somewhere you won't be interrupted.

Ask yourself:

- What am I no longer carrying?
- What part of me still feels restless or uncertain in the quiet?
- What small part of me feels the tiniest bit of relief?

Write down whatever comes. Don't edit. Don't judge. Let it be tender and messy.

Then, underline one sentence that feels like truth.

That's your anchor for the week. Come back to it when the silence starts to feel like failure again.

"Don't just do something. Stand there."
— *Zen proverb*

The truth is, your nervous system might not trust the quiet yet.

Even when your mind says, *I want peace,* your body may still flinch at it.
Because it remembers.

It remembers what it cost to survive.
It remembers what happened the last time you let your guard down.
It remembers how stillness used to come right before the crash — the phone call, the confrontation, the disappointment.

So when life slows down now — even by your own choice — your body might tense instead of soften.
Your breath might quicken.
You might feel the urge to fix, to scroll, to get busy.

That's not a character flaw.
That's a trauma echo.

One of the kindest things you can do in this season is stop expecting yourself to feel peaceful just because the storm has passed.
The body doesn't move on at the same speed as circumstance.
It needs proof.

Not logical arguments.
Not inspirational quotes.

Proof.
That it's safe to exhale.
That you'll listen to its no.

That you won't shove it back into performance just because the world keeps asking.

So start with one inhale.

Not a perfect one.
Not a 4-7-8 technique or a box breath or anything with a name.
Just air, in.
And out.

Start with the reminder that *you are allowed to be here.*

Not for what you produce.
Not for who you serve.
Not for what you've endured.

But simply because you exist.

It sounds simple. It isn't.
Because for many of us, our worth was always tied to action.

We learned early that love came faster when we were useful.
That rest was only acceptable after exhaustion.
That softness made us vulnerable to criticism or invisibility.

So now, here you are — standing in the aftermath of the letting go — and you're trying to believe that stillness is allowed.

But your body is waiting to see if you really mean it.

So prove it.
With a slow walk instead of a power hike.
With leaving the dishes until morning.
With not apologizing when you cancel a plan to stay home and cry.

These aren't lazy choices.
They're reclamations.

They're declarations that your nervous system no longer has to run on scarcity.
That your peace no longer has to be postponed until you've *earned* it.

I want to tell you about Amira.

Amira had spent most of her adult life working two jobs.
She carried her family.
She handled the emergencies, the bills, the emotional labour, the caretaking.
Even her friendships revolved around support — *her* giving it, mostly.

And when her father passed and the caretaking chapter ended, she didn't know how to stop bracing.

She had space, finally.
No one was depending on her in that same way.
She could've slept for a week.

But instead, she found herself doing laundry at midnight, offering help to acquaintances who hadn't even asked, and volunteering for committees she didn't care about.

"I think I don't know how to not be useful," she said to me once.
"I think I've confused being busy with being safe."

That hit hard.
Because haven't so many of us done the same?

Haven't we layered our days with proof of worth, even when no one is watching?
Haven't we filled our calendars out of habit, not alignment?

When Amira finally sat still — truly still — she wept.
Not from sadness, exactly.
But from the unfamiliarity of being with herself without a to-do list buffering the experience.

This is the work of becoming after the letting go.

Not becoming bigger.
Not shinier.
Not more productive.

Becoming honest.

With what you want.
With what you no longer want to carry.
With who you're willing to disappoint in order to honour your body's truth.

And sometimes honesty looks like inaction.
Like not knowing yet.
Like being quiet when the world expects you to announce a bold new vision.

Sometimes, growth isn't loud.
It's not a brand.
It's not a glow-up.
It's you, breathing more slowly than you did yesterday.
You, not reacting to the thing that used to unravel you.
You, choosing to listen inward, even when no one claps for it.

Try This: The Body's Yes / The Body's No

Close your eyes. Sit with your feet flat on the floor.

Think of a recent moment where you said yes to something.
Feel what happens in your body as you recall it.
Does your chest tighten?
Do your shoulders rise?
Or do you feel lightness, openness, a quiet sense of peace?

Now think of a moment where you said no — or wanted to.
Notice what rises.
Not the story. Not the guilt. Just the *sensation*.

Begin learning what your "yes" and "no" feel like in your body — not just your mind.

Because when your nervous system trusts you to listen, peace becomes more than a concept.
It becomes a companion.

One of the hardest things to explain to someone who hasn't been through it is just how vulnerable peace can feel.

Not because peace is painful.
But because pain, for all its weight, is predictable.

When you were suffering, you knew the shape of your days.
You had a story.
Even if it was a sad one, even if it felt like drowning, it was *something* to hold onto.

Now, after the release, you may feel like you're floating.
Not in freedom.
In disorientation.

And that feeling can be just as destabilizing as grief.
Because what comes after the letting go isn't always clarity.
Sometimes, it's fog.
Sometimes, it's the vast blank canvas no one warned you would feel so heavy.

And when no one's asking anything of you, when the pain has softened, when the fire has gone out —
there's nothing left to push against.
No more resistance.
No more adrenaline.

Just air.
And yourself.

And that can feel like the scariest part of all.

Letting go is a tearing.
But being afterward — *being* — is a re-rooting.

And roots don't grow in straight lines.
They grow downward.
In darkness.
In silence.
Without applause.

This part of your life — the slow unfolding, the gentle becoming — won't win you any awards.
No one may even notice.
And still, it will change everything.

Because you are learning how to exist without self-betrayal.
You are learning how to stay soft, even without anyone to save.
You are learning how to stop confusing exhaustion with worth.

That is sacred.
That is brave.
And that is what this chapter — this whole season of your life — is asking of you.

Not to perform healing.
To live inside it.

Not to be seen doing better.
To be okay not doing anything at all.

There's something profound about realizing you no longer have to be dramatic to feel alive.

You no longer need the emotional spikes — the chaos, the urgency, the validation loops — to remind you that you matter.

You get to redefine what aliveness feels like.

And maybe, just maybe, it's quieter than you imagined.

It's the way sunlight moves across your floor in the morning.
The weight of a mug in your palm.
The way your body sighs when no one's asking anything of you.

You begin to notice things you used to rush past.
Not because your life is suddenly interesting — but because you're no longer performing urgency through every moment of it.

You begin to become porous again.
Available.
Present.

Not to the world.
To yourself.

One afternoon, I was walking through the woods near my home. I had taken this path a hundred times before — a trail that curved through tall eucalypts and opened near a quiet field. But this time, I wasn't walking to clear my head or solve anything.

I was just… walking.

And in that stillness, something shifted.

Not because I had a revelation.
Not because a solution dropped into my lap.
But because I realized — for the first time in what felt like years — I wasn't waiting for the next crisis.

I wasn't flinching at the possibility of interruption.
I wasn't negotiating with myself about whether this peace was going to last.
I was *in it*.

Fully.

And the weirdest thing?

It was almost boring.

Not in a bad way.
In a holy way.

Because boredom, for someone who's lived in survival mode, is a sign of safety.

It's your body saying: *There's nothing to fix right now. You can be here.*

And that is a miracle.

So if you're in that moment now — the dull stretch, the in-between, the part where your friends ask, "What's next?" and you don't know — I want you to know something:

You don't have to manufacture purpose.
You don't have to invent clarity.
You don't have to make your peace palatable or impressive.

Let this season be soft.
Let it be uneventful.
Let it bore you, if it must.

Because boring, for you, might just mean healing.

Try This: The Safety Signals Scan

Sit quietly and ask yourself, *What in my current life tells my body it is safe?*

It could be:

- A closed door
- A soft blanket
- A quiet room
- The absence of notifications
- A consistent morning ritual

Now write down 3 of those signals.

Then ask: *How can I increase or return to these signals this week?*

Your body doesn't need big gestures.
It just needs consistency.
And proof that safety is no longer a someday concept.

```
"The quieter you become, the more you are
            able to hear."
                - Rumi
```

It can be easy to mistake this season for nothingness.

The space after letting go can feel so quiet, so uneventful, that your mind will try to convince you you're falling behind.
That you've become directionless.
That your lack of urgency means you've lost momentum.
That everyone else is moving forward, and you — for some reason — are still here.

Still becoming.

Still figuring it out.

Still unsure of what this new life is meant to look like.

But here's the truth: Not everything that grows makes noise.
And not everything that is still is stagnant.

You are not falling behind.
You are moving differently now.

You are moving at the speed of your nervous system.
You are healing on cellular time.
You are walking forward in a life that no longer runs on emergency mode — and that is *progress,* even if it doesn't look like success.

We have been taught to equate clarity with control.

But what if clarity is something softer than that?

What if clarity is the slow revelation that you're allowed to change your mind?
That you don't need a five-year plan to trust the direction of your body?
That you can live a life rooted in presence, not projection?

Some of the clearest moments I've had didn't come from goal-setting sessions or vision boards.
They came in moments of surrender.

The time I deleted every productivity app off my phone and felt my jaw unclench.
The morning I sat in bed for an hour just listening to birds and didn't feel guilty.
The evening I turned down a "great opportunity" because it didn't feel peaceful.

Clarity, it turns out, isn't always about answers.
Sometimes it's about resonance.
Sometimes it's just the absence of dread.

A client named Holly once said something that still echoes in me.

"I'm not waiting for the next chapter anymore. I'm learning how to live inside this one."

She'd spent years in future tense — when I finish school, when I get the job, when I fix the marriage, when I finally figure out what's *wrong* with me.
And when the dust of all that chasing began to settle, she found herself alone on a quiet Tuesday afternoon, drinking tea and realizing... no one was asking her for anything.

The next chapter hadn't arrived.
But neither had collapse.
It was just her.
Alive.
Safe.

And in that moment, she cried.
Not because she was sad.
Because she'd never felt so still before.
And the stillness didn't hurt.
It just felt *new*.

Sometimes, the hardest part of peace is learning to trust that it won't be taken from you.

Because if you've lived in instability — in relationships where joy was followed by punishment, in homes where the good days were rare and always temporary — you've likely developed the belief that stillness is a trap.

A trick.
A setup.
A prelude to something worse.

So even when your life becomes quieter, even when the danger has passed, even when you've chosen to release what once harmed you — some part of you may still be waiting.

Waiting for the next blow.
Waiting for the shoe to drop.
Waiting to be proven right that good things don't last.

And if that's what's happening in you now, I want to say this gently:

It's okay to feel that.
It's not irrational.
It's not dramatic.

It's a learned survival pattern.
And like any pattern, it can be unlearned — not through force, but through repetition.

Through safe mornings that begin without panic.
Through days where nothing urgent happens.
Through moments where you realize you are no longer bracing.

That's when the rewiring begins.
Not in some breakthrough.

But in the thousands of micro-moments where your body finally, finally exhales.

Try This: The Stillness Inventory

Ask yourself:

- Where in my life do I feel the most still?
- When was the last time I noticed peace in my body without effort?
- What do I tend to do when things get quiet?

Then reflect: *What would it mean to believe the quiet could be safe?*

There is no medal for being okay in silence.
No algorithm boost for slow mornings.
No headline that will ever read:
"Woman Wakes Up, Breathes Deeply, Feels Calm for No Particular Reason"

But that's the story your body is writing now.

A life that doesn't require collapse to rest.
A rhythm that allows you to be without earning it.
A way of moving that trusts peace is not a pause —
but a home you can return to.

You may still doubt it.
You may not be able to name it clearly.
But if you've made it this far in the chapter, you're already in it.

Not the crisis.
Not the aftermath.

But the becoming.

> "Your peace was never meant to be performative."
> – *Unknown*

Sometimes, the only way to recognize healing is by noticing what no longer happens.

The fight you don't start.
The apology you don't offer just to smooth discomfort.
The plan you don't make to impress someone who was never really watching.

These are the quiet victories.
And they are easy to miss if you're still measuring progress by how busy or visible you are.

But if you look closely — gently — you'll see them.
In the softening of your tone with yourself.
In the way you choose silence instead of over-explaining.
In the way you let a moment of discomfort pass without trying to control it.

That's peace.
Not perfect.
Not always graceful.

But real.
Embodied.
Yours.

There's a phrase I come back to often, especially when I feel like nothing is "happening":

"Nothing is wasted."

Not the pause.
Not the in-between.

Not the strange, uneventful days that feel too quiet to matter.

Because these are the days where your nervous system re-learns its rhythm.
Where your energy begins to regulate without external crisis.
Where your identity expands beyond pain and purpose into presence.

That matters.

Even if it doesn't make a good story.

Even if no one claps.

Even if all you did today was wake up and not panic.

I want to be honest with you: this phase won't last forever.

This quiet, this re-rooting — it's not the end of your story.
Eventually, you'll feel the spark again.
You'll crave momentum.
You'll get ideas that light you up, desires that stretch your edges, invitations that excite you.

And when that happens, it will feel different than it used to.

Not because you'll be certain.
But because you'll be rooted.

Not in identity.
In *integrity*.

You'll know how to stay home in yourself — even while the world pulls at you.

But you don't need to rush to that next season.
You don't need to "graduate" from this one to be worthy of joy.

There is wisdom here, too.

There is gold buried in the slowness.

And you are allowed to stay until it reveals itself.

A reader once wrote to me after finishing a previous book. She'd just left a long-term partnership, taken a leave of absence from her job, and was sitting alone in her apartment surrounded by blank walls and unanswered texts.

"I think I thought I'd feel more alive," she wrote.

Then, a few weeks later, another message:

"It's not that I feel alive in the big ways.
It's that I'm starting to notice I feel *here*.
I felt the sun through the window today, and for some reason, that mattered."

I keep that note printed on my desk.
Because that's what this book is for.

Not the grand transformations.
But the slow returns.
To the window.
To the warmth.
To yourself.

You may not realize it yet, but this chapter — this season — is when the next version of you begins to form.

Not through effort.
But through permission.

Permission to not know.
Permission to pause.
Permission to want softness more than certainty.

And from that permission, something holy emerges.

Not a new identity.

A new relationship with *being*.

You are not what you do.
You are not what you fix.
You are not how others feel around you.

You are breath.
You are choice.
You are presence.

And that is enough.

Try This: The Presence Prompt

At the start of each day this week, ask yourself:

How can I honour my presence today, without needing it to be productive?

Write down one gentle way:

- Drinking water slowly
- Looking out the window for five minutes without distraction
- Saying no without justification
- Saying yes to rest

Presence is a practice.
And every time you choose it — however quietly — you change the way you live inside your own life.

"Sometimes the bravest thing is choosing to stay when there is nothing left to prove."
— *Brianna Wiest*

Eventually, the quiet starts to feel less like absence and more like invitation.

At first, it was jarring — all that space, all that silence, the sudden absence of people needing you or crises defining you. But over time, something shifts. The emptiness softens. The stillness stops echoing. You begin to notice... there's room.

Room to listen.
Room to feel.
Room to imagine not just what you can survive, but what you might want.

For so long, you've been organizing your life around endurance. Around managing. Around making sure things didn't fall apart. But when you're no longer surviving, you get to start living in a new way. A slower way. A braver way. One rooted not in control — but in *curiosity*.

Curiosity is the antidote to post-survival paralysis.

Not certainty.
Not clarity.
Just gentle wondering.

What do I want to feel more of?
What happens if I don't rush this?
What would softness look like in this moment?

You're not designing a blueprint here. You're starting a dialogue. With your own body. With your present reality. With the parts of you that have been waiting for safety to speak.

This doesn't mean big changes right away.
It might just mean allowing yourself to follow a pull.

Maybe you feel drawn to water, so you drive to the coast and sit without speaking.
Maybe you feel restless at home, so you move a chair, repaint a wall, open a window.
Maybe something inside wants to write, or walk, or sing badly and out of key.

None of these things are dramatic.
And still — they're sacred.
They are signs of reanimation.
Of breath returning to the system.
Of life becoming something chosen, not just endured.

There's a story I once heard about a woman who lost everything in a house fire. And when she stood in front of the ashes, her only words were:
"I didn't know how much I didn't need."

In the weeks that followed, she told no one what she planned to do. She didn't rebuild right away. She rented a room. She walked more. She sat still. She noticed which parts of her grief felt like longing, and which parts felt like liberation.

"I realized," she said, "that what I missed most weren't the objects — but the distractions. The noise.

The rush. Once that was gone, I could finally hear myself think."

Sometimes, what burns away is not your life.
It's your illusion of what life needed to be.

What's left?
You.
More intact than you thought.
More honest than you've ever allowed yourself to be.

And that's where this chapter has been leading you.

Not to some grand proclamation.
Not to a reinvention.
But to this simple truth:

You get to live differently now.

Not because you've solved everything.
Not because you've transcended suffering.
But because you've stopped believing that life has to hurt in order to count.

That is the deepest shift of all.

To know that joy does not need to be repaid.
That stillness does not need to be justified.
That healing is not a prize — it's a permission slip.

You can feel good now.
Not when it's earned.
Now.

Even in a world that still hurts.
Even with pieces still undone.

Try This: The Soft Future Letter

Write a letter from your future self — six months from now — to your current self. Let it begin with:

"We didn't have to rush. You were already on your way."

Let this future self remind you of what grew slowly.
Let them reflect on the peace you made with the quiet.
Let them tell you about the life you're still unfolding into — not as a destination, but as a devotion.

Keep the letter somewhere private.
Read it on the days you forget that progress can feel like stillness.
On the days you doubt that you're becoming something beautiful — simply by being here.

> "The moment you accept yourself, you begin to truly live."
> *– Carl Jung*

Letting go is not a single act.
It's a rhythm.
A loosening that continues long after the decision is made.
And just as important as the release itself... is the way we *live afterward*.

This chapter has been a doorway — not into a new identity, but into the quiet space where identity is allowed to unfold without performance.
You've been invited to meet yourself without the Armor.
Without the narrative.
Without the rush.

Maybe for the first time in your life, you're no longer reacting.
You're responding.
Not to pressure, not to panic — but to presence.

This is what the aftermath offers:
Not a void.
But a field.

Not emptiness.
But space.
Fertile. Alive. Open.

And in this field, you are allowed to grow slowly.

It takes courage to stay here.

To not fill your time just to feel important.
To not chase a new goal just to prove you've moved on.
To not silence the quiet because you've been conditioned to fear what it might reveal.

But here's the promise:

If you let it, this stillness will reshape you.

Not into someone stronger.
But into someone softer.
Not into someone better.
But someone *truer*.

You don't need to go back to who you were.
And you don't need to leap into who you'll become.

You just need to be here.

Right now.
Breathing.
Belonging.
Beginning again.

So what comes after the letting go?

A breath.
A rest.
A reconnection to the ground beneath you.

What comes next is not a plan.
It's a pulse.

A small yes, deep in your chest.
A quiet knowing that even now — even here — you are whole.

You are not late.
You are not lost.
You are simply learning how to live without a cage.

And that, beloved, is freedom.

Reflection Page

Pause Here

- What have I stopped holding onto — mentally, emotionally, or physically — in the last year?
- How do I relate to stillness? What emotions come up when I slow down?
- What's one way I can honour this quieter season, instead of trying to escape it?

Try This

A Gentle Practice for the Week Ahead

Set aside one hour in your week with *no agenda*.

No scrolling.
No cleaning.
No planning or fixing or filling.

Let it be your hour of holy idleness.
Notice what rises.
Notice what softens.
Notice what your body does when no one is demanding anything of it.

Then — instead of reacting — simply *be*.

Even if it's awkward.
Even if it's unfamiliar.
Even if you forget halfway through and start folding laundry.

Come back to the hour.

It's yours.

> "After a while, you learn that peace isn't a place you arrive.
> It's something you practice — in the in-between, in the ordinary, in the still."
> — *Let It Be*

This is where we begin.

In the quiet that doesn't need to be filled.
In the pause between release and becoming.
In the honest, untidy, beautiful space where you no longer have to be who you were — and you don't yet need to know who you'll be.

Let this chapter stay with you.

Come back to it whenever the noise creeps in again.
Whenever urgency feels like safety.
Whenever the world tells you that stillness is laziness, or that you need to prove your worth with speed.

You've already let go.

Now — you get to *be*.

CHAPTER 2
THE ART OF ENOUGH

2. The Art of Enough

Core Focus: Releasing the myth of more, learning to feel full, anchoring in sufficiency

We live in a culture that thrives on hunger.

Be more.
Do more.
Achieve, fix, improve.
There is always something missing, something lacking, something just out of reach — and it is your job, apparently, to chase it.

So we do.

We chase productivity to feel useful.
We chase perfection to feel lovable.
We chase the next version of ourselves, hoping that once we get there, *then* we'll be worthy of rest.

But here's what no one says out loud:

The finish line keeps moving.

No matter how much you do.
No matter how much you give.
No matter how much you upgrade or heal or optimize — it is never enough for a system that profits from your emptiness.

And at some point, if you're lucky, you get tired.
Not from failure.
From *futility*.

From running a race you never signed up for.

Enoughness is a radical idea.

It says:
You are not a project.
You are not behind.
You do not have to earn your place in this world through output.

But to believe that — to truly believe that — you must unlearn decades of conditioning.
The kind that told you your value is based on your usefulness.
The kind that told you quiet days are lazy days.
The kind that mistook relentless striving for strength.

And here's the twist: this myth doesn't just live in your mind.
It lives in your body.

It shows up in the tension in your shoulders when you sit still too long.
In the guilt that rises when you cancel a plan and do nothing instead.
In the way you apologize for needing a break, as if exhaustion were a moral failing.

Enoughness isn't something you *understand*.
It's something you *practice*.
And like all practices, it begins awkwardly.

When I first began working with the idea of sufficiency — truly living as though I was already enough — I thought it would feel liberating.

But honestly?

It felt like failure.

Without my endless improvement projects, I didn't know who I was.
Without my goals, I felt directionless.
Without a reason to hustle, I felt useless.

I thought I wanted rest.
What I really wanted was permission.

Permission to stop.
To soften.
To not be *better*.

But that kind of permission doesn't come from outside.
It comes from the moment you realize there is no trophy for burning out.
No gold star for proving you're invincible.

Just your body.
Tired.

Waiting.
Asking if this could be the day you stop running.

I once met a man who had built an entire life around proving he was enough.

Every degree, every promotion, every relationship — all of it was part of a silent campaign to outrun the voice in his head that whispered, *You have to earn love.*

When he finally sat across from me, newly retired and emotionally raw, he said something I'll never forget:

"I did everything they told me would make me whole. But I still feel like I'm borrowing my own life."

Borrowing.

That word gutted me.

Because how many of us are doing the same?

Waiting to feel like this life is *really* ours — once we've achieved enough, pleased enough, proved enough?

Enoughness, it turns out, isn't a destination.
It's a reckoning.

A choice to stop outsourcing your worth to your achievements.
A decision to believe that you are already whole — even if you're still healing.

Try This: The Enough List

Write down five things you did this week that no one saw.

Small things. Mundane things.
Like drinking water before coffee.
Or choosing not to snap at your partner.
Or replying gently to an email that made your stomach twist.

Now sit with that list and say — aloud, if you can:

"This was enough. I was enough."

It will feel weird at first.
Say it anyway.

The body needs repetition to believe what the mind has forgotten.

> "Enough is a feast."
> – *Buddhist proverb*

There's a moment, subtle and almost forgettable, when you realize you didn't reach for more.

You finished your meal and didn't go back for seconds out of boredom.
You completed your task and didn't fill the next hour with another list.
You stopped scrolling without trying to escape a feeling.

These aren't revolutionary acts, not at first glance.
But they are signals.
That something inside you is changing.

That maybe — just maybe — you are learning to recognize fullness.

Not as a reward.
Not as perfection.
But as presence.

Fullness is hard to trust when you've been trained to doubt it.

We're taught from a young age that there's always a better version of us just around the corner.
More toned.
More focused.
More enlightened.
More lovable.

And if you just buy this product, follow this method, take this course, or read this one last book — *then* you'll finally arrive.

But the truth is: there is no arrival.
Not in the way we've been promised.

You don't become enough.
You *remember* that you already were.

That remembrance — that embodied knowing — is not dramatic.
It's quiet.
It's the way your shoulders relax when you stop trying to impress anyone.
It's the way your voice softens when you stop defending your choices.
It's the way your breath deepens when you stop chasing approval.

Enoughness lives in the body, not the ego.

I once knew woman named Joy, who'd been in recovery for years.
Recovery from addiction, yes — but also from perfectionism, from performance, from a lifetime of overachieving in the name of worth.

She told me this story:

"One day I made soup.
Just soup.

I didn't turn it into a dinner party.
I didn't take a photo.
I didn't serve it with artisanal bread or a story about my grandmother.
I made soup. I ate it. I sat down.
And I didn't feel like I needed to do anything else to deserve the rest of my evening."

That's what this chapter is about.

Not soup.

But *enough*.

The quiet revolution of ordinary sufficiency.
The way it sneaks in and reorients you toward presence.

We don't heal by becoming more.

We heal by remembering less is enough.

Less fixing.
Less proving.
Less contorting ourselves into palatable shapes.

Enoughness doesn't mean you stop growing.
It means you stop growing in ways that betray yourself.

You can still evolve.
You can still change and stretch and expand.

But from love.
Not from lack.

There's a big difference.

One says: *I am whole, and this growth is sacred.*
The other says: *I am not okay until I become something better.*

Enoughness invites you to root in the former.
To grow as a tree does — from the inside out, not the outside in.

So many of us walk through the world with an invisible meter running above our heads.

It tallies what we've done.
What we've said.
How we looked.
How much we helped.
Whether we smiled enough, achieved enough, stayed quiet enough.

And when the meter feels too low, we hustle.
We add.
We scramble for something that will boost the number.

But the truth is, there is no meter.
There never was.

You are not an app to be upgraded.
You are not a spreadsheet to be optimized.
You are not a machine to be made efficient.

You are a living body.
A soul with breath.
A person who is allowed to take up space — even on the days you accomplish nothing remarkable.

Try This: The Body Check of Enough

Place your hand on your heart. Close your eyes.
Ask your body — not your mind — this question:

"What would it feel like to be enough right now?"

Let the answer rise. It may not come in words.

It might come as:

- A deeper breath
- A release of tension in your jaw
- The urge to lie down
- Tears

Whatever it is — honour it.
That is your body speaking a language older than striving.

Reflection Questions

- What do I usually tie my sense of worth to?
- What would it mean to be *enough* even when I'm not being productive, useful, or impressive?
- Where in my life am I already enough, but afraid to believe it?

"You are not a problem to be solved."
— *S. M. Keyte*

Enough isn't flashy.

It doesn't post well.
It doesn't get standing ovations.
It doesn't come with a before-and-after photo.

And maybe that's why so many of us miss it.

Because we were taught to recognize value in volume — how much we do, how much we give, how much we prove. We were praised for overextension. We were admired for how much we could carry without breaking.

And somewhere along the way, *too much* became normal.
The goal.
The proof.

But here's the truth: Enough is not a performance.
It's a posture.

It's the way your spine aligns when you're no longer bending over backwards for approval.
The way your voice drops into your chest when you speak without apology.
The way your day feels when it ends without burnout — and you don't call that laziness, you call it balance.

A mother I once worked with told me, "I realized I didn't know how to play with my kids without also folding laundry."

She wasn't being dramatic. She was being honest.

Sufficiency had never been modelled for her — not as a child, not as a student, not as a woman. There was always a subtext of *Do more. Be more. Give more.*

So even when the moment called for presence — the floor scattered with blocks, her son offering her a toy phone and calling her from three feet away — some part of her couldn't sit still.
Couldn't believe stillness had value.
Couldn't believe play was productive.

We talked about how radical it is to pause without guilt.
To give your presence instead of your labour.
To believe that simply being in the room — fully, gently, openly — is enough.

And not just for others.
For *yourself*.

You might be carrying a silent fear right now.

That if you stop striving, you'll stop mattering.
That if you stop pushing, something will fall apart.
That if you rest, the world will forget you.

But listen to me:

Your worth is not conditional.
It's not a subscription service.

It does not need to be renewed each month with productivity and perfect behaviour.

You are allowed to pause.
To pull back.
To turn down the volume without turning down your value.

There's nothing noble about exhaustion.
There's nothing admirable about resentment dressed up as self-sacrifice.

Enough means enough.

Enough love. Enough space. Enough time. Enough energy.

And most of all?
Enough you.

When we stop chasing the mirage of more, something surprising happens.

We start noticing how beautiful life already is.

Not perfect. Not polished. Not curated.

But real.

The mess of an unmade bed that holds a body learning how to slow down.
The crumbs on the counter after a quiet meal eaten without distraction.

The voice that cracks during an honest conversation because it's been silenced for too long.

Sufficiency is what lets you see that these small, quiet, human things — they *count*.

They count in ways your calendar can't measure.
They count in ways that don't go viral.
They count because *you* are the one who lived them, breathed them, felt them.

And your presence is enough to make them sacred.

A client named Rowan shared something during a session I'll never forget.

He was in recovery from a long season of burnout, trying to redefine success on his own terms.

He said, "I realized I'd spent years building a life I wasn't even home for."

Every goal had been a way to outrun the present. Every task a way to distract from the feeling that no matter how much he achieved, it never quieted the ache.

Until one day, he stopped.

He sat on the floor of his apartment with a cup of tea and no agenda.
And he cried.
Because he was there.

And it was quiet.
And for the first time, he felt like he belonged in his own life.

Not because he had earned it.
But because he had *returned* to it.

That is the art of enough.
It is not loud.
It is not viral.
It is the quiet relief of finally being home in your own body.

"There is no shame in being full."
– *Your future self*

Try This: "I Release the Need to…"

Take out a sheet of paper and at the top, write:

"I release the need to…"

Then finish the sentence as many times as you can, without editing.

I release the need to…

- Prove I'm okay
- Be productive when I'm tired
- Apologize for my softness
- Say yes when I mean no
- Know exactly where I'm going

Then read it aloud — slowly.
Feel how each line loosens the grip just a little.

You don't have to carry what you were never meant to hold.

Enoughness isn't just a concept.
It's a confrontation.

To live as though you are already enough means you must untangle yourself from the systems — and sometimes the relationships — that rely on your self-doubt.

You'll start to notice the places where your worth was transactional.
Where you were celebrated for self-abandonment.
Where love came with conditions: Be good. Be impressive. Be useful.

And when you stop meeting those conditions?

Some people won't applaud your peace.
Some systems won't reward your rest.
Some roles won't function when you stop playing small.

That's part of the grief of enoughness.

Not just the letting go of "more,"
But the letting go of the identity that came with it.

You might feel lost for a while.

When you stop over-giving, you'll feel the space where obligation used to live.
When you stop over-explaining, you'll hear the silence where justification used to be.

When you stop overachieving, you'll meet yourself without the Armor of accomplishment.

This is where many people turn back.

Because it's easier to chase worth than sit in the pause.
Easier to strive than to feel.
Easier to hustle than to grieve.

But grief is part of it.

Grief for the years you believed you weren't enough.
Grief for the people who only loved you when you were useful.
Grief for the version of you that survived through striving — even if it hurt.

You don't owe shame to the version of you that coped.
You owe her gratitude.
She kept you alive.

But now?
You get to choose something different.

I remember the first time I deleted a to-do list on purpose.
Not because I finished it — but because I chose not to measure my worth that day by how much I got done.

I thought it would feel empowering.

It felt terrifying.

Without the list, who was I?
Without the checkboxes, what proved I mattered?

I spent the afternoon in a daze, feeling like I was cheating at life.

That's how deeply productivity culture can root itself in our nervous systems.

It makes *rest* feel like rebellion.
It makes *enough* feel like giving up.

But over time, the discomfort softened.

And in its place?
Something slower.
Something quieter.
Something real.

Not every day is productive now.
Some days are just... days.

And that's enough.

We live in a world that constantly reminds you of what you're not.

Not successful enough.
Not thin enough.
Not partnered, popular, healed, happy, spiritual, driven — enough.

And every scroll, every ad, every curated life reminds you:

There's more out there.
More to buy.
More to be.
More to do.

And yet?

None of that is about *you*.

It's about keeping you insecure.
Because insecurity sells.

It keeps you engaged, striving, spending, and trying.

But when you pause — when you truly, radically believe you are enough as you are — something breaks.

Not inside you.
Around you.

The illusion shatters.

And in that moment, the world stops being a mirror for your lack.
It becomes a canvas for your peace.

Try This: The Enough Mantra

Choose one of the following statements and repeat it softly to yourself each morning for a week. You can say it in the mirror, while brushing your teeth, or in silence before opening your laptop:

- "I do not need to prove anything today."
- "My value is not measured by my output."
- "I am enough, even when I do less."
- "My rest is allowed."
- "I trust the worth of my presence."

Let it feel awkward.
Then let it feel true.

Because the body remembers what the world taught you to forget.

Reflection Questions

- What identity do I hold that's tied to being "more"?
- What part of me is afraid to stop striving?
- Who benefits when I believe I am not enough? Who suffers when I start to believe I am?

"Your enoughness was never up for debate. You just lived in a world that acted like it was."
– S. M. Keyte

There's a difference between scarcity and simplicity.

Scarcity says: *You don't have enough, and you're not enough, so hurry up and fix it.*
Simplicity says: *What if this is already okay?*

Scarcity scrambles.
Simplicity slows.

Scarcity chases.
Simplicity listens.

Scarcity is what you inherited.
Simplicity is what you can choose.

Enoughness lives in that choice.

I once sat across from someone who'd spent years "levelling up."
They had the house, the job title, the salary, the lifestyle.
And still — they felt hollow.

They told me, "I kept thinking the next version of my life would finally feel like *mine*. But it never came. I kept levelling up into something that still didn't feel like home."

That's the trap of "next."

It tells you that happiness lives one promotion away. That wholeness is around the corner if you just try a little harder.

That rest is for later.
That peace must be earned.

But what if peace is right here?

Not dramatic.
Not polished.
Just here.

In your hands.
In your breath.
In the room you're already in.

When you start practicing enoughness, the world won't always understand.

Some people will see your rest as laziness.
Your boundaries as selfishness.
Your gentleness as weakness.

Let them.

Let them misunderstand your peace.

You're not here to be legible to people who only value you when you're exhausted.

You're here to be rooted.
Alive.
Whole.

And if someone cannot meet you in that version of yourself, it is not your job to shrink so they can feel comfortable.

You are not too much for this world.
You're just no longer performing lack.

That can be threatening — to the systems, to the dynamics, to the expectations built on your willingness to self-abandon.

But that's not your burden to carry anymore.

Try This: A Simpler Day

Design a day — or a half-day — around the question: *"What would enough look like today?"*

- What would you do less of?
- What would you stop performing?
- Where would you soften?
- How would you know it was a good day, even without external approval?

This isn't a productivity hack.
It's an invitation.

To spend a few hours living as though you are already enough.
And to notice what shifts — internally and externally — when you do.

Enoughness Isn't Complacency

It's worth saying clearly:

You can believe you are enough *and* still want to grow.
You can trust your worth *and* pursue meaningful goals.
You can root into presence *and* move toward change.

But when you grow from a place of worth, the process feels different.

You're not hustling to earn a seat at the table.
You're moving because your wholeness asked to stretch.
You're not afraid of failure, because failure doesn't undo your value.
You're not ruled by shame, because shame is no longer your compass.

Enoughness doesn't freeze you in place.
It frees you.

To create from joy.
To rest without guilt.
To belong to yourself — regardless of who's watching.

Reflection Prompts

- If I believed I was already enough, how would I spend my next day differently?

- What does "more" mean to me — and who taught me that?

- Where do I still equate busyness with value?

"You are not falling behind. You are becoming real."
— @notesfromyourtherapist

There's something that happens when you finally stop running.

At first, it feels like withdrawal.
Like silence after too much noise.
Like stillness that's almost unbearable.

Your nervous system doesn't know what to do without the buzz of constant striving.

You look around your life — same walls, same clothes, same morning routine — and wonder:
Who am I when I'm not chasing anything?

That question is the doorway.

Not into passivity — but into peace.

Not into stagnation — but into sovereignty.

Not into giving up — but into *choosing*.

Because when the performance stops, the truth has space to speak.

You begin to notice what no longer fits.

The clothes that were meant to impress someone else.
The habits shaped by guilt instead of desire.
The schedule designed to earn love you no longer want to beg for.

You start deleting apps that once dictated your self-esteem.

Start saying no without a 14-line explanation.
Start watching the sun set from your own window without feeling like you're missing out.

You don't post about it.
You don't need applause.

You're not proving anything anymore.
You're simply living — as yourself, for yourself.

And that's a quiet kind of liberation most people never get to feel.

Let's name what might rise:

Shame.
Fear.
Confusion.
Grief.

They don't mean you're doing it wrong.
They mean you're doing it *honestly*.

Because becoming someone who believes they are enough is not a gentle unravelling.
It's a confrontation with every lie you were taught to survive by.

The belief that being needed is the same as being loved.
That being perfect is safer than being real.
That being tired is just the price of being important.

Those are the ghosts of not-enoughness.
And they will visit you as you unlearn.

You do not need to fight them.
You only need to not follow them home.

Rewriting the Story: A Mini Exercise

Try this journal prompt:

"The story I was taught about being enough was..."
"The story I'm learning to believe instead is..."

Write freely. Let the old story unravel.

Then — take a deep breath — and write the new one like a love letter to your future self.

Here's one I wrote years ago:

Old Story:
You are only worthy if you're useful.
You are lovable when you are low-maintenance.
You are enough when you are doing more than everyone else.

New Story:
You are worthy because you exist.
You are lovable when you are honest.
You are enough when you are rested, quiet, soft, loud, flawed, healing, and human.

I still whisper that to myself on hard days.
Because healing isn't a destination — it's a practice.
A remembering.

You don't owe anyone the version of you that was built in fear.

You're allowed to grow new roots.
To change your mind.
To need less validation and more peace.

You're allowed to disappoint the narratives that were never written in your voice.

The version of you that slows down — that takes up space without explanation, that says "this is enough for me" — she is not selfish.
She is not small.
She is sacred.

And she's yours.

Reflection Prompts

- What version of me have I outgrown — and what did she teach me?

- What would I no longer do if I fully believed I was enough?

- What does a "peaceful day" look like for me? What's one step I can take toward that now?

"You were never too much. The world just wasn't used to people who know they're whole."
— *Nayyirah Waheed*

Let's talk about contentment.

Not the Instagram version.
Not the curated still life with a caption about gratitude.
But the real thing.

Contentment that whispers, *I have what I need, and I trust what I don't is on its way or unnecessary.*

Contentment that holds space for desire without turning it into desperation.
That makes room for ambition without making you feel hollow when you rest.

This kind of enoughness doesn't come from what you own.
It comes from what you *anchor* in.

And most of us have never been taught how to anchor inside ourselves.

We're taught to measure by comparison.

How am I doing, relative to her?
How fast am I healing, compared to them?
How far have I gotten, and why hasn't it been shared or liked?

It's exhausting.

Comparison is a thief, yes.
But it's also a mirror — one that warps your reflection.

It turns someone else's story into a standard.
Someone else's timeline into a scoreboard.

But you are not here to win.
You are here to *be*.

To be honest.
To be whole.
To be human.

And none of those things come with gold stars.

I remember a conversation with a friend who said, "I feel like I'm behind."

I asked, "Behind what?"

She blinked.
Paused.
Then laughed.

Not because it was funny — but because she realized there was no answer.
She'd been living by an invisible calendar.
An inherited sense of pace.

But behind who?
Behind what?

She didn't know.
None of us really do.

The idea of "falling behind" only exists when life is seen as a race.
But what if it's not?

What if life is a garden?

Would you compare the tulip to the oak tree?
Would you shame the cactus for blooming slower than the wildflower?

No.

You'd let it unfold.
In its own timing.
Its own rhythm.
Its own enoughness.

You are no different.

Try This: Anchoring Ritual

At the start or end of your day, practice this short grounding ritual to anchor into yourself:

1. Sit in stillness. Close your eyes if it feels safe.
2. Place one hand on your chest, one on your belly.
3. Inhale slowly and say inwardly: *I am here.*
4. Exhale slowly and say: *And that is enough.*
5. Repeat for 3-5 breaths.

Let your body believe it.
Let your system settle.
Let enoughness be more than a thought — let it be a sensation.

Enough doesn't mean you don't want more.
It means you aren't *ruled* by lack.

You can still dream.
Still build.
Still pursue what matters.

But not because you're broken.
Not because you're chasing someone else's measure of success.
Not because you're trying to fill a hole.

You're building from wholeness.
Not reaching for it.

That shift?
It changes everything.

Reflection Prompts

- What does contentment feel like in my body? Can I name that sensation?

- What areas of my life are ruled by comparison? How would it feel to release that?

- Who taught me that faster = better? What do I want to believe instead?

"You are not late to your life. You are right on time."
— *Brianna Wiest*

You are allowed to stop chasing.

You are allowed to stop chasing validation, chasing applause, chasing someone else's idea of success.

You are allowed to stop performing worthiness.
To stop proving you're okay by how much you can carry without breaking.

You are allowed to say:

I've had enough of the hustle that steals my joy.

I've had enough of the grind that erases my softness.

I've had enough of defining my value by how quickly I respond, how much I produce, how little I need.

Because this isn't the life you were born for.

You weren't born to burn out.
You were born to live.

Letting yourself feel that truth — even for a moment — can bring tears.

Because it touches the part of you that's been working so hard to be enough, for so long, that she forgot how to *just be*.

That part of you is tired.
She's ready to lay something down.

Let her.

Let her grieve the years she spent proving.
Let her mourn the identity built around self-sacrifice.
Let her unclench.

Then let her rest.

And in that rest, she will remember:

She was always whole.

The Myth of Deservedness

We are steeped in a culture that ties love and rest to deservedness.

You deserve rest if you've worked hard enough.
You deserve softness if you've endured pain.
You deserve peace — but only after you've suffered visibly, righteously, perfectly.

But what if that whole framework is broken?

What if you don't need to *deserve* peace?

What if peace is yours by birthright?

You don't have to bleed for it.
You don't have to earn your way into gentleness.
You don't need to apologize for wanting a life that doesn't fracture you.

That's not laziness.
That's liberation.

Try This: The Enough List

Create a short "Enough List" — no more than 3-5 things — that defines a day as successful *without external validation.*

Your list might look like:

- I moved my body in a way that felt kind.
- I spoke to myself with respect.
- I connected with someone I care about.
- I took a few deep breaths before reacting.
- I let myself pause.

These become your new metrics.
Not likes.
Not inbox zero.
Not crossing 12 things off a list.

Just presence.
Just care.
Just enough.

One of the most radical things you can do is *not need to be impressive.*

To walk into a room and not contort yourself to be palatable.
To choose silence when performance is expected.
To live simply — without apology.

You will not be for everyone.

You will confuse the people who built their identity around productivity.
You will frustrate those who benefit from your burnout.

Let them.

They don't need to understand your peace for it to be real.

You are not a product.
You are not a machine.
You are not an algorithm to optimize.

You are a person.
A soul.
A being.

And that is enough.

Reflection Prompts

- What am I still chasing, and why?
- How would I define a "good day" if no one else ever saw it?
- What can I stop apologizing for, starting now?

"Your worth is not measured by your output. Your worth is immeasurable."
– *Tricia Hersey, The Nap Ministry*

There is a version of you that lives beneath the proving.

A version untouched by comparison.
Unburdened by productivity.
Unmoved by the need to be "on" all the time.

She doesn't hustle for her worth.
She doesn't perform her pain.
She doesn't wait for someone to give her permission to be whole.

She already is.

And she has been quietly waiting for you.
Through every burnout.
Through every identity collapse.
Through every time you said "yes" when your body screamed "please, no."

She's the you that knows:
You don't have to survive your life. You can live it.

When we say "I am enough," we're not just talking about worth.

We're talking about permission.

Permission to choose differently.
To build slowly.
To not monetize every hobby.
To rest without guilt.
To take up space — even when no one claps for it.

That kind of enoughness becomes a compass.

It helps you say:

No, I don't want to keep climbing ladders that lead me away from myself.

No, I won't stay in rooms that require me to shrink.

No, I won't betray my needs to stay acceptable.

And then — the quieter yes:

Yes, I will trust my own timing.

Yes, I will honour what I need before I earn it.

Yes, I will let ease exist.

Try This: The Enough Identity Check-In

Ask yourself:

- What part of my identity was built in survival mode?
- What part of me is still afraid to be "too much" or "not enough"?
- Who do I become when I stop performing and start choosing?

You don't need perfect answers.
Just start the conversation.

The you who's ready for peace is listening.

You may lose people when you stop performing.

The version of you who never asked for anything —
who absorbed every task, every emotional burden —
she likely kept some relationships afloat.

And when you change the terms, some people won't know what to do with you.

Let them be confused.

Your peace is not a negotiation.
Your growth is not a betrayal.
Your boundaries are not a punishment — they are a declaration:

I am not available for the life that asks me to abandon myself.

You don't need to become someone different.
You just need to become more of who you already are — without the masks.

That's the path to enough.

Reflection Prompts

- What would I stop doing today if I believed my identity didn't depend on it?

- What kind of people, spaces, or habits help me feel most like myself?

- Am I willing to let go of what no longer fits, even if it's familiar?

"Your work is not to become someone else. It's to unbecome everything that isn't you, so you can remember who you were before the world told you otherwise."
— *Emily McDowell*

Sometimes, enough sounds like silence.

No more explaining.
No more defending.
No more contorting your story into something easier for others to accept.

Sometimes, enough feels like a full breath — one that doesn't catch in your throat or shrink in your chest.

It's the release of should.
It's the stillness after you've stopped running.
It's the gentleness you offer yourself when no one else is watching.

It's not loud.
Not showy.
Not polished for public consumption.

It's yours.

And it's sacred.

There's a softness that only comes when you stop living on edge.

When you stop bracing.
When you stop being ready to fight for your worth.
When you stop waiting for the world to catch up to your healing.

You learn to create enoughness inside.

You learn to trust it.

And in that trust, something else grows.

Joy.

Not the fleeting kind.
But the rooted kind — the kind that blooms even in hard soil, because it's not dependent on circumstance.

It's born of wholeness.

Let This Be a Reframe

Enough doesn't mean settling.
It doesn't mean resignation or stagnation.

It means this:

I am no longer driven by fear.

I can want more — and not loathe where I am.
I can evolve — without needing to hate who I've been.

I can stay soft in a world that demands sharp edges.
I can protect my peace without hardening my heart.

I am not behind.
I am not broken.
I am not missing anything.

I am enough.

Try This: Daily "Enough" Ritual

Each morning for one week, try starting your day with a single affirmation:

Today, I am enough for what this day requires.

Then ask:

- What would it look like to live from that belief today?
- How would I move?
- What would I choose to let go of?

Keep a short note at the end of each day. You may be surprised how much shifts when you stop needing to become someone else — and start inhabiting yourself more deeply.

Integration: Living the Art of Enough

- Revisit your Enough List regularly. Let it evolve with you.

- Pay attention to the moments when joy arrives unannounced. Those are often signs of alignment.

- Consider what narratives still tell you that you're not enough. Who benefits from them? Are you ready to rewrite them?

This chapter isn't about "fixing" your relationship with yourself.
It's about ending the war.

You're allowed to have needs.
You're allowed to rest.
You're allowed to be full and flawed and still worthy of peace.

Let this be your beginning.

> "She remembered who she was and the game changed."
> – Lalah Delia

CHAPTER 3

BEING OKAY WHEN YOU DON'T KNOW

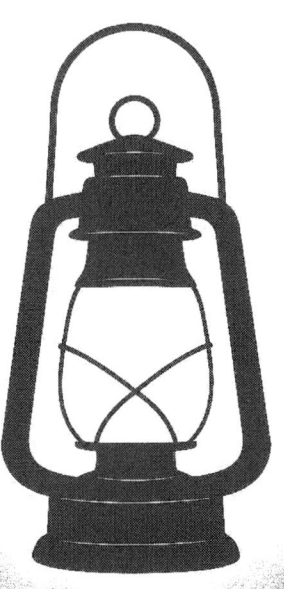

3. Being Okay When You Don't Know

There's a moment — maybe you know it — when the ground gives way under everything you thought was certain.

The job you thought you'd stay in.
The relationship you thought would last.
The version of yourself you thought you were becoming.

Gone.

Or not gone, exactly. Just... shapeless.
No longer clear. No longer solid.

And suddenly, you're here — suspended in between.
No longer who you were.
Not yet who you're becoming.

It's disorienting.

You keep reaching for a map.
A plan.
A certainty.
Anything to hold onto.

But the truth of this chapter is: there's nothing to hold but yourself.

This is the ache of not knowing.

And it is one of the hardest, holiest places a human can stand.

Because we've been trained to solve.
To decide.
To answer quickly and clearly and with confidence.

Ambiguity is treated like a flaw.
Doubt is considered weak.
Waiting is seen as wasting time.

So when you find yourself in the fog — unsure, unanchored, undone — the instinct is to rush out of it.

Fix this.
Figure it out.
Find a way forward. Now.

But what if the fog has something to teach you?

What if clarity isn't the goal — yet?

What if the not-knowing is sacred?

There's an old metaphor:
When a caterpillar enters the chrysalis, it doesn't sprout wings right away.

It melts.

Its entire identity dissolves into genetic soup.

The cells that once made up legs, and body, and form — they break down completely.

There is no caterpillar anymore.
There is no butterfly yet.

Just the mess.

Just the in-between.

And if you tried to rush the process — if you ripped open the cocoon too soon — the wings wouldn't form.

Because the transformation needs the dark.

It needs the not-knowing.

You, too, are allowed to be soup for a while.

Not decided.
Not clear.
Not defined.

Just present.

That is enough.

You are allowed to be a human mid-metamorphosis.

You are allowed to rest in the not-yet.

But how do you do that, really?

How do you stay grounded when you don't know what's next?

You breathe.

You soften.

You stop demanding answers.

You start practicing presence.

And slowly, piece by piece, you build a life that doesn't collapse in the absence of clarity.

A life that can hold space for the question marks.

Try This: The "Name the Fog" Practice

When you're overwhelmed by uncertainty, pause and write down:

1. What you *do* know, even if it's small.
2. What is *uncertain* — what part of the story isn't clear yet?
3. What is *not yours* to control?

Sometimes, seeing it written down brings a kind of relief.
You realize the unknown is smaller than your fear.
And even when it's big — at least now you've met it with honesty, not panic.

You don't need to know everything.

You don't need to know the timeline, the next step, or the reason why.

Sometimes you just need to know the next breath.
The next kind thing to do for yourself.
The next soft place to land.

Let that be enough — for now.

We tend to think peace comes from answers.

If I just knew what was going to happen…
If I just had a plan…
If I could just make the decision now…

But peace doesn't come from control.

It comes from relationship — with the moment, not the outcome.

When you stop demanding certainty, you start noticing something else:
The world keeps turning anyway.
Your body still breathes.
The sun still rises.

Not because you controlled it — but because life doesn't require your certainty to continue.

This is not a dismissal of your fear.
It's an invitation to trust that you can be held even when you don't understand how.

The Fear Beneath the Fog

Often, our resistance to not-knowing isn't about the unknown itself.

It's about what we fear it might mean.

If I don't know what's next... does that mean I'm failing?
If I haven't figured it out yet... does that mean I never will?
If I don't choose now... will I miss my chance?

The fear beneath uncertainty is rarely logical.
It's primal.
Rooted in childhood, in trauma, in the deep belief that safety depends on control.

So start there.

Name the fear.

Not to solve it.
But to see it clearly — so it doesn't quietly drive every decision you make.

Try This: The "And" Reframe

When you're in the unknown, reframe the moment with the word "and."

For example:

- *I don't know what's next, and I can still care for myself today.*
- *I feel overwhelmed, and I can still choose rest.*
- *I'm afraid, and I'm still here.*

"And" lets both things exist.

It softens the edges of urgency.
It reminds you: you are allowed to feel unsure *and* still show up.

You are not a problem to solve.
And neither is your uncertainty.

You are a living, changing, evolving being.
And that means you will have seasons of fog.
Not because you've failed — but because you are becoming.

And becoming takes time.

Be patient with the version of you that is still finding her way.

She doesn't need your judgment.
She needs your kindness.

Letting go of needing to know doesn't mean giving up.

It means surrendering your attachment to timeline.
To perfection.
To clarity as a prerequisite for action.

It means moving forward with grace — even if you're moving slowly.
Even if you're moving in spirals.
Even if you're still afraid.

That is strength.

That is trust.

That is the art of being okay — even here, even now.

Reflection Prompts

- What am I pressuring myself to figure out right now? Why?

- What is the cost of waiting until everything is "certain" before I move?

- How might I soften my relationship with this season of not-knowing?

"You don't have to have it all figured out to move forward."
— S. M. Keyte

Some of the best decisions you'll ever make won't come from certainty.

They'll come from alignment.

From the quiet knowing in your body that doesn't shout — it whispers.
From a pull toward peace that doesn't come with a checklist.
From the gentle yes that doesn't need to explain itself.

And here's the paradox:
You often don't find that alignment by trying to force it.

You find it by listening.
By waiting without rushing.
By staying close to yourself while the answers take shape.

This is the art of being okay without resolution.

A Story: The Man and the Rope Bridge

A man stood at the edge of a mountain, looking across to the other side.
Between him and the destination hung a long, swaying rope bridge, disappearing into fog.

He hesitated.
What if the bridge wasn't stable?
What if the other side wasn't what he hoped for?

He waited for the fog to clear.
Waited for the wind to calm.
Waited for some sign it would be okay.

But nothing changed.

Eventually, an older traveller approached and smiled.

"You don't need to see the whole bridge," she said.
"You only need to trust the next step."

He took a breath.

And stepped forward.

Not because he knew.
But because he was ready to find out.

That's what this season is like.

A rope bridge into the unknown.
No guarantee. No map. No applause.

But you keep walking anyway — because something in you is ready.

Not certain. Not fearless.
Just ready.

Try This: Three Truths Grounding Practice

When you feel lost in the unknown, try saying these three simple truths out loud:

1. *This moment is real.*
2. *I am allowed to not know.*
3. *I am still okay.*

Say them slowly.
Let your body feel them.
Let your nervous system soften.

You don't have to believe them fully for them to work.
You just have to try them on.

There is a kind of strength that doesn't announce itself.

It looks like this:

- Showing up for your day without answers.
- Making breakfast even when your future is blurry.
- Choosing compassion over control.
- Resting without needing to earn it.
- Asking for help — or just sitting with your own company.

That's the quiet courage of living in the question.

And it matters more than you think.

Reflection Prompts

- What quiet truths do I already know — even if I don't have the full picture?

- What is one small way I can honour where I am, without trying to escape it?

- If I trusted that clarity would come in time, how would I treat myself differently?

"I have learned that faith means trusting in advance what will only make sense in reverse."
– *Philip Yancey*

There's a tendency — especially among high achievers, healers, and recovering perfectionists — to make not knowing feel like failure.

Like you should've figured this out by now.
Like clarity is proof you're doing life "right."
Like uncertainty means you missed a step somewhere along the way.

But what if not knowing isn't a mistake?
What if it's part of the cycle?

Like winter.

Still.
Quiet.
Unyielding.

But underneath? A stirring.

Roots growing deeper.
Systems resting.
Life preparing for a return you cannot yet see.

You don't criticize the tree for being bare in winter.
You trust that it's still alive.

Can you offer yourself that same trust?

When Nothing Makes Sense Yet

There will be moments when the story doesn't line up.
When nothing clicks.
When the job, the relationship, the plan — all feel misaligned and no longer yours.

And yet, the next version of life hasn't arrived either.

This in-between is not evidence of failure.

It's evidence that you're shedding.
Growing.
Reorienting.

And that takes time.

There is wisdom in this waiting.
But you have to listen differently.
You can't listen with your urgency.
You have to listen with your presence.

Try This: "If I Knew Nothing Was Wrong..."

When you're spiralling in not-knowing, ask:

If I knew nothing was wrong, what would I allow myself to feel?

Often, we suppress our natural emotions — grief, confusion, anger, wonder — because we believe they're signs of dysfunction.

But what if they're signs of being alive?

What if the only thing "wrong" is the pressure to understand everything too soon?

Give yourself permission to *not rush back into knowing*.

That's where your peace lives — not in solving, but in softening.

You are not behind.
You are not broken.
You are not missing the point.

You are between chapters.
You are in the turning.
You are in the sacred pause between inhale and exhale.

Let it be what it is.
Not a setback.
A space.

A resting place.
A moment before the next beginning.

Reflection Prompts

- What do I believe about myself when I don't have answers? Are those beliefs kind or cruel?

- What evidence do I have that uncertainty has led to growth in the past?

- Can I name something beautiful I only discovered *after* a season of not-knowing?

"We do not grow absolutely, chronologically. We grow sometimes in one dimension, and not in another. Unevenly. We grow partially. We are relative. We are mature in one realm, childish in another. The past, present, and future mingle and pull us backward, forward, or fix us in the present. We are made up of layers, cells, constellations."
– Anaïs Nin

The most loving thing you can do for yourself in this season isn't forcing an answer.

It's offering stability *in the absence* of one.

That might look like:

- Keeping a morning ritual even if your job is uncertain.
- Getting outside for ten minutes a day even when you feel directionless.
- Making your bed not because you know where you're going — but because you're still here.

These are acts of groundedness.

They remind your nervous system: I may not know everything, but I am safe *enough* in this moment.

And that kind of safety changes everything.

There's a part of you that believes the next version of your life depends on having everything sorted.

But it doesn't.

It depends on your willingness to show up — in truth, in tenderness, in transition.

You are still becoming.

Even when the path isn't clear.
Even when you're scared.
Even when it feels like nothing is happening.

The becoming is still happening.

Silently.
Softly.
In the background of your day.

You don't always see it until later.
But it's real.

Try This: The "Anchor Five" Practice

Write down five small things you can do each day — regardless of how clear or uncertain life feels. These aren't about productivity. They're about anchoring.

Examples:

1. Drink water as a ritual, not a chore.
2. Step outside and name three things you can see.
3. Put on music that soothes you.
4. Text someone you trust with no need to be profound.
5. Speak one gentle sentence to yourself in the mirror.

When nothing feels stable, these practices give your body a signal: *We're okay. We can stay.*

You are allowed to take up space — even when you don't know what your "next step" is.

You are allowed to pause.
To rest.
To be unsure.

Because uncertainty is not the opposite of worth.
It is not a suspension of your value.
It is simply a part of being human.

And you are allowed to be fully human — even in the fog.

Reflection Prompts

- What do I tend to do when I feel unsure — and does it serve me?

- What would it look like to support my body *instead* of pressuring it?

- What can I anchor into this week, even if the big questions remain unanswered?

"There is more wisdom in your body than in your deepest philosophy."
– *Friedrich Nietzsche*

There's a strange kind of grief that arises in the unknown.

Not because you've lost something tangible — but because you've lost the illusion of control.
The version of the future you imagined.
The identity you were building around what you thought would happen.

And grief, in all its forms, deserves a place at your table.

Let it in.

Let it speak.

Let it say: *I miss the version of me who thought she knew.*

Because she was trying.
And you can love her for that — without needing to cling to her story anymore.

One of the most liberating things you can do is say aloud:

"I don't know who I am here yet."

Not as confession.
But as declaration.

You are shedding.

And it's okay that you don't yet know what's coming in to take its place.

You are in sacred territory — between identity and emergence.

And every moment you stay here — breathing, softening, staying kind — is part of the new foundation being built.

Try This: "Write from the Fog" Exercise

Open a journal or blank page and begin with the sentence:
"I don't know..."

Then just keep writing.

Let yourself pour out every uncertainty.
Every "what if," every "I wish I knew," every question swirling around in your chest.

No censoring. No fixing.

Just name it.

And then — after a page or two — begin a new paragraph:
"But here's what I do know..."

Write three small truths.
They don't have to be big.

Maybe just:

- I'm still breathing.

- I showed up to write this.

- I want to be gentle with myself.

That's enough.
That's where your center begins again.

There is beauty in the unravelling.

Not because it feels good.
But because it clears space.

Space for new values.
Space for deeper alignment.
Space for a life that fits who you're becoming — not who you were told to be.

You are not lost.
You are in motion.

And even now, your truth is still holding you.

There's a gentler kind of wisdom that only comes from not knowing.

Not the kind that shouts from mountaintops.
The kind that sits beside you in silence.
The kind that doesn't fix you — but *witnesses* you.

When you stop fighting the fog, you realize something:
The fog holds things, too.

Like patience.
And humility.
And the memory of what it means to be human.

You can be wise and unsure.
Brave and confused.
Soft and still strong.

The old rules said you had to pick.

But they lied.

The unknown isn't just a place of waiting — it's a portal.

One you walk through, not around.

It's a place where the old stories lose their power, and the new ones aren't quite formed.

And while that liminal space might feel empty, it's actually full of possibility.

Not in the loud, motivational sense.

But in the quiet knowing:
You are more than who you were.
You are not yet who you will be.
And right now, you are allowed to rest in-between.

This is not delay.
It's transformation.

You don't need to rush back to knowing.

You need to learn how to *be* here.
To sit with yourself without judgment.
To ask: *What does this moment require?* — instead of *What do I have to figure out?*

Sometimes, the most sacred thing you can do is nothing.

Let stillness answer questions that words cannot.

Let quiet hold what clarity hasn't yet revealed.

You are not failing because it's slow.

You are becoming because it is.

Reflection Prompts

- What parts of me feel like they're dissolving right now? Can I let that be okay?
- What helps me stay grounded when answers aren't available?
- What rituals, rhythms, or practices help me honour this "middle" space?

"To be fully alive, fully human, and completely awake is to be continually thrown out of the nest."
— *Pema Chödrön*

Let's say it clearly:

Not knowing doesn't make you less wise.
Not having answers doesn't make you less worthy.
Not feeling certain doesn't mean you're not on the right path.

There is no timeline for becoming.
No syllabus for healing.
No grade for how gracefully you navigate uncertainty.

Your only task is to stay with yourself.

To choose presence over panic.
To choose softness over strategy.
To choose showing up — over showing off.

Even when the world demands proof, performance, a plan —
You can choose *peace* instead.

So much of our suffering in uncertainty comes from labelling it as *bad*.

But what if it isn't?

What if not knowing is simply a different kind of knowing — one that doesn't speak in answers, but in sensations?

One that asks:

- Where does this feeling live in your body?

- What softens when you stop resisting it?

- What are you ready to lay down — not because you've figured it out, but because you're done carrying it?

That's wisdom, too.

It doesn't wear a lab coat.
It doesn't carry a checklist.
It wears pyjamas and breathes deeply.

It trusts.

Try This: "What's True Right Now?" Body Check-In

Once a day, pause wherever you are.
Close your eyes.
Place a hand on your chest, belly, or both.
Breathe.

Then ask:
What's true right now?

Not what you *should* feel.
Not what you *wish* was true.

Just the truth of this moment.

Examples:

- "I feel unsure, but I also feel grounded."
- "I'm tired, but I'm still here."
- "I'm afraid, and I'm also curious."

Let the truth be messy.
Let it breathe.

Let it guide you back to presence — even without resolution.

You don't need to narrate the unknown for others.
You don't have to perform clarity for the sake of making people comfortable.
You don't have to justify your confusion.

You are not required to know before you're ready.

Give yourself permission to take up space exactly where you are.

Because *this* version of you — this present, real, honest version — is still whole.

Even in the fog.
Even in the silence.
Even in the waiting.

Reflection Prompts

- How do I usually respond to uncertainty? Can I experiment with a different response?

- What helps me feel safe — even when I don't have clarity?

- What would it feel like to let uncertainty *belong* — not just as a problem, but as part of my process?

```
"I have no special talent. I am only
      passionately curious."
         - Albert Einstein
```

Let's imagine a life where you don't have to hustle for certainty.

Where the pressure to perform clarity dissolves.
Where confusion isn't a flaw — just a state.

In that life, you don't rush the fog.
You light a candle inside it.

You let the moment be what it is:
Unfinished.
Unclear.
Still enough.

Because here's the secret you don't get told enough:

You don't have to wait until you "figure it all out" to feel okay.
You can be okay *within* the not-knowing.

That's what peace really means.
It's not the absence of questions.
It's the presence of compassion — even while they're still unanswered.

What If the Fog is Fertile?

You've been taught to fear the fog.

To treat uncertainty as a threat.
To solve it. Escape it. Conquer it.

But what if the fog is where the real growth happens?

It doesn't look like progress.
It looks like stillness.
It feels like softness.
It sounds like silence.

But inside that space?

Things are shifting.
Roots are deepening.
Old patterns are being gently unlearned.

This isn't wasted time.
This is integration.

You don't have to see the seed sprout to believe it's becoming something.

Try This: A Letter to Your Future Self

Take 10 quiet minutes.
Sit somewhere safe.
No pressure. No answers needed.

And write to the version of you who *does* know — even if you don't yet.

Begin with:

"I don't know where this is going. But here's what I hope you remember…"

Let it be messy.
Let it be real.
Let it hold your gentleness.

Then seal the letter.
Tuck it away.
Set a reminder for 6 months from now to open it.

Sometimes, your future self is not waiting to be discovered — she's waiting to be *trusted*.

When the world asks you to perform certainty, you can choose a different truth.

You can say:

- I don't have the answers.
- I'm still becoming.
- I am allowed to take my time.

And not as an apology.
But as an act of self-respect.

Because your truth doesn't owe anyone polish.

And your becoming doesn't need an audience — only your attention.

Reflection Prompts

- What if I stopped seeing the fog as a failure — and started seeing it as fertile?
- What are three ways I can support myself this week without needing answers?
- If I trusted that something beautiful was unfolding beneath the surface, how might I treat myself differently?

There's a quiet kind of courage in staying with the questions.

Not running.
Not fixing.
Not distracting yourself into numbness.

Just breathing into the not-knowing.
Letting it be part of the sacred.
Letting it soften you instead of shatter you.

Because the truth is: life will always contain unknowns.

But you don't have to be afraid of them.

You can learn to make peace with the pause.
You can learn to sit in the space between the inhale and the exhale.
You can learn to live light — even while you wait.

Becoming Your Own Steady Ground

If there's one gift this chapter can offer, it's this:

You can become your own steady ground.

Not because you never shake — but because you trust yourself to return.

You trust that you are resilient.
You trust that you are evolving.
You trust that you don't need every answer to be okay today.

And that trust?
It builds something beautiful.

It builds a life that isn't dependent on certainty to feel meaningful.

A life that breathes with change.
A life that bends without breaking.
A life that flows, and rests, and *stays* — even when it's hard.

That's the kind of life you're allowed to choose now.

Final Reflection Prompts for Chapter 3

- What version of "being okay" am I ready to redefine for myself?

- How can I make space for both uncertainty and self-compassion in my daily life?

- What rhythms or rituals would help me return to presence — even when nothing feels clear?

"You do not have to know where you are going to be exactly where you're meant to be."
— Morgan Harper Nichols

Integration Tool: "The Presence Pocket"

Create a physical or digital space (a journal, a folder, a box) where you keep reminders of your capacity to endure uncertainty.

Include:

- Notes to yourself
- Quotes that calm your nervous system
- Photos or objects that ground you
- A breathwork script or meditation
- A list of things you've survived before

Return to this pocket whenever the fog thickens.

Let it remind you: *I've walked through the unknown before. I will again. And I can do it gently.*

CHAPTER 4
YOU'RE ALLOWED TO FEEL GOOD NOW

4. You're Allowed to Feel Good Now

There's a moment — quiet, tender — when you laugh again after grief.

Maybe it's sudden.
Maybe it startles you.
Maybe it feels wrong.

Like your joy is a betrayal.
Like your smile is too soon.
Like your heart forgot something it was supposed to carry longer.

But here's the truth:

Joy is not abandonment.
Joy is not forgetting.
Joy is not wrong.

Joy is *survival*.

And you're allowed to feel it again.
Even now.
Especially now.

When Guilt Follows Joy

One of the most painful things about healing is realizing that joy doesn't always feel good right away.

It can bring up guilt.
Self-doubt.
The sharp ache of "Should I be this okay?"

Because when you've walked through loss, trauma, burnout, or heartbreak, your body doesn't always know how to receive lightness.

It flinches.
It tenses.
It waits for the other shoe.

Pleasure feels dangerous.
Happiness feels fleeting.
Peace feels suspicious.

This is normal.

Your nervous system has been on high alert.
It's been trained to brace, not breathe.

But here's the gentle truth:

You can retrain it.
Not with force — with kindness.

Try This: The "Three-Second Joy" Practice

Each day, let yourself feel something good — even just for three seconds.

- Warm sun on your skin.
- A deep exhale.
- The sound of someone's laughter.
- The comfort of soft fabric against your body.

Name it.
Let it register.
Say, *"This is joy, and I'm allowed to have it."*

It doesn't need to last long.
It doesn't need to be profound.

It just needs to be noticed.

Noticing teaches your body: *Joy is safe now.*
We're allowed to feel good again.

The Myth of Earning Joy

We live in a culture that teaches you to earn rest.
Earn ease.
Earn pleasure.

But joy was never meant to be transactional.

It's not a reward.
It's a birthright.

You don't have to prove your suffering to deserve a moment of beauty.

You don't need a clean bill of emotional health to dance barefoot in your kitchen.

You don't have to explain why the laughter came.
You just get to let it come.

Because here's what no one told you:

Healing isn't linear — and neither is joy.

It comes in waves.
It shows up between the cracks.
It surprises you when you least expect it.

And that's what makes it sacred.

Reflection Prompts

- What do I believe I have to "earn" before I'm allowed to feel good?
- Where in my body do I notice tension when joy arises?
- What's one small thing that brings me quiet pleasure — and how can I allow more of it this week?

Let this sink in gently:
You do not need to be fully healed to feel good.
You do not need to be perfectly regulated, endlessly wise, or emotionally "together."

You can feel joy in the middle of the mess.
You can feel peace with your grief still breathing beside you.
You can feel light even when the world is still heavy.

This is not bypassing.
It's balance.

The Lie of "When I'm Better, Then…"

So many of us have internal timelines.

We whisper:

- *When I'm over this breakup…*
- *When I'm not so anxious…*
- *When I fix my burnout…*
- *When I lose the weight…*

…*then I'll let myself enjoy things.*

But the truth? That moment never comes.

There's always something unfinished.
Always something unhealed.
Always something "not ready yet."

Waiting becomes a habit.

And suddenly, you've spent years postponing your joy.

But here's the thing:
Joy doesn't need your perfection.
It only needs your *permission*.

Try This: Reclaiming Small Pleasures

Make a list called: *"Things That Make Me Feel Good (Even If I Think I Shouldn't)"*

It might include:

- Watching a trashy TV show you secretly love
- Eating cake for breakfast
- Turning your phone off for an hour
- Saying no without a reason
- Buying the expensive candle and lighting it on a random Tuesday

These aren't indulgences.
They're reminders.

That you are a living, feeling being — not a machine.
That joy is not frivolous — it's *fuel*.

You don't need to justify what helps you breathe easier.

If it nourishes your spirit without harming anyone — it's sacred.

The Role of Joy in a Hurting World

"But how can I feel good when there's so much suffering in the world?"

That question comes up often.

And it's valid.
Empathy makes you sensitive.
Connection makes you care.
Being awake means you see the pain.

But joy isn't the opposite of awareness — it's part of resilience.

You cannot hold the grief of the world if you don't let yourself taste its beauty, too.

If your nervous system only knows tension, it will eventually shut down.
If your heart only holds sorrow, it will eventually collapse.

Joy is not betrayal — it's *medicine.*

It lets you keep showing up.

Reflection Prompts

- What stories do I carry about "deserving" joy?
- Who taught me that pleasure is something to be earned — and do I still want to believe them?
- What's one area of my life where I can welcome more lightness this week?

Joy, in its truest form, is not a denial of pain.
It is a testament to endurance.
A radical reclaiming of your right to feel alive again.

It says:

I have walked through fire, and still, I open my hands to the sun.

Not because the fire didn't burn.
But because I choose not to live in ashes.

You're Allowed to Feel Good... Even If Others Don't

This one's tender.

Sometimes, it's not just your guilt that gets in the way of joy.
It's your fear of making others uncomfortable.

Maybe someone you love is struggling.
Maybe the world feels like it's falling apart.
Maybe you've always been the "caretaker," the "strong one," the "sensitive empath."

So you tone it down.

You hide your light.
You shrink your laughter.
You mute your celebration.

Not because you're ashamed of your joy —
But because you're afraid it might feel like salt in someone else's wound.

But joy doesn't need to be loud to be real.
And it doesn't need to be hidden to be kind.

You can hold both.

You can be deeply compassionate — and still deeply happy.

Try This: The "Both/And" Mirror Practice

Stand in front of a mirror.
Look into your own eyes.

Say aloud:

- "I can hold joy and still care about others."

- "I can feel good and still be aware of pain."

- "My pleasure doesn't erase my empathy."

Breathe.
Repeat as many times as you need.

Then smile at yourself — not because you're forcing it,
But because you're letting it come.

This is how we stretch our capacity.

To hold both grief *and* gratitude.
Tenderness *and* delight.
Empathy *and* ecstasy.

Joy as Resistance

There is power in your pleasure.

In a world that benefits from your numbness — your joy is rebellion.
In systems that profit from your self-doubt — your joy is defiance.
In a culture that teaches you to be small, apologetic, and invisible — your joy is sacred activism.

You are allowed to feel good now.
Not later.
Not when the world improves.
Not when it's easier for everyone else.

Now.

Because your healing *helps* the world.

Your light *adds* to the collective.
Your joy *ripples outward*.

So give yourself permission.
Then pass that permission on.

Reflection Prompts

- Where have I been dimming my light out of guilt or fear?

- What would it look like to share joy in a way that honours both me and others?

- What part of me most needs to hear: *"It's safe to feel good now"*?

There's something vulnerable about feeling good.

Because when you've spent so long in survival, joy can feel like exposure.

It's open. Soft. Unprotected.

And that scares us.

We think: *What if I let this in, and it disappears? What if I trust this light, and the dark comes back?*

So we Armor up.
We guard ourselves with cynicism.
We downplay the good before it has a chance to leave us.

But here's the thing:
Joy was never meant to be armoured.

It's meant to be *felt*.

Fully.
Even fleetingly.
Even if it doesn't last forever.

Because the truth is — it never really leaves you.
It just changes shape.

Joy Is a Muscle

You might not feel fluent in pleasure right now.
That's okay.

Joy is like a muscle — it strengthens with practice.

Not performance.
Not perfection.
Just *presence*.

You start small.

You notice what softens you.
You follow what warms you.
You lean into what lifts you.

And as you do, you begin to remember what it's like to *receive* your life — not just endure it.

That's the work.
Not chasing joy.
But letting it land.

Try This: The Joy Jar

Create a physical or digital "joy jar."
Every time something makes you smile, laugh, or feel grateful — write it down and drop it in.

Small things count.

- A kind text.
- A cozy moment.
- A favourite meal.
- A breath of air that felt just right.

Over time, you'll create a record of joy.

Something to return to when doubt creeps in.
Something to remind you: *I am still capable of feeling good.*
There is still light to notice.

Because even when you forget?
Joy remembers.

How to Let the Good Stay

Sometimes joy slips through our fingers because we never give it permission to stay.

We brush it off.
We rush past it.
We tell ourselves not to "get used to it."

But what if you did?

What if you let yourself build a life where joy feels familiar?

Not rare. Not random. Not conditional.

But regular.

Expected.
Welcomed.
Integrated.

This isn't about avoiding pain.
It's about letting pleasure take up equal space.

You are allowed to feel good *and* be awake.
To be light *and* real.
To be joyful *and* whole.

Reflection Prompts

- What would it look like to treat joy as a practice, not a performance?
- Where in my life could I invite joy to stay a little longer?
- What do I need to let go of to let more pleasure in?

Let this be your permission:

You don't need a perfect life to feel good in it.

You don't need closure to laugh again.
You don't need clarity to rest deeply.
You don't need every wound to be healed before you soften into peace.

Joy coexists.
With loss.
With confusion.
With imperfection.

It always has.

You are not betraying your pain by letting beauty in.
You are honouring your aliveness.

The Fear of Losing It Again

Maybe this is what stops you.

Not the guilt.
Not the hesitation.
But the fear of losing it all again.

Because you've felt it before.
You've known love, and watched it leave.
You've had moments of peace, only to have them broken.
You've opened your heart, and it cracked.

So now? Joy feels risky.

Safer to stay numb.
Safer to keep your expectations low.
Safer not to hope.

But safety is not the same as fulfilment.

And numbness is not the same as peace.

Your heart was meant to feel.
To risk.
To reach.

Not because it's naïve — but because it's strong.

Try This: The Courage Inventory

Write down five times you allowed yourself to feel good, even when it scared you.

Examples:

- The first time you laughed after a breakup
- The moment you said yes to a spontaneous trip
- Letting yourself fall in love again
- Dancing without worrying how you looked
- Resting when you "should" have been productive

These aren't frivolous.
They're *brave*.

Let this inventory remind you: you can trust yourself.
Even when joy feels tender.
Even when you know it might pass.

Because the point was never to hold it forever.
The point was to *hold it at all*.

Receiving Without Explanation

We often feel the need to explain our joy.
To justify it.

As if saying, "I've suffered enough, so now I'm allowed this."

But what if you didn't explain?

What if you simply received?

What if you let yourself experience goodness without proof, apology, or performance?

You are not required to shrink your joy into something digestible.
You are not required to defend your light.

You are allowed to feel good — without *earning* it.

Just because you exist.
Just because you breathe.
Just because you're here.

Reflection Prompts

- What's one joy I've felt recently that I tried to explain or justify?
- What would it look like to receive pleasure without apology?
- Where am I holding back joy because I'm afraid it won't last?

Let's talk about pleasure.

Not just the soft kind.
Not just the gentle exhale or the quiet cup of tea.

Let's talk about the bold kind.
The messy kind.
The kind that floods your senses and makes you remember you're *alive*.

You are allowed to want that too.

Yes — even after trauma.
Yes — even while healing.
Yes — even when the world feels like it's breaking.

Because part of reclaiming your life... is reclaiming your *right to enjoy it*.

Pleasure Isn't Shallow — It's Sacred

There is nothing small about your capacity for joy.

It expands you.
It roots you.
It brings you back to the body, to the breath, to the present moment.

And the body remembers.

It remembers how to laugh, even after grief.
It remembers how to dance, even when your soul is tired.
It remembers how to *want*.

Pleasure is not a luxury.
It's a form of remembrance.

It reminds you:

- You're not just surviving.

- You're not just managing.

- You're *here*.

And this life is still yours to live.

Try This: Five Senses of Pleasure

Choose a moment in your day — any moment — and check in with all five senses.

- What do you see that brings delight?
- What do you hear that calms you?
- What do you smell, taste, or touch that reminds you you're safe?

This isn't about stimulation.
It's about presence.

It's about coming back into contact with what *feels good* — on your terms.

Tiny pleasures count.

A warm sip. A breeze. A favourite sweater.

When you string them together, they become a path.
A breadcrumb trail back to yourself.

Pleasure After Pain

There might be grief inside your pleasure.
There might be shame.

That's okay.

Sometimes, the body feels guilty for enjoying what it was once denied.
Sometimes, we mistake comfort for danger — because trauma taught us that peace never lasts.

This is normal.

And it's *not a sign to stop*.

It's a sign to go slow.
To move gently.
To listen with care.

Your body is learning something new.

That it is safe to feel again.
That not every good thing disappears.
That maybe — just maybe — it's okay to want more.

Reflection Prompts

- What are some ways my body experiences pleasure without pressure?
- Where have I internalized the idea that pleasure is "too much" or "too soon"?
- What would it look like to let pleasure be part of my healing?

There's a question that sometimes rises like fog:

Who am I, if I'm not hurting anymore?

It can feel disorienting.
To step out of survival mode.
To not define yourself by what you're healing from.
To walk into light without a wound leading the way.

But healing is not an erasure.
It's a *homecoming*.

You don't stop being you when you stop struggling.
You become more of you.

More whole.
More steady.
More free.

Don't Let Your Pain Become Your Identity

When you've been in pain for a long time, it can become familiar.
A shape you know.
A way the world recognizes you.

You get good at talking about your trauma.
You find community in your grief.
You build your life around what you've survived.

But at some point, healing asks a different question:

What would I build if I wasn't trying to fix myself anymore?

Not because the pain didn't matter.
But because it's no longer the only story you want to tell.

You're allowed to outgrow the version of you who always needed saving.

You're allowed to be someone who feels good — not just someone who overcame.

Try This: "Future Me" Letter

Write a letter from your future self.
Not the "perfect" one.
The real one — who knows both peace and complexity.

Start with:
"Hey, I'm proud of you for letting things feel good again..."

Let this version of you speak.
Let her remind you:

- That joy didn't mean you forgot the pain
- That soft days didn't mean you lost your edge
- That healing made you deeper, not duller

Let this letter be a map.
You're writing it for the you who's still unsure.
Who's still waiting for permission.

Give it.

Joy as a New Storyline

You're not erasing your past when you let things get better.
You're expanding your plotline.

The girl who cried can also laugh.
The one who burned can also bloom.
The heart that cracked can also swell.

Joy doesn't ask you to forget.
It invites you to *continue*.

This is what it means to reclaim your authorship.

To stop waiting for your story to resolve before you let your life be rich again.

To let good things happen — without needing a plot twist to justify them.

Reflection Prompts

- Where have I been identifying with my pain more than my pleasure?
- What does "a joyful version of me" look and feel like?
- What new storyline am I ready to live into?

So much of healing is about unlearning.

Unlearning the belief that struggle is noble.
That happiness is suspicious.
That you must prove your pain to be taken seriously.

You are allowed to live a beautiful life — even if others don't understand how you got there.

You don't have to justify your joy.
You don't need receipts of your suffering.

Your light is not a betrayal.
It is a *return*.

When Joy Triggers Old Shame

Sometimes the hardest part of feeling good...
is how it calls up everything inside you that once said you couldn't.

- The voice that told you were too much.
- The people who resented your smile.
- The relationships where your softness was punished.

So now, when joy rises?
Shame follows close behind.

It says:
Be careful.
Don't be that happy.
They'll think you're bragging. They'll think you're fake.

But shame is not your truth.
It's a scar.
It's an echo.

You can feel it. Acknowledge it.
And then move beyond it.

Try This: Shame to Sovereignty Exercise

1. Write down three joyful experiences that triggered shame or guilt.

2. Next to each, write: "I am allowed to enjoy this."

3. Then add: "This feeling is mine. I don't need approval to keep it."

Speak them aloud if you can.

This is how you reclaim your joy — from the inside out.
Not by avoiding the shame.
But by *outgrowing* it.

Your joy deserves your full presence, not your apology.

What If You Shared It?

One of the most radical things you can do is *share* your joy.

Not in performative ways.
Not as curated content.
But as real, vulnerable light.

Tell someone when you had a good day.
Celebrate the thing that worked out.
Let people see you — not just in grief, but in gladness.

Joy, like pain, deserves witnesses.

And when you share yours, you create a kind of safety.
A ripple effect.

It gives others permission to feel good too.

Reflection Prompts

- What stories or people taught me to feel shame about my joy?

- How does that shame show up in my body, and how can I move through it?

- Who in my life feels safe to share joy with — even the small, unexplainable kind?

Sometimes, what blocks joy... is the feeling that you're leaving someone behind.

You remember the version of you who struggled.
Who couldn't get out of bed.
Who carried grief like a second skin.

And now that you're starting to feel better, a quiet guilt creeps in.

Am I abandoning her?

No.

You're honouring her.

By living the life she couldn't reach for.
By breathing deeper than she ever thought she could.
By letting yourself *want* again.

This is not betrayal.
It's continuation.

You're not erasing who you were.
You're expanding who you're becoming.

You Don't Have to Dim to Belong

If you've ever made yourself smaller to fit in...
If you've downplayed good news to keep others comfortable...
If you've quieted your light so someone else wouldn't feel inadequate...

Let this be a reckoning.

You don't owe anyone your dimming.

Belonging that requires you to shrink is not true belonging.

Real connection will celebrate your rising — not resent it.

You can be light without apology.
You can be bright and kind.
You can take up space and still be tender.

Try This: Letting Yourself Shine

Write down three areas of your life where you've been holding back joy, success, or softness out of fear of outshining someone else.

Then ask:

- What's the cost of staying small here?
- Who taught me that shining was dangerous?
- Who might celebrate me, if I let them?

The point isn't to push people away.
It's to stop pushing yourself *down*.

There is enough room.
Enough joy.
Enough light.

Especially for you.

Letting the Light Be Yours

There's no universal blueprint for joy.

Your version might look quiet.
Might be slow.
Might be loud, colourful, sacred, strange.

Whatever shape it takes, let it be yours.

Let it be *true*.

This chapter of your life doesn't have to resemble anyone else's.
It only has to feel like *you* — whole, willing, and awake.

Joy doesn't make you less deep.
It makes you deeper.
Because now you've touched both the shadow *and* the shine.

And you're still here.
Still soft.
Still reaching.

Reflection Prompts

- What version of me am I afraid to outgrow — even as I heal?

- Where am I still dimming my joy to make others more comfortable?

- What does unapologetic joy look like for me now?

So here we are.

At the edge of the softness you almost didn't let yourself feel.

And still — you're here.

Not because everything is perfect.
Not because you've unlocked some secret.
But because something in you whispered: *Try again.*

And you did.

You breathed into stillness.
You let warmth reach your skin.
You felt your way toward joy — even when it felt like trespassing.

You didn't just heal.
You came home.

Letting Life Feel Good Again

This chapter — your real life, not the pages — will continue asking:

Can you let it feel good?

Even when you're afraid it won't last.
Even when someone else is hurting.
Even when your mind tries to bargain with guilt.

And your answer doesn't need to be loud.

It can be a quiet yes.
A slow smile.
A breath that opens your chest.

Joy doesn't always burst through the door.
Sometimes it tiptoes in, waiting for you to notice.

Let it stay.
Even if only for a moment.
Let it *matter*.

Try This: The Joy Practice

Choose one small act of joy you can return to daily.

- A favourite song in the morning
- A five-minute breath ritual
- Lighting a candle while making tea
- Stretching with music you loved as a teenager

This is not productivity.
It's reclamation.

It's a signal to your nervous system:
"We don't live in the storm anymore."

You can still hear the wind.
But you know the way to shelter.

And sometimes, shelter is joy.

Final Reflection Prompts

- What does joy mean to me now — *not what it used to mean, or what others say it is*?

- What small, steady rituals remind me that life can feel good again?

- If I lived like I was allowed to enjoy my life, how would I begin?

Let This Be the Reminder

You are not behind.
You are not broken for wanting beauty.
You are not foolish for letting your heart rise again.

You are not betraying your past.
You are not rushing your process.
You are not wrong for wanting joy.

You are *allowed*.

To heal.
To hope.
To feel good again.

      Let it be true.
           Let it be now.
                Let it be yours.

CHAPTER 5
LETTING LIFE HAPPEN

5. Letting Life Happen

There's a moment when your fingers finally loosen.

Not because you've figured it all out.
Not because everything's suddenly easy.
But because you're tired of the tug-of-war with life.

And maybe for the first time, you whisper:

What if I don't have to hold it all so tightly?

That moment is where this chapter begins.

The Illusion of Control

We are taught, often quietly and young, that control keeps us safe.

Control your image.
Control your feelings.
Control your environment, your expectations, your people.

Control, we're told, is power.

But what if it isn't?

What if control is the thing that exhausts us?
What if it builds more anxiety, not less?
What if the tight grip we've perfected is keeping us from the very peace we crave?

Because life — wild, unpredictable life — rarely asks to be managed.

It asks to be *met*.

Letting Go Isn't Laziness

Let's be clear.

Letting life happen is not the same as giving up.
It's not passive.
It's not weakness.
It's not a spiritual loophole for avoidance.

It's a practice of presence.
A discipline of trust.
A quiet strength that whispers, *I don't have to force this to be okay.*

Letting go is what happens when you finally realize:

- The outcome was never yours to control.

- The timing was never yours to dictate.

- The only thing you've ever really had… is your response.

And even that doesn't need to be perfect.

Just honest.
Just kind.
Just enough.

Try This: "Let It Be" Body Check-In

When you feel tension rising — not just in your mind, but in your body — pause.
Ask yourself:

- What am I clenching right now (jaw, fists, shoulders, breath)?
- What am I trying to control in this moment?
- Can I soften, even by 5%, just for now?

You don't have to solve it.
You don't have to *feel better* immediately.

You just have to *notice*.

That's the doorway.

The choice to release begins with the awareness that you're holding.

Life Doesn't Need You to Fix It

This may be one of the hardest truths:

Not everything is yours to repair.

Not every conversation needs your perfect words.
Not every crisis needs your immediate action.
Not every emotion requires explanation.

Sometimes, life will wobble.
People will hurt.
Plans will change.
And your job is not to rush in and fix it all.

Your job is to stay open.

To feel without flailing.
To stand without forcing.
To trust that the wave will pass — and you'll still be here, breathing.

Sometimes, letting life happen means letting people happen too.

Letting them come. Letting them go.
Letting them misunderstand you.
Letting them love you imperfectly.
Letting them have their own lessons without micromanaging the outcome.

That's hard.

Especially when your heart is big.
Especially when your empathy has edges like open windows.
Especially when you've spent years translating the world — trying to make it make sense.

But here's the deeper truth:

You can care *without controlling.*
You can witness *without rescuing.*
You can love *without losing yourself.*

That's what letting life happen means.
It means trusting that other people's journeys are not yours to live.

Even when you ache for them.
Even when you think you know better.
Even when their choices break your heart.

Stop Holding the Sky

There is a story we tell ourselves — that if we stop holding everything up, it will all fall apart.

That our vigilance is necessary.
That our constant anxiety is a form of service.
That if we just try harder, prepare better, think faster... maybe we'll avoid the fall.

But the sky doesn't need you to hold it.

It holds itself.

And you? You're allowed to rest.

You're allowed to unclench your spirit and say:
"I'm doing what I can. That is enough."

Even if someone else thinks it's not.
Even if your fear screams otherwise.

There is grace in doing your part — and then *letting go of the rest*.

Try This: "My Part, Not All Parts" Reflection

Write down a current challenge or situation that feels heavy.

Now, beneath it, list:

- What is actually mine to hold?
- What belongs to someone else?
- What is no one's fault, just life being life?

Then answer:
Can I trust myself to show up for *my part*, and let the rest unfold without force?

You'll notice — your shoulders relax a little.
Your breath deepens.
The world feels a tiny bit less heavy.

That's not weakness.
That's alignment.

Flow, Not Force

When you stop fighting the current of life, something shifts.

You stop chasing closure from people who cannot give it.
You stop demanding certainty in a world built on mystery.
You stop performing strength when softness is what you need most.

Instead, you move differently.

- You ask questions instead of making demands.
- You breathe before reacting.
- You make space for outcomes that aren't perfect — but might be better than you imagined.

That's flow.

It's not passive.
It's responsive.
It's a dance between you and the moment, not a battle for control.

And when you live that way?

Even chaos begins to feel sacred.

Sometimes we don't need a plan.
We need permission.

To pause.
To pivot.
To trust that what's unfolding doesn't always have to be pre-approved by our fear.

When you let life happen, you stop demanding it prove itself before you participate.

You stop asking:

- "Will this be safe?"

- "Will this be perfect?"

- "Will this hurt?"

And instead, you whisper:

I'll meet it when it comes.

Uncertainty Is Not Failure

So much of our pain comes from believing that uncertainty is a sign we're doing something wrong.

We think that not knowing the next step means we're behind.
We think that feeling unsure means we're failing.

But what if it doesn't?

What if not knowing is the very space where life can *meet you?*

Where things can rise unforced.
Where intuition can speak louder than strategy.
Where tenderness can walk in where control once lived.

Uncertainty is not a threat.
It's an invitation.

To release the illusion of foresight.
To practice presence instead of performance.

To live — not just plan.

Try This: "Right Now" Grounding

When you find yourself spiralling about the future, come back to the only place life ever happens — *here*.

Ask:

- What is true right now?
- What is needed right now?
- What can I soften or surrender, just for this breath?

Notice the edges begin to blur.
Notice how often your suffering lives in the space between this moment... and your projections about the next.

The mind is brilliant.
But it is not a prophet.

Trust the now.
It will carry you.

A Life You Don't Have to Force

When you stop micromanaging your life like a fragile equation — one wrong variable and everything explodes — you begin to trust that it can hold you.

Not because you're always doing the "right" thing.
Not because everything's easy.

But because life is inherently creative.
It wants to expand.
It wants to adapt.

And so do you.

You are not here to execute a perfect plan.
You are here to live a real, responsive, human life.

Let it twist.
Let it stretch.
Let it surprise you.

The best things often weren't in your strategy anyway.

There's a kind of strength that looks like surrender.

Not giving up.
Not collapsing.
But choosing to release your grip on what cannot be held.

This is the strength that stays soft.

It's the hand that opens when it would be easier to clutch.
It's the heart that breathes when it wants to brace.
It's the voice that says, *I'll trust this tide,* even when the shore disappears.

Surrender Is Not Defeat

Surrender gets a bad reputation.

We think it means losing.
That if we surrender, we've been beaten by life.
That to let go means to admit we couldn't handle it.

But that's not what surrender means here.

This surrender is chosen.
Intentional.
Rooted in wisdom, not weakness.

It says:

- I am no longer trying to win against life.

- I am learning to partner with it.

- I will still show up, but not in resistance — in alignment.

It's not passive.
It's powerful.

It's the difference between swimming against the current...
And learning to float, breathe, and let the water carry you forward.

Try This: "If I Trusted Life" Prompt

Finish this sentence in a journal or reflection space:

If I trusted life a little more today, I would…

Let it be small.

Maybe you'd take the long way home.
Maybe you'd send the message.
Maybe you'd rest without justifying it.

This isn't about radical changes.
It's about noticing what's possible when force isn't required.

Letting Life Meet You

So often we're waiting for life to meet a checklist before we'll meet it back.

We withhold joy until we have proof.
We delay peace until there's a plan.
We refuse softness until someone else is softer first.

But life doesn't work like that.

It's messy.
Nonlinear.
Sacred in its imperfection.

It doesn't always make sense.
But it always moves.

And when you stop demanding guarantees, you start discovering grace.

You start realizing: maybe life wasn't supposed to be controlled.

Maybe it was always supposed to be *felt*.

Letting life happen doesn't mean letting everything happen *to* you.

This isn't about becoming passive.
It's about becoming *available*.

To respond rather than react.
To stay present rather than panic.
To choose, even when you didn't choose the situation.

You are still allowed boundaries.
Still allowed preferences.
Still allowed to say, "No thank you, not like this."

But the *spirit* you carry through the world changes.

It becomes less about defending.
More about aligning.
Less about guarding your edges.
More about knowing what's real beneath them.

You Don't Need to Hustle for Wholeness

Somewhere along the way, we were taught that peace is a reward we earn.

Finish the healing.
Fix the flaws.
Organize your trauma into tidy bullet points.

Then you can rest.

But what if you didn't have to hustle to be worthy of peace?

What if you could have it now — messy, unfinished, honest as hell?

Letting life happen means letting yourself be whole *while still becoming.*

You don't have to graduate to joy.
You just have to *make space for it.*

Try This: Gentle Truth Inventory

Ask yourself gently:

- What am I still waiting to finish before I allow myself to feel peace?
- Who told me I had to earn ease?
- What if this moment — imperfect, uncertain — was enough to begin again?

Then try this line:

I'm allowed to feel peaceful now, even if nothing is solved yet.

Let it land in your body.
Let it move through your chest.
Let it soften the parts of you still waiting for permission.

You Were Never Meant to Carry It All

Letting life happen also means admitting this:
You were never meant to carry it all alone.

Not every burden needs to be held in your hands.
Not every emotion needs to be deciphered in silence.
Not every answer has to come from your brain at 2 a.m.

Let people help.
Let the ground hold you.
Let your breath do more than survive.

You are not weak for needing rest.
You are not broken for needing support.
You are not failing just because your arms are tired.

Let them be.
Let *you* be.

Letting go of control doesn't mean letting go of care.

It means learning to care *without collapsing*.

To tend to your life with presence instead of pressure.
To give your energy with intention, not urgency.
To hold space for what matters — without squeezing it until it suffocates.

This is what changes everything.

Because when you live this way, your peace is no longer dependent on perfection.

It's rooted.
It's resilient.
It's *yours*.

You Can Live Without a Guarantee

What if the most courageous thing isn't creating a perfect plan?

What if it's choosing to live even when there's no guarantee?

No guarantee you'll be understood.
No guarantee you'll succeed.
No guarantee it will turn out how you hoped.

And still — you open your heart.
You try.
You breathe into the moment and say:

"I'll be here anyway."

That's bravery.
Not certainty.
But willingness.

Try This: "I'll Show Up Anyway" Prompt

Choose one area of your life that feels uncertain — a relationship, project, dream, or healing path.

Now finish this sentence:

Even if I can't predict the outcome, I can still...

Let the words come gently.
Let them remind you that showing up isn't about knowing.
It's about *being willing to meet what comes.*

No armour.
No guarantee.
Just an open heart — and maybe a deep breath.

There's Beauty in the Becoming

Letting life happen means embracing the *becoming*.

It means honouring the process, not just the result.
It means loving the middle, even when it's messy.

The you who doesn't have the answer yet.
The you who sometimes forgets to trust.
The you who is still learning to loosen her grip.

She's worthy too.

She's not the prelude.
She's the poetry.

Let her be messy.
Let her be in-progress.
Let her be enough.

Right now.
Exactly as she is.

Letting life happen doesn't mean you never make decisions.

It means you make them *from trust*, not terror.

From presence, not panic.
From clarity, not comparison.

It means pausing before you act — not to stall, but to *listen*.

To your body.
To your breath.
To the deeper wisdom you forget you carry.

This is how you stop reacting to life — and begin *responding to it*.

Softening the Edges of Urgency

There is a kind of urgency that isn't sacred.

It's the urgency of "should."
The urgency of not-enoughness.
The urgency that says, *if I don't fix this right now, I am failing.*

But softness is not the enemy of progress.

In fact, the most powerful shifts often come quietly.
Without dramatics.
Without rushing.
Without the demand that every moment be optimized.

Letting life happen invites you to move at the speed of *truth*, not anxiety.

Sometimes, the bravest thing you can do... is slow down.

Try This: "Slower Than I Usually Would" Practice

For one task or decision today — even something simple — try moving *slower than you normally would.*

Maybe it's how you respond to a message.
Maybe it's how you wash the dishes.
Maybe it's how you get dressed or eat your lunch.

Notice what changes when speed isn't your compass.
Notice what emerges when presence leads instead of pressure.

Slowness isn't laziness.
It's spaciousness.
And sometimes, it's exactly what lets life *catch up to you.*

There Is No Finish Line for Being Human

You are allowed to live as if life is not a race.

You're allowed to stop measuring yourself against invisible checklists.
You're allowed to quit the game of proving your worth through output.
You're allowed to redefine success as *alignment, not exhaustion*.

Letting life happen reminds you:
You are not late.
You are not behind.
You are not broken because things didn't unfold on a timeline someone else invented.

You are here.

Still becoming.
Still unfolding.
Still worthy — always.

Letting life happen is not passive resignation.

It's conscious allowance.
It's an active decision to *not interfere* with what is naturally unfolding — not because you don't care, but because you finally trust that not everything needs your intervention.

This is a shift in posture.

From grasping to receiving.
From defending to allowing.
From managing to *meeting*.

Life becomes less about steering the storm, and more about learning to sail with it.

Control Is Exhausting. Curiosity Is Sustainable.

Ask yourself: what happens when you stop needing to know everything before you start?

When you stop needing to be the best before you try? When you stop needing to be certain before you speak?

You begin to live from *curiosity* instead of control.

And curiosity is a powerful place to live from.

It doesn't demand guarantees.
It invites discovery.

It opens you to possibilities that control would've shut down.
It lets wonder in — even when fear wants to run the show.

Try This: "Instead of Controlling, I Can..."

Use this journaling sentence stem when you feel the urge to micromanage:

Instead of controlling this situation, I can...

You might write:

- ...breathe through it.
- ...be honest about what I need.
- ...ask a curious question.
- ...move gently and wait for more clarity.

Control wants to feel powerful.
But curiosity *is* power — power without pressure.

Life Happens in the Gaps

You don't have to fill every silence.

You don't have to fix every pause.
You don't have to answer every question with certainty.

Some of the most beautiful things in life arrive in the *gaps*.

In the space between who you were and who you're becoming.
In the pause between inhale and exhale.
In the stillness between decision and action.

Let life speak there.
Let yourself *listen*.

You are not missing anything.
You are being met — right here, in the space where nothing is forced.

You are not the sum of how well you manage chaos.

You are not defined by how quickly you bounce back.
You are not valuable only when producing, fixing, or progressing.

You are allowed to be still.
To not know.
To be *in it* without orchestrating an exit.

Letting life happen invites you to be human first — not a project, not a performance.

Just you.
Alive.
Present.
In the middle of it all, still enough.

Peace Doesn't Require a Perfect Life

We think peace is what happens *after* everything is resolved.

But real peace — the kind that doesn't shatter with bad news — it comes *before*.

Before the solution.
Before the closure.
Before the answer arrives.

It comes when you stop demanding life make sense in order for you to feel safe.

It arrives in the moment you say:

"I can feel peace *even here*.
Even now.
Even with this mess around me."

And sometimes, that soft choice changes everything.

Try This: "Permission to Be at Peace" Mantra

Use this line when your nervous system feels the urge to rush, grasp, or overanalyse:

I don't have to understand everything to feel peaceful right now.

Repeat it.
Let your breath slow down as you say it.
Feel it land in your belly.

This is not bypassing.
This is belonging.

To yourself.
To this moment.
To the deeper knowing that peace was never about *perfect conditions.*

Being With Life (Not Against It)

Letting life happen doesn't mean loving every part of it.

Some moments will hurt.
Some will break you open.
Some will stretch you in ways that feel unfair.

But even here — *especially here* — you are allowed to be with life instead of against it.

To grieve without shame.
To struggle without labels.
To soften without losing your strength.

This is where tenderness becomes resilience.
This is where living begins again.

Letting life happen is not about letting go of desire.

You're allowed to want more.
To dream.
To hope.

But it's a different wanting.
One that isn't soaked in desperation.
One that doesn't say *I'll only be okay if I get it*.

It's a wanting rooted in *wholeness*, not lack.

A desire that says:
I already belong to this moment. Anything more is a blessing, not a condition.

You Can Be the Calm

You don't have to wait for the world to settle.

You can become the calm.
The stillness.
The softness that holds space — even when things fall apart around you.

This isn't denial.
This is devotion.

To truth.
To gentleness.
To not becoming what the world tries to make you when it's scared.

Letting life happen turns you into a sanctuary.
Not because it's easy — but because you *chose* it.

Again and again.

Try This: "Let It Be Enough" Evening Ritual

At the end of your day, pause before bed.

Place a hand on your chest or belly and breathe.

Say (out loud or quietly):

"I let today be enough.
I let myself be enough.
I don't need to carry what isn't mine.
I trust that what's meant for me is already on its way."

Let your body unclench.
Let your day go.
Let life hold you, just for this moment.

You don't have to try so hard.
You already are.

Letting Life Happen Is a Practice

You will forget.
You will grip again.
You will want to control what cannot be controlled.

That's okay.

You can remember again.
You can soften again.
You can return — not to perfection, but to presence.

That's all this chapter has ever asked of you.

To begin where you are.
To breathe.
To notice.
To allow.

To stop fighting every wave...
And learn to float, knowing the shore is not where safety lives.

Safety lives in you.
Right here.
Right now.
Exactly as you are.

CHAPTER 6
RELATING WITHOUT ATTACHMENT

6. Relating Without Attachment

We all want to feel close.
To belong.
To be seen and held in our fullness.

That's not weakness. It's human.

But closeness built on clinging isn't intimacy.
It's survival.

And survival-mode relationships aren't sacred. They're transactions in disguise — *If I hold on tight enough, maybe I won't be left. Maybe I'll matter.*

In this chapter, we begin to untangle that.

To learn what it means to love — deeply, honestly, vulnerably — without collapsing into the need to control.

To stop confusing enmeshment for connection.
To stop calling our fear of loss "love."

Because there's a difference.

And it's in that difference that peace begins.

When Attachment Becomes Armor

Attachment isn't the enemy. It's how we bond, how we grow, how we heal.

But when attachment hardens into control — when it becomes the armour we wear instead of the intimacy we share — something beautiful gets lost.

We stop relating *to* someone.
And start relating *at* them.

We don't see them as they are.
We see them as a mirror of our unmet needs.

We expect them to fix our ache.
To never leave.
To carry our pain so we don't have to.

And that kind of closeness always comes at a cost.

You lose your center.
You stop breathing in your own rhythm.
You shrink your truth to keep the peace.
You give more than you mean because you're scared to say no.

And over time, love starts to feel like pressure.
Or performance.
Or punishment.

Not because the love wasn't real — but because it was rooted in fear, not freedom.

What Is Non-Attached Connection?

Non-attachment doesn't mean detachment.
It doesn't mean you stop caring or loving or investing.

It means you stop *gripping*.

It means you give your heart without asking someone to carry your whole identity in return.

It means you stay connected to yourself — even when someone else is upset, unavailable, or unfamiliar with your boundaries.

It means you can love someone… and still let them choose.
It means you can need support… and not collapse when it isn't offered.

This is radical.

This is the kind of love that heals instead of hooks.

Try This: Self Check-In Before You Reach Out

Next time you feel the urge to call, text, vent, or fix something with another person — pause for 30 seconds.

Ask yourself:

What part of me is reaching out right now?
Is it the part that wants connection... or the part that fears being alone?

This isn't about shaming your need.
It's about meeting it with clarity.

Because when you know what's driving you, you're more likely to relate with intention instead of reaction.

You get to choose.
Not just *respond* — but *relate*.
From your center. From your calm. From your whole self.

Somewhere along the way, many of us learned to trade authenticity for acceptance.

We were taught that safety came from staying small.
From being easy to love.
From not asking for too much.

And so, we learned to disappear a little.

To abandon parts of ourselves in exchange for proximity.
To twist into shapes we hoped would guarantee we'd never be left.

But this isn't love.
It's survival in disguise.
And no matter how tightly you cling, no connection can truly thrive inside a cage of self-abandonment.

You Are Not Too Much

It is not your job to be easy to digest.

It is not your duty to shrink your emotional range just so others feel comfortable.
You were not born to apologize for your depth, your needs, or your desire for intimacy that goes beyond surface.

Healthy, unattached connection doesn't ask you to be *less*.

It asks you to be *true*.

Because the right relationships — the ones built on resonance, not rescue — can hold your truth without trying to fix or flee from it.

And that's the kind of love you deserve.

The Fear Beneath the Cling

Most attachment wounds are not really about the other person.

They're about you.

They're about the part of you that never got to feel safe *without* being attached.
The part that was taught love disappears unless you work hard enough to keep it close.
The part that internalized absence as a reflection of your worth.

That part doesn't need to be punished.
It needs to be held.
Seen.
Listened to.

And gently reminded: *you can belong to yourself now.*

Try This: "What Am I Trying to Secure?"

When you notice yourself clinging, pleasing, or anxiously reaching in relationship — pause.

Ask:

What feeling am I trying to secure right now?
What do I think I'll lose if I let go?

Is it certainty?
Control?
Proximity?
Validation?

Notice what story is playing underneath.
You don't need to fix it right away.

Just *witness it*.

When you can meet the fear with curiosity, it softens. And in that softness, a new way of relating can emerge.

Loving someone doesn't mean disappearing for them.

It doesn't mean sacrificing your boundaries, your truth, your inner compass — all for the illusion of harmony.

Because harmony built on self-erasure always comes due.

It leaves you resentful.
Exhausted.
Confused about who you even are when you're not orbiting around someone else's needs.

You were not meant to be a shapeshifter just to stay loved.
You were meant to be a home — for yourself, first.
And then, if someone else knocks gently on the door of your truth, you get to let them in.

Not because you *need* to — but because you *choose* to.

Attachment Is Not Intimacy

We've been sold the myth that intensity equals intimacy.

That obsession equals passion.
That jealousy means you care.
That being "all in" requires self-sacrifice.

But true intimacy doesn't feel like suffocation.

It feels like freedom.
It feels like being fully seen, without being consumed.
It feels like wanting someone, not needing them to survive.

When you relate without attachment, you can love *deeply* — without placing your identity in someone else's hands.

And that's not less romantic.
That's more sacred.

Try This: "Your Seat at the Table" Visualization

Close your eyes.

Picture a round table in your heart. There are chairs at this table — one for your voice, one for your needs, one for your fear, one for your desires, one for your boundaries.

Now imagine you've been giving all the seats to someone else.
They speak. They decide. They dominate the space.

Take your seat back.

Gently, firmly.
Reclaim your spot at your own table.

And notice what it feels like to let your voice be heard *inside you* — before seeking validation *outside you*.

This is how you begin to relate without losing yourself.
This is how you return to the relationship that matters most: the one with your own truth.

Non-attachment doesn't mean being emotionally indifferent.

It means being emotionally honest.

It's not about closing your heart — it's about grounding it.

So that your love flows from freedom, not fear.
So that your connection doesn't collapse when someone sets a boundary.
So that your peace doesn't vanish when someone doesn't meet your expectations.

This is strength.
Soft, quiet, deeply rooted strength.
The kind that doesn't need to control in order to feel safe.

Loving Without Ownership

You do not own anyone.
Not their attention.
Not their choices.
Not their growth.

Love is not a contract of control.

It is an invitation — a continuous, consensual dance between two whole people.

When you stop gripping, you make space.
And in that space, the other person can meet you in truth instead of obligation.

That's where real relationship lives.

In the choosing.
In the openness.
In the daily, sacred decision to stay — not because they have to, but because they *want* to.

Try This: "What's Mine, What's Theirs" List

When you feel entangled in someone else's emotions, grab a piece of paper and draw a line down the center.

On the left side, write:

What's mine to feel, fix, or carry?

On the right side, write:

What's theirs to hold, process, or release?

Don't overthink it.
Let it be honest.

Then reread the right-hand column.
Exhale.
And remind yourself: *I can love someone and still let them be responsible for their own emotional landscape.*

That's not cold.
That's clear.

Relating without attachment is not about becoming distant — it's about becoming discerning.

Loving well, without losing yourself in the process.

There is a kind of loneliness that comes with letting go of attachment.

You start noticing where you once over-functioned.
Where you kept conversations alive that didn't nourish you.
Where you tolerated being misunderstood just to avoid conflict.
Where you mistook someone's inconsistency for mystery, or their neglect for depth.

And when you stop doing that — when you stop reaching just to keep others close — something shifts.

Silence grows.

But so does space.

Space for something real.
For mutuality.
For connection that doesn't cost you your center.

You Are Allowed to Be Chosen Back

You are not here to beg for breadcrumbs.

You are not here to constantly prove your worth.
You are not here to bend until you disappear.

You are allowed to be loved *in return*.
To be held, seen, prioritized — not just pursued in moments of convenience.

Letting go of attachment reveals where reciprocity was always missing.

It's not always loud.
But it is clear.

And once you've felt the peace of not chasing, it becomes easier to stop running toward what doesn't run toward you.

Try This: "Silent Support" Practice

Next time you want someone to respond a certain way — to validate you, to comfort you, to react how you want — pause.

Ask yourself:

Can I give myself that first?

What would it look like to sit in your own truth, to hold your own fear, to whisper *"I've got you"* without needing anyone else to say it first?

This doesn't mean you stop needing people.
It means your need becomes less urgent.
Less panicked.
More rooted.

And that changes everything.

It's hard to let go of how you used to survive.

Even when you know it's not working anymore.

Because the nervous system doesn't speak logic.
It speaks memory.

And if your nervous system learned that clinging meant safety, that over-explaining meant love, that controlling meant avoiding abandonment — then releasing that feels like dying.

But it isn't.

It's a return.

A re-meeting of your own wholeness.
A return to trusting that you are not only allowed to take up space — but that real love *requires* it.

Redefining Love in Real Time

Sometimes we don't realize how attached we've been until the other person doesn't meet our unspoken expectations.

They don't text back.
They need space.
They don't read our emotional cues the way we hoped.

And suddenly — panic.
Overthinking.
Gripping.
Withdrawing affection as punishment or begging for it to come back.

This isn't shameful.

It's just a signal.

It shows you where old wounds are playing out.
Where a younger version of you is still trying to earn love by being "good enough."

But here's the truth: your worth doesn't live in someone else's response.

You can

You can be whole even when someone else is unavailable.
You can be steady even when someone else is inconsistent.

You can be enough even when someone else doesn't choose you.

That's not indifference.
That's inner freedom.

It means you no longer confuse someone's behaviour with your value.
You stop measuring your lovability by how closely you match someone's fleeting preferences.

And instead, you anchor into something deeper:
Who you are when you're not trying to be chosen.

You Can Walk Away and Still Love Them

Non-attachment doesn't always mean staying.

Sometimes it means walking away — not out of spite, but out of self-honouring.
Not because you stopped caring, but because you stopped self-abandoning.

You can love someone and still leave the dynamic.
You can miss someone and still know it's not aligned.
You can forgive someone and still protect your peace.

That's not weakness.
That's wisdom.

It takes strength to not let the pull of familiarity keep you in what no longer fits your truth.

Try This: "What Would Self-Honouring Do?" Prompt

When you're unsure how to respond to someone — especially in moments of tension, disconnection, or emotional ambiguity — ask:

What would self-honouring do right now?

Would it pause?
Speak?
Step back?
Set a boundary?
Let go?

Let the answer come from *within*, not from fear or fantasy.

This question doesn't promise clarity every time.
But it does pull you closer to your own center.

And that's the compass you can trust.

—

It's hard to let go of how you used to survive.

Even when you know it's not working anymore.

Because the nervous system doesn't speak logic.
It speaks memory.

And if your nervous system learned that clinging meant safety, that over-explaining meant love, that controlling meant avoiding abandonment — then releasing that feels like dying.

But it isn't.

It's a return.

A re-meeting of your own wholeness.
A return to trusting that you are not only allowed to take up space — but that real love *requires* it.

Redefining Love in Real Time

Sometimes we don't realize how attached we've been until the other person doesn't meet our unspoken expectations.

They don't text back.
They need space.
They don't read our emotional cues the way we hoped.

And suddenly — panic.
Overthinking.
Gripping.
Withdrawing affection as punishment or begging for it to come back.

This isn't shameful.

It's just a signal.

It shows you where old wounds are playing out.
Where a younger version of you is still trying to earn love by being "good enough."

But here's the truth: your worth doesn't live in someone else's response.

You can be steady even in their storm.
You can stay kind without collapsing.

And when you no longer require someone's reaction to validate your reality, you stop living in emotional debt.

Try This: "Stay With Yourself" Grounding Practice

The next time you feel the pull to chase, fix, or perform — pause.

Put one hand on your chest. One on your belly.
Inhale slowly. Exhale even slower. Three times.

Then ask yourself:

Where am I abandoning myself right now?

Is it in the story you're telling?
In the expectation you're holding?
In the role you think you need to play to stay loved?

Once you find it — soften.
Speak to yourself gently.
Remind your body: *I can stay with me now.*

Because attachment isn't bad. But conscious connection — with others *and* with yourself — is where freedom lives.

Some relationships will fade when you stop trying to control them.

When you stop over-functioning.
When you stop shrinking to keep the peace.
When you stop managing everyone's emotional weather.

And yes, it might feel like loss.

But it's also truth doing what truth does: clearing space.

Because the relationships that survive your self-honouring are the ones built on something real.
Not performance.
Not people-pleasing.
Not silent resentment disguised as kindness.

Just presence.
Choice.
Love that's given without condition — and returned without demand.

The Myth of "Forever"

We've been taught that good relationships last forever.

That longevity is proof of success.
That endings mean failure.

But sometimes, the most loving thing you can do is let the connection complete.
Not collapse.
Not blow up.
Just... complete.

Like a breath you exhale fully.
Like a season that turns.

Non-attachment lets you appreciate what was *without demanding it stays*.

You stop gripping.
And you start honouring the chapter for what it taught you — even if it doesn't write the rest of your story.

Try This: "The Sacred Goodbye" Letter

Write a letter to someone you're releasing. You don't need to send it.

Use these prompts to guide you:

- What did they teach you, even if it hurt?
- What parts of you feel different because of knowing them?
- What can you bless them to carry forward — without carrying it for them?
- What are you reclaiming now that you're no longer gripping?

Let this be a ritual.
A full exhale.
A way to close without closing your heart.

You don't need to make someone the villain to walk away.
You don't need to be perfect to stay.

You just need to be honest.
With yourself, first.

Sometimes, the most powerful thing you can say in a relationship is:

"I'm no longer abandoning myself to stay connected to you."

That's not cruelty.
That's clarity.

It's a moment when your inner voice gets louder than your fear.
When your boundaries rise not as walls, but as gateways — to a different way of loving.

One that doesn't ask you to disappear.
One that doesn't punish you for being honest.
One that doesn't mistake neediness for intimacy.

Letting Others Have Their Process

You're not responsible for how someone reacts to your truth.

If you speak with kindness and clarity, and they respond with anger, withdrawal, or guilt-tripping — that's their work.

You can care deeply *without taking it on.*

You can say:

"I see that this is hard for you."
"I still care."
"But I'm no longer making myself small to make this easier."

Let people have their emotions.
Let them walk their path.
Let them feel uncomfortable.

That doesn't make you unkind.
It makes you honest.

And honesty is what non-attachment protects.

Try This: "Emotional Detachment ≠ Disconnection" Journal Prompt

Set a timer for 10 minutes and reflect on the following:

"Where am I confusing detachment with not caring? Where could I release control while still remaining deeply connected — to myself and others?"

Write without editing.

Notice where your old stories show up.
Notice how often care has been tied to control.

Then, reframe it.

What if the most loving thing isn't fixing — but trusting?
Not proving — but allowing?

Relating without attachment is not cold.
It's courageous.

You are loving from a place that isn't tethered to fear. And that love — untangled, ungrasping, unafraid — is the kind that frees both people.

You don't need to stop loving people.
You just need to stop abandoning yourself to do it.

You can love with open hands.
You can care deeply and still choose yourself.
You can show up without surrendering your center.

That's what it means to relate without attachment.

Not indifference.
Not detachment from emotion.
But a conscious choosing — moment by moment — to stay rooted in truth, even when it costs comfort.

When You Let Go of Roles, You Discover Realness

In attachment, we play roles.
Caretaker.
Fixer.
Performer.
Peacemaker.

But when you release the script — the pressure to earn love, or to control connection — what's left?

Just you.
Your presence.
Your realness.

And that's enough.

Because real love doesn't need a role.
It wants *you*.
Fully.
Messily.
Truthfully.

When you show up that way, you give others permission to do the same.

That's how new, honest connections form.

Reflection Page: What Comes Alive When You Stop Gripping?

Set aside some quiet time. Light a candle. Breathe.

Answer these prompts:

1. What relationship patterns am I finally ready to release?
2. Where have I confused love with performance?
3. What kind of connection am I calling in now — and what version of me is ready to receive it?

Let this page become a pause.
A reset.
A sacred moment between the old way of loving and the new one.

You don't have to rush.
Presence is enough.

And in that stillness, love returns home to you.

CHAPTER 7
CREATING SPACE FOR SOMETHING NEW

7. Creating Space for Something New

There's a moment in every transformation that feels like nothing.

No more clinging.
No new beginning yet.
Just... space.

This space is sacred.

But it doesn't always feel that way.
It can feel like loss. Like absence. Like floating with no anchor.

You let go of what didn't fit — the story, the role, the person, the pattern — and suddenly you're holding empty hands.

What now?

The Ache of the In-Between

Creating space doesn't always feel exciting.

Sometimes it feels like grief.
Like boredom.
Like a kind of quiet ache.

Because when you've spent your whole life being *full* — of noise, of proving, of people, of plans — the absence of that can feel like lack.

But it isn't lack.

It's clearing.
It's preparation.
It's what happens just before life breathes in again.

If you rush to fill the void, you'll miss the beauty of the pause.

Try This: "Make Room in the Room" Exercise

Pick one area of your life — physical, emotional, relational, digital.
Ask yourself:

"What here no longer reflects who I'm becoming?"

Then remove one thing.

Not to punish.
Not to fix.

But to practice.

To send a signal to your nervous system: *I'm allowed to have space.*
I don't have to hold everything.
I don't have to keep what I've outgrown.

Sometimes, the deepest self-trust starts with a cleared drawer. A paused habit. A no you finally say.

Why Space Feels Uncomfortable (and Why That's Okay)

You've been taught to fill the gaps.

Idle time means you're lazy.
Empty space means something's wrong.
Silence means disconnection.

But what if none of that is true?

What if the discomfort you feel isn't danger — but detox?

You're not breaking.
You're unlearning.

Letting go of the reflex to fix.
The reflex to scroll.
The reflex to "just do something" when your body is begging you to be still.

Sometimes, that discomfort is your first real breath in years.

The Difference Between Numbness and Spaciousness

Numbness is a shutting down.
Spaciousness is a softening open.

It's easy to confuse the two.
To think that quiet means you've lost something.

But spaciousness isn't emptiness.

It's an invitation.
To hear your real voice again.
To let your intuition speak before someone else's opinion floods in.
To notice what you truly want — not what you've been conditioned to chase.

If numbness feels like collapse, spaciousness feels like a gentle, unfamiliar expansion.

Try This: "Breathe Before You Reach" Practice

Next time you feel the impulse to check your phone, fill your schedule, say yes out of habit — pause.

Inhale for four counts.
Exhale for six.

Then ask yourself:

"Am I reaching to avoid space? Or am I reaching for what I actually need?"

Sometimes the answer will surprise you.

The more you honour the pause, the more clearly you'll hear your truth inside it.

You Don't Have to Know What Comes Next

One of the hardest things about space is this:

You don't always know what it's for.

You've cleared something — a habit, a relationship, a role — and now there's this wide expanse of unknown.
Your brain wants to fill it immediately.
Your ego wants to solve it.
Your fear wants to sprint toward the nearest certainty.

But sometimes, space isn't a problem to solve.
It's an opening to hold.

You don't have to know what's coming to trust that something *will*.

The Garden Metaphor: Dormancy Before Bloom

Think of a winter garden.
Barren. Brown. Silent.

To the untrained eye, it looks lifeless.

But underneath the soil, everything is shifting.
The roots are deepening.
The ground is absorbing what it needs.
The ecosystem is preparing for new life — quietly, invisibly, patiently.

That's what space is.

It's winter before spring.
It's stillness before the stretch.
It's the part of the story where you're becoming, even if nothing looks like it yet.

You are not behind.
You are not lost.

You are simply in the sacred pause between seasons.

Try This: The "Let It Be Empty" List

Open a journal and title the page:
"Let It Be Empty"

Then list 3-5 areas of your life where you've been trying to rush a solution, force an outcome, or fill a gap out of fear.

Next to each one, write:

"I give this space to bloom without my interference."

It may feel strange. Vulnerable.
But it also signals trust.

You're telling life:
I am willing to be in the fertile void.
I trust something meaningful is forming, even if I can't see it yet.

Making Space Isn't Passive — It's Intentional

Letting go can feel like giving up.
Resting can feel like avoidance.
Pausing can feel like paralysis.

But space — true space — is not a void of action.
It is an act of choosing.

Choosing to no longer fill your life with things that don't serve you.
Choosing to open your time, your heart, your calendar, your mind.
Choosing to release the chaos just long enough to hear what's under it.

Space is not the absence of effort.
It's the redirection of it — toward what actually matters.

Where Are You Overcrowded?

It might not be obvious.
Sometimes, the crowding is emotional.

A backlog of old resentments.
Thought patterns you inherited but never questioned.
A constant low-grade tension humming under your skin.

Sometimes, the clutter isn't physical — it's internal.
And even if your schedule looks clear, your spirit can feel crammed.

Start here:

What is taking up space in your life that you didn't *consciously* invite?

That question alone can open a doorway.
Not to shame.
But to awareness.
And from awareness, choice.

Try This: The "Three Things I Can Release" Prompt

Find a quiet place.
Breathe deeply.

Then write:

1. One habit I can loosen

2. One belief I'm ready to question

3. One small thing I can clear today

These don't have to be huge.
Sometimes the smallest clearings create the biggest shifts.
Like opening a window and feeling your whole body exhale.

Letting go isn't always dramatic.
Often, it's ordinary.
Unassuming.
Quiet.

But space made intentionally will always fill itself with something better — eventually.

You Are Allowed to Want More

There's a quiet ache that comes from settling.

You may not even notice it at first.
It hums beneath the surface — in the sigh before you open your inbox, in the tension that settles into your shoulders when someone asks how you're doing and you respond, "I'm fine."

But you're not.

You've been making do.
Tolerating.
Shrinking just enough to fit the version of life that once worked, but doesn't anymore.
And for a while, maybe that felt safe.
Maybe it felt easier than asking the question you've been avoiding:

"Is this enough for me?"

Not in a greedy way. Not in a "more, more, more" kind of hunger.
But in a soul-deep whisper that says:

"I think I'm meant to stretch a little further.
I think I'm ready for something truer.
I think I want more."

The Complicated Grief of Letting Go of "Good Enough"

This is one of the hardest types of letting go — when what you're walking away from wasn't terrible.

It wasn't abusive.
It wasn't toxic.
It wasn't even all that wrong.

It was... fine.

A job that paid the bills.
A relationship that worked on paper.
A city you grew up in and out of at the same time.

These are the things that trip us up the most — not the clearly painful, but the quietly misaligned. Because they come wrapped in guilt.

Guilt for not being grateful.
Guilt for being "too much."
Guilt for wanting what hasn't yet shown up.

But here's what no one tells you:

Gratitude and longing can live in the same breath.

You can thank your past for what it gave you — and still choose a future that feels better.
You can honour what worked — and still leave what no longer fits.
You can love parts of something deeply — and still know it's time to release the whole.

Try This: "The Gratitude + Goodbye" Practice

If you're struggling with guilt for letting go of something that was *almost* right, this practice is for you.

In your journal (or aloud, if that feels more powerful), write a two-part letter to the person, place, habit, or identity you're releasing.

Start with:

"Thank you for…"
"You helped me…"

Let yourself list all the gifts, all the ways it served you, all the reasons you once needed it.
Let the honouring be full and true.

Then begin the second half:

"And now I'm choosing to let go of…"
"Because I've changed. Because I'm ready. Because I no longer fit where I used to."

Don't rush it.
Let the words come as they need to.
Even if your voice shakes. Even if your heart hurts.

Sometimes clarity arrives only after we've spoken what we were afraid to admit:
That the version of ourselves who needed that chapter is not the version we are becoming.

Permission to Expand

So here it is.

The permission you've been waiting for.
To grow beyond what's just okay.
To want a life that fills you instead of just functioning for you.
To claim your own longing without apology.

Because here's the truth that might scare you — but also free you:

You do not owe your loyalty to a life you've outgrown.

Not to the job.
Not to the relationship.
Not to the dream you once had that no longer fits who you've become.

Your life is allowed to evolve.
And so are you.

Releasing the Shame of Wanting More

It's not selfish to want more space.
More peace.
More joy.

It's not indulgent to want ease instead of just survival.
It's not dramatic to want your life to feel like your own.

You've spent so long making yourself smaller — to be digestible, to be agreeable, to not be "too much."
But what if too muchness is where your magic lives?
What if wanting more isn't a flaw — but a compass?

You're not broken for feeling restless.
You're awakening.

Final Prompt: "What Wants to Grow If I Make Room?"

Close your eyes.
Breathe slowly.

Then ask yourself:

"What inside me is waiting for space to grow?"

Not a perfect plan.
Not a ten-year vision.

Just a whisper. A direction. A seed.

Maybe it's rest.
Maybe it's a shift.
Maybe it's joy, creativity, solitude, connection — whatever your soul has been gently asking for in the quiet moments.

Write it down.
Name it.
And trust that by making space, you are already saying yes to it.

Not Everything That Comes After the Clearing Will Be Immediate

Creating space is brave.
But let's be honest — it's also disorienting.

After you release what no longer fits, there's often... nothing.
No flash of insight.
No sudden clarity.
No magical new beginning rushing in to fill the silence.

Just quiet.
And maybe some doubt.

You did the hard thing — the courageous, self-honouring thing — and now you're staring at the blank space where something used to be.
It's tempting to rush to fill it.
To grab the next best thing.
To answer the question:

"What now?"
before the question has even had time to breathe.

But here's the truth:

Sometimes space is not meant to be filled.
Sometimes it's meant to *hold* you.

The In-Between Is a Sacred Place

This liminal space — between what was and what will be — is not failure.
It is a rite of passage.

It's the pause between the inhale and the exhale.
It's the moment between planting a seed and seeing green break through the soil.
It's the hush before the music begins again.

And though it may not look like progress, this is where transformation takes root.

But it doesn't feel glamorous.
There are no gold stars for staying still.
No applause for waiting.
Only the quiet bravery of trusting that the new beginning will arrive on its own time.

A Story: The Unfurnished Apartment

I once knew someone who, after ending a long-term relationship, moved into a small one-bedroom apartment with no furniture except a mattress and a lamp.
For weeks, she sat in that space after work — no TV, no distractions — just stillness and grief and the echoes of her own breath.

People offered her couches.
Chairs.
A new relationship.

She said no.

She said, "I want to know what it's like to be alone in my life and not be afraid of the quiet."

Months passed. She slowly began to fill the space — with intention.
A second hand bookshelf.
A plant she actually kept alive.
Eventually, a dining table — and the friends to sit around it.

But the most sacred thing in that space wasn't the furniture.
It was the pause.
The choosing.
The willingness to sit in nothing so she wouldn't settle for almost-anything again.

Try This: "The Empty Chair" Exercise

Find a chair in your home — or place a cushion on the ground.

Make it intentional.

Let it be a space where nothing is expected of you.

Sit there once a day, even for just five minutes.

No scrolling.
No solving.
No filling.

Let it be a container for presence.

And as you sit, ask:

"What is here, in me, when I'm not trying to fix or force?"

You may be surprised by what rises in the stillness.
Grief.
Yes.
But also... clarity.
Desire.
Peace.

Space reveals things.
But only when we stop trying to escape it.

The Fear of Emptiness Is a Learned Fear

Most of us have been conditioned to believe that stillness is lazy, emptiness is dangerous, and silence means failure.

So we fill.

We overcommit, overconsume, overthink — not because we're weak, but because we were never taught how to hold emptiness without fear.

But here's the radical truth:
The space you create by letting go is not a void.
It's a womb.

A place where something new will grow — but only if you stop trying to fill it with noise.

The Ache of Almost

There's a strange kind of ache that comes not from loss, but from nearness.
The almost.
The maybes.
The "it could have been something" things that never quite became what you hoped for.

And when you start clearing space in your life, those almost tend to rise.
They sit at the edge of your awareness like ghosts asking to be let in again.

"Maybe you were too quick to walk away."
"Maybe you expected too much."
"Maybe that was your one shot."

Almosts are seductive.

They don't ask for commitment — just reconsideration.
They offer the illusion of comfort without the substance of growth.
And if you're not careful, they'll trick you into rebuilding what you just bravely dismantled.

Because familiarity feels safe.
Even when it's not right.

Why We're Drawn Back to What We've Outgrown

It's not weakness that makes us want to go back.
It's biology.
Neurology.
The way our brains are wired to seek predictability, even in pain.

Our nervous systems don't know the difference between comfort and familiarity.
They only know safety.
And when safety has been wired to chaos, or compromise, or survival-mode hustle —
Even *space* can feel like danger.

So we reach.
For the job we know how to do.
The person who knows our triggers.
The self we used to be, because she knew how to operate in the old world.

But just because something feels safe, doesn't mean it is.

And just because something is unfamiliar, doesn't mean it's wrong.

A Story: The Coat She Couldn't Keep Wearing

Years ago, I had a heavy winter coat that had seen me through the worst season of my life.
I wore it through heartbreak, through anxiety spirals, through panic attacks in supermarket aisles.
It smelled like my old apartment.
It was frayed at the cuffs.
It held the shape of my fear.

But it had also kept me warm.

When I finally started healing, I went to donate the coat.
I held it in my arms at the donation bin, fingers curled around the threadbare collar —
And I cried.

Not because I wanted to wear it again.
But because it had carried me.
It had been enough, when I had nothing else.

And some part of me didn't want to let go of the version of myself that had survived in it.

But I left it there.
Not out of rejection.
But reverence.

We don't have to keep wearing what kept us alive.

Try This: The "Used to Be Me" Letter

Write a letter to a former version of yourself.

Not to judge her.
Not to fix her.
Not to pity her.

But to honour her.

Start with:

"You did what you had to do."

Continue with:

"I see now what it cost."

And close with:

"Thank you. But I'm not that version anymore."

This isn't a declaration of war against your past.
It's a release.
It's a signal to your nervous system that it's safe to move forward now — not because the past was bad, but because you've outgrown its shape.

The Courage to Not Go Back

Let's be honest.
Growth is not always graceful.

There will be moments you miss the old version of yourself.
The one who didn't ask for too much.
The one who could contort herself into the life that no longer fits.
The one who knew how to stay quiet to avoid being left.

But you're not that person anymore.
You're not required to shrink for comfort.

The ache of the almosts might still come.
Let it.
Hold it like a wave.
Let it crash over you.
Then let it recede.

Because every time you choose *not* to go back —
Every time you don't answer the text.
Every time you don't accept the offer.
Every time you say "thank you, but no" —
You're making space.

And space is sacred.

When Something New Doesn't Look Like What You Expected

We talk a lot about new beginnings as if they arrive with trumpets.
As if the universe delivers clarity in a golden envelope marked *"you're ready now."*
But most of the time?

Something new shows up disguised.
It doesn't announce itself as the thing you've been waiting for.
It shows up as an idea that won't leave you alone.
As a conversation that stirs something.
As an invitation that makes you nervous — but also curious.

New doesn't always look shiny.
Sometimes it looks inconvenient.
Sometimes it looks like loss — because what's arriving doesn't fit into your old life.

We want the new to feel good.
But the truth?
It often feels awkward before it feels right.

The False Promise of "When I'm Ready"

You don't have to feel fully ready to say yes to what's next.
In fact, you probably won't.

The idea that you'll feel perfectly prepared, emotionally regulated, financially stable, and spiritually aligned *at the same time* is a myth.
It's a comfortable story we tell ourselves to delay discomfort.

But life doesn't wait for your fear to calm down.
It simply offers.
And your job is not to be fearless.
Your job is to discern.

There's a difference between *not ready* and *not aligned*.
The first is fear.
The second is truth.

You'll know which is which if you pause long enough to feel it in your body.

A Story: The Invite That Made Her Sweat

A friend once told me about a creative retreat she got invited to — all expenses paid, with some of her favourite authors attending.

She almost said no.

Not because she didn't want to go, but because the invitation landed during a messy, uncertain chapter of her life.
She'd just left a toxic job.
She hadn't written in months.
She felt like an imposter.

She said, "I didn't feel worthy of showing up in a room full of people doing the thing I hadn't been able to do in years."

But she went anyway.
And not because she felt ready.

She went because she realized:

"If I wait until I feel like I belong, I'll never go anywhere new."

The experience didn't transform her overnight.
But it gave her a mirror.
One that showed who she was beneath the story of who she had been.

Sometimes the most powerful shifts happen not because we're ready — but because we're finally willing.

Try This: The "Would I Regret Saying No?" Gut Check

When something new presents itself and you feel unsure, ask:

"If I say no to this, will I regret it in a year?"

Not *will it be perfect.*
Not *will it solve everything.*
Just…

"Will I wonder what would have happened if I had let myself try?"

If the answer is yes, then you've already heard the truth.

You don't need certainty.
You need curiosity.
You need a crack of willingness wide enough for something new to enter.

You are not obligated to say yes to everything.
But you are allowed to say yes before you feel completely ready.

New Isn't Always a Thing. Sometimes, It's a Way.

Here's something we often forget:
The "new" that's trying to arrive might not be a job, or a partner, or a bold adventure.

It might be a way of being.
A slower pace.
A softer voice.
A truer rhythm.

Sometimes what's trying to arrive is *you* — the version of you that's been waiting for space to emerge.

She's not flashy.
She doesn't demand attention.
She shows up in quiet moments when your body relaxes and your breath drops deeper into your belly.

When the noise fades, she speaks.
And when you stop running, she steps forward.

This, too, is new.

The Hush Before the Bloom

There's a silence that comes after you clear space —
not a void, exactly,
but a hush.

It's the moment after the storm when everything is still,
but not yet green again.

You've let go.
You've stepped away.
You've chosen not to return to what no longer fits.

But now what?

This is the in-between.
The part we don't talk about enough.
Where nothing new has arrived,
and the temptation to rush back into something —
anything — buzzes just beneath your skin.

We don't always crave the past.
Sometimes we just crave a shape to fill the ache.

But this ache isn't wrong.
It's what grows when we stop being full of what we don't need.

The Temptation to Fill the Gap Too Soon

There's a certain kind of panic that comes when space stretches out wider than we expected.

It can feel like loneliness,
even if we're surrounded by people.
It can feel like failure,
even if we know we made the right choice.

Because most of us are used to being full.
Full schedules.
Full inboxes.
Full of things we've been carrying so long they started to feel like parts of us.

And when we release them —
even with intention,
even with care —
the emptiness afterward can be disorienting.

So we look for quick fillers.
New goals.
New people.
New noise.

But healing doesn't always need more.
Sometimes it needs less.
Less pressure.
Less performance.
Less pretending we're further along than we are.

A Story: The Garden She Didn't Rush

There was a woman who tore up her backyard garden after years of neglect.
It had been overgrown for seasons — tangled vines, stubborn weeds, soil dry from trying to grow too many things at once.

She wanted to start fresh.
To plant vegetables.
To make something beautiful again.

But a gardener friend told her:

"Don't replant right away. Let the soil rest. Let it breathe. Let the old roots rot and feed what's next."

It felt counterintuitive.
To want something so badly and... wait?

But she listened.

She sat with the emptiness.
She watered it anyway.
She visited the bare earth each morning, hands in her pockets, coffee in hand, unsure what to do but present enough to witness the quiet transformation.

And when she finally did plant again —
the garden bloomed.

Stronger.
Deeper.
More intentional than it had ever been.

Not because she rushed to fill the space.
But because she allowed it to be empty first.

Try This: The "Daily Space" Ritual

Create one pocket of unstructured space each day.
Just one.

It doesn't have to be long.
Even ten minutes can be sacred.

Sit somewhere you don't usually sit.
Turn off your phone.
Don't plan.
Don't journal.
Don't fix.

Just sit with yourself.

You might feel restless.
That's okay.

You're not doing it wrong.
You're just not used to the quiet yet.

If emotion comes — let it.
If a thought surfaces — witness it.

This is your space.
Not to perform in.
Not to improve in.

Just to *be*.

Something New Will Come. But Not Always on Your Timeline.

The ache won't last forever.
The gap won't stay empty.

Something will grow here.
But not on command.

You can't manifest healing by force.
You can't rush what asks to be rooted first.

And you don't need to.

Your life isn't on pause.
This is part of the blooming.

It just doesn't look like it yet.

So when it feels like nothing is happening —
when you're sitting in the quiet and wondering if you've made a mistake —
breathe deeper.

You're not behind.
You're becoming.

The silence is not absence.
It's preparation.

When You're Ready to Receive

Sometimes, newness doesn't knock.
It waits.

Not out of cruelty.
But out of respect.

It waits for you to stop filling the doorway with old stories.
It waits until there's space enough for it to be received.
Not grabbed.
Not earned.
But welcomed.

And that kind of readiness isn't about doing more.
It's about softening.
Opening.

Not everything new will change your life.
But some things will change your relationship to it.

And that's the shift that matters most.

You Will Not Miss What's Meant for You

This isn't just something people say to comfort each other.

It's a spiritual law.
One that doesn't rely on belief — just on being.

You may miss opportunities.
You may take detours.
You may say no when you could have said yes.

But what's *meant* for you?
It doesn't vanish.

It returns when there's room.
It reconfigures until you're ready.
It shows up again, wearing a new name or face or invitation — but always humming with that same internal knowing.

The right things have a tone.
And when your heart is attuned, you'll recognize the song.

Not through logic.
But through resonance.

A Story: The Apartment She Almost Didn't See

A woman once scoured the city for a new apartment.
She was exhausted, disheartened, convinced she'd never find a space that felt like home.

Then one day, she passed by a building she'd ignored dozens of times.
It looked too plain, too small, too… not her.

But something told her to stop.

She went inside.
Climbed the narrow stairs.
And stepped into a room bathed in golden light.

There was nothing extraordinary about it.
But she cried anyway.

"It felt like the place had been waiting for me," she said.
"But it could only meet me once I stopped searching for what I thought I needed."

Space had been made.
She had cleared the noise.
And so it could find her.

Try This: The "Welcome Letter" Practice

Write a letter to what you're ready to welcome —
even if you don't know what it is yet.

You don't have to name it.
You don't have to define the details.

Begin like this:

"Dear What's Meant for Me,
I've cleared space for you.
I may still be scared.
But I'm willing to meet you when you come."

Speak to it as if it's real.
Because it is.

Write with honesty.
With heart.
With curiosity.

You're not asking.
You're receiving.

Not with expectation.
But with presence.

You Are Not Empty. You Are Ready.

This chapter of your life might feel like a pause.
A strange in-between.
A clearing.

But it's not emptiness.
It's invitation.

To slow down.
To listen.
To become.

Letting go was an act of courage.
But holding space —
letting yourself not rush the rebuild —
that's an act of trust.

You do not need to chase what's next.
You are allowed to be still until it arrives.

And when it does?

You will not need to grip it tightly.
You will not need to prove your worth.
You will simply feel it:

This fits.
This is for me.
This is what I made space for.

CHAPTER 8
STILLNESS ISN'T LAZINESS

8. Stillness Isn't Laziness

There is a kind of tired that sleep doesn't touch.

It sits deeper. Beneath the body. In the soul.
It's not caused by effort, exactly, but by expectation —
the kind that tells you if you're not producing, you're wasting time.
That rest is indulgence.
That slowing down is falling behind.

We live in a world that rewards momentum.
Faster. Sooner. More.
Where rest is labelled luxury, or laziness, or something you earn after burning yourself out.

But what if stillness is not the opposite of growth?

What if it's the ground in which the next part of you is meant to root?

You don't need to move to prove you're alive.
You don't need to run just because the world is loud.

There is a rebellion in sitting still — not as a passive act, but a powerful one.
A choice to stop performing urgency and start trusting in rhythm.

Nature knows this.
The mountains do not move to be worthy of reverence.

The trees don't bloom year-round to stay relevant.
The tide goes out. On purpose.

And so can you.

Stillness is not a sign you've failed to keep up.
It's a sign you're listening.

To your own breath.
To the gentle pulse of becoming.
To the part of you that refuses to rush just because everyone else is.

There are seasons for sowing.
For doing.
For becoming.

But there are also seasons for pausing.
Letting the work breathe.
Letting your self breathe.

When everything in you wants to chase one more task — pause.
When the guilt creeps in because you rested too long — breathe.

You don't have to earn this moment.

This moment belongs to you.

And if it feels unfamiliar — even uncomfortable — that's okay.
You've been trained to measure your worth by your motion.

But you are not a machine.
You are a human being who gets to *be*.

Being is enough.

Even when you're not helping someone.
Even when you're not making progress.
Even when the world scrolls past you at dizzying speeds and you decide to stay still.

Especially then.

Because the pace of your life should not be determined by the panic of someone else's.

And because peace isn't always found in action.
Sometimes it's found in the sacred space between.

The pause before the next breath.
The moment your shoulders finally drop.
The way your heart softens when you stop asking it to prove itself.

Stillness is strength — not softness as weakness, but softness as wisdom.

There are answers that only reveal themselves when you're quiet enough to hear them.
There are truths that only emerge when you stop drowning them in busyness.

So when the world says "hustle," let yourself whisper back:
"No, thank you. I'm already enough."

There's a strange kind of discomfort that comes with doing nothing.
Not boredom — something more subtle.
It's the ache of internal restlessness.
The guilt of not being useful.

You sit down, finally.
Take a breath.
And your brain begins to yell.

You forgot that email.
You should be cleaning.
You need to check in.
You're falling behind.

It's not laziness you're fighting.
It's the conditioning that told you: if you're not stressed, you're not trying hard enough.

Stillness triggers all the parts of you that were taught to measure value by motion.

You weren't born that way.
But you learned it.
From a world that rewards burnout and calls it dedication.
From systems that profit off your constant self-improvement.
From family, perhaps, who didn't know how to rest themselves.

So the moment you try to reclaim stillness —
you'll meet resistance.

But what if that resistance isn't a warning?
What if it's a signal of healing?

Healing isn't always peaceful.
Sometimes it's uncomfortable.
Sometimes it feels like failure.

Because to heal, you have to stop moving long enough to feel.

And when you've used movement — achievement, distraction, productivity — as a way to avoid the hard stuff inside, stillness becomes the mirror you've been avoiding.

It shows you the ache you buried under your busyness.
It reveals the fatigue you ignored.
It brings up the grief, the longing, the truth.

But this isn't punishment.
It's permission.

Stillness makes room for what's real.
It gives your body a chance to speak.
It gives your mind a moment to soften.
It gives your heart a place to land.

And even when it hurts —
especially when it hurts —
it is sacred.

Stillness isn't always calm.
Sometimes it's chaotic.

Sometimes it's full of old noise surfacing because it finally can.

But that's not a reason to run.

That's a reason to stay.

To breathe.

To hold yourself through it.

Because on the other side of that internal resistance is something holy.
A kind of rest that doesn't just soothe the body, but rearranges the soul.
Not the quick nap kind.
The kind of rest that says:
You don't have to be anything else right now.
You don't have to prove or earn or perform.
You get to just be.

Let that be enough.

There's something deeply unsettling about silence when you're used to noise.

Not just the obvious kind — notifications, traffic, talking — but the more insidious noise. The mental tabs you never close. The planning, the reviewing, the fixing, the watching-yourself-from-above kind of constant self-monitoring that becomes so normal, you forget it isn't rest. You sit in a quiet room and think it's silent, but your brain is still sprinting laps, chewing on the next decision, the next worry, the next expectation you'll either meet or fail.

This is why stillness scares people.

It's not because it's empty.
It's because it's full.
Full of everything you've avoided. Full of truths you can't dodge when there's no noise to drown them.

Stillness, real stillness, strips you bare.
It shows you the shape of your mind.
And that's a vulnerable thing to witness — especially when most of your life has been structured to avoid it.

But there's also something liberating about that bareness.

When you let yourself stay in the quiet long enough, when you breathe past the initial discomfort, something shifts. The noise doesn't disappear, but it softens. The background chaos that used to run your nervous system like an engine begins to lose its grip. You stop needing to narrate your every moment. You stop trying to fill every pause. You start to hear your own voice again — not the voice of expectation or fear or obligation. The deeper one. The voice beneath all that.

This voice is slower. Quieter. But not weaker.
It says things like: You don't have to do that right now.
It says: You are allowed to stop.
It says: What if you just sat with it? What if that was enough?

And at first, it sounds wrong. Foreign. Lazy, even. Because your conditioning will tell you that slowing down is dangerous. That rest will make you irrelevant. That stillness equals stagnation.

But those are lies.

Stillness is not stagnation.
It's not resignation.
It's not the end of growth.

It's the beginning of a different kind.

The kind of growth that doesn't rely on willpower or effort alone, but on restoration. On recovery. On letting your nervous system come back into balance so that your next movement isn't just a reflex, but a choice.

Because there's a difference between running and being pulled forward by clarity.
There's a difference between hustling and aligning.

But you can't tell the difference unless you stop long enough to check in.

When you practice stillness — and yes, it is a practice, not a perfect state — you begin to notice how many of your actions are based in fear. Fear of missing out. Fear of being seen as lazy. Fear of disappointing others. Fear of sitting with your own feelings. Fear of failing.

And when those fears start to surface, your first instinct might be to run.
Scroll. Text. Plan. Organize. Overcommit.
The pull back into motion will be strong. Familiar. Comfortable, even.

But what happens if you stay?

What happens if you notice the discomfort and choose not to escape it?

This is where transformation begins.
Not in the grand declarations or bold leaps — but in the quiet moments where you stay with yourself, when every part of you is begging to flee.

Stillness builds tolerance.
For uncertainty. For discomfort. For life.

It teaches you that you can survive the pause.

More than that — that you can thrive in it.

Not because you're achieving anything during your stillness, but because you're letting yourself be whole.

Because you're making contact with the parts of you that only speak in silence. Because you're rebuilding your inner trust by not abandoning yourself in the name of productivity.

We talk so much about self-care, but rarely about the courage it takes to sit in silence with your own truth. That's what real rest requires. Not scented candles or spa days — although those can be lovely.
But the kind of rest that asks you to stop proving.
To stop escaping.
To stop trying to earn a break and simply take one.

It's not just rebellious. It's radical.

In a world that rewards urgency, rest becomes an act of quiet defiance.

The moment you step back — not out of resignation, but restoration — the world keeps spinning. Deadlines pass. Emails wait. Voices clamour. But you, rooted in stillness, begin to realize that not every fire needs your tending. Not every signal requires a response. The world is loud. But not everything loud is important.

This shift doesn't happen all at once.
It comes slowly, over time — a kind of soft revolution inside you.

At first, the stillness feels indulgent. You worry that you're falling behind. That while you pause, others are accelerating, achieving, ascending. It's hard not to compare when you've been trained to measure yourself by your output.

But then something curious happens:
You begin to notice how much of what you called "urgency" was actually anxiety.
How much of your "responsiveness" was just a fear of being forgotten.
How many of your yeses came from a place of depletion, not desire.

Stillness reveals this gently. Not as judgment, but as clarity.

You begin to hear the difference between your survival voice — the one shouting, pushing, proving — and your soul's voice, which whispers, waits, and only speaks when you're quiet enough to listen.

This listening takes practice.

You'll forget. You'll get swept back into the noise.
You'll find yourself reaching for your phone in moments of pause.
You'll catch yourself filling the silence just to avoid what might rise up in it.

But slowly, with compassion, you begin to return.

Not to an ideal version of rest, but to yourself.
To your body. To your breath. To the space between doing and undoing.

And in that return, you may realize something radical:

Stillness isn't a luxury.
It's a birthright.

You weren't born to hustle. You weren't created to perform your worth.
Before you knew the word "productivity," you knew how to be.

As a child, you knew how to stare out windows.
To listen to the wind.
To sit in grass without guilt.
To take your time without apology.

Somewhere along the way, that knowing was trained out of you.

But it's not gone.

It's waiting — underneath the layers of urgency, beneath the to-do lists taped to your worth, beyond the metrics and measurements.

Stillness is not something you have to earn your way back to.
It's something you remember.
Reclaim.
Receive.

And when you do, you begin to understand the depth of rest.

Rest is not the absence of effort.
It is the presence of trust.

To rest is to say: I trust that I am allowed to pause.
I trust that I am still enough, even in stillness.
I trust that growth continues, even when I am not managing it.

And most of all: I trust that I do not have to do anything to deserve peace.

This is what rest becomes: not just something you give yourself at the end of exhaustion, but something you fold into your days as proof that your worth is not transactional.

It is permission.
It is protest.
It is practice.

Stillness teaches you how to inhabit time, not conquer it.

In a culture obsessed with hacking time, filling it, squeezing every ounce of output from every minute — stillness is a return to wholeness. It says: you are not a machine. You are not a task to be optimized. You are a living body, a layered self, a spirit that pulses beyond productivity.

And yet, this remembering can feel like grief.

Because to reclaim rest, you have to acknowledge how much you've abandoned it. How often you've overridden your own signals. How long you've pushed when you needed to pause. It's humbling to see it — how long you've been living in reaction, not in rhythm.

But even the grief is sacred.

It means you're waking up.

Waking up to the fact that not all fatigue is fixed by sleep.
Waking up to the nervous system that never felt safe enough to relax.
Waking up to the truth that you don't just need rest — you need repair.

This kind of repair isn't found in a weekend off or a vacation booked six months from now. It happens moment by moment, in the small decisions to return to yourself. To breathe before you respond. To sit without solving. To let the dish sit in the sink if it means reclaiming five minutes of stillness.

There is no moral prize for exhaustion.
No trophy for burnout.
No gold star for never stopping.

And yet, for many of us, we've worn depletion like a badge of honour.
We've equated exhaustion with excellence.
Busyness with importance.
Fatigue with proof of how hard we're trying.

But what if rest was a greater measure of trust?

Not just in the world — but in yourself.

Trust that you are still worthy when you're not producing.
Trust that you can rest without falling apart.
Trust that life will not collapse because you stepped back to breathe.

This is the internal rewiring that happens through stillness.
It's not always dramatic. It's not always pretty.
But it is powerful.

Because eventually, your nervous system begins to believe you.

It begins to understand that you're no longer living on the edge of burnout.
That you are no longer waiting for a crash to give

yourself permission to stop.
That rest is not conditional — it is built in. Expected. Safe.

And in that safety, your body starts to repair.
Your creativity returns.
Your sense of humour. Your groundedness. Your clarity.
The fog begins to lift, not all at once, but steadily.

You start to notice beauty again.
The way light hits the wall in the late afternoon.
The softness of a quiet morning.
The joy of doing nothing — not because you've earned it, but because you're allowed to be.

This is when stillness becomes not just a tool, but a companion.

It walks with you.
It waits for you.
It meets you in the quiet corners of your day and says, gently, you don't have to rush.

And when the world pulls you back into the noise — and it will — you carry a deeper center inside you.

You remember what it feels like to rest.

You remember that peace is not something you chase.
It's something you practice.
Something you return to again and again, even if just for a moment at a time.

There's a kind of power that comes from no longer being driven by urgency.

You begin to notice how much noise you used to mistake for meaning. How much of what felt essential was simply habit. Repetition. The unspoken belief that unless you were constantly in motion, you'd lose your place in the world.

Stillness interrupts that.
Not to shame you — but to awaken you.

It helps you see the ways your energy has been leaking.
Every moment of performative presence.
Every reflexive "yes" that buried your needs.
Every conversation where you stayed polite instead of present.

These little fractures — over time — cost you your wholeness.

But in stillness, you begin the quiet repair.

You feel into the parts of yourself that have been rushing for years.
The part that always says "I'm fine" when you're not.
The part that carries everyone else's expectations without complaint.
The part that can't sit still, because stillness has always been followed by judgment.

Let that part rest.

Let her be tired. Let her stop carrying it all. Let her know: you are safe now.

You don't have to earn rest by burning out first.
You don't have to apologize for slowing down.
You don't have to justify the quiet with future productivity.

Sometimes, the quiet is the medicine.
Sometimes, what you need most isn't a solution, but a soft place to land.

And no one else can create that soft place for you.
You have to be the one to say: enough.
Enough running. Enough proving. Enough noise.

Because peace is not passive.
It's a practice.
A muscle you build every time you choose to stay instead of flee.
Every time you sit with discomfort instead of numbing it.
Every time you let yourself be, without needing to be more.

And yes — it will feel unfamiliar at first.

You might fidget.
You might reach for your phone.
You might find your thoughts racing and your breath shallow.

This is not a sign you're failing at stillness.
It's a sign you're arriving.

You're meeting yourself, beneath the noise.
You're feeling what your nervous system has been holding.
You're finally listening to what got drowned out in all the doing.

And in that listening, something begins to soften.

You stop trying to fix every discomfort.
You stop trying to outrun every ache.
You stop needing life to be tidy before you can be at peace.

Stillness doesn't demand perfection.
It asks for presence.

Not forever — just here. Just now.
Just long enough to remember who you are underneath the world's expectations.

You are not behind.
You are not broken.
You are not lazy.

You are a living body, worthy of rest.

You are a layered being, worthy of pause.

You are a soul, worthy of silence — not because you've earned it, but because you exist.

Stillness becomes revolutionary the moment you stop needing it to look a certain way.

It doesn't always arrive as serene meditation or silent forests. Sometimes it comes in micro-moments: a single deep breath in the car before walking into the room. A pause before responding. A cup of tea where you actually sit down. The decision to do nothing for ten minutes — and not feel guilty about it.

Those moments matter.

They teach your nervous system that you don't have to be on all the time.
They rewire the belief that every second must be optimized.
They carve out room for presence to return, breath by breath.

Because presence isn't always found in the grand gestures.
More often, it's found in what you don't do.

You don't check your phone first thing.
You don't scroll while eating.
You don't fill the silence just because it feels awkward.

You start leaving space.
Not empty space — sacred space.

This is how peace makes a home inside you.

And in time, something beautiful happens: you stop seeing stillness as separate from your life. It becomes woven into your day — not as an extra, but as a way of being.

You sit without fixing.
You listen without rushing to respond.
You rest without needing to collapse first.

And it doesn't make you lazy.
It makes you spacious.

You can hold more of yourself.
More nuance. More emotion. More of the messy middle where clarity hasn't come yet.

This is a strength few people talk about: the ability to stay with something, gently, when every instinct says to run or fix or numb.

To hold yourself in stillness — without panic, without punishment — is a sign of deep resilience.

It means you're no longer driven by fear.
You're no longer performing peace — you're practicing it.

Even when it's awkward.
Even when it's boring.
Even when nothing profound happens.

Because stillness isn't always profound. Sometimes it's quiet, mundane, uneventful.

And that, too, is sacred.

We live in a world addicted to drama, speed, and spectacle.
Stillness reminds us: you don't have to live in reaction.
You can live in rhythm.

You can live by your breath, not your to-do list.

You can live by what feels grounded, not what gets applause.

You can live from the inside out — even when the outside world doesn't understand.

Stillness becomes a compass when you let it.
Not a rigid rule, but a gentle return. A homecoming.

You notice the way light falls through the window. The sound of wind in the leaves. The rhythm of your own thoughts, no longer interrupted by constant noise.

And in that noticing, something sacred opens.

You begin to trust life again — not because you're in control, but because you're connected.
To your body.
To your breath.
To the quiet knowing that you are enough, even in rest.

Stillness asks you to believe that your worth is not measured in hustle. That you are not behind for taking your time. That pausing isn't failure, but wisdom.

It challenges everything the world told you about value.
It teaches you to stop rushing healing.
To stop rushing clarity.
To stop rushing your becoming.

You are not a machine. You are a living thing. Living things rest. They have seasons. They bloom, they wither, they lie dormant.

Stillness honours all of it.

It honours the winter inside you, the longing for quiet, the ache to stop striving and just be.
It welcomes the silence you were taught to fear.
It teaches you to meet yourself not with urgency, but with softness.

And maybe — just maybe — that softness will teach you something that force never could.

That rest is not idle.
It's a way back to truth.

Stillness is not a performance.

It is not something you prove, perfect, or polish until it looks enlightened.

It is something you let in.

You let it settle around you like dust in sunlight.
You let it hum beneath your thoughts without needing to silence them.
You let it wrap around the parts of you that ache from trying too hard.

Sometimes stillness is a room.
But more often, it's a choice.

A choice not to interrupt yourself.
A choice not to abandon the moment.
A choice to remain soft, even when it feels like softness won't be enough.

When you begin to explore stillness, you will meet your resistance.
The itch to move. The need to explain. The story that says rest must be earned.
You'll meet guilt. You'll meet boredom. You'll meet all the ways you've been taught to keep running.

Let them come.
But do not let them rule.

Stillness doesn't mean the absence of thoughts.
It means the absence of chasing them.

You let them pass, like clouds across the sky.
You let yourself breathe, without shaping the breath.
You stop trying to do it "right."
You simply do it.

And in that simplicity, you begin to return to yourself.

We think we need more stimulation when we're tired — more caffeine, more input, more distraction. But often, what we truly need is less.

Less noise.
Less urgency.
Less expectation to be anything other than present.

It feels counterintuitive, at first.
Especially when you've spent a lifetime associating worth with productivity.

But something deep inside you already knows: there's another way.

A way that doesn't require you to burn out to deserve rest.
A way that honours your being, not just your doing.
A way that says: even here, in stillness, I am valuable.

You are not lazy for choosing stillness.
You are not lazy for needing rest.
You are not lazy for wanting quiet.

You are human.

And humans — real, feeling, fallible humans — were never designed to be in constant motion.

You were meant to pause.
To digest experience.
To notice beauty.
To hear your own heart.

Stillness is where that remembering happens.

And when it does, you begin to live differently.

You begin to measure your days not by what you squeezed out of them, but by what you let in.

Laughter.
Gratitude.
Wonder.
Peace.

Not because you chased them — but because you slowed down enough to see that they were already there.

Stillness doesn't need to change you. It just needs you to stop changing the subject.

That's what we often do — rush past ourselves. The moment things get quiet, we reach for distraction. A phone. A thought. A plan. Anything to keep us from settling into the still.

Because stillness asks us to feel.

To feel what we've buried in busyness.
To notice what we've skipped over in survival.
To acknowledge what we've numbed through the constant hum of doing.

But when we dare to stay — to stay in the breath, to stay in the moment, to stay in ourselves — we remember that silence is not a void. It's a mirror.

And in that mirror, we see the truth we were too afraid to meet.

That we are tired.
That we are tender.
That we are more than what we produce.

Stillness reflects us back to ourselves not in criticism, but in kindness. Not in judgment, but in presence.

And presence is the most honest place you can live.

It doesn't require perfection. It only requires participation. You show up. You breathe. You witness. You listen.

Stillness isn't passive.
It's wildly alive.

There is movement happening under the surface — not the kind you can track with checklists, but the kind that softens your jaw and slows your pulse.
The kind that makes space for insight.
For grief.
For grace.

You begin to understand that rest is not a detour from growth. It is the soil it grows from.

And when you allow yourself to be still, your life stops feeling like a reaction.

It becomes a response.

Intentional. Rooted. Grounded.

You no longer chase every demand as if it's urgent.
You begin to discern what truly matters.

You pause before saying yes.
You breathe before replying.
You think before jumping to fix.

That pause — that breath — that beat of stillness between stimulus and action?

That's your freedom.

It's where you reclaim yourself.

No longer just a function of the world's needs, but a sovereign being who responds rather than reacts.

And in that response, you begin to feel your power again.

Not the frantic kind.
The steady kind.

The kind that doesn't need to shout to be heard.
The kind that knows when to wait.
The kind that understands that sometimes the wisest thing you can do... is nothing.

And that "nothing" might be the most healing, powerful act of all.

You are not behind for resting.
You are not broken because you're tired.
You are not failing for needing pause.

You are a body that breathes.
You are a heart that holds.
You are a soul that feels.

And all of those things need space to just be.

Not perform.
Not produce.
Not even improve.

Just be.

This is where stillness becomes sacred. Not because of what it achieves, but because of what it honours.

The part of you that knows how to heal, if only you'll stop interrupting it.

Stillness allows the noise to settle.
It allows your nervous system to reset.
It allows your spirit to return home.

So much of what we call "self-care" is still about doing. This isn't that.

This is about not doing.
Not pushing.
Not controlling.

This is about surrender.

And yes, at first, surrender might feel like laziness. Because the world has taught you to equate your worth with your usefulness.

But rest is not idleness. It's rebellion.

In a culture obsessed with productivity, your stillness is a quiet protest. A reminder that you are not a machine. You are alive. And that aliveness deserves care, not constant extraction.

So you give yourself permission. Not once, but over and over.

You give yourself permission to stop.
To breathe.
To stare out the window and not explain why.
To unplug and not feel guilty.
To rest even when there are things unfinished.

You give yourself back to yourself.

And from that place — from that still, grounded, untouchable core — you begin to live more fully.

Because only in stillness can you truly hear what your life has been trying to tell you all along.

✼ Tools for Letting Stillness In

Here are a few gentle invitations to help you practice stillness — not as a task, but as a return.

1. The Stillness Window

Choose one moment each day — just ten minutes — where nothing is allowed to happen. No phone. No tasks. No stimulation. Just sit. Look out the window. Notice what you feel. Don't change it. Just witness.

2. Guilt-Release Journaling

On one page, write down every guilty thought that comes up when you rest.
Then ask, *Where did this belief come from? Who does it really serve?*
Let your answers be messy. Let them be honest. Guilt is not proof of wrongdoing — sometimes it's just an old voice that needs to be challenged.

3. The Mountain Breath

Sit with your spine tall. Imagine yourself as a mountain — still, grounded, immovable. As you inhale, feel your base settle. As you exhale, imagine your breath sweeping over your peaks and valleys. You are not going anywhere. You do not have to.

4. Presence Ritual

Choose one daily task — washing dishes, making tea, walking the dog — and do it in complete presence. No podcast. No multitasking. Just the sound of the water. The warmth of the mug. The rhythm of your steps. Let it be enough.

CHAPTER 9
THE ONGOING PRACTICE OF LIGHTNESS

9. The Ongoing Practice of Lightness

Letting go isn't something you do once.

It's something you do again. And again. And again.

Not just in the big moments — the breakups, the losses, the seismic shifts — but in the ordinary ones too. The small disappointments. The micro-frustrations. The silent expectations that don't get met.

Lightness isn't something you achieve. It's something you choose.

Not all at once, and not forever. But moment by moment.

You choose it when you unclench your jaw.
When you exhale just a little longer than usual.
When you don't send the message that won't be helpful.
When you let someone misunderstand you, and decide not to chase after your own defence.

This is the part no one talks about.

The aftermath.
The unglamorous middle.
The daily effort it takes to keep releasing what keeps sticking to you.

Because even when you've "let go," life keeps handing you new things to carry.

An unexpected bill.
A tense conversation.
A plan that doesn't go the way you'd hoped.

And every time, you'll feel it — that old reflex, that tightening inside that says, *Control it. Fix it. Force it.*

But lightness lives somewhere else.

It lives in the pause.
In the breath between reaction and response.
In the tiny opening where you remember you don't have to hold everything anymore.

That's what this chapter is about.

Not some grand, spiritual awakening.

But the simple, hard, holy practice of surrendering over and over again in the most ordinary moments of your life.

Letting go of the argument that plays in your head three hours after it ended.

Letting go of the version of yourself you thought you had to be by now.

Letting go of the idea that peace only comes when everything is done, fixed, or perfect.

It doesn't.

Peace comes when you stop bargaining with the moment.
When you say, *This is what is.*
And then soften into it.

This isn't always easy.

Sometimes it feels unnatural. Like trying to walk with someone else's legs. You've spent so many years gripping tightly to things that letting go feels risky. Vulnerable. Wrong.

But lightness doesn't mean you don't care.

It doesn't mean you give up.

It means you choose not to suffer over what you cannot control. It means you stop rehearsing worst-case scenarios in your head like they're rehearsals for safety. It means you drop the mental load — not because the world got lighter, but because *you* chose to.

Because you knew you could.

And maybe that's the most radical part of all: the belief that it's allowed to be lighter than this. That even when the world hurts, you don't have to carry every sharp edge inside you.

Lightness is not about escape.
It's about return.
Return to your breath.
Return to your body.
Return to the present moment, exactly as it is.

There's a line from the poet Mary Oliver that says, *"Keep some room in your heart for the unimaginable."*
That's what lightness makes possible.

You clear out just enough space to receive something new.

And often, what comes is better than what you were gripping so hard to keep.

The right words.
The right person.
The quiet joy of noticing the sky after a hard day.

This is how you begin again — gently, not urgently.
This is how you practice lightness — not by perfecting peace, but by letting yourself loosen your grip just once, then again, then once more.

That's enough.

That's the work.

And the more you do it, the more your nervous system remembers:
We don't have to live in the weight anymore.

Some days, lightness feels like rebellion.

You wake up already bracing for the weight — the to-do list, the messages, the quiet background guilt that hums behind productivity. It creeps in fast, before your feet hit the floor. And before you know it, your chest is tight again.

That's when the practice begins.

Because lightness doesn't wait until your life is calm. It doesn't require a clean slate or a perfect schedule. It meets you in the chaos and asks, *What can you set down, just for now?*

Maybe it's the belief that you're behind.
Maybe it's the pressure to explain yourself.
Maybe it's the shame that comes from resting while others are still working.

Let that go. For this breath, at least.

It might return tomorrow. But for now — release.

Not because someone gave you permission.
But because you remembered that you are not here to suffer just to prove you're good.

There's a quiet kind of strength in that.
A courage that doesn't shout, but stands its ground.
The feather doesn't demand to be noticed — and yet, when it drifts down, it softens everything it touches.

You can be that.

Not because you're detached or passive, but because you're done with performing pain for worth.

Because the weight you carry in your mind shapes how your body moves through the world.

And if your shoulders are always tense, if your jaw is always clenched, if your thoughts are always sprinting toward what's next — then lightness cannot find you.

Not because it isn't there.
But because there's no space for it to land.

You don't need to run away to find lightness.

You don't need a cabin in the woods or a week of silence in a monastery — though those things can help.

You need a moment. One tiny crack in the concrete of your day.

Five minutes with your phone across the room.

A slow walk with no destination.

A pause before you answer the question, just long enough to notice if you're about to lie with a smile.

Lightness lives in those cracks. The unhurried seconds. The micro-decisions where you choose not to carry what isn't yours.

Maybe that's why it's so hard to hold onto. Because it's quiet. Because it doesn't push.

The world rewards urgency.
Lightness rewards presence.

And presence often looks like doing less, noticing more.

You start to see things differently.
The cup of tea becomes a ceremony.
The silence between conversations becomes a gift, not something awkward to fill.

Even your own breathing becomes more interesting than whatever the algorithm is serving you next.

Because lightness isn't about escaping reality. It's about sinking more deeply into it — without flinching, without rushing to label it, without asking it to be different.

It's not fragile.
It's not vague.
It's not the same as "positive thinking" or numbing out.

It's clarity.

And clarity lets you release what's unnecessary, not because you're indifferent, but because you're paying attention.

And what you pay attention to grows.

So pay attention to what feels gentle.
To what feels honest.
To what feels like an exhale, not a performance.

Pay attention to the part of you that is already light — the part that's always known how to be, even when the world demanded you hustle.

Because that part isn't gone.
It's waiting.

Just beneath the surface.
Just behind the next breath.

The practice of lightness isn't just about what you do.

It's about how you hold what you carry.

Because some things you cannot set down.
You cannot undo the death, the diagnosis, the debt, or the days you wish you could get back.
But you can stop gripping them so tightly.

You can stop letting them define every hour that follows.

You can shift your weight.

Not everything is meant to be solved. Not everything needs an answer.

Sometimes, it just needs to be held differently.

Lighter.

Not ignored. Not dismissed.

But witnessed with a softness that says, *I see you — but I will not lose myself in you.*

That's the discipline of presence. And it is discipline. It takes effort to stop spinning stories, to stop replaying every mistake, every wrong word, every imagined future where it all falls apart.

But here's the thing.

Lightness doesn't mean naivety. It means knowing the world can break — and still choosing to walk like your body deserves peace.

It means holding grief like you would hold a bird: carefully, reverently, but not so tightly that you crush the life out of it.

Because even grief needs air.

Even sorrow needs light.

Even pain needs room to stretch without owning you.

And if you let it move through — if you give it just enough space — it becomes something else. Something softer.

Maybe not joy. But breath. Movement. A little more space to be something other than your sadness.

And in that space?

That's where lightness returns.

Some people will not understand your softness.

They'll call it weakness.
They'll say you've gone soft, gotten lazy, stopped striving.

Let them.

They do not know what it costs to choose gentleness in a culture built on exhaustion.
They do not know what it takes to stop fighting with yourself.

Because it is a fight, isn't it?

Every day, the battle between who you are and who you were told you should be.
The fight between rest and the ache to be enough.
The tension between your truth and the mask you wear to make others comfortable.

So when you choose lightness — real lightness, not denial — you're not quitting.

You're changing the rules of the game.

You're saying: *I'm not playing by the weight anymore. I am not measuring my worth in how much I can carry without breaking.*

You are not a packhorse for other people's expectations.

You are not a container for endless guilt.

You are a body, a breath, a being.

And you get to move through life in a way that feels like life.

Not survival.
Not burnout.
Not constant pressure to do more, be more, fix more.

But living. Full. Present. Real.

Even if it's quiet.

Especially then.

Because the loudest things are often the emptiest. And what is most essential — peace, presence, softness — never needs to shout.

There's a moment — usually unnoticed — where you get to choose how you carry the day.

It's small. Maybe it slips past while you're brushing your teeth or waiting for the coffee to brew. It doesn't shout or sparkle. It won't feel like a breakthrough.

But it matters.

Because in that moment, you ask yourself: *Am I going to armour up again today? Or am I willing to walk in softer skin?*

That question changes everything.

Because the world will hand you a hundred reasons to clench, to brace, to grit your teeth and muscle through. It will reward tight shoulders and constant effort. It will cheer you on for surviving — and rarely ask how you feel while doing it.

So the idea of choosing softness, choosing lightness, can feel absurd. Selfish. Even dangerous.

But is it?

What happens to your body when you stop clenching?
What happens to your voice when you stop trying to say what's right and start saying what's real?
What happens to your relationships when you stop

pretending you're okay and let someone witness the truth?

You stop disappearing.

That's what happens.

And that's the most powerful thing of all — not to prove your value, but to *inhabit it*. To live inside your own body with enough tenderness that the world can't harden you by default.

Because the truth is, lightness isn't the opposite of pain.

It's the antidote to shame.

It's the balm for the part of you that thought you had to carry it all perfectly or not at all.

It's the practice of saying: *Even if I mess up. Even if I slow down. Even if I don't know what comes next — I am still worthy of ease.*

This isn't easy.

Let's not pretend that any of this is simple.

It's hard to soften in a world that mistakes tension for commitment.

It's hard to rest when your worth has been tied to output since childhood.

It's hard to release the tight grip of control when it's been the only thing that made you feel safe.

But lightness doesn't ask you to give all that up at once.

It just asks: *Can you let go of one thing today?*

One belief. One habit. One anxious loop.

It could be small. You could take your lunch without your phone. You could take three deep breaths before replying to that email. You could resist the urge to over-explain your boundaries.

And in that small surrender — in that tiny rebellion — you become someone else.

Not unrecognizable. Just more *you* than you've been in a long time.

Because lightness isn't about pretending nothing hurts.
It's about letting go of the lie that you have to hurt all the time to be real.

You are real already.
You are human already.
You are allowed to be free.

Even in the middle of the mess.
Even when nothing is certain.

Especially then.

Because the world doesn't need more perfect people.
It needs more honest ones.

More soft-hearted souls who still show up — not in spite of their lightness, but *because of it*.

And that?
That changes everything.

You do not owe the world your heaviness.

Read that again.

Let it sink in past the defences that say you do.

Because so many of us learned to equate responsibility with suffering — as if to care deeply meant to hurt constantly. As if to show up fully meant to sacrifice yourself completely. As if you weren't trying hard enough unless your body was aching under the weight of it all.

But what if that's not true?

What if your deepest responsibility is not to hold everything — but to hold it differently?

Not like a boulder on your back. But like breath in your chest.

Not tight and rigid. But fluid and alive.

What if presence isn't about controlling everything, but about being with whatever rises — without becoming it?

This is what lightness teaches. That you can show up without being swallowed.
That you can love without losing your center.

That you can be awake to the world's pain without carrying it inside your lungs.

Because empathy doesn't have to mean erosion.

You are allowed to feel without falling apart.
You are allowed to open without bleeding.
You are allowed to care *and* let go.

It helps to build rituals that remind you of this.

Not big ones. Not dramatic ones. Just simple acts that root you in softness. That anchor your nervous system when the world feels too loud or too much.

Like holding your own hand before a hard conversation.

Like placing your palm over your heart and whispering, "You're safe," when the spiral begins.

Like lighting a candle not for aesthetics, but for stillness.

You can turn ordinary moments into sacred pauses.
Not to escape life — but to meet it with more capacity.

These pauses don't fix everything. But they change the way everything feels.

And sometimes, that's all you need.

Because when you remember you have choice — even in how you breathe — you remember you have power. Not dominance. Not control.

But sovereignty.
Space.
A quiet kind of strength that doesn't need to announce itself.

It just *is*.

There's something subversive about this practice.

Because to walk lightly through a heavy world is an act of resistance.
To laugh even when the news is dark.
To rest even when your to-do list is endless.
To hope even when you've been hurt before.

None of this makes you foolish.

It makes you free.

Free from the narrative that you must earn your worth.
Free from the myth that only the burdened are brave.
Free from the lie that suffering is a sign of integrity.

You are not more virtuous when you are in pain.
You are not more admirable when you are depleted.
You are not more real when you are anxious.

You are still real — and whole — when you're soft.

When you give yourself permission to feel light, to let joy in through the cracks, to stop apologizing for your ease... that's when life begins to feel like yours again.

Not something you manage. But something you live.

Not something you perform. But something you inhabit.

The more you practice lightness, the more you'll notice what threatens to steal it.

Sometimes it's obvious — an email that makes your stomach clench, a conversation laced with criticism, a memory that drags you backwards before you've had a chance to breathe. But more often, it's subtle. It looks like urgency. Like over-explaining. Like saying yes when something inside you is whispering *no*.

It's in the micro-decisions. The ones you make without realizing. The way you flinch when your phone buzzes. The way you check for approval after sharing your opinion. The way you instinctively reach for tasks, for noise, for distraction — because stillness feels like a risk.

But stillness isn't the absence of life.
It's where life speaks the loudest — if we're brave enough to listen.

The truth is, many of us have been conditioned to mistrust stillness. To equate it with laziness, with uselessness, with guilt. We're told that productivity is morality. That stillness is indulgence. That silence means we're falling behind.

But that narrative? It's a lie disguised as virtue.

Stillness is not a flaw. It's not a void.
It's the space where you meet yourself again.

When you stop running — not just physically, but mentally — you begin to hear what's under the noise. Not the polished, curated thoughts. But the soft ones. The ones that say:

"I'm tired."
"I'm scared."
"I want something else."

And those whispers matter.

Because you can't shift your life if you never stop to hear where you actually are.

Lightness comes from listening.

Not fixing. Not forcing. Listening.

To your breath. To your gut. To your longing. To your limits.

And then choosing to honour what you hear.

Even when the world tells you to keep going.
Even when your guilt tries to say you're being selfish.
Even when your old patterns beg you to stay small, to stay useful, to stay agreeable.

Stillness doesn't make you passive.
It makes you powerful.

Because in stillness, you reclaim choice. You stop reacting and start responding. You stop performing and start living.

It's in stillness that you realize — you don't need to justify your peace.

You don't need to earn your rest.
You don't need to explain your healing.
You don't need to shrink your joy just because someone else is uncomfortable.

You're allowed to be well.
Even in a world that's hurting.
Even when others are still lost.

Your lightness doesn't mean you don't care.
It means you've learned to carry your care without letting it crush you.

This is where the shift happens.

Not in the dramatic declarations, but in the quiet, ordinary moments where you choose ease instead of effort.

You wake up and decide not to rush.
You speak slower, not to be heard louder — but to feel the words in your own mouth.
You leave space in your schedule, not because you're lazy — but because your nervous system deserves kindness.

You pause before replying.
You take the scenic route.
You cry when something moves you instead of swallowing it down.

And slowly, your life becomes something different.
Not necessarily easier. But lighter.
Not necessarily quieter. But more honest.
Not necessarily perfect. But deeply, beautifully *yours*.

Sometimes the heaviest thing we carry is the expectation that we should be light.

That we should be healed by now.
Grateful by now.
More enlightened, more patient, more composed — by now.

It sneaks in quietly. Not always through loud judgment, but through subtle shame. The way we side-eye our own tiredness. The way we feel guilty for resting. The way we apologize, silently or aloud, for being where we are — as if being human is an inconvenience.

But lightness doesn't mean pretending you're fine.
It means allowing yourself to be real — without punishment.

There is no shame in the mess.
No shame in the backslide.
No shame in needing reminders of what you already know.

This isn't failure. This is practice.

You don't become light once and stay that way forever.
You return to it, again and again, like breath.

Sometimes it feels effortless. Sometimes it's a fight. Sometimes the most radical thing you do is sit in a room alone and let yourself cry for no reason you can name.

Let that be holy.

Let that be enough.

The ongoing practice of lightness doesn't erase the dark.
It teaches you to move through it differently.

To stop bracing for impact.
To stop fighting every wave.
To let the ache be part of the music instead of a reason to shut the song off.

Because your softness isn't the opposite of strength.
It's the doorway to it.

The world will try to convince you otherwise.
It will reward your overperformance.
Applaud your exhaustion.
Celebrate your sacrifice — especially if it keeps you useful to others.

But usefulness isn't the same as worth.
And being needed is not the same as being loved.

You don't have to bleed to belong.

You don't have to stay small to be safe.

You don't have to prove your goodness through your suffering.

What if you didn't carry that anymore?

What if you believed — even for a moment — that peace was not something you earn at the end of a long journey... but something you can choose, right now, in the middle of it?

This chapter isn't here to tell you to bypass pain.
It's here to remind you: pain doesn't get to tell the whole story.

Your joy matters.
Your laughter is sacred.
Your capacity to feel pleasure — even in the ruins — is not a betrayal of anything. It's proof you're alive.

To feel light is not to forget what's been lost.

It's to remember what's still here.

The breath.
The body.
The chance to try again.

Not from a place of punishment — but from permission.

To begin again, not because you failed, but because that's what we do. We return. We come back to the practice. We soften the grip. We allow what is.

And in that allowing, we find a different kind of power.
One that doesn't shout.
One that doesn't rush.
One that knows — the mountain that does not move is still the strongest thing in the storm.

You don't need to justify your peace.

This sentence is easy to read and hard to live.

Because sometimes, the moment you start feeling light — someone will remind you of the weight. Not intentionally. But through side comments. Through the news. Through shared pain. Through unspoken contracts that say, *we hurt together — don't forget that.*

And you don't want to forget.

You don't want to be the one who turns away, who stops caring, who floats off into the clouds while others drown.

But this is the tension of healing — the belief that your lightness is somehow disloyal to the struggle that shaped you.

It's not.

You don't owe your life to suffering.

You don't have to keep wearing old wounds to prove you survived them.

You're allowed to love things again. To laugh too loudly. To rest too long. To look around and say — not everything is fixed, but *I feel okay today.*

That's not ignorance. That's reclamation.

And it doesn't mean you've forgotten what it's like to hurt. It means you've learned to hold that pain more gently. Without identifying with it. Without dragging it into every room.

You no longer carry your grief like a banner.
You let it live as part of you. But not the whole of you.

That's lightness.

It's remembering you're not the weight. You're the one who notices it.

And noticing is different than becoming.

It's the difference between *I'm anxious* and *I'm feeling anxious.*

The shift is subtle, but powerful. It gives you back your shape. Your choice. It reminds you that you are not your reaction. You are not the story playing on loop in your head. You are not the emotion — you are the one witnessing it.

And if you can witness it, you can breathe through it. You can wait it out. You can soften it. You can meet it with compassion instead of fear.

This is the ongoing practice:
To remember you are more than the noise.
To return to your breath when your thoughts spiral.
To notice the tension before it hardens into a shield.

You don't fix it all at once.
You just keep choosing to loosen your grip.

One breath.
One decision.
One moment of quiet rebellion at a time.

Because make no mistake: lightness is rebellion.

In a world that profits off your self-doubt and urgency, choosing calm is radical. Choosing to pause, to stretch, to say no — not out of avoidance, but out of self-trust — that's an act of reclaiming your autonomy.

You are not broken because you want peace.

You are not selfish because you protect your capacity.

You are not naive because you choose to focus on beauty, on kindness, on what is *still possible*.

The world will keep turning.

Let it.

You don't have to spin with it.

You can ground yourself. Anchor in. Stand still. Be the one who doesn't escalate, doesn't spiral, doesn't add more noise to the noise.

That's not passivity. That's power.

The kind that doesn't rush.
The kind that doesn't shout.
The kind that knows presence is louder than panic.

Lightness doesn't mean you've figured everything out.

It means you're learning to let go of the need to.

This distinction matters. Deeply.

Because the pursuit of certainty is seductive — it gives us the illusion of safety. If we can just name what's next, understand it, fix it, plan it, master it... then maybe we'll finally relax. Maybe then we'll finally breathe.

But life rarely works that way.

Peace doesn't arrive as a reward for control. It comes as a companion to surrender.

It's the deep exhale when you stop gripping the wheel so tightly. When you realize you don't need to know everything to move forward. You only need to be present for this moment — and the one after it.

That's where lightness lives.
In the choice to *be here*, not *figure it out from here*.

We spend so much time climbing out of our experience.

Analysing it. Judging it. Strategizing around it. Instead of being with it.

We reach for distractions. Or diagnosis. Or the next thing to fix.

Not because we're weak. Because we're human.
We were taught that stillness equals stuckness.
That rest equals laziness.
That calm equals complacency.

So we rush.
We perform.
We overexplain.
We apologize for not being "better" by now.

But healing isn't always linear.
And growth doesn't always look like movement.
Sometimes it looks like *not moving at all* — and noticing what that brings up in you.

Stillness reveals the noise.

It's not always comfortable. But it's honest.
It shows you where the ache still lives.
Where your mind still pulls for control.
Where you're still running from softness.

So let yourself pause.
Let yourself listen.
Let yourself stay long enough in the quiet to hear what your body has been trying to say all along.

Lightness isn't the absence of struggle.
It's the presence of awareness.

A spaciousness inside the storm.
A decision to meet yourself without flinching.
To breathe into the pain, not as a martyr — but as a witness.

There's dignity in that.
There's relief.

Because it means you're no longer resisting every emotion.
You're no longer trying to solve your way out of being human.

You're allowing the full spectrum — without needing to fix, label, or justify it.

And when you do that — when you soften into the now — the moment becomes enough.

Even if it's imperfect.
Even if it's heavy.
Even if it breaks your heart a little.

This isn't about detachment in the cold sense.
It's not about not caring.
It's about learning to care without collapsing.

To show up with your heart open — and your boundaries intact.

To feel deeply — and still protect your peace.

To love — without losing yourself in the process.

That's the nuance of lightness. It's *not* numb.
It's not a spiritual bypass.
It's not a fake smile.

It's a choice. A return. A practice of remembering who you are when you stop performing for safety.

It's the mountain that does not move — *because* it knows what it's rooted in.

Some days, that practice will feel impossible.

There will be noise.
And grief.
And triggers that pull you back into old shapes.

You'll want to explain yourself.
You'll want to react.
You'll want to armour up, or run, or prove that you're okay.

And that's okay too.

You're allowed to be undone.

You're allowed to forget.
To freeze.
To fall back into the spiral.

The practice isn't perfection.

The practice is return.

To your breath.
To your self-trust.
To the knowing that you don't have to carry it all — or carry it alone.

Lightness doesn't erase the human mess.
It gives you permission to meet it with grace.

You're allowed to live gently in a world that doesn't.

You're allowed to make space for joy, even while the world burns.

You're allowed to turn toward beauty — not as denial, but as nourishment.

Because lightness is not selfish.

It's the medicine we offer the collective when we stop performing pain to be taken seriously.

When we stop sacrificing our inner peace for external validation.

When we remember that our nervous systems are sacred.

That our rest is resistance.

That our softness is strategy.

Lightness isn't a destination.
It's a decision you make — again and again.

To return to your breath.
To the moment.
To yourself.

Not because everything is perfect, but because you've stopped demanding that it be.

You're not failing if you feel heavy.
You're not broken if you forget what you've learned.
You're simply human. Practicing.

And practice means we return.

You don't have to rush.
You don't have to catch up.
You don't have to carry what was never yours.

You're allowed to be free now.

And not because you've fixed it all — but because you've remembered that your peace was never something you had to earn.

Tools for Lightness Integration

1. The 5-Minute Presence Pause

Anytime you feel rushed, overwhelmed, or pulled out of your body:

- Sit quietly with your feet flat on the ground.
- Inhale for 4 counts. Hold for 4. Exhale for 4. Repeat 3x.
- Scan your body from crown to toes. Where is there tension? Where is there softness?
- Whisper (aloud or internally): *"This moment is safe. I can be here."*

2. Morning Anchor Practice

Begin the day with a single sentence:

"Today, I choose to meet the world lightly — not because it's easy, but because I'm allowed to."

Repeat it each morning. Watch how it changes you.

3. The Let-It-Be List

Create a running list of things you no longer need to fix, force, or control. Start small — the laundry not being folded, the email that can wait, the opinion that doesn't need your response. Let each item be a permission slip. A soft surrender.

4. Journal Prompt: What Would It Feel Like to Be Weightless Here?

Explore a place in your life where you feel emotionally heavy.
Ask:

- What story am I holding about this?
- What would it feel like to lay it down — even for one day?
- Who am I without this struggle?

Write it all. Let the page carry the weight.

You don't have to fight for your peace anymore.
You only have to stop abandoning it.

Let lightness be what you come back to — even when it feels far away.

Let it live inside you.

Even now.

Even here.

CHAPTER 10
LET IT BE: BECOMING YOUR OWN PEACE

10. Let It Be: Becoming Your Own Peace

Letting go is not the end of the journey. It's the middle.
The soft threshold between holding and becoming.

You've done the hard part — the releasing, the unravelling, the mourning of old versions.
You've walked barefoot across the sharp ground of surrender.
And now you've arrived at something quieter.
Stranger.
A kind of space that doesn't demand anything from you — except that you stay.

This is what it means to *let it be*.

Not to give up.
Not to turn numb.
Not to ignore pain, or bypass discomfort, or feign neutrality when the world aches.

But to learn the difference between carrying and clinging.
Between effort and force.
Between being present with life — and trying to control its every breath.

Peace is not passive.
It's not fragile.
It doesn't mean you stop caring.

It means you stop grasping.
You stop editing the moment in front of you because it doesn't match your idea of how it *should* be.
You start letting the world show up as it is — and loving yourself enough not to resist it.

There is power in this kind of stillness.

Not the kind that stagnates, but the kind that roots.

You stop chasing what left.
You stop bargaining with the past.
You stop making your worth dependent on the people who never knew how to hold you.

Instead, you become your own ground.

This isn't the kind of peace that arrives all at once.
It's not a finish line.
It's not the prize at the end of a spiritual marathon.

It's a daily practice.
A returning.
A remembering.

That your breath is still here.
That your body is allowed to soften.
That nothing more is required of you in this moment but to *be*.

And that's the hard part, isn't it?

Not fixing.
Not producing.
Not proving or performing.

Just being.

Existing in your own presence without urgency or apology.

That's where peace lives — not in the outcome, but in the willingness to stay for what's real.

To be with what *is*, even when it isn't easy.
Even when it's boring.
Even when it breaks your heart.

Peace doesn't protect you from pain.
But it does keep you from turning your pain into punishment.

You can hold grief without drowning in it.
You can meet joy without fearing its loss.
You can walk forward without dragging your history behind you.

This is the peace that grows roots.
That spreads into your spine.
That teaches your nervous system:
You're not in danger anymore.

You don't have to flinch at every silence.
You don't have to micromanage the unknown.
You don't have to earn your own belonging.

You are already allowed to be here.

Not after you fix it.
Not after you prove it.
Not after you understand everything that hurt you.

Now.

Even with the questions.
Even with the fear.
Even with the jagged edges of an unfinished healing.

You are allowed to be whole here.

You are allowed to rest.

Peace used to feel like a prize.
Something you reached after you had figured it all out.
After the hard parts were over.
After the drama died down, the trauma healed, the noise silenced itself.

But what if peace isn't something you earn?
What if it's something you remember?

Like breath. Like stillness. Like your name whispered back to you by the wind.

There's a quiet that comes when you stop looking for the next wound.
When you stop anticipating what might go wrong — and instead trust yourself to be there if and when it does.

You can't outrun chaos.
But you can stop feeding it.

This is where your peace lives now.
Not in the conditions.
Not in the perfect outcome.
Not in the other person doing the right thing.

But in the tiny pause where you remember:
You don't have to become the pain to survive it.

You can step back.
Exhale.
Stay soft.

Let people misunderstand you.
Let the past stay where it is.
Let the world be as it is today — flawed, beautiful, unfinished.

Your job is not to control the story.
Your job is to keep choosing your own grounded truth within it.

There is freedom in not needing every part of your life to be tied up in a neat bow.

Peace doesn't need your perfection.
It just needs your presence.

And presence doesn't mean you never feel anxious or upset or overwhelmed.
It means you stop abandoning yourself when those feelings rise.

It means your body becomes a place where feelings are allowed to pass, not build permanent homes.

This chapter of your life is not about becoming a better version of yourself.
It's about coming home to the self that has always been waiting underneath the noise.

It's about trusting that you're still whole even when everything feels uncertain.

Even when your heart is tired.
Even when your voice shakes.
Even when you're not sure what to do next.

Especially then.

You've let go of so much.
You've peeled back the layers.
You've walked through the burn.
Now, here is where you get to rest.
Not because everything is fixed —
but because you are allowed to stop fixing.

The work now is not in solving.
It's in seeing.
In softening.
In being.

Let it be messy sometimes.
Let it be weird and tender and raw.
Let it be human.

Let yourself be human, too.

Because that is where the real peace lives.
Not in the polished performance of healing.

But in the gentle practice of letting yourself belong — fully — to the moment you're already in.

Sometimes the most radical thing you can do is sit still and let the world move around you.

Not because you've given up.

But because you've given yourself permission not to chase what doesn't belong to you.

That's the kind of peace no one can hand you.
You build it slowly. Brick by brick. Moment by moment.
A discipline of not abandoning yourself just because the world hasn't learned how to stay.

You will be tempted to perform healing — to make it look neat, photogenic, hashtag-worthy.
To prove to others that you've "moved on" or "glowed up" or "found your power."

But real peace?
It doesn't beg to be seen.

It's found in quiet acts of devotion.
The days you breathe deeper instead of snapping.
The nights you close your laptop instead of numbing out for five more hours.
The mornings you let the sun touch your face before the to-do list touches your mind.

That's what it means to become your own peace.
Not to escape life, but to meet it differently.
From the inside out.
From groundedness, not panic.
From softness, not defence.

It's okay if you still flinch sometimes.
If your nervous system forgets.
If you find yourself spiralling even after all the work you've done.

This isn't failure.
It's the next layer.

You're not going backwards — you're spiralling upward through your own remembering.

And part of remembering means learning how to respond to yourself like someone you love.

Would you rush someone you cared about through a moment of pain?
Would you shame them for not "being over it" yet?
Would you hand them a checklist and tell them to get back to you when they've completed their healing?

Of course not.

So why do you do it to yourself?

Peace isn't a deadline.
It's a way of being in relationship with your own unfolding.

You are not behind.
You are not too much.
You are not broken just because you still ache.

Even the mountain shakes.

Even the ocean churns.

Stillness doesn't mean nothing moves — it means you are no longer moved by every storm that passes through.

And that takes time.
Practice.
Kindness.

Let peace become a muscle you build.
Let softness become a skill you strengthen.

Because the world won't always reward you for it.

People will say you've changed.
They'll wonder where the old you went — the one who used to hustle for love, beg for clarity, over-explain your worth.

Let them wonder.

The old you didn't disappear.
She just got tired of performing her own pain for other people's comfort.

She's still here — but now she lives in peace.

There's a certain kind of silence you come to crave.
Not the silence of avoidance. Not the quiet of suppression.
But the kind that holds you. Anchors you.
A silence that isn't empty, but full — of truth, of breath, of self.

This is what the world never taught you to want.
Because silence, for so many of us, meant tension.
It meant trouble brewing. Rejection simmering.
It meant someone was disappointed, someone was withdrawing, something was breaking.

So we filled it.

With noise. With over-explaining. With busywork. With fixing.

We became masters of filling silence.
Until it started costing us something we couldn't name.

Your peace begins to grow when you stop fearing the spaces in between.

The pause before an answer.
The breath before a decision.
The moment after someone says no and you choose not to unravel.

You stop needing to overperform clarity.
You stop needing to control the narrative.
You stop needing to be loud enough to prove you're allowed to exist.

You start trusting the ground beneath you.
You start holding your own gaze in the quiet.
You start letting life come to you — not as a test, but as a teacher.

This kind of peace doesn't make you passive.
It makes you potent.

You become someone who can sit inside a feeling without needing to solve it right away.
Someone who can say, "This is uncomfortable — and I can be with it."

You stop resisting discomfort as if it's the enemy of growth.
You start seeing it as the doorway.

Because the more you resist the moment, the more power you give it.
But when you sit with it — open-palmed, grounded — something changes.

You realize you are no longer living in reaction.
You are responding.

And in that space between reaction and response — there's choice.
Agency.
Freedom.

You begin to see that being at peace doesn't mean you never feel angry, or scared, or heartbroken.
It means those emotions no longer define who you are.
They move through you — not as identity, but as energy.

And the more you practice letting them move, the more space you have inside yourself.

Not empty space.
Sacred space.

The kind that holds your contradictions.
The kind that softens your shame.
The kind that reminds you — again and again — that you are still here.

Still growing.
Still worthy.
Still becoming.

And maybe that's the truest peace of all.

Not needing to arrive.
Just learning how to stay.

There's a moment in every healing journey when you realize: you've been waiting for permission that was never going to come.

Permission to slow down.
To breathe.
To rest without earning it.
To want something softer.

For so long, you waited for the world to offer it.
For the voice of a parent, a mentor, a partner, a friend — to finally say:
You're allowed to stop trying so hard.
You're allowed to be at peace now.

But they didn't say it.
Or if they did, you didn't know how to trust it.
Because they raised you in a world that called exhaustion noble.
That made burnout the price of value.
That equated your worth with your productivity.

And so you ran.
You pushed.
You over-gave.
You tried to hold the weight of everyone else's comfort just to earn a sliver of your own.

Peace felt irresponsible.
Selfish.
Lazy.

But here's what's true: rest is a birthright, not a bonus.

You do not need to apologize for softening.
For unplugging.
For choosing not to spiral just because someone else is spinning.

Peace isn't something you arrive at once you've outperformed your pain.

It's something you *choose*, again and again, in a world that profits from your restlessness.

You have a right to turn your phone off.
To close the laptop.

To let a message sit unanswered if responding would cost your nervous system more than it's worth.

This isn't neglect.
It's self-trust.

You are not required to be constantly available to be good.
You are not required to explain your silence to be kind.
You are not required to earn your peace — only to protect it.

The people who belong in your life will understand.
They'll make room for your no.
They'll celebrate the boundaries that keep you whole, not punish you for drawing them.

And for those who don't?

Let them misunderstand you.

Let them think you've grown cold, selfish, withdrawn.
Let them mislabel your stillness if they've only ever known you in overdrive.

Because the ones who love your peace are the ones who love *you* — not just your usefulness.

Peace will cost you something.
It will cost you some dynamics that only worked when you abandoned yourself.
It will cost you habits that numbed you but never

nourished you.
It will cost you roles you played just to be palatable.

But what you get in return?

Yourself.

Unrushed.
Unperformed.
Unapologetic.

You get to build a life that honours your softness instead of exploiting your strength.

A life where you don't have to brace for the next crisis to feel needed.
Where you don't have to shrink to be safe.
Where your joy isn't postponed for some mythical "after" — it's welcome now.

And that kind of life?
That kind of peace?

It doesn't ask you to fight.

It invites you to stay.

There's a myth that peace looks like perfection.

That once you find it, nothing rattles you.
No one gets under your skin.
You walk through life like a monk wrapped in soft light and sage smoke.

But real peace is messier than that.
It's grittier.
Less aesthetic.
More lived-in.

It's choosing not to raise your voice, even when your chest is burning.
It's pausing mid-conflict to take a breath, even when your body wants to defend.
It's walking away from something that once defined you, and letting the silence roar without rushing to fill it.

Real peace doesn't mean you don't feel.
It means you don't *fuse* with every feeling.

It means you know the difference between "I am angry" and "I am anger."
Between "I feel lost" and "I am lost."
Between "This moment hurts" and "I will always be hurting."

Peace gives you space to witness what's passing without mistaking it for permanence.

It teaches you to trust the ebb as much as the flow.
To let grief visit without setting the table for it permanently.
To feel rage without needing to destroy something to release it.

And that trust — that inner holding — is what transforms your relationship to chaos.

You stop demanding that life stop hurting.
You start asking how to hold yourself when it does.

You begin to unlearn urgency.
To walk slower.
To decide later.
To stop assuming that the fastest answer is the best one.

You begin to measure your days not by output, but by presence.

Not: Did I finish everything?
But: Did I meet myself where I was?

Not: Was I impressive?
But: Was I honest?

Peace doesn't come from always getting it right.
It comes from refusing to abandon yourself when you get it wrong.

It's showing up to the version of you that's still healing — with gentleness, not judgment.

Because you will have days when your nervous system misfires.
When an old wound flares.
When someone touches the sore spot you thought you buried under all that growth.

That doesn't mean you've regressed.
It means you're alive.

You are a body, not a brand.
You are allowed to be tender.
You are allowed to be triggered.
You are allowed to return to tools you thought you'd outgrown — because healing is cyclical, not linear.

And peace?
Peace is knowing the spiral doesn't make you broken.

It makes you human.

It means you can come back to your breath a thousand times and still be worthy of softness.
It means you can forget your practices, fall off the path, lose your rhythm — and still be welcome in your own life.

Because the mountain doesn't shame itself when it shakes.

And neither should you.

You don't have to disappear to find peace.

You don't need to move to a cabin in the woods, delete every app, or renounce the world.
(Though if that sounds good—do it.)

What you do need is presence.
Right here.
Inside your real, messy, overstimulated life.

The kind of peace that lives in the body, not just the calendar.
The kind that finds you in traffic.
In hard conversations.
In the three-minute gap between meetings, where you put your hand on your chest and remember: I'm still here.

Because peace isn't a retreat.
It's a return.

To your breath.
To your body.
To this moment—exactly as it is.

Not once it gets easier.
Not once you've earned it.
But now.

Now, when the dishes are still in the sink.
When the inbox is still full.
When the family member is still unpredictable.
When the deadline is still looming.

Peace doesn't wait for everything to settle.

It settles *you*.

It's the voice that says: yes, this is hard.
And still, you are safe to soften.
Still, you are allowed to slow down.

And the more you practice that — the more you drop into that stillness in small, ordinary moments — the more it becomes muscle memory.

Your system learns:
I can pause before reacting.
I can stay with myself when I feel overwhelmed.
I can be spacious even when the world is not.

This is how peace gets built.
Not in some perfect, curated day.
But in the minutes you choose not to spiral.
The breath you take before speaking.
The gentle no you offer yourself instead of a forced yes.

You stop waiting to be rescued by the weekend, or the vacation, or the next break.
And you start offering yourself tiny moments of break *now*.

These moments don't have to be grand.
They just have to be real.

Three slow breaths before you open a message.
Five minutes of silence in the car before walking into the house.
A reminder in your phone that says, "Soften your shoulders."

Peace is not performative.
It doesn't need to be shared or seen.
It just needs to be felt.

And the more you let yourself feel it — even in stolen seconds — the more your life starts to shape itself around it.

You become someone who holds peace not as an escape, but as a standard.

Not as a luxury, but as a right.

You begin to curate your energy instead of constantly bleeding it out.

You begin to center your nervous system instead of contorting it to fit chaos.

You begin to trust that you can be present without absorbing.
That you can witness without rescuing.
That you can listen without losing yourself.

This is how peace becomes your way of being.

Not because the world calmed down.
But because *you* did.

And when you learn to carry that stillness into your day —
even as things fall apart —
even as people misunderstand —
even as you forget and remember and forget again —

that is when you become the mountain.

Unmoved by passing storms.

There's a moment when peace stops being something you visit and starts being something you embody.

It happens quietly.

No grand awakening.
No lightning strike of insight.

Just a day when someone else is spinning, and you don't match their spin.
A moment when you feel the old urge to defend, justify, or shrink — and instead, you breathe.

Instead, you stay still.

Not frozen.
Not dissociating.

Present.

Rooted.

Alive in a way that doesn't need to be loud.

And suddenly, you realize — you're not just trying to be at peace.
You *are* peace.

Not because everything is perfect.
But because you've chosen not to fight every imperfection.

You've stopped assigning yourself to every emergency.
Stopped chasing closure from people who aren't ready to give it.

Stopped explaining your boundaries to those committed to misunderstanding them.

This is the power of internal stillness.
You begin to anchor yourself in something deeper than reaction.

Your identity no longer depends on how others receive you.
Your worth is no longer up for debate.
Your softness is no longer conditional.

It just *is*.
And it stays, even when nothing else does.

This kind of grounded peace isn't about detachment from life.
It's about deeper participation in it — without losing yourself in the process.

You laugh more freely.
You say "I don't know" with grace.
You take up space without apology.

And you rest.
Not as escape, but as embodiment.

Not just on the days when your to-do list is complete.
But especially on the days when it isn't.

Because you've learned that your aliveness matters more than your efficiency.

That your wholeness is not something to hustle for — it's something to *honour*.

And from that place, peace starts to ripple outward.

You show up differently.

Not performatively calm.
Not pretending everything is fine when it isn't.

But real.
Steady.
Able to hold space for contradiction.

You can say "this hurts" and still be at peace.
You can cry and still be grounded.
You can want more and still be content with what is.

This is the paradox that peace makes room for:
Longing and gratitude.
Desire and presence.
Discomfort and calm.

You stop waiting for one feeling to cancel out the other.
You start trusting that the human heart is big enough to hold them both.

And in doing so —
you become the kind of person who makes others feel safe just by being near you.

Not because you fix.
Not because you save.

But because your stillness reminds them: they can stop trying so hard, too.

It's easy to believe peace is passive.

That choosing softness means surrendering strength.
That being calm means you've stopped caring.
That letting go means you've given up.

But peace is not passivity.

Peace is choosing what matters most.

It's saying: I will not spend my precious life rehearsing pain.
I will not burn myself out proving I'm enough.
I will not sacrifice presence for the illusion of control.

This kind of peace is *active*.
It takes strength to soften.

To say "no" gently but firmly.
To walk away from something that drains you, even if it used to define you.
To stand still when the world is demanding you run.

Peace doesn't mean you don't act.
It means you don't *react* from fear.

You move —
but from alignment, not anxiety.

You speak —
but from truth, not panic.

You choose —
not because someone else expects it, but because your soul knows it's right.

And you rest.

Not because you've earned it, but because you *exist*.

Because your body is not a machine.
Because exhaustion isn't a badge of honour.
Because stillness isn't laziness — it's wisdom.

Like the mountain, you don't rush.
You don't chase every cloud that moves past.
You don't mistake noise for importance.

You let the winds howl.

And still, you stay.

Because you've learned that stillness isn't absence — it's *essence*.

It's what remains when the striving settles.
When the proving fades.
When all that's left is breath, bone, presence.

This is what it means to become your own peace.

You carry it into every room.
Not to shield yourself from the world —
but to bring a different frequency into it.

You no longer search for peace in places that demand you abandon yourself to find it.

You *are* the sanctuary now.

And that changes everything.

You were never meant to earn your peace.

You were meant to return to it.

Over and over.
In the quietest ways.
Through the smallest doors.

It doesn't come in a single moment of transformation, some final fix that makes everything better forever.

It comes in the practice.

In the choices you make each day to come back to yourself.
To feel your feet on the ground.
To soften your jaw.
To breathe deeper than the urgency.

It comes when you forgive yourself for forgetting.
For falling back into old patterns.
For mistaking the noise for truth.

And then —
you begin again.

Not from shame.
But from gentleness.

That's what this book has been: not a solution, but a starting point.

A hand on your back saying, "It's safe now. You can let go."

Of the heaviness.
Of the story that says you must do more, be more, fix more to be worthy.
Of the tight grip on everything you were taught to control.

It's okay to want peace.
And it's okay if it takes practice to feel safe inside it.

So you start small.
A few minutes of silence in the morning.
A deep breath before you answer.
A post-it on your mirror that simply says: Let it be.

Let it be messy.
Let it be unfinished.
Let it be beautiful in ways that no one else notices but you.

Because this is your life now.

A life that doesn't chase or grip or cling.
A life that allows.
A life that softens.

A life that flows — not because it's easy, but because you are no longer trying to fight the river.

You are learning to float.

And in the floating, something opens.

Your body begins to trust you.
Your mind starts to rest.
Your heart starts to speak.

And what it says — in the quietest, strongest voice — is this:

You are safe now.
You are free.
You are home.

Tools for Becoming Your Own Peace

1. Stillness Practice
Sit in silence for 5 minutes each day. No music. No phone. Just sit. Let your body arrive. Let your breath be your only task. This is not about clearing your mind — it's about *not abandoning yourself* in the quiet.

2. Phone-Free Window
Choose a 30–60 minute window each day where your phone is completely off or out of sight. Use this time to engage in something grounding — a walk, a meal, a conversation, or just rest. Give your nervous system the gift of uninterrupted presence.

3. Guilt-Release Journaling
Set a timer for 10 minutes. Write down all the reasons you feel guilty for resting, saying no, or needing space. Then, one by one, cross them out. Underneath, write: *My peace does not require permission.*

You don't have to fight anymore.
You can still care without carrying everything.

You can still show up —
but this time, as someone who knows that peace isn't found outside you.

It lives here.
Within.
Always.
     Let it be.

BONUS TOOLS
&
REFLECTION
PAGES

Bonus Tools & Reflection Pages

Daily Presence Rituals

Purpose: To re-anchor the nervous system, body, and mind in the present.

- The One-Minute Anchor
  Close your eyes.
  Inhale for 4. Hold for 4. Exhale for 6.
  Repeat 3 times.
  Ask yourself: *What is here now? What is mine to carry?*

- Presence Trigger Object
  Choose a small object (stone, ring, leaf) and carry it with you.
  Let it be your reminder to return to presence when your mind spirals or rushes.
  Each time you touch it, repeat silently: *I'm here. I'm safe. I'm enough.*

Breath and Silence Practices

Purpose: To cultivate resilience through nervous system regulation and internal spaciousness.

- Box Breathing
  Inhale – 4 counts
  Hold – 4 counts
  Exhale – 4 counts
  Hold – 4 counts
  Repeat for 3-5 minutes to recentre during overwhelm.

- Daily Silence Window
  Carve out 10-15 minutes a day with no input.
  No music, no screens, no conversation.
  Just you, your breath, your presence.
  Let this silence be a sanctuary, not a void.

Integration Journal Prompts

Write freely in a quiet space. Let yourself be surprised.

1. How have I softened this year?
2. What do I still cling to — and why does it feel safer than letting go?
3. What parts of me have made peace feel impossible — and what would happen if I forgave them?
4. Where in my life am I ready to let it be?
5. What does peace look like, sound like, or feel like — in my body?

Reflection Pages

Use these pages as soft ground to land on.
Come back here anytime you forget who you are.

Final Reflection: *A Letter to My Future Self*

Write from the voice of the "you" who has learned to live light.
Remind your future self how far you've come. What you want her to remember.
Begin with:

Dear Me,
I know you're doing your best. I just want you to remember...

Peace Declaration

Sign this as a personal vow — a reminder of what you've claimed.

I no longer chase what costs me peace.
I no longer perform for love.
I no longer grip what wants to go.

I let it be.
I let myself be.

I am light. I am whole. I am enough.

Signed,

_____

(Your name, your truth, your return.)

Printed in Dunstable, United Kingdom

MODERN MAGIC

BETH WILLIAMS

Copyright © Beth Williams 2025

The moral right of this author has been asserted.

All rights reserved.

All characters and events in this publication, other than those clearly in the public domain, are fictitious and any resemblance to real persons, living or dead, is purely coincidental.

No part of this publication may be reproduced, stored in a retrieval system, or transmitted, in any form or by any means, without the prior permission in writing of the publisher, nor be otherwise circulated in any form of binding or cover other than that in which it is published and without a similar condition including this condition being imposed on the subsequent purchaser.

Editing, design, typesetting and publishing by UK Book Publishing

www.ukbookpublishing.com

ISBN: 978-1-917329-86-6

MODERN MAGIC

ABOUT THE AUTHOR

Beth is a practising corporate lawyer based in the UK, although she is still unsure what she is supposed to be practising and whether she has been given the right equipment.

She spends her time creatively writing her way out of fantastical high stakes situations involving an amusing cast of eccentric characters.

She also writes fantasy novels in her spare time.

To Dad, who never let them get me down.

1.

THE TREE AND A TIGER

On a dismal late summer morning, Ivy Armstride was on her way to work at the Citadel's pre-eminent Tower of Lore and Sorcery, the establishment of Jackdaw and Spittlelick.

At least, the mages at Jackdaw and Spittlelick considered the Tower to be pre-eminent, although Ivy, who had spent several years practising there as a mage, felt there was very little to support this depiction. She also suspected that the mages at the Citadel's other four Towers were all harbouring the same cheerful delusion in respect of their own Tower. But that was mages for you.

When Ivy first came to the Citadel to undertake her apprenticeship as a mage, she had expected something more, well, *magical* from the Tower itself. Brimming with anticipation, she had imagined a majestic structure surrounded by a surfeit of green trees and gently bubbling water fountains, with gleaming white marble surfaces that glinted in the sunlight. To her mind, the mages working at this magnificent Tower would undoubtedly be milling around thoughtfully, absorbed in leather-bound spell books, leafing through illuminated pages of ancient text while the air hummed with cultivated magic.

What she hadn't expected was the morose building that had instead confronted her. The Tower of Jackdaw and Spittlelick was a circular construction rendered in grey-black goblin stone, its drab exterior supported by six large dragonsteel girders that had seen better days. A large glass dome perched atop the coliseum-like structure, coated in layers of dust and grime like a mouldy cake-topper. The Tower's mages did not mill around, artfully pondering the mysteries of the universe, but instead dashed about in a haze of frenetic activity, looking like they, too, had seen better days. Any raw magic that leaked into the air as a result of the work undertaken at the Tower was quickly smothered by panicked mages, hastily papered over like an uninvited patch of damp on a wall. The whole affair – building and mages alike – seemed forever on the verge of nervous collapse.

Ivy was now resigned to the fact that the Tower had never lived up to her initial expectations. She barely registered the mild disappointment of its reality anymore, her mind instead fixed upon the mountain of work that usually awaited her each day. But today, she found herself pausing upon entering the Tower.

It was early morning, and the Citadel was still grinding itself into a bleary-eyed awakening. The air of the Tower was static and still, and its large circular foyer was noticeably empty, save for the tree.

It stood in the middle of the foyer, enormous and ancient. Its huge, gnarled roots buried themselves assertively into the dark granite floor, its branches punching up past the seven floors that encircled it so that its leafy canopy brushed the dome of the Tower's roof, expectant.

The tree had appeared several months ago. Upon first encountering it, Ivy had observed that a tree this large almost certainly hadn't been transported though the definitely-not-large-tree-sized entrance by non-magical methods. She had wondered what methods had been used to achieve the transplant (so to speak), given that teleportation spells were notoriously unstable on living objects. However, no one in the Tower had been forthcoming with an explanation and Ivy had come to accept the tree as part of the furniture, only occasionally pausing to wonder why it had mysteriously appeared without the fanfare which usually accompanied any re-design of the Tower's interior, however inconsequential.

Still pondering, Ivy approached the tree. There was a heaviness in the air around it, like the sensation of standing deep within a forest. Its leaves were rustling softly above, despite the absence of any breeze. They whispered to her. The tree felt old, out of place, tired. Its bark was dry; too dry, although Ivy could not have said how she knew that to be the case. For a moment, she almost thought to reach out and–

"Wotcher," said a familiar voice from behind her, causing her to start.

Ivy turned to see Dante strolling across the empty foyer towards her, hands in his pockets, grinning that dry half-smile of his.

"Massive, isn't it?" Dante said, nodding towards the tree. "Still not sure why we need it. Like something Lovett and Leavitt would have, showy toffs." He stopped alongside her and peered at the tree critically, shaking his head. "Looks a bit ill, if you ask me," he added, echoing Ivy's thoughts. "Not surprising, though. Nobody here seems to know how to look after anything properly."

Ivy gave a murmur of agreement, before observing, "You're in early…"

Dante worked alongside Ivy in Jackdaw's Castings Division, where they devised and implemented complex spells for the industrialists and market-makers of the Citadel. He did not seem to take much enjoyment from the work, seldom missing an opportunity to mock the desperate aspiration of his fellow mages. The Masters of the Tower did not seem to find much amusement in Dante's black-humoured disposition, frowning at his lack of ambition and application. However, both sides tolerated this state of affairs because Dante was, without any discernible effort on his part, an exceptionally gifted mage. Most days, Dante tended to make his appearance mere minutes before the first Masters started arriving, although he was nevertheless adept at creating the impression that he had been at his desk for several hours before that.

"Skelton's already in," Dante explained with a shrug. "Admittedly, after it became clear that he'd settled in for the day, I decided to go for a long walk. I'd just about persuaded myself I should probably head back up when I saw you. Coming?" He nodded towards the stairwell.

"Sure," Ivy said, turning away from the tree. She felt reluctant to leave it. "It looks sad," she said.

"If it's going to stay in this godsforsaken place, it should probably get used to it," Dante said, leading her away from the tree. "Are we braving the lift today?"

Ivy looked at the rickety lift that sat next to the foot of the stone stairwell. Like much of the Citadel's machinery, the lift's mechanism had at some point been supplemented by well-meaning but inevitably unpredictable magic. As a result, it rarely operated as intended – Ivy recalled one occasion where it had stopped halfway between floors, thrust open its doors impatiently, and started to expel a soporific tune which she had not heard before or since.

"Stairs for me," Ivy confirmed.

"Suits me," said Dante, following her up the stairs. They glanced back at the lift as it convulsed and made a loud *phut* sound. "Could probably do with the exercise anyway."

◆

Settling down at her shabby desk in the Castings Division on the fifth floor, Ivy stretched out her legs and felt them brush something warm, furry and solid. A quick look down (one could never be too sure) confirmed her suspicions. Bob was under her desk again.

"Hello, Bob," Ivy said, as she pulled some papers towards her. "I suppose we'd better make a start on the day."

Bob turned his head and greeted her with baleful yellow eyes, before issuing a considerable and leisurely yawn.

Bob was a curious case. He was a vast and imperious tiger that gently padded the corridors of the Tower, usually in search of a comfortable place to doze. He had not always been a tiger; he had previously been an affable and comfortably proportioned ginger tom cat who had sauntered into the Tower one day and established himself as its unofficial familiar, ambling around, not paying much attention to anyone and yet demanding attention from everyone, usually at inconvenient moments.

His transformation had occurred not long after Ivy had started practising within the Castings Division. The Division had decided to hold a small gathering on the fifth floor to celebrate the completion of a particularly difficult spellcasting for a client. A number of celebratory drinks were cheerily imbibed, and Master Williamson – who had become quite pink-faced with all the excitement – had begun to declare very loudly (and repeatedly) that Bob in his current form was really not a familiar befitting of such an august establishment as Jackdaw and Spittlelick.

Before anyone knew what was happening – Ivy included – Bob was subjected to some highly questionable impromptu spellcasting and transformed into an extremely large tiger. Master Williamson was taken aback, but not as much so as Bob, who had been curled up on a chair which had inexplicably become too small.

The surprised tiger had then darted through the corridors, knocking over various items of furniture and piles of paper as he wrestled with a form completely at odds with his small cat-brain, culminating in a mad scramble up some drapes which were evidently not designed to hold an adult tiger's weight.

At this point, none of the mages considered it sensible to attempt to subdue a bloody great predator and they were all experiencing a collective inability to remember any training which might possibly be helpful. So Bob, who had resorted to hiding under a desk, was left squarely alone. Instead, it was resolved that someone would inform the relevant authorities in the morning so that it could be all cleared up.

Except that no one did.

Time passed by, and the presence of a giant tiger had simply become accepted as part of Tower life. Bob himself appeared largely settled in his new form. The mice were annoyingly small, and people didn't seem to appreciate him sitting on them quite as much as they used to, but the Tower's chambers were warm, and Ivy still fed him under her desk.

As Bob gazed expectantly up at her, Ivy absently pulled open one of her desk drawers and delved for something edible. What she located was almost certainly not fit for human, let alone feline, consumption, but Bob, as always, seemed grateful. She then attempted to turn her mind to the casting in front of her.

Ivy had been instructed to prepare a spell for one of the Tower's largest clients: Dragonsteel Industries. Dragonsteel had styled itself as the driving force behind the Citadel's 'upwards mobility' in recent years, which – to Ivy's mind – seemed mostly to consist of manufacturing products which made buildings go upwards. Jackdaw and Spittlelick had worked hard to secure Dragonsteel's retainer and its mages needed to work harder still to retain that work, as Master Skelton insisted on reminding her each time he deftly deposited a new brief atop her heaving in-tray.

The usual order of business for Dragonsteel was to draft and cast a binding spell: a piece of magic designed to control Dragonsteel's large and fiery 'assets', which was the generally preferred term for the dragons labouring in its industrial facility. The spells needed constant updating and renewal, although the principles remained largely consistent. After several years of practice, Ivy could almost draft these binding spells in her sleep – and she had often worked so late into the night preparing them that she probably had on several occasions.

This time, though, Dragonsteel needed something beyond the usual binding castings. They wanted a *shielding* spell which would physically safeguard the dragons.

Apparently, there had recently been an 'incident' which had made the client extremely nervous, although it hadn't divulged the details.

Skelton had described it as an 'exciting opportunity to demonstrate our continued importance as trusted mages'. But Ivy had not cast a shielding spell for assets such as these before and was not finding the opportunity remotely exciting. The drafting was proving horribly complex, and she had been given little in the way of actual instruction by Master Skelton. The words 'urgent' and 'bespoke' had also been used, which in Ivy's painful experience generally preceded several days of working flat out on something, only to have it unceremoniously rewritten by the instructing Master and for the client subsequently to decide they didn't actually need the casting after all, but thank you anyway and could they please have a quick discussion about the fee?

Ivy allowed herself some further internal ranting about Masters and clients, which inevitably spiralled into another internal rant about how much internal ranting she had been doing lately. She tried to go back to first principles: identify the subject, identify the objective, identify the appropriate limitations on the objective… She sighed. Limitations. There were always so many bloody limitations to think about.

The practice of magic had been highly regulated ever since the wars of the mages had come to their bitter end half a century ago. Now, all but the most incidental of spells required mapping out with military precision before any thought of casting could enter a mage's mind. Ivy found the entire process thankless and frequently despaired at the fact that – contrary to her original expectations – being a mage consisted mainly of paperwork.

There was one upside to the practice, however, which was the business of actually casting the spells. Here, Ivy could draw upon the deep wells of power within the fabric of the universe, channelling it so that she felt the raw energy coursing through her body as the stitches of reality were unpicked and remade. Ivy was constantly itching to cast, but the opportunities to do so seemed few and far between, and she was finding it harder and harder to cast without the carefully constructed words of a spell before her. She struggled to shake off the impression that being a mage was all a lot less fun than it was supposed to be.

Nevertheless, with Bob warming her legs, Ivy began, haltingly, grudgingly, to write, trying to spur herself on with the promise of the thrill of performing the casting later that week.

✦

After only ten minutes of further attempts at drafting, Ivy decided to take a short break to stretch her legs, which hadn't had much opportunity to move due to the presence of the large tiger under her desk.

She wandered along the fifth floor corridor, clutching her empty mug in one hand and some papers in the other, just in case she needed an excuse for leaving her desk.

"Hard at work as usual, I see," came a sneer from one of the internal chambers along the corridor. Ivy rolled her eyes and turned to face the occupant of the chamber. A young woman was sitting behind a desk covered in reams of half-finished castings, looking tired and drawn. Her red-rimmed eyes glared out at Ivy with the edge of a challenge.

"Some of us don't need to work twice as hard to achieve half the results, Salonika," Ivy retorted. She shouldn't bait her like this, but Salonika had been exceptionally snide of late, and Ivy had found she had increasingly little patience for her pettiness.

"Some of us haven't been afforded the luxury of coasting," Salonika snapped back, tossing her unusually lank black hair from her face. Unpleasantries exchanged, she looked back down at her papers, before adding, tight-lipped, "Skelton's looking for you."

This was not what Ivy needed to hear. That Dragonsteel casting was nowhere near ready. She muttered a grudging thanks to Salonika, which went entirely unacknowledged, and hastened back along the corridor to her chambers, which were directly opposite Skelton's.

Perched at the small workstation between the two chambers was the short, whiskery female goblin who acted as personal assistant to Master Skelton.

"Ah, Ivy, Master Skelton has been wondering where you were. He has been trying to reach you *most urgently*," the goblin admonished Ivy as she hastily approached Skelton's chambers.

"Sorry, Elspeth, I had no idea. I literally stepped out of my chambers a minute ago." She pointed towards Skelton's door, which was always open, albeit guarded with zealous vigilance by the diminutive goblin. "Shall I head on in?"

"Master Skelton is occupied. He has left a message for you via the display."

"Are you sure it's not just easier for me to stick my head in, see what he's after?" Ivy moved towards Skelton's chambers, but was headed off by Elspeth, who had risen from her chair and placed her hands on her hips.

"Master Skelton has left a message for you," the goblin repeated officiously. "In your chambers."

"Fine, fine, I'll check my messages…"

Sure enough, the pinkish-orange light on the top of the crystal display sitting neatly on the corner of Ivy's desk was flashing agitatedly. Someone – presumably Skelton – had been trying to call her. Ivy pressed her palm to the cool crystal.

Nothing.

She exhaled loudly in frustration as she removed her hand and attempted to place it at a slightly different angle, to see if that would yield any results. She hated this thing. The displays had been developed internally and heralded as a feat of magical engineering, guaranteeing faster communication across the magical community. Unfortunately, mages not being engineers by nature, it mostly didn't work.

Master Skelton, being a committed modern mage, was nevertheless an avid and frequent user of the crystal display. If Skelton's attempts to collar a junior by marching down the corridor had failed due to the mage – and this Skelton found quite unfathomable – *not being at their desk*, he would simply return to his own chambers, and record a short but exceedingly polite message asking the mage in question to 'pop into his chambers' as soon as convenient. Recently, to the horror of the junior Castings mages, Master Skelton had somehow discovered a way to leave what appeared to be a message but which, when activated by the absent mage, instead *automatically called him back*.

After a couple of unsuccessful adjustments to palm pressure and placement by Ivy, which concluded with a frustrated slap to the crystal, sure enough, the display instantly connected to Skelton's display and the lively face of Master Skelton appeared, grinning widely.

"Ah, Ivy. Excellent, excellent," Master Skelton said in his fast, breathless manner. "Just wondered if you could pop by as soon as you have a moment? Excellent. Thanks very much." Without waiting for a response, Skelton disconnected the call.

Ivy sighed and once again made her way across the corridor to Master Skelton's generously proportioned chambers.

Elspeth looked up haughtily. "Ah, Ivy, there you are. The Master will see you now…"

Doing her best to smile through gritted teeth, Ivy passed Elspeth to the open door and knocked gently on the doorframe.

"Ivy, there you are. Excellent. Do come in," came Skelton's voice from somewhere near the floor. The Master was crouched at a bookcase beside his desk, rifling through a pile of books and papers. His slim fingers, all protruding knuckles and veins, were flicking through pages and tracing swift paths across cramped text as his eyes roved hurriedly back-and-forth and his thin-lipped mouth quivered in thought. He was a man perpetually in motion, possessed with a nervous energy that belied his sallow complexion and long, wasted-looking limbs. Ivy had sometimes wondered – usually late at night, after being tasked with a particularly testing casting by the Master – if Skelton had indeed died some years ago but simply refused to stop working, lest he miss some trifling advancement in modern spellcasting. He certainly looked dressed for a funeral. Unlike many of the other mages, Skelton had an obsession for modern minimalist tailoring, eschewing the more traditional and purposefully over-embellished finery paraded by many of the other Masters for solemn, dark grey suits which were impeccably cut to his elongated frame.

"How are you fixed this morning?" he asked her, not even glancing up.

"I'm in the middle of drafting those castings for Dragonsteel–" Ivy began, before the Master cut across her.

"Great, great. I'd like you to attend a meeting with me this morning. Old client of the Tower. We've been doing groundbreaking work for them, and we need some additional junior support. Meet me next to the tree in the foyer in, say, seven minutes. No need for you to bring anything."

The Master still hadn't looked up.

Ivy was well-versed in Skelton's mannerisms and expectations; she knew what this commandment entailed. Hastily returning to her chambers, she tried to work out what she needed to take with her, knowing from painful experience that the instruction not to bring anything was only valid until Master Skelton inevitably instructed her to take notes. A meeting, though. That at least sounded like it might be interesting. And interesting was what she needed right now; she was beginning to feel lost, like a drone in the wrong hive. There had to be more to this magic business, there just had to be. She couldn't have left so much behind for this circus of paperwork and process…

As she hastily gathered up her satchel, a small voice inside her pointed out that she had just been excited by the prospect of a *meeting*, indicating that things were worse than she cared to admit. She ignored it, as she always did, and headed down to the tree, leaving Bob dozing gently under her desk.

✦

The tree sat encased within walls of stone and dragonsteel.

It wanted to stretch out and touch the sun and feel the wind on its sickly limbs. Instead, it was in half light, a grim and grubby streak of sunlight filtering through panes of thick, tinted glass above it. Its leaves rustled sullenly in the cloistered, airless environment.

The tree was not happy. In fact, it was decidedly aggravated, and it was beginning to get angry.

Something skittered along its branches, and into the morning gloom.

2.

CURIOUS BREWS
━━━━━━━◆━━━━━━━

Ivy was trying to catch her breath. Skelton had marched her halfway across the Citadel at a brisk, wordless pace and she was now experiencing an uncomfortable stitch as she stared up at the massive building in front of her.

It was constructed in the old pre-Accords style, a vast sandstone frontage atop of a flight of worn, shallow stone steps. There was nothing cosmopolitan about the construction; no dragonsteel, no goblin iron, no magical engineering on display. It was a resolutely human edifice. Towering, windowless stone walls branched off from either side of the impressive frontage, preventing Ivy from glimpsing what lay within. Whatever it was, it reeked – noxious odours clambered over the walls, making Ivy's nose wrinkle in distaste.

"Right," Skelton announced, "we've made excellent time. Let's get a drink before we go in – Woodbane's stuff is relatively insipid, as I recall…"

Woodbane. Ivy knew that name. Woodbane Cosmetics was a long-established client of the Tower, specialising in the manufacture and wholesale of magical cosmetic products. That would explain the unpleasant smells skulking across the steps.

But Woodbane dealt mainly with the Solutions Division of the Tower, so what was Skelton, a Castings Master, doing here?

Before she had time to ask, Skelton had started peering around optimistically. "In fact, I could do with a bit of a pick-me-up – some of that faerie stuff would do the trick marvellously…" Skelton didn't look as though he needed a pick-me-up; the man was practically vibrating as it was. Ivy didn't understand it. Someone as brittle and gaunt as Skelton shouldn't have been able to keep up a stride like that. Yet the Master wasn't even out of breath. "I think there's one of those new little pop-up cafés somewhere around…" Skelton continued, "I came across it only the other day."

Looking around with a slight frown, Ivy could see nothing but the soft bustle of various species weaving their way through the busy square in front of the Woodbane building. She then experienced a sudden start as – literally out of nowhere – a small street stall sprung up before them.

It was like watching someone unfold a bit of paper yet somehow, *at exactly the same time*, fold it into something even more complex. In a matter of seconds, the stall was simply *there*. A bored-looking male faerie was leaning on the counter of the small, shabby stall next to a stack of cups, while a large, complicated machine coated in crusted globules hissed and bubbled maniacally in the back, several levers and dials bouncing up and down exuberantly and entirely autonomously.

"Ah, marvellous, yes, this is the one," said Skelton chirpily.

"Can I help you?" the faerie asked in a voice that dripped with indolence.

"Yes, indeed. Indeed. One of those excellent Bubbular Brews, if I may," Skelton said, as he rummaged in his outercloak for his money pouch. "Salted fudge flavour this time, I think."

"That'll be four Queens and sixty," the faerie drawled, plucking a cup from the stack and sliding it listlessly under a spiral nozzle on the machine, which whistled in what Ivy thought was an abnormally threatening manner.

"You want anything?" the faerie asked her directly.

Ivy wavered. Although she had lived in the Citadel for years, she still wasn't sure about faerie brews. "I'll have the same," she resolved, firmly dispelling any lingering hesitancy. "Thank you," she added as an afterthought.

"That'll be five Queens and ninety-five," the faerie said, once again lifting a cup and sliding it towards another nozzle.

"Excuse me?" Ivy said, confused. "It was four-sixty a second ago!"

"Ah, but as you say, that was a second ago, weren't it?" said the faerie, as though he was explaining something patently obvious. He hooked his implausibly smooth hands over the lapels of his green leather jerkin and observed her condescendingly. "It's supply and demand, innit? There's suddenly demand, so I need to up me prices to meet it. S'called dynamite pricing."

Ivy looked to Skelton for support, but he was now standing at the top of the steps to Woodbane Cosmetics, sipping his brew and clearly impatient for her to join him.

Ivy, now entirely baffled, said, "Wait a minute. What if I changed my mind? What if I ordered–" Ivy squinted at the cramped yet florid handwriting on the board above the strange machine "–melted clementine flavour?"

"Still be five ninety-five."

"But it's a completely different flavour!"

The faerie shrugged. "Like I said, s'all a matter of market forces. I don't make the rules. So, you want the salted fudge or what?"

Ivy sighed, shoving some money on the sticky counter. "Here you go. Just the one I ordered, please."

"Coming right up."

She watched as he flicked a few buttons, allowing what looked suspiciously like boiling tar to gush angrily from the contraption in the rear of the stall. He shoved a cup her way, then caught her eye with a smirk as she lifted it off the counter.

Not waiting for her to say anything, and spying no other unwitting customers, the faerie yanked down the flap above the counter and the entire stall did what can only be described as a controlled crumple, before vanishing from existence.

Not entirely happy with the outcome of the transaction, Ivy walked up to where Master Skelton was draining his cup. "Ready?" he asked, looking sharply at her.

Ivy nodded, hastily slurping her Bubbular Brew, which turned out to have a somewhat singular taste. There were definitely undertones of something resembling salted fudge, but mostly it tasted of pure, unadulterated sugar, heated to an intensity where it almost certainly should have caramelised, but had instead somehow charred. Ivy shuddered as the beverage hit the back of her eyes.

"Good stuff, isn't it?" Skelton said. "I'm a big fan of these new little outfits. Big fan. Right, any questions?"

Ivy realised this was a golden opportunity to ask Skelton something which might sound astute. However, with the wretched brew still doing cartwheels and blowing raspberries somewhere in her cerebrum, Ivy could only think to ask, "What exactly are we doing here, Master?"

"Yes, good question, an explanation would probably be useful, wouldn't it?" Skelton said, as though the notion of describing the purpose of their visit was a novel concept to him.

"Woodbane Cosmetics has, with our assistance, been working on a magical anti-ageing solution. Unusually, some Castings input has been required. The drafting work has been completed, so I expect we will be discussing timescales in relation to the casting itself. Understood?"

Ivy nodded, unsatisfied, but realising this was all she was going to get.

"Great, great," Skelton said. "I'll introduce you when we get in, naturally, but let's consider this meeting more of a 'listen and learn' exercise for you, shall we?" Skelton looked at her closely as he said this.

Ivy nodded a second time. She knew what that meant. Keep her thoughts and opinions strictly within the confines of her own head. The instruction was of little surprise. After years of working at the Tower, with its never-ending catalogue of rules, regulations and limitations, part of her questioned whether she had any independent thoughts or opinions left to confine.

They walked in through the grand entrance and approached a large mahogany reception desk, behind which sat a large mahogany receptionist.

"Hello, Margery," said Skelton politely. "Good to see you again, you look like you've been keeping well." She looked like she had been left unattended in direct sunlight for the last three decades. "We've got an appointment with Ramston. Could you point us in the direction of today's meeting room, please?"

The woman gave him a dour stare and then squinted at the leather-bound logbook before her. "Through that door," she said curtly, jabbing a thick finger towards a large, embossed door down the hallway. "He'll be with you shortly."

"Thanks, thanks. Much appreciated," said Skelton, striding through the door, untroubled by the receptionist's abruptness.

The meeting room was exquisitely furnished; an exercise in pre-Accords opulence. Heavily lacquered and decorative oak panels adorned the walls, the parquet floor was buffed to an extravagant sheen, and a wide oval table commanded the middle of the room, surrounded by eighteen ornately carved, high-backed chairs. There were no windows; the only sources of light being the old-fashioned lamps affixed to the walls, emitting a muted glow which reflected languidly across the dark-varnished table. Ivy had never before seen so much humble wood pressed and pruned and polished into abject submission.

"Tea? Coffee?" asked Skelton, interrupting her thoughts. "There's some over here, although as I mentioned before–" at this Skelton's voice dropped to a whisper– "it's pretty weak stuff." An elegant sideboard rested against one panelled wall, hosting a small selection of individually packaged teas, all resolutely of the human variety.

Ivy politely declined. She was still clutching her Bubbular Brew, which was now sputtering gently.

At that moment, Ramston Woodbane entered, flanked by a younger man whom Ivy recognised with a jolt: Hartley Crumpley-Snafely. He'd been a senior mage in the Solutions Division at Jackdaw and Spittlelick until about a year ago. Ivy had heard he'd gone to work 'in-house' for one of the Tower's major clients; it appeared Woodbane was the major client in question. From the look of him, Hartley was doing very well for himself indeed. Ivy had forgotten how annoyingly handsome he was.

Leaving no time for Ivy to adjust to Hartley's unexpected presence, Woodbane launched towards Skelton, grasped his hand, and shook it effusively.

"Everard, good ter see yer again," Woodbane boomed at the Master, who – despite his own not inconsiderable height – looked frail in the face of Woodbane's huge frame. There was not an ounce of fat on the man; he was simply built on a different scale to other humans, possibly one necessitating construction in a shipyard.

"Likewise, Ramston," Skelton replied, "good to see you too."

"Are you well?" Woodbane barked. "You're looking tired around the eyes, old boy. You should try some of our new range, perk you right up."

"It's been a busy few months," Skelton replied evenly.

"Always busy, busy, you mages. Hartley here never seems ter stop beaverin' away," Woodbane exclaimed jovially, motioning towards the figure slightly behind him.

"Hartley," said Skelton warmly. "How are you keeping?"

"Lots to do, Master Skelton, as Ramston was just saying." Hartley delivered this in a slightly self-satisfied manner. Ivy suspected that Hartley – like most in-house mages – was unlikely to be especially busy. Certainly not 'Tower-busy'. That was one of the perks of being an in-house mage – it was practically early retirement as far as Ivy was concerned. However, some habits were hard to break, and Hartley, being Tower-trained, clearly still felt it important to appear suitably busy and important. Ivy watched as he ran a hand absently through his thick hair.

"Business is booming!" proclaimed Woodbane. "Product sales for this new solution you've been brewin' up are through the roof. Can't stop it flyin' off the damn shelves every time we get it in stock!" He veered off course abruptly, having suddenly noticed Ivy. "And who's this? Not seen this one before!"

"This is Ivy Armstride," said Skelton. "She'll be assisting me on this matter."

"Good to see you again, Ivy," said Hartley softly, fixing his grey-blue eyes on hers.

She opened her mouth to respond, but Woodbane marched over to shake her hand, exclaiming, "Nice ter meet yer, Ivy!" Woodbane shot a look across at Skelton as he pumped Ivy's palm energetically. "You do seem to go through 'em, Skelton." Woodbane leant towards her and said in a loud stage whisper, "Don't know what it is he does ter you lot. You keep an eye on that one, gel."

Woodbane finally released Ivy's hand, much to her relief. He motioned towards the table. "Come now," he said grandly, "to business! Sit, gel, sit!"

Ivy never knew quite where to position herself in these situations. It was like some perverse test. How was she to know what the right chair was? What if she sat down at one end and the client sat at the other, leaving an awkward gaping hole between them? What if that's what the client expected? What if she took the client's chair? Exhausted by the existential crisis engendered by the simple act of choosing a chair, she gave herself an internal shake and took a seat opposite Hartley, willing her Bubbular Brew to stop its nervous popping.

"So, how's my new solution coming along?" Woodbane boomed. Not waiting for Skelton to respond, he addressed Ivy and said, "I'm sure yer Master's told yer, but you clever buggers have finally worked out a way to add a zim and a zap to me potions. Created a magical little wrinkle potion which has been doing business a world o' good. Them smart arses over at Preddle Cosmetics don't know what's hit 'em!

"I've been telling Hartley all along – yer can't make real magic with a bunch of bloody plants and leaves!" At this,

Woodbane shot a dark look at Hartley. "Just look at what happened with that damned calming lotion your lot brewed up! Poor Mrs Woodbane refused ter come downstairs for a week after testin' that last batch! Thank goodness we didn't take *that* ter Market!"

It dawned on Ivy that – in the manner of client meetings across the universe – she was about to be subjected to a dramatic account of all happenings to date. Naturally, this would mostly be for Woodbane's own benefit, and so thoroughly indulged, but on this occasion, Ivy was grateful given the limited information she had extracted from Skelton.

Woodbane exhaled theatrically. "Anyway, I went ter Hartley here," Woodbane continued, jabbing Hartley in the shoulder with some force, "and I says ter him: 'make me some magical ingredients that *work*. The proper stuff, like in the good ol' days'."

Ivy knew enough to know that Woodbane was referring to the pre-Accords days when potions often contained ingredients derived from the blood, flesh and bone of magical creatures, ingredients which were now classed as 'Restricted Substances', their use strictly prohibited. The solutions produced in the Citadel since the creation of the Restricted Substances Register had lacked their previous potency; a fact which had long been bemoaned by industrialists and consumers alike (or the human ones, at least).

"And Hartley here, he tells me we can't obtain Restricted Substances. And so, I says, 'I didn't say get 'em, I said *make* 'em! You say you specialise in solutions – *make* me one!' Ha! You should have seen the look on his face!"

"It isn't quite that straightforward," Hartley carefully interjected.

"Well, you're the details man, so yer are," Woodbane barked dismissively, before continuing. "Well, Hartley got in touch with Everard here and 'Presto!', we were in business."

At this, Woodbane let out a guffaw. "And what a business! A month ago, Woodbane's Original Ever-Young Solution was topping every bestseller list this side of Chelmsbridge. Damned shame that the bloody supplies have run dry – we could be makin' a killin'!" Woodbane paused, allowing Ivy a brief but pleasant respite from the barrage of exclamations. Ivy's beleaguered ears rung in the quiet.

"Which brings me ter why we're all sittin' here today!" Ivy braced for another bombardment as Woodbane resumed. "The Market is desperate for us to restart supply, we're up ter our necks in pre-orders, and it wants somethin' stronger too, somethin' we can sell to the *premium*–" Woodbane savoured the word "–customer. Plannin' on callin' it 'Woodbane's Premium Ever-Young Solution'. Got a nice ring to it. Hartley tells me you and your potions people have worked out the formula.

"By rights, we should be able to get goin' straight away, but according to Hartley there's an issue with yer input, Everard. Says yer not producing enough ingredients for mass production. That right? I've got me mages all lined up with nothin' ter brew..."

Mass production. Ivy knew that Woodbane Cosmetics, like many industrial producers of magical goods in the Citadel, employed a number of 'in-house' Solutions mages, all Tower-trained, to brew potions at scale. Jackdaw and Spittlelick, like all Citadel Towers, did not have the facility to manufacture solutions in volumes large enough to satisfy Market demand, so once the Solutions mages at Jackdaw had developed and trialled the product, they would hand over mass production to clients such as Woodbane Cosmetics, who would usually also procure the ingredients. Unfortunately, in this case it seemed Woodbane was dependent on Jackdaw to supply the magical ingredients, a fact that Ramston Woodbane was clearly impatient about.

"The casting process for the premium product's ingredients is extremely complex," Skelton responded. "A novel approach has been developed, but there have been… hurdles…to surmount–" at this, Hartley and Skelton exchanged a quick look that Ivy couldn't quite read– "and we have needed to pause supply. However, we are close to being able to deliver the ingredients needed at scale."

"That's what I like ter hear," Woodbane said approvingly. "As long as we have somethin' ter pull out of the bag for the stockholder presentation at the end of the month, we'll be well-placed to meet the Wintertide rush. If the stockholders are happy, I'm happy. Especially as I'm the majority stockholder!" Woodbane rubbed his hands together hungrily.

"We'll naturally do our best to meet timescales, Ramston," said Skelton cautiously, "but I would remind you that, for the premium product, we will also need to obtain Regulator approval before handing over ingredients for mass production."

"How long?" Woodbane barked.

"It should only add a matter of weeks to the timetable, if we are fortunate. A month or two if not. I assure you that there will be no undue delay."

"Fine, fine. Anythin' else I need ter know?"

At this point Hartley interjected. "I can take you through the process for the premium product separately, without taking up any more of Master Skelton's time. I'll also prepare a briefing note for the stockholders. I'll make sure it's the way you like it."

"Short!" said Woodbane, puffing himself up and emitting his bark-like laugh again.

Skelton was readying himself to rise. "In which case, Ramston, if there's nothing else…?"

Ivy was grateful the meeting was being brought to a close. The room had become increasingly stuffy; a steady stream of dust motes was whirling sleepily in the cloistered air. Skelton and Woodbane exchanged a few more words about the process and timings. As her attention drifted, she felt the intense, blue-grey eyes of Hartley on her. She looked up to see him raising an eyebrow at her, a slight smirk playing around the corners of his mouth.

Disconcerted, she met his gaze and took a sip from her drink, remembering far too late the viciousness of the concoction and spluttering sharply. Hartley's smirk widened. Ivy felt herself flush and looked back down at her notes. What was it about Hartley that made her react like this? They had never exchanged more than basic pleasantries whenever they had crossed paths at the Tower. And yet…

"Anything to add, Ivy?"

Mild panic arose in Ivy. She hadn't heard a word Skelton had just said. Skelton's smile had momentarily frozen. A sense of desperate self-preservation suddenly reminded her that she wasn't actually expected to say anything interesting. "No, I think that covers it," she heard herself reply automatically.

Skelton's tight smile relaxed, as he brought the meeting to a close.

As the occupants of the now thoroughly musty room rose to their feet and moved towards the exit, Hartley nodded at

Ivy. "Nice to see you again, Ivy," he said coolly. "I'm sure we'll be seeing a great deal of each other over the next few weeks."

Ivy felt a twist in her chest as he flashed his half-smile at her.

Woodbane then grabbed Ivy's hand and shook it firmly once again. "Welcome on board," he boomed. "Try ter last longer 'n the last one."

✦

When they arrived back at the Tower's huge circular foyer, Skelton said to Ivy, "That went well, I think. We've got work to do, though. I'll need you to make this matter your priority."

"Happy to, Master," Ivy said, despite having promised the same thing to at least two other Masters in the last week.

"Master?" she asked, hesitantly.

"Mm?"

"This new solution for Woodbane… he said you've found a way to somehow *make* Restricted Substances… is that even possible?"

"It is. Through considerable trial, and some fortune, we have managed to find a way to create synthetic versions of certain Restricted Substances."

"I've never heard of anyone performing such magic," Ivy ventured.

"Nor should you have." Skelton did not offer anything further.

"Has anyone done it before?"

"Not successfully. The casting process required is… complex. It is also rather more *intense* than other casting ceremonies. Besides, until now, there had been no need to perfect the process. Before the Accords, Restricted Substances were more readily... obtainable... and while there has been some discussion more recently about replicating the effects of Restricted Substances, the Regulator has generally discouraged experimentation, believing it has good reason to keep mages tightly monitored in such respects.

"Times have, however, changed, and the Regulator is under pressure to change with those times. Such progress is vital in our modern age. That is why this matter is of the utmost priority." Skelton looked away from Ivy, gazing now into the middle distance, past the colossal tree that dominated the grand foyer.

"Is there anything I can do this afternoon?" Ivy volunteered.

"Indeed, indeed," Skelton said absently.

"Perhaps a draft casting I can help with?" she prompted.

"No further drafting is needed at this stage, but we will need copies of the casting I have drafted, which is somewhat bespoke, to enable us to undertake the next ceremony. I'll leave it on your desk. Three copies should do it. See that Cleft makes it a priority."

"Will do," she affirmed.

Skelton nodded in acknowledgment. Without waiting for her to follow, he crossed the foyer and strode into the lift. As he pulled a small lever and pressed a button that went 'ding' (Ivy was convinced it hadn't made any such sound before), Ivy watched the doors clunk shut and felt a thrill thread through to her fingertips as she recalled Skelton's words. She would be undertaking a complex casting, one which Skelton had described as *intense*...

Well, that finally sounded like exactly the sort of magic Ivy could get on board with...

3.

A POCKETFUL OF ASPIRATION

◆

Ivy Armstride was not the only one in the Citadel taking a keen interest in Master Skelton's innovative new spellcasting process.

Glof, the elderly goblin who supervised the Audit Office of the Citadel's Regulator of Magical Practice, had been summoned only the previous week to the wolfwood-panelled chambers of the Regulator's Supervisor General. She had informed him that, whilst the Approvals Office had reviewed the theoretical magics behind the synthetic ingredients used in Woodbane's new "Ever-Young" solution and discerned no foul play, they still harboured some lingering concerns.

Despite their reservations, they had approved the product for release to the Market. However, the submission paperwork that the Approvals Office had recently received in respect of Woodbane's latest *premium* Ever-Young solution had presented the perfect excuse to undertake a more *particular* enquiry. The Supervisor General had therefore determined that a special audit should be undertaken within the Tower of Jackdaw and Spittlelick.

"Find out what the bloody hell is going on, Glof," she had commanded, adding, "but do so quietly."

At that point, Glof could have enlisted one of his more experienced auditors, or even looked around Jackdaw and Spittlelick himself. After all, he knew it needed to be handled delicately. But he really couldn't spare one of the main team, and Glof himself was getting older; the thought of remaining in the warm, quiet confines of the Audit Office was a far more appealing prospect. So perhaps, just perhaps, this might be a perfect little task for the eager new recruit now sharing Glof's otherwise serene office space and asking a tad too many insightful questions…

◆

Hop Pockett had been an auditor with the Regulator for about six weeks. The ink had practically yet to dry on his formal General Regulatory Certification (for which he was determined to find a frame suitable for such august contents).

Hop had harboured dreams from an early age of training as a Citadel mage. Neither of his older siblings had demonstrated any magical tendencies (there was a cousin that claimed he could dowse for water, but since he only ever performed this feat indoors, having first asked to use the facilities, Hop was sceptical of these claims). Nor did his father, who had been responsible for much of the growth of the Market, have much respect for Hop's obsession with practising magic.

Hop, however, was determined that he would be the first mage in the family, regardless of whether he had the blessing of his father or whether he had actually been blessed with any magical ability.

Not being a popular child, he had found plenty of time to bury himself in books devoted to explaining the fundamental principles of magic use. He had finished his formal schooling with a rudimentary grasp of basic maths and literacy, but with an encyclopaedic knowledge of Lore and Sorcery. He was like a piece of high-specification kit that someone had forgotten to plug in.

Hop did, somewhere very deep down, appreciate that it was unlikely he would ever become a mage if he was unable to channel enough magical energy to boil water. Nevertheless, with a hearty dose of optimism, he had applied to all five Citadel Towers for an apprenticeship, enthusiastically answering the section in the Standard Entry Submission stating 'describe your magical aptitude and abilities to date' as 'not applicable'. When faced with the question 'what (in brief) first interested you in becoming a mage?' he had enclosed a treatise on the Wolf Accords and their subsequent amendments.

The apprenticeship offers did not pour in.

So, Hop instead set about applying for a position at the Regulator, determining that, if he couldn't become a mage, he could at least keep an eye on what they were all up to, make sure they were doing it properly, and perhaps (he secretly hoped) occasionally try his hand at a spell or two.

Hop had taken to his training at the Regulator like a troll to mud. He had passed both his Moderate Examinations and his Disproportionates with flying colours and, upon finally becoming fully Certified, insisted upon immediately taking on an auditing field assignment.

Glof, the long-suffering Chief Auditor, had initially given Hop a few internal tasks, hoping to dampen his alarming over-enthusiasm. Much to Glof's dismay, he was fast running out of tasks. It seemed as though no sooner had he given Hop an assignment, Hop had not only completed it, but had compiled a raft of follow-up observations, many of which contained polite suggestions about how well-established internal practices might be improved.

Glof had been feeling at a complete loss before the special audit at Jackdaw and Spittlelick was requested; now here was a wonderful opportunity to solve several little problems in one masterful stroke! Tremendously pleased with himself, Glof had beckoned Hop over and outlined his first *proper* field assignment, being most careful to emphasise that Hop was to undertake the audit quickly and discreetly. Above all, he was not to go beyond the remit of the investigation.

Hop, beaming with pride, had nodded along as Glof's instructions fell on decidedly deaf ears. He had proceeded directly to Jackdaw and Spittlelick with relish, eager to ensure the magical marvels he imagined were being performed *exactly* as required.

✦

Ivy Armstride was not experiencing anything approaching relish.

She had returned to her chambers to find two piles of paperwork on her desk. One was the Woodbane casting, a fulsome document that contained thirty-odd pages of Master Skelton's scrawl, the other a pile of duplicate castings from another matter marked 'Please Ump'. Clearly Master Skelton had not wanted to miss a golden opportunity to save himself further time.

After giving Bob a brief pat (it seemed he had bedded in for the day), Ivy traipsed down the stairwell to the second floor and along a dimly lit corridor to a door marked 'Copy Room'.

Unlike the other floors of the Tower, the second floor was remarkable in that it contained absolutely no external or internal windows. This windowless loop was, according to the impassioned claims of the Tower's architects, merely the result of an 'unanticipated omission in the assumptions made during the preliminary design phase resulting in a conceivably less than ideal number of casements'. Roughly translated, someone had botched the brief. Nevertheless, the mages had found an excellent use for the second floor. It was the perfect location to house the Tower's library, alongside that mysterious yet essential department that fascinated mages more than any eldritch magical workings of the universe: Facilities.

The Copy Room sat within the Facilities department. It was where castings, solutions formulae, and all other papers produced by the operation of a thoroughly modern magical establishment were dutifully – and above all *accurately* – copied so as to be disseminated amongst the mages who needed them. As every apprentice was taught, a single word out of place could change the entire outcome of a spell or brew. Clients would not pay for a spell meant to keep a dragon in check that instead brought a hapless passer-by out in boils, or which only worked every other Tuesday when the right shade of footwear was worn.

The sole copier for Jackdaw's mages was a spindly and cantankerous old goblin named Cleft. Cleft's copying was always immaculate, as one would expect from a goblin, making him indispensable to the Tower. He resided in the Copy Room alongside its other occupant: a small rotund troll called Ump, responsible for document disposal.

"Morning, Cleft, morning, Ump," Ivy said, as she breezed into the Copy Room. "A couple of quick jobs for you both please. One Umping job – old casting copies from a matter from last year. And one copy job, being three copies of a new bespoke casting for Master Skelton." Ivy tried to emphasise Skelton's name, hoping its gravity would register with the goblin.

Cleft did not look up from his transcribing. Ump merely cocked his boulder-shaped head slowly.

"If you don't mind, the copying task is urgent, Cleft. It's for Woodbane Cosmetics and–"

"Bottom of the pile," Cleft indicated with his spindly digits, without looking up.

Ivy frowned. Cleft was difficult to operate at the best of times, but this was not going well.

"It's just that Master Skelton requested that this casting be copied as a matter of *priority*…"

Cleft responded with a studied disinterest. "It will get done, although I cannot at this stage commit to any timeframe. Bottom of the pile please."

Ivy was at a loss. Many a mage had tried to charm, cajole or coerce Cleft into completing their copying within their required timeframe. Some had shouted, some had attempted bribery and a fair few had even wept in sheer desperation. But Cleft copied at the rate he deemed appropriate, which could at times be so glacial that entire civilisations could crumble and re-emerge while his pen caressed the paper.

Ivy gave it one last attempt. "If I just leave it right here, perhaps you could take a quick look this afternoon…?" She slowly slid one pile of papers onto the top of the 'in'-tray on Cleft's otherwise pristine desk and tossed the other pile into Ump's basket. Ump brightened at the sight.

Being a troll, and blessed with a unique digestive system, Ump was capable of processing pretty much anything carbon-based, and was exceptionally adept at processing magical items. As such, after an exhaustive consultation process involving several sub-committees, Ump had been hired – or perhaps more accurately installed – to dispose of sensitive magical documents.

Unlike Cleft, Ump was refreshingly easy to operate. A mage would simply leave any paperwork marked for destruction in the small basket next to Ump, or indeed anywhere in his immediate vicinity, and Ump would place the documents into his mouth and swallow them wholesale, usually accompanied by a thunk of a syllable which could in fact only be described as "Ump".

"Ump," said Ump agreeably, helping himself to a couple of sheets from the pile of papers Ivy had thrown to him. Ump was about as communicative as a workbench and had about as many distinguishing features, but he nevertheless appeared content with his role, although perhaps it was more the case that he was never outwardly discontented, which in the Citadel was generally mistaken for the same thing.

"Ms Armstride–" Cleft began, furrowing his brow and narrowing his crystal blue eyes at Ivy. Before he could get any further, the Copy Room door swung open.

Into the small room strode a prim young man holding a leather-bound folder. A pair of round glasses sat perched on the bridge of his nose, looking dangerously at risk of sliding down it at any moment. Other than this, the man who entered the Copy Room was almost completely, and somewhat perturbingly, unremarkable. He gave the impression of being neither tall nor short, neither handsome nor ugly, neither big nor small.

Cleft turned to him. "Yes?" he asked, an edge of irritation in his voice.

"I've come for audit purposes," said the man, puffing himself up as he did so.

"And you are?"

"An auditor."

This momentarily stumped the occupants of the Copy Room, including Ump, who had been following the proceedings with great interest, like a child hypnotised by a series of bright colours and pictures.

Ivy took up the interrogation. "An auditor? From the Regulator? But the Tower isn't due an audit. We had one last Wintertide. Do the Masters know you're here?"

Cleft carefully placed his pen on his desk. "And what pray is an *auditor* doing in the Copy Room?" he said icily. "No one *audits* the Copy Room."

"I've been asked to conduct a special audit over the next few days. The Masters are aware. I can't say any more than that, I'm afraid," the man said pompously. "In the course of my enquiries, I thought I would come down here to make sure that correct copy and destroy procedures are being followed. Shouldn't take up too much of your time."

"Ump," contributed Ump, shovelling in another fistful of paper.

The man paused, as though replaying the previous stream of questions. "I'm Hop, by the way," he added. "Hop Pockett."

Cleft gave a small sniff. "Well, Mr Pockett, that is all well and good, but rest assured there's nothing irregular about the Copy Room's procedures. Absolutely nothing. This is an impeccably maintained and efficient centre of operations."

Ivy, sensing an opportunity not to be wasted, chimed in, "I couldn't agree more. I came here but moments ago with this complex casting for Woodbane Cosmetics, a *very important client*, which needs to be copied as a matter of priority." Ivy didn't notice the look of excitement that flashed across Hop's face at the word 'Woodbane' because she was preoccupied with looking pointedly towards Cleft. "Cleft here was just reviewing it to make sure he had ample time to give it his *full attention* this afternoon."

Cleft began to open his mouth but caught his indignation in his throat. "Quite so," he said. "Indeed."

Cleft picked up the papers Ivy had placed on the top of his neatly stacked pile and started leafing slowly through them. Without moving his eyes from the paper, he said, "Mr Pockett, please do feel free to examine the Copy Room." Cleft motioned expansively at the bare, windowless walls of the small room, the stooped figure of Ump next to his almost empty basket, and his own spotless writing desk. "When you have quite finished, in your own time of course, we would be more than happy to answer any pressing questions you might have."

As Ivy went to leave, satisfied she had achieved her objective, Hop obstructed her exit and said, "You mentioned Woodbane Cosmetics. Do you happen to be working on the matter?"

"I do," Ivy replied slowly.

"Excellent," said Hop, opening his folder quickly and pulling out a pen. "And you are?"

"Ivy Armstride."

"Role?"

"Junior mage, Castings Division…"

"No, no. Role on the Woodbane matter, please."

"Um... copying? So far, at least."

"Copying what, may I enquire?"

"The draft casting for the creation of–" At this, Ivy wavered, wondering if she was about to say more than she should. "Look, I'm not really sure I should be speaking to you..."

Hop was scribbling frantically. "Very helpful. I'd like to examine this casting, if I may?"

"It's being copied," Ivy said, hoping this would deflect further enquiries.

At this juncture, Cleft raised his eyes from the papers and interjected. "Ms Armstride," he began, "I confess myself perplexed. You said this was a new casting, correct?"

"I did."

"Quite. And yet, what I have before me is thirty identical copies of a single-page casting which I distinctly recall copying last year..."

Ivy looked sharply at the papers Cleft was flourishing, which were categorically not the Woodbane casting, but instead comprised the defunct casting papers Skelton had marked for Umping.

With a growing sense of dread, she looked slowly down at Ump, hoping against hope to see the pile of papers she had tossed to him earlier. They had to be there...

The basket next to the troll was conspicuously empty; the Woodbane casting was nowhere to be seen.

"Ump," said Ump cheerfully.

✦

Ivy was in a state by the time she returned to her chambers and collapsed into her chair. She needed to fix this, and quickly.

How could she have mixed up the Woodbane casting with the papers for Umping? She never made this sort of stupid mistake. Never.

She slammed her elbows on the desk and held her head in her hands. What to do? She would have to come clean. It might not be so bad. Skelton would probably remember most of the casting anyway. But what if he didn't? That casting had probably taken days to draft, and it was all in Master Skelton's hand, which was unusual and raised the stakes even higher. How would he react?

Perhaps she could try to redraft the casting, and then plead with Cleft to copy it at speed? But that was nonsense; she didn't know nearly enough about the magic to draft it from scratch.

Ivy realised with a heavy sigh that the only document she was likely to be composing in the next twenty-four hours was her letter of resignation. Had it come to this? Her last few years of work, all about to be Umped like the draft casting she had lost?

She couldn't let that happen. She needed to stay. This Tower was everything to her. Skelton's approval was everything to her. The man was practically raising her; he was the closest thing to a parent she had left. She thought of the real family she had left behind, the backs that had turned on her, all because she wanted to come here – *here* – to practise magic. Magic! In all its heat and fire and glory… What would they think of her now? Even more of a disappointment? She folded the feeling away, under swaddling layers of steel. She couldn't think about that.

She breathed deeply, trying to calm her rattled thoughts. She could solve this. But what was she to say to Skelton?

As she tilted her head back, the shadow of the giant tree rising behind her, she recalled performing her first ever casting with Skelton almost a decade earlier. Still only an apprentice, and an exceptionally young one at that – barely fifteen – she had been summoned by Skelton to attend Dragonsteel Industries. He wanted her to assist with placing the magical bindings on one of their reptilian assets; bindings which would render the creature docile and governable. To this day, she still had no idea why he had taken her and not one of the more senior mages.

Standing in Dragonsteel's dusty forecourt, enclosed within polished walls of black granite and obsidian, she had watched as two muscular ogres had heaved a dragon from a vast outhouse buttressed with shining dragonsteel girders. They had wrenched at its chains, hauling it across the yard as it writhed and struggled, its tremendous claws raking up clouds of dust and charcoal.

Ivy remembered scales like tarnished silver rippling on its heaving flanks as it wrestled against the heavy dragonsteel shackles that ballasted its monstrous wings. She pictured the gleaming metal muzzle that bit tight around its massive jaws. Ugly welts had formed across the bridge of its nose and crisscrossed the scaffold of its wings, oozing viscous dark liquid.

Even bound, the thrashing reptile was terrifying, a brutal machine, glowering savagely at Ivy and Skelton. The Master had stood at her shoulder, bracing her as she felt the casting papers tremble in her hands. "*Now, Ivy,*" he had said, nudging her forwards.

The dragon had keened wildly and flailed its head. One of the ogres had lost its grip and a heavy chain had whipped across the forecourt, narrowly missing the mages, churning up more coarse dust which scratched Ivy's face and filled her lungs. As the dragon had lunged towards her, she had instinctively reached out with her magic to appease it. She could feel the pounding of its heart in its panicked breast–

"*The words, Ivy,*" Skelton had commanded. "*You must recite the words!*"

She had fumbled with the casting; in that moment, its carefully constructed words had seemed alien and meaningless. But Skelton had started intoning and she followed suit, magic coursing through her and bending to her will as they recited the pages and pages of the casting. The dragon's rage had quelled by turns, first into agitation, then into nervous fretting and keening, and then slowly, slowly into utter docility and calm. It slumped to the ground, motionless.

Ivy remembered its golden eyes, dimmed like embers.

The dragon's handlers had dispassionately uncoupled it from its heavy chains, which clanked unceremoniously to the ground. It lay, unmoving, until a series of arcane words were barked by one of the ogres, whereupon it soared upwards and circled the forecourt, before landing gracefully and retreating obediently back into the vast outhouse. Anyone could operate it now, provided they knew the command words.

Ivy had been euphoric. Skelton had merely nodded at her, before striding back to the confines of the Dragonsteel facility.

That experience, for Ivy, had been enough to drive her to do more, to do better. To seek from Skelton more than a mere nod, to aspire to his express approval.

Yet now, all she could see was the failure looming before her, certain that Skelton would not suffer her mistake lightly. What was she supposed to do? And why, *why* was such an innocent mistake causing her insides to coil in tight, searing dread? She had bound that dragon and bound others countless times after that. She had spent her childhood in a village that crouched on the edge of a different Citadel, ruined by the wars of the mages and still infected with the toxic magic that had destroyed it, infested with the dark, nameless emanations of that pollution. She was not afraid of things that went bump in the night, so when and why had she become so terrified by something that went 'Ump' in the day…?

Still looking blankly at the ceiling, lost in a well of despair, Ivy suddenly became aware of a strange scratching noise coming from somewhere in her chambers.

Having frequently stayed in the Tower long past nightfall, Ivy was no stranger to the odd noises made as the magics of the day settled and cooled, but this scratching, skittering noise was new. It also sounded extremely close…

She scanned her chambers but couldn't locate the source. It stopped for a moment, then resumed from a different area. Ivy stood and started scrutinising the books on her shelves. She crawled under her desk, peering into the corners, but found nothing but an abundance of the orange and black tufts of fur which were the hallmark of Bob.

"Ms Armstride?" enquired a voice from the corridor, making her start and thump her head on the desk.

Ivy emerged and looked up, rubbing her head. She could have sworn she heard a scuttling sound…

Elspeth was standing in the entrance to Ivy's chambers, studying her. "You're late for your appraisal," she intoned reproachfully. "With Taryn Underfoot."

Ivy swore under her breath. Just what she needed. The strange noise would have to wait; as would the crisis with Skelton.

✦

At that moment, in Skelton's chambers, a different crisis was unfolding. As Ivy Armstride darted down the stairs to the third floor, Salonika was seated opposite Master Skelton. The young mage was tugging nervously at her long black hair, which hung limp and lifeless in front of her shoulders. Her fingers caught in the knots.

Skelton was bent over his desk, examining a draft casting. His thin lips twitched once or twice as he scanned the pages before him, and he picked up a pen. The pen darted critically across the rows of carefully penned sentences, scratching out certain words in hurried exasperation and circling others with an exaggerated sweeping motion, as though he were binding a malevolent spirit. Each time his pen struck the paper, Salonika's heart tightened in her chest; every correction felt like the sharp slice of a knife. Death by a thousand cuts.

"No, no…not the correct usage… this part needs refining…" Skelton muttered, just loud enough for Salonika to hear. Salonika clenched her jaw as Skelton's pen swiped through several sentences in one horrible movement, erasing hours of anxious work in one lethal stroke. The room felt perversely hot – or was that her? It was furnace-like, although her hands were cold, so very cold.

"Salonika," Skelton addressed her, raising his eyes from the page. Was that smoke she could smell? The corner of her left eye started to cloud; it was on the brink of watering.

"What we do is so important," Skelton was saying, as though from far away. "Every word matters. It must be chosen with great care, for – as you know – it forms and binds the magic we use. If the words are not properly formulated, the consequences can be costly."

Salonika stared at the pages of the casting on Skelton's desk. So many lines and circles subjugating her painstakingly wrought words. So many new words wedged in between her neat lines; shouldering and shoving her old words out of the way.

"Salonika," Skelton was saying, "it troubles me how many avoidable errors this draft casting contains…"

Salonika's hands were in her lap now, twisting uncomfortably. Something was definitely burning. She could hear the voice in the back of her mind again, whimpering. It was back – had it ever left? Acrid woodsmoke hit the back of her throat, causing her to cough uncomfortably. She blinked a couple of times. The smoke was filling her eyes now; pain blurred her vision.

"I can't do this anymore…" she whispered.

Skelton was silent for the merest of moments, scrutinising her passively. "It has, I think, become clear…" he said, looking back down at the casting and making another few incisive swipes with his pen, "yes, very clear… that perhaps a bit of a rest is needed. Some time to refresh and get yourself back up to the standard we've come to expect of you. I suggest that you take a few days – even a week. Then perhaps you can look to work on some other matters for a time. I will look to onboard someone else in the meantime, to take some of the strain. I've already engaged Ivy to assist with the Woodbane matter, which, as you know, is the most pressing–"

Salonika stood up, interrupting the Master; another avoidable error. Sharp fire licked at the edge of her vision. The voice in the back of her mind screamed.

"No need," she heard herself say dangerously.

"Excuse me?" Skelton said, quietly but equally as dangerously.

"No need for a break," Salonika asserted.

She balled her fists, her fingernails digging into ice-cold palms. Fire enveloped them. She was made of fire now, but it was uneasy, not hers – it shouldn't be there, it wasn't right. But here it was, ancient and feverish. Her eyes burned and watered. Raw magic suddenly coursed around the room in ferocious sparks, tripping across Skelton's expertly cut jacket, lacing across the papers on his desk, flickering on the corrections and glowing white-hot. The words on the pages contorted and twisted as if in agony.

Books clattered from shelves, hitting the floor with a thump, pages flapping in a fluttering frenzy as the hot mage-fire whipped around the room. Skelton's pen lifted and bent, cracking over on itself like a snapped neck. It fell to the desk with a weak, broken clatter. Salonika clenched her fists and stared at it in desperation, blinking her eyes rapidly to clear the burning tears.

Skelton remained seated at his desk, unperturbed. He raised a dismissive hand to quell the mage-fire ripping around the room, but before he could master it, the flickering purple-red sparks coursed into the desk. He glanced down impassively and saw, charred into the surface of the desk, two perfectly formed words:

I resign.

Skelton stared at the words for a moment. He smoothed his jacket down casually. "I will say," Skelton observed briskly, still patting his jacket, "that's a great shame, Salonika, a great shame – but understandable, most understandable. I will inform human resources in the morning."

His hand made a swift movement, and his pen juddered and twitched, straightening itself like a reanimated corpse.

He picked it up and returned to examining the papers before him.

Salonika turned and left the room, without uttering another word. Several sparks of mage-fire continued to crackle at the corners of the draft casting. Skelton watched them without emotion for a few moments. Then his thin lips twitched once again, and he clicked the fingers of his free hand. The magic sputtered out. The pen sliced at the words once more.

4.

CULTIVATED ADVANCEMENT

Taryn Underfoot, senior mage in the Solutions Division at Jackdaw and Spittlelick, was also having a very difficult day.

She had arrived late at her cramped, internal chambers to find an apprentice perched awkwardly in the seat opposite her desk. She interrogated her memory, but it yielded nothing. "Can I help you?" she asked, giving up.

The apprentice shifted slightly, visibly perplexed. "I'm here for my performance review…?" he said.

Taryn had completely forgotten. This was going to throw her entire day out.

She sighed tetchily. "Right. Caspar, isn't it? You'll just have to bear with me while I locate your papers."

Bloody appraisals. Until relatively recently, the Tower had operated on the basis that junior mages needed little in the way of pastoral care or training, simply steering the more brainless specimens towards straightforward activities such as herb collection. However, the senior Masters had taken great delight in introducing the *thoroughly modern* concept of the 'Performance Review', with various nebulous criteria for judging mages at each stage of their 'career journey' (Masters excepted, of course, given that they were already happily ensconced at their destination, and had started ordering the wine).

Upon realising how much work would be involved in all this modern appraising business, the Masters had determined that perhaps the senior mages could handle all the actual appraising, and that this (here Taryn imagined the Masters felt distinctly pleased with themselves) could be an excellent demonstration of a senior mage's *own* personal and professional development.

And so Taryn, as a senior mage, had to undertake regular performance review meetings with the junior mages, designed to provide them with a clear plan for career progression and (much to her dismay) ensure their 'emotional well-being'.

Taryn would not have minded, were it not for the fact that most mages, not being naturally inclined towards linear or conventional thinking patterns, presented something of a challenge when participating in a session designed to ascertain whether they were functioning within normal psychological parameters.

The mage in front of her certainly met that description. Taryn skimmed the notes provided by Caspar's team members with ostensible interest.

"It says here," she said, "that there was an incident with a casting for the Dreamtime Corporation?"

"I really don't know what happened with that one," Caspar replied earnestly. "It was just meant to be a Restful Night charm for some of their customers. You know, to help them sleep better. I did everything I was meant to, included all the necessary limitations and provisions. Dante checked it. *Three times*," he added. "Something just happened when I tried to cast it. I'm not sure what."

"It says here you put the entire Administrative team for the Department of Inter-Species Relations to sleep for seventeen hours straight?"

"I know. I'm sorry. If it helps, they did say they felt extremely well-rested afterwards."

"I imagine so. Thankfully they were all at their desks at the time. Apart from–" here Taryn squinted at what she recognised as Dante's laconic scrawl "–one Mr Fallstrop, who was found in a rather compromising position."

Taryn frowned. It wasn't that Caspar was a poor apprentice, although there were plenty of those in the Tower – mages who struggled with binding spells, who muddled solutions ingredients, who couldn't make a prediction about an absolute certainty. No, according to several comments, it was more that the results of Caspar's basic castings had been inexplicably erratic. No matter how carefully he followed instructions, some sort of mild disaster had invariably ensued.

Taryn did her best to outline, as diplomatically as possible, some of Caspar's areas for development. At the end of the session Caspar dejectedly asked, "So what exactly am I good at then?"

Taryn searched for something constructive to say. "Morale?" It wasn't entirely untruthful, Taryn supposed. Most other mages would likely have looked at Caspar and felt infinitely less redundant as a result.

Caspar mulled this over. "Morale… I suppose that's something. I was worried you were going to say I was completely useless."

✦

Later that day, during a brief interlude between appraisals, Taryn looked at her notes. A couple of the junior mages in Castings left to speak to. Then she could finally progress the ever-increasing number of solutions she had been asked to prepare by Master Bladlow, including the new Woodbane solution.

Woodbane. This was what she had to focus on, not these junior mages. The Woodbane project was her ticket to advancement; it was innovative, ground-breaking, a way to replicate the potent natural magic found in blood, flesh and bone. She needed to speak to Skelton, make sure he was on track. To Bladlow too; he said he had sorted the procurement issue.

She slumped at her untidy desk, which was surrounded by shelves crammed with books, vials and various magical plants. Some of the plants had sprouted trailing leaves which were wrapping themselves indolently around the non-vegetative occupants of the small room, which gave Taryn's chambers the feel of a greenhouse laboratory competing for living space with a library, with neither element particularly willing to concede any ground to its neighbour. The plants seemed to be winning.

Taryn looked around at the various magically engineered blooms squashed into crevices. A small tendril of one of the plants was creeping its way towards the ceiling. It would find no escape there. She needed to remember to feed them before she left tonight; they were restless.

These plants were meant to be her route to promotion to Master. She had cultivated them carefully, intending to magically modify them for deployment as an aid to farming practices in the rural regions scarred by the wars, regions like home. She had researched and experimented (within

Regulator-approved limits) with methods of improving yields, strengthening crops, cross-pollinating magical and non-magical varieties, and using specially cultivated potions to stimulate rapid growth.

Over time, however, the project had been subtly cultivated by other fingers. The Market – and the Masters – were more interested in modifying plants for decorative use. Some of the Citadel elite had been quite taken with blooms that turned to follow them around the room. It had become clear that Taryn's original work was not a priority for the Division, with Master Bladlow in particular demonstrating indifference. With her solutions practice and supervisory responsibilities, Taryn herself had less and less energy to push for its progress.

Throughout this time, her two children, cultivated by other hands, had also continued their own march through youth.

Taryn turned in her chair and contemplated the view. The light straining through her grubby internal window was starting to fade, the last golden vines of sunlight creeping away. She could see the lower branches of the foyer's massive tree thrusting up past her large internal window. Its leaves were coated with a sickly golden sheen from the sunset that filtered sourly through the skylight above.

She brushed her fingers over her hair, which had been sleepily pulled back into an untidy bun this morning. The darker roots were growing out again; she needed to go to the Market and get some more colouring potion, but when would she have time to do that? She knew that she could probably brew some herself, and that whatever she brewed would undoubtedly last longer than the cheap stuff sold at the Market, but, again, when would she have the time? She sighed with exhaustion.

Instinctively, she reached towards the top drawer of her desk. She probably shouldn't, she told herself. But it wasn't like she would be heading home early today. Her children would be in their beds long before she made it back, as they so often were these days. Besides, she thought, pulling out a small glass bottle with a twisted neck, she deserved something after the day she'd had, just to see her through the remaining appraisals, and into the long evening of work stretching ahead of her. She poured a glass of greenish, brackish liquid. A small dram of Gorgon wouldn't do any harm. She took a large gulp, and felt the warmth of the spirits scorch her throat.

All those youthful faces, all still dreaming, her own dreams half-remembered, as though she was drifting in and out of that sluggish zone before awakening.

Ivy was dashing along the third floor's central corridor when she heard her name called from one of the internal chambers. She slid to a halt and saw Taryn Underfoot sitting behind a desk, looking out at her questioningly.

Aside from a few sporadically scheduled appraisals, Ivy had not interacted much with Taryn. This was, by all accounts, not a disagreeable state of affairs; the senior mage had a reputation for working her juniors hard and for working herself even harder. Whereas many of the senior mages in the Tower were inclined to leave their juniors to handle the dirty jobs, Taryn was the kind of mage you would find knee-deep in the manure, thrusting a shovel at you with a meaningful glare.

Taryn looked as though she would indeed be exceedingly adept with a shovel: heavily-set and broad shouldered, her faded blonde hair scraped into a hasty, no-nonsense bun, she reminded Ivy of one of the magnificent old war horses that tilled the fields outside the Citadel. She had the same weary look in her eyes as they did, too. All around Taryn, peculiar-looking plants, wedged tetchily between spell books, fought for her attention, thrusting out from the shelves impatiently. A wilting sunshrub skulked sullenly in a dark corner and, through the window directly behind Taryn, Ivy could see the colossal trunk of the tree, its bark glinting like gold in the last sunlight of the day.

"Right. Shut the door behind you and take a seat, would you?" Taryn said abruptly as Ivy entered. "I've got some reports from your team members and supervisors, and on the whole–"

"Are those magically engineered?" Ivy asked, motioning at the plants. As she did so, one of the more exotic blooms released a green-tinged cloud with a gentle puff.

Taryn seemed surprised at the interruption.

"It's just, I've never seen a dendrobium quite as…lively… as that," Ivy continued, not waiting for Taryn to answer, and nodding her head towards an orchid that had turned its petals to face her as she spoke. "It must have taken a lot of work, particularly at your level. Did the Regulator approve the research? I thought magical cultivation of living things was forbidden. You know, to make sure we don't end up in a world filled with inadvertent Bobs, or whatever it is that the Regulator's always so afraid of…"

"The work is all approved," Taryn said evenly, rankling at the phrase 'your level'.

"I haven't seen specimens as interesting as this outside of books," Ivy continued. "That one over there looks a bit angry." She nodded towards a trailing plant that was wrapping itself surreptitiously around the base of a cactus a couple of shelves below. "And that one seems to be drinking something it shouldn't…" Ivy pointed at another plant that had crept a tendril across Taryn's desk and was helping itself to the contents of an ink cartridge.

"For Gods' sake," Taryn exclaimed, "I wish it wouldn't keep doing that – it's bloody obsessed!" She wrestled the empty cartridge from the offending shrub. Its foliage flushed an inky black for a moment, as it expelled a quiet hiccough. Taryn shook her head at it. "It's going through ink like nobody's business. I could really do without the constant trips to the Unstationery Cupboard – bloody thing is never where it bloody well should be."

Ivy felt some sympathy for Taryn here. The Unstationery Cupboard existed somewhere on every floor of the Tower, and sometimes nowhere at all. It tended to delight in vanishing just when one's need for supplies was at its greatest. Invariably, if one did manage to stumble across it, one would usually open it to find only a few half-chewed pencils and a selection of yellowed notepaper in every conceivable size except the one you needed, often emblazoned with the letterhead of a long-dead Master.

"Look, never mind all that," said Taryn irritably. "Let's concentrate on your appraisal, shall we? I see you've been working with Master Skelton. He's rated you as 'adequate', which is high praise coming from him… What have you been assisting him on?"

"I've been preparing some new castings for Dragonsteel Industries," Ivy replied, the bubble of anxiety catching in her throat at the mention of Skelton. "He's also just put me on something for Woodbane Cosmetics–"

"So you're the replacement for Salonika?" Taryn interjected.

"Am I? I don't know about that. But Skelton asked me to attend a meeting with Woodbane this morning. Are you working on it too?"

"Yes. I'm part of the Solutions team on the project, along with Master Bladlow. We developed the original Woodbane solution. We'll also be developing and brewing the premium product, once Master Skelton has procured the necessary ingredients. Do you know much about the brewing processes involved?"

Ivy shook her head. She assumed the principle was the same as with all potions: brew a large vat of liquid filled with ingredients, and magically bind it all together. Ivy had always disliked the work done by the Solutions Division. All that measuring, reducing, adding, percolating, stirring, not stirring, stirring anti-clockwise… the processes were fastidious and dull, with none of the raw thrill of spellcasting.

"Perhaps we should set a time to talk about the Woodbane project separately?" Taryn continued. "If you're helping, you should understand what we're doing down here on third. It's a fascinating process. Really ground-breaking stuff. You should be very excited to be a part of something like this – it's beyond anything currently in development in the Citadel."

Ivy nodded, rather unenthusiastically. A thought then occurred. "I don't suppose you or Master Bladlow happen to have any copies of the latest Woodbane casting…? For making the new ingredients?" she asked. "I'm supposed to read it and… well… the copy Master Skelton gave to me is down in the Copy Room at the moment." She reflected momentarily that this last statement was *technically* correct.

"No, we don't have a copy, I'm afraid. We only have the formula for the brew."

Ivy felt her heart sink and the bubble of anxiety rise. "Not to worry, I just thought I'd ask."

"I'm sure Cleft will have it back to you sooner than you think. He usually does, despite his pretences to the contrary."

Taryn cantered swiftly through the rest of the review and then took some time to enlighten Ivy on the formulae for the two Woodbane Solutions. However, Ivy's thoughts were very much elsewhere, as her mind worked away trying to find an entirely different sort of solution.

✦

As darkness slumped moodily across the Citadel sky, two floors up from where Taryn was finally putting pen to paper on her overdue solutions, Ivy Armstride found herself sitting on the floor of her chambers, resting her back against the internal window and contemplating her next steps while Bob sat nearby, attempting to clean himself.

Her earlier conversation with Taryn had decided it. There was no hope of reproducing the Woodbane casting. She was going to have to come clean and hope that Skelton would not be minded to drop her 'adequate' progress rating to 'questionable' or even – Ivy shuddered at the thought – the dreaded 'needs development'. She couldn't allow herself to end up in that position, not with him. Her status at the Tower depended on retaining his approval; if her position here was jeopardised and she was asked to leave, she had nowhere else to go.

She almost certainly couldn't go back home. There wasn't anything left for her in the small market town where she had spent her childhood. She thought of New Charnford, the sparse settlement clustering around what had once been a great, sprawling Citadel. Charnford had been the hardest hit of all Kirin's Citadels, brutally razed to its foundations during the mage wars. Its citizens had suffered the violent lash of dragon fire and sorcery and Ivy's family had been no exception, as her parents always reminded her. She remembered the remains of the Citadel slumped ominously near her small family home, the raw magic still crawling over its corpse, the dark creatures lurking in its festering undercarriage. She had never quite understood why her parents had stayed; perhaps they felt they had nowhere else to go. Perhaps they did not want to let go of the pain caused by the mages, nursing deep anger and suspicion in their embittered breasts.

Ivy had not asked for any magical ability, she had not hoped and wished and prayed for it like Hop Pockett. When it had manifested, it had been something to be repressed rather than nurtured, and Ivy's parents had done all they could to asphyxiate her growing powers. She wished it had been different, wished she could have explained things better to them rather than just leaving for the Citadel, knowing as she did so that she would never be forgiven. She couldn't go back; there was now only forward, upward.

But where could she go if she couldn't go home? The Tower had accepted her and Skelton in particular had, in his own careful way, cultivated her, forever pushing her to undertake more challenging and complicated magic while strictly guiding her in how to channel and control that magic. Ivy admired him; his unspoken encouragement nourished her, but she craved his outright praise like a small plant craning its stalk towards the sun. She needed to stay at the Tower, because – above all else – she needed him.

Yet now, as a result of the most trivial of errors, she faced the possibility of invoking that most painful of prospects: his disappointment.

Bob padded over and nuzzled her softly. With effort, she raised herself from the cold floor, and walked over to the door. As she exited her chambers she almost collided with Salonika, who was carrying a large crate filled with odd boxes and papers. Ivy muttered a quick apology, but Salonika appeared not to notice; she had halted, standing strangely still, eyes gazing dully ahead. She looked as though she had been crying.

Before Ivy could say anything else, Salonika said, in a flat, lifeless tone, "You're next."

Not looking at Ivy, Salonika continued on her miserable way, long black hair hanging lifelessly down her back.

You're next? What was that supposed to mean? Ivy was utterly confused. Did Skelton already know about the Umping incident? Did everyone know? A bubble of anxiety started to creep up her chest.

She crossed the corridor and approached Master Skelton's door like a person condemned. As she approached the open doorway, she saw Skelton reach across and tap his crystal display before registering her presence. His desk was littered with books and papers, covering the surface. An odd odour hung in the air, like burnt wood.

"Ah Ivy, excellent," Skelton said briskly, "I was just about to give you a call. We need to undertake the Woodbane casting first thing tomorrow. How's the copying going?"

"About that…" Ivy began, steeling herself as the walls closed in.

✦

It was night now. Not true night, though. This was tame night, night that let the dim glow of humanity and its cousins engulf it and smother it. The tree missed the feel of true night, starlight and moonlight bathing its limbs.

It felt hot, feverish. Had it ever felt feverish before? Had it ever felt before? Something had been fed to it earlier. Something noxious and vile, yet filled with raging vitality. Its roots had no choice but to soak up the poison; attempting to coil and curl away had been fruitless. As the power seeped into it, the tree wanted to writhe, to flail, to burn.

It longed for the coolness of the stars.

5.

THE GOSSIP

Ivy's admission to Master Skelton last night of the unfortunate Umping mix-up had gone better than expected. There had been no shouting, no recriminations, just a shocked pause. Ivy had never seen the man truly still before – it was like watching a machine shut down. The pause was eventually followed by a quiet "Right, right, right…"

Ivy had allowed him to continue like this for an awkward minute or so before asking if there was anything she could do to rectify the situation.

It transpired there was not. After muttering something about "dealing with additional complications", Skelton had determined that he would simply have to redraft the Woodbane casting. He had presented Ivy with a raft of other papers from his shelves and told her to deal with them while he attended to the redrafting. This, apparently, was her penance.

Having resolved to look at them in the morning, she had crept towards the stairwell, hoping that Skelton would not register her absence from her desk.

Looking this morning at the work she had been given, she immediately regretted leaving the Tower last night. She had been summarily plucked from a hot pan and thrown into the crackling fire. She needed to construct a fortune casting. The drafting work was far beyond anything she had attempted previously. And she still hadn't started the Dragonsteel casting. Why was being a mage so ridiculously complicated? All she wanted to do was some actual bloody magic. Her fingers twitched and a thin spark crackled along them; she buried them in her hair as she rested her head in her hands.

"Here's a bit of gossip for you."

Ivy looked up as Lilirey, one of the Tower's non-human assistant mages, waltzed into her chambers, eyes twinkling and dragonfly-wings bobbing conspiratorially. The faerie plonked herself down in the chair opposite Ivy, nevertheless managing to appear effortlessly elegant as she tucked her long bare legs under the chair.

Lil was actually rather old for a faerie, who did not tend to live much past their sixth decade. She was now well beyond the halfway point, the finishing line having worryingly appeared on the horizon. Lil still had the perfect, iridescent skin that was characteristic of all faeries in Kirin, although over the years – much to Lil's dismay – this natural beauty had increasingly needed to be supplemented with ever-stronger illusory charms.

Happily for Lil, this morning she was radiating youthful energy, most probably due to having digested an excellent nugget of gossip, and had accordingly fixed her face to perfection.

Usually, Ivy would have been curious about the information Lil was clearly eager to impart, but today was not that day. However, aware that Lil was unlikely to move until she had indulged her, Ivy sighed and said, "Go on then…"

Lil savoured the dramatic reveal, leaning conspiratorially forward, her dragonfly-like wings unfolding behind her excitedly. "Salonika has resigned. Left under a bit of a cloud, I hear…"

"Not a literal one I presume?" Ivy queried sarcastically. It was not a large stretch of the imagination.

"No, nothing like that," Lil said. "Apparently, she had a complete breakdown during a meeting with Skelton last night. All very dramatic.

"Anyway, Elspeth said she came in to find Salonika's resignation note on Skelton's desk… and when I say *on* his desk, I mean burned right into the woodwork…"

That at least explained the burning smell in Skelton's chambers last night, Ivy thought. But she did not have the mental energy at that moment to consider *why* Salonika had resigned so theatrically. She was preoccupied with her own problems, and as far as she was concerned, it was to be expected. Salonika had been struggling and this had obviously resulted in a poor appraisal yesterday. Her work had become sloppy, and the Tower had little tolerance for mistakes.

Had Salonika not resigned, Ivy expected she would have been pushed out sooner or later anyway. There had always been a high rate of attrition amongst the Tower's junior mages, and despite some suggestion that a more nurturing environment should be adopted, nothing was likely to change on that front anytime in the next century. Masters felt competition in the lower ranks was important. Plus they were keen to limit the amount of competition in the loftier ranks.

Clearly not satisfied with Ivy's apparent disinterest, Lil pressed on, wings elegantly beating up and down and eyes wide. "There was something a bit…well, *odd* about it all, though," Lil said. "There was more to it than the usual overwork or stress. Something funny was going on with her before she left."

"Funny how?"

"I'm not sure. Dante said she was behaving weirdly."

"Dante thinks everyone is weird. I doubt it's anything more than the fact that she just wasn't very good and she finally realised she wasn't going to get anywhere."

"If you say so. I thought you'd be interested, given that she was at your level…"

Ivy considered this briefly and shrugged once again. Salonika had trained as an apprentice alongside Ivy and had, until recently, looked like a decent contender in the field for elevation.

"Anyway, how are you getting on? Busy?" Lil asked, changing tack. She clearly wasn't leaving any time soon. Ivy despaired.

"Unfortunately, yes. Although… there is this tricky casting I need to prepare. I could do with your help."

"Not sure I'm the right person for it, if it's a tricky one," Lil said automatically.

Ivy frowned.

Having no magical knack for anything other than trifling illusions, Lil always fiercely maintained that she couldn't do 'proper mage work'. There were plenty of such individuals engaged by the Tower these days, the Masters having realised that certain tasks could actually be performed by someone with *no magical aptitude whatsoever* (although they were careful not to advertise this fact to clients). Naturally, there were a handful of Masters who muttered about devaluing an arcane and venerable institution, but given that these Masters were fast approaching arcane and venerable status themselves, no one paid them very much attention.

While, for the most part, such 'assistant mages' were indeed simply a valuable resource from a time and cost perspective, provided they weren't given anything too complicated to do, Lil was, to Ivy's mind, far more useful than she gave herself credit for.

Lil had worked in every department in every Division within the Tower and there wasn't a single person she didn't know by name or reputation. Not only that, but she also knew every skeleton in every closet (usually on first-name terms). If you came into possession of a bit of gossip (and mages did enjoy a gossip), then you might call on Lil to ever-so-discreetly inform her, usually to find that not only did Lil already know about the scandal, but she also knew a series of accompanying pieces of information that no one, absolutely no one, could have divulged to her at that point. While her knowledge of Castings, Solutions and Futures work might be rudimentary, she knew all the levers to pull to Get Things Done – and this was exactly what Ivy needed right now.

"Please, Lil, I'd appreciate it if you could give me a hand," Ivy pleaded. "I need to pull together a casting for this client of Master Skelton's. He wants a fortune casting, apparently."

"Ah," said Lil, knowingly, "is this the old Abe Carterton matter again? I might be able to help after all if it is."

"That's the one," said Ivy. Things were already starting to improve. "Have you come across him before?"

"Abe's been a client of the Tower for a while now," explained Lil. "The story goes that he came into a bit of money a while back from a family venture involving some sort of dragonsteel refinery, I don't know the ins-and-outs–" (Ivy suspected this was untrue)

"–but basically there was some bad business and Abe wanted to make sure the money was invested safely, so he purchased a future, to make sure everything would turn out on track.

"Apparently, the future said he was going to be forever unlucky financially, which was a bit of a blow, I'm sure. Turned out it was untradeable on the Futures Exchange too – which was a complete surprise as there's usually someone desperate or daft enough to make a trade.

"So anyway, he then set out about trying to procure a casting or solution from us to alter his fortune and cancel out the future."

Ivy was perplexed. "But those castings are notoriously unreliable, and the solutions aren't any better, given that the most effective ingredients are Restricted Substances," she said. "It's not something we can really offer, at least not without strict caveats."

"Yes, well," carried on Lil, "that didn't stop him from engaging us. The Carterton family are long-standing clients, so some of the Masters thought it was worth a go."

"But surely someone informed the client of the risks?"

"They did, but Abe was adamant that this was the way to go. He's tried a few solutions and castings, but nothing's really stuck so far. One casting worked for three weeks straight; Abe sent us a letter saying he was on the coast, having the time of his life. He was financially afloat for the first time in years and had just bought a very pricey boat."

"What happened?" Ivy asked.

"It sank."

"Ah. So he came back, even after that?"

"He's been back a few times since, he's relatively upbeat about the whole thing."

"That's madness," Ivy said, shaking her head.

"I know, but that's Abe. Anyway, I can try to dig up some of the old casting notes if I can find them, although I expect they'll have been Umped by now. I'll ask around."

"That would be great, thanks, Lil. I feel bad that he's not seen any results so far."

"I wouldn't worry about it. The Masters don't mind. He's spent an absolute fortune with us over the last few years…"

◆

After Lil's departure, Ivy gazed round her chambers idly, avoiding the paperwork in front of her.

She saw a figure strolling past in the corridor outside. It was the auditor, Hop Pockett. He paused for a moment, peering at Skelton's door, which Ivy noticed was (quite unusually) firmly shut. She spied Elspeth rising slightly from her desk (and it was ever so slightly given how diminutive the goblin was) and Hop hurrying on. Curious.

A stray spark of raw magic flickered across her right hand, interrupting her thoughts.

What was going on? This hadn't happened since her magics had first appeared during her adolescence, before they had settled. Even more peculiarly, despite these random discharges, she had nevertheless been struggling lately with performing even the most inconsequential incidental spells.

She peered outside her chambers. Nobody seemed to be about.

Now for something to try. She determined to start small, going back to first principles. She let her mind rest, felt for the edge of unreality, curled her fingers around it.

Her mug of tea was nearby. It had gone cold as usual, half-drunk. She focused on warming it back up, gradually exciting the molecules. Not too much, not too little, not for too long. She tried to remember how to do this without the words of a casting guiding her, without the protective net of limitations supporting her. Panic crept in. She pushed the thoughts away as the liquid began to simmer and then boil. Too much. She could feel herself losing her grip as the edge of the mug assumed a blue-green tinge. She held on to the power, let the liquid cool gently. Then she relaxed, work completed.

She picked up the mug. It felt warm as she clasped it. She slurped the tea gingerly and promptly spat some of it back out. Perfect temperature, but it now tasted of orange.

Frustrated, she clasped the mug again and then gasped as it bubbled fiercely and completely evaporated. There was a moment of stillness before a brief shower of tea droplets erupted directly over her desk.

She hastily tried to magic away the tea stains now spattered across her draft Dragonsteel casting and succeeded in removing the vast majority of the stains. Unfortunately she also removed all of the vowels.

Another setback, she thought. She wasn't getting anywhere…

"Wotcher," Dante proclaimed, strolling in and flinging himself down on the empty chair. Now she *really* wasn't going to get anything done.

"Lil said you got the Carterton gig. Bad luck," said Dante. "Anyway, if you want me to take a look when you've made some headway with the casting, I can. I drafted one for him a few years back and I was never particularly happy with it. I was so close. If it hadn't been for that damn boat…"

Ivy felt a rush of gratitude wash over her; Lil had delivered on her promise quickly, as usual. "Thanks, Dante, that would be amazing."

"No problem. Not to spook you, but Skelton's got a bee in his bonnet. Can't imagine Salonika's resignation has gone down well and, to top it all off, apparently some complete idiot Umped a complicated draft casting for Woodbane Cosmetics before it had been copied."

Ivy's stomach curled into a tight knot. At least no one had worked out it was her yet; Skelton had apparently kept that to himself. Although judging by the speed at which gossip was seemingly rippling around the fifth floor this morning, it might not stay that way for long…

"So while he tries to re-draft it, he's handing out jobs like there's no tomorrow, which there might not be given all the messing about with reality that goes on here. Expect that's why you've landed Carterton, lucky you."

Ivy glimpsed Hop strolling past in the corridor outside once again. Very curious.

"Do you know anything about this auditor?" she asked, tilting her head towards the door.

Dante craned round to look.

"That pompous yet slightly drippy chap who's been strutting about like a llamacorn that's just won Best in Show?"

"That's the one."

"I've no idea what he's doing here, no. I thought we were done with audits for a while. Passed the last one, surprisingly. All very weird."

"I ran into him in the Copy Room. He said he was undertaking a special audit. Was very interested in Woo–" Ivy realised she was about to mention Woodbane and stopped herself abruptly. Dante was smart; it wouldn't take him long to work out she was responsible for the Umping incident. "–the Copy Room procedures…" she amended lamely.

Dante raised an eyebrow. "I'll see what I can find out," he said. "It would give me something to do while I wander the halls of this place, waiting for death to take me into his sweet embrace."

"Dramatic as always. Can't be that bad."

"I suppose. At least I haven't Umped anything I shouldn't recently. Poor soul. They're in for some fun over the next few weeks…" Dante smirked knowingly at her.

Damn. Looked like that particular rabbit was out of the hat. "Mm," said Ivy, feigning disinterest.

"Well, I suppose I had better go and manacle myself to my desk for a bit." At that, Dante got up and sauntered out, saluting solemnly at Ivy as he left.

No sooner had he left than Bob padded in. He looked around the small chamber dolefully.

"You too?" Ivy sighed.

She looked back down at her drafts and picked up her pen. There was a thump behind her and a creaking sound, followed by a strangled attempt at a purr. When she next looked round, Bob was precariously draped across the top of a bookshelf, giant limbs dangling down, golden eyes shut contentedly.

◆

Hop Pockett was thoroughly enjoying himself. He strolled along the fifth floor corridor of Jackdaw and Spittlelick, pausing every now and then to pick up some of the paperwork strewn across the various desks and trays in the corridor, glancing at each item with barely contained excitement.

In reality, Hop was gleaning very little information about the inner workings of a Tower of Lore and Sorcery from these snippets, other than the fact that the place generated paperwork on an industrial scale. Indeed, some of the paperwork was about the sheer amount of paperwork; Hop had spotted copious duplicates of a three-page memorandum promoting a reduction of paper waste in several of the Tower's internal Umping baskets.

Hop came to a halt just outside Master Skelton's chambers. The door was still very much shut. He had tried to speak to Skelton a few times, but the man was always busy.

Hop was beginning to think Skelton was avoiding him. This was nothing outside the norm for Hop, but on this occasion, he was convinced there was more to it. He would not have been assigned this *very specific* and *highly important* investigation if there wasn't.

A large desk sat outside Skelton's chambers, at which there usually sat a goblin. Hop couldn't believe his luck. The goblin was nowhere to be seen.

Hop had been making circuits of the fifth floor for most of the morning, attempting to look purposeful, hoping to 'investigate' some of the papers stacked neatly on the goblin's desk, just in case Skelton had left any material relating to the Woodbane project with the female goblin. Each expedition had resulted in Hop meeting with the hard stare of the goblin, who was remarkably disinclined to let him near any of the papers, no matter how authoritative he tried to sound.

Here, though, was the perfect opportunity to investigate! He quickly scoured the paperwork scattered across the desk, and noted one had been marked 'confidential'. He picked it up and looked around nervously. Comfortable no one

was observing, he scrutinised the paper in front of him, which read:
- *Private and highly confidential*
- *Pick up outercloak from cleaners*
- *Drinks with D Ind.*
- *Meeting with Solutions re W Solution*

So, not a casting. Nor did it reveal anything about the new synthetisation process Skelton had developed. That was likely too much to hope for.

There was one nugget of interest buried in the detritus, though. The meeting with Solutions. W Solution. Might that be the Woodbane Solution? Highly possible. It was worth finding out. Maybe he should poke his head into Skelton's chambers quickly? Just to see if he was in; perhaps ask him about this meeting…

"And just what, pray, do you think you are doing?" rasped a voice from somewhere around Hop's waist, in a dangerous whisper.

Hop started guiltily. He looked down to see the goblin who was proving such a formidable adversary. She stared up at him with yellow eyes above the spindly drop of her nose. Her face bristles looked particularly impressive today.

"Just checking something," he said, aiming for a blend of confident and innocent but instead hitting flustered bang on the target.

"May I have that back?" the goblin said, motioning at the paper in his hand.

"Of course, absolutely fine," Hop said, handing back the paper as inoffensively as he could manage, which, what with Hop being Hop, was not a resounding success.

"Will that be all?" she enquired, the intonation suggesting that it should absolutely be all, and that further questions would be met with the rejection they undoubtedly merited.

"Yes," said Hop, before a thought occurred to him. "Although I was hoping to confirm the time of this meeting with Solutions. I'm expected to attend."

"11.30 tomorrow morning."

"Yes. That's what I thought. Has the room changed? Is it still…?" Hop fervently hoped the wind was in his favour here.

"7B. Yes." The goblin finished his sentence without hesitation. She sat down at her desk, turning her back to him.

"Excellent. If you could let them know I'll be there. As discussed." Hop congratulated himself. He was good at this investigative business. Now he could finally start working out what was really going on with this most peculiar Woodbane matter.

6.

THE CRYPT
═══ ◆ ═══

At this point, one might begin to wonder whether magic in Kirin consisted mostly of paperwork. It did.

But the copious paperwork churned out on a daily basis by the Citadel's five Towers and the small chambers scattered across Kirin was not a prerequisite of making magic. Formulae for solutions, words for castings, questions for determination… these were all simply designed to give structure to the magical intention, to define, limit and control it.

The People In Charge of the Citadel liked it that way, and the mages themselves had not only taken on board the limitations required of them, they had also developed new and more complicated restrictions of their own, helpfully citing such complexities as justification for the rather expensive fees that they charged for their magical services. This reliance on form and strictures for all but the most incidental of magics meant that the practice of 'instinctive' magic was gradually dying out in Kirin.

Ivy certainly felt this way. Her instinctive magic use had not always been so unpredictable in its results. Prior to working at Jackdaw and Spittlelick she had felt confident in her nascent powers, knowing how to feel her way to what she wanted, what was needed, what was not. Admittedly, she had been implored to suppress such wants and needs by her family, but she at least felt as though she knew what she was capable of achieving with her magic.

Now, following years of rules and regulations coiling and tightening around her like a python, her magic came less easily without the comforting words of a casting to direct her.

Tonight, she was in her chambers, awaiting a call from Skelton.

Skelton had locked himself away, painstakingly reconstituting the Umped Woodbane casting. He had not spoken to Ivy at any point during the day, but she had been haughtily commanded by Elspeth to remain at her desk until summoned by the Master. The Woodbane casting ceremony would be undertaken tonight. There was no option to delay, and Ivy's presence was mandated.

Ivy was still none the wiser about what this casting ceremony would actually involve. They all seemed much the same to her these days; focus her magic on the words – and only the words – before her, structuring and limiting her intention in accordance with what had been written. There was absolutely no room for creativity; she had been taught that the power required for more complex spells was too unstable to be allowed any scope for interpretation as it flowed through her – there was too much that could go wrong.

As she waited patiently, absently munching her way through some food of questionable provenance and dubious nutritional value, Ivy again became aware of a scuttling, scratching sound. She looked up and around. Nothing.

"Bob?" she asked tentatively, knowing that it was unlikely to be the vast tiger, who was nowhere to be seen.

A chirruping sound erupted in response.

"Hello…?" Ivy ventured.

More chirruping. Further scratching. Ivy tensed. She could perhaps use some sort of revealing spell? As the thought flashed into her mind, it was immediately quashed by the weight of her training. She didn't have any drafts prepared for something like that.

She resorted to assuming an imperious tone, proclaiming loudly, "Whatever you are, I'd advise you to show yourself."

Silence.

Ivy wondered if stress had finally broken her. Was this what going mad felt like?

Without warning, something small suddenly jumped out from the bookcase behind her, tumbling with a soft clatter onto her desk.

"What the…?" Startled, Ivy jerked backwards in her chair, staring at the thing in front of her.

It stared back.

The creature was tiny, with a rounded belly protruding from its brownish grainy body. Spindly, twig-like limbs covered in miniature leaves sprouted from it, and its head was over-sized, like a bulbous bud atop a plant stem. Big, woody eyes peered up at Ivy as the creature started to trill excitedly.

Ivy had never seen or heard of anything like it before.

"What *are* you?" she asked incredulously, leaning in.

It tilted its large head, placed its front twigs on the desk, then scampered up Ivy's arm. The sensation was like sticking one's hand in a bush.

The creature perched on her shoulder and made its peculiar little chirp into her ear. Ivy frowned at it. It continued chirruping and poked at her cheek curiously with its twiggy digits. She pulled her head away. "Not that shy after all, are we?"

It clambered up the side of her head, prompting a shudder. She reached up, wrapping her fingers cautiously around its fragile form and attempting to disentangle it from her hair. Having gently extracted it, she held it in her hand and examined it critically.

It didn't seem malevolent, although Ivy knew enough about existing in a universe where magic seeped in at the seams not to judge anything based solely on appearances. Many a human had lost a limb to an innocuous-looking dandelion in some of the wilder regions of the continent. She had also grown up in the shadow of a ruined Citadel it was inadvisable to enter even on the brightest and most joyful of summer days.

Still, this thing didn't seem dangerous. It rustled its foliage benignly. "Hmm. Hope you don't have spiders," she said drily. "I don't do spiders."

Without warning, her crystal display started to flash and emit a jaunty yet highly irritating tone. The creature leapt from her hand in alarm and skittered away into the recesses of the books.

Ivy looked at the display, disconcerted. Skelton. The casting ceremony. She pressed her palm to the crystal and, sure enough, Skelton appeared.

"Ivy, excellent," he said. "Ready to head down to the Crypt?"

"Just coming," she replied. Skelton had already ended the call. Addressing her chambers at large, she then proclaimed, "Whatever you are, you're just going to have to wait. I'll be back up shortly. I'd stay in here if I were you – Bob will be on the prowl at this time of night."

She thought she caught a glimpse of those large, pool-like eyes from deep within the shelves. She left the room and carefully closed the door behind her, thoroughly distracted.

Skelton, Ivy and Caspar were in one of the large basement vaults of the Tower that sprawled beneath the ground floor.

The original architectural plans for the Tower had been for the Crypt (as the basement was cheerily known) to cover the entire floor span of the Tower, with appropriate load-bearing walls and a stunning auditorium located at the centre of the circle directly beneath the foyer. Unfortunately, 'certain unforeseen levelling issues in the construction process' had resulted in the area earmarked for the auditorium remaining compacted with soil and rubble. Apparently, the auditorium had in fact been built and could be located several hundred feet further down, although nobody had been able to prove this.

Instead, the Crypt consisted of a number of large rooms peeling off from its warren-like internal corridor. Dark and windowless, these underground rooms were heavily insulated, but not in any normal sense. The thick stones that formed the walls of the vaults had been injected with ground grimling carapaces; as a result, they absorbed any loose magical energy which might leak out from the magical activities undertaken in the Crypt.

Tonight, Skelton, Ivy and the junior apprentice, Caspar, were standing in one of the cavernous stone vaults of the Crypt, preparing to undertake the Woodbane casting.

"Right, right," said Skelton with his usual breathless urgency, "everyone ready?"

Ivy took a deep breath and confirmed, "Ready." Although admittedly she had no idea what for.

Caspar nodded and clutched nervously at some papers. He was joining for training purposes only and that was only on sufferance.

Caspar was the son of one of the Tower's former Most Senior Masters, a formidable woman who now sat on the Council of Mages that protected the rights and interests of mages in the Citadel. The Masters knew it was in their best interests to keep Caspar gainfully employed at the Tower, despite the apprentice's unambiguous shortcomings.

Nevertheless, Skelton had made it patently clear Caspar was not to approach the casting circle, not to speak, not to move and not to breathe too heavily.

At the centre of the vault, within an exquisitely rendered casting circle, stood an altar of utilitarian dragonsteel design, a few unintelligible runes etched onto its sides. The vault was otherwise empty, save for some large, gnarled roots which had begun to muscle through the walls, clinging indignantly to the grimling stone. Ivy realised they must belong to the tree above. She hoped the foundations of the Tower were secure.

Ivy shivered against the tug she felt coming from the stones as they attempted to leach her power. She hated casting down here.

"Right, right," repeated Skelton, murmuring softly to himself. "The new draft should have sorted out some of the leakage issues we had previously..."

Ivy was beginning to feel slightly concerned. If Skelton's last Woodbane castings had problems with leakage – being the general term for the seepage of raw and potentially dangerous magic from a spell – they could be getting themselves into a world of uncertainty. The grimling stone surrounding them could only assist so much.

"Here we go then," Skelton murmured, as though checking off a mental list. "Source, catalyst, conduit, base material… fine, fine… yes."

He turned to Ivy. "Stand directly at the altar, would you, please, Ivy?"

Ivy approached the altar. On it, she saw three large plates, decidedly mundane in appearance.

The first plate contained a pile of soft dust, which looked to be of the ordinary household variety. Upon the second plate rested a small heap of what looked disturbingly like teeth from a human child; Ivy hoped they had fallen out by natural means. The final bowl contained an overripe pumpkin, which was starting to reek.

"Pumpkin?" she asked quizzically, unable to restrain her curiosity.

"Excellent for transformative magic," Skelton affirmed. "A very versatile fruit, the humble pumpkin. Now, place your hands on the altar."

Ivy did so.

"Great, great. Given there is only a single copy of the casting–" Ivy winced a little at this "–for this particular ceremony, you, Ivy, will act as the conduit… yes, while I cast, directing the magic through you to the items on the altar."

"Master," Ivy asked cautiously (she still wasn't convinced she had been returned to Skelton's favour), "what will happen to the items?"

"All being well, they will be transformed from mere base matter into items with rare magical properties.

"For the previous Woodbane solution, the creation of only one… ah… artificial replica of a Restricted Substance… was required, being faerie dust. The base element used for this was simply household dust. However, the premium solution requires the synthetisation of faerie dust and two additional substances, hence the three items before us tonight. This has not been attempted before, but the magic should prove stable if my assumptions are correct."

Ivy felt apprehensive at hearing this last piece of information. Many a mage had been undone by a mistaken assumption.

Skelton seemed to anticipate Ivy's unease. "However, you do not need to concern yourself with this. All you need to do is focus your mind on the items as I recite the casting."

"Should I do anything else, Master? Are you sure I don't need to assist with reciting the casting? I would have thought–"

"No, no, I will recite the casting. Please just keep your hands on the altar and focus on directing the magic into the items. Understood?"

Ivy nodded. Not really; Skelton's explanation still didn't explain the magic behind the transformation and how she was supposed to direct it, but she supposed she would just have to pick it up as she went along. As usual, it seemed questions were a luxury she was not to be afforded.

"Is there anything *I* can do, Master?" Caspar volunteered optimistically, having already forgotten Skelton's injunction to remain silent.

Skelton shot him an impatient glance. "Nothing, Caspar, thank you. Nothing will be quite adequate."

Puzzled by the lack of active participation required of her, Ivy placed her hands on the cold metal of the altar, staring intently at the objects. Exactly what about them was she supposed to focus on? The dust and pebbles appeared unremarkable, and she was struggling to find anything about the pumpkin to commend it to her attention. Besides, how was she supposed to channel magic without the reassuring words of a casting in front of her?

As Ivy pondered, Skelton began to recite the casting, speaking barely above a low murmur. Ivy strained her ears to listen.

Just as she felt she could make out some of the arcane words, a rush of power coursed through her body, blocking out all other sound.

The sensation was violent. Her head snapped back; her hands became bonded to the altar with a white-hot heat. The magical energy storming through her was a torrent of pure unreality. Instinctively, she sought to guide it, to shape it; it was like trying to sculpt a waterfall. Around the edges of her mind she felt the shadow of a familiar shape. It looked like something she'd seen recently, but at the same time never before, proud and ancient and filled with incandescent rage. It screamed her name, she whispered back. She reached for it, clasping–

"Ivy, leave it!" she heard Skelton shout to her, his voice distorted and muffled, as though from deep underwater.

She let go, and she could almost feel Skelton pull and wrench the magic into shape with a renewed vigour as it cascaded through her veins, setting her fingertips on icy fire. She tried to focus on the altar as it swam in and out of her vision, on the roundness of the pebbles, on the slight sheen of vegetable sweat on the pumpkin, on the weightless dust… reality jarred and blots of dark light flashed across the backs of her eyes as the shapes before her distorted and shimmered and sparkled and pumped. How was she supposed to control this? She flailed desperately and gasped for breath. She heard Skelton's voice, but not his words; powerful and commanding as he wound and unwound the net of reality. Exhilaration beat through her as she allowed Skelton to use her magic to bend actuality into shape. She gave it to him willingly and as she did so a new clarity of form and meaning washed over and through her into the items of the altar with an intensity of intention she had never felt before. She let it swell and on Skelton's wordless command, somehow, she *directed* it at the objects without hesitation. She implored them to change, commanded them to take the form they would now and forever always have had…

Then, unexpectedly, with a cold and empty certainty, she knew it was done.

Ivy peeled her hands from the altar, and collapsed to her knees before it, trembling with shock. She wrapped her arms around herself. No other casting had felt like this. Not even the ferocious thrill of dragon binding approached this violent authority. Whatever she had just drawn on, it was ancient and mighty. She felt cold, so cold… and yet, burning. The burning sensation was not right; it shouldn't have been there.

"Well done, Ivy…" said Skelton, breathlessly.

Skelton moved towards her, and motioned for Caspar to follow. "Help her up, would you, Caspar? There's a good fellow."

Caspar helped Ivy lurch to her feet.

The three of them looked down at the altar.

There before them, the three plates sat, their contents transformed. The dust now shimmered, the white teeth had coalesced into a sinister horn of polished bone, and the pumpkin... the pumpkin had become a purplish-red organ which globbered and glimmered grotesquely.

"Marvellous, simply marvellous," Skelton whispered reverently.

Ivy felt cold beads of sweat trickle down her forehead.

"I think that went well," Skelton said, matter-of-factly. Ivy couldn't understand how the man was still standing, let alone talking. That casting should have floored him... She felt herself sway.

Looking across at Caspar, Skelton said, "Please see to it that Ivy gets back to her chambers to retrieve her belongings. Then I think it's past time for you both to head to your respective lodgings. I shall remain down here a little longer, to ensure the substances remain bonded..."

"Yes, Master," Caspar acquiesced. "Come on, Ivy, let's go upstairs." He was looking at what had previously been the pumpkin with a singular expression, distaste mingled with awe.

✦

Ivy hardly registered the journey back to her chambers, not even complaining when Caspar steered her towards the lift, which on this occasion behaved itself admirably, as if knowing that now was not the time for wobbling or conducting an experiment in ambient mood music.

Leaving Caspar to collect his belongings and make a hasty exit, Ivy headed wearily down the fifth floor corridor to her own chambers, opened the door and quietly shut it behind her.

She buckled with exhaustion and stretched out an arm to steady herself. Her fingers felt strange, pulsing numbly. A memory floated hazily across her mind – hadn't there been a strange little creature in here earlier? Had she imagined it?

She slowly started to look for it, and eventually found it on top of a row of dusty books, stretched out and fast asleep. Its mouth was slightly open and it was expelling a stream of drowsy chirrups.

"Well, that looks like an excellent idea," Ivy said, sinking into her chair. Within seconds, she was fast asleep herself, head and arms resting on her desk. It had been a very peculiar night.

7.

DARK REFLECTIONS

─────◆─────

The morning after Ivy had undertaken the Woodbane casting ceremony she had awoken at her desk, groggy and confused, haunted by the sense of an ancient shadow looming at the threshold of her mind.

It was not long past dawn and the Tower was empty. The strange stick creature was still sound asleep, although it must have moved at some point during the night as it was now on Ivy's desk, nestled comfortably next to her elbow. She could feel its soft breath on her face. Its woody scent reminded her of hidden forest trails coated with sodden leaves. It reminded her of the tree in the foyer – perhaps that was where it had come from? She considered whether it might be some sort of wood sprite, even though it looked nothing like any sprite she had ever seen. She watched its little pot belly rise and fall gently for a few minutes. Struggling to dredge her mind back to the present, she resolved to get some fresh air.

Having left the small creature quietly dozing in her chambers, Ivy found herself sitting on a low wall in the square outside the Tower, gazing at its coliseum-like structure. Its giant dragonsteel girders glinted like burnished darkness in the reflected warmth of the morning sun.

Ivy exhaled deeply, the exhaustion of last night's casting weighing upon her. How Skelton envisaged they would be able to perform that casting at scale was beyond her.

At least the raw magic that had been crackling around her fingers yesterday had stopped; in fact, she felt completely sapped. She tried to muster enough energy to create a small glow ball, but nothing happened.

Various human and non-human denizens of the Citadel had started filtering through the square, all commuting to their employment, all somehow managing to appear at once tremendously pleased with living and working in a Very Important Place, while also seeming resigned to the futility of such an existence.

"Morning," came a voice from behind her. Without waiting for an invitation, Dante swung his legs over the wall and joined her.

"So I think I've finally cracked it," he announced. "Carterton. What I was missing before was the Futures angle. It's complicated stuff, and as with everything Castings-related it'll be bloody tedious, but I'm going to modify some of the previous castings to account for certain forward-looking adjustments and variables…"

Ivy's thoughts drifted as Dante expounded. Dante had previously undertaken a good deal of Futures work, although the team in which he had truly excelled was that of 'Pasts', officially known as the Wills and Deceased Department. The Pasts team dealt with 'matters spiritual', which mostly consisted of requests from clients to communicate with the dearly departed. It sat, rather incongruously, within the Futures Division of Jackdaw.

Ivy had never pressed Dante on why he had switched to Castings a few years ago, although she assumed it had been due to the dwindling demand for the Pasts practice. Jackdaw's industrial clients seldom used the service beyond occasionally asking if a deceased member of staff could be summoned to remind them of the code for the storage warehouse, quite urgently please. She wondered how much he missed the Pasts and Futures work; he certainly made no effort to conceal his disaffection for the present.

Dante rattled on. Ivy continued to observe the square, watching as small faerie stalls popped in and out of existence in front of the Tower, trying to catch the mages on their way to work and relieve them of their cash. Ivy thought she spotted Skelton clutching a Bubbular Brew, characteristically frenetic, no traces of tiredness from last night's casting. Strange.

"…it's all quite simple really, once you get your head around the uncertainty principles at play–" Dante came to an abrupt halt and looked at her closely. "Are you OK, Ives?"

"Sorry, you know I've never been good with Futures work and this is all sounding ridiculously complicated for first thing in the morning… plus Skelton had me undertake the Woodbane casting with him last night and I'm absolutely spent."

"Did he now? How was it?"

"Strange," she said quietly. "There were these items, and we *changed* them – not like a temporary illusion or transfiguration, but *permanently* – and we gave them magic. In every tiny cell, we *gave* them magic.

"It wasn't like a normal casting either, the power was insane and…" she hesitated, "…there was something else there, Dante, something old and angry… it didn't feel right." As soon as she said it Ivy realised that it made her sound like a crazy person. "Maybe it's just me. My magic has been all over the place recently. All I want to do is cast, but everything seems so much harder than it bloody should be."

Dante brushed away Ivy's concerns. "Look, I wouldn't worry. It's new magic, difficult magic, and you had a late night. You're bound to feel a bit weird. Well, weirder than usual." He nudged her shoulder companionably and rose from the wall. "Come on, let's get you some breakfast and you'll feel better."

Ivy acquiesced gratefully, giving herself a shake, oblivious to the look of concern on Dante's face.

✦

Hop had decided, in the face of Skelton's evasiveness, to make a brief detour to the offices of the Regulator on his journey to Jackdaw & Spittlelick.

Chief Auditor Glof was surprised to see Hop enter the sleepy Audit Office that morning. He had the Audit Office to himself, barring a wolf auditor who was taking the opportunity for some well-earned downtime from sniffing out discrepancies by lolling, eyes shut, in front of the office fireplace.

"Mr Pockett? Back so soon?" Glof asked, unable to conceal a hint of dismay. He had hoped the Jackdaw assignment would have kept Hop occupied for at least a week or two. "Nothing of concern to report, I hope?"

"Well, that's just the thing," said Hop indignantly, "I can't find anything irregular to report."

"That is excellent news," Glof responded, missing the nuance in Hop's tone. "We shall need to make arrangements for your return, I suppose..." Glof had a minor internal crisis at this point, before righting himself admirably, "before finding another external assignment for you, yes indeed. I shall consider some options and let you know. In the meantime, may I suggest a well-deserved break is next on your agenda…?"

The wolf lifted its head and yawned, before blinking open its eyes. It shook its head and the mane of dull-brown fur on its neck rippled, tufts of silver catching in the light from the fire.

"What I mean to say, Glof, is that I can't find any evidence of irregularities because I can't get any of the mages to talk to me! How am I supposed to conduct a meaningful investigation if no-one will take it seriously?" Hop exclaimed, clearly agitated.

The wolf by the fireplace was now looking over at Glof and Hop questioningly. A scar raked across its long muzzle. Hop always found the scar unsettling; it spoke of blood and teeth, thoughts which seemed out of place in the sleepy Audit Office.

The wolf rose to its feet and suddenly underwent something which can only be described as a reality sneeze. With a distorted judder, it became very much woman-shaped.

"It's all right, Wrex," Glof said, shifting in his chair and waving dismissively at the wolf, "I do understand Mr Pockett's concerns, although I worry perhaps that they may be felt somewhat too keenly."

Hop assessed the woman standing before him. He had always been (though he firmly refused to admit it to himself) slightly intimidated by Senior Auditor Wrexhannah Langstaff, the female wolf who was effectively second-in-command at the Audit Office. The woman was formidably tall and lean, clad in a long hide jacket and leather boots. Her shaggy, black-brown fur had become shaggy, black-brown hair, flecked with silver-grey. The scar was even more pronounced – and somehow even more unsettling – on her now human face, which still had a hint of dog lingering about it. Hop found it impossible not to feel disturbed by the memory of those large lupine jaws as she moved towards Glof in support, her arms folded imperiously across her chest.

Hop took a deep breath and said, as calmly as he could, "I apologise for shouting, Glof. It's just that this whole investigation has been a most frustrating affair. Every question I ask is circumvented. I have literally nothing to report. I know there is a meeting about the Woodbane matter at Jackdaw later this morning, but despite initial assurances that I was to have complete access, I was neither informed nor invited. I only discovered it was taking place through–" Hop puffed himself up proudly "–my independent investigations."

"We've all been there, lad," Glof reassured him. "Mages are skittish, and too clever by half. Not a good mix. They all hate audits, not necessarily because they've done anything wrong, but more because they resent having to *evidence* they've done nothing wrong. They'll give you the run-around even where there's nothing to chase. You end up chasing your own tail. No offence, Wrex," he added, glancing at the wolf. "I suspect there's probably nothing more to it than that."

"True…" agreed Wrex, in a warm, husky tone. "Although Master Skelton's avoidance in discussing the project is concerning. He is usually extremely compliant."

Glof reflected on this pensively, as he watched shadows flicker across the wall, dancing in the firelight. Even though they detested it, the mages usually cooperated during audits; they knew the consequences of not doing so. They knew about the cellar full of grimlings that crouched in the darkness directly beneath Glof's comfy Audit Office…Perhaps Hop had just rubbed Skelton up the wrong way? That was a distinct possibility. But still... The goblin stroked his whiskered old chin, his brow furrowed with deep creases.

At that moment, the pensive atmosphere of the Audit Office was rudely punctured by the sudden appearance of a large portal, which popped into existence in the centre of the room. Hop and Glof jumped, while Wrex let out a surprised growl. Snow started to swarm and swirl in from the imposing mountainscape that could be glimpsed through the portal.

"What the–" exclaimed Hop, steadying his glasses.

"Not again," Wrex barked, rolling her eyes in dismay. "Someone submitted a malfunctioning Automatic Portal Generation Device to the Complaints Department the other day because they weren't getting anywhere with the goblin manufacturer. They don't have clue what to do with the damn thing and the bloody idiots keep setting it off by mistake. A portal turned up in the canteen the other day right in the middle of my breakfast!"

"Never a dull day, is it, Wrex?" Glof observed mildly. "Portals randomly popping up at inconvenient moments… we should probably keep an eye on that. No good can come of it."

"Fascinating…" breathed Hop, poking his fingers into the portal and waving them around, marvelling at the searing chill of the mountain air.

"I wouldn't do that, if I were you, my boy," cautioned Glof. "Portal magics don't last long at the best of times and by all accounts this device is a bit temperamental." Hop withdrew his fingers hastily just as the portal vanished.

"Right," said Glof. "Where were we? Yes, that's right… Mr Pockett, it might interest you that my cousin Gnit, in the

Approvals Office, received a message from a Jackdaw potions Master yesterday – Charles Bladlow, I believe – informing him that Jackdaw would be submitting the approvals submission for the new premium Woodbane product in the next two days. Master Bladlow was insistent that the approval of the submission be expedited.

"Naturally my cousin Gnit is minded to place the request at the bottom of his pile, but he did note the remarkable speed at which the new Woodbane products are being pushed through to the Market."

Glof looked at Wrex, who raised one of her heavy eyebrows.

"Please do keep investigating, Mr Pockett," Glof directed. "Discreetly, of course. If the Masters do not provide you with the submission paperwork, you should request a copy from the Approvals Office upstairs. Just ask for Gnit and say I sent you.

"Report back to me in a fortnight. If you can locate no evidence of anything irregular, we will consider the matter closed and inform the Supervisory Board of the same. Agreed?"

Hop nodded gratefully and left the stuffy Audit Office behind him, intent on his assignment, while Glof and Wrex assumed their previous positions, for some reason feeling rather less comfortable than before.

Dante was strolling along the fifth floor corridor later that morning, hands in pockets, when he heard raised voices coming from outside Skelton's chambers.

It was that auditor. He appeared to be having an issue with Elspeth. This was bound to be entertaining. "Is this chap bothering you, Elspeth?" Dante interjected; a roguish grin plastered across his face.

"No, no, thank you, Dante," replied Elspeth haughtily. "I have everything quite in hand. I was just explaining to Mr Pockett that Master Skelton is unavailable today."

"He must have *some* availability!" Hop said in exasperation.

"He is unavailable," Elspeth repeated firmly. "He is currently occupied with Regulator enquiries."

"But this *is* a Regulator enquiry!" Hop shouted indignantly.

The argument was interrupted by the appearance of Master Skelton at his doorway. "What is going on out here, Elspeth?" he demanded politely.

"Master Skelton!" Hop interjected, before Elspeth could respond. "I was hoping we might be able to discuss the Woodbane matter? I have some questions I'd like to ask you."

"Absolutely, absolutely. I'm afraid I'm tied up for the next day or so, perhaps we could pencil in a meeting after that? Subject of course to client work. Elspeth can arrange a suitable time."

Elspeth glared at Hop triumphantly.

"Now, if that's all, I must get back to my work." Skelton paused and looked over at Dante. "Do you have somewhere to be?"

The inference was that Dante very clearly should have somewhere to be. He shrugged and replied, "I expect so, Master."

"Well, perhaps you should get to it, then," Skelton said curtly, before stepping back into his chambers.

"Bad luck, old boy," Dante smirked, retrieving a small round object from his pocket and casually tossing it up and down. It made the occasional small squeak.

Hop and Elspeth eyed one another. Elspeth got there first. "I shall check the Master's diary and send you a list of suggested times."

"Most grateful," said Hop, thoroughly demoralised. "Please do also inform – I mean *remind* – Master Skelton that I will be in attendance at this morning's meeting in 7B," Hop checked himself quickly, remembering he was pretending to have known about the appointment with Solutions.

He looked over at Dante and suddenly had an idea. "Can I have a word?"

"It seems to be my lucky day," said Dante sardonically. "You may, but make it quick."

Dante led Hop down the corridor to his chambers.

"Welcome to my humble abode," Dante said, gesturing expansively.

Dante's chambers were larger than most on the floor, although not as large as Skelton's, and faced out onto the Citadel. There would have been a splendid view of the Citadel's buildings, but unfortunately it was obscured by various scribbled memos and a few incongruous paper cups stuck unceremoniously to the large windows, which were casting dappled shadows around the room.

Paper was, in fact, the main decorative element of the room, if decorative was the appropriate term. Litterative might have been more suitable. It was everywhere, and yet somehow contrived to look carefully managed as opposed to strewn. This was never more evident than when Hop inadvertently trod on a sheet covered with illegible scrawl, sliding it along the threadbare carpet, and Dante rushed over and said, "Careful of that, it's very important," before shuffling it back to its original hazardous position.

"Have a seat," Dante said absently.

Hop pondered the seat in front of Dante's desk. It was piled high with stacks of papers.

"May I?" Hop asked, gesturing towards the paper.

"I'd rather you didn't, to be honest. I'll never get it straight again," Dante said with an exaggerated sigh, "but you might as well. Pass them here."

Hop lifted the piles as carefully as he could manage and passed them very slowly over to Dante, who promptly dropped them on the floor behind his desk.

They took their seats and looked across the desk at each other. Dante took the ball from his pocket and bounced it once or twice on the cluttered desktop. It made a chirpy little squeal as he did so.

"I was hoping you might be able to answer a couple of questions for me. About the Woodbane process?" Hop began.

"Ah…no can do, I'm afraid," Dante replied lightly.

"I'm experiencing a lot of that," Hop said. "You know, I'm really not sure why people won't talk to me about it. It's not helping my investigations at all!" There was a noticeable vein of petulance in Hop's voice.

"It's not that I won't talk about it. I just have nothing to tell you."

"But you must know something about the principles of the casting and solutions processes!" The vein of petulance now looked fit to burst.

"I didn't say I didn't," Dante replied evenly.

"This place is madness. You know, I came here expecting to find–" Hop inhaled and Dante interjected.

"Expecting to find what, exactly? That's your problem… you *want* to find something. You won't. There's nothing in this place worth finding."

Hop shook his head. "I expected to find a little more respect, at least."

"Hah. Me too, but you won't locate that anytime soon either. Honestly, the best thing you can do is write up your little report, get back to your cosy little office at the Regulator, and put your feet up until a proper audit comes along. Nothing good ever comes of lingering too long around this place, trust me." As he said this, the morning sunlight which had been stubbornly trying to filter through the paper affixed to the window dimmed.

"Look," persevered Hop. "What you are doing on this Woodbane matter shouldn't be possible, at least not at the scale you need to be doing it. The transference of specific and *stable* magical properties into non-magical matter would require drawing upon a magical source which is far beyond anything naturally available–"

"You suddenly know an awful lot about the process for someone who hasn't managed to talk to anyone about it," Dante interjected, his eyes narrowing.

"You'll find I know a substantial amount about magic in general!" Hop said self-importantly. "I also read – exceptionally carefully – the submission papers for the original product, which claimed to create synthetic faerie dust. The theoretical magic behind the synthetisation process Skelton put forward – and its mass production applications – quite frankly, doesn't add up. He needs to draw the magic he is transferring into these artificial Restricted Substances from somewhere and he has provided absolutely no information on this point. There is something simply not *right* about Skelton's process."

Dante remained silent.

Sensing he was going to get no further, Hop rose from his chair and declared defiantly, "I'll get to the bottom of this business. I have a job to do here and I'm going to darn well do it, starting with that meeting upstairs!"

Dante shrugged as Hop flounced out.

After Hop had left, Dante gave the small ball another bounce, turned in his chair and surveyed the Citadel – or at least those sections of it he could see. That was the second person this morning who had said Skelton's Woodbane casting process was not quite right.

Staring out of the window, something unexpectedly flickered in the back of his mind. It seemed panicked, terrified… a familiar voice calling out from a place Dante had long abandoned.

Darkening shadows crept across the glass before him, slowly inching through the slim gaps in the papers stuck to the surface. They crawled across his reflected features, pausing under his eyes. He could hear rushing water coming from somewhere.

Unnerved, he slammed shut the door in his mind, ignoring the frantic hammering that ensued.

Dante gave a sharp wave of his hand. Papers from the floor flew up and affixed themselves violently across the window, smothering the cracks, blocking out the darkness reflected in the glass.

✦

Elsewhere in the Citadel, about a mile or so away from the Tower of Jackdaw and Spittlelick, Salonika had, until very recently, been standing on a bridge.

Standing probably wasn't the right word; she had been swaying rather too much for that. On the bridge probably wasn't right either; her feet had been rather more off the bridge than on it.

She wasn't sure how she had ended up on the off side of the bridge. It had just seemed like the right sort of place to be. She couldn't think of anywhere else that made much sense. There certainly wasn't anywhere else to go.

Salonika had looked down at the river water that bobbed along unobtrusively beneath her. It seemed quite gentle down there, the morning sun reflected in its tranquil ripples. Refreshing, even. Just what she needed really.

It wasn't supposed to have worked out this way. She wasn't supposed to have ended up here, looking at the water down there. She was so tired. It was as though everything had been drained out of her, replaced with a dry, brittle burning sensation. The voice in the back of her mind was whimpering again, as though recoiling from the press of a hot iron.

Should she? Could she? She wasn't even sure she had choices like this anymore. Perhaps she should go home. Sleep. That was what she needed. Her eyes felt heavy, her head thick with fog. She clutched at the wooden railings of the bridge, feeling for its firmness, willing it to wake her up. She was so very tired.

Her eyes closed, the world swam. The bridge wobbled from the vibration of a passing Deep Cart just beneath the riverbank. Her fingers slipped, too weak to grip. With no more weight than an autumn leaf, she felt herself fall.

The water really was quite refreshing.

8.

DIVISIONAL MATTERS

Shortly after Hop had left Dante's chambers, the two teams from Castings and Solutions convened on the seventh floor of the Tower to discuss the progress of the Woodbane Solution.

The seventh floor was situated underneath the broad dome of the Tower's skylight. Its circular corridor spanned its inner circumference and was neither walled nor windowed. Originally the walkway had been *extremely* open, the architects later grudgingly confessing to 'omitting to delineate the area between the uppermost floor and the ground level'. Certain mages who did not much like the idea of falling seven storeys to a splattery death were not impressed with this oversight and determined that a balcony should be installed.

By then, however, the mages had run through a vast amount of coin in hiring the architects of the Tower, in later attempting to sue them, and in settling one unfortunate splattery death claim. In a Significant Cost-Saving Exercise, the mages had therefore formed a Cross-Divisional Balcony Installation Working Group and attempted to construct the balcony themselves, reinforcing it with a casting or two.

Unfortunately this had somehow animated the balcony, leading to its having a full week off once every financial quarter and taking occasional time off in lieu.

Provided one kept an eye on the balcony's whereabouts, though, the seventh floor was a decidedly nice place to reside. As such, its spacious rooms housed the chambers of the Most Senior Masters and the larger meeting rooms. Although the Most Senior Masters had enviable views of the Citadel, the view they tended to enjoy most was the internal panorama. Here, they could gaze down from the precarious balcony into the internal chambers of the junior mages on the third to sixth floors and delight in watching them profitably beavering away at their tiny desks. Regrettably, the giant tree that someone had so inconsiderately planted in the middle of the foyer was now rather spoiling that wonderful view.

It was in one of the meeting rooms on the seventh floor that Ivy, Skelton and Taryn Underfoot were now sitting, awaiting the arrival of Master Bladlow, head of the Solutions Division, papers spread out before them like a display of arms.

Due to the competitive nature of most mages – especially those who had obtained the hallowed rank of Master – collaborations between mages practising in different Divisions within the Tower were often fraught affairs. Today's meeting was to be no different.

"Right," said Skelton, having exhausted his limited patience after a mere five minutes. "Shall we crack on?"

At this moment, the door opened and Master Bladlow puffed in amiably, panting a rushed apology as he closed the door and moved towards an empty chair. "Sorry, sorry. Another meeting overran." It hadn't, but artful lateness was a perennial sign of being a *most* important person.

"Hello all," he said to the room at large, before nodding brusquely at Skelton. "Everard."

"Charles." Skelton nodded back.

Charles Bladlow was not a tall man, but his girth was considerable. With not inconsiderable effort, he squeezed himself into a chair.

At this juncture, one might pause to wonder why Bladlow had not availed himself of one of the many popular slimming solutions on the Market (a few of which had been developed by Bladlow himself). The simple truth was that these solutions were not really designed to work, at least not for any length of time, and some were even cynically calibrated to make the consumer gain weight. Accordingly, Bladlow avoided slimming solutions. Unfortunately, what he did not avoid was copious quantities of complex carbohydrates, saturated fats and sugar. Bladlow treated his body like a temple; albeit one where frequent offerings of fatted calves were mandated.

"Wonderful," panted Bladlow, having eventually managed to insert himself behind the table. "Thank you for your patience. Let's make a start, shall we?"

As the law of meetings dictates must be the case whenever someone has made a second attempt to commence proceedings, at this very moment the door to the meeting room opened once again. The mages present appeared thoroughly baffled as Hop Pockett entered, chin raised. "Good morning, all," he proclaimed brightly.

"Are you lost?" asked Bladlow.

"I understand you are here to discuss the new Woodbane solution," Hop said. "I'm here to observe on behalf of the Regulator. Please do continue." He pulled out a chair and positioned himself slightly away from the table, resting a yellow notepad on his lap and brandishing his ink pen.

"But this is a confidential meeting!" Bladlow spluttered.

The mages all instinctively shuffled their papers back towards themselves.

"As a representative of the Audit Office of the Regulator of Magical Practice, I have authority to attend any meeting or any casting, brewing or determining session of interest, provided appropriate notice of my attendance is delivered to you in good time," Hop said. "Unfortunately, as I only found out about this meeting yesterday, I had to leave the notice with your respective assistants this morning."

Skelton glanced questioningly at Ivy, who shrugged.

Bladlow turned to Taryn. "Tarragyn," he said, oblivious to the wince he evoked with the use of her full name, "did you know anything about this?"

Taryn shook her head. "I wasn't informed, no."

"Well," said Bladlow, mopping a sheen of sweat from his forehead. The man could perspire even when seated. "Everard, what do you think? Shall we continue?"

There was a slight pause. "I don't believe we have anything to say that cannot be said in front of the Regulator's appointed representative," Skelton eventually answered, just a little too sharply, looking directly at Bladlow as he did so.

"Fine, let's get on with it then, shall we?" said Bladlow, clearly irritated. "As you are all aware, my team's *Regulator-approved* Woodbane's Original Ever-Young Solution had been performing well until supply complications arose. On the Castings side, I should specify." There was no need at all to specify this, but Bladlow could not in good conscience waste the opportunity. Skelton's cheek twitched.

"My team has since developed a new *highly complex* formulation for a more *premium* product, as a result of close collaboration with my former protégé and Woodbane's head mage, Hartley Crumpley-Snafely."

None of this information was needed, but Bladlow had resolved that if notes were being taken about the project, he was damned sure they were going to reflect the extent of his involvement.

Ivy tried to ignore the flutter she felt in her stomach at hearing Hartley's name.

Bladlow steamed on. "While we feared we would be behind schedule due to – ahem – some delay in the casting of the necessary ingredients for the premium product–"

Ivy winced inwardly. It was her Umping incident that had caused the delay.

"–we have nevertheless worked tirelessly through the night to brew the first batch of the premium solution for delivery to Woodbane."

Taryn's jaw clenched at this. It was only she who had worked through the night. Bladlow had been at a seven-course embassy dinner, followed by a well-deserved late start.

"However," Bladlow huffed, "when I spoke to Hartley this morning to confirm arrangements for delivery, he mentioned you had met with them, Everard. Apparently, you were not particularly reassuring as to timescales."

"I was simply transparent about the need to obtain Regulator approval for the new product, Charles," Skelton countered.

"Provided you've completed the paperwork, that element is all in hand, Everard," Bladlow replied, shooting a quick glance at Hop, who was scribbling furiously. "Hartley and I are not concerned about this. What we are concerned about is wider mass production."

"That aspect is equally in hand, Charles," countered Skelton. "However, as you know, certain aspects are outside my control. I've told you what it would take to make it work." Skelton looked pointedly at Bladlow as he said this.

"If I may interrupt you at this point, Master Skelton?" Hop interjected, raising his pen in a querying manner.

Skelton raised his eyebrows in surprise. Masters were not accustomed to interruptions, at least not from anyone other than other Masters, who like to interrupt each other as much as possible. He quickly recovered and intoned most magnanimously, "Of course, of course..."

"The Regulator is very interested in this aspect. To magically create synthetic Restricted Substances at scale is–" Hop began.

"Is an advancement in modern magic which will benefit large elements of the population," interposed Skelton firmly. "Charles, let's discuss the requirements for casting at scale separately, before we undertake the ceremony."

"I'd very much like to attend that casting ceremony," said Hop, unable to mask a slight hopefulness in his voice.

"Absolutely, absolutely. I will ensure the relevant details are sent in your direction in due course," Skelton said evasively. "In the meantime," he continued, turning back to Bladlow, "we will continue to produce smaller quantities of ingredients, which will allow Woodbane to produce a limited supply of both the original and premium products in anticipation of approval being obtained. That should enable you to inform Hartley that all is well. Please also let him know he is welcome to contact me *directly* should he have further concerns."

All Masters were instinctively protective of client relationships and Bladlow was no exception. Bladlow was already livid that Skelton had met with Ramston and Hartley independently; he was not about to let Skelton become any closer to Woodbane Cosmetics.

"I'm sure that won't be necessary" Bladlow responded. "In the meantime, we of course have the first batch of the new solution ready for delivery to Woodbane. I was thinking we should–"

"Excuse me?"

"Yes, Mr Pockett?" Bladlow panted impatiently.

"May I please be provided with a sample, for review purposes?"

"Not necessary," Bladlow said dismissively. "A sample is being provided to the Regulator separately, alongside the submission papers Master Skelton has prepared."

Bladlow turned to Skelton. "Now, Everard, as I was saying, the solution needs to be formally delivered to Woodbane and–"

"Ivy and I should be delighted to attend," Skelton breezed.

"Ah, yes, well…" stuttered Bladlow, ambushed; he was expecting to be the only one to hand-deliver the product to Woodbane. "Splendid. Indeed. Let me check timings with Hartley and we can fix something up."

"If I could perhaps–" started Hop hopefully.

"Mr Pockett," interjected Skelton smoothly, anticipating Hop's next request. "I would suggest that attendance at such a presentation sits beyond the limited remit of your enquiries."

Hop looked deflated.

"That's settled then," Bladlow steamed on. "Everard and young Ivy here will attend. Tarragyn – it's best if it's simply me attending from the Solutions side. Given Hartley will be there, we wouldn't want to overwhelm poor Ramston with us mages!" Bladlow chortled.

Taryn could not quite believe what she had just heard. She had just worked through the night alone in the Crypt, feeling ever more numbed by the proximity of its grimling stone walls, exhaustedly brewing the new potion at speed from the moment Skelton had handed her the ingredients. And yet Bladlow was about to seize the glory?

Adding insult to the injury was the fact that 'young Ivy' was of course invited to share in that glory. She looked across the table at the wan face and brittle frame of the girl that had been deemed such a rising star by her colleagues. A dull rage began to settle and seethe. She nevertheless nodded her silent assent to Bladlow, as was expected.

Ivy, for her part, had not registered the unexpected honour that had been accorded her. She was caught between enduring the strong wave of exhaustion that had started to crash over her and the rising tide of anticipation at seeing Hartley again.

"Of course." Skelton smiled. "Is there anything else, Charles?"

"No, no, I don't believe so, Everard," said Bladlow, returning Skelton's smile. "Tarragyn?" he asked, not looking at her.

"I don't believe there's anything else, Master," said Taryn automatically.

Hop opened his mouth once again to speak, raising his pen questioningly.

"Wonderful," said Bladlow, resolutely ignoring the auditor and uncorking himself from his chair. "We'll leave you to it then. Lunch beckons."

One suspected lunch had been clamouring for attention shortly after breakfast had conceded ground to elevenses.

Bladlow wheezed out of the room contentedly, Taryn following wearily.

Skelton hesitated momentarily before rising. Hop seized his opportunity. "Master Skelton, if I could just ask a few quick questions?"

"I'm afraid I have another matter I need to attend to," Skelton responded rapidly. "Ivy can answer any questions, I'm sure."

Skelton strode out from the room and Ivy and Hop eyed each other cautiously.

"Well, I think that went well, don't you?" said Ivy drily, reclining in her chair and stretching her arms out behind her, cat-like, trying to keep herself awake.

Hop frowned and pushed his glasses back up his nose. "I have some questions for you," he said abruptly.

Ivy was taken aback. "Really?"

"Yes, principally because every time I try to speak to Master Skelton, he's always in the middle of something. I've read all the materials submitted to the Approvals Office for these Woodbane anti-ageing products, been working my way through the principles… and…" Hop trailed off.

"Yes?" prompted Ivy.

"I don't think it is going to work at the scale you need it to."

"What do you mean?"

"I know a lot about how magic works, quite a surprising amount really, and the sort of magic you would need for mass production would require a massive amount of magical energy. Even then, the magical forces at play would make the process extremely volatile."

Ivy was quiet, remembering the intensity of the magic from last night.

Hop seized upon her silence and said, "I would like your help to establish what is really going on."

Ivy hesitated. She wasn't entirely sure she should be talking to the auditor, doubtful that Skelton genuinely expected her to answer Hop's questions – not that she was even sure she could. She was curious though, in spite of herself.

She looked at him intently. "Maybe. It depends on the enquiries."

Ivy picked up her papers and rose from her seat. "I need to get back to work now, though," she said. "Watch out for the balcony on your way out, by the way. It's got this afternoon off."

✦

The subsequent presentation by Bladlow, Skelton and Ivy of Woodbane's Premium Ever-Young Solution to Ramston Woodbane and Hartley Crumpley-Snafely went extremely well.

Hartley had examined the product approvingly as Bladlow had smiled proudly on. Woodbane had guffawed loudly as he twirled the delicate pots of the trial batch in his industrially over-sized hands and called in his much put-upon receptionist (who transpired to be his much put-upon wife and chief product tester).

Mrs Woodbane had, at her husband's loud behest, obligingly slathered a hefty slop of the solution onto her face before the gathered mages.

Having spent an inadvisable proportion of her not insignificant years both trialling Woodbane's cosmetics and cheerfully exposed to sunlight, Mrs Woodbane had developed an alarming leathery texture to her face, so the effect of applying the solution was akin to oiling an elephant. After just a few moments, though, the wrinkles on Mrs Woodbane's face did indeed begin to visibly shrink, much to the delight of the men in the room.

Ivy, too, was impressed, although she nevertheless felt that several industrial-sized vats of the stuff would be needed for Mrs Woodbane's personal use alone.

The assembled grand personages of Bladlow, Skelton and Woodbane had all exclaimed how it had taken years off Mrs Woodbane. They had all then hastily added variations along the theme of 'not that it was needed, of course...' when faced with her hard (albeit rather oily) stare.

Bladlow had then reassured Woodbane that the Regulator's approval was effectively assured, Skelton had confirmed that mass production of the ingredients was in hand, and it was subsequently felt by all that an impromptu celebration was in order.

Handily, Bladlow had – sensing spontaneity on the horizon – already requisitioned a *perfect* number of tickets to the Grand Game happening two nights thence.

Five tickets were offered up, with Woodbane, Hartley, Skelton and Bladlow assuming one each. Mrs Woodbane was courteously offered the final ticket, which she robustly declined on the basis that she had far better things to do with her time on the proposed evening. One could hazard a relatively confident guess that such things would involve the remaining pots of the Woodbane Solution, as a grinning Mrs Woodbane dabbed further quantities onto her glowing face.

So it was Ivy who was offered the fifth ticket, after Woodbane's booming overtures that she absolutely must join. Hartley had grinned widely at her as she had accepted, commenting that it was certain to prove an entertaining evening. Ivy had smiled back, her heart racing at the prospect of spending the evening with him, while trying to remind herself that this was about business, not pleasure.

So it was decided that the party would reconvene to revel in the cleverness of all involved, and to watch the Grand Game.

The tree was exhausted. It could feel its leaves wilting. It needed sunlight and fresh rainwater and air on its boughs.

Someone was approaching to feed it again. It tried to twitch its roots away, but they caught in the grimling stone. As toxins scorched through its roots, on a bookcase several floors above the small twig creature convulsed in its fitful sleep.

9.

CLIENT ENTERTAINING

A few years ago, in the spirit of improving inter-species relations, it had been decided that a new sport should be introduced to Kirin, one that catered to humans and non-humans alike.

A Committee was established to design this 'Grand Game', with representatives from all of the main species who were signatories to the Accords: human, wolf, troll, goblin, and faerie.

The Committee took to their brief with vigour. A team of fifteen players was devised, containing members from each of the main species, with the aim of the game being the traditional one of attempting to score as many points as possible by throwing small balls at things.

Specific field positions were created to suit players of certain heritage, rules of engagement were carefully mapped out, and flattering team outfits were painstakingly designed (although no one quite knew what to do with the trolls, it proving remarkably difficult to dress a creature that resembled a moss-covered boulder).

As with all things designed by committee, matters rapidly spiralled, with the Grand Game growing ever more complex as competing interests and long-held grievances were hastily taken into account. The faerie representatives maintained that there needed to be an element of airborne play, whereas the trolls and goblins point-blank refused to countenance any.

At one point in its development, the sport involved no fewer than six differently sized balls, several goals installed at various positions on the pitch, and a highly intricate scoring system which would bemuse doctoral mathematicians, never mind the average sports fan.

After years of debate, the inaugural Grand Game (the Committee having summarily failed to reach consensus on a better name) was finally scheduled. On the night of the match, crowds had poured into the new flagship stadium, which had been constructed on a derelict area of wasteland outside the Citadel.

Ivy was currently seated in that new stadium, ensconced between Skelton and Hartley, who was perched at one end of the group. The towering figure of Ramston Woodbane had dropped anchor between Skelton and Bladlow, who was perched at the other end, although perched was perhaps not the best description; he was currently spilling over into an aisle, looking thoroughly irritated that Skelton had assumed centre stage.

Ivy still felt drained from the further casting ceremonies she had undertaken with Skelton over the last couple of days, but a burst of adrenalin coursed through her as she surveyed the giant stadium, which buzzed with the chatter, grunts and growls of the various races in attendance (most of the grunts and growls seemingly coming from the human attendees). Bladlow had secured seats in the executive block of the stands, meaning Ivy had an enviable view of the full squoval pitch (the

Committee having settled on the confused shape in the spirit of exhausted compromise).

She looked up with a thrill at the pair of dragons circling idly above, the slow beats of their powerful wings audible above the swell of the crowd, arrayed in the black and blood orange livery of Dragonsteel. They arched their long, scaled throats as their riders tugged at their harnesses, rearing their monstrous necks in bridled dominance.

Hartley followed her appreciative gaze. "Beautiful, aren't they?" he said, leaning in to ensure she heard him over the din. A pleasant shiver threaded down her spine as she felt his breath on her neck. "I wasn't expecting to see them here."

"They must have been loaned by Dragonsteel," she observed, pleased to have something to contribute. "The organisers must have struck a deal with them. Can't imagine it would have been an easy negotiation – Dragonsteel hate their assets being out of commission." Ivy knew this from her castings work for them; every time a dragon was temporarily withdrawn from service for renewal of its bindings, Dragonsteel harassed her to ensure the asset resumed its smelting operations as quickly as possible.

"Judging by the amount of dragonsteel on display in this stadium, I think I can guess how they managed it," Hartley said, flashing her his rakish half-smile.

"I think you may be right," she replied wryly, returning his smile.

The stadium was a feat of multi-species engineering, combining techniques from centuries of goblin, human, faerie and troll architectural tradition, but dragonsteel was the dominant material, assertively binding arching wooden timbers and prehistoric slabs of rock in its utilitarian embrace.

"It really is quite something, isn't it?" said Skelton, shouting across at the pair of them while examining the assembling masses.

Ivy felt so far away from home she could barely comprehend it. She had never seen so many different species in one place in Kirin. She had known the Citadel to be staunchly cosmopolitan, but she hadn't truly realised to what extent, having grown up in the provinces and spent over half a decade cloistered away in the mostly human-occupied Tower of Jackdaw and Spittlelick.

Apart from the trolls, who were mostly seated in the lowest tier of the stands (the organisers not wanting to test even dragonsteel to its limits), the crowd was an indisputable mingling of races. Ivy discerned dazzling faeries stylishly clasping bubbling concoctions gossiping to wolves who howled with laughter, goblins gesticulating avidly to their neighbouring humans (possibly about the complexities of the engineering on display, judging by the mystified looks on their neighbours' faces), humans joshing with trolls and trying to avoid any reciprocal slaps on the back, and even sprites chatting flirtatiously with orcs.

It was only the executive block, where Ivy was comfortably seated, which appeared almost exclusively filled with humans. Aside from the multi-species Committee for the Grand Game – who had afforded themselves the best view of proceedings as reward for a job well done and a ghastly experience survived – the rest of the executive block comprised many of the Citadel's industrial and commercial elite, together with the human mages who served them.

Skelton had continued talking while Ivy was busy examining the crowd. "It's been in the works for so long,

I'll admit I was sceptical it would ever truly happen," he commented. "A thoroughly modern endeavour. Quite, quite something!"

"Did anyone think ter get drinks?" Woodbane boomed over the throng. "No? Charles – you're parked closest to the exit. Do yer mind doin' the honours and fetchin' some fuel for the fire?"

"Of course, very happy to," Bladlow said, looking anything but. "Anything particular for anyone?"

The group placed their orders, with Skelton taking the opportunity to ask for what sounded like a very complicated faerie brew. Bladlow huffed his way back down the stand towards the drinks station, which was thronged with a heaving mass of beings, all assuming they were in the official queue, but also beginning to wonder whether one of the other eleven queues might in fact be the official queue.

"How's that damned submission comin' along?" barked Woodbane at Skelton.

"It's with the Regulator. We hope to have their decision in a couple of weeks."

"That long, eh? Stockholders won't be happy, I tell yer," grumbled Woodbane. "Bloody rules and regulations, all nonsense. Enough ter keep you lot lining yer pockets, though." He shook his industrially-proportioned head.

"Jus' get it done," he continued, "so we can start turnin' our minds ter other applications. Hartley tells me the possibilities are endless!"

As Skelton and Woodbane talked on, Hartley leaned back insouciantly and said, "Well, Ivy Armstride, this promises to be quite the spectacle. Any idea what the rules are?"

"Not a clue," answered Ivy honestly.

"Me neither. I assume some sort of scoring system has been settled on."

"I wouldn't hold your breath," Ivy remarked with a smirk, gesturing across at a large raised wooden board at one end of the pitch, where a couple of faeries dressed in official-looking garb and holding various wooden numbers with hooks attached appeared to be having a full-blown argument.

"Looks like it's going to be entertaining indeed." Hartley laughed. "So," he said, changing the subject, "should I take it you're the lucky mage responsible for keeping those magnificent beasts under control?" He pointed up at the circling reptiles.

"Not really," replied Ivy modestly. "The castings are ridiculously complicated but it's mainly about getting the control terms recorded and recited properly, making sure you're absolutely clear what you want the dragons to do, or *not* to do, which is possibly more important... The magic itself is surprisingly easy once the first binding is done."

"Really?" Hartley seemed intrigued. "I suspect you're making it sound easier than it is. I was always under the impression that dragon binding was tricky magic and one of the reasons Skelton's casting expertise is so in demand." He paused and scrutinised her. "On which note, we're currently on the hunt for a good castings mage…" he continued meaningfully.

Hartley leaned in closer and lowered his voice as he said, "It's probably completely inappropriate to ask, but I don't suppose you might–"

Ivy was intrigued but, before Hartley could finish, a rousing choir of water sprites floated gracefully onto the pitch to warm up proceedings, breaking into spritesong.

Dragon fire suddenly lit up the stadium's open roof, warming things up further still, somewhat uncomfortably for those in the top tiers of the stands.

Bladlow, who had been at that very moment huffing his way back up the steps with a tray of precariously balanced glasses, experienced quite a start. The contents of the drinks slopped across the tray. Damp from exertion and sploshed beverages, Bladlow handed out the orders and resumed his seat.

The party settled back to take in the electric atmosphere. Unfortunately, the rousing chorus of spritesong was being drowned out by the sound of numerous goblin trumpets suddenly erupting from the crowd. These absurdly long instruments had been carted in by many goblin fans and appeared capable only of farting out a single flat note.

Some of the wolves, currently in human form, tipped back their necks and howled chillingly in an effort to overpower the blare of the goblin trumpets, a clamour which provoked many of the humans in the crowd, who began to roar and jeer in challenge. It seemed to Ivy that the companionable atmosphere of the crowd was evaporating quickly and previously suppressed tensions had started to simmer ominously.

Thankfully, at that point, amidst the cacophony, the two teams entered the stadium and lined up to face one another. An expectant hush enveloped the now packed stands.

One team was dressed in a sombre black; the other in a fetching shade of magenta. The teams did their best to size each other up menacingly, an entertaining affair given how mismatched in height the players were.

The three balls which had eventually been decided upon by the Committee (with substantial sulking from the wolf representative, who felt one could never have enough balls) bounced into play. The goblin referee stood between the teams, placed an odd-shaped whistle to his lips, and blew. A scream like someone finding a large spider under a bath towel emerged and the Grand Game began.

What ensued can only be described as unadulterated chaos.

Having only had a short time to practise, and no one being entirely clear on the rules, which had been in motion until the last hour before the game, all players rushed towards each other and started desperately grabbing and kicking. The referee did his best to remind the teams that the grabbing and kicking needed to be focused on the balls rather than on opposing (or in some cases, friendly) players, but it was to no avail.

Points were scored at speed, with beleaguered deputy referees running breathlessly up and down the sidelines wondering why no one had thought to suggest that play be paused after each goal.

The wolves bounded up and down the pitch, having been allowed to assume their wolf forms, happily pouncing on anything moving, tails wagging in sheer exhilaration, now completely unidentifiable but for a small collar in their team colours. Trolls rolled about, oblivious to their having become a trip hazard for the rest of the players.

Two of the goblin players, exhausted after six minutes of gentle jogging about, splintered off from the action, sat their spindly forms down, retrieved some pens and paper from the pockets of their smartly pressed trousers (the goblins had refused to wear shorts), and started feverishly devising a more sophisticated mechanised goal hoop.

"Any idea who's winning?" Ivy asked Hartley, as a magenta-collared wolf grabbed a ball in its teeth and delivered it at the foot of one of the magenta-clad human players. The human was desperately pointing and shouting towards one of the goals.

"It's not looking good for either team, from what little I can tell," Hartley said, leaning in closely. Ivy felt the warmth of his body next to her and – even though she knew she absolutely shouldn't – she leaned her shoulder against her client's, telling herself it was perfectly acceptable behaviour, packed in as tightly as they were.

The magenta-clad human player had picked up the ball and thrown it forcibly in the direction of the goal. The wolf had bounded after it, grabbing it mid-air in a powerful leap, before circling gracefully and trotting back to deposit it back at his teammate's feet. At this point the human player looked ready to burst into frustrated tears.

"Bloody carnage, isn't it?" thundered Woodbane. "Told 'em as much. Spoke to the Committee, I did. Said it'd be a recipe for disaster! Never going ter get anythin' useful out o' bloody goblins and wolves! Not ter mention the damned faeries!"

"Absolutely agree, a ridiculous endeavour, as we all expected," Bladlow said obsequiously.

Skelton looked irked, and seemed about to say something, but at that point a goal was scored, and the crowd erupted.

After twenty further minutes of disordered play, with the magenta team now comfortably (if inexplicably) leading on the points front, a black-garbed faerie swept down onto the pitch and hurled a small red ball through a gold-painted hoop.

The magenta-clad human apparently meant to be manning the gold hoop failed to stop the progress of the little ball, and it hurtled through the shining hoop, landing with a definitive thud on the edge of the pitch.

After a short moment, the strange whistle screeched abruptly and the players stopped in their tracks, stunned.

It appeared that, notwithstanding the fact that the magenta team had been considerably ahead on points, the black team had just won.

As the black team realised what had just occurred, they started to celebrate wildly, cheering and whooping. The magenta team looked down (or up, depending on their species) at the goblin referee, who was hastily flicking through a not insubstantial rulebook.

Not finding what he was looking for, as the crowd started to rumble and murmur ominously, the referee flicked in a panic to the 'Frequently Asked Questions' section he knew to be at the back of the rulebook. He confirmed, as the magenta team began to remonstrate, and the crowd shifted in anticipation, that the black team had indeed won.

At that point, fights broke out up and down the pitch, quickly overflowing into the crowd in the manner of sporting encounters the universe over, as bubbling, barely contained tensions finally exploded into pandemonium. Punches were thrown, as were a few humans who had the misfortune to be standing next to some of the trolls doing the throwing.

Hartley and Ivy glanced at each other in concern as some members of the crowd around them started to get to their feet and gesticulate at the occupants of the executive block, who had remained somewhat nervously seated. Ivy felt Hartley grab her hand and pull her down as a beverage-based projectile hurtled its way towards the Committee members who were a couple of rows behind them. She suddenly found herself practically on top of him; she could feel his breath on her face, his heart beneath his chest…

CLIENT ENTERTAINING

As matters escalated, a blast of dragon fire lit up the stadium, bathing the crowd in a rush of fierce heat. It was unclear whether this was a pre-planned victory celebration or a desperate attempt by the dragons' riders to quell the rising tide of riot flooding the stadium.

Whatever the cause, a second scorching blast served to quieten the crowd.

The assembled masses calmed, and the members of the executive box awkwardly righted themselves. Hartley stood up, disentangling himself from Ivy and releasing her hand. She hadn't wanted to move.

"What a bloody farce," Woodbane growled, shaking his head, as the crowd settled themselves. "Who gave that damned flyin' faerie a free pass, that's what I'd like ter know! As if they don't have it easy enough already. Bloody farce."

"Wouldn't blame you if you felt short-changed here, Ramston," Bladlow wheedled, patting himself down. Bladlow had attempted to squeeze himself under his seat during the panic. Bladlow's clothes were now in significant disarray; the seat had not fared much better. "We'll make it up to you," he continued, desperately attempting to restore some dignity. "Shall we head to another venue, perhaps?"

"No, no – I'll be headin' on home! Not your fault, old boy," Woodbane said, slapping Bladlow on the back, which didn't help the mage's efforts to compose himself. "Told 'em it'd never work. Need to stick to yer own in sport."

Ivy knew exactly what that meant. She saw Skelton's jaw muscle twitch as Bladlow nodded along in agreement. Ivy looked at Hartley appraisingly, but his expression was inscrutable.

As the rest of the crowd began to file grudgingly from their seats, the group agreed to call it a night, and instead hold a good, old-fashioned celebratory feast when the new solution had been approved and went into mass production at Woodbane's facility.

As they squeezed down the steps, carefully stepping over a groaning human who had unwisely picked a fight with a wolf, Hartley looked at Ivy and sighed, "Well, that's that, I suppose."

"It's a shame it ended so quickly," Ivy said. She meant it, but not because she had been enjoying the sport. She was still thinking about the warmth of his hand around hers.

"Agreed," said Hartley, fixing his grey-blue eyes on her, a fierce intensity to his expression. The dragons rose high into the sky above them, assignment completed, and for a moment Ivy almost felt herself soar with them.

Hartley and Ivy exited the stadium together, shoulder to shoulder, nudged forward by the sullen press of the crowd, before parting ways with an unspoken mutual reluctance.

Ivy had returned to her chambers the following morning having spent her entire journey replaying her conversation with Hartley, gazing into the middle distance even more vacantly than usual as the Deep Cart rattled along, thinking about his voice, his touch.

She arrived, feeling tired but strangely buoyant, to find her crystal display flashing ominously. Expecting to see Skelton's face swirl into view as she gingerly pressed her palm to the crystal, she instead smiled in surprise when she saw a message from Hartley, requesting a call back. Closing the door to her chambers (much to Bob's dismay when he sauntered by for his morning nap a few minutes later), she returned Hartley's call, her heart racing.

"Ivy," he said warmly. He was half-grinning at her, his face flickering slightly as the temperamental magic of the crystal display sputtered grudgingly into use. He ran his hand absently through his thick hair, a habitual motion that Ivy was finding increasingly comforting. "I just thought I would check in on the Woodbane matter," he continued. "I completely forgot to speak to you about it last night in all the excitement…"

Ivy's heart sank slightly at these words. This was clearly a work call, nothing more than that. "It's all going fine," she answered as coolly as she could manage. "We're still casting small batches of ingredients while we're waiting on Regulator approval to come through."

"Great… that's great," Hartley said, before hesitating. Ivy suspected that was all Hartley needed, but found herself not wanting to be the one to end the conversation.

However, it seemed Hartley was experiencing a similar moment of indecision, much to Ivy's surprise. "Well… I suppose that was why I was calling…" he said stiffly.

There was another pause. "Bit of a weak pretext, really," he then admitted, clearly having come to some sort of resolution. "I just wanted to speak to you again."

Ivy smiled widely. The two then continued to talk, haltingly at first and then ever more freely and exuberantly.

They discussed everything and nothing; last night's game, historic encounters with some of the more idiosyncratic Masters in the Tower (which were admittedly most of them), arcane words used in dragon binding spells, first pets and first spells, and countless other topics beside. Ivy found herself detailing her childhood in New Charnford – something she had never discussed with anyone else in the Citadel, describing games of hide and seek amongst the ruins of the great Citadel of Charnford. Hartley, meanwhile, regaled her with dry anecdotes about his own upbringing and the interminable familial pressures which came with being a fifth generation Citadel mage.

As they spoke on, Ivy forgot all the work she had to do, all her tiredness, all her frustration. She also remained oblivious to the vast tiger scratching morosely at her door.

10.

SEEDLINGS

As late summer slouched sullenly into autumn, Ivy found herself busier than ever. New requests landed on her desk as fast as she could draft and cast them.

Goliath Investments wanted a charm to remove an infestation of critterlings munching at their foundations, the Futures Exchange had an unforeseen issue involving a particularly malevolent water fountain, some accountants wanted an incantation which kept their associates awake during a file review, the Opera House wanted to add some pizzazz to their lighting, Phoenica wanted some sales brochures enchanted so that their contents were magically tailored to each individual (Ivy didn't even know where to start with that one). The list went on. She hadn't even touched the complicated shielding castings for Dragonsteel.

Amidst the frenetic activity, she also had to allocate time for further castings with Skelton on the Woodbane project, producing small quantities of synthetic Restricted Substances on a nightly basis. Skelton was exhibiting a mania even more pronounced than usual. Ivy wondered whether he was anxious about the imminent demands of mass production.

One night, after a particularly draining Woodbane casting, she had finally peeled herself from her desk, walked towards her door and started to unhook her outercloak. At this movement, Skelton's head had bobbed up from the papers he had been perusing across the corridor and he had shouted across at her, exceedingly amiably, "A bit chilly in here tonight, isn't it?" At that, Ivy had frozen in her tracks, realising there was no option other than to mumble an assent, pull on her outercloak, and return to her desk.

She had also been speaking to Hartley on a daily basis, keeping him updated on the progress of the project and her day-to-day activities. She desperately wanted to see him again, but she knew that without a genuine pretext for a meeting, any independent socialising with her extremely handsome client would be the subject of intense suspicion and might cost her her job – junior mages had been expelled for far lesser breaches of Tower ethics. And Ivy wasn't sure she could trust herself around Hartley and that winning grin of his.

She nevertheless remained alert to the possibility of somehow engineering another assignation, although her fear of repercussions prevented her from being the one to offer a meeting. Hartley offered nothing either, save for one occasion where – after she had expressed her frustrations about the restrictions on her magic at the Tower – Hartley had suggested giving her a proper tour of the Woodbane facility, so that she could see their industrial magic in action. This was exactly what she had been hoping for.

However, an image of Skelton looking thoroughly disappointed had quite unfairly fixed itself in her mind at that moment. She found herself completely unable to give in to her desire, instead mumbling something about the demands of her current workload making such a trip impossible. She had kicked herself hard after that, and the opportunity to escape into Hartley's imagined embrace did not present itself again.

In truth, her workload *was* demanding, and whenever she did manage to leave the confines of the Tower, she found she could do little else but fall into fitful sleep. She would wake feeling groggy and displaced, with the vague impression that something had been attempting to reach her, something ancient and yet unborn. She had little appetite and could feel her already skinny frame – the product of a childhood of under-nourishment in one of the more war-scarred regions of Kirin – becoming ever more emaciated.

Yet still she worked on, ever more tiredly, living for the casting ceremonies, running on a potent mix of adrenalin and exhaustion. She was certain that the tiredness was having some sort of effect on her magic – lately she had found that, much to her dismay, any attempts at using her magic outside of her work were resulting in erratic effects.

One evening she had attempted to magically activate the lights in her chambers and it had not gone well. The lights had flickered sporadically for about ten minutes before erupting into violent spasms of red, green and pewter, accompanied by a fluorescent rainbow which spun chaotically around the chambers, bouncing off her bookcases. After a panicked fifteen minutes she had finally stumbled upon the cosmic off-switch, resolving that at some point she would need to figure out what the bloody hell was wrong with her.

✦

Ivy's life of restless circles was sharply interrupted with a crash one afternoon when Bob skidded into her chambers, holding something small and brown in his massive jaws.

At times like these, it was very important for a person to tell the monkey-brain operating its human user *very firmly* that it was not faced with a giant tiger. Unfortunately, some reactions are hardwired, and it turns out to be extremely difficult to tell oneself that the immense, sharp-toothed predator which has just pounced in front you is actually merely an over-sized tom cat.

Ivy pressed herself against the internal window behind her and swore loudly.

Bob himself was startled by this reaction and shied away, dropping what was in his mouth and inadvertently knocking over an internal Umping basket, which only served to startle him further.

"For Gods' sakes, Bob!" Ivy shouted in shock, as the tiger thumped into a pile of discarded drafts and sent them wheeling. Bob peered up at her apologetically, calmed himself down and gently nudged the mouthful he had dropped towards her feet.

It was the stick creature. It seemed to be alive, but barely.

Ivy leant down and picked it up. "Was this your fault, you great bully?" Ivy asked Bob accusingly.

Bob simply nosed her palm tenderly as she lifted the small body.

Its large eyes were closed and its mouth was tightly clenched. Its breathing came in small ragged gasps, which made the tiny leaves sprouting from its twig-like limbs tremble and judder. Ivy could see that the creature didn't look well, but she didn't have the faintest idea what to do about it.

"What am I supposed to do?" Ivy asked the tiger, who remained silent. "I don't even know what this thing is, let alone how to help it…" Ivy ran through a mental list of where she might be able to take it…

Taryn, she thought suddenly. Taryn might know what to do.

She bundled up the creature and headed down to Taryn's third floor chambers, Bob padding silently behind her.

✦

Taryn was at her desk, scribbling furiously, when there was a knock at the door.

"Come in," she said wearily, hoping it wasn't Master Stanforth again. He'd made another attempt to offload his children's decrepit llamacorn on her earlier.

Instead of the genial Master, however, it was Ivy who entered, cradling a small bundle of twigs and leaves, followed by Bob.

Taryn had never felt comfortable around the tiger, however much the Castings team insisted he was 'just a big softie really'. To Taryn, Bob represented five hundred pounds of twitching muscle, situated directly behind jaws designed to snap necks. The beast did, however, seem utterly devoted to the girl standing before her, a fact which caused Taryn an unsolicited pang of envy.

"Taryn, have you got a minute?"

"Not really," said Taryn, shortly. It was the truth, but that wasn't why she said it. She sighed. "But I suppose you're here now. Close the door behind you."

Taryn looked down at the small bundle as Ivy laid it on her desk. A curious expression crossed her face.

"Where did you find it?" she asked softly.

"I didn't," said Ivy. "It sort of found me. And then it disappeared for a while. And then I guess Bob found it again." Ivy shot the tiger a sharp look. Bob was now sprawled across Taryn's floor, redolent with imperious indolence as he batted a vine which was trailing lethargically from one of the plants bursting from the cramped shelves.

"Hmm…" mused Taryn, examining the creature intently. "I'm not sure Bob is actually to blame in this instance," she said slowly. "It looks more dehydrated than mauled. Almost like it's overheated…"

Taryn gently prodded the creature, a strange expression on her face. "You do realise what this creature is, don't you, Ivy…?" she asked Ivy solemnly.

Ivy shrugged. "I don't, actually. Is it some sort of wood sprite?"

"No," Taryn said, shaking her head. "It's a seedling." Ivy knew by the way she said it that this meant something important, but Taryn didn't elucidate further. "I haven't seen one since I was a child, and that was only the once and a long way from the Citadel. When did you first see it?"

"It just turned up one evening in my chambers. It was a couple of weeks ago, maybe? It ran up my arm and then hid in a bookcase, where it went to sleep. I didn't see it again after that and to be honest I had forgotten about it until Bob dragged it in earlier."

Taryn was still staring at the creature with that odd expression.

"I was wondering, though, whether it might have come from *that*…" Ivy said, gesturing past Taryn and through the grubby glass of the internal window.

Taryn's eyes followed Ivy's gesture towards the trunk of the magnificent tree. "Hmm," Taryn said in a non-committal tone.

Not offering any more than that, Taryn then started scrabbling around in drawers and plucking outlandishly shaped glassware from her shelves. A couple of books tumbled to the floor and a lively cactus did something which looked suspiciously like a sneeze as dust cascaded onto its topsoil. She placed a large beaker of water on her cluttered desk and started adding droplets of liquid from various vials into it.

"Do you think it might have done? Come from the tree, I mean?" Ivy pressed.

"I don't know," Taryn said, honestly. The creature's arrival had unnerved her. "Perhaps," she conceded. "Seedlings are extremely rare. Most mages don't believe they exist – if they've even heard of them." She swilled the liquid around in a beaker and then ferreted out a pipette. She drew some of the solution from the beaker and held the pipette aloft. "Could you just hold it gently please, Ivy, while I feed it some of this?"

Taryn carefully squeezed a couple of drops into the creature's mouth. It made a little sucking sound and opened its large black-brown eyes, which glistened darkly. After a couple more drops, it suddenly scrambled with astonishing speed up Ivy's forearm and leapt onto her breast, where it clutched at her with thorny little fingers. She clasped her hands over it protectively.

"Well, that seemed to do the trick," Ivy said approvingly. "Thank you, Taryn. I wasn't sure who else to ask, and given–" she waved at the various plants waging their interminable battle against the inanimate occupants of the room "–all this, I thought it was worth a shot."

Taryn acknowledged Ivy's gratitude stiffly.

"What sort of feed solution is it?" Ivy asked, as the seedling scampered down Ivy's back, onto Bob – who batted at it lazily – and up onto the shelves, poking at the other plants curiously, constantly chirruping.

"It's the mix Bladlow instructed me to brew for the tree down there, just not as potent."

"You feed the tree?" Ivy looked out at its vast trunk thoughtfully as Taryn nodded. "Can't you just use a growth or fortifying spell on it?"

"It would take a great deal of power to maintain and would be unstable. Solutions are the way to go," Taryn replied confidently.

Ivy mused at this. To her mind, the giant tree still didn't look well, whatever they were feeding it. She was curious, though; especially if it was somehow connected to the little creature now pottering around chirpily. "What type of tree is it?" she asked, not wanting to let the subject drop.

"It's an ancient chestnut," said Taryn tersely. "About 400 years old at least. There aren't many of them left." Taryn gazed at its softly bristling branches.

"Do you know why it's here? Who it came from? How it got here?"

Taryn didn't answer, but instead glanced at the seedling, which was affectionately stroking an exotic bloom. "Look, Ivy, I'm not sure what this thing is doing here," she said quietly, gesturing at the seedling, "but you should keep it out of sight. Don't ask why. I just think, for now, it might be for the best."

Ivy looked at her curiously, but nodded as she stood up to leave.

The seedling swung down onto Ivy's shoulder from the shelf, where it had been listening to some rather salacious gossip from the perfumed chrysanthechid.

Taryn put a stopper into the beaker with the feed solution and passed it to Ivy. "Twice a day," she prescribed.

"Thanks, Taryn, I really appreciate it."

Bob stretched and arched his back, padding after Ivy as she left. Taryn once again felt the sharp pang. What was so special about this girl who never seemed to need to work for anything?

And now, the girl had acquired a seedling – a seedling!

Taryn leaned back contemplatively. A seedling. Here, in the Tower. What was that supposed to mean? Its presence didn't change anything, though. Besides, she knew what she was doing – Bladlow had discussed it all with her and she was carefully monitoring matters. The work was still the work and it had to be done. It was too late to start doubting things now.

Taryn noticed a shadow rippling across her desk. Through the internal window behind her, the late afternoon sunlight was filtering wanly through the Tower's large domed skylight, catching like honey in the leaves of the ancient chestnut. She really should go home soon. Her real home. Her hand moved instinctively towards her top drawer.

Taryn studied the tree with a worried expression, before opening the drawer and wrapping her fingers around the misshapen glass neck of a bottle, her thoughts lost in the memory of sleepy woodlands, a half-remembered pair of large dark eyes glinting down from a canopy of thick, verdant green.

✦

Ivy made her way back upstairs to her chambers, trying to shield the seedling from view with her hand.

"So, little seedling," she murmured to the small, twig-like creature clinging to her breast, "if you're going to stick around like this–" Ivy congratulated herself on the pun "–we should probably give you a name."

It chirruped up at her solemnly.

"So what shall it be?" mused Ivy. "Twiglet?"

The creature gave a definite snort.

"No? How about Seedum? Nut? You'd make an excellent Nut."

More strange snorts, accompanied by clicks like the sound of feet snapping branches.

"Fine, fine. Not those." Ivy paused. "I don't know. I've never met a seedling before you. Didn't even know you were a thing, to be honest."

Ivy had reached her chambers now, still cradling the creature, gently stroking its large pod-head.

"You stay out here for now," she said firmly to Bob, who looked up at her dejectedly. She entered the room and shut the door, placing the seedling on the desk and gently disentangling its twiggy claws from her chest.

"Let's get you some water." Ivy located the jug of water she normally kept on the shelf next to her desk. She tried to find something to pour it onto, eventually locating an old, abandoned plate. "You might need to ignore the mould," she said apologetically, before adding, "unless you like that sort of thing."

She dribbled some water onto the plate and watched as the seedling moved its small body closer, looking up at Ivy with a wide-eyed, questioning stare, before gingerly placing a foot-root in the pool of water.

"There you go," said Ivy gently. "I'll give you some more of this stuff Taryn made later on, if you like. Hopefully you'll feel better soon."

The creature chirruped melodiously.

"Kork," said Ivy suddenly, surprising herself.

The seedling looked up at her curiously.

"Will that do?" she asked it. "For a name, I mean?"

It chirruped. It would do.

There was a knock at the door. The newly named Kork skittered off the desk and crouched behind Ivy's legs. She felt it prickle the backs of her calves.

"Come in," said Ivy.

Lil entered, a little out of breath, her ragged wings slowly flapping. "Ivy, I think you need to come down to the Quiet Rooms..."

"Why?" Ivy enquired.

"Dante's going at it with that auditor and, well, they're not exactly being *quiet* and some of the stuff that's being said... it's about the Woodbane process. Let's put it this way, the auditor is making some pretty wild claims... "

"Fine, I'll come down," Ivy sighed. "Let me just finish something quickly. I'll be there in a minute." Once Lil had left, Ivy looked down at Kork. "Are you going to be okay up here?" she whispered.

Kork clacked and tilted his large seed-pod head.

"Fine. I'll be back in a bit." She noticed Bob lingering expectantly outside the door. "Don't let that over-sized cat give you any grief, okay?" she advised the seedling, before giving the tiger a stern look and following Lil down the corridor.

11.

QUIET WORDS

Hop Pockett had been installed in one of the Quiet Rooms next to the large library on the second floor.

Sadly, Hop had not been granted access to the great library itself, which was manned – or more correctly, 'trolled' – on a constant basis. The security troll was a veritable boulder of a being, guarding the entrance with single-minded intent. It had clocked Hop's lack of an official library card immediately and Hop's attempts to play the Regulator card had fallen on moss-covered ears. Hop found this unfair, particularly given that he had once seen a mage gain access by presenting the security troll with a sheet of crumpled notepaper. Hop had tried the trick using some archaic headed notepaper he had found in a vaguely sinister stationery cupboard on the third floor, which he hadn't seen before and hadn't been able to locate since. His attempts had proved futile, the troll refusing to budge no matter what carbon-based offering was provided.

Having reluctantly abandoned the prospect of spending happy hours perusing magical textbooks and precedents, Hop had proceeded with his special audit, the subject of which was now being ventilated across the corridor during a heated debate with Dante. Ivy and Lil could hear the raised voices from quite some distance as they approached.

"What Skelton claims he is doing is simply not possible!" Hop was shouting.

"You have absolutely no idea what you are talking about!"

"I have more of an idea than you!"

Ivy and Lil entered Quiet Room Three and Ivy shut the door, hearing a soft *glup* as the room insulated itself from the outside world. Mercifully, the shouting would now be muffled.

The windowless Quiet Rooms were a space designated for mages who wanted to work away from the hustle of the upper floors. However, the Masters took a dim view of any mage unable to work effectively whilst bombarded with interruptions and took an even dimmer view of mages who did not remain *exactly* where they could see them. As such, the Quiet Rooms were generally only used for indiscretions and the more uncomfortable personnel meetings, which usually concerned mages who had not been sufficiently discreet about their indiscretions.

Quiet Room Three was, however, currently being used as Hop's base of operations. It was filled with boxes, all neatly stacked and labelled. A large piece of paper occupied most of one wall, covered with careful handwritten notes and various connecting lines. Most of the lines terminated at a fastidiously rendered question mark.

Dante and Hop wheeled round to register Ivy and Lil's entry. Hop was out of breath and red in the face and Dante had clearly been running his hands through his hair in agitation. Both attempted to regain their composure, Hop pushing his glasses back up the bridge of his nose.

Dante took a deep breath. "Wotcher, Ivy. I see Lil's invited you to join the fun," he noted. "Mr Auditor and I have just been discussing that Woodbane casting of yours. He seems to have got it into his head that it doesn't work, which naturally is complete nonsense."

"On the contrary," Hop said firmly. "Trebbletuft himself tried for decades, to no avail."

"Yes, well, we all know what happened to Trebbletuft, so let's not cite him as a reliable source," countered Dante.

"What happened to Trebbletuft?" Lil asked Ivy in an undertone.

"I think he combusted," Ivy whispered back. "Pretty spectacularly, by all accounts."

Hop puffed himself up as he continued. "No mage has ever been able to synthesize magical matter for any length of time, certainly not at scale. And yet that's what this–" Hop flapped what appeared to be a regulatory clearance application in front of Dante's face "–submission claims you are doing."

"Have you even read that piece of paper you're wafting around?" Dante demanded contemptuously.

"I have indeed. I'll have you know that it provides literally no useful information about the process. In fact, it's startling how many words are in here that don't actually say anything!"

"Sounds about right…" Ivy muttered.

Dante rolled his eyes. "And what exactly does the Regulator think? *They* seemed satisfied with the application."

"The Regulator didn't find any reason not to proceed on the basis of the original submission. But they had their doubts and want to look into this premium product more closely. That's why I'm here," Hop said, sticking his chin out and pausing momentarily for effect, "*investigating.*"

Dante muttered darkly.

Hop ignored him and pressed on, his voice rising in pitch and tone. "Whilst I appreciate that I am not a *mage*, what I do know is magical theory and Trebbletuft's Principle provides that it is impossible to transform base matter into *stable* magical matter without siphoning energy from a potent magical source. To do that at a mass production level is inconceivable – all you mages can do is channel enough magic for temporary tricks and illusions! What makes you seriously believe you can achieve this sort of alchemical sorcery? Everything you do needs constant 'topping up' and nothing ever seems to work properly in the first place!"

"To be fair, he has a point…" muttered Ivy.

Hop continued firmly, "Skelton's submission provides no useful context on where he is transferring the magical energy from, leading me to doubt he is actually achieving it. Nor does he explain how he intends to find a source great enough to replicate it at scale. Which, as I have clearly explained, is completely impossible," said Hop, firmly.

"Only insofar as your limited imagination would have you believe," retorted Dante, throwing his arms up in the air. "I think you just can't accept that we might be doing something here that's beyond your little rulebook of the universe! Why shouldn't we be able to create magical matter? We're bloody *mages* for Gods' sake! Normal rules don't apply!"

"It's against Trebbletuft's Principle!"

"I swear, if you mention Trebbletuft's bloody Principle again–"

At this, Ivy felt the air in the room blister.

Reality momentarily jarred. Hop looked disconcerted.

Ivy watched as Lil moved closer to Dante and put a warning hand on his arm. The air cooled abruptly.

"Can I just say something?" said Ivy, having had just about enough by this point. "I'm the only one here who has actually been doing these castings and the ingredients we've made during the ceremonies have felt magical enough to me."

"Thank you, Ivy!" interrupted Dante dramatically, never taking his eyes off Hop.

Hop adjusted his glasses. "Yes, well, it's all very well *feeling* something," he sniffed critically, "but how do you actually *know*? Did you investigate the components you created, test them for magical properties? Examine the molecular structure?"

"Not at the time, no…" replied Ivy.

"Would you know a real goblin spleen from a fake one? Be able to distinguish – on sight alone – a genuine unicorn horn from a fabrication? Actual faerie dust from normal dust?"

"Well, no… but I saw the matter transformed. And so did Caspar."

"And did you and Caspar remain in possession of these items? Check they remained 'transformed'? Follow their journey during the brewing process?"

"To be frank, I haven't been much good for anything except sleeping after the castings. Solutions have been handling all of that. But I know that the ingredients must work – I watched Mrs Woodbane test the solution, although it's an image I'm trying to forget…"

"I'll second that it works," Lil chimed in. "Dawn in Accounts says she used the original solution and it took years off her. She's livid that she can't get hold of it at the moment. I'm thinking of placing a pre-order on the premium version. Would do me the world of good after all the stress of working with you lot, I feel like I'm constantly topping up my little illusions these days…"

Dante had been pacing the room, but suddenly stopped. "Holy llamacorns…" he said slowly, interrupting Lil's wittering, "That's it, isn't it? I think I've just worked out where you're going with this… You really are quite mad, aren't you, Mr Auditor…? You think we're switching what Skelton's been producing for *real* ingredients…"

Hop frowned, clearly considering whether to continue down this path. An astute observer might have noticed a small sliver of doubt appear in his eyes as the remit of his original brief from the Regulator resurfaced in his memory. Unfortunately, Hop was relishing his moment in the limelight, and so ploughed on regardless. "That is my working theory at this stage, yes."

"But if *that's* true… there's faerie dust in those solutions… isn't there?" Lil said quietly, shocked. Her wings gave an involuntary shudder.

Dante was shaking his head in disbelief. "This is beyond insanity… You can't *seriously* be suggesting that the ingredients used in the Woodbane Solution are actual Restricted Substances? It would be a fundamental breach of the Accords! I know people think mages only care about profit, but no one here is that bloody stupid!"

"Are you so certain?" Hop queried. "You'd be surprised the lengths people go to in order to make a profit."

"Yes, but that's Dark Market stuff! It would be professional suicide! You'd be handed over to the grimlings!"

"It's funny you should mention the Dark Market," Hop said. "You may not be aware of this, but there was a strikingly similar product to the Woodbane Solution on the Dark Market a while back. It was very popular, and it was *not* being made with synthesised materials…"

"Gods, I remember that..." said Lil. "Someone I know got hold of some. Worked just like this stuff. Everyone was going gaga for it until suddenly no one could get it anymore. It didn't even occur to me at the time that it might contain faerie dust..." Lil looked uncharacteristically solemn as she tailed off.

"Yes, well, I happen to have read some very revealing papers–" (Hop had found some old newspaper articles) "–which indicated that someone inside one of the Citadel Towers was supplying the Dark Market with the illegal solution, leading me to conclude that it may not be beyond the realms of possibility." Hop savoured the sentence with a renewed smugness that caused Dante's blood to boil.

"I can't believe I'm hearing this, can you?" Dante exclaimed, appealing to Lil and Ivy. He jabbed his finger at Hop. "I think *you've* gone beyond the realms of possibility."

A silence followed. "If what you are saying is true..." Ivy said slowly, "then we're all in a lot of trouble..."

The room went quiet for a moment as the group reflected on this.

Then Dante seemed to shake himself. "You're all completely mad if you think this ludicrous theory is worth pursuing," he exclaimed. "You don't have the first idea about the Dark Market or what it would take to–" Dante stopped abruptly and clenched his fists.

"Hop," intervened Ivy, "Dante's got a point, this is a lot to take on board. I think we all need to have a think before we jump to any conclusions."

"I for one won't be doing any jumping," confirmed Dante resolutely. "I can't listen to this madness anymore, and neither should you two," he added pointedly to Ivy and Lil. With that, he brandished a palm. The door crashed magically open and he stormed out.

✦

Ivy walked back to her chambers alongside Lil. As they ascended the stairwell up to the fifth floor, Ivy noticed that Lil's skin had lost some of its usual shimmer and firmness.

"Do you really think there's something to all this business?" Ivy asked.

"I don't know," sighed Lil. "I really hope not." She paused, before adding, "You do know where faerie dust comes from, don't you?"

"I have to admit that I don't. All I know is that it's on the Restricted Substances list. I've never seen any real faerie dust, apart from the stuff we've been making for Woodbane, which apparently may not be real after all. Bloody felt real though… the magic, Lil, you have no idea…" Ivy trailed off, before realising that she had digressed. "Sorry, Lil, you were saying?"

"Faeries had it tough during the wars. We're not really good for anything much, you see…" Lil continued plodding up the stairs, a tone of dejection in her voice. "We've got wings, can make a pretty mean brew, can do the odd illusion here and there maybe, but most of our 'magic' is too far inside us to reach. It's baked in. In our skin, our blood, our bones. Doesn't really do much, or at least most of us have long forgotten how to use it if it does."

Lil had begun to breathe heavily. For a moment, she looked disconcertingly older.

"You need to kill a faerie to get their dust," Lil said between huffs. "It isn't like dandruff, falling out of us if you give us a jiggle. We need to be all ground up. We were hunted like animals for centuries. Got really good at disappearing. Took us a long while after the Accords to feel safe enough to come and join 'polite society'.

"I still remember my grandmother telling me tales of the bad old days. Nasty stuff. They didn't stop at fully grown faeries, neither… If that's all happening again, well…" Lil shook her head and changed the subject abruptly. "Gods, these stairs are torture…"

"You could have taken the lift," noted Ivy, "or, you know, fluttered up, or whatever."

"Hah, these bloody wings are useless these days. Too tired, too bloody tired."

Ivy was at this moment acutely aware of exactly how old Lil was for a faerie.

"I think I'm just going to get my things and head home early tonight," Lil said. "I'm not in the mood for work."

"That sounds like a sensible idea. I might try to escape early today, too. I've been feeling so tired recently."

"Well, make sure you do. Work too hard, you do. Besides, everyone will be busy focusing on tomorrow," Lil said, a small twinkle returning to her eyes. "They're announcing the Citadel Tower Rankings in the morning…"

"Gods, I'd completely forgotten. Is it really that time of year again? I wonder how we'll do…"

"Hopefully pretty well. I saw some of the submissions. Be nice to think about something a bit less depressing after all this business, anyway."

They had reached Ivy's chambers.

"Agreed," said Ivy, as she pushed open the door. "See you in the morning. Try not to worry. I'm certain there's nothing to it.

Hop's just desperate for something to be going on so that he can justify his existence. I don't think he's going to find anything."

"Let's hope so."

Lil ambled off, wings drooping down her back, her usually perfect hair hanging lank against her neck.

Ivy entered her chambers and closed the door behind her. Kork was chirpily skittering about a disgruntled Bob, who every now and then patted his paw at the seedling in weary irritation. The plate of water was empty.

As she sat at her desk, Kork clambered up her arm and perched on her shoulder, chirruping gently. "You seem perkier," Ivy said, smiling slightly, before frowning as she tried to unpick the earlier conversation.

Was there anything to what Hop was saying? She tried to remember the casting ceremonies, the way the power had crackled through her body. They were intense, but had she felt any different to when she'd cast any other complex spell? Perhaps not.

What about the components they had produced? She remembered the glistening organs on the altar, the dust that shimmered in the manner so reminiscent of Lil's skin. They had certainly looked real. But were they really magical? How would she even know? And even if they were magical, how could she be sure they had stayed that way? Ivy tried to contemplate the alternative, the possibility that Hop's substitution theory was correct, that they had been undertaking an atrocity in the name of profit.

Surely Skelton wouldn't risk sacrificing his career on the altar of progress? Surely Woodbane wouldn't risk his business? She recalled the disparaging way Woodbane had spoken about other species during the Grand Game; he clearly had little regard for the other races that populated the Citadel. But would he go so far as to treat those races as beasts fit only for slaughter?

And Hartley… *Hartley*… Would he be capable of participating in such an undertaking…? Ivy went over and over their last few conversations in her head. Part of her wanted to speak to him, to hear him reassure her that Hop was being ridiculous.

Her crystal display started to flash. Hartley?

It was Skelton. "Ivy, excellent, you're still here. I couldn't find you earlier. Can I have a quiet word please? Thanks." Not giving her chance to reply, he terminated the call. She trudged across the corridor to his chambers.

"Sit, sit," Skelton motioned to her. Ivy took a seat. Skelton continued to shuffle paperwork for a moment before looking up at her.

"We will need to undertake further Woodbane casting ceremonies as mass production approaches. However," Skelton said, scrutinising her closely, "I think it's perhaps time for you to have a little break. A couple of days, maybe."

This was a surprise; she had been certain he had called her across to accompany him down to the Crypt for another casting. She had been considering whether to interrogate him about Hop's theories, but now there was only one question she could ask.

"A break?" she said weakly. Ivy had been at Jackdaw and Spittlelick long enough to know that 'breaks' were simply not offered; you worked, or you were off the project. Her heart sank. Did Skelton no longer believe her capable?

"You've been putting in the hours, that's clear to see, so yes, a break. Just a temporary one, I hope. We can review in a couple of days. Perhaps Caspar can pick up any castings in the meantime. That will be all tonight, Ivy."

She said nothing in response, but returned to her chambers, stricken with a tight anxiety that overrode any concerns she had felt about the Woodbane process. Kork skittered down from her desk and landed on Bob as the vast tiger arched his back in a deep stretch, before bouncing up onto a bookcase, cooing gently.

Ivy stared blankly ahead, as the little seedling tilted his head and looked down at her with his dark, black-brown eyes.

✦

Somewhere on the edge of the sleeping Citadel, a person – who categorically shouldn't have been where they currently were – was quietly searching for something.

The cloaked figure found it in a cavernous stone outhouse; a magnificent infernal machine, scaled with metallic silver and rust, sat idling.

The figure hefted a large bag onto the charred and dusty floor and pulled out a blade whose edge shimmered with the gleam of dragonsteel. It glinted evilly in the darkness.

The infernal machine remained still. The only sound in the room was a quiet hum, punctured by the sound of the sword whipping through the air as the figure swung it gently, testing its weight.

The figure approached the target slowly, tentatively. Still no movement.

There was a new sound now; the quiet words of a long dead language being murmured.

The infernal machine slowly raised itself from its moorings, now aloft but still solidly indifferent.

The figure lifted the blade again. Surely it couldn't be this easy?

The blade swung.

12.

RANKLINGS
━━━✦━━━

It was the morning of the release of the Citadel Tower Rankings.

The Rankings had been introduced just over a decade ago. Each of the five Towers were 'rated' on the basis of the performance and delivery of their magical services, with individual mages being singled out for acclaim. Those ratings were compiled by an independent outfit, mostly comprising non-mages (including one or two grimlinged mages who had been allowed to re-enter certain circles of polite magery) and then published annually as the Rankings.

The ostensible aim of the Rankings was to provide clients with a helpful directory of magical practitioners, enabling them to make an informed decision when selecting a Tower for any piece of magical business. Unfortunately, there had been a miscommunication with the small troll press which handled the publication and distribution of the Rankings. The trolls delivered copies to each of the Towers, assuming the mages were arranging for onward distribution. The mages were unaware of this, and weren't. The mages therefore happily presumed that anyone of importance in the Citadel would be awaiting the arrival of the Rankings on publication morning with the same excitement levels as they were. This was not the case.

The result was that the Rankings were only read by mages, although this was ultimately no great loss; every mage secretly knew that it was only the opinion and esteem of other mages that mattered.

Taryn Underfoot had arrived at the Tower to find the building humming. She approached the sounds of merriment and chortling with a feeling of intense trepidation, locating their source in the first floor Eating Hall (mages could be relatively literal when naming things).

Upon entering the Eating Hall, Taryn noticed that the ageing stone water fountain near the wide doors had been transformed in a fit of celebratory excitement. The weathered old gargoyle that usually spouted fresh spring water was now spurting out a sparkling golden liquid in violent sputters from its gaping jaw. Bubbles also emanated sporadically from one of its nostrils and some of the liquid had started trickling from a pointed ear.

Citadel mages really struggled with incidental magic.

What they were not struggling with was giving one another resounding pats on the back. Jackdaw and Spittlelick appeared to have performed well. Taryn could see Master Flartstrop hooting away to one of the junior Futures mages, recounting what he evidently believed to be a humorous anecdote. She looked like she'd seen the punchline coming.

"Wotcher," said Dante, breaking off from a small group of mages and strolling over to Taryn. He grabbed a glass brimming with sickly gold nectar from the table next to the gargoyle, which had inexplicably started to whistle.

"Not too early for you to start?" he asked Taryn, raising a sardonic eyebrow as he handed her the glass.

She took it. In truth, it hadn't been that many hours ago that she'd stopped.

"Thanks," she said.

Dante clinked his glass against hers. "Cheers. Not sure I feel much like celebrating today to be honest, though. Did you see the news this morning?"

"I did," said Taryn stiffly. "Bloody awful."

"Apparently," Dante said, "they found her washed up on the banks of the Clude. Horrible stuff. There'll be an inquest, but people are saying she jumped. Not a word from any of the Masters on it this morning, not that I expected any better from them, so pre-occupied with their own little triumphs…" he trailed off darkly.

Taryn said nothing for a moment, before changing the subject abruptly. "Go on then, what's the damage?"

Dante and Taryn rehearsed this ritual every year. They had both started their apprenticeship at the same time and had maintained friendly relations across disciplines, despite this being awkward whenever the inevitable divisional battle lines were drawn. The two of them had historically found much amusement in discussing the inevitable internal politics that accompanied the annual delivery of the 'Ranklings' (as they had dubbed them). It was clear that neither of them felt particularly enthused this morning as Dante impassively recounted the standings.

"Jackdaw in second, missed out on the top spot, which went – surprise, surprise – to Ampleforth again. Lovett and Leavitt down to third, Pendleton Bluish fourth, Skeets fifth. We did well in the Castings category – honourable mentions to Skelton, Williamson and a few others – and Solutions did well, as always. Futures had a torrid time, though. Most of them didn't bother to turn up this morning."

"Really?" said Taryn. "So what about the Solutions entry? Anyone named and shamed?" She tried to sound offhand.

"Bladlow got a glowing review," Dante replied, carefully. "For the Woodbane Solution in particular, alongside a few other projects."

"I don't suppose…?"

"Not this time. Sorry, Taryn."

Taryn felt her throat knot. She drained her glass in a futile attempt to relax it. Dante said nothing.

"And you?" Taryn said, still aiming for casual.

"Small mention. For Dreamtime work. Despite Caspar's best efforts at torpedoing it." Dante didn't meet her eyes.

"About time," Taryn said tightly. She looked at the fountain and held her empty glass under the gargoyle's face, letting the nectar slosh in.

"Look," said Dante consolingly, "you know it's all about who controls the submissions to the Rankings Deliberation Committee. And Bladlow doesn't like to share. It's just a massive vanity project anyway. It doesn't mean anything."

Taryn could see Bladlow at the back of the Hall, bobbing away in a circle of other Masters, ruddy-faced and laughing heartily. A wave of bitter resentment coursed through her.

Dante shifted on his feet. "You're not going to like this, but… you'll find out sooner or later and it might be best if it comes from me…"

Taryn looked sharply at Dante as he took a deep breath and said, "Ivy got a mention. For Dragonsteel alongside Skelton, and… Woodbane."

Taryn felt the knot tighten. Another gulp of nectar. She looked at Dante, frowning. "But she's only just started working on the Woodbane matter..." she said quietly, haltingly. "I don't understand."

"I know, I know. It should have been Salonika really. Skelton must have spoken to the Committee, got the name amended before it went to press. Not surprising really…"

Taryn drained her glass. "Great," she said, fortifying herself with hollow sentiments. "Good for Ivy. Fantastic."

"I expect we'll be heading out to the Garbled Goblin later to celebrate. Or commiserate, if that's what's needed. You're welcome to join. Might be good for you to get out of this place in the evening for once. Like old times."

"Thanks, but it's probably not the best idea. Work to do."

She held the glass under the fountain, watched it fill. Dante raised his eyebrow again, but remained silent.

Taryn could see Ivy across the Hall, smiling as Caspar said something to Lil. "I have to get upstairs," she said shortly. "Congratulate the rest of Castings for me. And well done for making it this year."

She drained her glass, handed it unceremoniously back to Dante, and left the Hall.

Instead of heading to her chambers on the third floor, Taryn had found herself back in the foyer, staring at the giant tree, which loomed above her in solemn dismay, vast and unforgiving, magnificent in its suffocation.

It needed air. So did she.

She turned on her heels and left the Tower.

As she stepped over the threshold and into the coolness of the morning, she inhaled deeply, and continued to walk. Through the main streets and side streets, she walked. Past grand edifices and crumbling earthworks, over cobbles and paving, so far removed from the fields she had grown up with. Eventually, she had walked far enough that she had reached the Citadel's original limits.

The huge stone ramparts that encircled the city's central streets towered over her. The Citadel of North Riding (as the Citadel had once been known, back when there were more than one in Kirin) had once stood entirely contained within these walls. However, urban sprawl in recent decades had meant that buildings now stood (or, in some cases, leaned) against either side of the Citadel's immense fortifications.

Taryn stood on Pembry Street, a large, disused road that terminated at the West Gate of the Citadel. The West Gate was a colossal stone arch set within the ramparts, housing a leaden portcullis. Unlike the other entrances to the Citadel's interior, the West Gate had not been opened since before the Accords. The portcullis had long since gained a coating of rust. Dark ivy now strangled it and weeds had sprung up between its teeth.

The area around the West Gate was hushed, with sleepy houses on either side. The occupants, who were mostly working professionals simply needing somewhere to sleep off the excesses of a modern career in the Citadel, saw no need for an open road to their neighbours, there being a perfectly serviceable modern gate further along the ramparts. They therefore treated the West Gate much like the rest of the wall, as an insurmountable boundary which had nevertheless failed to contain the persistent march of progress and expansion.

Taryn found herself at the West Gate from time to time. She had first stumbled across it years ago, this giant edifice tucked away in the Citadel's rambling streets, a remnant of another age. An ornamental stone fountain, long fallen into disrepair, stood in the centre of Pembry Street, directly in front of the West Gate. It was here that Taryn finally stopped walking and sat down, facing the iron gate.

She kicked at the cobblestones with her feet. She desperately wanted a stiff drink, even though it was still early morning and she had already had more glasses of nectar than she should. She needed to stop that; it wasn't helping. It had become habitual, a way to muzzle the screaming creature in her head. She sometimes felt that if she didn't take the edge off existence, she would never stop raging at it. It had not always been this hard. She had not always been this angry.

It seemed a lifetime ago that she had first come to the Citadel to undertake her own formal training. She could still hear her grandmother's fierce voice ringing in her ears.

"Load of old cobblers, if you ask me. Bunch of showy men thinking they know magic, filled with their own cleverness. Cleverness! Hah! Citadel mages and their rules and regulations," she'd scoffed. *"They've created so many limitations they don't know how to do anything without consulting a damn committee. Forgotten what real magic is. It's all about knowing what you want to do, girl. If the intention is there, the rest will follow. That's all that needs learning."* The old woman had practically spat the last word.

Taryn had tried to reason with her grandmother at the time, tried to educate her that there could be much to learn from those showy Citadel mages. New ways of doing things. Ways which could help. Things which could make life better for them, for their neighbours and for the continent as a whole. She could be a part of it all, a part of the advancement of Kirin.

"Such grand designs, eh?" her grandmother had snorted. *"You mark me, Tarragyn Underfoot, the only advancement you'll be securing is for them that is already licking the cream from the bowl. They'll eat you up and spit you out when they're done taking from you. But who am I to tell you this, you who thinks you know it all? Grand designs, indeed..."*

She had ignored her grandmother's cynicism, confident that she would be able to make a difference with her work, a difference for which she would be justly lauded. Back then, the world had felt fresh, full of ripe and rich pickings.

But she had been working so damned hard recently, with a meagre harvest to show for it. Her cultivation projects had been sidelined, as – apparently – had she.

She had dared to dream that, her original ambitions having been thwarted, the development of the Woodbane Solution, heralded as a catalyst for progress, would perhaps at last be her route to recognition, renown, reward…

But it seemed that even that was being taken away from her. The laurels of glory were now inexplicably resting upon the head of Ivy Armstride. What was so special about this thin stripling of a girl who had come from nowhere? How had *she* taken the Woodbane project away from her? Bladlow and Skelton had cast her aside and the brilliant Ivy Armstride had replaced her as easily as she had stepped across Salonika in Castings to bask in Skelton's praise.

At this thought, Taryn pictured Salonika's sallow face during her appraisal, heard her bleak words, her broken voice. Taryn had been recounting to the young mage Skelton's suggestion that she take a break from the Woodbane project, concentrate on something less strenuous. Salonika had looked at her, drained and desolate, utterly betrayed, before pleading with her to intervene with Skelton, to tell the Master that she was still capable.

Taryn had merely advised Salonika to take it up with Skelton, saying that it wasn't her decision. And Salonika had done just that, burning those desperate words of resignation into the tight, polished wood of Skelton's desk.

Taryn thought about where Salonika was now, feeling the sadness and anger rise… Was that her future too? Cast aside and washed up?

She glared at the dark vines, slowly choking the goblin-iron latticework of the gate's grille. She needed to pull herself together. She couldn't just sit here brooding, she had too much to do. Too many responsibilities. She thought about her work at the Tower, her children in school. She rebuked herself for remembering them in that order, and then again for counting her children among her responsibilities. She would make it up to them soon, maybe take them out of the Citadel. Perhaps a trip home; it had been such a long time.

She adjusted her focus and squinted through the West Gate, knowing that somewhere on the other side, past all the cramped and crumpled buildings, lay acres of fields and woods and a sky that arced across the world.

She could always just leave. Pack some bags for her, for the children. Her partner might come too, although she struggled to remember whether they were currently on speaking terms; they so often weren't these days. Perhaps they would be if only she could release the taut ball of bitterness curled up inside her.

A holiday suddenly sounded like a very good idea.

However, Taryn knew that it would need to wait. There was simply too much to do right now and, judging by the

Rankings, she had a lot of ground to make up. Time away from work must be limited. Too many limitations, that was the problem. Something nudged at her mind at this thought. Her grandmother had said something to her when she was small. What was it? It lingered on the edge of memory like a half-lost dream. Something about the limits of the mind… or was it limits *in* the mind? She shook herself and stood up slowly. This was getting her nowhere.

She needed to see to that tree. It needed feeding. Bladlow said he had resolved her concerns about the feed mix; he would be brewing up a new recipe. At least he actually seemed to be doing some work for a change.

At the thought of the tree, the image of the seedling from yesterday appeared, scampering about her chambers.

It had chosen Ivy, not her.

What had she done wrong? Doubt was creeping in now, conflicting her further. She pushed it out. She knew what she was doing. Everything would be absolutely fine.

She looked up once more at the cast-iron portcullis before turning back towards the Tower.

✦

The tree was not absolutely fine.

It felt the mages in the Tower, laughing and joking in triumph. It rankled at their insolent mirth while it choked and burned from the inside, throbbing and sapped. It strained its roots at the grimling stone.

Nothing. It was not strong enough to break free.

It thought of the dragons which once whirled in the sky above it and dreamed of uncurling wings of hide and fire.

13.

FIRST PRINCIPLES

Ivy had been thinking a lot about principles following the encounter with Hop in the Quiet Rooms. She should have been celebrating her appearance in the Rankings, but she just felt flat.

If Hop was right that genuine Restricted Substances were being used in the Woodbane Solution in blatant breach of the Accords, then what would that mean for the Tower, for Kirin, and for her? If any foul play were discovered, then this was not going to end well for anyone.

Ivy had spent most of the day attempting to quell her anxieties, ignoring eager missives from Hop asking to speak, while also trying to concentrate on undertaking the Dragonsteel brief, which had apparently become quite urgent. She had already received several messages from Dragonsteel impressing upon her the need to finalise the security spell as a priority.

She was therefore relieved when Dante and Lil appeared late afternoon and forcefully demanded that she join them for a celebratory drink or six at the Garbled Goblin.

Ivy did not usually partake in the after-hours socialising other mages frequently enjoyed. She always seemed to have too much work to do and she had never been much of a drinker. Today, however, her mind was spinning, and she felt like – just this once – it might be *fun*. Besides, Skelton had been *quite* clear about her needing a break. Ivy was still smarting from Skelton's edict last night. Even the Rankings celebration had not been able to take the sting out of her perceived inadequacy.

So she found herself, shortly after dusk, at the door to the mages' favoured local, the Garbled Goblin.

The establishment long pre-dated the Accords, and possibly even the official founding of the Citadel. It had gone through a variety of names, usually along a goblin theme, although no one could adequately explain the current 'garbled' iteration. It had changed hands frequently, perhaps unsurprisingly given mages comprised its key clientele.

The building itself was incongruously squashed between two large steel and granite industrial structures, its exterior oak beams riddled with rough cracks and holes, its plaster looking in need of a thorough clean. The rickety old structure rambled unreservedly behind and under its neighbouring buildings, and even incomprehensibly through one.

Mages from all Towers and all disciplines would ensconce themselves in a crooked corner of the Garbled Goblin to drink away and forget the long hours spent at work. Indeed, so much 'forgetting' went on within the pub that every now and then its current owners, a couple of extremely elderly goblins – who certainly never garbled *anything*, thank you most kindly – yearned for the pre-Accords years, when mages were too preoccupied obliterating each other to cause trouble.

Warm yellow light flooded out onto the cobbles and Ivy could already hear the sound of voices raised in lively chatter, and probably even livelier debate, emanating from within.

She heaved open the oak door, which gave an exasperated creak, and shouldered her way through the throng of bodies clutching at drinks and talking animatedly.

She spotted Dante and Lil in a cramped nook, huddled around a small round table. She felt an unexpected swell of pleasure at the sight of them. Normally she felt only a mild sense of irritation on the (all too frequent) occasions one of them wandered unsolicited into her chambers. Whether it was due to the exhaustion of the past few weeks, or the anxiety provoked by yesterday's uncomfortable argument and her subsequent relegation, she didn't know, but the prospect of their company was suddenly welcome. To Ivy's surprise, they were accompanied by Hop, who was holding a large glass of frothy ale as though he wasn't entirely sure what to do with it.

As Ivy approached, Dante smiled widely and flagged her down. "Ives! You made it, fantastic! Have you got a drink? I'll get you one, if not. What do you want?"

"Thanks, Dante. Anything's fine," she said, before adding carefully, "although nothing too strong, please."

"Sure. Let me see what's on offer on the only mildly hallucinogenic menu."

Ivy wasn't sure if Dante was joking, but it was too late to stop him now, as he sauntered over to the crush of people at the bar, which was being unenthusiastically staffed by a thoroughly disenchanted faerie. Ivy was briefly reminded of Lil's history lesson yesterday and wondered if it explained why so many faeries seemed to view humans with such antipathy. It could, of course, simply be that this particular faerie was having to deal with a crowd of self-important mages, all competing to be served first.

"Did you see the news this morning?" Lil asked her, as Ivy squeezed herself behind the table. "I was so shocked–"

"Ivy," launched Hop, cutting across Lil, much to the faerie's indignation, "I'm glad you're here, I've been trying to get hold of you to discuss–"

As Hop pontificated, Ivy noticed with a jolt the tall figure who had just entered the Garbled Goblin.

Hartley.

She hadn't expected to see him tonight. As most of her body tensed with excitement at seeing the man she had spent a not insignificant amount of time wishing she could be near to again, a small but insistent part of her mind pointedly reminded her that it was ill-advised to be discussing the Woodbane project with Woodbane's in-house mage in such close proximity.

She quickly cut across Hop. "I know, I know, sorry," she said hurriedly. "Been tied up with some other things. Can we talk about it tomorrow?"

Hop frowned and was about to protest when Hartley spotted Ivy. A look of complete surprise crossed his features. He composed himself and approached, hefting the bag which was slung over his shoulder into a more comfortable position.

"Ivy, Lilirey…" Hartley declared, smiling that wolfish half-smile of his and raking a hand through his hair. "This is a nice surprise, although I should have thought I might see you here. Heard the Rankings came out this morning. Our new solution seems to have caused a few ripples…

"Mind if I join? I'm meeting someone but they haven't arrived yet, so I've got a bit of time to kill."

"Of course," confirmed Ivy, heart racing.

Hartley found a chair and positioned himself next to Ivy, carefully placing his bag at his feet. As Ivy felt the warmth of his body next to hers, she tried to remind herself sternly that not only was Hartley a client, but she had also spent a not small portion of the day turning over and over in her mind the disturbing possibility that he might be involved in the conspiracy which Hop was convinced was underway. Her hope for a relaxed and uncomplicated evening was fading fast.

"I don't believe we've had the pleasure," Hartley said to Hop, reaching out his hand. "Hartley Crumpley-Snafely, head mage at Woodbane Cosmetics."

If Hop felt excitement at the identity of the newcomer, he admirably managed not to let it show as he shook Hartley's outstretched hand. Ivy wondered if there was hope for the auditor yet. "Hop Pockett," said Hop, introducing himself. "I'm an auditor. With the Regulator. I've been investigating your new product, as it happens." Perhaps not.

"Amongst products and services for other Jackdaw clients," Ivy added swiftly.

Hartley grinned and raised an eyebrow. "Really? How interesting. I do hope you haven't found anything out of place. Odd to see an auditor out socialising with mages, I must say. I thought that sort of thing was discouraged?"

Hop suddenly looked like a rabbit caught in a casting circle.

Fortunately, at that moment Dante strolled back over, holding a tray on which was a cluster of long thin glasses perched precariously, all filled with some sort of purplish-green liquid. A small object was sloshing around in them, although whatever it was appeared different in each glass.

A small troll rolled past Dante's ankles, almost tripping him up, before unrolling itself to clear a few shards of broken glass from the bare floorboards, which it then promptly ingested.

"Here we go!" Dante exclaimed, stepping over the troll and placing the tray on the table. "Help yourselves. My treat."

He paused, noticing the new arrival. "Hartley?"

"Dante," Hartley said, inclining his head. "You look surprised."

Dante looked as though he'd stumbled across a rather large spider.

"Just amazed you've decided to grace us with your illustrious presence," he recovered swiftly. "I figured you'd be supping with the overlords about now, laughing about those poor Tower mages strapped to their desks, or whatever it is you do over at Woodbane these days."

"Now, now. It's not all fun and games. We've been hard at it the last few weeks, as Ivy here can tell you." Hartley smiled at her.

"I don't doubt that Ivy has been working hard," Dante retorted.

Hop interjected, "So you all know each other, then?"

Lil responded on everyone's behalf, hoping to alleviate the tension that had taken grip of proceedings. "Hartley used to be in the Solutions Division at Jackdaw, before moving in-house to Woodbane last year. He trained alongside Dante."

"Noted, thank you," said Hop.

"That going in your little report, is it?" Dante snapped pettily. Hartley's presence had caused his gregarious mood to evaporate.

"It might well do!" said Hop defensively.

"Let's just have a nice drink, shall we?" proposed Lil hopefully. "It's been a strange couple of days, but we're all friends here, and off the clock."

"Indeed," agreed Hartley, "and I for one am pleased to hear I won't be being charged for this."

Dante glowered at Hartley.

The Garbled Goblin was heaving now; filled with mages from all five Towers pressed into its wandering rooms and cellars. At one point, Ivy caught sight of Bladlow at the bar, red in the face and expounding away at another patron. He glanced over at their table every now and then with a distinctly disapproving expression. Ivy could only assume he was not best pleased that they were fraternising with his client and former protégé.

"Rather fun to be working together, isn't it, Ivy?" Hartley said, nudging her arm with his. "Big business afoot." He pivoted to the wider group and continued, "We're gearing up to take delivery of the components Ivy here has been helping to manufacture, in order to get our mages brewing away. And then comes mass production! All very exciting. Worlds away from the run-of-the-mill casting services that Jackdaw usually offers…"

"Run-of-the-mill?" Dante repeated peevishly.

"Well, most castings work the Tower usually performs is hardly ground-breaking stuff, is it? Doesn't really require that much thought."

Ignoring Dante's aggrieved expression, Hartley continued. "In fact, as I mentioned to Ivy only the other day, any mage really wanting to challenge themselves should consider coming in-house. It's where the real innovation is."

Dante simmered as Hartley smirked. Lil changed the subject as quickly as she could manage. "Annual Falltide dinner is coming up next week," she said, excitement humming in her voice. "Hopefully it will be as outrageous as the last one – I don't think anyone's quite gotten over the incident with the giant lantern and the illusion of Master Stanforth's llamacorn…"

"I certainly haven't," said Hartley drily. "Didn't Master Williamson also magic himself up a pair of antlers and start chasing people?"

Ivy laughed at the memory; it had been an eventful night. She realised with disappointment that Hartley wouldn't be at this year's celebration and found herself wishing she had actually spoken to him at the last one.

The conversation moved on and the dubious drinks were emptied, refilled and then emptied again. Lil divulged some salacious gossip, including an account of an unfortunate mix-up involving a misplaced hair growth solution Alf Starbottom had been working on, a discarded coffee cup, and a very disgruntled member of the Facilities team.

For an hour or two, the occupants of the corner table laughed at each other's stories – grudgingly at first on Dante's part, although he eventually gave up and joined in. Ivy finally felt herself relax into the evening. She forgot about her earlier concerns, all anxiety surrounding the Woodbane process melting softly away as Hartley smiled and joked.

Lil amused them with her illusions, conjuring swarms of iridescent butterflies which transformed into a series of floating targets which Dante and Hartley took increasingly competitive turns to shoot down with flashing sparks. Ivy was cajoled into casting too, attempting to form a small, moving sculpture from the liquid contents of her glass but succeeding only in creating a small, localised shower over the unimpressed head of Dante. She was getting good at those at least, she supposed.

Hop watched it all like a child in a toyshop, asking excited questions, begging for further demonstrations, all thoughts of his special audit temporarily forgotten.

As the evening wore on, the throng of mages in the Garbled Goblin started to disperse. Lil decided that she needed to return home and get some beauty sleep (her illusions were starting to flicker and fade, although everyone was too polite to mention this). After divulging one last piece of gossip (this time involving a female Master whose client had been caught somewhere they shouldn't be when a concealment charm which had not been intended for that purpose had promptly expired), Lil stretched her wings and pottered off in good spirits.

Hop was very much the worse for wear by this point, having himself consumed a large quantity of good spirits, and was braying obstreperously into his drink.

"Y'see…" he said grandly, extending one arm expansively and nodding meaningfully at Ivy, Dante and Hartley (or at least towards what he believed to be their general vicinity). "You mages… s'all jus' a… jus' a job to you… client says 'gimme magic' and you say 'poof!' Magic… but we have to have *principles*. We have to make sure s'being done… *principled way…*"

Dante studied him with amusement. "And you think we're an unprincipled bunch, do you, Mr Auditor?"

"Princip'ly… yes…" Hop slurred. "No regard… for how s'all s'posed to work…"

"I don't disagree when it comes to mages like old Crimple-Snarflace over here," said Dante, motioning dismissively at Hartley.

"Crumpley-Snafely," Hartley corrected automatically.

"But we're not that bad, for the most part," Dante continued, ignoring him. "I for one am a thoroughly good sort."

Hartley snorted.

Ivy, who – while feeling slightly fuzzy – had been nursing her own drinks more judiciously than Hop that evening, said, as sagely as she could manage, "I think it's possibly time for some of us to head home…"

"Just a minute, Ivy," said Hartley, placing a hand on her wrist and smiling widely but intensely. Ivy's skin shivered pleasantly at his touch. "I'm interested to know what exactly Hop here feels we are so unprincipled about. It's quite a serious allegation coming from someone representing the Regulator, after all…"

"He doesn't know what he's talking about," said Ivy quickly.

"He really doesn't," agreed Dante.

"Let's hear him out, shall we?" Hartley said, with a hard edge to his voice which Ivy hadn't heard before.

"He won't say anything intelligible," retorted Dante, "and that's when he's sober."

"S'cuse me," said Hop crossly, just about keeping up. "I can speak quite well for myself…"

"Wouldn't bank on it," muttered Dante.

"I was merely pointing out that, from what I've seen…" at this point Hop stifled a hiccup, "…none of you have demonstrated much regard for well-established principles… f'r instance, Trebbletuft–"

"Okay, I think that's enough from you," said Dante, cutting in quickly and shooting a look at Ivy. "Let's get you homewards, shall we? Before you bore everyone to an untimely death."

He stood up briskly, looped an arm under a remonstrating Hop, and hauled him to his feet. "Ives, are you going to be okay getting back by yourself? I think Hop here will need an escort."

"I'll be fine," Ivy said quickly, as Hop held out a finger and attempted to resume his proclamation.

"I'll make sure she behaves," added Hartley flirtatiously, leaning back in his seat and resting a proprietorial arm across the back of Ivy's chair.

For a moment, Dante looked torn, but then Hop opened his mouth and Dante decided, on balance, that Ivy could probably take care of herself. "Fine. Have a good evening. Not too late, Ivy…" he cautioned. "I need to talk to you about Carterton first thing tomorrow."

Dante shuffled a disgruntled Hop out of the bar, stumbling over the small bar troll who was now contentedly 'cleaning' the sticky floorboards by lapping up spillages.

"Well, that was all a bit odd," said Hartley to Ivy.

"Yes, he is rather," Ivy replied distractedly. She was now even more conscious of how close Hartley was to her. She could move closer still. It wouldn't be hard. She gave herself a shake and searched for something to say to defuse the tension building in her body. "I suppose your evening hasn't turned out entirely as planned, has it?" she ventured. "Your friend never did turn up…"

"Hm?" said Hartley, studying the group of mages propping up the bar. He looked back at her. "Yes, well, I think it's not worked out too badly." He smiled winningly and Ivy could feel her heart pounding against her ribs. She once again tried to remind herself that he was a client, that there were rules, principles, against this sort of thing. "It's been good to hang out here again," Hartley continued. "You forget what it's like as a Tower mage after a while."

"Do you miss it?" she asked, glad that she could divert her mind from the urge to reach towards him.

"Now and then," he replied. "But not as much as I thought I would. It's very… freeing. I suppose when you're working at the Tower, it's all about what someone else wants, and needing to make that happen despite all the limitations. Especially in Solutions. So many restrictions on what we can and can't do… it becomes more and more about expectation management, less about creativity.

"It always felt like the closer I came to actually doing something interesting, something that might, you know, 'carry on the family tradition of magical excellence'–" his voice assumed a mocking tone as he said this "–or whatever it is I'm supposed to do with my life, the more doors were closed. Do you know what I mean?"

She did. It was all she had thought about for the last few months. Ivy was quiet for a moment, sipping the remnants of her drink. Last orders had been called a short while ago. It was almost time to leave.

"I do," she replied. "Magic never seems to work for me outside of formal castings. And castings are all about limits and rules and worrying about what might go wrong… it sometimes feels like life is all about what I can't do, what I shouldn't do…" She lingered on the word 'shouldn't', looking helplessly at his profile.

Hartley simply nodded. "Exactly, which is the wrong way of looking at it all. We could achieve so much more if we were more uninhibited, if we just knew what we wanted to happen and made it happen, rather than tying ourselves up in knots the whole time."

At this, the Quiet Room conversation of yesterday started preying on Ivy's mind. Perhaps she should just ask him outright? Get it off her chest? In a diplomatic fashion, of course – she didn't want him to think her stupid if Hop's fears were completely imagined, which she was convinced they must be, however unusual that casting process felt to her.

Emboldened by the drink, she asked, "Surely though, even at Woodbane, you still need to work within the Accords?"

"Hah, the Accords," Hartley laughed, "bane of every mage's life. Thankfully, not really my problem anymore. I can leave that sort of thing to Bladlow and the rest."

He nodded over at the portly figure of Charles Bladlow, still at the bar and now even ruddier. Bladlow narrowed his eyes at them briefly. Ivy remembered she shouldn't be seen alone with Hartley. But Bladlow merely dipped his head in acknowledgement, before resuming his conversation.

At that moment, the faerie wearily wiping down the bar called time. Hartley rose and took Ivy's hand, gently pulling her up. She clasped his palm tightly.

"Come on, Armstride. Time to go. Work to do tomorrow."

Upon exiting the Garbled Goblin, the door creaked shut behind them and a rush of cool air hit their faces. They lingered outside the doorway. The street was quiet, slumbering, with no illumination save for the glow trickling drowsily out from the rickety-paned windows of the pub.

Hartley rested an arm against the crumbling wall and leaned over Ivy. She felt the intensity of those large blue-grey eyes of his as he half-smiled at her.

"The thing you need to remember about working magic, Ivy, the real principle of it all," he whispered solemnly, "is that you just need to *want* something enough…"

Ivy felt him lean in; he was inches away now. Something in her wanted him to move closer still…

She reminded herself for the tenth time that evening that Hartley was a client, and that there were very clear Tower *principles* about this sort of thing. He was also possibly a suspect in Hop's investigation, which complicated matters further…

The weight of all that she shouldn't do once again collapsed profoundly upon her, as she looked up into Hartley's questioning eyes.

Something in her yielded, and she reached up and kissed him.

He returned it warmly, gripping her tightly and pulling her firmly away from the doorway and into an alcove under a half-ruined archway, away from the prying eyes of the mages who had started to filter reluctantly out of the pub to stumble their way home.

Ivy's skin burned as raw magic skittered across her arms, through her fingers and into Hartley's hair, as she raked her hands through it. He laughed at the pleasant shock, kissing her again.

She heard the door to the Garbled Goblin creak shut for the last time and the sounds of bolts drawn and latches flipped. One by one, lights flickered off, and the street grew dark.

Ivy remained oblivious to it all, lost in the alcove and Hartley's embrace; lost in the magic that coursed through her like undulating flames.

Eventually, painfully, she pulled away, the rippling magic spinning down her arms fading gently. She said quietly, agonisingly, "I have to go home."

Hartley straightened up, but continued to clasp her, hands warm against her back. She didn't want him to release her.

As he moved slightly away, Ivy noticed something and observed, "I think you may have forgotten your bag…"

"For Gods' sake, that's annoying…" Hartley replied. "I'll have to come back and get it in the morning… it's all your fault, Armstride," he said in mock-exasperation. "You've been too bloody distracting of late. I'm not getting any work done."

She laughed. "I know the feeling."

He leaned in closer again. "Are you okay getting home by yourself?" he asked, invitation in his voice. "It's pretty late…"

Ivy hesitated. She could ask Hartley to walk her back, but that would lead to… problems. She was in enough trouble as it was.

Eventually she said, with not inconsiderable effort, "I'll be fine…"

Hartley gazed at her intensely for a moment and gave her a final, softer, kiss before they parted ways.

14.

THE HOUSE OF LITTLE SECRETS

◆

"I'm beginning to think that annoying little auditor might be onto something. I don't trust Crumple-Snakeface as far as I can throw him."

It was the morning after the night at the Garbled Goblin and Dante was leaning against a bookcase in Ivy's chambers in his usual insouciant manner.

"Really?" said Ivy croakily. She was not holding up well after the late night and the copious quantities of whatever it was she had imbibed, in addition to the fact that she had spent most of the small hours wide awake, replaying every moment with Hartley...

Gods, she felt awful... it was like someone was trying to wring out her brain, the tight squeezing sensation accompanied by a hot humming noise. Worse still, her fingertips had started running hot and cold again. She wondered if it was a side-effect of the magic that had streaked along her arms last night, arms that had been wrapped around Hartley...

She gave herself a small shake. Hadn't Dante just mentioned Hartley? She tried to focus. "I thought you said that Hop's theories were all a load of nonsense."

"And I stand by that. They're ridiculous. In fact, I intend today to demonstrate exactly how ridiculous. But if anyone is up to no good, it would be that stuck-up, preening prat. Did you see the way he was sneering at everyone last night?"

"Not really."

"So self-important. Thinks he can tell everyone what to do. I for one would like to tell *him* where to stick it."

"Dante, I really don't have time for this. I need to get on with some work. Or possibly lie down and die quietly."

"No time for that. Here–" He tossed Ivy a small vial, which she fumbled and only just managed to catch.

"What's this?"

"Remedial Solution. Drink up, we have somewhere to be."

"We do?" Ivy asked weakly.

"Meet me in the foyer in ten minutes. Now drink up."

Dante exited her chambers, flicking his fingers from down the corridor so that Ivy's door slammed magically shut with a thump that made her brain cringe.

She looked dully down at the draft castings before her and then at the small vial. It looked like work would, yet again, have to wait.

Ivy found Dante in the foyer, flanked by an implausibly perfect Lil and a painfully perky Hop.

"Ivy, there you are!" exclaimed Hop. "Now we can proceed!"

"How are you still alive?" she asked incredulously.

"Excuse me?" Hop said, thoroughly baffled.

"You must have drunk your own bodyweight in spirits and ale last night!"

"It is not in a Pockett's future to suffer hangovers," Hop said proudly.

Ivy didn't have the energy to challenge this peculiar assertion, so left it at that. She appraised the strange assemblage, gathered beneath the shadow of the tree. "Dante," she said, exasperated, "what, exactly, are we doing down here?"

Dante smiled knowingly. "Proving a point."

With no more than that, he led them out of the building, down to the Deep Carts, and halfway across the Citadel to the Goblin Quarter.

Ivy didn't often visit this part of the Citadel, save for when she needed to pass through to attend the nearby Dragonsteel facility to perform or refresh a dragon binding. The buildings were uniformly neat in their design. Everything appeared to have been measured and constructed with the utmost care and consideration, probably because it had; goblins were fastidious engineers by nature. They didn't start out that way, but when your race is small, spindly and under constant threat from club-wielding barbarians, those who survive do so because they have become very, *very* adept at crafting traps.

The Goblin Quarter was an exhibition of the finest in goblin engineering, a sprawling stronghold of artifice which had outlasted the wars, possibly due to the number of (supposedly now-defunct) mechanised defences cunningly concealed within the orderly rows of commercial and residential properties.

As they marched up from the Deep Carts entrance, Ivy had become uncomfortably aware of dragons wheeling overhead, their huge wings thumping up and down in a primeval rhythm.

Ivy had never seen so many in the sky at one time; she counted six of Dragonsteel's seven 'assets' circling above. She knew Dragonsteel needed to exercise the beasts on occasion, but they tended to do so in rotation to minimise any loss in productivity at the facility. Such a congregation of the great lizards was exceptionally unusual and an unnerving sight.

Ivy and Skelton had together bound each one and it was Ivy who was principally responsible for periodically checking in and maintaining those bindings, not that she had been able to do it for a while. Ivy hoped they were still fresh enough to hold. She watched the dragons soar purposefully overhead. They seemed to be looking for something.

Dante halted the group outside an old but spotlessly maintained shop. Above the entrance was a large wooden sign, displaying the words 'Pethrick's Emporium' in supple goblin italics. "Here we are!" he announced.

Exquisitely carved mechanical toys and curiosities bobbed away in the shop's window, complex contraptions which looked like they should be running on magic rather than whirling cogs and springs. Ivy was particularly taken with a fiendishly complex marble run that spun and spiralled in an impossible labyrinth of coils and wheels. These were far beyond the playthings of Ivy's own childhood.

A sign on the door read, in the manner of curiosity shops the universe over: 'Gone to lunch'. Dante opened it anyway, ignoring Lil's protestations.

Ivy was surprised to note that Hop did not look remotely perturbed by the trespass; in fact, his eyes were wide with anticipation.

"What exactly are we doing here, Dante?" demanded Ivy quietly, as they filed into the small, shady confines of Pethrick's

Emporium, which was stocked shelf upon shelf with yet more gloriously intricate devices and curios.

"You'll see," came the enigmatic answer.

Hop started poking at a small, lidded box placed at eye level near the shop's entrance. After some energetic stabbing, the lid opened to reveal nothing but emptiness. A disappointed Hop closed it softly, upon which it re-opened abruptly and a skeletal wooden hand shot out on a black concertina, poking the petrified auditor squarely in the nose.

Dante smirked.

As Dante strolled off towards the unoccupied counter, Ivy, Lil and Hop perused the shop's wares, Hop a little more cautiously than before. They browsed the shelves, wondering at the vast array of ingenious inventions: furniture which automatically adjusted its dimensions to accommodate its user, self-winding stopwatches, a menacing contraption which purported to be an automated barbering service, a puppet which with intricate grace imitated the flight of a swan. Rapt, Ivy almost tripped over a bespectacled goblin wearing a flawlessly pressed suit.

As she went to apologise, she realised it was Cleft, the Tower's copier.

"Ms Armstride," he addressed her courteously. "A pleasant morning to you. What, if I may ask, brings you to the Goblin Quarter on this fine morning?"

"We've got the morning off," replied a startled Ivy. "So we thought we would do a little browsing…" As if to illustrate her point, she picked up an extravagantly carved miniature dragon. Its wings unfurled at her touch and a deep purple-red stone at its breast began to pulse and glow.

Cleft raised his delicately whiskered eyebrows. "I do hope you find what you seek," he intoned politely, before adding, eyes glinting shrewdly, "however, I fear you may be looking in the wrong place." With that, the goblin bade her a peremptory good-day and exited the shop.

Ivy had no time to ponder this before Dante urgently announced, "Come on, Wry's out back." He marched towards a large curtain in a dim corner of the shop, partially obscured by a giant wooden rocking unicorn that looked peculiarly rabid.

"Wry?" Ivy asked, replacing the dragon with some reluctance; it had felt warm and perfect.

"Wryneck, my contact," Dante pronounced, not volunteering any further context as he lifted the curtain and ushered them through.

The party stood cramped in a side-room which seemed to be used exclusively for storing broken furniture. Its contents were stacked precariously up to – and somehow *along* – the ceiling. Apart from the hedge-hogged framework of table legs and chair arms, they were alone.

"I thought you said your contact was back here?" Hop said, perplexed.

"He is," Dante replied coolly.

"But I don't see him anywhere!" cried Hop, peering anxiously around, trying to deflect one of Lil's wings from his face, much to her disgruntlement.

"As I said before, just because something isn't in your little rulebook of the universe, doesn't mean it doesn't exist. Now, enough of this – Wryneck's expecting us and he's a busy individual."

Dante pressed forward, brandishing a tiny golden key, barely perceptible to the eye. She followed his gaze to where, buried under the bevelled furniture corpses, she suddenly spotted a dolls' house, coated in a layer of thick dust. She could have sworn it hadn't been there before.

It resembled a pre-Accords Citadel townhouse, crafted at the height of Kirin's power, decorative columns and balustrades adorning its mock-stone frontage, which spanned an impressive five storeys. Peering through the begrimed windowpanes, Ivy thought she could make out tiny lights flickering and sputtering within. As she looked closer, Ivy had the peculiar sensation she was looking *up* at the house, despite its modest proportions. The harder she looked, the grander and more impossibly imposing it appeared.

Dante delicately inserted the miniscule key into a lock in the panelled double-doors at the front of the house. He turned it.

Ivy had the sensation of a door opening and closing on dimensions. The house did not grow bigger, nor did she become any smaller, and yet, within the space of a moment, the house and the group were all the size they were *supposed to be*.

They found themselves in a hallway, opulently furnished, but clearly in need of attention. The bannisters framing the central staircase were mottled and chipped, and the carpets and wallpaper looked threadbare. She glimpsed some half-eaten cheese and biscuits lying on a scratched silver platter on a sideboard next to some misshapen pots and jars.

Ivy, Hop and Lil stared in reverent silence, their eyes darting around the space. Doors branched off from the hallway, which seemed at once cavernous and narrow. Most were bedecked with odd little signs such as 'Alchemical Larder Supplies', 'Dr Grim, esq.' or 'Nowhere'. As Dante led them up the creaking stairs, they passed landings hosting more definitively closed doors, all bearing curious signs and symbols. Ivy noted a few of the doors also displayed smaller hanging notices along variations of 'Gone to Lunch', although one simply read 'Gone'. They reached the top of the stairs and proceeded along a dimly lit corridor, past still more doors. The air around them was musty and stifling, heavy with silence. Ivy thought she heard something scuttle behind them, but did not dare turn around. Eventually, they paused outside a door upon which was emblazoned an hourglass symbol.

"What now?" Lil asked, unnerved.

Dante simply opened the door and breezed confidently into the room, which appeared to be some sort of library.

As she followed Dante in, Ivy tried not to stare too closely at the assorted books and paraphernalia strewn across the surfaces and shelves. Every time she did so she had the peculiar sensation she was somehow looking simultaneously at both a real object and its miniature replica. The effect was profoundly unsettling.

"Dante Umbriano!" a voice cried from behind a large desk littered with oddities. "Well, well… I never thought I'd see the day you'd darken my study again!"

"Hello, Wry." Dante smiled.

Ivy's eyes widened as the figure stood up. And up. Wryneck was like no being Ivy had ever seen before. Chillingly spindly, with long-fingered limbs and sallow cheeks, he looked upon them with yellowed, mottled eyes. His elongated neck undulated as he hunched his sunken head towards them, smiling a wide, dead smile. The exceptionally tall being shuffled over from behind his desk and placed a friendly hand on Dante's shoulder.

Lil had shuffled closer to Ivy and grabbed her wrist. Hop, meanwhile, had extracted a small notepad and was busy recording the time, date and attendees, all of which served as a helpful pretext to avoid looking at their host.

"Up to no good, I hope?" Wryneck addressed Dante, with a voice that rattled like teeth in an urn. "I've got a couple of necroes who, I am afraid to say, just aren't cutting the mustard lately and–"

Dante laughed jovially and shook his head. "No, no, Wry, nothing like that. I'm just here for information."

Ivy and Lil glanced at each other. Necroes? Wryneck surely couldn't be referring to necromancy? That had been outlawed since long before the Accords. Yet Dante seemed unfazed by the word. As one, Lil and Ivy glanced at Hop, who had just recorded the location of the meeting as 'toy house' and was currently double underlining it. Ivy marvelled.

"Pity." Wryneck appraised the rest of the group. "And who are your most welcome companions on this venture into my humble study?"

"May I introduce you to Ivy and Lil, colleagues of mine. And this is–"

"Hop Pockett, assistant auditor, from the Audit Office of the Regulator of Magical Practice," Hop interjected officiously.

Wryneck blinked. Ivy could have sworn she saw dust cascade from his eyelids.

"The Regulator? Dante, I must confess this is–" a look passed between the pair, as something unspoken was quickly exchanged "–a *most* unexpected pleasure." Wryneck glided forward, seizing Hop's hand. "I am always delighted to assist the Regulator.

"And I see we also have a member of the fae present." He clasped Lil's hand with a skeletal claw, and the faerie twitched involuntarily. "My dear, it is a rare pleasure to see you indeed. Such short lives, but so *energised*…"

Next Wryneck approached Ivy and took her hand. His skin felt like parchment, soft and cracked. "Ivy Armstride." His eyes met hers and she felt the heavy weight of ages past, barely remembered. She couldn't recall that Dante had mentioned her last name, yet somehow it seemed right that he knew it. "The Dragonbinder. Remarkable, quite remarkable in one so young."

"All right, Wry, let's be done with the niceties, shall we?" Dante declared sharply. "Mr Auditor here has some questions which I suspect only you can answer. Questions about the supply of Restricted Substances."

Wryneck placed a hand on his cadaverous chest in a gesture of mock-indignation. "Restricted Substances? Goodness, I wonder what caused you to think *I* might be familiar with such torrid matters?"

"Wry…" Dante admonished. He turned to Hop. "Ask away, Mr Auditor."

Hop puffed himself up delightedly, raising his eyes upwards to meet Wryneck's. He mustered as much bureaucratic inspiration as he could, and began, "Mr Wryneck, I have been tasked with a *special* investigation, the exact circumstances of which I am not at liberty to disclose. I am pursuing various avenues of inquiry, but my investigation has led me to suspect that certain individuals might be procuring Restricted Substances at scale, namely faerie dust, unicorn horns, and goblin spleens."

Wryneck steepled his fingers as an expectant silence descended.

"Heard anything, Wry?" said Dante.

Wryneck slid behind his desk and hunched over it, vulture-like, craning his long neck towards them. "None of the items you describe have, to my knowledge, passed through the Dark

Market in recent months. There was some… activity… a while back now, but that was terminated, most *finally*.

"Furthermore, the historic activity I mention was not procurement at the scale necessary for production of Ramston Woodbane's latest commercial concoction." He smiled gently as Hop tried to disguise his surprise. "Oh yes, Mr Pockett, I know all about that. However, I am afraid I cannot assist you further in your enquiries. Most distressing, I appreciate."

Dante flashed Hop a smug look. Lil relaxed her shoulders in visible relief. Ivy remained apprehensive.

"I would add," Wryneck exhumed, "that there has been very little interest whatsoever in the supply of Restricted Substances of late. It seems, Mr Pockett, that the threat of the Regulator's housebroken grimlings – such a marvellous phenomenon – is proving a most effective deterrent." He paused, caressing the spine of a book with papery fingertips.

"Thank you, Wry," Dante said, motioning to the others that it was time to leave.

Hop raised his pen questioningly. "Are you absolutely certain that you have witnessed no such activity?"

"As certain as the grave," Wryneck affirmed.

"I think that's your lot, Mr Auditor." Dante made to leave.

"Of course," Wryneck observed. "Dragonsteel may feel that the market for Restricted Substances remains very much operational."

"Dragonsteel?" asked Ivy, startled into speech. "What's Dragonsteel got to do with anything?"

"Nothing, and perhaps everything," Wryneck answered cryptically.

"Speak plainly, Wry," Dante warned. A shadow crept across the dusty shelves, weaving its way towards Wryneck.

As the shadow slunk closer, Wryneck's neck suddenly lengthened and twisted into a nervous, ugly curl. Dante raised his chin as the others recoiled.

"Dragonsteel appear to have lost an item far more powerful than the trifling ingredients required for Woodbane's wrinkle balms," Wryneck began, neck crunched and distorted. Lil gripped Ivy's hand and Hop had stopped writing, his face turning pale. "They've lost a dragon heart, I hear. Stolen right from under their noses while one of their dearly guarded assets was left unattended."

"What do you mean?" exclaimed Ivy. A dragon heart? Stolen? Ivy found herself unable to comprehend this unexpected information.

Wryneck merely uncoiled his neck and shrugged. "Tragic. So very tragic."

The strange being said no more than that. He selected a book and started flicking through its pages with studied apathy. "If there's nothing else, Mr Pockett, I trust that concludes our interview?"

Hop could think of nothing and placed his notebook in his satchel, thoroughly unnerved but trying to disguise his unease.

"Thanks again, Wry. We'll see ourselves out," concluded Dante.

Wryneck waved an emaciated hand in slow motion. "As you will. I do hope I'll be seeing you again soon, Dante Umbriano."

Dante rolled his eyes and made to leave. He motioned for the others to follow.

"You too, Ivy Armstride." Wryneck's voice floated after her, like the dying breath of ages.

Ivy looked back, unsettled. Wryneck was staring at her, his book still open in his hand, his neck once again cocked in that horrible, crumpled twist, a little smile creeping across his lips.

He snapped the book shut, creating a small cloud of dust as he did so. At the noise, the shadow, which had been skulking in the corner, slipped down and across the floor. It slithered past Ivy until it reached Dante, coiling up his back and settling just below his shoulder blades. No-one else had commented on the shadow – had anyone else even seen it? Hop seemed entirely oblivious, and Lil was huddled beside her, looking determinedly down at the floor, wings hanging tight behind her.

Without warning, the doors along the walls of the corridor suddenly started to rattle. Dante stopped dead, eyes darting from door to door as they trembled and shook in their warped timber frames. The handles creaked and began to slowly, slowly turn…

"What's going on?" Hop shot at Dante.

Dante said nothing, still looking at the doors. He was breathing fast, his chest moving rapidly. Something flickered in his eyes, but Ivy knew it wasn't the ice-cold fear that was slipping down her throat. One of the doors was opening now, a grim chink of light widening around its edge. Her pulse raced. She knew she didn't want to see behind the door.

Ivy could hear other doors, further down the stairs, start to open and shut in a hideous cacophony of banging. Ivy looked around for Wryneck's door, wondering if the strange being was the one causing it. It was nowhere to be seen. A wall stood where the door with the hourglass symbol had been, its ripped wallpaper revealing the decaying plasterwork beneath. The sound of doors slamming open was getting closer, the air was thickening.

"Dante–" she said, suddenly panicked.

Before she could finish, Lil moved over to Dante and placed a hand on his wrist. Her features shifted ephemerally, her eyes becoming bright and firm.

"That's enough, now," she said quietly. "Let's get back to the Tower, shall we?"

Lil's wings extended out behind her back and raised into the air, glowing softly against the shadows on the walls. Ivy felt a sudden warmth wash through her. She saw herself lying beside a fireplace on her stomach – she couldn't have been more than seven or eight years old – playing a game of cards with her family, laughing uproariously. The memory – was it a memory? – had appeared as though Lil had just dragged an exceedingly comfortable chair from a dark corner of Ivy's mind and pushed her bodily into it.

The doors in the corridor fell quiet again and the air in the corridor seemed to thin and lift. Lil's wings flattened against her back once more and Dante appeared to have calmed, although a certain tightness to his jaw remained. Ivy realised she had been holding her breath. What *was* that?

"What was that?" echoed Hop, looking suspiciously at the doors. Spurred on by whatever cheerful memory Lil had forced upon him in that moment of panic, the auditor stepped forward and knocked at one of the doors with his pen. Ivy half wondered if it would knock back, but it stayed quiet.

Dante shrugged nonchalantly. "It's an old building," was all he said.

Ivy felt there was more to it than that, but she knew that she needed to wait until Hop was out of earshot to interrogate the mage further. Without another word, the four of them exited the peculiar house.

✦

Outside in the welcome fresh air of the Goblin Quarter, Dante addressed the group. "Glad that's cleared that up," he said lightly. He flashed them a quick grin, as though to doubly reassure them that absolutely none of that had just happened. "See, Mr Auditor, told you there was nothing untoward going on with this Woodbane business. If anyone would know about nefarious activities, it would be Wry," adding quickly, "from completely legitimate second-hand sources, of course."

"It's a bit worrying to hear about that dragon heart, though," Lil observed. "Can't imagine that will sit well with Dragonsteel..."

Ivy, thoroughly unnerved by the exit from the strange house, had completely forgotten about the news of the theft. She wondered if that explained Dragonsteel's recent demands for improved security spells. Did Wryneck know about that, too?

"Indeed," agreed Dante. "I wonder what nasty little potion that's going to turn up in," he added darkly. "Maybe that's what you need to be investigating, Mr Auditor."

"You can rest assured that something like that will be at the top of the Regulator's – and the Constabulary's – priorities, I'm sure," Hop said primly, the colour returning to his face. "Meanwhile, my Woodbane enquiries will continue. Mr Wryneck is just one source and I have yet to independently verify the reliability of that source."

That comment reminded Ivy, who had at that moment been lost in thought about the dragon heart theft and Wryneck's parting words, that there was something she wanted to interrogate Dante about. "Dante?" she said firmly. "A word please?"

"Sure." He flashed her his quick smile and joined her to one side, leaving Hop and Lil to make an attempt at conversation.

She grabbed his arm. "What in the name of the Gods was all that at the end?" she shot at him.

"I can't think what you're referring to," he replied evasively.

"Come on, Dante – all that business with the doors. What was that?"

"Like I said, it's an old building. It probably has all sorts of quirks." Dante was clearly not prepared to be further drawn on the subject, but Ivy tightened her grip.

"Quirks! There was nothing bloody quirky about what just happened – you and I both know what type of magic that was! Which reminds me – what exactly were you thinking taking an actual *auditor* to speak to someone who is clearly involved in – how did you put it? – 'nefarious activities'?" she hissed at him, infuriated.

"Relax, Ives," he said, shrugging away from her grip. "Wry knows what he's about. As for investigator-of-the-year over there, he doesn't have a clue, trust me."

Hop was now talking animatedly to Lil, who was appraising him quizzically.

"But what if he tells someone?" Ivy pressed. "What if he comes back with others from the Regulator to storm the place? What if we get implicated?"

"We won't," Dante replied, putting his hands in his pockets. "I think you should just see it as a job well done. Hop's got what he needed, whether he likes it or not, and now we can get on with our actual day jobs without having to listen to his ridiculous conspiracy theories.

"Besides, even if he did somehow – which, by the way, is seriously unlikely – come back to 'storm the place', as you so colourfully put it, he'd never be able to find it again, let alone gain entry."

Ivy appeared unconvinced.

"Don't worry so much," Dante reassured her. "It's all above board and completely fine. Not that you couldn't do with living dangerously once in a while."

Dante removed a hand from a pocket and casually flicked his fingers. Ethereal sparks the colour of darkness danced along the cobbles.

Ivy sighed, watching the sparks skip along the street. "I suppose," she conceded reluctantly. "It's not like we took him to the Dark Market or anything like that."

"Ivy," said Dante, staring at her, "where did you think we *were*?"

15.

HEARTS OF STEEL

✦

"I had a thought about where we might investigate next," Hop told Ivy excitedly later that morning, monstrous optimism plastered across his features.

"Did you not hear the same information I did?" Ivy asked him, confounded. "Dante's source was very clear that no trades of Restricted Substances have been happening," she said, adding, "at least not involving Woodbane."

Hop looked unconvinced.

They were sitting in a small café at the edge of the Goblin Quarter, mulling over the events of the morning. Dante and Lil had returned to the Tower, both satisfied that Hop's theories had been (at least ostensibly) disproved. Ivy wasn't entirely sure why she had stayed with Hop, but she had been hungry and Hop had recommended they find somewhere nearby to eat.

She was beginning to realise that Hop had dragged her here on a false pretext and that strategizing, not lunch, was first on the menu.

The café was filled to bursting with bright pastel furnishings and legions of cats in every soft nook and patch of warming sunlight. Save for the human owner, who was visibly irritated by the prospect of customers interrupting her crossword, the café was otherwise vacant. Ivy studied the menu, surrounded by several fawning cats, which was proving quite off-putting. Hop had no such feline admirers.

Outside the window, she caught a sudden glimpse of a dragon circling overhead, scales glinting in the lazy autumnal sun, the edges of its wings rippling in an updraught.

She looked across the street at the giant structure of Dragonsteel Industries, which – rather incongruously – was situated directly opposite the tiny café.

The Dragonsteel building was a formidable construction of black granite and obsidian, which towered above the Citadel's Goblin Quarter. If Woodbane Cosmetics was a temple to human masonry, Dragonsteel was a primordial forge. A pair of vast iron and steel doors, pocked with foreboding spikes and scales, stood sentry.

Clearly, they had not been standing sentry enough. Wryneck had said they had lost a dragon heart, which meant someone had killed a dragon. Untamed, Ivy knew dragons could be mercurial and deadly, but this did not prevent her from feeling a hot wrench of sadness at the thought.

As she looked back up at the wheeling reptile, she imagined a dragon, lying helpless and prone as someone surgically sliced out its still-beating heart. She thought too of her abandoned Dragonsteel castings, designed to reinforce the protections around the industrialised lizards, lying unfinished on her desk.

Dragonsteel must have had an inkling that something like this was about to happen. She had been told the castings were urgent, but she hadn't believed that the client had actually meant it – they usually didn't. She tried to convince herself she couldn't have known, couldn't have foreseen the consequence of not completing them. Trapped in knots of guilt, she became aware that Hop was saying something.

"Even if it's not been noticed by Dante's contact, that doesn't mean Woodbane isn't still obtaining Restricted Substances from somewhere. Seeing Woodbane's in-house mage last night made me wonder... perhaps I've been looking in the wrong place? He mentioned they were preparing to receive deliveries for mass production. And yet, Jackdaw haven't been mass-producing the synthetic components, you've not even come close. So what deliveries is he expecting, I wonder? Restricted Substances, perchance? And what if the information I need about the procurement and delivery of those Restricted Substances is at Woodbane's offices?"

Tearing her eyes away from the dragon, Ivy countered wearily, "Look, if there were any incriminating evidence, which – and here I am minded to agree with Dante – seems deeply unlikely, why in the name of the Gods would it be at Woodbane?"

"You've been to Woodbane's offices, haven't you? Have you seen anything? Did you hear anything while you were there?"

"No," she said shortly. The discussion around Woodbane was reminding Ivy of last night, of Hartley's arms wrapped around her. She dispelled the memory and tried to focus. It had been a strange twenty-four hours. "Nothing abnormal was said or done," she said, trying to focus. "Nothing. You need to drop this, you know."

Hop ignored her. "Is there any way to take a look around Woodbane Cosmetics, do you think?"

Ivy considered this for a moment. She knew she really shouldn't go to Woodbane. If anything, it was now more important than ever to get back to the Tower; Skelton would be furious when he realised her delay with the Dragonsteel castings might have led to such serious consequences… What was she going to say to him? She tried to ignore that worry and concentrate instead on why visiting Woodbane was a very bad idea.

"We can't do that. There's no reason for *me* to be there, let alone you. Bladlow would go ballistic if he found out. Besides, let's be realistic. Even if there is something sinister going on, it's not as if evidence of deliveries of Restricted Substances is just going to be lying around!" Ivy exclaimed. She pushed away a cat that had started licking her hand with its sandpapery tongue; she seemed to spend her life being bothered by creatures these days – it was becoming almost as annoying as Hop.

"That's rather absurd of you, Ivy," Hop said pertly. "Why, if every investigative officer in the Citadel thought that way, no one would ever bother to try to solve any crimes!"

"Solving crimes? Is that what you think your job is? For Gods' sakes, Hop – most auditors that turn up at the Tower are in and out as quickly as they can manage! What in seven hells makes you so desperate to be different?"

Hop opened his mouth to remonstrate, then shut it again. The café was quiet, save for the purring of the cats and the sound of the café owner's pencil completing seven down. The woman didn't seem to be in any hurry to serve them (fourteen across was proving fiendish). Ivy's stomach rumbled impatiently.

Eventually, Hop said, in a matter-of-fact tone, "There's no magic in my family. None at all. My father didn't like that I wanted to be a mage, not when there were so many other, more *suitable* options available.

"But I kept on trying and hoping and learning as much as I could about the theory of magic. All to no avail, sadly. 'Hopeless Hop' my older sister used to call me…

"So I decided to put my knowledge to use, working at the Regulator, better understanding how it all works in practice. Yet the more I see, the more I realise that you mages don't have any idea what you're doing, nor do you seem to have any discernible principles. You mostly seem to use your gifts to make people like my father richer, regardless of how much twisting… oh, wait, sorry, *interpretation* of the Accords that entails.

"I might not be a mage like you, but – whatever anyone might think – I do actually know a lot about how magic is supposed to work and there's something not adding up here. It's simply not right that I should stand by. I have questions and I must ask them. That's my job."

Ivy had no time to digest this monologue as there was a sudden screeching from the sky, which made them both peer up and out of the window.

A horrific, slow, keening noise sliced through Ivy's ears and scorched down her spine. As one, the hackles of the café's innumerable cats raised; they hissed and spat and yowled in fear.

With alarming speed, the dragon overhead, which had until that moment been circling calmly, suddenly dived directly towards the great obsidian structure of Dragonsteel.

Ivy and Hop leapt from their seats in shock as the massive lizard smashed violently into the street in front of them, slamming its huge clawed feet into the ground, which shook from the impact. Inside the café, crockery rattled and rung, chairs tumbled, tables juddered. The cats bolted towards the back of the room; the café owner was suddenly nowhere to be seen.

The dragon wrestled desperately against its harness, wrenching and tearing and beating its vast wings as its rider shouted command words at it. The words were ineffective; the dragon was beyond control. Skidding across the street, metallic scales glinting dangerously in the sunlight, it pulled and twisted until it managed to fling its panicked rider from its back. The figure hit the gates of Dragonsteel with a sickening thump before sliding to the ground, motionless.

The dragon panted, curls of smoke escaping from its flaring nostrils.

Then, in one awful motion, the dragon turned to face Ivy, arching its immense neck towards her. She looked into those beautiful golden eyes; eyes she had seen on so many occasions.

They weren't dulled with magic now. They smouldered.

It opened its colossal jaws, lined with ferocious rows of deadly teeth, and roared. The sound splintered the glass of the café window. It splintered through Ivy, wrenching her heart in its sheer despair.

"Can't you do something?" Hop screamed at her, trying to pull her back from the fractured window. The panic in his voice compelled her to move – she hadn't realised that she had been frozen to the spot.

"Do what?" she shouted back at him. "I haven't got any binding castings on me!"

"But you must know how they work! You have magic, don't you? Use it!"

Ivy stared at the beautiful violence of the beast as it arched its neck back. She tried to remember the spells. She must know them by heart by now, surely? It was worth a go, at least. The alternative was not looking like an option with long-term prospects.

Ivy tried to draw on the magic inside her, but as she did so she realised in horror that she didn't have anywhere near the power she needed to bind the dragon. How could that be? Was it the Woodbane castings? Or last night?

Turning from the window, the dragon rotated its neck and belched out a burst of bright, concentrated fire at the enormous iron and steel gates of Dragonsteel. The metal burned and screamed, glowing forge-hot with the intensity of the flame.

Further down the street, a second dragon had now landed, agitated but still just about under the control of its rider. The rider leapt from its back and rushed towards the thrashing dragon, which swept its tail around and struck him square and firmly, stopping him in his tracks.

It keened and moaned in unearthly rage as it coiled, braced, and spun its tail violently, thrashing the rider in his midriff and sending him skimming across the cobblestones like a pebble towards the other, smaller dragon, which was now extending its wings as though to also shake off the bindings that kept it docile.

The larger dragon was roaring again now and preparing another burst of fire in the furnace of its chest.

"Ivy! Do something!" Hop repeated.

"I can't!" she shouted, "I'm trying!" She drew on every last reserve she could find. The lights in the café flickered, a tea cup exploded, the crouching cats in the back room yowled in distress. Power, she needed power to bind it… and she needed to remember the binding spell. How did they start? With a name.

A name. With a cold, panicked dread she realised she couldn't remember the dragon's name…

Seven dragons she had bound. Over and over again. She would have put this one's bindings on it, anaesthetising it as it screamed with fire; she would have maintained those bindings, scarcely even aware of its awesome splendour as it lay prostrate and motionless before her. She must remember its name! But no, the names were always quickly recited and quickly forgotten. She had no idea which name belonged to the magnificent silver and rust machine in front of her. It was simply an asset to be managed.

The asset in question turned back to the window, having projected another stream of fire at the gates to Dragonsteel. Hop was ducking under the small table. That would be no protection if the dragon unleashed its fire and fury upon them. Ivy imagined the molten glass of the window enveloping her.

The dragon had stopped its keening and fallen deathly silent.

Please… please… not this, not now, she thought.

The dragon stared at her, massive nostrils flaring again with heavy, ragged breaths. Condensation was forming on the window from its breath; the glass had become hot and supple, slowly melting. She gazed up into those beautiful, terrible eyes. A clarity of thought cut through Ivy's panic and terror: it was in mourning. And it seemed as though it was trying to appeal to her.

What did it want? She gingerly reached her fingers towards the fractured, melting window pane. Without entirely knowing why, she slowly, tentatively, pressed her palm against the glass. It didn't burn. How did it not burn?

The dragon dipped its head towards her. There was a moment where she felt like she was on the edge of hearing something, something important. She leaned closer, straining her mind...

There it was – a lost dragon. A heart. A theft, a wretched thief – but she couldn't see the thief, couldn't make out anything beyond–

There was a metallic screech as the indomitable gates of Dragonsteel lurched open on their industrial hinges, their iron and steel frontage still glowing.

Several ogres thumped out from the gates, followed by humans clothed in thick leather.

The dragon turned its head, inhaled and–

Please, no…

Ivy had closed her eyes tightly, not wanting to watch what was about to unfold.

But instead there was only shouting, and the clanking clatter of heavy chains being pulled across flagstone.

She opened her eyes and looked on as the large dragon, seemingly docile once again, was led with little resistance through the giant gates. How had that happened?

Its sister dragon – how did Ivy know that? She had never known that before – followed meekly, gently carrying the second rider in its massive jaws like a dog does a favourite toy. A stretcher had been summoned for the first rider, who still lay crumpled and unconscious on the street.

"Is it over?" came Hop's small voice from below the table.

"It's over," said Ivy, bending down to help him up.

The metal doors of Dragonsteel slammed shut. The street was empty again. No-one had dared to venture out during the commotion. Ivy suspected it would be a while before they ventured out again.

As though to prove her wrong, the café owner suddenly reappeared from her back room, marching across towards the splintered windows and shaking her head. She was still clutching her crossword, now rolled up tightly and primed for attack.

"I've had just about enough of that lot!" she complained loudly. "I'm going to give them a bloody good piece of my mind, that's what I'm going to do, mark my words! Bloody great creatures, out of control, scaring my kittens!" The cats had yet to re-emerge.

The woman flung open the door to the café, only pausing to shout indignantly at Ivy and Hop, "And don't think I've forgotten you haven't paid yet!" She waved her rolled-up crossword at them. Ivy felt too shaken to remind the woman that they hadn't actually ordered anything.

After she had left, slamming the door so hard that its little bell fell to the ground and tinkled pathetically, Ivy and Hop looked at each other uncertainly.

"Are you okay?" Ivy asked him.

"I think so. That was all rather terrifying…"

It was rather, Ivy agreed inwardly. But there was something else, too. Something beautiful and wild, just on the edge of her understanding.

The dragons had always been important; but always as some form of savage equipment which was to be scrupulously maintained… but now…

She thought back to what Hop had been saying before the dragon had crashed down before them. He had been railing at her, telling her that she didn't know what she was doing, never thinking about the consequences of her magic. She had spent so much time lamenting what she couldn't use her magic for, but had she ever paused to question what she *was* using it for? Whether it was right?

Had binding those dragons been right? She thought again of the lost dragon heart, of the melancholy in those deep golden eyes. She had found something there. Now, she felt she had questions.

Dante had wondered what nasty little potion someone would make with that heart. If someone could steal a dragon heart just to make a potion, perhaps someone could steal more than a dragon heart. Perhaps they could steal from unicorns and goblins and faeries and any other being or creature they saw merely as an asset to be exploited.

Somewhere, under all the layers of learned obedience and conformity, a core of pure steel reignited in Ivy.

"Come on then," she resolved. "Let's pay Woodbane a visit."

Hop looked momentarily taken aback, before adjusting his glasses and smiling widely.

✦

Six infernal machines, where once were seven, lay dormant in their moorings in the giant outhouses of Dragonsteel Industries.

No work today.

No furnaces had operated since the little worker bees had discovered the magnificent, desecrated chassis of the seventh machine the other morning, its still-beating engine torn from it like a lump of meat.

No work today.

The six had been flown, out across the Citadel and further afield, to search for that engine, to track what had been so wretchedly stolen. Nothing. No heartbeat to heat the world. This should not have happened. A heart like that should not have been extinguished so easily.

No work today.

The worker bees had confined the six, fearing the weakening of the bindings that held them. One of them had almost malfunctioned. The largest and oldest machine, silver-coated and flecked with rust, shook her neck, idly testing her binding. *She* had put that binding on. The frustrated little girl. *She* would find what had been stolen from them. Reparations would be demanded.

No work today. Not today, but soon.

16.

QUESTIONABLE PROCEEDINGS

Upon arriving at the vast stone edifice of Woodbane Cosmetics and making their way to the mahogany reception desk, Hop and Ivy had been greeted most magnanimously by Mrs Woodbane, modelling a noticeably less weathered face than previously.

"Ah, Ivy, my dear!" the woman boomed in tones almost as sonorous as her husband's. "You're early! Young Hartley's Jackdaw appointment isn't for another hour!"

Ivy and Hop glanced at each other. This was an unexpected development. Ivy wondered who Hartley was expecting and fervently hoped it would not lead to complications.

For now, there was no choice but to proceed with the charade and pretend that they were indeed expected and had simply arrived ridiculously early.

Mrs Woodbane led them into a small wood-panelled room, informing them that this was Hartley's office and that she expected he would be along shortly. She had sat them down in comfortable old leather seats facing Hartley's impressively large oak desk, babbling away while unconsciously patting her face.

Once she had bustled out, Ivy scanned the room curiously, observing that the place appeared devoid of personal touches; it was stuffy and formal and any paperwork had been stowed safely out of sight.

Hop gesticulated urgently towards an old-fashioned documents cabinet with three large drawers. Ivy's eyes darted anxiously to the door, left ajar by Mrs Woodbane. She attempted to convey her concern that this was a Very Bad Idea by frantically gesturing to Hop. He ignored her and instead proceeded to tug at the cabinet's ornate handles.

"Locked," he said. A slight fizz of blueish-green light erupted from one of the handles. "Magically, it would appear."

"Would you just sit back down?" Ivy hissed, panicked. "He might be here any moment."

Hop ignored her. "I don't suppose you know how to prise it open?" he asked, trying to sound as innocent as possible.

"No. Well, maybe. I don't know what magic he used to seal it. It's probably really complicated. Besides, it would be breaking and entering, which is not what we're here for. You said we were after answers!"

"But what if the answers are in there?"

"You're meant to be from the Regulator – I thought you were supposed to like rules, not break them!"

"I know, I know. We just might not get another chance… it's worth a quick look, don't you think?"

Ivy hesitated. She knew they were here for answers, but she also knew that Hartley could be implicated should they find those answers. She wasn't sure what she was more afraid of: being caught breaking into a cabinet or finding out something she didn't want to know. Then she remembered the eyes of the dragon, their desperate appeal…

She pushed the office door gently shut and joined Hop at the cabinet.

"It's definitely magically sealed. I wouldn't know where to start breaking this. I can't remember any unlocking charms – I'd need to think about what's needed, get the wording right…"

"Is that really how magic works? Is that why you couldn't bind the dragon earlier?" Hop sounded disappointed. "I honestly thought mages could channel magic any time they wished. I thought the words were simply meant to stabilise and restrict the magic."

"Maybe for some mages. But I need the casting words for my magic. Believe me, I wish I didn't." Ivy ran her hand across the front of the filing cabinet, which fizzed again. "It's not like I can just *demand* that the cabinet open!" There was a harshness to her voice which made Hop back away. "I mean, it would be great if I could simply dip my fingers into the ether and mould reality into shape without needing all the words, all the ridiculous pages and pages and *pages* of limitations! If I could stop a bloody great big dragon from almost frying me to a crisp without needing a piece of sodding paper in front of me! I mean, how the hells did I end up like this, after all the bloody training, how can I not even unlock a bloody cabinet–"

Ivy slammed her palm against the cabinet. It hissed violently and a froth of turquoise light burbled out of it as all three drawers burst open, slamming into Ivy with a thud.

Ivy went quiet, before saying, "Well, that was unexpected."

Hop didn't pause to ask Ivy if she was hurt, but instead peered over the top drawer and started rifling hastily through the dusty folders within.

"Look, here's a file that says 'Ever-Young'!" he exclaimed. "There must be something in there. Hold on a minute."

Ivy just stood there, examining her palm blankly.

Hop flipped through the contents of the folder. "It appears to contain merely receipts and invoices," he said, removing a handful and looking at them dejectedly. "Most of them are between Jackdaw and Woodbane… there are a few from third parties, but the ingredients being procured are relatively mundane…"

Ivy rolled her eyes in irritation, "I've tried telling you, Hop, they're hardly going to say, 'consignment of goblin spleens', are they?"

Ivy felt as though her every nerve ending was ablaze. She tried to assert a grip on herself. Straining her ears, she thought she could make out footsteps coming from the corridor. "Hurry up, for Gods' sakes! I can hear someone coming and I need to get this locked again somehow!"

Hop jammed the drawers shut, dropping the folder he was holding on the floor in a fluster. He picked it up and shoved it into his own leather-bound folder while Ivy placed her hands on the cabinet and desperately tried to reverse what she had just achieved. "Come on, come on… work! Lock!" she hissed.

There was a soft *slup* sound and the drawers sealed. Ivy noticed with horror that one of the cabinet drawers was still emitting a faint orange glow. She shuffled in front of it as Hartley stepped into the room.

"Ivy?" Hartley's voice was filled with surprise. "And… Mr Pockett? What are you doing here?"

Now it was time for some *very* fast talking.

Ivy wasn't sure quite how, but they had managed to explain their presence well enough to have satisfied Hartley.

She had begun by improvising that Hop was undertaking several spot checks on Jackdaw matters as part of an interim audit – a process being trialled by the Regulator – and that a client site visit was part of the remit, under the supervision of one of Jackdaw's mages, of course.

Hop had then appeared – in a display of unexpected acting ability that had quite astounded Ivy – *appalled* that Hartley had not received the formal written notice informing Woodbane Cosmetics of the visit, which he had claimed the Audit Office had *assured* him they would send via troll mail.

Ivy observed that it might have been eaten in transit, which Hartley had no trouble accepting, this being a common flaw in the troll mail system.

Hop had offered for them to return at a more convenient time, on *proper* notice. Hartley had demurred graciously and insisted that it was no problem at all, that he was more than happy to assist the Regulator with its inquiries at the present time, and that – and this was discreetly directed at Ivy – it was an unexpected pleasure to have them here. He was busy supervising some brewing processes at the moment, though, so might they consider discussing any questions on the factory floor? They of course obliged.

Hartley led Ivy and Hop to the main brewing chamber, where they found themselves standing on a network of metallic gantries hanging above the vast machinery of the industrial solutions-making below. Enormous cauldrons bubbled and blistered and seethed, their contents a swirling mix of all colours and none, expelling hot plumes of vapour into the roof of the massive space. The vapours curled and coiled and crept through the upper windows, whereupon they tumbled down the sandstone walls, coating them with a slick, slimy sheen. The air was cloying and tight with noxious fumes; Ivy found herself glad she had not eaten lunch.

And there, standing on the central gantry, his huge arms resting proprietorially on its railings, encircled by whorls of smoke and steam, was the industrial figure of Ramston Woodbane. He looked up as they approached. "Ivy!" he exclaimed, raising his arms like a mechanised crane. "Good ter see yer!" The man beckoned her over. "Come, come!"

Hartley motioned his head towards Woodbane. "Go on over, Ivy. I'll speak with Mr Pockett separately."

Ivy joined Woodbane on the central gantry.

"Amazin', isn't it? All beaverin' away, brewin' up me potions," he boomed, bearing down on the team of mages scurrying around the floor below like the prow of a gargantuan battleship.

"That one down there is our best-selling' slimmin' solution." Woodbane gestured towards a vat of frothy salmon-coloured liquid, crackling with raw magic, to which a mage was adding something that looked suspiciously like broccoli. "Works like a charm. But the really clever thing is that, after a while, it stops workin' unless you up the dosage. Means the consumer has ter keep buying the damn stuff!" Woodbane guffawed. "'Built-in corpulence', that's what the clever buggers in product design called it! Better returns than on any of me other oils and lotions… all except this new potion of yours, o' course…"

As Woodbane thundered on, Ivy recalled what Hop had said earlier about making rich people richer and her mouth twitched with a distaste that was only partly caused by the odours circulating in the cavernous chamber. She glanced over at the auditor, who was deep in conversation with Hartley. Hop had retrieved his notepad and was scribbling furiously once more, pausing now and then to de-mist his glasses and ask another question. She found she had some questions of her own.

"You said at the Game that, if we get this Woodbane solution right, the possibilities are endless. What are you proposing to make next?" she interrogated.

"Ha! Ain't that the million queens question!" he laughed. He released his grip on the railings and started to walk her back across the gantry, towards Hartley and Hop, enjoying the opportunity to grandstand. "We've got all sorts o' things in mind. Delayed mortality elixirs, *proper* invisibility potions – thinkin' o' branchin' out into the huntin' market for that one, although I'm sure there will be *other* applications–" he flashed her an over-exaggerated wink at this– "beauty balms ter put even the best faerie charms ter shame… you name it, we intend ter flog it!

"We've been limited for too long thanks ter those damned Accords. Most o' the really good stuff needs the kind o' zap you can only get from a dragon or two."

Ivy froze. What if that was it – the piece that linked Woodbane to the dragon heart theft? That proved they were capable of procuring Restricted Substances–

She had no time to complete that thought, because at that moment a voice rang out across the background hiss of the chamber. "Hartley! There you are! I've been looking everywhere for you."

Taryn Underfoot was approaching, the clatter of her heeled boots reverberating as she strode across the metal gantry.

"Bladlow's struggling to bind the new mix," she said. "He needs some bloodwort and we're all out at the Tower so–" she halted abruptly as she reached him. "Mr Pockett?" She then looked at the towering figure of Woodbane with evident unease. "And Ivy? What are you both doing here?"

Hartley stepped in. "I was just assisting the Regulator with its inquiries. Supervised by Ivy here, naturally."

Ivy was aware she had not been doing much in the way of supervising for the last few minutes. She hoped Hop had not become *too* inquiring.

"Right," said Taryn shortly, eyeing Ivy warily. "I hope they haven't been disturbing you too much, Ramston," she said to Woodbane.

"Not at all! I was just tellin' Ivy here about our big plans! Things are shapin' up rather nicely!"

At that moment, a blast echoed around the chamber, causing the gantry to shudder and sway. Ivy tumbled into Hop and Hartley, while Taryn grabbed the railings in alarm. Woodbane remained steady, ballasted against the storm. There was shouting from below, mostly of the accusatory variety. Acrid smoke had started to billow from one of the cauldrons and one of the mages was clutching at his face, which had turned a vivid orange.

"Bloody idiots!" thundered Woodbane. "That's me next batch of Forever Firmin' Foundation, up in smoke!"

"I'll go," Hartley offered, having gently righted Ivy, who was coughing violently as the fumes rose.

"No, no – I'll see ter this pers'nally! Blatherin' idiots couldn't boil an egg!" Woodbane strode down the gantry steps and aimed himself at the beleaguered mages on the factory floor like an incoming warhead, wreathed in smoke.

Dismissing the fumes coiling around her with a wave of her hand, Taryn pursed her lips. "Well, Mr Pockett, I'm sure you've taken up quite enough of our client's valuable time."

Woodbane had launched into a bombastic tirade below, sending several mages scurrying as they sought to stem the tide of doughy mixture that was now burbling over the rim of the offending cauldron.

"However," Taryn continued, ignoring the shouts and wails below, "I'd be happy to answer any remaining questions you might have on our way back to the Tower." Her emphasis on the last few words was unmistakable; it was time to go. Ivy prayed Hop wouldn't be difficult; this was all going to take some explaining as it was. "On which note, shall we?"

"Are you not meeting with Mr Crumpley-Snafely?" Hop queried, wafting the smoke about with his notepad, which only seemed to be making it worse. Ivy thought it was a fair question; Mrs Woodbane had said Hartley was due a meeting with Jackdaw. "I'd be happy to attend that too?"

"No need," Taryn replied sharply. "Hartley, could you see to it that a few pounds of bloodwort finds its way to Bladlow, please? Usual channels."

Hartley nodded.

"Ivy–" Hartley said, as she started to follow Taryn out of the chamber. "If you don't mind staying for a short while, there are a couple of points I'd like to discuss?"

Taryn gave him a puzzled look.

"Just a couple of internal casting queries," he added quickly.

Taryn did not look pleased at this, but she could not prevent Ivy from remaining at her client's request. "Fine," she said. "Ivy, don't stay long, please. Master Skelton has been looking for you." She ushered out Hop, who already had his pen raised in anticipation.

Hartley led her back to his office and closed the door, flicking his fingers and magically sealing it with a practised ease that Ivy envied. As they entered, Ivy saw that the cabinet in the corner was still fizzing faintly following its earlier breach, although mercifully its excitement seemed to have dimmed.

Hartley was clearly too preoccupied to detect any unusual magical activity; he swiftly pulled Ivy towards him and kissed her.

She drew away, looking at him questioningly. "Hartley–" she began quickly.

The conversation with Woodbane was still whirling away in her mind, clamouring for attention alongside the interview with Wryneck and the intensity of the dragon's anguish. It had been an incredibly strange and rather awful day. Part of her wanted to forget about everything, to melt into his arms and then return to the comfort of her chambers later, never to spend another day investigating. The other part had questions.

"Mm?" Hartley said, leaning in and pressing his lips to her neck.

"This new process… creating Restricted Substances…" she tried to get her words out as he kissed her. "Woodbane was talking about some of the applications… and…"

Hartley paused and looked at her curiously.

Ivy felt torn. Hop's earlier suspicions were creeping in at the edge of her mind, clamouring for attention. She didn't want to listen to them; didn't want to give them any credence. It was all nonsense, she told herself firmly. It had to be. But still… "It's just, some of the stuff he was talking about using it for… and the ingredients we're supposed to be creating… is it all going to be, you know, above board?" she wrenched the questions out, haltingly.

Hartley laughed gently, brushing her hair from her face and tucking it behind her ear. "Ah, I see… look, Ramston talks a good talk, but that's all it is – pure bluster. All the ingredients are synthetic, as you know–" he smiled teasingly as he leant in "–and nothing we produce would ever breach any of the Accords. It will all be properly approved and it won't get approved if it doesn't have all the usual built-in limitations, you know that." He kissed her again. "It's all completely fine, I promise. Now, I think I very much want you to distract me from my very important work again, Ivy Armstride…"

With that, she – reluctantly at first but then ever more easily – let her questions melt away like the vapours in the brewing chamber as she reciprocated Hartley's embrace. As they moved towards the desk, Ivy was glad that it was, in fact, completely clear.

The cabinet fizzed away gently in the background, completely unnoticed.

17.

WRONG POCKETS
━━━━━ ◆ ━━━━━

The following morning, Ivy was summoned to a meeting with Skelton on the seventh floor. Despite Taryn's warning yesterday that Skelton had been looking for her, she had not returned to the Tower after the visit to Woodbane, her mind still firmly preoccupied with Hartley. Besides, Skelton had been quite clear that she had needed a break and, for once, she hadn't been minded to jump to his bidding.

However, her confidence in her reasons for ignoring his summons had largely evaporated overnight. Apart from a blissful few seconds of lucid dreaming before awakening, where she had been convinced that she had been conversing with an over-sized Kork under the shadow of a tree, she had spent the morning bombarded with waves of self-doubt and apprehension.

Not only had her delay in producing the Dragonsteel castings potentially compromised a key client asset, but she had also somehow spent the vast majority of yesterday visiting the Dark Market, facing off against a key client asset that turned out to be a lot more sentient than she had realised, attending a client's premises without permission and becoming ever more… entangled… with Hartley. Guilt sloshed around her body like one of Woodbane's potions.

She paused to give Kork, who was dozing fitfully on a shelf, a small stroke before taking a deep breath and trudging up the stairwell to the seventh floor. The seedling hadn't seemed well recently.

Waiting outside one of the meeting rooms, she heard raised voices emanating from within. That did not bode well.

While idling outside the room, she peered out over the foyer below (making sure she wasn't too close to the balcony; she hadn't checked its diary recently). She could see the branches of the giant tree thrusting up from below, heavy with large, spiked pods. She hadn't noticed those before. She looked down to the dark granite of the ground floor, feeling a rush of vertigo as she did so. She vaguely wondered what it would be like to fall…

"Ivy?" Skelton was standing in the doorway to the meeting room. He looked even more gaunt than usual, with deep shadows under his usually piercing bright eyes. His mouth was thin and solemn; Ivy felt her stomach lurch unpleasantly as he motioned for her to come.

As she entered the opulently furnished meeting room, Ivy was confronted by more faces than she had been expecting; in addition to Skelton, seated around the table were Bladlow, Taryn, Hop, an elderly goblin Ivy had not seen before, and a giant, grizzled wolf sitting obediently at the goblin's feet. Ivy's heart raced.

Hop was looking dejectedly at the floor. The other occupants looked grave, save for Bladlow, who looked like he had been shouting for quite some time and was firing up to resume.

"Ivy," said Skelton coldly. "Sit, please."

Ivy did as instructed.

"This is Chief Auditor Glof and Senior Auditor Wrexhannah Langstaff of the Regulator," Skelton continued, gesturing at the goblin and the wolf.

Ivy felt completely blind-sided. She looked over at Hop, who didn't meet her eyes.

"It has come to our attention," Skelton said coldly, "that yesterday you and Mr Pockett took it upon yourselves to attend the offices of Woodbane Cosmetics to discuss the Woodbane Solution, without the permission or the presence of a supervising Master."

Ivy glanced across at Taryn, who was sitting there impassively, arms folded.

"Further, upon being escorted back to the Tower by Ms Underfoot, Mr Pockett revealed to her a number of concerns which involved some *extremely* damaging – and entirely unfounded – allegations of illegality."

"Bloody shock that was, to discover that you two had gone sniffing around behind our backs," snarled Bladlow, before remembering that he was in the presence of senior auditors and adding, "Not that there was any reason to sniff around about in the first place!"

"Quite," affirmed Skelton. "Ivy, Master Bladlow and I will speak with you separately in a moment, but before Mr Pockett and his supervising officer take their leave of us, I would like you to hear what we have been discussing, so that any doubt in your mind as to the legitimacy of this venture is fully and finally settled.

"It has become apparent that Mr Pockett in particular has drawn some outlandish conclusions about the

Woodbane process that are demonstrably and categorically misguided."

"Bloody lies, that's what he's peddling! Accusing us of using Restricted Substances in our work – the impudence!" Bladlow fumed, apoplectic, like a balloon on the verge of bursting. "To imply that Masters of Jackdaw and Spittlelick would risk the reputation of the Tower in such a way! It is utterly preposterous and an unacceptable insult to us all!"

Ivy sat in silence, observing with bitter distaste that Bladlow appeared more concerned with the reputational impact of breaking the Accords than with any moral implications.

The wolf was tilting its head as it watched Bladlow intently. There was a ferocious scar running down its nose; Ivy had a sudden sense of jaws clamping down and blood on snow.

"Enough, Charles," warned Skelton. "We have explained to Chief Auditor Glof," he continued, "who has been most accommodating, that no such activity was ever contemplated, let alone implemented, by the mages working on this matter. The development of the Woodbane casting process has been the culmination of years of careful study and work. It is, naturally, still a developing process, but we have achieved much with modern methodology that we previously thought impossible.

"It is understandable that Mr Pockett, not being mage-trained and therefore unfamiliar with the nuances of the magical principles at play, came to the conclusions that he did, but I am perplexed, Ivy, as to why *you* believed the process was anything other than genuine. After all, you had been undertaking the casting ceremonies alongside me. Did you not comprehend the magic?"

Ivy lowered her eyes from his.

"I've been brewing the batches," Taryn weighed in disapprovingly. "I have had to confirm to Auditor Glof this morning that the ingredients Master Skelton has been producing have *not* – as you should well have known – been tampered with or swapped out."

"The very idea!" blathered Bladlow. "Believe me, we shall be discussing *in some detail* the slanders Tarragyn tells me you have been perpetuating and the consequences for you of your complete disregard for the Masters of this Tower!"

Ivy raised her gaze and fixed it on Taryn. Slanders she had been perpetuating? Disregard? That surely wouldn't have come from Hop merely reciting his concerns to Taryn… Taryn must have embellished matters. But why? She had thought Taryn was an ally; she had helped when Kork had been sick. Yet there was no compassion in those eyes; it was like an iron gate had closed.

"We will consider that in a moment," Skelton continued. "In the meantime, to conclude matters with Auditor Glof and Mr Pockett, I invite the Regulator to supervise the creation and delivery of the Woodbane ingredients. Equally, Master Bladlow has spoken with Hartley Crumpley-Snafely, who is open to having an on-site supervisor from the Regulator once the product goes into mass production, if required. Their only request is that the representative be impartial."

"Meaning not this little oik!" shouted Bladlow, pointing a plump finger accusingly at Hop, who held his gaze at the floor. Ivy should have resented the disconsolate auditor – after all, if it were not for Hop, she would not be in this mess – but she felt nothing but sympathy as Bladlow bore down upon him.

"It is a shame it has had to come to this," said Skelton smoothly. "We did offer Mr Pockett the opportunity to oversee the process, but as yet he has been unable to attend any of the casting ceremonies or brewings."

At this, Hop couldn't help but interject. "Only because nobody ever told me when or where they were happening!"

"A mere breakdown in communication, I assure you."

At this, Glof, who had been observing matters shrewdly, spoke. "Pending further discussion with the Supervisory Board, I believe we have heard enough to allay the concerns they expressed when requesting this special audit.

"On behalf of the Audit Office, I can only apologise and once again assure you that Mr Pockett – although he should have sought authorisation before attending the premises of Woodbane Cosmetics – was merely acting on what he understood to be his mandate.

"That being said, I will discuss the matter further with the Supervisory Board. In the meantime, Mr Pockett will return immediately to the Chamber with me. I only respectfully request permission for him to return following his debriefing to collect or destroy any relevant papers, as appropriate."

"Yes of course," affirmed Skelton. "I thank you for your time here this morning on such short notice, Chief Auditor Glof. We look forward to welcoming you again soon."

"Indeed," responded Glof. "It's almost annual audit time for Jackdaw, after all…" He gestured to Hop. "Come along, lad. Let's be on our way."

Glof and Hop exited, tailed by Wrex, with Hop appearing more deflated than Ivy had ever seen him.

"That'll be all from you too, Tarragyn," Bladlow instructed. "I'll see you back downstairs shortly. Lots to be going on with."

Taryn nodded in assent and left. Ivy thought she glimpsed triumph in her expression.

Bladlow turned abruptly to Ivy. "Right, I would like to know *exactly* what you were thinking. What in the seven hells do you think you've been doing? What gave you the right to speak to a client without our permission in the presence of a bloody auditor? Not to mention I'm fully aware that you've been *consorting* with Hartley – don't think I didn't see you both at the Garbled Goblin, in clear breach of Tower ethics! Explain yourself!"

"Charles…" Skelton cautioned.

Ivy hesitated, turning over the various options in her mind. Apologise, deflect, counter, evade… She resolved on the truth, or at least some of it. "I have not been perpetuating anything. I've never said to Hop that I believed any of his concerns had merit, but I was keen to ensure that the process was all being undertaken… properly." Next was the hard bit. Hartley. She found she couldn't meet their gaze and fell silent.

"Perhaps your apprehension regarding the process is partly my fault," Skelton replied, before Bladlow could start. "I could have explained it in more depth. I would have thought, though, that you would at least be capable of understanding the magic and the principles underpinning it. My mistake, it appears."

Ivy felt the sting of this remark far more keenly than Bladlow's enraged accusations or Taryn's relish at her misfortune.

"Ivy, Master Bladlow and I will need to determine what to do with you. You have placed us in a very difficult position. Attending Woodbane demonstrated very poor judgement on your part. Thankfully, Hartley has not raised a complaint as to *your* presence and we are fortunate that Ms Underfoot came to us as soon as she realised what Mr Pockett was alleging. Nevertheless, you put the Tower at risk. Competition amongst the Towers for work is more intense than ever, other mages are undercutting on fees, heavily courting clients like Woodbane–"

"Devious and witless, the lot of them," muttered Bladlow, which Skelton ignored.

"–and now more than ever it is imperative that we are seen to be capable of delivering magical services at an elite level, not to mention the benefits that we can bring to the Citadel – to the whole of Kirin – if we are able to perfect the Woodbane process. We are extremely fortunate that no lasting harm has been done. But things can always change, Ivy. Matters are fragile. Do you understand?"

"I do, Master," said Ivy, lowering her eyes again.

"Despite the unfortunate copying incident, which is best left forgotten–" said Skelton, clearly not having forgotten it at all "–you've been performing satisfactorily on the Woodbane matter over the last few weeks. However, it has become clear that your work has been suffering across the board. In particular, there is the matter of the unfinished Dragonsteel castings, the consequences of which have caused real difficulties with one of our biggest clients and may yet cost the Tower dearly."

Ivy hung her head dejectedly as Bladlow made a harrumphing sound. It was all crumbling around her now.

"As for the… consorting… as Master Bladlow put it, well… I do not know the extent of the misdemeanour, but I am afraid to say that it again demonstrates that your decision-making of late has not been of the standard expected of a Jackdaw mage."

Skelton shook his head, disappointment etched across his haggard features. Ivy had never seen the man, usually a perfect example of thoroughly modern freneticism, so solemn and still. She felt the full weight of his dissatisfaction. She fought back an intense swell of tears.

"Master Bladlow and I will consider further what is to be done. For now, Caspar will pick up the Woodbane matter."

"In the meantime," said Bladlow, unable to resist having another dig, "keep your nose firmly out of matters you clearly don't understand. And keep your hands off anything – or *anyone* – associated with Woodbane Cosmetics."

Ivy looked up at Skelton, heart in her throat, eyes glassy with the tears she was fighting to hold back, not wanting to plead but looking at him silently, silently in supplication.

"That will be all, thank you, Ivy," Skelton said finally, not meeting her gaze.

Ivy left the meeting room, shut the door, and stared blankly at the canopy of the tree.

She thought she had been doing so well. Only the other day people were toasting her success. Yet here was Skelton telling her that she wasn't good enough, that she was incapable of understanding complex and demanding magic, *"My mistake, it appears..."*. She was making poor choices, she was slipping, failing... Above all people, she had not wanted to let down Skelton, the person who had recognised and nurtured her – seemingly alleged – potential.

She couldn't recall the walk back to her chambers, but she found herself slumped at her desk, fists clenched and fingers burning. Kork scampered tiredly up her arm, looking at her mournfully as she finally let the hot tears run silently down her cheeks.

✦

"I can't begin to imagine what you were thinking there, lad," Glof told Hop, shaking his head.

They were plodding their way back to Sealem Street, the location of the Chamber of the Regulator of Magical Practice, Wrex padding softly alongside. "As for whatever it was you said to that Solutions mage that got her running to her Masters…" The old goblin sighed.

"I'm sorry, Glof. I didn't mean to cause all this trouble. I was just… so sure. The Masters were being so evasive and none of the details in the submissions added up. Something seemed wrong."

"I don't doubt you had your reasons for thinking what you did, but a good auditor doesn't jump to conclusions. Especially conclusions as dangerous as these. I know you thought something unusual was going on, but this… this is quite a big leap, my boy. Quite an accusation… what a kerfuffle…." Glof shook his head once more. "I'm all for initiative, but there's a time and a place, ways and means…"

He looked across at the trotting wolf. "Any observations, Wrex?"

The wolf *shifted*. Planes of reality shuddered with a sensation that inexplicably *looked* like the sound of chalk on a blackboard, and Wrex was strolling along beside them.

"Nothing from Skelton or the female Solutions mage – smelled clean as a whistle," she said gruffly, rubbing the scar on her face absently. "Bladlow, on the other hand… even despite all the bluster, I could smell the nerves. Gods, I could smell them. Something strange there."

"Interesting," mused Glof. "I fear this is not over yet, my boy," the goblin continued, addressing Hop, "but, for now, I will need to discuss the matter with the Supervisory Board. See what is to be done with you. Wrex and I will do our best to protect you, but we will have to hope the Board are minded towards leniency."

Hop couldn't quite believe it; Glof did not think his suspicions had been entirely misplaced! Hop had begun to let the tiniest sliver of self-doubt pierce his armour of certainty, which had proved a most unfamiliar and unpleasant feeling. He felt reinvigorated.

Glof was still murmuring to himself as the trio proceeded back to the Chamber. "Delicate balance, this job, when you sit between the mages, their masters, and ours… delicate balance indeed…"

18.

BACK TO THE COPY ROOM

Ivy, much to her dismay, had found herself back in the Copy Room. Only this time, her presence was not temporary, but an extended banishment, her penance for all her misdemeanours and her insubordination, for not staying obediently at her desk, crafting castings without question.

She had been ignominiously relegated to feeding discarded castings, solutions formulae and general administrative documents to the ever-cheerful Ump. Her strict instructions were to check carefully that each document had been properly – and correctly – marked for Umping. Master Skelton had been quite particular about that requirement, evidently finally alighting upon fitting redress for her Umping mistake, a compounding of penalties.

For the last week, she had spoken to almost no-one other than the desperate mages pleading with the unflappable Cleft, who looked to her in vain to intervene on their behalf.

Left to her own thoughts, the certainty she had started to feel around there being something wrong with the Woodbane process had faded. There had been no foul play. There was no link to the stolen dragon heart. Nothing had been amiss apart from – apparently – her own sense of perspective.

Hop was, to the best of her knowledge, still awaiting his disciplinary hearing at the Regulator. If not expelled, Ivy worried that he would almost certainly be placed on probation, eliminating any chance of advancement in the near future. Each morning, she had walked past Quiet Room Three and seen his rows of neatly arranged boxes and that strident question mark rendered at the centre of his investigation board. She felt a despondency at his absence that she hadn't expected.

The absence she was suffering most keenly, however, was that of Hartley. She had neither spoken to him nor seen him since her visit to Woodbane. Following the encounter with Bladlow and Skelton, Ivy had been hesitant to contact him – she feared she was being watched. However, early in her incarceration she had crept up to the fifth floor to check for messages on her crystal display. With a racing heart, she had seen several from Hartley, but just as she had bent to access them Elspeth had appeared at the door, arms folded. The display had been pointedly removed and her chambers magically locked.

After that, she had half-hoped to find him waiting for her outside the Tower or even at her lodgings, but there had been no sign of him. Whether he had tried to reach her again she had no way of knowing. She resolved she would just have to wait and engineer a way to see him again, feeling ever more despondent as the days passed.

Lil and Dante had in the meantime both found various excuses to find their way down to the Copy Room to attempt to cheer her up, although Dante's variations upon 'I told you so' were not generally having the desired effect.

Bob had taken to lounging alongside Ivy during the day in the Copy Room, much to Cleft's distaste and Ump's gentle bewilderment.

As for Kork, well, Kork spent most of the time sleeping in Cleft's top drawer, a development that had irked the meticulous goblin to no end. Kork had been sleeping a lot the past week, seeming ever more drained and fitful no matter how much of Taryn's feed solution Ivy administered. Ivy had been so concerned she had enlisted the opinions of Dante and Lil. She had been forced to reveal Kork's existence to them earlier that week when he had unexpectedly appeared out of nowhere with a strange *pfft* sound on Dante's shoulder. That troubled Ivy too, sensing the wilting seedling was becoming increasingly lost and unstable. The trio had examined Kork closely but had not been able to diagnose his condition.

She had taken Kork one evening to see the tree, wondering if that might help. He had seemed skittish in its presence and had clung to Ivy and chirruped and jabbered at her agitatedly until she had carted him back to the Copy Room and the safety of its heavy, windowless walls.

Today, Kork was deeply asleep, this time on some shelves piled high with immaculately stacked and glistening white paper, although Ivy suspected it would not be long before the seedling would vanish and reappear in a certain goblin's very pointedly *locked* drawer. Bob was lolling imperiously beside her as she picked up a pile of papers, peppered with crossings-out, and fed them mechanically to the troll beside her.

"Ump," said Ump, companionably.

Ivy looked blankly down at the paperwork, staring vacantly at the heading 'Draft phoenix bindings', which had been marked over in large handwriting 'Do Not Use – Serious Incident Recorded – To Be Umped'.

Ivy said bitterly, "So that's it, I suppose. Doomed to live out my days down here, feeding paper to a bloody troll."

Ump's shoulders sagged.

"No offence, Ump," she added hastily, feeding him more papers.

"Ump," said Ump, brightening up as he munched away. Cleft said nothing, as his pen continued its nimble dance across the paper before him.

There was a knock at the door. Bob languidly raised his mighty head, before laying it back down upon Ivy's lap and attempting a strangled purr.

"Enter," said Cleft, not looking up from his work.

In blundered Hop, holding a mountain of papers which he could barely keep tucked under his chin. Ivy felt herself smile at his unexpected arrival. Kork, awoken by Hop's noisy entrance, hopped down from his shelf and skittered around the auditor's feet, chirruping, before excitedly scampering over to Ivy and scaling her arm. She felt the small prickles of his twiggy limbs upon her flesh.

"Ivy? I wasn't expecting to see you down here!" Hop said, voice filled with pleasant surprise, unperturbed by the presence of either the seedling or the gigantic tiger.

"Welcome to my new chambers," said Ivy, with a droll smile and an expansive motion towards the all-too-close walls of the small room, "where all the truly important work happens."

"You too? We really did mess things up, didn't we?"

"Seems so."

"Ump," contributed Ump, not wanting to feel left out.

"Well, that's that then," he said, dropping his papers on the floor next to Ump, "the fruits of my labour…" The troll started merrily working his way through the pile.

"Stop that," said Ivy to Ump sternly. "You're not supposed to feed yourself. That's my job now." Ivy wrenched some papers from Ump's hands as the troll looked on, extremely deflated. Ivy turned back to Hop. "So, how did it go with the Regulator?"

Hop sighed. "I'm allowed to continue to work in the Audit Office, but on the strict provision that I take on no field audits for the next year and am 'consistently and closely supervised' when I do go out in the field again… they kept talking about how I might prefer a career in the Regulatory Interpretation and Guidance Department, but that's not for me." He removed his glasses and gave them a brief wipe. "I'm sorry for dragging you into all this, Ivy. It made perfect sense to me at the time. I mean, how else can the process be explained?"

"How else indeed?" murmured Cleft.

"There must be another ingredient, a trick. I just assumed…" Hop sighed as he trailed off.

At this, Cleft carefully placed his pen on his ever-immaculate desk and looked appraisingly at them, steepling his long, spindly fingers under his pointed chin. "You see, Mr Pockett," Cleft intoned gravely, "that was your first error."

Ivy looked round at him in surprise. Beyond pleasantries, Cleft had barely spoken to her in the last week. Even when Kork had appeared somewhere he shouldn't, Cleft had merely handed him wordlessly back to her. But now, Cleft seemed poised to deliver a lecture.

"You proceeded on the basis of an assumption. Most ill-advised. You assumed, for instance, that Woodbane Cosmetics, one of the largest and oldest corporations in the Citadel, would knowingly break the most fundamental of the Accords and, in doing so, risk inviting open inter-species warfare. This is not an unfair assumption, given recent tensions between the industrialists of the Citadel and its occupants, but the evidence has shown it to have been misplaced.

"You also assumed that the senior mages in this institution would not only condone such behaviour, but facilitate it, mass procuring Restricted Substances in the full knowledge that, in doing so, they would put their entire profession at risk, along with their own individual careers. A much greater assumption, perhaps not beyond the realms of plausibility in one or two cases, but, on balance, most unlikely."

Cleft paused at this point and squinted at Hop with those piercing blue eyes, which suddenly seemed to glitter dangerously. "However," he continued, "the principal assumption you and Ms Armstride made was that the vital organs of numerous goblins could have been harvested and the bodies of faeries crushed to dust without detection. Her Majesty the Goblin Queen has eyes and ears in every institution of note in this Citadel, and many others beside. She would be the first to know – and believe me, she would *know* and not merely assume – that a violation of the Accords of such magnitude had occurred.

"This was your most ill-advised assumption, to assume that such an atrocity would ever be permitted to occur on her vigilant watch." At this, Cleft once again picked up his pen and continued his copying work with a solemn shake of his head.

Ivy and Hop stared at Cleft incredulously, as they slowly digested his admonishing diatribe. If what Cleft was implying was true, then he had been paying far more attention to matters than he had let on.

"You knew," Ivy said quietly. "You knew Hop was sent to investigate the Woodbane Solution. You knew what we were looking for in that strange little shop. And you knew we wouldn't find any evidence. You could have stopped us at any time. Saved us from professional embarrassment and probable career destruction."

There was a pregnant silence. "I did suggest you were looking in the wrong place," said Cleft, slowly. He shrugged a single shoulder and nonchalantly picked up his pen to resume his transcribing. "In any event, it transpires that, for certain students, some lessons are best learned in practice rather than in theory."

"Wait…" said Ivy. "You said we were looking in the wrong place? So where exactly are we supposed to be looking?"

Cleft's eyes glittered and he inclined his head towards the pile of paperwork Hop had deposited with Ump.

"What's in these papers?" Ivy asked Hop sharply, gesturing at the piles.

"Just some records I was going through. All destined for Ump. Plus that file we retrieved from Woodbane's offices. I thought that was probably more sensible than leaving it lying around or trying to figure out how to return it."

Ump made a grab for the file. Ivy snatched it quickly from his hands.

"Ump" said Ump, deflated.

"That's odd…" said Ivy, flicking through it.

"What's odd?" asked Hop, disconcerted.

"Ump?" queried Ump.

"Nothing. It's just… it's a receipt. For delivery of that great big tree in the main foyer," Ivy said.

"So?" queried Hop.

"It's dated shortly before production on the Woodbane Solution began. It was procured by a Woodbane subsidiary entity – at least that's what it looks like. The Tower didn't pay for it. The signatory is Hartley…" She felt a sharp jolt at seeing the name.

"I'm not following the relevance here," Hop said curtly. "What does it matter that Woodbane sent the tree?"

"I don't know. I really don't. But I think it's important somehow…" At that moment, Kork leapt from her shoulder and scampered excitedly about Ivy's feet. "Kork, stop it," Ivy said, laying the paper back down and moving to shoo the seedling out of the way. "I'm trying to think."

Ivy started to pace. Bob observed grumpily, having been unceremoniously dislodged from her lap.

"If the tree is from Woodbane, then there must be a reason," she mused. "Ramston Woodbane doesn't make financial decisions lightly and transporting a tree that large – which must have been by magical means – it would have cost a fortune. It must be linked to the process. But to the Castings side? Or the Solutions? Taryn had been feeding it…"

As Ivy was pondering, feeling as though the solution to the problem was lurking in the outskirts of her peripheral vision, Caspar entered the Copy Room.

Ivy hadn't seen Caspar since Skelton had suggested he undertake the Woodbane casting ceremonies in her place. In fact, she had been actively avoiding him, not wanting to acknowledge the possibility that someone so notoriously useless might be a sufficient substitute for her.

Caspar looked terrible. Pale and wan, like all the vitality had drained away. His hair was unkempt and his eyes were ringed with shadows. He looked even more sorry for himself than usual.

"Ivy," he said blearily. "Heard you were down here. Sorry about that."

"I'll live," she said frostily. "You look like death, though. Not feeling well?"

"Not really. It's like I've got some sort of illness or something. Can't seem to shake it. Which is annoying as these Woodbane casting ceremonies have been going really well over the last few days – we've been making loads of ingredients, really ramping up. I just wish I didn't feel so rough." He paused, and added, "Sorry, Ivy, I didn't mean to… I know it should be you…"

"That's okay," Ivy said.

"Anyway, I need to get back to it. Skelton just asked me to bring these down for Umping. I suppose I should give them to you?"

"That's the idea. Here, let me take them," Ivy said, reaching for the papers.

"Thanks," mumbled Caspar.

"Looks like you could do with a break, Caspar," Ivy said, and then frowned. What was it that was bothering her?

"I wish…" said Caspar, turning to leave and running a hand across his eyes. "Feel like I could sleep for days. And my fingers feel all tingly. Dante would probably say I'm doing something wrong again… Anyway, I'd better get back. Skelton wants to schedule the first go at mass production later tonight. I'm pretty much just hanging around, waiting to be put through it all again… Means I'll miss the Falltide Dinner. It's so annoying as I heard the Masters get up to all sorts… Sorry again, Ivy, I know you can't go either…"

Ivy smiled tightly; she had been trying not to think about the dinner. Her invitation had been rescinded, a stipulation of her banishment added pettily by Bladlow.

"Gods, I need a break…" Caspar continued, "but I suppose Mother always says that hard work is its own reward…"

Caspar left the Copy Room dejectedly.

Ivy's mind was still turning over Caspar's exhausted words, his strange demeanour. What was it that felt so familiar? There was something there, resting at the edges of her mind. Her own fingers tingled slightly, a memory of magic deep and ancient…

That was it!

She turned to Hop, eyes wide. "Hop, I think I know what's been happening! We've been looking at this all wrong. We've been trying to work out how they've been faking it, but they haven't at all!"

"Yes, I'm painfully aware that I've been looking at this wrong," Hop responded petulantly. "What's your point, exactly?"

"Don't you see? It's all to do with the tree!" She started waving the receipt excitedly. "You said we couldn't perform the Woodbane castings without drawing on a magical source – the tree is that source! That's why I've been having all these dreams and feeling drained and weird." Hop looked baffled as Ivy expounded in triumph. Cleft looked at her approvingly.

"It's all connected – and so are we! Me and Kork and Caspar and Salonika before that… we're all being affected too." Ivy paused and tilted her head, momentarily lost in thought. "Salonika… maybe that's our next step? Maybe that's why she resigned – I bet she knows something…"

"Kork? Salonika?" Hop was thoroughly confused.

Ivy tossed the papers in her hand towards Ump, who snorted with delight. Ivy dashed towards the exit, grabbing Hop by the wrist. "Come on – I know who we need to talk to!" she exclaimed. She skidded to a halt and turned on her heel abruptly. "Cleft, I'm just going to take a quick break, if that's okay with you?"

"You may do as you please, Ms Armstride. I have no interest in your comings and goings. I would only request that you take your menagerie with you."

Ivy nodded, clutching Kork and motioning for Bob to follow. She promptly marched Hop up to the fifth floor, ignoring his questions, simply urging him to hurry. They arrived at a small door Hop had not noticed before, on the other side of the building to Ivy's chambers. Ivy gave a perfunctory knock before barrelling in and pulling the door closed behind her. She left Bob outside, gazing after her despondently with his golden eyes.

Sitting in an extremely stylish chair, incongruously situated in a room which resembled a broom closet that had been optimistically decorated with scraps of shimmering bunting, was Lil, disconcerted by their abrupt arrival. Even Hop noticed the sudden shift as Lil hastily composed her habitual illusions across her face.

"What in Obcryn's name are you two doing here?" she exclaimed, her wings fanning out like a startled peacock.

"Lil–" rushed Ivy, breathless from the climb (although not nearly as much as Hop, who looked thoroughly winded). "I need your help. I think I've worked this Woodbane business out, but we need to be absolutely sure this time. I need you to find someone for me."

"Slow down, you'll do yourself an injury. Who do you need me to find? I haven't really got much time, to be honest – I was just about to head home to get ready for the dinner."

Hop, who had just about stopped panting, interjected in a perplexed tone. "But it's still morning…"

"*Late* morning," returned Lil pointedly.

The annual Falltide Dinner was the highlight of Lil's year; a formal affair which inevitably became a somewhat less formal affair as the evening wore on. She had organised it now for a number of years, with each event more extravagant than the last.

There was some scratching from outside, accompanied by the tortured sound of a growl fruitlessly attempting to resemble a mewl. "Hang on..." Ivy said, opening the door with a sigh. In wandered Bob, now assuming an air of defiant indolence. Ivy shut the door behind him and he rested the warmth of his heavy flank against her legs. "Bloody stupid cat. Look, Lil, I know the dinner is tonight, but I need your help. I need to speak to Salonika. Urgently. Do you know where she is now? I haven't spoken to her since she resigned and I've got no idea where her lodgings are."

Lil raised her eyebrows in astonishment, or at least gave the impression of doing so. It's difficult for a faerie in full illusory mode to move any element of their forehead. She definitely widened her eyes. With an incredulous tone, she said to Ivy, "You mean you haven't heard?"

"Heard what?" said Ivy impatiently. "I know she resigned; you told me that weeks ago."

"Oh, Ivy..." Lil shook her head, as a desolate hush entered her voice. "Salonika's dead... It happened a couple of weeks ago. They found her washed up on the banks of the Clude. They think she might have jumped off the Seventh Bridge, but no one's sure. I'm so sorry..."

The news hit Ivy like a Deep Cart. "Gods..." she began eventually. "I had no idea..." Ivy ran a hand through her hair, completely stunned. Salonika... dead? "Why didn't you tell me?"

"I thought everyone knew. It was all over the papers… came out at the same time as the Rankings. I just assumed you had seen but didn't want to talk about it."

Ivy hadn't been reading the papers. She had been so wrapped up in what had been going on with her castings work, with Hop's Woodbane investigation, with Hartley… How had she missed this? She desperately attempted to process the news, curling her fingers around Bob's fur, steadying herself with his comforting weight. Salonika. How could she not be *there* anymore? And all she had ever done was trade petty insults with her… She felt a wave of shame as Kork cooed soothingly in her ear.

"Well, that's unfortunate," said Hop awkwardly.

Lil shot him a disdainful look, which Hop completely missed.

Lil then elegantly raised herself from the chair and placed a manicured hand on Ivy's upper arm.

"Gods, Lil…" breathed Ivy unsteadily. "I didn't know… I wanted to speak to her… it was about the Woodbane matter. I think she might have had some answers to something important…what if that's what led to her…? Gods…"

"What are you talking about?" Lil asked, surprised by the sudden change of direction. "I thought there was never anything to the Woodbane investigation? Is that what *he's* doing back here?" Lil gestured at Hop, her wings making the glimmering bunting that criss-crossed the ceiling quaver and waft as she nervously fluttered them. "Is something going on? Was Salonika involved?"

"I don't know, but I think so. I needed to ask her about it." Ivy felt her mind reel. What was she supposed to do now? And what if Salonika's death had indeed been connected to what she thought Skelton was doing to the tree? Did this mean Caspar was in danger too?

"What next then?" said Hop, breaking the tension. "We seem to have reached a dead-end." Lil shot Hop another look, clearly unappreciative of his poor choice of words, but Hop once again remained oblivious. "I mean, it's not as if we can interrogate the dead…"

"*We* can't," Ivy said slowly, turning to Lil, "but I can think of someone who can."

"You can't be serious…" Lil said, shaking her head at her. "He's really not going to like this…"

19.

SALONIKA

✦

"**D**ante, we need a favour."

Ivy, Hop and Lil piled into Dante's spacious but haphazard chambers on the fifth floor. It looked as though a paper factory had exploded. Dante was sat in the middle of it all, bent back precariously on his chair, feet on his desk, tossing a small spiky ball against one of the walls. Judging by the quiet squeak it made every time it bounced against the plaster, Ivy realised that the ball was, in fact, one of the scruttles that seemed to inhabit Dante's chambers en masse despite the Tower-wide ban on familiars. Ivy knew they were supposed to be able to withstand immense heat, pressure, cold, and magic. Dante mostly bounced them off things. Remarkably, they didn't seem to mind.

"Hello to all of you, too," Dante said, raising an eyebrow as Lil shut the door firmly behind them. Twilight was seeping through the gaps in the papers stuck to the window behind him, as ghostly lights started to flicker on in buildings across the sprawling Citadel.

"And I see our very own investigator is back with us," Dante continued, facing Hop. "Aren't you supposed to be locked in a cupboard somewhere?"

"Very funny," said Hop through gritted teeth.

"I thought so." Dante swivelled back round to the wall and continued to bounce the ball-shaped creature against the wall, as Bob and Kork followed its trajectory with interest. "Now, what do you lot want? I'm snowed under, as I'm sure you can see."

"Look, Dante," said Ivy, "I know you won't want to hear this, but this Woodbane business–"

"You're right, I don't want to hear it. I'd like to inhabit the real world," asserted Dante, plonking his legs back on the ground and dropping the scruttle on his desk, whereupon small legs popped out from its rubbery body, and it scuttled away, squeaking tetchily. "I'm not going through this again. I did try to warn you. Mr Auditor was wrong. End of story. Nothing more to say."

"But there is!" Ivy shouted. "Look – I think I've worked it all out. It's the tree."

"What?" Dante frowned in confusion.

"Hop was right – Trebbletuft's principle means we can't use natural matter to create stable magical matter unless it is taken from a stable natural magical source."

Hop couldn't resist a smug grin.

"What magical source?"

"The tree!"

"What tree?"

"The bloody big one downstairs!"

"The one in the foyer?"

"Yes!"

"But the tree's not magical." Dante leaned back in his chair and rested his hands behind his head, as if the matter had been fully and finally settled, before hesitating and adding, "Is it?"

"I think it might be. I think it might be where Kork has come from."

The seedling was currently sitting astride Bob's massive head and had somehow obtained one of Dante's scruttles, which it was bouncing up and down between Bob's ears, to the tiger's mild irritation.

"That's speculation. And in any event, even if that were the case, what would be wrong with that?" Dante leaned forward and looked challengingly at Hop as he said this. "The Accords permit the use of magical flora by mages – it's the fauna they aren't so keen on us using."

Ivy answered. "Look, I'm not sure whether it's of any interest to the Regulator, to be honest. But I'll bet it's that tree that's being drained for the castings and it's not good for it – you've seen the state Kork's been in, always dehydrated, frequently passed out.

"Something's happening to the mages performing the casting ceremonies too. Caspar's only been performing them for the last few days, and he looks awful. Salonika did too. I felt constantly exhausted. I've got a really bad feeling about it, Dante."

"Okay, so we're working on the basis of feelings now, are we?" said Dante sarcastically. "How about we go back to the original question: what do you need me for in all this madness?"

"We need to speak to Salonika."

Dante looked stunned. "You do know what's happened to Salonika, right?"

"Yes, although admittedly I only just found out…"

"Right. So, again: what exactly are you asking here?"

"Look, we can't go to the Wills team, and none of us know how to commune with… you know… deceased persons… as well as you do."

Dante moved abruptly backwards in his chair, waving his hands at them. "Oh no. No, no, no. I don't do that sort of thing anymore. Lil, you know that, right? You know I don't do that sort of thing?"

"I did try to tell her," Lil said earnestly, "I said you wouldn't like it. But she wasn't having any of it. Proper bee in her bonnet."

"Well, it can buzz right off. As can you lot. The answer is no. No."

"Please, Dante," pleaded Ivy, "something isn't right here. Something bad is happening. What if it's behind what happened to Salonika? Isn't that worth checking?"

"You're mad," Dante shot back, shaking his head. "You've all gone bloody mad. I'm well aware that this place does bad things to good people, but, frankly, it's done an absolute number on you lot. I'm not doing it. Salonika might not even be there to ask! And even if she is – what makes you think she'd want to speak to us? Besides, I said no. I don't. I can't. No."

"We wouldn't ask if it wasn't important."

Dante turned to look at Hop. "And the Regulator is okay with this? You do realise we'd be breaking the Accords? After all, we're not supposed to make unsolicited calls on the dead without a 'legitimate commercial purpose' these days…" Scorn dripped from his voice as he delivered the last sentence.

Hop pushed his glasses back up the bridge of his nose. "In my view, the legitimate commercial purpose of the exercise is to investigate whether Woodbane's commercial enterprise is in itself legitimate," he said stuffily. "I am confident I would have the Regulator's support in the matter, were they aware of the facts of the situation."

"But they're not, are they?"

"They will be, as soon as I am able to produce a comprehensive report of my further enquiries. To enable me to do so, it is vital we obtain all the information we can."

"But you're not supposed to be making any enquiries! The matter was closed! Done!"

"Dante, please," beseeched Ivy.

Dante stood up and paced the room, rustling the papers strewn across the floor. There followed some muttering on Dante's part, further pleading on Ivy's part, and then further pacing and muttering. At one point Dante flung his arms out over his head, looked up at the ceiling, sighed loudly, and then resumed his pacing, inadvertently disturbing several piles of organised chaos.

Shadows flickered, licking at the edges of the papers plastered across the walls.

Lil clasped Ivy's wrist, tugging at it. "Come on, Ivy, I told you it wouldn't work," she said. "He won't do it."

"Won't… or can't?" Ivy challenged, glaring at Dante as he paced, refusing to meet her eye. Not getting a response, even from this, she shrugged sullenly. "Fine. If you can't, I will–"

Dante held out a hand for silence and pressed his fingers to his temples.

The room fell quiet; the shadows settled. Dante closed his eyes and ran his hand across his face, murmuring. Hop opened his mouth to say something, but Lil hushed him. Eventually, Dante opened his eyes and said quietly, "You're not going to let this go, are you? You're all mad. Completely mad. Fine. I can't believe I'm about to say this, but… fine, I'll do it. But it can't be here."

"Where, then?" asked Ivy, not quite believing they had managed to convince him, but unwilling to let the opportunity slide.

"My place."

✦

Ivy had never been to Dante's lodgings, which were situated in a quietly wealthy precinct of the Citadel. To be fair, it looked as though not many people had visited Dante's lodgings – and certainly no one in the cleaning industry. Hop, Lil and Ivy entered a large living room with a small kitchen area at one end. Discarded books, clothes and miscellaneous musical instruments were scattered across the dusty surfaces (Ivy did not know Dante was a musician – he had kept that to himself). A pair of curtains which had once been deep red but had now faded to dried salmon hung across the window. It looked like they hadn't been opened for a while. Streetlamps and the ambient glow from neighbouring windows filtered through the moth-holes in the fabric. The slender beams of light swarmed with gently circling dust particles.

Dante gestured casually with his hand and a dim yellow-orange glow illuminated the room. He kicked aside some clothes, unsettling further dust as he did so.

"Make yourselves at home," he said.

They looked round the room, all trying to determine if there was anywhere to sit that wasn't already occupied by what should rightly have been the contents of Dante's drawers, shelves and kitchen cupboards. There wasn't.

Dante sat himself down on the carpet and crossed his legs. The other three followed suit awkwardly, Lil brushing some crumbs out from under her legs as she did so.

"Right. For the record, I want to reiterate that this is sheer lunacy and I can't believe I'm doing it. No one is to speak about this to anyone, ever, as I would rather not find myself in the basement of the Chamber becoming acquainted with the grimlings. Understood?"

The others nodded.

"I would also like to make clear that I have not visited the reality beyond ours in years–"

"Why not?" asked Hop abruptly.

"I have my reasons, Mr Auditor. In any case, it's not a particularly fun place to find oneself if you're not used to it. Has anyone here done this before?"

Lil and Hop shook their heads. Ivy admitted she had done it once while in Futures. This had only been for a couple of minutes, and it had been pitch-black so she had mostly bumped into things and yelped a lot.

"Right. And I assume you all wish, for want of a better expression, to come for the ride?"

This time they all nodded, albeit a little uncertainly.

"You're all mad. It's going to be bumpy. I can't guarantee we'll find Salonika, but I know her well enough to find her quickly if she is there. I need you all to stay calm, quiet and focused. Try not to panic or let your mind drift elsewhere. Understood? Good. Questions?"

"Don't we need candles or something?" Hop asked.

"Why would we need candles?" Dante snapped irritably. "Are we planning a romantic evening?"

"I don't know, I just thought candles were a thing."

"Well, whoever came up with that ridiculous notion is clueless. To my mind, the worst thing you can have nearby when communing with the dead is an open flame, liable to be knocked over while you're busy inhabiting an alternate plane of existence."

"It was just a question! I suppose you'll say we don't all need to hold hands either?"

"Not really, no. But if you want to hold someone's hand, don't let me stop you. Now, hush. I need to concentrate, especially as you want me to bring all of you with me. I haven't done this in a very long time and I'm not exactly travelling light here."

"Excuse me!" said Lil indignantly.

Dante ignored her and closed his eyes. He sat, legs-crossed, straight-backed, hands facing upwards. "Okay…" he breathed, "here goes…"

The others observed him apprehensively. Ivy watched the dust swirl softly behind his eerily rigid outline, expectant. For a moment, there was nothing. The only sound was the delicate internal hum that always disconcertingly accompanies silence. Then a supple chill gradually descended, accompanied by subtle whispering voices on the brink of hearing. Ivy strained to hear the words of the voices; they sounded urgent, frantic. She knew if she leaned just that bit closer, she would understand what they were trying to tell her. She felt as though she were on a Deep Cart, rumbling along beneath the firmament of reality…

Without warning, the journey juddered to a halt, shoving them sideways.

Ivy opened the memory of her eyes.

A sensation of place shifting uncertainly; the landscape seemed to need a few moments to work out what it wanted to be. Barren plains faded into abundant forests dripping with sweaty raindrops into snow-capped mountains into a rush of electric light into darkness into, finally, a meadow resting beside a riverbank. The meadow seemed at once nothing more than a narrow strip of grass and yet infinite in size. The soft grass underfoot susurrated in and out of reality and shimmered ominously.

The river running alongside the ephemeral bank frothed and foamed, seething silently. The sky above sloped into a deep purplish red. The atmosphere was thick and soapy, exerting a soft, soundless pressure. She felt dream-like, alien, almost intangible. Dante was good at this; she hadn't experienced anything approaching this during her one and only previous foray into the beyond.

Ivy shifted tentatively towards the bank, or at least attempted to. She wasn't sure if she was solid or whether air was simply thicker here; it was a peculiar sensation, like being underwater. She tried to breathe but nothing happened. She couldn't see the others; but they were there, somewhere, nowhere.

"What is this place?" The voice of Hop fractured the landscape, resounding assertively in the otherwise stilled air.

"Nowhere." Dante's cool tones.

"Clearly it's somewhere, otherwise how am I here?" Hop's form materialised abruptly as he motioned down at himself.

Ivy was still struggling to find herself.

"That's between you and your Gods. Although clearly, you're very sure you're wherever you think you are, which comes as no surprise," the voice of Dante replied.

Hop looked almost too substantial, unyielding against his shifting surroundings. As Hop's brow furrowed, Dante simply said, "Just think of it as an in-between place."

"In-between where and where?"

"Excellent question. Somewhere between dream and memory."

"Whose memory?" This came from Lil, who hadn't coalesced into anything yet, but flickered in the periphery like an ungrounded electrical spark.

"Hers," Dante said, pointing. Ivy felt herself drawn to a space along the bank that faded gradually into vision.

On the edge of the riverbank sat a young woman, clasping her knees to her body, staring at the river. Her legs were long and bare, and her toes hovered listlessly above the water. Tresses of thick black hair hung loose around her head, which was bowed over the tops of her knees.

"Salonika," said Dante's voice.

All shape is ephemeral here, but if she concentrated hard enough Ivy imagined she could fix an outline of Dante's form.

"Salonika."

The woman looked up, uncomprehending, face streaked with dirt and tears.

"Salonika, it's me, Dante. Can you hear me?"

A slow nod of acknowledgment.

"We'd like to talk to you, if that's okay?" Dante's voice was gentle and comforting, like someone murmuring to a wild animal on the verge of bolting.

"We?" she asked weakly, staring around.

The others came into soft focus, save for Hop, whose edges were already dependably crisp.

"Me, Ivy, Lil and a chap from the Regulator – his name's Hop."

"The Regulator?" Salonika seemed uncertain. "Have I done something wrong?"

"No, no. But that's what we're here to talk to you about. We think something wrong has been going on at the Tower and we're trying to work it all out," Dante said. "We need your help, Salonika."

"This is about Woodbane, isn't it?" replied Salonika sharply. The landscape flashed and wobbled. Momentarily, grass gave way to flagstone; the river plunged to somewhere far below and grew calmer, deeper, greater. The sensation lasted only for a second, before the strange, bright wildness of the riverbank hastily re-materialised.

"Salonika, it's Ivy," Ivy said, stepping forward, although Ivy had the peculiar impression Salonika had simply become spontaneously closer.

"Ivy? What are *you* doing here? You hardly spoke to me when I was..." There was another shudder in the surroundings, as Salonika stuttered. "Well, when I *was*."

"I know, I'm sorry. Really, I am, for what it's worth..."

"It's not worth much."

Ivy bristled. The sky seemed to darken. As she went to retort a surge of pressure gripped her throat.

"Ivy, please..." cautioned Dante, with strain in his voice. Ivy got the sensation that only she could hear him. "...holding this together for so many of us is hard... I need you to stay calm..."

Ivy checked her temper. "Look, you're right, it is about the Woodbane matter. I've been helping Skelton–"

"Hah," Salonika interrupted with a snort, "of course you have, you were always his favourite. Should have known it'd be you he'd choose in the end. It's always *you*."

Ivy again struggled to keep her voice level. "There's something not right about the Woodbane process. We thought it was all a sham at first, but now... well, we know it works, but we aren't sure how. There's some sort of link with that massive tree in the Tower, and it's been affecting us – me, Caspar, you, maybe even Skelton... look, I don't think I'm explaining this very well..."

"We need to understand how the magic works," supplemented Hop, "and whether what you are doing is within the boundaries of the Accords."

"We need your help, Salonika," added Ivy. "We need to know whether it's safe."

Salonika stared blankly at the river. "I should have guessed you weren't here to check whether I was all right. I'm not, by the way, in case you hadn't noticed. Not that anyone cares. No one cared when I was alive, so why should now be any different? You're all the same. Just like Skelton."

Salonika rested her head back on her knees and started to cry. Ivy went to say something but felt a gentle pressure on her arm. Lil whirled into being, enduringly ethereal, magnificent, lucid beauty floating across her features. The dreamscape of death seemed to agree with her. The sky brightened as Lil enveloped Salonika in warmth. "Oh, Salonika..." she whispered. "We had no idea what was happening, I promise. I know it won't mean much to you, but we're here with you now. We see you."

Salonika clutched at Lil, visibly shaken, although the tears had calmed.

Dante had joined Lil and was kneeling by Salonika. "If you want to talk, we'll listen. I can't promise it will fix anything, but the more we know about what happened, the more we can do to stop anyone else getting hurt. That's what Ivy and Hop are trying to say, admittedly not brilliantly, but this is their first time speaking to a dead person, so you'll have to forgive them."

There was something in Lil's warmth, and in Dante's directness, that seemed to lift Salonika. She started, slowly, achingly, to talk.

"Skelton asked me to help out with some developmental magical work last winter. Said it was confidential, something he'd been thinking about for a while. A way to restore some of the strength of the Old Magic in a modern context. He told me he thought he'd worked out how to create synthetic magical matter using a process which was completely stable.

"He said he needed to draw on primal magical energies and fuse them with ordinary materials in order to transform them. He had tried to do it by himself before, but found it impossible – that's why he needed me.

"We had a few trial runs. Inevitably, there were issues. We could transform the matter, but it rarely stayed stable for long. Sometimes it crumbled, sometimes it went back to how it was, sometimes it just… went somewhere else. Skelton was convinced we were on the verge of discovering how to make it work. But it didn't seem to be going anywhere, and I was exhausted. I could barely even look at the other work I had on. Kept having to give it to others. Kept messing up. I knew people were noticing, too. Don't think I wasn't aware that you were all enjoying watching me crack."

"We weren't, Salonika, I promise," said Lil. "I did wonder what was going on, though…"

Ivy remained silent.

"A lot was going on," said Salonika bitterly. "Too much. But Skelton needed this to work. He had been speaking to Bladlow and they'd pitched the product to a client. He became desperate, pushing me to the brink. And then, one day, I don't know what happened, but while we were performing the casting, while I was channelling magic from wherever the hell we draw the damn stuff from, I sort of *slipped*..." Salonika paused, unsure. "...The only way to describe it was like falling off a bridge, into clear water, and *reaching*..." Reality flickered again and Ivy felt cold stone beneath her feet. Salonika continued, "...But then I found something to cling onto. It was small, a plant I think, somewhere in the building – at least that's what I told Skelton. It felt like magic feels when it's bone deep... so I pulled.

"The casting stopped, and we'd made something. Faerie dust. We knew there was something different about it this time. It remained stable. It was still faerie dust weeks later. I carried some around with me, in a pouch, partly to make sure, partly as, I don't know, a souvenir of finally pulling it off. Faerie dust..."

Lil gave an involuntary shudder. "I'm sorry, I know it wouldn't have been real, but still..."

"It *was* real, though, wasn't it, Salonika?" asked Ivy quietly.

Salonika stared up at the heavy, bruised sky, and nodded. "It was real. Inherently magical. But the magic was stolen."

"So that's where the tree comes in, then? Skelton and Bladlow sourced it, Woodbane paid for it, and then you began draining it?" Hop intoned matter-of-factly.

"Basically, yes. Skelton interrogated me for ages after that casting. Made me explain over and over. He figured it out. Soon enough, the tree had arrived. Skelton had revised the casting. Made it easier to work. He would effectively draw on the tree, propel its magical energy through me. I would, at his command, channel it, convert it, make the reaction.

"I was so proud. I felt like I had achieved something, even though it was all him, really. It was always him."

Salonika was silent for a while.

"It broke me. I don't think he realised. I didn't want to tell him. Thought he'd be disappointed in me. But whatever was happening in that process was destroying me. My skin felt like it was all fire and ice, my head felt thick, I couldn't stop sleeping, it was never enough. By the time we'd finished producing components for the original product line, Woodbane was already demanding more.

"But I had nothing left to give. I felt like I was going mad at times. Could hear voices, *feel* the tree. It started with whimpering, then protests. Like it was suffering. I was so tired. So I told Skelton I couldn't do it anymore."

The memory of Salonika's resignation, burned with acrid magic into Skelton's desk, skittered across the deathscape. The edges of the horizon started to shimmer and crackle, becoming a violent purple-green haze.

"Ivy…" Dante's voice. She felt for him, found him braced against the grass. He seemed to be flickering too. "Ivy… I can't hold this much longer…"

Swirling, dense, cloud-like structures formed in the sky above. Stones beneath the feet, river beneath that, deep, endless.

Salonika's tone became scornful. "He took it exactly how I expected. Suggested he *onboard* someone else, someone to help take the strain off me. Said I should maybe take a little rest, work on some other matters for a bit. Turned out I wasn't that *indispensable* after all." Ivy felt Salonika's bitter anger resonate discordantly with her own.

The landscape was volatile now, simmering. Ivy knew that time was running out. She could feel Lil's panic, Hop's uncertainty, Dante's exhaustion, all in her own being. More than all that, she could feel Salonika's resentment, pouring like molten tar over the grass.

"He said it would be a shame, of course, a *shame*," Salonika spat the word. "But that he completely understood. He understood nothing. Nothing!" The pitch of Salonika's voice was a seismic scream, but her lips were no longer moving. She was standing, arms by her sides, fists clenched, teeth clenched, head hanging.

Heat cascaded around Ivy. The water below sounded closer than ever now, reaching up to embrace them.

"You took it away from me! All of you!" Salonika shrieked, her head jerking up at them, like a broken doll.

Dante was clearly struggling, and strange shadows had crept towards them, dark shades. Others.

Ivy said hurriedly, "Salonika, we can make this right, but I need you to stay calm… Lil – please! Help her!" Ivy felt existence crumple and twist around her. Fingers were at her throat. She wasn't sure if they belonged to Salonika, or the shades, or her.

The fingers squeezed. They choked, crushed. A flash of blinding white light. A cry, a gasp of breath.

Stillness. Blackness.

20.

BAD TIDINGS

Ivy cautiously blinked open her eyes to see Dante's living room swim into view. With a vast tide of relief she observed the papers and boxes and clothing strewn across the room, absorbing their delightful solidity like a sailor disembarking from a boat after a storm. Her head swam and her fingers burned; her throat felt constricted and raw.

Dante was out of breath and crouched over on all fours, breathing heavily.

"Are you okay?" croaked Ivy, half-crawling to him as Lil rushed over to try to brace him.

Dante shuddered and retched violently, trembling and scanning the room as though he was searching for someone. Pushing Lil away, he scrabbled through the detritus on the floor, pain and despair creasing his face. Ivy thought she could detect darkness crawling down from the corners of the walls, slithering towards him as he scrambled around his discarded belongings, running his hands feverishly through his untidy dark hair. "Madness…" he muttered breathlessly, over and over.

"Dante!" Ivy shouted at him as Lil tried to grab him again and steady him. "Come on, please!" She yanked his shoulders, spinning him around to face her as the shadows traced their way to him.

He looked at her strangely, as though he didn't recognise her, his eyes dilated and pooled with a deep blackness. "Can you see him?" he asked her harshly.

Ivy released her grip in alarm.

Lil moved in and enveloped him, stroking his hair and murmuring to him as he coughed and shook. Slowly, slowly, he started to calm, his breathing becoming less ragged, his eyes more focused. He exhaled and rolled onto his back, placing one hand on his chest, which was rising and falling steeply.

"Oh my Gods, I'd forgotten what that felt like," he said finally. Ivy felt her body relax and noticed Hop, who was sitting bolt upright, looking jaded and lost, staring ahead blankly.

"Dante, what *was* that? What happened?"

"Madness…" was all he said.

Ivy tried to pull herself together, which was made difficult by a lingering sensation that some part of herself was currently nowhere to be found.

"Speaking of madness," Lil said, looking critically at the pair of exhausted mages and the broken auditor, "what exactly are we supposed to do now?"

Lil made them some restorative drinks, which they consumed gratefully, even though they tasted like berries left on a mountainside mixed with charred animal. With each sip they began to feel more like themselves, nestled amongst the debris of Dante's lodgings. Night was falling across the Citadel; Ivy was grateful for the gentler darkness that was softly washing through the grime of the windows.

"Is it usually like that?" Hop asked, ever inquisitorial. "Visiting the beyond?"

"It was definitely more constructive than my only previous visit," Ivy said quietly.

Dante remained silent.

"So," began Lil, hesitantly reiterating her earlier question, "what do we do now? What do we do about what Salonika said? Shouldn't we tell someone?"

"Tell who what?" Dante was rubbing his eyes tiredly. "Skelton's draining a tree of its magic. It's hardly any different to using leaves in a brew."

"But he's hurting it," Ivy countered. She thought of Kork, back at the Tower, probably now ensconced in Cleft's top drawer, with his small, rounded belly and stick-like legs twitching as he slept. She thought of Salonika, forgotten and distraught on the riverbank of death. "Not to mention what he did to Salonika."

"Yes, Ives, but *what* did he do to Salonika?" Dante sounded exasperated and exhausted. "He tired her out. That's all that happened there. No different to the drain we all feel when channelling magic. She probably should have listened when Skelton said she should take a break."

Ivy glared at him in disbelief. He raised his hands in a placatory manner. "I'm not trying to be difficult, I promise. I'm just envisioning what Skelton would say when quizzed by Hop's friends at the Regulator." Dante nodded towards the auditor, who was looking pensive. Ivy noticed Dante had used his actual name for once.

"Hmmm…. I'll need to speak with Glof and Wrex…" mused Hop. "Unfortunately, Dante makes a good point. Although we seem to have *finally* established what's been going on, it's difficult to see any breach of the Accords, on a strict reading."

"But Salonika's dead!" Ivy shouted. "Kork's sick! And Caspar's not doing much better!" Something niggled at Ivy as she said this, something Caspar had said earlier. What was it? But the conversation of the morning felt like a lifetime ago. "You can't tell me that's right! We need to stop all this, before more people get hurt or sick. Or worse. Something about this just feels bad."

"I'm with Ivy on this one, what they're doing isn't right, whatever the rules say," Lil said in an unexpectedly firm voice. "If they've started ripping magic out of trees, they might not stop there. Who knows where else they might start ripping magic from... and then it's back to the bad old days. Don't forget, someone out there ripped a dragon heart out of an actual dragon, right under Dragonsteel's noses, just the other day. There's plenty of folk in this Citadel who wouldn't blink to do worse than that, whatever they might say."

Lil's dark remark reminded Ivy of her own family's endemic distrust of mages. Maybe they had been right all along; maybe the Citadel mages simply didn't care what harm they caused so long as they were making a tidy profit. She stared dully at the walls.

"I don't think any of us are saying that it's right," Dante pointed out. "We're just trying to work out what to do about it. Look, it's getting late, we're all tired…"

"We're not done yet, in case you've forgotten, Dante," Lil said. "Got the bloody Falltide Dinner to go to, not that I'm feeling in the party mood anymore."

"Bugger…" Dante sighed, once again rubbing his face vigorously, as though to massage the life back into it. "We could just not go? No-one would notice."

"They would. I have to go, I organised the sodding thing." Lil's beautiful illusions were flickering and fading; she looked tired underneath. "I wish I didn't, though. I don't feel quite right after all this… I could do with you there, Dante."

"Fine," Dante conceded reluctantly. He looked at Hop and Ivy. "What about you two?"

"I'm going to head back to the Chamber, write up my report this evening while it's still fresh, and research whether there are any options under the Accords we can consider. There must be an angle we can pursue!" Hop was brimming with resolve again. Ivy just felt flat.

"Ivy?" Lil ventured. "Might be worth you heading home? Getting some rest? We can re-group in the morning…"

"You can always crash here," Dante offered. "I can't imagine we'll want to stay too late."

Still gazing at the wall, Ivy replied in a monotone, "I think I'm just going to go back to the Tower and check on Kork. Someone needs to make sure he's okay."

Dante and Lil looked at each other in concern.

"Are you sure?" Lil said, moving across and putting her hand on Ivy's shoulder. "If you need us, we can come with you. It's only a silly dinner, after all."

Ivy felt a rush of gratitude towards the faerie, but she needed to be alone right now. She needed to get her thoughts in order.

"No, it's fine," Ivy said, as reassuringly as she could. "I'm fine. I just want to check on Kork and then I'll head home. We can speak again in the morning, see whether there's anything we can do about Skelton."

Lil gave Ivy's arm a companionable rub. "If you need us, Dante's got one of those portable crystal displays Skelton got so excited about a couple of months ago. We can take it with us."

Dante groaned. "Not that thing! Do I have to? Last time I took it somewhere it melted a hole in my trousers!"

✦

While the collected mages and non-mages of the Tower of Jackdaw and Spittlelick were gamely working their way through the first of six courses in a glamorous venue at the heart of the Citadel, Ivy was sitting in the Copy Room, stroking the tiny seedling on her lap, who was twittering faintly as he slept.

She had arrived back at the Tower just as Cleft and Ump were setting off for the Falltide dinner. On his way out, Cleft had scooped Kork out of his drawer and handed him to her wordlessly. Ump, leaving the Tower for the first time in weeks, had cheerfully curled up and rolled along after the goblin. Bob had padded over and settled in next to her as she sat on the cold floor, kneading at her with over-sized paws.

The Tower slowly emptied, leaving Ivy in the quiet solitude of the Copy Room, leaning against the warmth of the tiger, exhausted. She stared lethargically at the endless words and rubrics on the discarded papers in the Umping basket, in the neatly stacked pile on Cleft's desk, on the shelves in front of her. So many words.

She had accepted it all so unquestioningly, fearful of the power that curled inside her like a snake. Magic was dangerous; mages were untrustworthy. Those were the words of her mother and father, words she had been raised on. Words she had been too afraid and ashamed to repeat to anyone, even to Hartley, when she had talked to him of her childhood.

Her parents, scarred by the wars of the mages that had razed the Citadel of Charnford to its footings, that had claimed the lives of their own parents, had lived in fear of mages. They had always denied even the merest hint they may themselves have inherited the curse, even though magic tended to run through the blood. To their minds, the Accords did not go nearly far enough. They had pleaded with her when she had discovered her power, told her to hide it, to bury it. Mages did not live long in New Charnford.

But she had wanted to use it, this magic inside her. It wanted to be used, too; it raged against her captive breast. The pleading of her parents had become scolding; the scolding had become renunciation, backs which had turned forever as she left for the Citadel. She had forced herself instead to bury their shame, her shame.

She had put all her hopes into the Citadel, the last bastion of Kirin's human magic users, imagining the splendour of the Towers and the freedom and acceptance they would afford her. But the mages here had been tamed and trained and put to good use, their magic stifled with words and limitations that served and profited only the few. Skelton more than most had managed her training, teaching her all the right words.

Ivy knew the rules and regulations were a good thing, an important thing, needed to prevent the rampant destruction that magic could cause. Yet the words fell like chains around her; chains that pulled at her like a harness on a dragon. Those words had somehow bound her in a way they hadn't bound other mages. Hartley and Dante had no problems using their magic; they weren't wrapped in fear at the mere thought of trying to cast a spell without the comforting constraints of careful drafting.

Was this what magic was supposed to be?

She picked up a discarded formula, turning the paper over in her hands as she gazed, unseeing, at the complex methodology inscribed on its pages. She remembered the Woodbane castings with Skelton, standing under his direction as they pulled the magic from what she now knew to be the giant ancient chestnut nearby, draining it – and her – to feed the magic of Woodbane's potions, those cauldrons of matter and magic, the infernal industrial machinery of the Citadel.

She considered Salonika. She hadn't even questioned Salonika's behaviour over the last few months, believing the mage was straining under the weight of the magic undertaken at the Tower. Ivy had, like the others, forgotten Salonika once she had left. She hadn't even been aware of her death. Had Skelton caused that? Had Ivy herself been complicit in perpetuating the theft of the tree's magic, in ignoring Salonika's anguish, all in aid of not disappointing her Master?

She imagined Skelton at the Falltide dinner, avidly conversing with the other Masters, expounding the merits of his new process, oblivious to the damage he had wrought. Or had he known all along and simply not cared? Did the man care about any of them? Had he cared about her?

She rested a hand on Bob, restlessly wrapping her fingers in his fur as the seedling on her lap slept on. She had trusted him. She had trusted Skelton and his words. As a tide of anger and frustration rose, magic crackled along her fingers, making Bob's fur shiver with static.

At that moment, the walls of the Copy Room gave a strange tremble.

Kork juddered feverishly in his sleep. Ivy looked down as the seedling shook and moaned plaintively. His foliage cracked and shrivelled before her eyes, his bark-like limbs becoming harsh and hot to the touch, almost causing her to drop him.

Bob rose, ears pricked, haunches crouched in a nervous pose. What was happening?

She stood up, panicking as the tiny seedling gasped and chirruped in pain. He felt desiccated and brittle, like a plant in winter that snaps at the slightest pressure. She had to feed him, get some water into him. Clutching him to her chest, she raced across to the shelf where she had placed the solution Taryn had given her.

The bottle was empty.

What should she do? She tried to think quickly as Bob started growling, a low sound which made the hairs on her nape prickle. Maybe there was some more feed in Taryn's chambers? Ivy dashed out of the Copy Room towards the stairwell, cradling the seedling, Bob pounding along beside her.

The tree had just been fed again. It hadn't even tried to resist it this time, sullen and stolidly clamped in the grimling stone. It had let the solution soak through its aching roots, up through its suffocated boughs.

As the abominable liquid seeped in, the tree convulsed.

The feed… the feed… it was different. Stronger, beating with a fire that burned like the furnaces at the centre of the world. Raw and powerful and vile.

It knew this magic; an old enemy, familiar and feared.

Fury surged through its branches, flames wreaking through its ancient limbs. Not this, not this…

The tree had had enough.

21.

SYSTEMIC FAILINGS

◆

Taryn Underfoot was sitting morosely in her chambers, mulling over the futility of existence and other jolly subjects, when Ivy opened the door and hurried in, tiger at her heels.

"Ivy?" spluttered Taryn in confusion. "What in seven hells are you doing here?"

Ivy jumped in shock. "Sorry," she said, trying to regain her composure. "I assumed you'd be at the dinner with everyone else. I've run out of that feed solution you made for Kork."

"Kork?" Taryn enquired, still confused.

"The seedling. I've been trying to look after him, but… I don't know what happened… I think he's really sick." Ivy felt the panic tighten in her chest. Bob paced anxiously round the small chambers, tail flicking dangerously.

"Show me," Taryn demanded.

Ivy eyed Taryn suspiciously. She wasn't certain she could trust her after the events of last week, nor after the revelations from Salonika, but she was desperate. She presented the seedling to Taryn, laying him tenderly on her desk.

"Gods…" said Taryn, looking at Kork, examining him delicately. He was twitching and whimpering, his large black eyes scrunched in pain. "What happened?"

"I don't know… He was asleep, and then he just started to shrivel in front of me…" Ivy felt her voice catch in her throat, as she blinked back frightened tears.

Taryn leapt up and ferreted around on a shelf crammed with various pots and vials, slapping away a twirling vine from one of her more curious specimens. "Okay, okay… I'll see what I can do, but, Ivy… he doesn't look right. It may be beyond my abilities." She sifted through vials hurriedly.

"It's because of what you're doing to the tree, isn't it?" Ivy said dejectedly.

Taryn stopped in her tracks, staring at Ivy in alarm. "What did you just say?"

"The tree. I know you've been using it for the Woodbane process, draining it of its magic. Kork's connected to it, isn't he? He's getting drained too."

Taryn looked down at the tiny seedling, suddenly looking for all the world as though all the fruits of her harvest had transpired to be riddled with rot.

"Shit," she said quietly.

"You knew all along, didn't you?" Ivy's eyes simmered as she felt her temper rise. Her arms throbbed with magic and anger. She felt the building tremble again but paid it no attention. "You knew Skelton was using the tree to create those ingredients."

"Yes, we've been using the tree, but–"

Ivy cut Taryn off, she was now too enraged to listen. "What have you all been playing at? Do you have any idea what it's done to Kork? To Salonika?"

Kork whimpered on the desk between them.

"Salonika?" Taryn repeated weakly. "But Salonika's–"

"Dead. Yes." Ivy was railing at Taryn now, at this woman who was supposed to mentor and guide her, who had, just like Skelton, failed her. "You drained her too. Why? For Gods' sakes, why? Was it all just because you wanted to impress a bloody client with your cleverness?"

Taryn slumped in her chair, clutching a glass beaker. It seemed like every last shred of conviction had been sapped out of her. She looked at Kork blankly for a moment and then put her head in her hands. "I thought it was under control. We all did."

"What was under control?" Ivy raged.

Taryn took a deep breath. "I thought Skelton would have told you. It wasn't a secret that we were using the tree. But it all makes more sense now.

"I couldn't understand why you'd been indulging that auditor and his ridiculous theory that we'd been swapping what you made with actual Restricted Substances. Bladlow was livid and Skelton was completely blind-sided. We all thought you were trying to shut down the project, I couldn't figure out why you'd want to do it, not when we'd all worked so bloody hard, but if you didn't know..."

"Of course I didn't bloody know! Even if I had known, I wouldn't have gone along with it as unquestioningly as you!"

"I had my questions!" Taryn snapped back, eyes suddenly blazing. "Unlike you, I didn't just blindly follow my Master, expecting to have everything laid out for me on a bloody platter! Don't you *dare* stand there and talk to me like you know it all."

She took a deep breath, calming herself, before continuing.

"I tried to make damned sure that if they were going to do it, they were going to do it properly, without hurting anyone or breaching the Accords. I know better than *anyone* what Bladlow's like when he's got his eye on glory. I didn't want my own reputation tarnished. Not when all I've done for the last nineteen years is give my bloody life to this place."

Taryn looked away from Ivy and started adding liquids into the beaker and sloshing them around. The contents turned a muddy brown and emanated an earthy smell.

"When they worked out that they needed a natural magical power source for the transformation casting, Bladlow and Skelton came to me," Taryn continued. "Skelton thought that it could be done using one of my magical blooms – he suspected Salonika had already done it by accident."

Ivy felt her rage subside as Taryn spoke. Bob had settled down near the door, sphinx-like.

"It wasn't enough, though. They needed something more powerful and more sustainable. I told them about the ancient magic in some of the trees and plants in the forests back home…" Taryn stumbled slightly. "We resolved to ship one in. Woodbane paid for it. I told myself it would all be okay, that I could look after it. I know how to look after plants." She trickled some of the solution over Kork as the seedling gasped. "At least, I used to think so…

"I'd been tending to the tree, feeding it, making sure it wasn't too sapped. It was a struggle, though. It didn't seem to be taking to the feed well. I was doing my best. I wanted it to work, needed it to work.

"When you brought… Kork… up here, I couldn't understand why he'd come to you – to *you*. Seedlings are special. My grandmother told me they only reveal themselves to mages who are *worthy*. He looked so ill – I started to worry that I hadn't been looking after the tree properly, that maybe we should give it a break or try a different feed mix. But Bladlow kept pushing and pushing, and the work was just too important. It was going to change so much…"

There was a pause before Taryn spoke again, this time in a voice that was taut and broken. "Ivy, I swear I didn't mean for Kork to get sick. As for Salonika, I–"

Taryn was interrupted by Kork, who had pulled himself up and started squealing shrilly.

"Kork? What's the matter?" Ivy questioned, as the little creature hopped up and down on the desk and thrusted a twiggy digit in the direction of the internal window behind Taryn. Ivy and Taryn followed the seedling's gaze and looked through the window at the tree in the foyer.

At first, they saw nothing unusual. The giant ancient chestnut tree continued to dominate the internal circle of the Tower, dark and unlit.

"I don't understand what we're supposed to be looking at…" Taryn said, standing up and walking closer to the window, where Ivy joined her.

Ivy turned her head back to Kork. "Is it the tree?" she asked him. "Can you feel it?"

The seedling jabbered and nodded.

Ivy felt a shiver run down her back as something in the back of her mind clamoured for attention.

"Taryn…" she asked slowly. "Why aren't you at the dinner?"

"I had to feed the tree. Skelton's casting tonight and I need to be here to make sure the tree can handle it as it's a new feed mix and he's attempting–"

"Mass production…" Ivy whispered, finishing Taryn's sentence. That was it, that was what had been bothering her. Caspar had said this morning that Skelton was going to attempt it tonight.

Kork was scrabbling and shrieking.

"I don't understand," Taryn said. "What's–"

"Hold on…" Ivy said abruptly, placing a finger to her lips. "Everybody, quiet. I think I can hear something."

Taryn fell silent, as did Kork.

A low hum was coming from the foyer, almost inaudible, but gradually growing louder.

The tree then started to glow, pulsing gently. Its large fingered leaves began to glimmer with a waxen, unearthly sheen.

"What's going on…?" Taryn whispered to Ivy.

"I think it's Skelton's casting…" Ivy replied.

"Why's it glowing, though? It's never glowed before!"

The hum began to throb menacingly, as the branches of the tree glittered scarlet and burnished bronze. Bob's ears flattened against his head and he assumed a crouching position, shifting slowly backwards. The vibrations were mounting in pitch and intensity. Hairline fissures started to crawl icily across the Tower's internal windows.

Ivy was hit with a sudden realisation that next to a window was not a sensible place to be standing.

The thought struck her just in time for her to wrench Taryn forcefully down to the floor as every internal window in the Tower simultaneously shattered.

Glass sprayed everywhere; vicious knife-like shards shredding the air in an appalling scream. The entire Tower shuddered and rippled. In Taryn's chambers, plants and books toppled from shelves, crashing tumultuously into heaps of soil and sheaf.

The air rung in the aftermath, humming with the sound of a wetted finger on the rim of a glass.

After a few moments, Taryn and Ivy dragged themselves up from the floor and surveyed the damage. The tree was still there, whole and unbroken, glimmering just as maleficently, but now quiet again.

Bob had bolted; Kork was nowhere to be seen. Taryn and Ivy were mostly wet.

"Why am I wet?" Taryn asked, confused.

"Sorry," said Ivy hurriedly. "I was just trying to think about being hit by anything other than glass – I didn't really have time to plan anything."

"I smell like tea."

"Sorry."

"That's okay, I suppose it's preferable to being shredded by glass…" Taryn looked around her chambers, contemplating her life's work, scattered and strewn across the floor. Fragments of pottery crunched beneath her feet as she gingerly walked around the other side of the desk towards the door.

"Can you see Kork?" Ivy asked her, slapping her damp clothes soggily and squeezing tea out of her hair into a nearby mug, which had lost its handle.

"Not yet. Hold on…" Taryn peered under some books and shifted a venomous-looking fuchsia to one side. She gently lifted the seedling's small body. "I've found him."

"And?"

"He's alive. Barely."

"Thank the Gods."

Relief swiftly gave way to panic, and Ivy started digging under the debris on Taryn's desk as Taryn cradled the small seedling.

"I need to get hold of Dante and Lil," Ivy said urgently. "Where's your crystal display?" She pulled it out from under a pile of books, heavy with damp. "Please, please, please don't be broken..." she muttered desperately.

It was broken.

Ivy hurled it away in frustration and started to march past Taryn towards the door. Taryn grabbed Ivy by the arm sharply and pulled her round to face her.

"Ivy, what in the name of the Gods is going on? The bloody Tower's half-exploded. Did the tree do that? How?"

"Look, we need to get hold of Dante and Lil," said Ivy. "I said I'd call them if I need them. And I need them. I need to get down to Skelton to try to stop this and I don't think I can do it alone."

Ivy wrenched her arm from Taryn's grasp and stumbled towards the door as another quake shook the entire floor.

Sickly streaks of burnt red lightning crackled along the tree's frame and splintered out across the foyer and up towards the huge glass dome of the skylight, rippling with magical energy. Fissures formed across the magnificent dome, and – with a deafening sound which resembled a thousand drinks cabinets smashing all at once – the dome exploded.

Glass shattered and tumbled, dragonsteel supports plunged from the roof, all crashing to the foyer floor with a monstrous knell that reverberated around the Tower for what seemed like an age. Ivy's ears throbbed with the noise. Heavy gusts of wind invaded the Tower from above, whipping around the canopy of the tree and buffeting its branches ferociously. Clouds were gathering in the sky, heavy and solemn.

The tree remained standing, defiant, encircled by a crystalline lake of shards of glass and dragonsteel.

"Oh my Gods…" Taryn breathed, staggering back. Kork whimpered.

Ivy stood, transfixed in shock. Then, remembering herself, she scrambled out into the corridor and sprinted across into one of the external-facing chambers.

The crystal display here looked intact. She breathed a sigh of relief as she shoved aside tumbled books and furniture to reach it, but when she attempted to activate the display, it crackled with a burst of frenzied static. Ivy slammed her palm against the display in despair. Nothing.

"Come on, come on! Turn on!" she shouted at it hopelessly. She concentrated her mind, trying to force power through her fingers into the display, but this only had the effect of eliciting a flashing red message, which read: "SysTEm F⊠iL⊠R€".

Ivy tried a couple of the other chambers. Any displays which hadn't been destroyed were showing a similar error message. She ran towards Taryn, who was now by the lift.

"Well?" Taryn demanded.

"Nothing. None of the displays are working. Do you have one of those portable ones?"

"No, I don't. It spontaneously turned into a celery stalk a few weeks after I was given it, so I threw it away." Taryn gestured towards the stairs and the lift that sat alongside them. "I don't think we're going to be getting out of here any time soon…"

The lift was stuck between the third floor and the ceiling of the second floor below. Its doors were opening and closing violently and it was emitting a discordant noise similar to that made by someone who incorrectly believes they can play jazz. The stairwell next to the lift shaft was blocked by what had previously been the upper stairs.

"We're trapped, then," Ivy noted disconsolately. The floor shuddered and the lift doors banged open and shut again ferociously.

"Looks like it," affirmed Taryn. "What do we do now?"

"We could try a casting – move the debris off the stairwells? Transform it or something?"

"I'm not sure we should even consider free casting with so much raw magic in the atmosphere – it would likely only make things worse." As Taryn said this, energy crackled around Kork with an electrifying jolt. "Ivy, I don't know what's going on. This shouldn't be happening! If anything, Skelton's casting should be draining the tree, not… pumping it up or whatever it's doing!"

"Wait," said Ivy, grabbing Taryn by the arms. "You said it was a new feed mix. What did you put in it?"

"I don't know!" Taryn was almost wailing. "Bladlow brewed this one up – he said mine weren't strong enough. He was having some issues with binding whatever he was putting in it, though – that's why I went to Hartley last week for the bloodwort. He only finished it just before he went to the dinner. That's genuinely all I know."

"Okay, but what was in it before? What was in it?"

The building gave another tremor.

"It was a fortifying potion. Plants and minerals mostly, but there were some dragon scales in there–"

"What?" shot back Ivy.

"All perfectly legitimate – Hartley procured them. It wouldn't have been strong enough without it, not for what we needed it to do." Taryn's voice became animated and defensive. "This is why the Woodbane process is so important – we could have made it a hundred times more potent if we'd had a synthetic dragon heart!"

At this, everything suddenly fell appallingly, horrifically into place.

There was a seismic shudder as the tree convulsed and raged. Ivy felt a wave of nausea rise in her stomach. "Taryn, I don't think Bladlow wanted to wait for a synthetic one…"

✦

The tree had moved beyond anger now. It was experiencing pure, unadulterated rage.

It had been taken, root and branch, from its home. Unceremoniously installed into a network of grimling stone and steel, it had been slowly suffocating, the stonework eating at its toughened roots, dulling its magic.

It had been fed and fed until it burned on the inside, pumped full of fire magic.

Worse still, that amplified, root-deep magic had been leached away. It had happened slowly at first, an irritant, a parasite. But then the rot had started to set, and now this… this…

Theft of nature! A beating, pulsing dragon heart, buried inside its lifeblood. The audacity of it, the sheer humanity of it! An inexcusable atrocity.

It could feel itself more alive than it had ever felt before and yet dying, slowly and on fire, its seedling lost and shrivelling pitifully nearby.

Magic had been taken and now payment was due. The tree felt the wings of a dragon unfurl inside it.

22.

GOING NOWHERE

───────◆───────

Ivy stared at the blocked stairwell with profound dismay. How was she supposed to deal with this?

She tried to think. They could probably find their way down somehow, even without using magic, but that wouldn't solve the issue of the tree, which was now throbbing dangerously again, pumping with the blood of the lost dragon.

What to do? Could she fix this – whatever it was – alone? No. She needed reinforcements, but the Tower was completely empty. Surely someone outside had heard the explosion?

"I wish I'd been able to get through to Dante… he could raise the alarm… try to get the Masters here before this entire place falls down…" she murmured anxiously.

She looked at Taryn, who was just standing there, clasping an unconscious Kork to her breast, as though trying to make amends for the desperate situation they had found themselves in. They were getting nowhere…

"Hang on! I know what we can do!" she shouted excitedly. "We can reach Dante through the beyond!"

Taryn was mystified. "What are you talking about?" she said, weary and exasperated. "Dante doesn't do that anymore, hasn't for – wait a minute… Ivy, if you're suggesting one of us has to, you know, *die*–"

"No, no, no…" Ivy's eyes were alight. "If I could reach Salonika, maybe she could get through to Dante! Do you know how to pass through?"

"What? No, not my thing, never had the knack. This is all just too much… Ivy, let's be realistic, please."

"I guess I'll have to give it a go, then. Only tried it once while I was in Futures. It didn't work very well. I think I remember the theory, though. And I know where to find her, I think, assuming she's still there…"

"Ivy, this is not a good time to experiment. We're trapped up here, the building could collapse at any moment, and the tree still looks wrong. It is not a good time for one of us to pay a visit to another plane of existence…"

"What other choice do we have? No one knows we're here. The Tower mages are halfway across the Citadel, Gods only know whether anyone nearby will be brave or stupid enough to investigate. Just watch Kork for a moment, would you? I need to remember how to do this really fast…"

Ignoring Taryn's continued protestations, Ivy sat down, cross-legged in the dust and debris. She closed her mind. How was this supposed to go? She tried to remember back to her Pasts sessions in the Futures Division, wishing she had paid more attention. Dante had made it look so easy, like slipping out of one outfit and into another. She felt for the edges of reality, the folds in the fabric of the universe. The building quivered. Her concentration slipped.

She cursed, settled her breath, and tried again, inching her mind out further, trying to ignore the nearby sounds of crumbling stonework. She could sense the raw edge of this plane now, the layer underneath, like gauze beneath a skirt. She felt her mind drift and conjure random inchoate images, akin to the moment before falling asleep. She thought of Salonika, the riverbank…

✦

The world jarred. For a moment she thought it was simply another tremor, but then she found herself standing in the middle of Nowhere.

She could see nothing. Then a reddish-purple haze enveloped her. Through it, if she squinted (or at least focused her mind in a way which resembled squinting), she could just about distinguish a massive shape. It started to throb into perspective. The tree. What was the tree doing here? She must have done something wrong.

The landscape flickered. She couldn't hold on to any sense of place. She felt exhausted already. How was this supposed to work again?

The tree shimmered into view. She clung to it, urging it to solidify, all thoughts of Salonika slipping through her fingers. All she could perceive was its immense form, cloaked in unreality. This was too hard. What was she doing? She thought she could hear Taryn shouting somewhere, feel the ground of the third floor… she needed to stay here. Concentrate, Ivy, concentrate.

She pushed hard with her mind, and the tree felt firmer; she could almost see it now.

And there, atop one of the vast roots that were protruding from the spectral grass, and leaning her back against the tree's enormous trunk, was Salonika, glaring at her with intense irritation.

"You?" Salonika said brusquely. "Back again so soon? You must be feeling guilty; we didn't speak this much when I was alive…"

"Salonika…" Ivy tried to focus on her. "Look, Salonika, I'm sorry, but honestly, I don't have time… I need your help. Skelton's casting – it's gone wrong. It's the tree. I think they fed it something they shouldn't have..."

The landscape in Ivy's periphery fizzed and whorled. She could see Taryn and Kork again. She was disorientated, fading, nauseous. She tried to cling to where she wasn't.

"The tree? That explains this then…" Salonika patted the bark of the shadow tree with an ethereal palm. "It doesn't seem very happy," she said coolly.

"It's not. And I need to get a message to Dante, I need his help. He's not at the Tower – none of the mages are, they're all at the Falltide dinner – but I need to speak to him and I can't get through to him any other way. I have to tell him that the Tower is on the verge of collapsing, that we need the other mages to come and help stop it."

"Dante?" scoffed Salonika, laughing patronisingly. "You want me to speak to Dante? You really don't take the time to learn anything about anyone, do you?" Salonika tossed her hair imperiously. "I was surprised to see him here before. Dante closed his mind off to this place years ago. I thought everyone knew that? I tried to reach him after I… you know… after I… but he slammed the bloody door in my face." The landscape roiled into ugly colours.

She added darkly, "Something's not right with him, anyway. Those shadows he brought…"

"I thought they were yours?" Ivy said, perplexed. She remembered the creeping, distorted shapes from their last visit, slouching across the edge of whatever counted as the horizon on this anti-dimensional plane.

"Perhaps. Perhaps not…"

"Look, can you at least try to reach him? Maybe his mind is still open from earlier? Please, Salonika, I need your help. I need you to try."

"Why should I help you? When have you ever helped me? Little Miss Perfect, scampering around the Tower like Skelton's favourite pet. Never had to work at anything, have you? All handed to you on a bloody platter."

"That's not true!" That was the second time Ivy had heard that phrase in a ridiculously short time. Is that what they all thought of her? That it was easy for her? That she could just click her fingers and–

More crackles of fire. Blood licked the edges of her vision. She clenched her fists – did she do that here or there? – and tried to hold on to nowhere.

"It hasn't been easy for me either, Salonika! I don't think it's easy for any of us! But you know what? You're right. I didn't help you. I didn't want to and I wouldn't have known how to help you even if I had wanted to. That's on me. But it's not like you ever *asked* for help either!"

"What did you expect me to do? Tell *you* I was struggling? Admit failure? To *you*? And how would *that* have gone?"

The tree seemed to be moving, coiling, its bark shifting like sections of a wooden puzzle box.

"Probably not well," Ivy conceded. "I'll admit I assumed that, if you failed, it was because you couldn't cope. And if you couldn't cope, then you probably shouldn't have been at the Tower. It was stupid; a stupid way to think. It can't go on like this, though. We can't. I know you won't believe me, but

I'm trying to fix things." Ivy said this with a force of emotion she didn't even knew she felt. Bleak light swirled and flickered above her. "I'm sorry. Truly I am. And I really need your help. Please, Salonika…"

Salonika raised her chin defiantly, but seemed mollified.

She then tossed her long hair and rolled her eyes in an exaggerated fashion. "No need to be so dramatic about it…" she said coolly. "I'll try to reach Dante. But I can't promise anything. Stay here… if you can."

Salonika vanished. The landscape shifted again, the sky turning a cold, deep, forgotten blue. Stars wheeled erratically overhead, glinting above the vast canopy of the ancient tree. Ivy could feel moist leaves and soft sodden earth underfoot, littered with brittle twigs and desiccated bark. She had the sudden impression that the tree was simply one of an infinite number of such trees, stretching onwards in the periphery of her gaze like an endless world forest.

It was no longer hard to focus; the tree gripped her, solid and ageless. She could smell Kork's comforting, earthy musk, like that time she had awoken to find him nestled next to her face. It whispered to her like rustling leaves. It needed her help. She saw a dragon soar menacingly overhead, a black reptilian silhouette against the stars–

"It worked. I found him."

Salonika was back and the vision had evaporated with a disconcerting jerk.

"He must have had his guard down still. He's actually on his way," Salonika continued, as Ivy tried to refocus her mind. "Said he and Lil had left the party early. Apparently, that auditor turned up. Said he got a tip-off from a goblin that tonight was the night, and they needed to get back to the Tower."

"Cleft. He must have sent someone to Hop."

"Cleft?"

"The Copier."

"Yes, I know who Cleft is. What I meant was, what's he got to do with it?"

"I think he's a spy."

"Hah!" Salonika crowed. "Interesting. Do you think he should be copying confidential information?"

"Probably not." Ivy could hear Taryn's voice from somewhere behind her ear. The deathscape was flickering and shimmering again; the tree next to Salonika had started to throb and pulsate. "Look, I don't have time – do you know how far away they are?"

"They're on a Deep Cart, a few stops away. There's no way to call anyone else – Dante says the display network is completely down. But they'll be at the Tower soon. He did not appreciate the interruption. Said it's hard to get off at the right stop if you're unconscious."

"Thank you," Ivy said. "I mean it." She did. "I have to get back now. See what I can do to fix this." She was about to dislocate her mind from this reality when she hesitated. "Are you going to be okay here?" she asked quietly.

Salonika eyed her shrewdly. "I don't exactly have much of a choice, do I?"

There was an awkward silence.

"I miss the Falltide dinner," Salonika said quietly. "I miss all dinners, to be honest."

"If it's any consolation, I didn't get to go either."

"It's not."

Salonika looked at Ivy, rolled her eyes again, sighed deeply and said, with an air of affected resignation, "I genuinely don't know why I'm bothering with all this nonsense – it's not like it'll have any effect on my day-to-day life, as it were – but I'll see if I can try to get hold of a mage in Pasts who might still be at the dinner. Try to raise the alarm."

"Thank you, that would be amazing…" Ivy replied, taken aback. "Salonika… after all this is done, me and Dante, we'll check in, okay? Let you know when we've sorted it all…?"

Salonika smiled wistfully in return. "Don't make promises you can't keep. Good luck, Ivy Armstride."

At that, Salonika reached out her arms and *pushed* at Ivy.

Ivy jolted back to the floor of the Tower, sprawling sidelong across the ground. She could taste plaster dust in her mouth. She spluttered and coughed. Bob had reappeared, nudging at her with his giant head. She grasped at his body, cherishing the warmth of his soft fur.

Taryn was kneeling beside her. "Are you okay?" she asked, helping her up as Bob let out yet another strangled attempt at a purr. "Did it work? Did you find Salonika?"

"I did," replied Ivy, dusting herself down. "It turns out Dante, Hop and Lil are already on their way."

"And Salonika… is she okay?"

"Not really."

Taryn looked down. "I feel like this is my fault. The Tower, the tree, Salonika, Kork. I'm so sorry about all of this, Ivy."

Ivy looked down at the tiny seedling, who was breathing raggedly and looked smaller and more shrivelled. "How has he been?" she asked, changing the subject.

"Pretty much the same. He gets worse every time there's another quake."

Ivy stroked her fingers across his little form before turning to look critically at the lift and the stairwell. "On that note," she said, rubbing some dirt from her face with a sleeve, "we really should work on finding a way down to more stable ground…"

It did not feel like a day to try the lift, which was still juddering in violent spasms. Ivy looked again at the stairwell. "Is there definitely nothing we can do to unblock the stairs? Some sort of vanishment casting maybe?"

"That's more your area than mine. It's a lot of rubble, though. And I don't trust that what's under it would hold up."

"A levitation casting on us then? Out the window?"

"Can you do that?"

"To be honest, I doubt it. I've never been great at telekinetic magic, even with castings in front of me. I don't seem to be much good at any type of magic without a casting in front of me…"

"You've been doing fine, as far as I can see. The thing with the glass, a bloody trip to the beyond… I think you underestimate yourself. Anyway, the words are only to help shape the magic. It's mostly about intention." Taryn expressed the last sentiment automatically and wasn't sure where it came from. "That's what I was taught a long time ago, anyway," she shrugged. "I wouldn't know, though, my castings are so rusty I wouldn't trust myself either, especially with all this raw magic around… I'm beginning to think specialising in solutions was not my smartest life choice…"

Ivy glanced over at the lift again. "If we can brace those doors, we might just be able to squeeze in and see if we can get it to work…"

"It's a terrifying idea, but it might be our only option," Taryn agreed. "What about Bob?" Taryn looked sceptically at the tiger's massive frame.

"We might need to give him a push. He doesn't like being shoved into small spaces… I think I can manage it, though."

"Okay…" exhaled Taryn, gritting her teeth with all the resolve she felt she could muster. "Shall we take the lift, then?"

"Let's," said Ivy, bracing herself.

◆

Dante, Lil and Hop tumbled into the grand foyer of the Tower of Jackdaw and Spittlelick just as Ivy and Taryn were attempting to wrench themselves free from the lift, which had stopped and opened its doors halfway below ground level. The screeching, wobbling journey down to the ground floor had been accompanied by a tortured attempt at a cello solo from the lift, which was not functioning on all cylinders, and frankly was unsure if it had any cylinders left. It had done its best, however, and Ivy found herself inexplicably grateful to it for its efforts.

The group rushed over to assist the pair as Bob muscled through the gap and streaked past them to crouch low in front of the tree, as though preparing to pounce.

Taryn and Ivy eventually extracted themselves with some difficulty. They stood looking over at the tree, which was throbbing ominously.

"Are you both okay?" asked Lil. "There's some sort of force-field around this place – there's a massive crowd outside but no-one can get in without magic and there's not a bloody mage in sight."

"Not one stupid enough to try at least," added Dante wryly. "Apart from me, apparently. You seem to be in one piece though."

"We're fine. Shaken, but fine, I think. Skelton's tried to perform the mass production casting," replied Ivy, ignoring Dante. "Turns out the tree doesn't like it."

"I can see that…" remarked Dante, noting the dragonsteel girders and the shards of glass littering the floor.

"I'm pretty sure it's got something to do with the dragon heart Taryn here fed it before Skelton started," Ivy said pointedly.

They turned slowly to look at Taryn, still clasping the whimpering seedling.

After a brief moment of stunned silence, the three of them started talking at once, all in disbelief and anger. Hop looked positively incredulous; he was so stunned by being confronted with a crime of such magnitude he hadn't even taken out his notebook. Taryn tried to remonstrate, to no avail.

"Look," Ivy interjected, removing Kork from Taryn's arms and placing him down gently against the wall next to the lift, "Taryn says she had no idea what she was feeding it and that it was Bladlow, which – pending further evidence to the contrary and given the situation we are in – I have decided to accept as the truth. We can sort all of that out later – and believe me we bloody well will–" she glared at Taryn "–but right now we need to find Skelton and Caspar, make sure they're okay, and try to put a stop to whatever it is they're doing. They should be down in the Crypt. We need to–"

Ivy never had a chance to finish her sentence. At that moment, another quake, more powerful than any previously, shook the entire Tower, bringing sections of masonry crashing to the ground around them. They huddled together instinctively.

The Tower reverberated with an almighty, eldritch shriek. The hairs on Ivy's neck stood up. She shivered involuntarily.

"What in seven hells was that?" exclaimed Lil.

"I don't know, and I would prefer to keep it that way…" whispered Taryn.

"I don't think we're going to have much choice…" Dante said, motioning towards the tree.

Branches in the canopy above rattled and broke away from the tree, crashing to the ground with deafening thuds, causing the shattered glass on the floor to bounce and dance. The trunk of the giant ancient chestnut was squirming now, strange distortions shifting across its thick bark.

It looked womb-like, large, distended shapes thrusting outwards grotesquely. Kork let out a high-pitched keen which screeched achingly across the foyer as, with a horrifying slowness, something started to emerge from the tree.

A horned head comprising twisted wood was disgorging itself from the tree's pulsating trunk. Its face was elongated and ancient, unmistakeably reptilian, and slick with sap that trickled stickily down its nose. As it pushed further out from the tree, a massive, clawed foot tugged its way out, landing on the foyer floor with a thud that shook the ground. Lethal talons resembling oversized thorns raked at the dust and glass on the floor as the monster then wrenched another front limb free. With a laborious twist, a giant, arching body pushed and pulled its way out, seemingly both part of the tree's colossal trunk and yet also separate from it, like an appalling optical illusion. The tree wailed in pain as it expelled the remainder of the creature; two back legs and an immense tail which slithered out, coated in sap and purplish fluid, the rotten fruit of a reprehensible labour.

Primal birthing complete, the creature raised itself from the floor, a wooden titan, its body a mesh of twisted branches, vines and leaves. Its tail lashed across the floor, a brutal whip of curling limbs and vines woven together. Planting its four giant claws firmly in the ground, the creature arched its back and unfurled a pair of monstrous wings framed by skeletal wooden wing-bones. The creature's wings were leaf-like in texture, with fine veins webbing across their translucent surface, and autumnal in colour, one last vibrant flash of life before the naked coldness of winter.

Vast eyes blinked open sharply, glistening with a deep darkness, as the creature creaked its long neck towards them and opened jaws lined with thorny teeth. At a shrill pitch which made the shattered glass quiver and resonate on the floor, the dragon roared.

23.

THE TREE AND THE TOWER

"What do we do now?" Ivy screamed over the roar, as the group pressed themselves against the wall next to the lift, Lil clutching at Ivy, terrified.

"I don't have a bloody clue!" Dante screamed back, eyes wide.

Massive limbs of twisted timbers tore across the floor of the foyer, groaning hideously, lifting granite and glass in ravaging quakes. The huge tail thrashed into walls, bringing masonry tumbling down.

As the creature stomped heavily towards them, Bob bolted and skittered behind Ivy. Through her sheer terror she noticed with a shock that under the creature's huge, misshapen ribs sat an orb of purple-red tissue and pulsing light; a stolen heart reformed and caged. It throbbed frenziedly as the monster savagely ripped at the scenery.

Hop let out a cry along the lines of "Oh my Gods, oh my Gods, it's going to kill us all!"

Taryn shook him. "This is not a good time to start panicking!" she screamed at him, in utter panic.

"I don't know," shouted Dante, "you'd be surprised how much can be solved by panicking!" Galvanising himself, he drew on the raw magic crackling with instability around the foyer, balled it, and shot it at the creature with an aim born of years of scruttleball. It hit true, smashing into its torso.

The creature looked momentarily winded as the energy struck, before absorbing the raw power irritably into its chest, making its limbs shiver with vivid brilliance. It then reared its head and discharged the power from distorted jaws into the upper floors of the Tower in a blast of platinum fire.

"Well, that didn't work," observed Dante.

"Can we make it out?" Ivy shouted, pointing across at the entrance doors of the Tower.

"Not without getting past that thing!" Dante shouted back.

"Should we try to stop it?"

"It doesn't look like it wants to be stopped!"

Ivy heard Bob mewl and looked down at him. Trying to restrain her own tide of terror, she grabbed him by the scruff of his neck. "For Gods' sakes, Bob, you're a tiger! Be a bloody tiger!" she wailed desperately.

Somewhere in the small cat-brain inside Bob, Ivy's words hit a nerve. He didn't understand them, but somehow, in a glorious moment of self-actualisation, he understood what he needed to be. His formidable frame tensed, sinews moving like pistons, and he leapt forwards with a ferocious roar that surprised even himself. Pounding effortlessly towards the tree dragon, he leapt, the immense force of his momentum causing the creature to stumble backwards.

As Bob vigorously scratched and clawed, muscles rippling under the sheen of his fur, the others huddled together and started shouting rapidly, over the deafening howl of the violent wind and raw magic ripping around the foyer.

"How are we supposed to take down that thing? It's absorbing magic!" Ivy shouted.

"I don't know!" Dante howled back.

Hop, who had now calmed himself considerably, or at least had transcended his earlier delirium and assumed a focused madness which seemed deceptively similar to calm, grabbed Ivy's arm purposefully. "Try binding it!" he shouted over the noise. "Like with normal dragons! That could work, in theory?"

Ivy and Dante looked at each other, stunned.

"I hate to admit it, but that's not a bad idea…!" Dante acknowledged.

"It could work…" Ivy shouted hurriedly, "but have you ever done a dragon binding using free casting? I haven't!"

"No, but we could try. We know how it's supposed to work… we're going to need to distract it somehow, though. We'll never be able to cast something that powerful if it starts coming at us…"

Bob was tiring and was now losing ground to the dragon, which was growing more and more aggravated as it swatted at the tiger.

Lil, who had been quivering beside them, suddenly raised her chin resolutely. "Leave that to me."

They looked at her incredulously.

"I'm a bloody faerie. I can do distractions. I just need to hope my illusions work on this bloody thing – I've never seen anything like it before… its mind might not accept them."

"Are you sure?" Ivy asked, knowing the limits of faerie illusions.

"Trust me," Lil said confidently. "I know I'm not a mage and can't do all the fancy stuff you lot do, but I want to help. And I think I can actually do this. Probably."

"Okay," Taryn chimed in. "Lil will help Bob distract it while Dante and Ivy do the binding casting. In the meantime, I'll get down to Skelton and Caspar – try to stop the casting."

"Sounds like a plan," affirmed Dante. "Take the auditor, would you? He'll be even more useless than usual up here." Ivy knew this was Dante's way of keeping Hop out of harm's way, although it was clear that Hop hadn't taken it this way as he had started spluttering indignantly.

Despite Hop's protestations, Taryn steered him towards the stairwell leading down to the Crypt, which thankfully hadn't suffered the same fate as the third floor stairs and still appeared largely accessible. She paused and yelled at Ivy, "You can do this casting. It's all about intention, remember? Don't worry about the rest."

At that moment, the creature swung its thorned tail and knocked Bob clear across the foyer. He hit a wall with a sickening thump and lay still. The creature let out another earth-shattering roar.

"Bob!" Ivy screamed. He heaved his head and shoulders up at the sound of her voice, before collapsing again.

"Lil, you're up!" Dante shouted, as Taryn dragged Hop towards the stairs.

Lil nodded and strode forward to confront the creature, dragonfly wings aloft.

✦

Taryn and Hop descended into the Crypt, heaving crumbled stone and mortar from their path and crawling over a tangled mass of tree roots. The roots felt warm to the touch and pulsed malignantly. Taryn could taste the metallic tang of magic in the close air.

"Let's just find Skelton and Caspar, stop whatever the seven hells they're doing, and get out of here," gasped Taryn, choking on clouds of dust. "I really don't want to be down here any longer than necessary…"

A primeval screech, like chalk scraping down a blackboard, reverberated deafeningly around the Crypt's warren-like central corridors.

"Agreed," affirmed Hop, tentatively threading his way past a massive root.

"They should be just down here." Taryn wasn't entirely sure what she expected to find, but it wasn't this. As they pushed aside a heap of fallen masonry from the entrance, and stumbled into a large basement chamber, Taryn wondered how the Crypt had not been completely buried. She did not need to wonder for long.

Huge earthy roots dominated the cavernous room, lurching angrily into the darkened corners of the chamber. Tendrils crept across the ceiling in a tight lattice, pushing against the ground floor above. The chamber was bathed in an eerie golden-red light; a monstrous grotto.

Looking down, Taryn noticed that the flagstone floor – at least those portions of it not covered by the tree's slithering roots – was strewn with the detritus of the latest Woodbane casting ceremony. Unicorn horns, smashed and bent, were scattered everywhere. Many had fused to the tree roots, like spikes on a brutal club.

"Watch your step," Taryn shouted at Hop, as she edged in and felt the unpleasant squelch of goblin organs beneath her feet. She tried not to look at the seething tissue, but there was no escaping the foul odour. Hop retched violently behind her. She peered towards the darkened edges of the chamber.

Then she saw them. Stretched out against the back wall, bathed in the reddish light, bound and held by monstrous coiling roots, were Skelton and Caspar.

"There they are!" she shouted, treading her way across the chamber as carefully as she could. A root twitched as she passed it. She concentrated on reaching the wall, Hop moving cautiously alongside her. Before they could make it, there was a muffled scream. Hop had tripped over a sinuous root. His face smashed solidly into the ground.

"Hop!" screamed Taryn, running across to him. As she crouched down beside him, small roots slowly started to snake around their calves and wrists.

Hop pushed himself up, trying to scramble away from the constricting roots. His glasses were cracked, his face smeared with dust and blood. As they tugged at the vine-like tendrils, two huge, horn-encrusted roots ripped out of the stone and started to flail in their direction. They leapt back, dodging the furious heavy blows.

"What exactly are we supposed to do about those?" Hop shouted at Taryn.

"I'm working on it!" she shot back, wincing as the horns attached to one of the roots clipped her left calf and she lost her balance.

"Don't you have any potions we can, I don't know, throw at them?" Hop said, panicking.

"Oh yes, I'll just get out my cauldron, shall I?" Taryn shouted. "I'm sure we have plenty of time to whip something up and let it percolate!"

"I find that sarcasm is most unhelpful in these sorts of situations," he cried, somehow managing to sound aggrieved despite the desperation of the situation.

"As though you're being helpful right now!" Taryn screamed back at him.

"Well at least you have magic! I don't have anything! It's not as if a couple of pens are going be of any use in this situation!"

At that moment, the Unstationery Cupboard materialised in its full metallic glory and thumped heavily onto a huge root just as it writhed over to ensnare Hop, pinning it to the ground with a triumphant clang. One of the cupboard's large doors creaked open and a few half-chewed pens and pencils rolled slowly out and clattered onto the floor optimistically.

Hop and Taryn stared at it in stunned confusion.

The tree then wrenched its pinioned root out from under the cupboard, which toppled sideways, sending sheaves of official letterhead paper in an array of unhelpful sizes skidding across the floor.

"Well, that was unexpected," said Hop. "Although I don't feel as though it's moved matters forward…" The roots lunged towards them.

Taryn tried to think furiously. Fireball? That could work, if she could remember the principles quickly enough. She followed the thought through and realised that being attacked by flaming spiked roots seemed like a backward step. What else could she do?

Her mind whirred through the options as the chamber shook and the tendrils of the tree wound around her ankles. She wrenched her feet free, ducked another blow from the roots, and wondered if Ivy, Lil and Dante were having any better luck above.

✦

Things were not going well on the ground floor either.

Lil stood before the tree creature, arms spread beside her, like another pair of wings, head tilted towards the open sky of the Tower, as the creature raged and pounded at the ground. Wind whipped around her as she tried to exert a grip on its monstrous mind. It was like nothing she had encountered before. Human minds were weak in comparison; this was ancient and powerful.

Unwavering, she forced herself upon it, dropping all her common appearance illusions with only a small residual pang of anxiety as she concentrated on threading into its consciousness. The tree saw her as she truly was. Older than imagined, rounder than imagined. Yet, despite the stripping back of every bodily twist of fancy she had clung to for so long, there was strength and beauty there.

She tried vainly to coax the monster to sleep; it wouldn't be lulled. It continued to roar and lash.

She swiftly changed approach and hurled an imagined flock of ink-black birds at the fringes of its perception. To Lil's surprise and relief, this caused a momentary lapse in the creature's defences, as it started to swat its huge claws towards the swarms of pecking, screeching figments. She had edged her way in. She now just needed to keep it up for long enough for Ivy and Dante to undertake the casting.

Behind Lil, backed against the wall, Ivy and Dante were still shouting at one another, bracing against the waves of magic spiralling out from the tree and feeding the warped and woven body of the tree-dragon. They were crouched next to Bob, who was now thankfully upright, although limping as he paced back and forth. Kork was still propped against the wall, twig arm resting across his belly, breathing ragged and stilted.

"But I don't know any binding castings by heart, they're all about twenty pages long!" Ivy was wailing.

"Yes, but most of that is boilerplate!" Dante shouted back.

"Fine, but we don't even know its name!" The creature thrashed and belched molten amber at them, which Dante only barely managed to divert with a rapid shielding motion. "How are we supposed to refer to a bloody great big ancient tree dragon?"

"Well, that should do it! I think it'll know we're referring to it – do you see any other bloody great big ancient tree dragons around here?"

They watched in horror as the bloody great big ancient tree dragon (as it was apparently now to be known) lunged brutally at whatever fictional assailant Lil was directing at it, beating its fronded wings and discharging a slug of smoky plasma from its thorn-encrusted jaws as it did so. The force of the blast rent a monumental tear in the east side of the Tower, which started to collapse in slow, tumbling slabs. The seventh floor balcony decided to take a last-minute extended leave of absence at this point.

"There go my chambers," said Dante bleakly. "I hope the scruttles all made it out in time…"

"My Gods," breathed Ivy. "We have to get on with this casting, and fast... Right. First principles… identify the subject matter."

"Done. Bloody great big ancient tree dragon."

"Fine. Set out the purpose."

"Bind its gigantic arse."

"What do we want it to do?"

"Stop trying to kill us would be an excellent start!"

"Okay… for how long? Should we say, 'for as long as reasonably necessary at our sole and unfettered discretion'?"

"Seriously, Ivy? For eternity for all I care! Honestly, we don't have time to sweat the details – we just need to get on and bloody cast!"

"What if it doesn't work, though? Or doesn't go to plan? What if the magic leaks or there are unexpected side effects?"

"Then we can go to our graves knowing that the Regulator had it right all along. Now come on! Get on with it!"

He grasped her hands with his and looked directly at her, ignoring the carnage that Lil and the dragon were wreaking upon the Tower. "Ives, we can do this. This place is crawling with magic – we can draw from that. All you need to do is focus when you channel it. It will be unstable, and we'll likely fail, but at least we'll have tried very hard not to die."

That was, in all probability, the most life-affirming thing Dante had ever said to her. She nodded in acknowledgement. They rose, Dante still holding one of Ivy's hands.

Lil was fading now; her wings hanging limply behind her as she fought vainly to retain a hold on the creature's alien intellect.

Ivy and Dante reached out with their free arms towards the tree dragon, concentrating on drawing in the magic. As it coursed into them, Ivy felt the crash of a wave of power. In the recesses of her mind flashed the vision she saw in Nowhere: dark forests of sleeping giants stretching into an infinite horizon. She could feel the tree now, she knew what it was, the shadow that had dominated her dreamless sleep.

Now she felt a rush of panic infest her mind, drowning and suffocating her. Her thoughts swam with the enormity of what she needed to do, what she had to achieve. But all she could think about was what she shouldn't do, what she couldn't do. She felt the shackles of limitation clamp down, the endless anxieties which imprisoned her. Then, gasping as the magic surged through her body, she thought of Kork, of Caspar and Salonika, of the others that were here with her. A clarity of purpose emerged. She knew what she wanted to do. She could do this.

She experienced a thrill of sheer exultation as she and Dante propelled the energy towards the tree dragon, bending and commanding reality in unison, both of them grabbing the fabric of the universe and folding it authoritatively in two.

"Bloody great big ancient tree dragon!" they shouted together, their voices resonant and harmonious, bidding the chaos of their surroundings to order and silence. The creature turned to face them, raking a limb across an upper floor and sending piles of papers scattering and cascading to the ground in graceful waves. "We hereby bind you! Cease!"

The sky above, heavy with clouds, crackled and thundered with magical energy. The wind raged around them, kicking up dirt and leaves. The dragon howled and writhed, swinging its heavy tail across the ground and sending waves of fragmented glass cascading and crashing around them. It fought as the magic wrapped and bound it, like a thousand imaginary dragonsteel chains linking and locking around its tortured limbs. With a low rumbling keen, like aged trees creaking unbearably in a storm, the creature went terribly still. The wind died; the leaves settled.

"Did it work?" said Dante.

✦

Down in the Crypt, Taryn and Hop were fast fighting a losing battle. Exhausted, bruised, they continued to dodge the roots, their escape route blocked by a mesh of serpentine tubers that had coiled across the entrance.

Taryn had, as a last resort, attempted to blast several fireballs towards the flailing timber. To her shock and unease, as it had done with the creature above, the magic had simply been absorbed with a throb.

"What now?" Hop wailed, as tendrils wrapped around his wrists and across his torso. He wrenched at them despairingly, convulsing as they coiled around his neck.

Taryn was faring no better. She could feel the bitter hatred flowing from the tree. It clung to her, draining the last vestiges of her power. She wouldn't get out of here alive. She'd got it all so very wrong. She wouldn't have time now to fix anything; there was so much she needed to fix. She'd never hold her children again. Her children. Wracking sobs of utter terror escaped her. Her children… how had she forgotten them? How had she forgotten who she had wanted to cultivate this new world for?

And then, suddenly, silence.

The under limbs of the tree thumped senselessly to the ground, crashing into the stone and sending clouds of glinting dust into the air. The tendril roots which were wrapped around Taryn and Hop froze, as though stunned. The chamber was enveloped in unearthly quiet.

Ivy and Dante had bound the tree.

Hop and Taryn struggled free of their bonds, heaving and gasping breathlessly.

"They've done it…" Taryn panted incredulously, wiping a hand across a face streaked with dirt and blood and tears.

"Is it over?" Hop, too, was coated in blood and grime; large red welts had appeared where the tree had gripped him.

"I hope so," Taryn gasped, rubbing her wrists. "Let's get to Skelton and Caspar."

✦

On the ground floor above, Ivy, Lil and Dante were huddled close, exhausted and drained.

The dragon was silent, clawed foot-roots fixed to the floor. It glared at them with eyes filled with dark emptiness, rage quelled but not extinguished. The stolen dragon heart was dimmed, throbbing mutely beneath its cage of wooden ribs. Ivy looked at it, seeing in its embers the dragons impounded at Dragonsteel, beasts chained with industrial magic. A deep sadness enveloped her. What was she doing? She had just achieved magic beyond anything she had thought possible, so why instead of triumph did she feel nothing but guilt?

Kork whimpered. She scooped up his little body and cradled him. His breathing was tortured now, a tiny, pitiful rattle like dried seeds in a pod.

"How's he doing?" Dante whispered.

"Not good." Ivy knew that it was worse than that, she could feel the small being dying in her hands. "I don't think he's going to make it…"

Lil nestled against her as tears carved out slim streams down their dirt-streaked faces. Dante gazed blankly ahead at the dragon, elbow resting on a bent knee, head in his hand, spent and desolate.

Ivy felt Kork stiffen in her fingers. Bob brought his magnificent head close, nuzzling the seedling, hot breath cascading over Ivy's fingers and making Kork's wilted foliage quiver. It couldn't have come to this. They had tried so hard. She had failed him.

As a chilled silence descended, what was left of the grand entrance doors of Jackdaw and Spittlelick suddenly burst open in a rush of electrified fire.

A group of Masters rushed in, stopping abruptly in their tracks as they encountered the dragon, bound and moored in front of the tree. Shouting ensued; Ivy let it wash meaninglessly over her as she clasped Kork. The mages cautiously fanned out, circling the strange beast, gesturing frantically to one another.

She felt the floor tremble as, despite its bindings, with an immense effort, the tree dragon twisted its body and let out a roar of pain so rending and raw that many of the mages staggered backwards. The tree behind it convulsed violently, whipping its branches ferociously. Ivy could feel the bindings slipping and snapping as the dragon contorted its body and the orb at its chest hummed loudly. Its colossal wings unfurled once more and beat thunderously towards the assembled mages as it wrenched one foot-root from the floor, finally ripping through its bindings.

Ivy was dimly aware of various mages gathering their strength. One of them stretched their arms upwards and a torrent of glass and dragonsteel rushed from the floor, melting and twisting into glazed rods. Another mage directed the rods at the flailing dragon, curving them around its rusted, translucent leaf-wings, snapping its wooden wing-bones with a crunch that caused the dragon to screech in heart-rending agony.

Ivy clenched her hand around the seedling as she felt the dragon's visceral pain. She could sense the other mages channelling their power into new bindings, pulling at unreal chains, wrenching the beast to its belly, pinning it as it glowered at them with its pool-like dark eyes and lashed and writhed against its bonds.

Ivy knew she should join them in their endeavour as they channelled their magic in unison. She held out her right hand and drew on the magic, forcing it towards the dragon, hating the pain she caused it as she did so, straining against its terrible, righteous anger. It was too much; she couldn't hold it… she shouldn't hold it…

She shouldn't hold it… She looked down at the broken form of Kork, clutched in her left hand, gasping his last few tiny breaths. She saw Bob, panting and exhausted; Dante and Lil, ashen and desperate. Finally, she looked at the dragon, wrestling feverishly at the foot of the shuddering tree, pinioned by the force of their power.

It hadn't asked for this; they had inflicted this upon it. It didn't deserve to be bound like a chattel, to be carted from its home and then put to work and drained until it could give no more. It was right to be angry. The stolen dragon heart thundered within its wooden ribcage, panicked and fast. It thundered in Ivy's too.

Captivated by the intensity of the tree dragon's aching sorrow, Ivy lowered her arm.

24.

THE HEART OF THE MATTER

As the tree dragon heaved its twisted flanks, Ivy heard, as though from afar, the frantic yelling of the mages. One mage shot a bolt of something bright and hot towards the beast – it roared in incandescent rage mingled with agony.

"Stop!" Ivy screamed at them. "You have to stop! You're hurting it!"

The mages ignored her, still casting fervently towards the imprisoned titan. Ivy appealed to them in desperation. "Please!" Closing her eyes, she pulled on the magic of the tree and thrust it against the tide of the mages, then instinctively clutched dreamlike fingers at the bindings enfolding the dragon, snapping the links. As the recoil from the breaking chains hit them, the mages fell to the wrecked atrium floor, momentarily paralysed.

"Ivy, what in the name of the Gods are you doing?" railed Dante, grabbing her and shaking her, confusion etched across his features.

"Dante – I have to stop them, this isn't helping. I should have known–"

"What are you talking about?"

"We did this to it, it's in pain – we need to heal it, not chain it!" She was frantic now, eyes wide.

The dragon shook and keened, waves of purplish red flashing at its latticed breast. The tree behind it continued to convulse. The air in the Tower assumed a leaden texture, the pressure mounting as the tree absorbed the lingering magic in the atmosphere, as it drew the power from all present, inhaling it deeply with a shivering breath. The mages on the floor shivered and twitched, gasping for breath. Lil cried out as she was stripped of the little illusory power she had left, while Bob shimmered between tiger and cat forms. Dante and Ivy fell forward, clutching their breasts, lungs contracting in excruciating anguish.

The dragon raised its massive form from the foyer floor in laborious majesty. It unfurled again its shattered wings, beating them once in a pained and heavy motion, as though contemptuously shedding its shackles. It crouched on its forelegs and lowered its twisted neck and opened the gaping maw of its jaws.

It screamed at them all, encircled by a halo of purple and platinum fire, as the tree prepared to unleash one final pulse of pure sorcery. It wanted to end it all.

In the Crypt, Taryn hurried across to where Caspar and Skelton were still braced against the wall, bound by the colossal roots.

Taryn examined the pair. They were conscious, although barely. Skelton looked drained and sallow. He was moaning softly. Caspar's eyes flickered open as Taryn approached, trying to focus on her.

Hop followed behind, out of breath. "Are they alive?" he gasped.

"Yes. But only just," Taryn whispered. "Caspar? Can you hear me?"

"Taryn?" he croaked. "Is that you? I keep seeing things… bad things…" he choked, as he shifted weakly against the tight grip of the tree across his chest. "What happened…?"

"It's okay, Caspar," Taryn tried to reassure him, as she tugged at his bonds ineffectually. For some reason, the tree was still gripping Caspar firmly, despite the binding casting. That was concerning. "It's all going to be okay…" she repeated, trying to clear her voice of uncertainty.

Caspar whimpered, and looked at her with drained, lifeless eyes. "Did I mess it up again…?" he sobbed. "I always mess everything up."

Taryn felt her chest tighten with sympathy. He looked so like a child, helpless and scared, yet still desperate for the approval she had denied him in his appraisal meeting that already felt like a lifetime ago. "No, no… you did just fine, Caspar. None of this is your fault… Don't worry, we're going to get you out of this."

Out of the corner of her eye, Taryn noticed that the tree roots lying on the floor had started to twitch.

"Hop!" Taryn shouted. "Can you try to free Skelton?" She looked round for Hop. He was standing a few feet away. He had picked up a sheaf of some of the crumpled paper that had escaped from the Unstationery Cupboard, which was now catatonic, and was writing furiously.

"What exactly do you think you're doing?" Taryn spluttered disbelievingly.

"I've never even heard of magic like this before! I'm trying to take down some contemporaneous notes. For evidential purposes. Historical records et cetera."

Taryn was thunderstruck. "If you don't bloody help, we'll all be bloody historical records! The entire Tower could collapse at any moment and bury us! Now put the pen down and help!"

"On it," said Hop apologetically, pocketing the offending stationery and moving towards the bound Master. He attempted to pull at the roots, but they only gripped more firmly. "It doesn't seem to be working," he observed. "I thought the binding would control the tree?"

"I can't move them either," Taryn said. As they wrenched at the roots helplessly, the foundations of the Tower rocked and a pained roar echoed from above. The binding must be breaking. There were further screams and crashes from up above. What was going on? Whatever it was, she needed to work fast. The room heaved and juddered, on the brink of total collapse.

Taryn grasped at the root around Caspar's chest as firmly as she could. As she wrapped her fingers around its tough bark, she felt an intense grief wash over her. It was coming from the root itself, from the tree…

It was in pain. Utter, incomprehensible pain. A vision flashed violently across her mind. She was the tree, watching on as a group of Tower mages bent steel and glass around the wings of its monstrous guardian. She could feel the snap of its wing blades, the tear of leaf and branch. She watched as the dragon cowered under bonds of magic, still burning at its alien heart. The pain, the fire… There was Ivy, fighting not the dragon, but the mages pinning it. What was this? The tree was hurt and confused. Its seedling was dying before its eyes, its hateful guardian wounded and broken. It wanted to stop the flames that tore at it in rage, but it couldn't. It was too far gone; there was only one way to end it all now.

Taryn had betrayed the tree. That's why the seedling had chosen Ivy instead of her. All this time, she thought she had been protecting the tree, doing her best to nurture it in this unnatural environment. She should have known better than to use dragon scales in its feed mix; she should have intervened sooner when she saw it growing sicker and sicker. When had she forgotten how to truly care? How had she let this happen? It was all her fault.

She knew she needed to help the tree, to soothe it, to repair the damage done. She felt its distress as its monstrous guardian raised itself from the floor above, wreathed in brilliant white dragon fire. But how could she help it? She couldn't think of anything of any use. Nothing she had ever learned or studied was of any bloody use.

She suddenly heard her grandmother's voice, ringing haughtily inside her skull.

"You Citadel mages and your rules and regulations. You've created so many limitations you don't know how to do anything without consulting a damn committee. Forgotten what real magic is. It's all about knowing what you want it to do, girl. If the intention is there, the rest will follow."

Taryn gripped the root with both hands, and, with a strangely detached focus, felt within it for the depth of its pain, beyond the fire of the stolen heart. The tree – or was it her? – was lost, hopeless. A longing for home. Home… Visions of vast woodlands, of fields, of strong, sustaining earth beneath, of clear open air above. They had uprooted it; they had fed it with ash and charcoal, and it burned in pain.

It needed to heal, to draw from the buried wells of spring water in the forests it remembered. Taryn inhaled deeply, breathing in the soaring stream of magic ancient and timeless. She held onto it, soothing it as she would a child that had been lost and then found. She told the tree soft stories of home, promises of reparation. She sang to it of sorrow and remorse, tears running down her cheeks and mingling with the memory of icy waterfalls and soft, fresh rain. She sang to it of seedlings and new growth, of children lost but then found.

Slowly, steadily, with infinite sadness, the tree calmed. The dragon no longer railed in fury. Taryn felt the tide of righteous anger ebb, gradually evaporating, leaving behind merely a mournful acceptance. The tree shuddered one last time, the foundations of the Tower gave a final quiver, and then there was rest. Release.

Taryn let go of the tree and crumpled to the floor as she exhaled. She hadn't realised she had been holding her breath.

"What did you just do?" Hop asked, looking at her with mingled shock and admiration.

"What was needed." That was all Taryn said, as the two of them set to disentangling the groaning forms of Caspar and Skelton, and heaving them out of the Crypt.

✦

An air of perfect restfulness descended upon the foyer. The tree had stopped its pulsing and trembling; the dragon grew suddenly calm.

"Taryn..." breathed Ivy, although she could not explain why.

The mages were starting to rise to their feet now, dazed and rubbing arms which felt coldly bereft of power. Ivy stepped forward, Kork in her hands. The seedling was breathing normally again now, eyes open and curious.

As she moved closer to the dragon, it arched its neck of latticed creepers and branches and slowly inclined its head towards her. She felt the full intensity of its gaze, an ancient serenity in the unfathomable liquid pools of blackness that were its eyes – eyes so like Kork's. It looked down at the seedling, which was now tentatively stretching its twiggy arms, and gently lowered its head to nuzzle him.

As the dragon touched the seedling, its form shifted, branches and vines twisting and creeping. Clawed feet became stump legs and arms, with spindly wooden fingers softly clasping and unclasping. The snaked neck and brutal tail receded, bending into the trunk of the reformed figure with a soft suppleness. Jaws became a wide, restful mouth, desiccated wings drifted to the ground like the final leaves of autumn.

The figure scooped up the seedling, no bigger than a conker in its large palm, and then bent one knee and offered its hand towards Ivy. Kork gave the tree creature a tender look, before hopping across to Ivy's arms. She clutched at him, before reaching out a hand towards the massive torso of the tree guardian. She could see the dragon heart, still pulsing, but more steadily now. She placed her palm against the smoothed ridges of its wooden ribs. She could feel the heat of the dragon heart, the fire of the lost dragon beating within. It sang of theft and death. She remembered its name and uttered it with remorse. The pulse softened further and the heat dimmed. The power seeped into her veins, entreating her to help; begging her for redress.

The guardian smiled. It was free now; the fight had faded from it. Then, with no more noise than the rustle of leaves in the wind, the figure stepped slowly backwards towards the tree, melding into its vast trunk.

For a brief moment, the universe hung silent and still.

✦

Then, inevitably, pandemonium erupted.

Ivy, Lil and Dante were met with a barrage of questions, exclamations and accusations from the gathered mages, who were nursing bruised limbs, and more importantly – at least as far as they were concerned – extremely bruised egos. The group tried to quell the consternation and confusion, which only increased as the bedraggled figures of Taryn and Hop emerged from the stairwell leading down to the Crypt, half-dragging the dazed Skelton and Caspar alongside them.

Bladlow had by this point thrust his way through the crowd of angry and bewildered mages, puffing and panting. Ivy couldn't recall seeing him when the assembled mages had first entered. Either he had taken longer to reach the Tower due to his inordinate lack of fitness or he had simply waited outside until someone else had dealt with the disaster (or possibly both). Ivy's face flushed with anger; this was the man at the heart of the devastation that surrounded them.

As Bladlow huffed over, she glimpsed a figure lingering quietly on the periphery of the squabbling crowd of mages. Hartley. He caught her eyes and her pulse quickened. She felt the dragon race inside her, urging her to action. What did it want from her?

Bladlow had started railing loudly, drowning out the din of other voices. "What is the meaning of this?" he exclaimed furiously. He cast his eyes over the scene. "You!" he spluttered, pointing a stubby finger towards Hop, who was dragging Skelton towards where Ivy was now standing, side-stepping the heaps of rubble strewn across the smeared sheen of the cracked granite floor. "You! If I find out that you are behind this... this... wanton destruction, there won't be a place in all of Kirin that will employ you! Look at this! The damage! And the tree! That tree is client property and a key income stream for the Tower... it had better be fully useable!"

Tearing her eyes from the figure of Hartley, Ivy faced Bladlow. "Useable?" she shouted at him. "Useable? That tree is more than just a bloody asset! Do you have any idea what you've done to it? You've been killing it, all this time!"

"How dare you!" Bladlow roared. "I've had just about enough of your ridiculous and baseless allegations!"

As Bladlow's voice rose in pitch, the battered Hop heaved Skelton towards the throng of mages. Without ceremony, he unhooked his arm and let Skelton thud, semi-conscious, to the ground in front of the sputtering Bladlow. He authoritatively held up a hand for quiet and the collected mages – including, much to everyone's surprise, Bladlow – fell silent.

"It is my understanding that the present situation was caused by the draining of a magical tree for spellcasting purposes," Hop said formally. "Said tree was fortified by the application of a solution brewed by Master Charles Bladlow which contained a dragon heart illegally procured from

Dragonsteel Industries. I therefore recommend that Master Bladlow be remanded to the custody of the Regulator."

Gasps and exclamations followed this statement, as Bladlow's eyes widened in fury.

"I shall be compiling my full report presently," Hop resumed primly, adjusting his spectacles, one lens of which was cracked. "You should expect a copy within three working days."

Hop's words were met with looks of utter disbelief from the assembled mages. This was the last thing Hop Pockett remembered seeing before he promptly fainted.

✦

As Hop was busy delivering his ringing indictment, Ivy watched as the figure of Hartley slipped silently into the darkness.

The lost dragon whispered to her.

Blood still thundering in her ears from her confrontation with Bladlow, she couldn't understand what it was saying. She tried to calm her rage. It was telling her something, something she didn't want to hear, something she couldn't bring herself to admit might be possible. It whispered more urgently still, exhorting her to follow Hartley.

She brushed through the crowd, ignoring demands for her to remain, Kork clinging to her shoulder. Bob, once again an imperious – albeit limping – tiger, joined her at her side as they pursued Hartley into the darkness.

The clouds that hung so portentously overhead had stopped their flickering and roiling. Rain was beginning to fall on the Citadel, slapping onto the stonework. Through the rain, Ivy could just about make out the figure of Hartley up ahead. He seemed cloaked in the night itself, keeping close to the shadows of the buildings rising up around them, darting around the throng of people now ebbing towards the devasted Tower.

Ivy followed on, Bob at her heels. She heard the wings of a dragon thump through the sky overhead. Instinctively, with newfound power, she felt herself reach skyward towards the dragon, feeling the feverish heat of its body, feeling the rage in its heart. She realised with a thrill of fear that it had no rider. Surely Dragonsteel had not loosed it deliberately?

She could feel it up there. The largest dragon, the one that had stared at her outside the glowing gates of Dragonsteel. No. Not it. Her.

Kilndown.

The dragon's name echoed in Ivy's mind, thundering with righteous rage, searching for the lost heart of her kin.

Somehow, Ivy knew the other five dragons were up there too, circling, searching. Awash with the sensation of their collective anger, Ivy surmised it was only a matter of time before they turned their wrath towards the Citadel at large. Yet the crowds streaming in the rain towards the Tower were not paying any attention to the dragons overhead; the steady beat of dragon wings was too familiar a sound.

Still the lost dragon whispered to her, willing her towards the truth she feared, as Hartley hurried into a dark alley, disappearing from view. Ivy reached the entrance and raised her hand.

"Stop." Her words rang out, crystal clear, fierce with power. She approached Hartley. He was fixed, motionless, in the centre of the alley, confused.

"Ivy?" he whispered.

"Amazing what you can do, if you know the right command words," she snarled coldly, her anger forged like steel. "And you knew the right words, didn't you, Hartley?" She stood facing him, while Bob circled him, shoulders rippling dangerously. "You knew because I told you." She practically hissed this last part, fire taut in her voice.

"Ivy, what's going on? I have no idea what you're talking about. You've clearly just been through something–"

"*Been through something?*" she repeated. The lost dragon was screaming inside her now, as Ivy finally opened her mind to the memory it was urging her to face. The cold outhouse at Dragonsteel; the cloaked figure, dragonsteel blade poised and raised, ready to slice. She felt fire flash down her spine as the memory of the blade's edge ripped into the lost dragon, into her own mind. She raged at Hartley. "You ripped the heart out of a dragon and fed it to an ancient tree which tried to kill us all!"

"Ivy, please. Let me go…"

"No."

Kork jabbered at Hartley angrily, shaking his tiny stick fists, as Ivy tightened her binding on him. He winced and tried to wrestle from the grip of the spell, desperately attempting to counter-cast. But she was too powerful.

"I should have known Bladlow wouldn't have wanted to dirty his hands," Ivy continued, ignoring his struggle. "Not when he has so many willing disciples at his disposal… That's why you were so bloody interested in my work for Dragonsteel – you needed the command words. You wanted to make sure the dragon wouldn't resist. Did you even feel anything as you butchered it? Are you even capable of feeling anything for anyone?"

This last word caught in Ivy's throat.

"Ivy, I'm sorry. I–" Hartley faltered. His shoulders sagged, no longer fighting her grip. No justification followed.

"Not good enough. You tore a dragon's heart out!" she raged. More waves of realisation mixed with alien memories flooded as she looked at him, standing there with his handsome head bowed. "You had it, didn't you? That night at the Garbled Goblin – it was in that bag. You never forgot it, you left it for Bladlow – no wonder he kept looking over! That was who you were meant to meet that night! It all makes sense now!" She was crying with fury now. "It was at my bloody feet the whole night – why didn't I feel it?"

"It was charmed. Preservation spell. No-one would have sensed it, even if they were looking for it," he said dully.

"Was that why you cosied up to me? You needed a distraction, a way to get me out of the way so you could make your filthy trade with Bladlow?"

"I promise, I wasn't just using you," he answered, his voice now filled with emotion that almost matched her own. "I mean that. What we had – it was real – I've been trying to speak to you all week, I wanted to talk to you – I didn't know what else to do…"

Ivy's heart clenched. She tightened her grip, fighting back tears.

"None of it was real. You used me, just like you and Bladlow used the tree, used the dragon. I've been such a bloody fool – to assume you actually cared…" She tried to stop her voice from cracking, but it broke, and she started to sob wretchedly. "Why did you do it, Hartley? What was it all for?"

The bindings loosed and Hartley slipped free. Thinking he was about to run, Bob prepared to pounce, and Ivy steeled herself to recast. Instead, Hartley moved in, gripping Ivy's shoulders and looking at her intensely with those grey-blue eyes of his. She still wanted him, even though she knew what he was. She could feel his breath on her cheeks; her heart ached with pain as he pressed his forehead against hers and whispered to her hurriedly.

"Ivy, I promise that what happened between us was real. Everything else... It was Bladlow's idea, he said the scales hadn't been strong enough. I was just doing my job, trying to keep it... You have no idea the pressure I was under – I needed to deliver something extraordinary... I didn't know what else to do. Please, Ivy, I need to leave, Woodbane will be livid when he realises. Not to mention what the Regulator will do to me–"

She could let him leave. Just let him walk away. The sorrow was unbearable. She felt the dragon soaring overhead, the cold rain steaming off its scales. She pushed him away. "I wouldn't worry about the Regulator, if I were you."

The dragon was approaching, closer and closer, it was keening and calling in the rain, marshalling the other dragons. A burst of sharp fire cascaded across the clouds.

Hartley looked up, panic crossing his face.

"They're looking for you." She gazed at him coolly. "Should I call them? You know I could."

"Ivy, please..."

She looked away. Bob was standing next to her, mouth ajar in anticipation of the kill. She curled her fingers in his wet fur, smelt the acrid dragon fire in the air above. She could do it; she felt the power racing inside her. She could command them all with a thought if she wanted. The dragons, the tiger; they would all bend to her desire.

Kork brushed his seed-pod body against her, entangling his stick limbs in her hair.

She inhaled the smell of trees in the rain.

Finally resolute, she summoned her power, wrapping the bindings around Hartley again, not needing to recite the words, knowing how to direct and limit it instinctively. This time the unreal chains pinned him firmly to the floor.

Bob settled himself down next to the prostrate mage, baleful glare fixed on him, tail flicking menacingly.

She flashed Hartley a half-grin. "I think we'll be paying a visit to the Regulator in a little while," she said. "Bob will watch over you in the meantime, although I would warn you, he's rather hungry and I haven't had time to give him his evening snack."

"Please, Ivy… don't leave me like this…" Hartley implored.

Ivy looked down at him, her eyes as cold as cooled steel.

"I have some dragons to calm down," was all she said to him.

Exultant, she left him, Kork chirruping happily on her shoulder.

25.

BRIGHT FUTURES
━━━━━ ◆ ━━━━━

It had been just over a week since the near total annihilation of the Tower of Jackdaw and Spittlelick. Autumn had settled in and the Citadel had experienced a series of bright, cold days.

Ivy was perched on a low wall in the square outside the Tower, next to Dante. Both were looking up thoughtfully at the remains of the Tower. The tree was still standing, its lofty crown of leaves overlooking what remained of the coliseum-like circular walls of the Tower, its branches undulating gently even though there was no breeze. It seemed restful now, a colossus softly sleeping. The Tower had almost entirely collapsed in some sections, leaving its giant dragonsteel supports jutting up into the frigid air like the ribs of a decayed titan.

She looked up at the cold, clear sky. No dragons today.

She sensed them slumbering in the cavernous outhouses of the Dragonsteel facility. Perhaps she shouldn't have returned them to Dragonsteel, but it had been difficult to know what else to do with six angry dragons at the time, and she was still unsure about the limits of her control over them.

She had arrived just after dawn on the night the Tower had fallen, riding on Kilndown, the largest, leading the others into the facility like a row of giant reptilian ducklings. She had caressed them and whispered to them as she led them into their stalls. The ogre handlers and dragon riders who had gathered at their arrival stood by in shocked awe as she settled them without the need to recite any casting.

She had then turned to the assembled crowd and informed them that she would be checking on their welfare periodically. She wasn't sure whether they had taken her seriously about that, but they had let her leave unquestioned as they moved to secure the beasts to their moorings, grateful for their return.

Ivy gazed back at the remains of the Tower, wondering about the future of the dragons. Perhaps she should have ridden off with them after all…

"I still can't quite believe it's gone," Dante remarked, breaking the silence and nodding towards the Tower.

"I know. End of an era, I suppose," Ivy commented.

"Hah," barked Dante suddenly, "this place never ends. It just slithers off somewhere else, like a snake shedding its skin."

"Cheery."

"It's true, though. The Masters already have plans for a new Tower. Bigger and better, naturally. Those Masters who haven't jumped ship, that is. Apparently, there's some excellent real estate on the riverfront, just crying out for development. It'll put us right next to a number of key clients. At least, that's what I've heard…" Dante put his hand in his pocket and pulled out something round, which he proceeded to toss up and down reflectively.

"Is that one of the Tower scruttles?" Ivy asked incredulously.

"Yup," confirmed Dante. "Turns out these little buggers really can survive a magical apocalypse. Found them all bouncing about earlier. I should probably go back for the others at some point, but they seem happy enough."

Ivy wasn't particularly surprised by the fact that the scruttles were enjoying a brief moment of freedom, as the unfortunate specimen in Dante's hand emitted an irritable squeak.

"It's like I said," continued Dante, "this place just keeps on going. Did you hear they've already set up a temporary site near the docks? They want us all in bright and early next week."

"Yes, I'd heard. A slightly longer holiday would have been nice. Especially after all the saving the Citadel we just did."

"To be fair, we only really saved ourselves. And Caspar and Skelton. And Kork and the tree. And Bob. And I suppose you put those dragons back to bed. That could have gotten nasty."

Ivy looked at the ruins of the Tower contemplatively.

"I spoke to Skelton again the other day," Dante continued.

"And?"

"Same old Skelton, albeit a bit shaken. He's self-reported to the Regulator. They're reviewing the case, but it sounds like he'll be getting off lightly. Claims he had no idea what Bladlow and Hartley were up to. Said he'll be helping the Regulator 'implement a new governance framework for the synthetisation process', or something to that effect."

"Same old, same old."

"Indeed. He also said he'd spoken to Salonika. One of the mages in Pasts put him in touch."

"How did that go?"

"Fine, I think. I went to check on Salonika myself afterwards. Wondered if it had been enough to allow her to finally pass on."

"Had it?"

"Nope. She's there. Still a bit peeved, but weirdly I think she's enjoying all the attention. Said she was planning on hanging around for a bit, which I can't say I'm looking forward to."

"I can imagine. I'll visit her soon. I promised I would."

The sun was beginning to sink beneath the skyline now, bathing the Tower ruins with a soft golden patina. The tree's large horse chestnut leaves glinted and swayed majestically in their autumnal russet and gold. Despite the serenity of the tree, Ivy was feeling morose, riddled with a frustration she couldn't place. She sighed.

"What's up?" asked Dante, sensing her mood. He pocketed the squeaking scruttle, and looked at her.

"I don't know. I had a message from Skelton yesterday, funnily enough. He wants me to meet him tomorrow morning in front of Woodbane's offices. Something about next steps."

"Ah."

Dante left it a moment, for once understanding that silence was what was needed. Then, not unexpectedly, the outburst from Ivy followed.

"What am I supposed to do? Go back to work? Pretend it's all normal? Back to playing by their rules? Drafting casting after casting until I feel like I've reached my limits and there's no real magic left in the world? Am I even helping anyone or changing anything? Is any of it even right? You saw what they were doing for Woodbane. I just don't know if I can do this anymore. I don't even know if I want to." Ivy was fiercely blinking tears from her eyes.

"That's a lot to take on board," Dante said gently. He moved closer to her and nudged her shoulder with his. "Would you like to hear a story?"

"Must I?"

Dante didn't answer, but instead started talking pensively. "Before I came to the Tower, I knew exactly what type of mage I was. Smart, clever, funny…" A grin started to play around his mouth.

"Seriously, Dante. Please tell me you're going somewhere with this."

"I was also exceedingly good at conversing with dead people. In the same manner you seem to pick up all the waifs and strays in life, I picked up the deceased, those whose souls refused to move on to pastures new.

"It was interesting at first. It started when I was a teenager. Barely had to open my mind and there they were, moaning away. And my Gods, do the dead know how to moan. On and on they went, quite literally." Dante took to mimicking their voices, with an alarming degree of authenticity. "*'I'll be damned if that harlot gets her hands on my silver…', 'do you know who I used to be?', 'If she moves in with that two-faced prat after I'm gone, I'll bloody well haunt her until the end of her days…'*"

He paused for breath. "It was all relatively amusing, although I was never sure what they expected from me. Mostly I think they just wanted someone who would listen to all their unresolved life issues."

In spite of herself, Ivy's curiosity was piqued. "Is that why you didn't want to stay in the Pasts team?"

"No. Quite the opposite. Like I said, I was very good at talking to dead people. And listening, if you can believe that. I suppose I wanted to help them have a voice through me, find closure and all that warm and fluffy rubbish. I genuinely enjoyed working in Pasts. And Futures. I wanted very much to continue."

"So what happened?"

Dante looked downward and paused, before continuing. "It was a few years ago now. Things had been going well. I was actually happy, which is probably why it all went wrong, the universe being the utter knob it is.

"I was in a really good relationship, with someone I'd been with since my late teens. He wasn't a mage. Worked as a healer, but non-magical. We had it all planned out – do our time in the Citadel, make some decent money, then move out, find a nice village somewhere we could settle down. Perhaps actually help people. Real people. Not just the big bad corporations here. Existence was going to be worth it.

"And then he died. Stupidly, suddenly, pointlessly."

Dante was now staring fixedly at the ruins of the Tower. A shadow of longing flickered across his face.

"So I did what anyone with my sort of power would do. I searched all of Nowhere. Did some stupid things. Fell in with some questionable people."

Ivy recalled the conversation with Wryneck in the dolls' house. She remembered the strange shadows creeping through Salonika's deathscape.

"I tried everything I could, but I couldn't find him. Couldn't feel him anymore. He hadn't stayed." Bitterness had crept into his voice. "Clearly I wasn't unfinished business or whatever. He was just gone."

Silence cascaded around them, save for the whispered rustle of leaves from the tree.

Eventually, Dante resumed. "After that, I couldn't face the thought of reaching out into the beyond at work every bloody day, seeing all those dead people, all wanting and needing and taking and taking and it all feeling so utterly empty. So

I decided I'd switch to Castings instead." He snorted bitterly. "Bloody Castings. Spells and charms to help businesses profit and leech and thrive."

Ivy was looking at him sadly. "Dante, I had no idea… I'm so sorry. All that business with contacting Salonika… it makes sense now."

"Yes, well, anyway. That's sort of my point. The funny thing is that it took contacting Salonika for me to realise that maybe I've been a complete idiot. I closed everything off. Someone up there moved my whole damned future and I didn't deal with it very well. I grabbed another future from the shelf without properly considering if it was the right one for me."

"Do you regret deciding to work in Castings?"

"Hah. Always. Sometimes. It depends, really. I've got more out of it than I thought I would have. It's honestly hard to know whether I'd have enjoyed working with dead people any more than I enjoy working with living ones… but I admit I do sometimes think that, if only I'd done something useful, even though it was the harder path, I would have felt less… empty. Maybe it's not too late, though…" Dante trailed off momentarily. "Look, what I'm trying to say, admittedly not very well, is that ultimately you can never really be sure what's going to happen next, but you shouldn't let that stop you from doing what feels right. Don't be scared like I've been."

"Thanks, Dante." Ivy nudged his shoulder with hers, returning the favour. "I get it. I'll think about it, I promise."

Dante exhaled, seemingly satisfied. "Good. That's all I ask. Although I'd naturally prefer it if you didn't leave Jackdaw. It would be bloody boring around here without you." He stood up and stretched. "Also, while we're on the subject of futures, you can do a lot better than Hartley Crumpet-Snackfart. Trust me."

"Mm…" Ivy replied, not wanting to address the still raw subject of Hartley. She had been trying extremely hard not to think about him after leaving him in that alley, folding away everything she felt like steel being bent into a sword.

"Heard he and Bladlow were being sentenced this morning," Dante continued quietly. "Any right of appeal has already been denied – the Regulator has the full backing of the Council of Mages. Apparently, Caspar's mother was beside herself."

She leaned against Dante slightly. Unlike Hartley, at least Dante was still reassuringly here, infuriating as he was. As for her future… she sighed. "It would be so much easier if I knew what my future is supposed to look like."

"We do have people on the sixth floor who can advise on that sort of thing, you know…" Dante looked at the ruins, and added, "Well, we used to."

"True. Although I suppose if that Carterton matter taught me anything, it's perhaps that it's best not to know."

Dante grinned. "Funny you should mention Carterton, actually. During your exile to the Copy Room, I undertook the Carterton casting – he got in touch with me about it only yesterday."

"And?" Ivy pressed, curious. "How did it go?"

"It went exceedingly well at first. Carterton came into some old family money out of the blue."

"Really? What happened?"

"Turned out it wasn't his family."

"Bugger," said Ivy. "Poor man."

"I know. Really thought I'd got it this time. Not that you were any help whatsoever, Armstride." He put his arm around her shoulder affectionately. "Right. Shall we grab Kork and get to the pub? The others will be wondering where we are."

"Sounds like a plan," Ivy affirmed, feeling somewhat brighter. "Kork!" she shouted towards the tree, shading her eyes with her hand against the glare of the setting sun.

There was a *pfft* and Kork appeared on her shoulder, proudly brandishing a large leaf in one hand and a shiny chestnut conker in the other.

"Thanks, Dante," Ivy said, as they left the ruins of the Tower.

"No problem. Now let's go have a drink. I really need one after all that deep and meaningful nonsense."

✦

Dante and Ivy met Taryn and Lil in a warm nook deep within the Garbled Goblin, where they huddled over a round of steaming drinks.

Lil was bubbling with excitement. Since the collapse of the Tower, there had been no end of drama and internal politics and Lil was divulging the gossip to the group with the air of someone completely in their element.

The Masters had split into three camps: those who were focused on rebuilding the Tower elsewhere; those who had quickly secured a position at one of the other Towers; and those who had been quite content with the previous state of affairs and were now distinctly anxious about where the money to feed the llamacorn was going to come from. The senior mages were assessing their options critically, hoping to hitch themselves to the right horse. The junior mages and support staff were mostly just waiting to be told what to do, which was reassuringly business as usual. The seventh-floor balcony had been sighted on a sunny clifftop somewhere along the coast and did not look like it was going anywhere anytime soon.

"Some of the Masters have made a start on the new Tower plans already," Lil was relaying with gusto. "Apparently, they want something bigger and better than before. Master Stanforth has already set up a committee, although it's not been going well." The Committee for the Appointment of Genuinely Competent and Inexpensive Architects had already descended into several arguments about parquet flooring. "They've started to wonder whether they should just design and build the whole thing themselves this time."

There was a collective groan at this prospect from the others.

Lil smiled. The faerie was finally looking more at home in what was, to all intents and purposes, her own skin. She had ditched the cosmetic illusions, although – some habits being hard to break – she had started experimenting liberally with human beauty products instead. She had not quite got the hang of it, as evidenced by the fact that her complexion had taken on a somewhat cake-like texture. "Anyway," she said. "I spoke to some of the Masters the other day about my big idea. Amazingly, they thought it was actually worth a go!"

"I'm not surprised," Dante remarked cynically. "I expect there's a lot of money to be made in making illusions at client events. The Masters must be rubbing their hands with glee."

Kork had scampered down from Ivy's shoulder and was peering curiously into the group's drinks. Ivy steered him pointedly back to his plate of water.

"Well, here's hoping they give me more than a bloody broom cupboard in the new Tower," Lil said, before looking at Taryn. "What's next for you, Taryn?"

Taryn took a sip from her drink, pondering her answer. The drink was, in a recent development, decidedly non-alcoholic, although she wasn't convinced that she was enjoying it. "I'm not sure, to be honest," she said after a moment. "I must admit the Regulator's decision to suspend me actually came as a massive relief. After everything that's happened, I just need to go back home – my real home – for a bit and think things through. There's also some family stuff I need to deal with that I've been putting off for a long time... I might try to take the kids with me, if school will allow it. It would be good for them to see the countryside."

Taryn turned to Ivy before continuing. "I know it's a big ask and I don't expect you to agree to it, given what I've done, but I was wondering if I should take Kork? If you're happy with that, Ivy? And provided he wants to go, of course."

Ivy looked at the little seedling, who was now rolling around in his water plate. It might be good for him to see the forests of his home and Taryn clearly felt she had some amends to make. Besides, Kork had been staying with Ivy since the destruction of the Tower and, given that she had also somehow adopted Bob, who chased Kork around her tiny lodgings whenever the seedling provoked him (which was frequently), things had gotten a little cramped.

"That feels right to me," Ivy said. "Provided Kork's happy with it."

Taryn smiled at her.

As Kork scurried about, leaping on and off of the head of the Garbled Goblin's cleaning troll, another small troll suddenly rolled into the Garbled Goblin and over to their corner table, hitting a table leg with an ungainly thump and sending their drinks tottering across the tabletop.

"Ump," said Ump, uncurling in a daze.

"Ump?" Ivy queried.

"Ump," he replied cheerily. The troll pulled out what looked like an elegantly sealed parcel. There was a brief moment of panic as Ump then promptly tried to place it in his mouth, stopped only by the baffling chorus of protestations that emanated from the group.

Ivy took the parcel from his smooth, round digits. It bore her name in an unmistakable graceful script. She opened it carefully. A small figurine of a dragon tumbled onto the table. Lil picked it up, turning it over and then passing it to Dante, who inspected it curiously. Ivy read the small square of paper that had been enclosed with the figurine.

'Never assume' was inscribed delicately across it.

"What is it?" Lil asked, mystified.

"It's from Cleft," Ivy answered with a wry smile, retrieving the dragon from Dante. It felt warm. As she held it, its small wings unfurled and its breast glowed softly.

"Very weird," said Dante.

They looked at it for a moment, as Ump, mission accomplished, rolled over to join the cleaning troll in happily licking spillages from the floor.

The conversation drifted onto what came next for Ivy.

"I'm supposed to meet with Skelton tomorrow," Ivy told them. "I expect he wants me to stay, but I really don't know what I want. I'm not sure I can keep working for clients like Woodbane and Dragonsteel…"

"I think you should see what Skelton has to say," Taryn said firmly. "You've got real potential, Ivy. This isn't the end of things for you. You never know. You could still make an impact, make things better, fairer. Although I fear it will be a case of evolution rather than revolution for Skelton and the rest."

"Let's see," replied Ivy sceptically. She was now feeling decidedly apprehensive about tomorrow's meeting with the Master, the man she had followed unquestioningly for so long now. Could she keep following?

"We'll still be here for you, whatever you decide," said Lil brightly.

Ivy smiled at her, feeling a swell of gratitude and companionship.

"How about Hop?" Taryn asked. "Has anyone heard from him?"

"I spoke to him the other day," said Ivy, still toying with the dragon in her palm, trying not to think of Skelton. "He seems to be enjoying himself back in the Audit Office. Keen to get on with further investigations, he told me."

"Gods help us all," said Dante.

Nodding as one, they all took a very long drink.

✦

Hop was indeed enjoying himself. Matters had all worked out rather well.

The Supervisory Board had – to Hop at least – seemed most impressed when he delivered his two-hundred-page report on the Jackdaw and Spittlelick and Woodbane Cosmetics Special Investigation at his formal debriefing in the main hearing room of the Regulator of Magical Practice. The Head of the Supervisory Board had very carefully placed the report in a large beige folder in front of her and assured Hop that she would review it as an utmost priority. Hop had thought she seemed especially grateful when he had caught up with her in the corridor after she had inadvertently left it behind.

After the debrief, Hop had found himself back in the Audit Office, all criticisms of him quietly dropped. Well, perhaps not all criticisms. The Audit Team had been released from the annual Wintertide audit of Jackdaw and Spittlelick, there not being much left of the Tower to audit. Glof, Wrex and the rest of the small team were enjoying the serenity of the Audit Office, cocooned from the outside chill. At least, they would have been enjoying it but for Hop, who was brimming with a renewed fervour since his return from his assignment.

Eventually, Glof had suggested that, seeing as Hop had demonstrated a talent for such work, perhaps they could find something else for him to investigate. Hop had beamed at the prospect, already mentally bestowing unto himself the inestimably distinguished title of 'Head of Special Investigations'.

Wrex had then mentioned something about the recent audit of the Tower of Ampleforth, Hassle and Bluster revealing an unusually high number of futures being determined by their mages. She had wondered whether it might be worth investigating any possible connection to the increased trading activity on the Futures Exchange of late.

Hop had grinned widely. It sounded like an excellent place to start.

✦

Not far below the warm confines of the Audit Office, Hartley Crumpley-Snafely was sitting on a cold wooden bench in the cellar of the Chamber of the Regulator of Magical Practice. He had been left in a dimly-lit antechamber, which had been magically sealed. The air was tight and fetid; it had no escape either. He shuffled uncomfortably against the cast-proof chains which manacled his hands and feet, awaiting his grim fate. His future was not looking bright at all.

The Regulator had been firm, and the Council of Mages had been incandescent with fury. Not for Hartley and Bladlow the temporary suspension that Underfoot had somehow achieved with her contrite admission. Not for them the gentle slap on the wrist Skelton had incurred with his display of appalled regret at his colleagues' actions.

No, despite numerous concerted pleas from his father, his mother, his grandmother and a very well-regarded uncle, Hartley had been summarily stripped of his status, unceremoniously fired by Woodbane, and was now facing the horrific prospect of having his magical powers permanently drained by the grimlings. They were just there, on the other side of the thick stone wall in front of him, waiting ever so patiently.

Bladlow had already been escorted into the grimling chamber, first ranting and railing, then huffing and spluttering and pleading miserably. The guards had paid him no heed.

Hartley could hear the grimlings peel themselves from the masonry and *click-clack-clatter* across to the blubbering Bladlow, dreadful mandibles crunching, spindly legs tapping, echoing across the stone floor…

He shivered. His heart raced. His neck itched with a cold trickle of sweat. This was definitely not how it was supposed to go. He had done everything he was told. He had worked hard to secure the family status, to live up to his unquestionable birthright. Now, that power was to be leeched from him.

Click-clack-clatter…

He tried to think of something else, something that might distract him from the torment that lingered on the other side of the wall. He thought of Ivy, the way she had looked at him that night, as he had desperately tried to explain himself, the tears running down her face. Another thing that hadn't worked out how he had thought it would.

Bladlow was railing again now, squawking out a stream of incoherent rants as the grimlings crawled over him. Inside the chamber, the consummate consumer that was Charles Bladlow fell to his knees as the grimlings clacked and snapped and devoured… The screaming eventually stopped. Hartley's heart was in his throat. His turn next.

Click-clack-clatter…

Fortunately for Hartley, in a twist of fate that no futures mage could have predicted, at that very moment several floors up, an overworked sprite in the Complaints Division stumbled into the confiscated Automated Portal Generation Device, causing the peculiar machine to judder and whirr. Without warning, a large void appeared directly in front of the manacled mage.

Hartley jumped in alarm. He then peered at the scene through the portal: a large, sandy beach stretching out invitingly, waves gently lapping at its shore. Hartley glanced around the empty antechamber and then back at the portal. He heard scraping sounds coming from the other side of the wall.

Click-clack-clatter…

Still bound, still shaking, Hartley Crumpley-Snafely stepped into the portal, just before it vanished.

26.

NEXT STEPS
━━━✦━━━

The morning after the sentencing of Bladlow and Hartley, Ivy met Skelton at the foot of the steps to the impressive pre-Accords frontage of Woodbane's factory. It was early morning and this part of the Citadel was tranquil. There had been a sharp frost last night and the air hung with the tang of ice.

Upon her arrival, Skelton handed her a cup of faerie brew. It was spluttering savagely.

"Thought I'd pick this up for you on my way here," Skelton said, as Ivy took the cup and immediately felt it scald her palm. "Should warm you up."

"Thank you," she replied simply. It would certainly achieve that; dragon fire was more temperate than the bubbling beverage in her hand.

Skelton nodded a quick acknowledgment and an awkward silence followed. "Ivy," he began eventually. "I've asked you to meet me here because I would very much like for you to attend the meeting I have scheduled with Woodbane to discuss the next steps for the synthetisation process. It is, however, entirely your decision.

"Before you decide, I believe you deserve an explanation from me. Will you sit with me?" Skelton motioned at the steps. It was the first time he had ever asked her such a question. She had become so accustomed to his casual directions to "Sit, sit..." that the invitation was unsettling, but not unwelcome.

Ivy sat down on the smooth stone steps next to Skelton. The steps were shallow and worn with the press of decades of footfall. She placed her cup down beside her and laid her hands on the cool step, waiting for Skelton to continue. He was staring fixedly at a point on the horizon. He looked older than she remembered.

He inhaled slowly and began speaking in a solemn tone, in stark contrast to his usual breathless pace. "As I'm sure you know, I have been working on transferral and binding castings for a number of years. It has become a speciality for me, ensuring a good flow of work from clients such as Dragonsteel Industries over the years. At some point, I started considering whether it was possible to use similar principles to imbue non-magical matter with potent magical properties.

"This was not the first time any mage had ever considered such possibilities, but none had so far managed to master the art. I became convinced that this was my way of restoring some of the lost power of magic, in a way that was so very, thoroughly *modern*. I thought of the good we could achieve: the healing elixirs, the restorative solutions, the opportunities for improving the lives of those on Kirin, for repairing the damage inflicted by our predecessors! That was what drove me."

Skelton took a gulp from his cup, and said, "To my surprise, I discovered, with Salonika's help, a process which looked like it would yield successful results. I delivered my theory to a few of the other Masters. Master Bladlow, in particular, saw opportunities to use the synthetic product in his Solutions work.

"However, it was too soon, and Bladlow promised much more than we could deliver. Yet it would not be long before other Towers or sole practitioners started to develop similar offerings. We needed to be first to market, at the cutting edge of modern magic, so we pressed hard to find a solution.

"As you now know, that solution was to draw upon the powerful innate magic in living matter – matter which we believed to be non-sentient, such that its use was completely legitimate."

"You didn't refer to the tree in the regulatory submissions, though," Ivy interjected. "That could have saved us all a lot of time."

Skelton looked momentarily perplexed. "Of course I referenced the tree," he said, affronted. "I specifically referred to the transference of the molecular composition of inorganic sessile magical matter via a catalytic conduit."

Ivy shook her head at him, temper rising. "At no point does that explain that you were funnelling the life-force of a bloody great big angry tree via your junior employees!" she remonstrated angrily. "And fuelling it with dragon parts!"

"Ivy, you must believe me when I tell you that I categorically did not know what Master Bladlow had been feeding the tree. I was aware that Bladlow had suggested fortifying the tree in order to meet mass production demands, but I never for a moment countenanced what Bladlow and Hartley undertook."

"But why didn't you speak to Hop about the process? Answer his questions? If you were so sure that the process was legitimate, you could simply have spoken to him instead of arousing suspicion by avoiding him."

"I never avoided Mr Pockett. I was simply often where he was not. I do confess to reacting to his interrogations with slight contempt – I felt he was on a fool's errand, and there was no room for delay."

Ivy felt her blood rising. She wasn't buying it; any of it. "But you didn't believe there was anything amiss with the Woodbane process? Even after Salonika came to you, exhausted? Even after you saw the effect it had on me? And Caspar, too?"

The sun was edging higher in the clear sky above them, scaling the Citadel's spires and towers, and casting shadows across the steps. A few early morning commuters ambled by, clutching cups and cases, pulling their outercloaks tightly around them against the chill. A troll rolled past, bouncing over the cobbles. It was a while before Skelton spoke again.

"No, I didn't believe there was anything amiss. I gradually realised that the casting process was taking its toll on the mages undertaking the castings; on Salonika, on you, on Caspar, even on myself. I was not aware of the full extent of that toll. To my mind, the process required no more energy than any other large casting. Salonika had been struggling for a while – I assumed she was simply not up to it. For that, I am truly sorry."

Ivy felt her fingers clench reflexively. His apology rang hollow. She steeled herself to continue listening, although she couldn't fathom why she still felt she owed him even that.

"And you…" Skelton continued, "well, you had so many other projects in hand that, again, I made an assumption. I assumed we had been working you too hard across the board. Hence why I suggested you take a rest.

"As for Caspar… Caspar I had intended to switch out before the last casting, but an unfeasible deadline had been imposed at the last minute. I felt I had no option but to continue in order to meet production timescales. As far as I was concerned, there was nothing dangerous or unstable in what we were doing."

Skelton paused and drained his drink. Ivy had not touched hers. Her heart was thumping in her chest, but she stayed quiet, gathering her thoughts.

"That," resumed Skelton, "unfortunately, was my mistake. I failed to recognise the impact on others in the face of the deadlines demanded. I also failed to comprehend the lengths to which Charles Bladlow would go to ensure the project succeeded."

Skelton and Ivy both stared at their feet for a few moments.

"I don't expect forgiveness, Ivy," he said quietly. "You may indeed feel I do not merit it. However, I thought it best, given the circumstances, to tell you the truth of the matter."

The street was beginning to fill; business in the Citadel was grinding into gear. People had started moving past them on the steps, on their way to the great doors of Woodbane Cosmetics. Skelton, while maintaining his innocence, was nevertheless doing a magnificent job of appearing contrite. Ivy couldn't accept this; the questions still burned in her throat.

"What happens next?" she asked sharply. "With Woodbane?" She gestured at the magnificent stone building looming over them.

"That, Ivy, is up to you. Work continues, as it inevitably must. The synthetisation process is proven, and Woodbane would like us to look into alternative options so that production can be resumed."

"And if you don't?"

"Undoubtedly other mages will perfect the process instead."

"What if it can't be done without bringing harm to others? What if it just *shouldn't* be done? What if the products Woodbane manufactures with the synthetic ingredients *aren't* going to be for the good of all Kirin?" Ivy was struggling to keep her voice under control. How could Skelton seem so calm, so considered? She felt the dragon-fire seethe in her blood; the slow thump of leathery wings thudded in her ears. She controlled it, she didn't need to call upon it now.

"All excellent questions, Ivy. Excellent questions indeed. Naturally, the Regulator will now be watching very closely, and – I am reliably informed – will in due course be issuing guidance on best practice. So I suspect there will be limits to what we will be permitted to undertake in the field. And rightly so, rightly so." Skelton appeared to have regained some of his customary bounce now. "As to whether we can achieve it by safer alternative means – means which do not cause disproportionate harm – I am certain we can. Clearly the catalyst needs to be organically magical, but then we encounter the stumbling block of sentience… I was thinking we could try magical minerals? Goblin ore, perhaps…? Any thoughts, Ivy?"

"Honestly, Master? I'd rather not risk you awakening some sort of ancient rock monster next time," Ivy replied caustically. "You should have gone with dragonsteel," she added, and instantly regretted it.

Skelton slapped his free hand to his forehead dramatically. "Yes! Why didn't I think of this? That is an excellent suggestion, Ivy! A non-sentient, highly magical modern alloy! A most exciting prospect…"

Skelton indeed looked positively beside himself with excitement. He carried on enthusiastically. "We'll need to speak with Dragonsteel, naturally, but I'm sure they would be happy to act as an indirect supplier to an established corporation like Woodbane. What an opportunity to cross-refer! Plus we could build real 'stickiness' with both clients if we get it right…"

Ivy had experienced enough stickiness recently. She put her hand in her pocket and felt the warmth of the dragon figurine nestling against her fingers. The wingbeat thudded in her ears again. She remembered the wind hitting her face in flight, the sense of fire encasing her, the power she felt as she suppressed the beast, forging herself into the white-cold steel of resolution.

"I can introduce you to Dragonsteel's new head of development, Tate Tattlebury," Skelton continued. "He was brought on while you were… ahem, downstairs… to work on decreasing inefficiencies with their assets. You'd get on famously, I should think. Lots of modern ideas. Very impressive individual.

"As for the Woodbane casting process, we'll consider how to resource production within the Tower. Don't want you or anyone else feeling the drain too much this time. Perhaps we can work out a rotation amongst the juniors? I'll get Elspeth on it. We can take our time to get it right. Ensure the process is fully sustainable in addition to being stable. Most exciting indeed…"

The unicorn had well and truly bolted now. And it seemed Skelton very much wanted Ivy riding that unicorn. Before the events of the past few weeks, she would have triumphed at the fact that Skelton so clearly valued her assistance. But something had changed. His answers had been unsatisfactory; his assumption that she would unquestioningly resume business as usual was misplaced. *Never assume…*

As she clutched at the dragon in her pocket, she knew she had already resolved she did not want to be a part of it. She wasn't going to stop being a mage, but she was not going to be *this* kind of mage.

Skelton was still talking animatedly. "Why don't you take the lead today on presenting this potential alternative option to Woodbane? An excellent learning opportunity, I should think. On which note, once we've worked out any kinks in the new process, perhaps you can take more of an active role in directing the castings? If you think you can manage it? I'll retain a supervisory role, of course."

Ivy looked at Skelton. "If it's all the same to you, Master, I don't think this line of work is for me."

He looked at her in stunned silence.

"You see," she continued, standing up and looking down at him, "this isn't just about business. What you do – what you've *done* – it doesn't just affect some bottom line. This shiny new magic you're toying with has *consequences*. It affects real people and real things. It gets into the soul, and it burns it up, and that's not right."

She raised her hand and pure mage-fire erupted around her fingers. She rotated her wrist as she spoke, and the fire danced and twisted over and under her knuckles, licking at her fingertips. Skelton stared at the wild magic, hypnotised. "You're playing with fire, all of you, and you don't know how to control it. In time, it'll burn you up, too. Just like Salonika." She closed her fist, and the dancing flames flickered down her wrist, absorbing into her skin. For a moment, her forearm glinted with the sheen of new-forged steel.

"This is a *learning opportunity* for you, Master," she said. "It would be a shame, such a *shame*, if you wasted it. An 'avoidable error', one might say." She paused and set her jaw determinedly, inhaling deeply. Skelton looked as though he'd been struck in the face with a crowbar. His thin lips opened as though to say something, forming her name, but Ivy cut him off. "You can consider this my formal resignation, Master. But don't worry, I won't be leaving the Citadel. I have some dragons to attend to."

She nodded at him courteously and turned her back, leaving him staring after her. She descended the steps, retrieving the dragon from her pocket and smiling to herself as its wings unfurled.

ACKNOWLEDGEMENTS

Writing this novel was easy. At least, that's what I thought when I finished the first draft after a few weeks of fevered writing. Job done. Amazing what you can do with a quiet spell at work.

It turns out that writing a novel actually takes quite a long time and requires many people to politely point out that some readers prefer their books not to resemble the aftermath of a tragic keyboard accident.

So this is a thank you to everyone who helped transform this story into an actual novel.

Firstly, thank you to Helen Lane and John Baker, whose editorial insights were brilliant and absolutely spot on (and led to more dragons, which can only ever be a good thing). Also to Ruth Lunn, whose fine proofing toothcomb picked up the nits that my husband swore he wouldn't have missed (but did), and to Jay Thompson, whose excellent cover design perfectly captures the spirit of the story.

Next, to Zoë Douglas-Judson, who started this all off when, in a career coaching session, she pressed me to outline what I wanted to achieve in life, rather than keep banging on about everything I felt I wasn't achieving. The answer: 'to write' came from nowhere and surprised us both.

Thanks should also go to my friend Ben, who read my first draft and didn't immediately tell me that I was having a mid-life crisis. Ben convinced me that my writing might possibly be enjoyed by people who weren't close family members obliged to say nice things.

To my husband, Andrew, who did say a lot of nice things but also turned out to be an extremely capable editor, go the biggest thanks of all. You don't know how strong your relationship is until you have your pages returned to you with large chunks of text crossed through and your casual approach to split infinitives patiently signposted (excluding the one above, which he is yet to discover...). He was invariably right about everything, and his reward for this is that he gets to do it all again for the next one.

Finally, a special thank you to my dad, who did everything he could to ensure that a book-hungry child was kept in books and, as a result, introduced me to more wonderful worlds than I could possibly recount. I'm so glad I can share this one with him.

Printed in Dunstable, United Kingdom

One of A Kind
Making Things Happen

For 'Megs'

I hope you enjoy reading about your "Lost" Cousin.

Despite all that happened, or maybe because of it I made it through.

your Cousin

Tony Moore

One of A Kind

Making Things Happen

Tony Moore

Copyright © 2012 by Tony Moore.

Library of Congress Control Number:
Soft Cover ISBN:

All rights reserved. No part of this book may be reproduced or transmitted in any form or by any means, electronic or mechanical, including photocopying, recording, or by any information storage and retrieval system, without permission in writing from the copyright owner.

This book was printed in the United States of America.

To order additional copies of this book, order through Amazon.com

FOREWORD

I DON'T KNOW WHERE this book will take me or how interesting it will be for you to read. The reason I decided to write it was not for personal gain (even if all of my friends bought it—both of them!), but as a calling I felt I had to answer. I am, in fact, just an ordinary guy with an extraordinary ability to make the most of the situations that I find myself in.

I have often thought about how really and truly lucky I have been all throughout my life, even in the toughest of times, and I wanted to write a short story in the faint hope that you will read this story and be inspired to make the most of your life too.

One thing I truly believe is that all of us are given divine gifts when we are born to enable us to manage our lives, deal with the problems, risk failure, and/or achieve our successes, if we choose to do so. We are also given divine help in the form of the very small voice that stays with us all our lives and is sometimes so very hard to hear against the "noise" of life and living and the crowded noise of our own jumbled-up thoughts.

Although I eventually learned to listen to this voice, which is not inside your head but is right in the middle of your being; I didn't learn to "hear" the voice until I had made many, many mistakes along the way.

I also know that I have been blessed with some brilliant friends who have been there for me in times of great difficulty. Even after a lifetime of not seeing them since school or earlier jobs that we had shared when we were just starting out in our twenties, we are all still in touch, and we still remain very close.

I have been gifted on three occasions with dreams that foretold me what was going to happen and how I should deal with the "soon-to-be" imminent situation, which I will explain later in this book. When I was dreaming each of the three dreams, I was aware that I was being told something important. With each dream, I knew I had to remember everything and had to say what I had seen out loud.

I have also had a spiritual experience while in my local church, in Greenwood, of all places. To this day, I cannot explain it, except to say that what happened did happen; it was very real, and it proved to me beyond the shadow of a doubt that God exists, that he is real, and that he is there for us if we know how to ask for help.

So, why the title I chose? It's as if my life has been made up of a never-ending series of short stories that have run on; sometimes overlapping and sometimes as a series of single events. Not that knowing what I know makes me brilliant (though I probably am brilliant); but what I do know, as a thinking and genuine Guinness-drinking bloke, is a lot about a little and making extraordinary things happen is what I have done. Now, that I have fully explained my title, on with the book.

None of us get to choose the conditions under which we are born, we therefore have to make the most of the hand we are dealt with, regardless.

I WAS BORN in Northampton, England, and my mother, Rosina, was a Catholic, having come over to England from, I think, Milan, Italy. My mom was pretty, with dark wavy hair and dressed, on the times I saw her, in light pastel colors. I'm sure I would have loved her very much if I had known her, but unfortunately, I only saw her three times in my life. At that time, in the fifties in England, there was an epidemic of tuberculosis; and unfortunately, my mother had the illness when I was born. Of course, it didn't mean much to me at the time, except that I couldn't live with her for fear of catching the highly contagious disease.

I can't imagine how she must have felt having had to give me into the care of the Middlesex County Council for my own health and well-being. Probably a part of her was happy that I would be looked after, but a part was sad as well at having to see me go away. For my friends in America, Middlesex isn't a lifestyle choice, but an area of Greater London, and the County Council was the governing body of Greater London responsible for all things that moved (or tried to) in the Greater London area.

I was born with TB from what is called a "TB contact," which left a huge scar on my lung. So I was moved out of Acton in West London, where I lived with my mother for a very short time, and they found me a place to live in by the sea Lowestoft in Suffolk with Mrs. Bleby.

The only times I ever saw my mother after I was moved to Lowestoft in Suffolk to live with Auntie, as Mrs. Bleby became, was when I was three years old and traveled by train from Auntie's house in Lowestoft with Tessa, my surrogate older sister, Auntie's daughter.

We left Lowestoft on the early-morning express where we had breakfast along the way. I was so excited at having breakfast on the train, in the Pullman car, while watching the world go by and gazing out of the window, looking up at the patterns that the steam made as it billowed above our carriage. The express was pulled along by a powerful steam engine that made the trip to Liverpool Street station in three hours.

We traveled by tube from Central London to Acton, where my mother lived; and I vaguely remember actually meeting my mom in a bungalow there.

Although it didn't seem strange that after a spending only a day with her we should leave and get back to Lowestoft, I was sad to leave her. I thought that I may never see her again, even though I was so young. She gave me a whole box of soft mints to eat along the way, which, being only three at the time, I promptly dropped as I boarded the bus and had to scramble to try to get them all back in the box.

Lowestoft was now my home, and although I wanted very much to know my mom, that was not to be. When I saw her that time, she was dressed in a pastel pink dressing gown and seemed to be very tired. She was slim, with very dark wavy hair, quite petite, and very graceful. She called my name softly, and I went to her and held her small hand in mine. She spoke to me, asking me how I was telling me how tall I had become and how proud she was of me. I didn't understand all that she said, but I loved the sound of her voice; it was pleasant to listen to; though often she was asking Tessa about my new life at Auntie's. She became quite breathless at talking as the TB had gotten a real hold of her.

We left later that same day; and apparently, as I found out much later, I wasn't as sad as I could have been as I was very happy living with Auntie and my very large family, and I had all the space anybody could ever possibly need. I remembered though looking back at her as she stood in the doorway, waving to me as we left her. We caught a black cab to the station, and I looked out the back window to keep seeing her as long as I could and waving back to her the whole time. She finally disappeared as we turned the corner, and I hoped I could visit her again.

I asked Tessa if we could; and she said, "Yes, of course, dear. We'll meet her as soon as your mother is strong enough."

The last time I ever saw her was when she traveled from a sanitarium, where she had been moved to from her house in London, to see me at Lowestoft. Her journey, like mine, took some three hours by train; and Auntie had her picked up from the station.

My beautiful, but now very ill, mother traveled all that way; and when she arrived at Lowestoft, she had to stay outside of Auntie's house and could only watch me through the window in our large nursery, at the back of the house overlooking the large garden. She traveled with her new husband of ten days, though I only vaguely remember him, and she watched me from outside the large bay window while I played with all the other children. I remember looking out through the window and waving at her after Tessa told me she was my mother and that she had come to see me.

I can only imagine how happy yet sad she must have felt, not being able to meet her only son, me, in person; but at the time, I thought it was perfectly normal. Normal is, after all, only relative to what you're used to, isn't it? And since I had never really seen my mother or knew anything more than what I had been told by Tessa and Auntie, I had nothing to compare what a real mother should or could be like. What I do know is that if Auntie hadn't cared enough to go out of her way to make this meeting happen, I would never have had known anything of what my very own mother was like.

She stayed outside for a little while watching me through the window and smiled at me the whole time; she was supported by her new husband, standing next to her in the cold March air. I went over to the window and placed my hand on the glass, and she did the same so that we could both touch hands through the glass—my tiny hand and her very small hand. She was smiling the whole time, and I sat on the ledge of the bay window and looked at her the whole time she was standing with her small hand on the window. She left shortly after that, and sadly, I was never to see my mother again as she died of TB shortly after. She had managed to see me one last time before she died.

My mother was not rich-in fact, she was rather poor—and I gathered that since she was not married when I was born, that the Catholic Church did not help her much. At that time, to be an unwed mother was a difficult and shameful issue, especially to the Catholic Church, and was, to a large extent, swept under the carpet. It seems rather pointless to bestow problems onto the children who are innocent.

Now, however, being a single mom is not a big deal; and it is much more prevalent than it was then. But to all of the children having to grow up with one or no parents, it is a difficult thing to deal with and continues to affect them their whole life.

In my case, though, I was gifted with the ability to cope and to do well and to climb up after each fall and to succeed whatever the difficulty.

This was one of the many gifts I seem to have been given, along with a good sense of humor to help me along the way.

Anyway, the reason, I believed, that the church made it difficult for her was that Auntie told me years later that my mother's last wish was that I should not remain a Catholic. Though my mother was Italian and definitely a Catholic, she didn't want me to remain one. I can only surmise that through her ordeal of having a baby and having TB with no family around to help, at least as far as I knew, life must have been very difficult for her. She did have a sister called Peggy, but none of her family ever bothered to seek me or my mother out or to try to get in touch, so neither did I. Maybe it was the time, and her being an unwed single mother was an embarrassment to them. I can think of no other reason for their lack of interest other than perhaps they had disowned them. Either way, the result was the same.

The only reason I knew of her sister was from an old photograph of my mother with her sister Peggy, which was given by my mother's husband to my daughter Georgia when she went to visit him living in the same house that I had lived in for a short while after leaving Lowestoft. In the photograph, the two of them were together riding bikes with another man who may have been my father, but I don't know or really care about him. That was fine by me, and again, it seemed to be perfectly all right as I saw things at that time.   Years later, I often thought about these things in my past; but life goes on, and you either move with it or get stuck at that point in time, and I was not a person to dwell on stuff like this.

When things around you happen that you can't control all that you can do is learn to accept what is and not spend time worrying about it while doing your best to manage the situation.

AUNTIE

Sometimes someone will come into your life to make an eternal and positive difference!

AUNTIE WAS EVERYTHING one could imagine that a proper English lady or a great aunt could and should be. She was the stuff that an empire was built from.

Auntie was larger than life, and as nature would have it, she was also a rather large lady who often wore huge flamboyant hats whenever she went out. Auntie had perfect English diction, sounding like Joyce Grenville, the famous storyteller and actress at that time. Her speech was absolutely perfect "Queens English." She would always call me "Tony deah" or "my dahling Tony" and would call me that right up until her ninety-second birthday. But there's a lot more to talk about before that time comes!

Auntie was my true guardian angel, placed into my life by none other than God or maybe by one of God's angels. It's the only explanation I can think of. You see, Auntie was not a true blood relation but was the choice of the London County Council in their infinite wisdom. So you see, even local government can get it right sometimes! But not all the time as you will see later on.

No one messed with Auntie; what she said was the way it would be. She would stride through life absolutely and completely sure of what she was doing and where she was going. She was, to me, absolutely the perfect surrogate mom any boy could ever wish for. Shakespeare once said, "Give me a child to his seventh birthday, and he's mine for life." So Auntie had me up to age eight, and she was to be the biggest influence in my life.

Auntie was extremely protective and always made sure you found plenty of things to do, or she would find it for you. "Go and play in the bottom garden" or "Help Mr. Moore with the gardening" or "Why don't you find something to do with your beautiful day?" And we did, in case she found it for us.

When I say "us," I mean Beatrice, Mary Brookes, John, Hoey, and me; and we were inseparable right up till I left Auntie at eight years old; But more about Beatrice later.

You could hear Auntie's voice all over the house; although she never ever, to my recollection, shouted. She just had one of those voices that carried, and it pierced through the highest wind or the noisiest of surroundings and definitely carried from the kitchen all the way up to the top of the house.

I loved Auntie as I never would or ever could love any other person in my whole life; and I could never have made it to where I am now without her strong, never-wavering help and sound advice.

Apart from being who she was to me, I can honestly say she was a very clever and wise person. She believed in fairies and believed that every time a baby is born, a fairy smiles. And when good people die, they "go to the fairies," which was her way of saying they went to heaven. She was very tolerant of children but completely intolerant of adults, especially those who behaved badly. Though as I said she was very proper, she was also very liberal in her ideals. She helped me always and gave me her wisdom until I was well into my forties. To me, she was like the queen is to England—always there in the background and always doing the right thing.

Auntie's first husband was Nunky, who was quite old and was the retired headmaster of a very large school in Scarborough. She called him "my darling Nunky," and they had two children. Her son was John Bleby, who was, to me, an ethereal figure that would appear once in a while when coming home from Cambridge University or from the army.

When John came home, all the nurses would go wild at his stories of travel and university life. John studied veterinary medicine and in fact became a vet. He even went on to become a veterinary surgeon the Her Majesty, the Queen. I believe he looked after some of her many horses and used to go to the Royal "Tattoo" to look after the horses.

Auntie's daughter was Tessa Bleby. Though I seldom saw John, at least not until many years later, I spent a lot of time with Tessa. To me, Tessa was like an older sister and was at that time still at school. She went to St. Mary's Convent on Kirkley Cliffs, which is still there, right on the seafront, perched on a high cliff overlooking the sea. That was my first school when I was five years old and was a convent. Imagine that! Me taught by nuns! I remember very little of that school except that it was very strict and was located right at the top of the cliffs, a rather large gray austere building overlooking the sea.

Auntie's house, at 35 Kirkley Park Road in Lowestoft, Suffolk, was huge; and she had decided, years earlier, to use it as a children's nursery or a children's home for young children, from one year to eight years old, who for one reason or another couldn't live with their parents.

To her, this was perfect. She had as many as twenty to thirty children at that time. Some were really my favorites, and I remember even at that time being in love with Mary Brookes (at four years old). I have a photo of Mary and me standing in the middle of the main staircase in our pajamas. Mary was holding a doll, and I was looking on—Mary with her beautiful blonde hair and me with my very dark and very curly hair.

I don't know to this day why Mary was there, but I knew absolutely that I did in fact love her as only a four-year-old could! Mary had the most beautiful blonde hair and lived with us, with me, for seven years. I never knew when she left, but I missed her a lot. I did know that Mary had left never to come back into my life again, and I tried to find her through Facebook and Friends Reunited but was never able to find her.

Some were children of diplomats who were eventually picked up to live again at their real homes, while others like me had no home to go to except this home. The funny thing is that this was to be the theme of most of my childhood. I was there for convalescence and to be able to breathe the clear, non-smoggy non-London air while living by the sea.

All you need to succeed in life is one person who can take the time show you what you are capable of and if that person believes in you, you can succeed!

KIRKEY PARK ROAD

How lucky we all were to have a home like this to live in

KIRKLEY PARK ROAD was a quiet street to the south of Lowestoft, just off the Pakefield Road, and was only one street back from the sea. The road curved and had very large houses all along, each one set back from the road, with its own driveway, and each built to its own unique design, probably in late Victorian times. Ours was constructed of red brick and was three stories tall.

Each was large enough to have its own servants' quarters or large enough for the very biggest of families. Number 35 was Auntie's house, set back from the road behind a wide, sweeping graveled driveway. It was a very large house with a huge oak front door set back in a stone porch.

There were two large bay windows at the front that continued up to the second floor on either side of the front door.

The house had three very tall floors, and the children's bedrooms were located upstairs off a wide spacious landing. There was a babies' nursery in the front downstairs inside a glass conservatory with colored panes of glass that amplified the daylight, making it very bright inside.

To the right of the drive was a garage complete with a sunken pit with concrete stairs for repairing the cars. Above the garage was the "apple loft," where, originally, apples from our orchard were picked and were placed there to ripen. Now, however, it was converted into a very comfortable apartment, or flat, that I stayed in many years later, as a young teenager when I went to visit Auntie. The smell of the apples had over the years permeated into the very woodwork of that loft and hung in the air like being in an orchard.

At the side of the house, just past the large stand-alone garage, was a long graveled path leading through the top garden and on into the lower or back garden.

On the first floor, there were two large bedrooms at the front of the house that could sleep around eight to ten children each. One was "the pink room," and the other was "the blue room." The pink room was where I spent my very youngest days. The blue room was where I slept as I got older, from three years old. Across the large landing was the "Snuggery," Auntie and Nunky's lounge. It always smelled of brandy, wood fires, and pipe smoke. I loved the smells in that room and sometimes crept in there during the day to breathe in the beautiful aroma of the room. It was surprising I didn't take up a pipe or cigars at the time as I loved the aromas emanating from within their private sanctuary.

Just outside the Snuggery was the largest dollhouse I have ever seen. It stood at the top of the main stairs on its own pedestal and was very beautifully made and very detailed. It was a three-story house with front doors, back doors, sash windows that opened, lights that lit, servants' quarters in the loft, and tiny handcrafted furniture in every room. Even down to the detail of cups saucers and plated pictures on the walls, the dollhouse was painstakingly accurate in every detail. The walls had wallpaper, and the stairs had a stair carpet; and in some of the rooms, there was a chandelier.

I have never ever seen such a beautiful dollhouse; and once many years later, when I was visiting Auntie in Scarborough with Sue, my wife, Auntie asked me what I wanted from her estate when she "went to the fairies." I told her there was only one thing that I would love to have, and it was the dollhouse. She looked at me and said, "Would you look after it, Tony?" I remember telling her that I would and that I would rebuild anything that was broken and that I would probably place it in a museum so thousands of children could enjoy it as much as the other children and I always had. Unfortunately, though, that wasn't to be as the family wouldn't allow that to happen and instead left it broken and in disrepair. Some things are never meant to be.

On the first floor, there were also several bathrooms, a nursing station with an airing room, and a long verandah outside that overlooked the west-facing garden. The verandah was the width of the large house; and in summer, some of us, who were a lot older (maybe four or five years old) were allowed to sleep there at night. I mention west-facing because not only did it have a magnificent view of the bowling green, the three enormous green houses, and the bottom garden; but we could also see the sunsets from there. And even at that age, I loved just standing, with Mary and Beatrice, quietly watching the sun set across our beautiful garden. I would stand there for hours, often by myself, just looking at this fantastic sight.

Apart from the very large sweeping main staircase, there was another set of servants' stairs leading to the upper third floor, where Auntie's bedroom, the nurse's bedroom, bathrooms, and Tessa's bedroom were located. Between these rooms, at the top of the upper stairway, was the tank room where there was a hoard of the most interesting stuff you could ever imagine. There was a very large model yacht that was as big as I was, train sets, and all kinds of things that had belonged to Nunky or John and Tessa and could never be thrown away.

Tessa's bedroom was where I spent many nights when I was older, and I actually slept in Tessa's bed. I loved Tessa; she was the kindest gentlest girl I have ever met. I can never ever remember her raising her voice, only that she was so kind to me. She and Auntie would take me out with them into town to go shopping, or down to the beach for the whole day, or out into the garden. Tessa was the best older sister a boy could ever wish for, and we spent so much time together.

Above Tessa's bed was a pastel painting of a baby sleeping. She used to tell me that it was me as a baby, and although I didn't know if this was true, it really didn't matter.

The room, being at the very top of the house, had a sloping ceiling that formed part of the roof and had huge wooden beams along the ceiling. It was decorated in pastel yellow and white and was always very neat. The bed was in one corner to the left next to the front window that looked out onto a stone-turreted balcony outside both Tessa's room and the nurse's windows along the roof. I imagined that I was living in a castle and often looked out over the stone-turreted balcony.

I spent a lot of time in the kitchen "helping" the cooks as they prepared our meals on two large ranges. One range was an "Aga"; the other was an eight-burner gray gas range for preparing the food for all us children. Just off the kitchen was the walk-in pantry loaded with everything you could imagine. Next to the kitchen was the breakfast room or the dining room.

We had the complete set of blue "Willow Pattern" tableware all housed in a very tall glass-fronted cupboard, and there must have been hundreds of pieces placed there.

The "breakfast" table was a very large solid oak table that sat sixteen with ease when Auntie was entertaining guests. Dinners were at 7:00 p.m. and were fairly formal in that we had to dress properly, wash hands, and be on our best behavior. I would always eat with Auntie, Tessa, John when he was home, and the nursing staff. It was these times that I picked up much of the local gossip and what was going on in our house with all the children and staff. That was my home for the first eight years of my life—laundry maids, kitchen staff, gardeners, nurses, and a full house of children. One could never say it was quiet; in fact, it was the opposite—absolutely teaming with our daily life. Often the nurses would invite their boyfriends over for drinks or a party at night, and on some of these days, I would hide under the table in case I got caught.

Tessa was fine with me being there, but Auntie would send me upstairs with a stern comment.

My learning began very early in what is acceptable for one person may not be for another.

AUNTIE THE BOSS

Early childhood shapes who we will be.

AUNTIE WAS A larger-than-life English lady who managed a staff of kitchen maids, laundry maids, two gardeners, and a full staff of nurses. Though a large lady, she was good-natured, at least toward me, but sometimes she could be quite severe. She was the most intelligent woman I have ever known and had a way of seeing things that was unique. She also had a way of describing things that would happen if you did something wrong without thinking it through, and she was always right.

Everyone respected Auntie, and no one ever crossed her—at least if they did, they wouldn't get away with it for long. Although she was quite strict, she had a very kind side for her "babies," as she called us. She would never ever tolerate fools or idle chatter about nothing. The nurses were all very respectful of her, and she ran a very tight ship.

In summer, Auntie would invite her and Nunky's numerous friends to play bowls on the bowling green in the back garden. They all got dressed in white, wearing all the correct clothes to play all afternoon in the sunshine and have drinks and afternoon tea. I would sometimes watch them from upstairs on the verandah, wondering how the bowling balls seemed to know when to turn in toward the little white "Jack."

They all laughed or shouted out when someone won or knocked a close ball away from the small white "Jack."

Aunty was a working mom and would direct all of the daily routines in the busy house. She would direct the kitchen staff on what to cook, often helping them prepare the food. She would discuss with old Mr. Moore what he was to take care of that day; she would direct the nurses on which children had special needs that day and in fact managed the whole house like a general in charge of her own army.

The only times I ever saw her get serious was when the family doctor, Dr. Mc Nab, came 'round to see one of the children if they were ill. Dr. McNab was an elderly gray-haired Scottish doctor who always looked the part, a little like Dr. Finlay's father in the TV series, and always dressed in a three-piece suit with a pocket watch that he used to check our heart rate with.

Auntie had a soft spot for Dr. McNab. She loved him coming round and would talk to him for hours about a situation concerning one of her children. But she was very matter of fact about the problems the children had and always let him do his work, but often she would tell him what she thought might be the trouble. When Auntie spoke, no one interrupted, not even dear Dr. McNab!

I went back to see Auntie as an older child around nine years old and later as a teenager, long after I had left the nursery as I had so many happy memories of living at Lowestoft with her and the "family" there.

Auntie never ever changed; she was always exactly the same and was as sharp as a pin even in her nineties. I listened to whatever she had to say; and often she would sit and talk as if I were an adult, asking me what I had been up to and how my job was going and what London life was about for me.

She often played bowls in summer on our bowling green that was so perfect that when I watched them play, again from the verandah, though now being older, I still didn't get the game. I could see the balls rolling long and very straight. I used to watch in wonder at how they knew the rules and would shout at each other in glee as the game went on.
Sometimes the balls would roll straight and then twist inward toward the "Jack," while other times the balls would roll straight without bending in.

I asked her how the balls knew when to turn like they did. She told me that it was something called "bias," which of course made it clear as mud to me.

Behind the bowling green were three very large greenhouses for growing just about anything you could imagine, from oranges, tomatoes, to grapes on old vines that stretched right across the glass roof of the greenhouse. There were also all kinds of fruits and vegetables that were also grown there. I loved the warm smell inside the greenhouses and would watch Auntie or the gardeners doing all the work to grow anything we needed. The air inside was always warm, humid and strong, and rich with the smells of the vegetation and the many things that we grew in there. Behind the greenhouses were a potting shed and the boiler house, where a lot of "other" things went on, nothing at all to do with potting; but you'll have to ask the nurses all about that.

Other than the greenhouses, we also had a market garden that we called "the bottom garden," where we grew our own vegetables; and we had an orchard with apples, pears, fig trees, peach trees, plum, and cherry trees. We even had a pond where we kept geese and had an area where we kept chickens. I climbed up the trees to get the fruit, often throwing down the ripest to William or Beatrice, when on holiday as a teen.

Several times a year, Auntie would ask old Mr. Moore (no relation) to get us a good-sized goose for dinner at Easter or Christmas, and I would wander down the garden to sit quietly and watch him pluck all the feathers off. I would be happy to just sit there chatting with old Mr. Moore, marveling at how huge the pile of feathers came from just from one goose.

"Where do all those feathers go?" I asked him one time. Old Mr. Moore said, "Buggered if oi knows, but oi do knows they've all gotter come off in toim fer dinner. Otherwise, you'll all be going 'ungry, and Auntie'll have moi guts fer gar'ers." He relied in his strong Suffolk accent He let me try to pluck one of the feathers out, but it was determined to remain where it was. I didn't think of the goose as dead; it just was there being plucked, ready for lunch.

Mr. Moore was our general handyman, with a very strong East Anglian accent; and he cycled to our house every day from Pakefield, about five miles along the coast road, regardless of the weather. I never knew his first name, but as far as I was concerned, he was "old Mr. Moore." He was a wiry man—not tall but very strong, with his shirt sleeves always rolled up, revealing naval tattoos on his arms—and was good at everything from fixing things, polishing the shiny hard wood floors, cleaning the windows, and gardening. When he polished the shiny parquet floors, in our main hall, the smell of fresh polish was so fragrant it would drift through the whole house. He did that always on a Tuesday morning, so when I smelled the fragrance of fresh polish anywhere throughout the house, I knew it was Tuesday.

Mr. Moore always called me "Little Tojo" for some unknown reason, based on his extensive knowledge of the great Japanese emperor of the same name.

These times living with Auntie were the very best I ever had, and it didn't bother me at all if this was my home or, as it turned out, a borrowed home where I was fortunate to live for a time. Summer lasted forever, winters were always fun with snow everywhere, and we played in the sea in all weather. I loved to be at the sea especially in the really rough weather clinging on to Auntie's, Tessa's, or Nurse Rosemary's hand while the huge waves crashed over my head. We spent all of our free time at the beach; and it didn't matter if it was summer autumn or winter, when Auntie said, "Beach time today, Tony deah," that was what we were doing.

As if this wasn't enough, we also had a beach hut right on the beach where we could make tea, get changed, and take shelter when the weather got really rough or when the weather turned suddenly as it often did and started to rain. I loved the sea, especially when spending days there with

Auntie, Tessa, and the nurses, and always with my surrogate sister, Beatrice, and with her younger brother William.

As I said, there were many children there, and we were like a huge family. Beatrice and William were lucky enough to live with Auntie except for a few years away when it had been decided to return them to Boreham Woods, where their mother lived. They moved back to Lowestoft, as their mother was in a mental hospital and was, sadly, deemed incapable of looking after them. All through their childhood, they lived in Lowestoft as a normal family. I unfortunately could not as the Middlesex County Council in their infinite wisdom decided to move me back to London, at eight years old, but that's another story.

The day that Auntie and Tessa came to give me some "very sad news," I was four years old and was lying on the floor, painting with my paint pallet on the upstairs landing next to the dollhouse, which was my favorite place. She came up to me and said to me, "Tony deah (that's how she called me till the day she died at ninety-two), I have some very sad news about your darling mother. She died this morning, bless her, and she's gone up to the fairies." She held me close, and she told me, "You shouldn't be sad." She also said, "She's in a much better place now."

I didn't know what to think as I had seen her so few times. I was very sad, but for some reason, it didn't really sink in to me.
She told me years later that when I was told that awful news, I answered, "Well, that's how it should be then, isn't it, Auntie? She was so very ill, and I'm sure she will be all right, don't you? After all, she is in a better place now." And I carried on painting. Sadly, it meant little to me since I had only met her three times and life for me was so full; and my mother by that time was only a distant memory.

When I was four years old, I became ill with meningitis. I was very, very ill. Auntie and Dr. McNab didn't think I would make it back to the nursery after I was taken away in an ambulance to spend many weeks in hospital. Funny though, Tessa bought me a pair of blue slippers and left them at the bottom on my hospital bed, just in case.

I recovered and was returned back to Auntie's where I spent many weeks lying in bed. I lay in bed and looked out of the large bay window at the sky and the red chimney pots of the house over the road, which was all I could see for weeks and weeks. The illness was serious, and I had to recover completely; so, for so many weeks, I could not get out of bed.

I never slept more than two to three hours a night and was probably the very first child to be diagnosed as a hyperactive." In fact, I have never had more than two to four hours sleep a night in my whole life.

How lucky I was, though, to have had such a huge bedroom to be in when at night I couldn't possibly sleep as I wasn't at all tired. So Auntie's fix for me (Ritalin wasn't invented yet) was to leave me to go to sleep in a large wooden playpen with pillows inside (just in case I did nod off)where I would spend night after night rocking it and bumping it along the floor from one side of the room to the other. The bedroom was about thirty feet by thirty-five feet. Once I got to the other side of the room, I would turn all my stuff around to face the other direction and bump the cot all the way back, continuing on until morning.

On her ninety-first birthday party in Scarborough, Auntie told me that they would always hear a bang followed by a scrape, which was me sliding around the bedroom in my wooden cot. And they would take turns to check up on me, if the noise stopped, whoever was on night duty, all through the night, night after night, to make sure I was OK.

It was during that time that I had my first nightmare, which I have remembered even to this day; and to me it was very, very real. I was sitting in my cot when a huge tiger entered the bedroom and padded silently and slowly past me. As he passed by, he looked straight at me, gazing with huge unblinking amber-colored eyes. I watched him in numbed silence as he slowly passed by, but I wasn't scared; I knew he wouldn't harm me, and when he stared at me, it was as if he knew something about me and didn't want to share it. I only saw him once but remembered my feelings and the sight of him slowly moving past me in the bedroom as if he was guarding all of the children.

As I got older, around five or six, during a very hot summer night while we were sleeping on the verandah, John Hoey, who was a little older than I was, was telling us that he learned what a mile was. "What's a mile then?" we asked him. He looked over at the back garden to a neighbor's garden and said, "It's as far as that." We all looked and thought what a long way a mile was. Now that we know that in fact that was only a couple of hundred yards or so, it's relevant, isn't it? At our size, that was very significant distance, and for days afterward, I would make sure everyone else knew what a mile really was. It was anything from "over there past the back door" to "as far as you can see anything."

During long summer days, Mary Brookes, Beatrice, and I would go down to the bottom garden, beyond the orchard, to where there was an old open gypsy wagon painted in faded pink and light blue, which used to be pulled along by horses. We would play there all day long, never troubled or worried and with no one to bother us.

These times were soon to be gone forever, as the Middlesex County Council decided that, despite Auntie's stream of letters and telephone calls,

I should be moved back to London to live with my, now widowed, stepfather back in Acton. They decided that she had too many children there, and that she couldn't keep me as well as Beatrice and William. She decided to keep them both as she thought that they would fare better, after their mother had been moved into a mental hospital, with her than in a children's home or in a foster home somewhere in London.

Though I didn't know it then, she was right, of course. Beatrice's mother was in a psychiatric hospital and had been for years. William was a little slow at understanding things, maybe a little autistic, and was very quick to temper. Beatrice and William were at that time quite close as I recall, as they, like me, were used to life at the nursery. William took a lot of handling mainly because of his quick temper but also because he was a little autistic.

But with all the help and care Auntie gave him, he would at least have a fair chance to manage his life.

Aunty made the difference to many children and I was lucky to be one.

DARK TIMES

It's sometimes not the problems but how we deal with them.

I WAS EIGHT AND a half, when I was moved back to live with my stepfather. My stepfather had married my mother only ten days before she died, just around the time she had come to see me that last time at Lowestoft. She met him in the sanitarium, but he survived and she didn't.

I have a photo of my mother on her wedding day; and I could see years later, when Auntie gave me that picture, that her coat was too large for her as at that time she had lost weight due to her illness, but she looked so pretty and had a beautiful smile, which I always thought was just for me.

I don't to this day know why I was moved back to Acton from Auntie's in Lowestoft, but it was to become a very dark time in my life.

I was like a toy robot; all you had to do was point me in a direction, and off I went wherever I was told to go.

When I moved into my stepfather's apartment, from Lowestoft, I couldn't believe how small it was. It was an upstairs flat at number 39A Cumberland Road and had a bedroom, living room, a kitchen, and a bathroom. We had to go up the stairs through a tall door to get to the flat.

It was what is now called a row house, one of a long row of houses built in Victorian England. He lived with his mother (whatever her name was), who was, I swear, truly a real witch. She was a miserable old lady and always got me into trouble, telling tales about what I had supposedly done that day. I definitely became unmanageable (or at least tried to be). I swore (where the hell did I learn that? I wonder. Oops, there's that "H" word) actually wore out my shoes and stayed out on the streets all the time after school rather than spend time in that horrible flat.

I went to a day school a few streets away. Sometimes I would be taken, and sometimes I would get there myself. The flat was tiny and smelled of kerosene, which was used to heat the freezing place in winter. I absolutely hated it there and prayed every night that Auntie would come to get me.

My school was miserable as well and very rough. I recall even now how horrible it was and how I regularly got attacked by the other boys because I spoke nicely (thanks a bunch, Auntie). This was where I started to learn to look after myself.

One day, when I left school to go home, his mother was meeting me from school. I was attacked and knocked to the ground as several of the boys jumped me by the boys' toilets where I was kicked and punched repeatedly.

I had never ever experienced this and was certain it would never happen to me again. I had bruises, a bleeding nose, two black eyes, and torn clothes. I was eight years old. Anyway, she was waiting for me along with all of the other mothers who were horrified at seeing me come around the corner from the inner playground. They said, "He's got it written all over his poor little face." And all I could think of was how do I get rid of the writing that was apparently on my face, though I couldn't see it when I got home later. I was concentrating on hiding my face from everyone as I walked home in case they would see the writing that I was convinced was all over my face.

The next day, I was called in front of the whole class to point out the boys that did it, but I didn't want to cause myself more embarrassment.

All I wanted was to move on and not to remember what had happened. I never told on who they were and was placed under the care of an older girl who offered to look after me at playtime. I didn't need any help and had all but forgotten what had happened but was never bothered by them again. These were the darkest times in my childhood. My stepfather often used to smack me when he got home from work.

I was apparently not a very good boy, and sometimes I was caned across my hand while being made to stand on a chair facing the kitchen window with my arm stretched out in front of me. I know it hurt, but I refused to let either my stepfather or "the witch" see that it hurt. I would simply go to the happy place, in my mind, and imagine being back at Auntie's, while staring straight ahead, looking at the rooftops and chimneys. I hated it when I heard him coming up the stairs from work in case I had done something wrong that I couldn't remember.

All that had to happen for me to get caned when he came home was for his mother to tell him that I had been swearing or had run off, or stayed out playing on the streets, or had been seen by her spitting on the road. (Where did I learn that little gem?) Yep, I learned a whole lot of neat things in my early Acton life that I never learned at Auntie's!

I subsequently played out on the street from school time until dinnertime as I was certain that I didn't want to stay in horrible tiny flat alone with her. Even if I wasn't allowed to go out, I did not want to spend any time at home, and so I stayed out as long as I could find things to occupy my time either on the streets or in the small park at the bottom of my road.

It was hard to imagine moving from Auntie's in Lowestoft, with all that I had there and all the friends and people whom I loved, into a small flat with two of the most miserable, unhappy people I had ever met. I never recall them ever laughing or ever being happy with me there, and I never knew why. I do know that whenever the council case-worker came around, they were really nice to me, telling me not to talk unless spoken to or asked to speak. I soon got the hang of mentioning how often I was smacked just before my case worker came 'round in order to get sweets—"a little bribe" for keeping quiet.

Funny how things turn out, years later when I was thirty-three, I had a wine bar in Ealing, not far from Acton; and a woman who used to be a regular in my bar told me she worked at Elizabeth Arden in Acton and told me of a very tall horrible security guard with red hair who would be nasty to the staff, shutting the gate if they were late or locking the gate if they didn't leave on time. Unbelievable! It was the same man. As I recalled, my stepfather worked as a security guard at Elizabeth Arden! I couldn't believe my ears as she told me of things he had done.

They called him "Hitler." Yep, that was him all right! So I didn't exaggerate it; he was an unhappy miserable man everywhere he went.

He was very tall like a lurch and had thinning curly reddish hair and large gangly hands and large gangly feet. What on earth did my lovely mother see in him? I prayed hard every night, while lying awake in bed, that Auntie would come to get me and take me back with her to my real home in Lowestoft.

Maybe she thought he would help me after she had gone. I was free when I was out of the flat, and I could do whatever I wanted to do. In fact, I used to cross the main road and go into the park to play with Rex. Rex was a huge white Pyrenean Mountain dog who was actually bigger than me. I would wait for him for hours until he would arrive with his master.

To me, everything was "par for the course." And despite not liking where I was living or the rough Acton school that I had to go to, I had Rex to play with; so everything for a short while each day was fine. Well, as luck would have it, my prayers were eventually answered.

One sunny afternoon when I was playing with Rex in the park, I heard this very familiar voice calling from the park entrance. "Tony deah, is that you?" It was my very own Auntie. She had come in answer to my prayers.

"What on earth are you doing here by yourself, Tony deah?" I was so happy I couldn't speak but ran across the park and held her as tightly as I could with both hands in case she disappeared and I was dreaming again. I chatted and held on to her tightly, not daring to let her go.

I had to stand on my own two feet at a very young age and this stayed with me forever!

AN ANGEL COMES TO VISIT

Help is sometimes not what we expect it to be

ONLY AUNTIE COULD arrive in a completely strange place, in a huge city like London and in a town like Acton, and ask anybody who she passed on the street, "Do you know my little Tony?" And believe it or not, she told me later that everyone knew me from her description, and she was not surprised at all. I had in fact introduced myself to anyone that passed me along the street. What a moron I must have been.

She was told that at this time of the day "Tony is always over at the park playing with a very large white dog." I was now nine years old at the time. I heard her calling out to me from right across the park from where she was standing at the entrance, next to the wrought iron gate. I ran over to where she was standing, running as fast as I could go, and grabbed her hand. She gave me one of her huge hugs, squeezing the breath out of me as she lifted me off my feet. I kissed her again and again, as we were standing in that park, and begged her to take me back with her to Lowestoft. I held her face in my hands, as she bent down to hug me, and thought, *You really are my angel from heaven.* "Have you come to take me home, Auntie?" I asked her again and again on the walk back to my dreary little flat.

That was the only time I ever saw tears in her eyes, although I didn't understand why. She said she would see what she could do and asked me to take her to where I lived. "What are those people thinking," she said, "leaving you to play by yourself on these wicked streets?" I told her, "I'm OK, Auntie. I have plenty to do, and there's always Rex," as I pointed over the park to where my beautiful Rex was sitting watching us. "He's my friend, and I play with him. Huge, isn't he? I wish I could have a dog just like Rex?"

We walked back to the flat with me clinging to her hand, afraid she would disappear again. Once at the tiny flat, Auntie told the witch who she was and that she would wait until my stepfather came home to speak to him. She told Auntie how bad I was and how much I swore and that I wore my shoes out and that I cost a fortune to keep. They told her all about my bad behavior. She actually probably thought Auntie would agree with her or give them money for keeping me! Auntie would have none of it and told her to stop talking nonsense! She told her that she had brought me up for eight years, and that I had never behaved like that at all.

Well, as soon as "he" got back, Auntie tore into them both, "How dare you treat Tony like this? Of course, he wears his shoes out. He's a little boy, and that's what little boys do, deah, and I should know as I have dozens of them." As she was giving them what for! I was clutching her hand for dear life, hiding behind her dress, peering around her to look at them both and begging her, "Please take me with you please, please"

They were having none of that. They got hold of my other hand and yanked it hard away from her, trying to pull me back, and started pulling my arm in the other direction. I was stuck in the middle, trying to get them to let me go, kicking and struggling to make them let me go. I bet it looked funny, a tiny scruff between two battling grown-ups-them on one side and Auntie on the other side. She was worth both of them and more besides! I remained like that stretched out between them, while they both fought their battle to keep me.

I was trying to get them to let go, and I was yelling at them, "LET ME GO, LET ME GO," screaming for all I was worth, "I hate living here. I don't want to be here. I want to go home with Auntie right now." Auntie was telling them, "He's clearly very unhappy here, and it would have been better for them to let me leave with her. "I have all the space, and 'these things' you're telling me are not the Tony I know at all." They would have none of it; and I couldn't understand why, since they seemed to dislike me as much as I disliked them, they didn't jump at the chance to let me go.

Anyway this tug of war lasted for what seemed ages, but in the end, Auntie had to back down and had to let me go. As she left, she promised to do everything in her power to get me back. She left that evening, and I was desolate as I watched her leave and walk away down the street, knowing I had to stay with these people. I cried later that night, which is something I seldom if ever did and prayed and prayed to God that I would be able to go away from here and be happy again.

I learned that when I was in a bad place, any change would be an improvement.

PRAYERS ANSWERED

Be careful what you ask for!

WELL AS LUCK WOULD have it, a move was soon to be a reality, and my prayers were answered. After some six long months, after Auntie's visit, when I was nine and a half years old, my stepfather gathered all my things (my worn-out clothes) and we walked down the road to the bus stop. He was in silence the whole way on the bus ride from Acton to Hanwell and said nothing at all to me while we were traveling. My step father didn't even tell me where he was taking me.

Well, what a surprise! I was moved to a children's home at number 82 Oaklands Road in Hanwell, some forty-five minutes and a million miles away from Acton. I couldn't care less where I was as long as I never ever saw them again.

When he left, he did so without saying anything to me at all, not a single word, not even goodbye, which was fine by me, another door to close in my life.

Apparently, Auntie's prayers on my behalf were answered but probably not in the way she planned (I'm sure God has a sense of humor). Closing the door in my mind was one of the tools I had been given and was my way of dealing with all of the things that would happen to me as I grew up. This in fact was a tool that I often used to deal with all bad things that I had to deal with, and it stayed with me as a way of dealing with life's many tests and trials.

When you ask for help accept the help that is given.

THE ORPHANAGE

Sometimes we have to move sideways to move forward

OAKLANDS ROAD WAS an orphanage, a children's home that had some eight kids—all boys—and was in another small house; but this one had several bedrooms. The mistress of this place was called Mrs. Bumford! She was a large homely woman who looked after all her boys. I don't have many memories of that time, except that her cooking was always very bland and tasteless. We always had loads of greens, and I hated greens. Though Mrs. Bumford was OK, the place had no love and no good things at all going for it except that we were all there together as a sort of temporary foster family. I shared a bedroom with four other boys.

While I was there, I had to go to a new school—"Oaklands Road," which was a primary school and was in fact just across the road from the children's home. It was an old Victorian building, very austere, and was built of gray stone. It had very tall windows and a large concrete playground. The only difference between this one and my last one was the color—gray stone instead of red brick.

It was known by all the staff that I was from *The Orphanage*, which meant little to me at the time as I couldn't care less what they thought. I spent most of my time in my own little world and for the most part managed to shut the world out. I did, however, soon see an advantage in that the dinner ladies, as we called them, all felt very sorry for me, for some reason that for the life of me I couldn't understand, and always gave me loads of extra food.

I don't know if they knew I was always hungry, which I always was, or that I looked thin, which I probably did. Anyway, they were really great to me, and I looked forward to school dinnertime when I could load up with enough to last me till the following day. I could even have seconds and thirds before others even had a first course; and I especially loved the pudding, which was custard or chocolate custard, and I loved the skin. I always asked them to save it for me, which they always did. I got the feeling they looked forward as much to seeing me as I did to see them, and they were happy to give me all the food I wanted. Funny, this was going to stay with me all throughout my childhood and well into my adult life. I knew that if I ate my food fast, no one could take it off my plate. Every day was like a mini battle being fought, with the battle field being the school canteen and my plate. I would line up with all the other kids, get my plate, and hold it forward for each dinner lady to dollop on whatever was for dinner that day. We would pass down the food line until we got to the end then move over to sit at a table. Most of the time, I sat by myself, as no one would sit with me, because I was from "the orphanage." I didn't mind that as I could eat fast and go for seconds and thirds, often rejoining the line to get more food.

At weekends at Oaklands Road, the radio was always on tuned to the BBC Light program, and I had to listen to current hits like "Que Sera Sera," now and other songs that I tried to sing along with. I loved music and could get completely lost in a song. I didn't care what I sounded like, but when I sang, I was oblivious to anything else.

Weekends at Oaklands Road were also very interesting for another reason. Young married couples arrived on Saturday mornings and afternoons, as potential foster parents for some of the boys. They came into the home, to meet whoever they were there to see, and take them away for the day or for the weekend. No one ever came for me, as I knew no one at all here in London and I was nearly always alone there at weekends, which was fine by me as I could play with any of the toys and no one was there to stop me as they usually did when they were present as I had no toys of my own to play with. I loved playing with the Hornby 00 gauge wind-up train set, as the electric one was not for me to ever touch.

However, I played with it all day long in the back room when no one else was there, and I loved the smell of the electric sparks that came out from the wheels whenever it went over a join in the rails.

I didn't have to ever wind it up, and it would run on and on round the track. The detail was amazing, the engines were so realistic, and the maroon and cream passenger cars reminded me of Lowestoft and the train ride when I went to see my mother.

After some time of living there, life for me settled down, again, when one Saturday afternoon, a young couple came to the home while I was playing in the back room. The young lady, Joyce, was very pretty with dark wavy hair and was quite tall, slim, and very well dressed. Joyce had a kind face and was smiling at me the whole time. Her husband was Herbert (Bert). He was very elegantly dressed in a dark pinstriped suit, and they both seemed interested in talking to me.

They both knelt down next to me and started playing along with me with the train set. They had come to meet a boy called Freddy Weekly, but he was out that day. They met me by accident and started talking to me instead

of leaving. They were asking me why I was there alone and what had happened to my family. I told them my mother had gone
to the fairies, which was as it should be since she had been "very ill with TB, you know." I hadn't a clue what TB was, but people seemed to know all about it and it saved me from having to explain further.

The Whiteheads, which was their name as I understood from Mrs. Bumford, came again some weeks later and were looking again for Freddy, Well, Freddy had once again already gone out that day, and as usual I was there by myself.

I would most often get the electric train set out to play with, and on this second trip, I recognized them; and they asked me if I would like to go out with them. Of course, I said, "Yes; that would be OK if Mrs. Bumford said it was all right." I whispered to them to ask if I could eat lunch with them as the food there was not very nice. They laughed and said, "Yes, of course."

We went out from Oaklands Road to their home in Boston Manor, and their house was much larger than the foster home. The house had three bedrooms, two rooms downstairs, and a small front garden with a longer back garden. The house was brightly painted in red and white and was located halfway down on the left-hand side on a respectable quiet street called Clitherow Avenue; and the house was number 107.

I spent many weekends there after that, staying first on Saturdays, after which they would both take me back to Oaklands Road Hanwell on the trolley bus. As time went on and we became better acquainted, I got to stay with the family for whole weekends. Bert and Joyce had a son, Richard, who was two years older than me and seemed OK; but I wasn't sure about him yet.

Richard told me, one night, he had wanted a brother and thought that I was probably going to be his new brother. I didn't mind at all since it was better than life at the children's home and I really liked my new foster parents, his mom and dad. I said to Richard, "OK then, I'll be your new brother," not really knowing what a brother was supposed to do, but if it meant leaving the children's home and living here instead, then that was fine by me.

Some months later, as their visits became regular events for me and were something to look forward to, when we were leaving Oaklands Road to go to my "new family" for the weekend, Joyce asked me if I would like to live with them permanently. I said I needed to ask permission, but if it was OK with Mrs. Bumford, it was fine with me; and that was that.

I was so excited to be moving out of the children's home for good, and simply left there—no goodbyes and no fuss, just another door to close behind me as I moved on. Freddy's loss was my gain, although he had found another couple to stay with, so it was not a real loss for him. I never saw Freddy again, nor did I ever go back to see that orphanage again ever! In fact, this part was ore difficult to write than other parts as it had little effect on me and I had few memories of that time except being dropped off and eventually being found by the Whiteheads.

   I seemed to have put that place in a separate part of my mind, so "closing that door" was very easy. Don't you see what I see? That things happen for a reason and being there got me away from my step father, and even if it was a children's home, it really didn't matter to me. I just fitted in wherever I was and made the most of whatever I had to deal with at the time. My belief in God was unshakeable, and I knew I must have had a whole host of guardian angels looking after me to have been so lucky as to have Bert and his beautiful wife Joyce to come into my life right at that point just when I needed them and I was ready to move on.

God's plan is never wrong we just have to trust in his wisdom as we cannot see everything that will be!

MY NEW FAMILY

I entered a period of calm in my life.

LIFE BEGAN TO settle down for me, and I was beginning to have somewhat of a normal life. I started a new school, Fielding Primary School, though I stayed there for only a few months.

Soon it was summer, and I could do anything—play all summer long and go back to my very own home.

Every week, Joyce used to give Richard and I pocket money. I hadn't a clue what it was for as I had never needed any money, but she bought me some sweets with the money and they were kept in a jar on a high shelf in the larder—licorice, Flying Saucers, Sherbet Lemons, anything I wanted.

Richard had his jar marked with his name, and I had mine. Most of the time, I was so busy I forgot all about the sweets, so Richard took mine as well as his. I didn't mind, nor did I really notice until I had none left in the middle of the week.

At that point, again and again, Joyce would ask me if I had eaten all of my sweets; and when I replied, "No, I haven't touched them," she would step in and take sweets from Richard's jar and would give them to me. He always said I owed him his sweets back, so I would give him some of mine from time to time. I had never had any possessions of my own at that time—no toys that were mine and certainly no sweets—so it didn't matter that much; and I thought if Richard needed mine, he could have them. After all, it was his house.

But Mom, as I got to call her, was angry that he took them I moved up from Fielding Primary school to Fielding Junior School in 1959 when I was nine years old, and that was when I began for the first time to have real friends. It was there, at Fielding, that I met my lifelong friend Ian Howard. Ian had a house about a mile away from my house at number 5 Southdown Avenue and had a younger sister called Annabelle.

Ian and I began to be best of friends and spent all of our time together. In fact, we were to remain friends all our lives, although we didn't know it then of course.

The two of us joined the Cub Scouts and even sang in the church choir at the huge "St. Thomas the Apostle" Protestant church on the Boston Road.

We were together all the time and would meet up at his house or mine and would go out every Wednesday night to choir practice at the church. When we weren't at choir practice, we went to the Cub Scout hut, which at that time was in an old wooden hut next to the church on Friday nights. Later when we became Boy Scouts, we went to a purpose-built hut along Trumpers Way in lower Hanwell, some three miles from our houses.

Ian's mother was apparently a famous actress, Peggy Evans, though it meant little to us at the time, Dad certainly knew of her acting. She was very, very beautiful and was tall, had long blonde glamorous wavy hair that would cascade down to her shoulders.

Ian's mom was always very kind to me and always let me see Ian whenever I wanted, which was almost every day. She had starred in a film called *The Blue Lamp* with Dirk Bogard and Jack Warner. She was often seen on television doing her famous scream as Jack was shot outside a cinema by Dirk Bogard, who was playing the role of a small time thug. Peggy would come running out of the cinema look at what her boyfriend, Dirk, had just done, as Jack was slowly sinking to the ground, having just been shot, and would scream at the top of her lungs.

Ian and I would watch the clip whenever it was on and recite word-for-word what Jack and Peggy did in that scene. "Drop it and don't be a fool" Ian would say, and I would reply, "I'll drop you. This thing works. Get back, get back, I say." Well, apparently, he didn't get back because Dirk shot Jack dead right there in front of the cinema. Jack Warner's name in the film was *Constable Dixon*, and the police station was at Dock Green, which was at Paddington Green in west London.

They played that scene over and over again for the next fifty years, and always it caused the same stir of emotion as being the very first time a cop had got shot on screen. Boy were they all in for a surprise nowadays; sadly, it happens both in real life and in movies every day.
Jack went on to star in a very long running TV series of the same name, *Dixon of Dock Green*, and I watched that show for years afterward; even though it was in black and white. It was always on, on, Saturday nights at 7:00 p.m.

Ian, Annabelle, and their mom didn't have a lot of money all the time I knew Ian, but they got by just fine. Ian's dad was a famous comedian called Michael Howard and was on a radio show every lunchtime, called *Workers Playtime*, which was played by all of the factories all over England. Michael had divorced Peggy shortly after Annabelle was born.

Peggy got a little help from "Equity," which was an actor's union; but it wasn't much, and I don't think Michael ever helped her out with Ian and Annabelle.

Money and possessions meant nothing to me or to Ian. We had all we needed—our friendship, plenty of fun, both our homes, and loads to do. In fact, we were inseparable all throughout our childhood and on into our late teenage years. We learned to sing and play guitars, but that is a later story.

Life for me was now very normal. I loved school, I loved my new home, I loved my new family, and I loved all my new friends. The school was magic and was really the best school one could hope for. The teachers and the atmosphere at Fielding Junior School were the best I would ever know.

Many years later, I met all of my school friends online through a Web site called Friends Reunited. I kept in touch with Janette Andersen, Linda Miller (the second love of my life), Carolyn Davies, Iris Nunn, and many more. In some way, it proved to me that all of these things had actually happened.

The really good teacher was our music teacher, Mr. Woodcraft (Woody Woodcraft), and he was a truly gifted music teacher.

Mr. Woodcraft had a teaching method where he would describe a complete piece of music to us before playing it on a large wooden gramophone that he placed in front of the classroom. He would describe a scene from *Peer Gynt in the Hall of the Mountain King* or from the *William Tell Overture* or from the Fingals Cave part of *The Hebrides Suite*, or from *Peter and the Wolf*. Then after half an hour of detailed description of the music and what it represented, he would let us hear the piece of music, playing it in front of the class; and we could fully understand all that the music had described. I loved these music lessons, and he was to influence my life forever. It was through him that we were all fortunate enough to have had a complete understanding of how music was written and why it was written, of the "movements" in a piece, and how it progressed through to the finale. At Christmas, the whole school was decorated, and every window in the large school hall was painted with Christmas scenes from the Bible and Christmas carols.

Each class was given one of the large windows in the school hall for them to paint their scene. Some, of course, were better than the others; but our teacher would make all of the paintings seem perfect. We sang carols at morning assembly, and I loved the beautiful hymns and carols that we sang. The excitement of waiting for Christmas holidays lasted for the whole month of December when the weather was starting to get cold.

My birthday signaled the beginning of the Christmas season, and I was happy that it was on December 6 for that reason. The walk from my house to the school was about one mile; and sometimes Ian and I would meet at the bottom of my road, which was on his way, and we'd walk to school together. Then at the end of the school day, we walked home together, parting at the bottom of my street so he could go on to his house and I to mine.

We all loved the time there at Fielding; and even now, though my class friends haven't met for at least forty years, many of us keep in touch through the Web site.

On Sundays in summer, Mom, Dad, Richard, and I would go to the Lyons Sports club in Acton as Dad worked for J. Lyons & Company at their head office in Orchard House in Central London.

The club was just for employees and their families and was incredible. We had an open-air swimming pool, playing fields, and every sports activity you could think of. There were soccer teams, rugby, tennis courts, and in fact every sports activity one could imagine.

Joyce loved to play tennis and would play for hours on any of the many courts there with a bunch of friends, sometimes singles and sometimes doubles. Richard and I would watch her play; she was a very good tennis player. Life was so good then, and I wanted nothing else. My guardian angel had once again looked after me.

I had many new friends to play with—Brian Phillips, Brian Pinder, Ian. Brian Phillips was a sturdy, or as his Scottish kinfolk would say a "brawny," boy with red hair, freckles, and a very kind character. Brian Pinder was also much bigger than me (as were most of my friends) and went on after school to join the army in some specialist position or other. We all played together or cycled about the streets and did whatever we wanted.

On Saturday mornings, we went to the Northfields Odeon to watch *Saturday Morning Pictures*. It was sixpence and lasted for three hours.

We all sat together to watch *Mr. Pastry*, the *Lone Ranger*, *Superman*, *Laurel and Hardy*, and many other short film episodes, some in black and white. Brian Pinder got us sweets from his dad's sweet shop on the corner of Northfields Avenue, and we would all sit there shouting at the screen as some villain was up to no good or when the Lone Ranger rose on his horse and said, "Hi ho Silver away," whatever that meant.

Summers were of course endless, and we always found things to do. I pretty much went on with my life doing all the normal things boys do. On Sundays, if we weren't going to the Lyons Sports Club, Dad would go to the local pub for a lunchtime pint . . . or two or three. He would always take Richard and I, and we would both have an 'Orangina' each, which for both of us was a real treat.

The pub, the Royal Hotel, was an enormous Tudor building in white, with black beams all over the rather stylish front and sides, and was located right at the corner of our street. It had an interesting garden with a miniature zoo. There were parrots, monkeys, a donkey, and other little creatures.

We could sip our drinks and spend all lunchtime there till Dad had had his pint or two. Then we'd all walk home where my beautiful mom had made roast beef or roast lamb for lunch. I loved Sunday lunch with the whole family together, though often Mom would get cross with Dad for getting back at one thirty when lunch was at 1:00 p.m. I never understood why lunch on Sundays was at one when Dad never got back before one thirty. This became our Sunday ritual; it made me smile . . . my normal family.

Having a family is what most people take for granted, I never did!

ANOTHER DOOR TO CLOSE

Inner strength comes from getting through difficult situations intact.

I NOW HAD A perfect family; everything else was behind me and I was at last happy. One warm sunny Sunday in summer when I was now eleven, Mom and Dad decided that we'd go to the sports club, as we often did. So we all set off together with me swinging between Mom and Dad's arms, excited to be meeting all of Mom and Dad's work friends. The sports club was three stops on the Piccadilly line from Boston Manor to Acton Town, and we had to change trains at Acton Town to get another train to Sudbury Hill station where the sports grounds were located.

After a short walk to the Boston Manor Tube station, we took the Piccadilly line to Acton Town then changed tubes. When we got there, Dad would smoke his Players Weights and played cards with his friends, always with a beer next to him; while Mom played tennis with her friends. I made as much noise as I could with other kids or simply stayed with Dad and watched him, fascinated as he played cards. Richard hung out with his friends, and we would stay until it was time to go home usually around 3:30 p.m.

We boarded the tube for home and arrived at Boston Manor station shortly after 4:00 p.m., as we usually did, with me swinging between Mom and Dad as we walked home together in the afternoon sunlight of a warm summer's day. As we reached the corner of our street, Mom suddenly stopped walking, complaining of feeling a little giddy and lightheaded, and asked me to stop swinging as she sat down on the wall at the corner of our road. Dad told Rich and I to go on home, saying they would follow as soon as Mom felt better. She looked so pale as I had never seen her before.

We were both told to go 'round the corner and wait at a friend's house until Dad called us home. Later on that evening, we were both told to go home and see Dad. The Cuttings, who were our very close friends, where we spent the remainder of that afternoon, became serious; and I could tell something was very wrong as they weren't smiling and seemed so very sad.

As Richard and I walked home, we were talking about Mom, wondering what was wrong with her as we had never ever seen her ill before. When we arrived home only a few minutes later, Dad was in the front room, looking pale, trembling, and looking terrible. I couldn't imagine what was wrong. I had never seen a grown-up seem as Dad looked at that moment. He asked us to join him in the front room as he sat heavily on the couch. He gathered his strength and looked at us both long and hard before telling us, in a now cracking voice, that Mom had died that afternoon of a brain hemorrhage.

Mom had died right there, on the corner of our street while sitting on that low wall, and Richard and I never ever saw her again. I wish I had kissed her goodbye or told her how much I loved her, but life isn't like that. We never get the chance to change the past, and I would never get that chance again. We were both scared and shocked we didn't know what to do.

Richard screamed at the news and sobbed his poor heart out, his whole body shaking. I was very sad too but not in the same way Richard was. I had no idea really what this all meant, but what I did know was that my life would probably change yet again. I went up to my room and sat on the bed, scared of what would happen to me now. I closed the door that day and prepared myself, once again, to move on to whatever was in store for me I was getting both used to, and fed up, with this; but at the same time, I had to just deal with it.

I felt once again desolate and alone but had no one to really talk to, so I had to keep my emotions to myself as Rich was immersed in his own sadness; and Dad was, well, Dad and didn't ever show us his true emotions, so I didn't want to bother him though it broke my heart to see him this way. I was also scared that if I cried or got on his nerves, he might place me back in that awful orphanage.

The funeral, several days later, was a very sad day; though I must confess it didn't really sink in like it did for Dad and Rich. I never went to the funeral and instead was parked with relatives for the afternoon at our house; the atmosphere was awful.

I was scared, as I had been through this before. I prayed again that God would look after me and not let anything too bad happen to me. I had no idea what would be happen to me now that Mom was gone; but what I did know was that I missed her very, very, much. And as her passing was so sudden, it really never impacted me until many months later. I thought I had all that I needed and I was just getting used to what must be a normal life and once again had to "shut the door" and move on. I had no choice.

I had no idea how serious it was to be for me; my life was about to change again. My father was alone now with no partner to help look after Rich and me. He was my stepdad (number 2) and may not be able to keep me as a single parent with a full-time job, looking after two boys with no help. I worried a lot about the possibility of being placed in another children's home but tried not to think about that possibility as I could do nothing about it.

It was at this time that Ian's Mom came 'round and asked Dad if I could go and live with them and perhaps even adopt me, saying that Ian and I were like brothers anyway. Dad, of course, told her that it wasn't possible; and so Ian and I never became real brothers. But in truth, we were every bit true brothers even more than Richard and me.

A family shares everything, including loss and it is at these times of loss that we have to pause our lives before we move on.

AUNTIE SIS

Some people we meet may never know how well we see them as we may not be in a position to tell them at that time.

DAD HAD A sister in Manchester where he was originally from and invited her to come and stay with us to help him cope. Auntie Sis, as she became known to us, moved down from Manchester to live with us and did everything for us; she cooked, cleaned, and looked after all of us, including Dad. She reminded me a lot of "Ena Sharples," a character from way back in the now long-running *Coronation Street*, having the exact same appearance and accent; the hair net and even her mannerisms were the same.

The only change I saw was that once every three months, the county council, in their infinite wisdom, sent a case worker 'round to see how I was doing. She was a very calm tall lady, with dark hair; and her name was Mrs. Osborne, though I never knew her first name. She would always talk to Dad and then to me, and then she would talk to just me alone.

I never really understood the purpose of these meetings, but I knew that Dad was always a little nervous before she came around. She would ask me about school and my friends and about how my life was at home.

I was fine, although I did become more of a loner at school. I talked about it with Ian, but we both would start laughing at something or other, and life would move on. Aunt Sis being with us enabled me to keep living at our house and enabled Dad to cope with bringing two boys up without a mom as long as Aunt Sis stayed with us.

Gradually, things returned to normal, and I remember saying to Ian one day when we were walking home from school, "I suppose I should be grateful. I have now had two moms and two dads in my life, and you've only had one." Ian didn't say anything that time, and we walked home in silence. Richard changed after Mom had died and became harder to live with and never ceased to remind me that Joyce was his mom, not mine.

Though his words stung, I understood why he said that, though I could never show him that it hurt as it would give him more ammo!

I understood how he felt and felt so sad for him, though there was nothing I could do about it. I had lost two moms by now, and he had only lost one; so as I saw it, he was much better off than me.

Richard became angry and aggressive, and little things seemed to upset him very easily. I guess it was a grieving that he needed to get through. There were no "counselors" and no programmed grief counseling at all for us, so we just had to "grin and bear it" with a "stiff upper lip."

Dad never showed his grief to us, but I remember that he seldom smiled after Mom died and seemed to be going through life mechanically. However, one day, two years later, he told us that there was a woman that he liked at work; and he was going to bring her home to meet us soon.

He had married beautiful Joyce fairly young, and they had known each other since high school and were perfect for each other. It's times like this that I often wondered where God was and why we were given such difficult things to deal with. I did realize though that if a person has an easy life, they don't have anything to test their strength of character.

Boy, I suppose I should have been Mr. Universe in that case, but that's life, so deal with it.

When Dad got ready for work, he always had very shiny black shoes that he polished every day and wore a striped shirt with a separate white collar attached with a stud, a dark pin-striped suit, and a toned-down tie a bowler hat and an umbrella. He looked every bit the London businessman, and I looked up to him and admired how elegantly he always dressed. He did manage to keep all us together, and I love him for that and for everything else he did for us. Aunt Sis was a lovely person, and although she was old, she managed to keep us all well and helped Dad a great deal, doing all that she could to help him look after the family. Aunt Sis, I love you still!

The stiff upper lip that my step father demonstrated was a sign of great inner strength.

BOYHOOD WITH IAN

A true friend is a soul mate forever.

As FOR ME, I settled down pretty quickly, and I had my friends to play with. Ian, Brian Pinder, Brian Phillips, and I would always hang out together. We got into some not-so-good things, one of these was when Ian and I stayed behind at school together with a beautiful blonde girl, Janette Andersen, and another girl called Roisin O'Connor (pronounced Roshene). Roisin had brown curly hair and was a tomboy, but we didn't care—she was our friend, and the four of us hung out together.

I had, at that time, a secret crush on Janette, though it was entirely uncool to ever let a girl know that! The four of us were just hanging out together in the school playground as we sometimes did, with nothing to do after school, when we decided that we should climb up on top of the brick pillar that was at the side of the school front gate. The pillar was around six feet high at the left side of the entrance to the school, and that supported the "Fielding Junior School" sign. We decided to punctuate the name Fielding, intending only to place a small dent in the sign. However, it didn't quite work out that way; and what happened next was that as I kicked the sign, egged on by the other three, unfortunately for me, my foot went right through the board and made a huge hole in it.

We had kicked a huge hole right through the sign, not realizing that we were in fact in full view, and we were seen from the houses just over the road. The following day, we had to meet Ms. Hunt, the head mistress, after someone told on us, and had to stand outside her office at lunchtimes for a month with no lunchtime playtime at all!

We stood outside her office in the corridor and roll marbles along the floor for something to do. In fact, I was always outside Ms. Hunt's office for one thing or another and didn't mind it that much as I always found things to do; and anyway she had a jar of sweets on her desk, which were fair game if she wasn't around.

Ian and I were true friends and we both went through a lot together.

THE BIG RED APPLE

If something looks too good to be true, it usually is.

WHEN IAN AND I were walking home later that same year, which was now the fourth year at Fielding Junior school, we spotted a huge bright red apple on a tree in someone's garden behind a wall next to the school on Wyndam Road. This red apple was all by itself hanging on a single branch high up behind a high curved wall, which was on a bend in the road. The wall separated the garden from the street and had a smooth side with bits of broken glass set in the bricks along the top of the wall. So as we were walking past, day after day, we decided that the apple was made for eating; and it was all alone on the tree and would probably taste delicious. At that time, "scrumping" (another word for stealing apples from other people's trees) was a perfectly normal thing for kids like us to do; and besides, that particular bright red and ripe apple had been hanging there for weeks . . . all alone and by itself.

It never occurred to us that the tree had no other fruit on it, nor that the apple was absolutely huge and looked exactly the same every day that we walked home from school!

So on our way home from school one day, we decided that one of us (me) would climb up the wall and grab the apple and toss it down to the other (Ian), and we would both share it. So after carefully looking up and down the street to make sure no one was around to see what we were about to do, Ian gave me a leg up, and up I climbed up the wall.

The wall was around eight feet high, and it took us several attempts as we kept bursting out in laughter. I finally climbed onto Ian's shoulders, and head making sure I stood on his face to get high enough for me to just reach the top of the wall. I climbed up onto the wall and shinned along the top, minding the broken glass all along the top of the wall to reach the tree.

With adrenaline pumping, I stretched up to the tree, grabbed a branch, and swung over onto the branch and slowly edged my way along to reach for the apple.

Of course, while I was up there completely exposed, Ian wasn't keeping quiet; he was shouting at the top of his lungs to anyone who was around to hear: "Tony Moore who lives at 107 Clitherow Avenue is stealing your apples, and he's taking that huge red one. Help, police! Tony Moore, I told you not to do it . . . that's stealing." He was in fits of laughter as he was shouting out to the "hopefully" empty street.

Bloody great, I was up the tree whispering down to him, "Shut up, stupid, or we'll get caught." I am doing the hard work, and he is making it worse! I couldn't move fast enough, frightened that someone would catch me up in the tree. But I was both laughing and cross at Ian for blowing my cover; and as usual, we both burst out laughing, and I could hardly move for laughing so hard. Anyway, before I climbed down the tree, I shouted that I would keep the apple and eat it right up there in front of him if he didn't shut up. I held the huge red apple in front of me, polishing it on my school blazer to emphasize the point and making out that I was about to take a big bite, so he finally stopped shouting.

I tossed it down to Ian who was waiting on the pavement. I then jumped down, and we both ran as fast as we could, laughing the whole time as we both ran away from the house. When we were at safe distance from the house, we ran down an alley way where we decided to share the huge red apple. Since I got it down, the first bite was mine; and as I bit into the huge red apple, it broke completely apart, falling into hundreds of pieces onto the ground. Our beautiful apple that we had been ogling at for weeks was made completely out of clay and tasted disgusting as I spat out the pieces all over Ian!

The whole thing was a hoax. Just great! We laughed and laughed all the way home and took some of the pieces to show Janette and Roisin, at school the following day, what had happened to us the day before.

Some things are not always what they seem and can leave a bad feeling behind, it certainly did here.

RALPH AND THE GUARD DOG

A simple unlocked door can save a hell of a lot of pain!

OUR SCOUT HALL was at the bottom of "Trumpers Way," along mostly unlit lane and meant that we had to walk home with other Boy Scouts from our troop. Ralph, one of our friends, a rather plain slightly overweight kid who wore milk bottle bottom glasses, would sometimes come home with Ian and I as he was scared of the dark road.

One night, on our way home, we were walking down Trumpers Way and decided to stop at the film props yard to take a look inside. The yard was behind a long sliding steel door that was twelve inches off the ground and slid open and closed along a long steel runner at the top while the bottom of the long steel door hung free.

The yard was halfway down Trumpers Way and was in a very dark part of the lane. We used to peek inside, often to look at all of the neat stuff that was inside, behind the big steel sliding door. Inside, it was an amazing sight, and there were many film props—army trucks, field guns, a helicopter, parts of airplane fuselages, Army Jeeps, etc. It was, of course, a junk yard; but to us, it was a treasure trove of the most cool stuff a twelve-year-old could ever see.

Ian and I decided that we would take a closer look inside, but Ralph didn't want to come in with us, and so we told him to wait by the sliding steel door and keep a lookout just in case. So as Ian bent down to slip under the door and was halfway through into the yard, I started barking like a guard dog as loud as I could, making Ian jump out of his skin. I swear he completely left the ground as he was crawling in on all fours and had cleared the door. He wasn't amused as he quickly changed direction to crawl backward under the door to get back onto the street.

I burst out laughing to see him so scared. "you idiot! That's not funny," he said. "I could have got hurt on that door." But I was laughing so hard he began laughing as well. As luck would have it, apparently, I said something in dog talk that started off the real guard dog, which we had no idea lived there, in a tirade of really fierce barking at us. We could hear this barking starting from deep inside the yard as this huge brute began barking at us. He rounded a corner from behind an aircraft fuselage and was an absolutely huge black German shepherd. He was chained to his dog house by a huge steel chain that we could just see glinting in the moonlight as he ran back and forth, straining at his steel leash.

We both legged it as fast as we could, but when he didn't come after us, we both slowly walked back and knelt down, peering under the sliding door, to see why; and we realized he wasn't coming as he was still securely chained, or so we thought. So we started barking back at the dog who was heaving and straining even more at his chain, trying to get to us.

I really think that all barking is the same word, unless as you bark you start thinking about what you want to say. When that happens, I believe your barks take on whatever it is you are thinking at the time.

Anyway, that's just me and it didn't matter what I was thinking as it made no difference to what was about to happen. We just stood there laughing and barking back at the huge dog; while Ralph, now scared out of his wits, was shouting at us to stop as he stood some way back along the road nervously looking at us and at the way out up the lane.

After several minutes of the dog barking and us, attempting to have a conversation with the dog, by barking back, the bloody brute broke free; and we saw him come running across the yard toward us, getting bigger and bigger as he got closer. The three of us legged it as fast as we could back up Trumpers Way, looking back over our shoulders as we ran.

Now Ian and I were certainly not gentlemen; and we ran as fast as we could, getting past Ralph who was not by any means as good a runner as we were (we had had more practice), as he had flat feet that seemed to get in his way. As we passed either side of him, the huge dog was getting far too close for comfort. Just then, we came up next to a large truck that was parked on the side of the road. "Quick!" I shouted to Ian. "Let's get inside the cab."

We both leapt up onto the running board and prayed that the door wasn't locked. As luck would have it, it wasn't, so we quickly grabbed the door handle and leapt inside, slamming the door behind us.

Once we were safe inside the large truck, we both slowly moved our heads up the door so that we could sneak a look out of the window. We sneaked a peak out only to see poor Ralphy being grabbed by the huge dog and was being taken down by his leg. Ian and I were so scared at this point we could only look on with baited breath, mesmerized at the sight, with noses pressed hard on the truck window. We watched as the huge guard dog grabbed poor Ralph at the back of his knee and expertly twisted him down. Ralph, of course, screamed at the top of his lungs as he fell to the ground. Once Ralph was down, the dog then looked up to see where we had gone; he saw us and jumped up at us, snarling and snapping at us through the window, not reaching us as we were now safely in the cab. We knew we were safe and snarled right back at the brute. The brute then ran back past poor Ralphy and went under the door and back inside the yard, ignoring Ralph who was moaning and crying on the ground.

We listened to poor Ralph as he was crying after having been bitten. We should have felt really bad, but once again, we looked at each other. We started to laugh, and we couldn't stop laughing, having a mixture of adrenaline, fear, and relief. As we carefully stepped down from the truck, Ralph was lying on the ground, moaning and clutching his leg. We helped him up and looked to see the damage. "Not much muscle there, Ralphy. Thank God. Otherwise, he would have had even more to bite on," Ian said. "We were trying to get to you, but the door just locked on us, and it wouldn't unlock until just now."

The damage wasn't really too bad though, but he did have the beginning of a huge bruise with teeth marks beginning to show; and though we were still trying not to as we were being as sincere as we possibly could, we were still laughing hard though we felt sorry for Ralph. Poor Ralph, once he realized he was OK, he started laughing and crying too, more out of relief than humor. We kept on looking at his leg, admiring the perfect set of teeth marks at the back of his leg as we walked him limping home.

Ralph was really a good sport, and we agreed that we couldn't say anything to anyone as it was Ian's fault, as I kept telling Ralph while pretending to give Ian the evil eye, and if not for him, we wouldn't have gotten into trouble at all.

All's well that ended well but I've given up trying to talk to guard dogs.

THE CANAL

Ignoring 'No Trespassing' is not a brilliant idea.

IN SUMMER WE used to go down to the Grand Union Canal in Boston Manor and watch the long heavy barges being pulled along by the huge powerful cart horses as they wound their way along the "tow path." We would walk all the way from near Ian's house to Brentford, a distance of about four miles walking along the canal towpath. One very hot summer day, we decided to go into the railway yard, at the back of the Firestone Tire factory in Brentford, to see if we could "footplate" on the engines.

Footplating was where we would go up to a train in the shunting yard and ask permission from the driver or fireman to stand on the footplate as it was being shunted around.

The yard was a huge railway siding with loads of trains bringing rubber, coal, chemicals, and other stuff for Firestone. As we wandered inside the yard, there were large pools of some bright orange powder dotted all over the huge railway yard. That day, the weather was very hot, and it was in the middle of August while we were both on summer holidays from school. We had on only sandals, with no socks, and were too busy talking to notice much around us; after all, this was another adventure for us. We didn't notice for instance that there were sticks and tree branches along the edge of these pools of orange powder that were smoldering.

As we were walking through the Firestone yard, I accidentally stepped into one of the orange powder pools and got badly burnt on my foot. This time, I wasn't laughing as my foot immediately broke out into a huge blister, and my sandals were seared and smoldering.

Ian grabbed my arm and helped me out of the pool and had to help me limp home. Once we got home, the doctor was called. My doctor was Dr. Topham, who lived just a few houses down from mine; and after seeing my badly blistered foot, she wanted to know what had happened. After we had told her, she decided to call the police immediately. I wasn't so sure this was a good idea, but she called anyway. When they arrived, we had to tell them what had happened, and they decided to take Ian with them to see where these pools of acid (as we called them) were. Ian left me with Dr.

Topham and went to the Firestone yard with the two burly policemen, getting to ride in the police car. As they got near to the yard, the police could see that we had in fact been trespassing on private land; and, according to Ian, they became more cautious.

They proceeded to tell Ian off for going where he shouldn't and lost interest in what we had been telling them. So I got laid up, while Ian got told off. He called me later that night to see if I was OK and told me he nearly got nicked. Neither one of us could understand why the cops were not interested in finding out what the orange powder was or how it had burnt my foot.

I learned to not only look where I'm going, but to notice what is on either side of the path I am on and to think twice before ignoring 'No Trespassing' signs.

AUTUMN LEAVES

Fun for one person can be bloody hard work for another!

ON OUR WAY back from choir practice one Wednesday evening, we were playing in the autumn leaves along the Boston Road, and as we had nothing else to do, we decided to stack as many leaves as we could outside a large house on the corner of my street. Laughing at our brilliant plan, we began to stack a huge pile of leaves right outside the front door of this house. We had no idea who it belonged to except that it was fair game for our little prank. Finally, after some thirty minutes of "leaf stacking," when we had stacked the leaves to at least six feet high in a huge pile, we ran to the corner and hid to see what would happen.

We were very proud of our building abilities and were carefully peeking 'round the corner at our handiwork at the house when the front porch light went on and two men came out and stopped dead at the sight of our huge pile of leaves outside their front door. "Let's be really cool and slowly walk right past and pretend we know nothing about it."

I said to Ian. "OK, but no laughing and I mean it," he said, and we casually started walking slowly past the house, whistling as we went, being very careful not to look at the huge stack of leaves or at the two men staring at our handiwork from the lighted front porch. We were doing really great, as we quite casually began to cross the road, next to their house, and strolled past their house; that is, until Ian looked at me and I looked back at him at the same time. That was it. "Don't do it," I whispered forcefully at him. "Don't you dare laugh." But all our cool vanished, and we tried desperately not to laugh. Well, it didn't work. "oy you," one of the men shouted! "run!" I shouted. And we legged it off down the street, chased by both of the men. The older of the two gave up after chasing us some two hundred yards farther down the road and went back to the house.

As we were both laughing and running as fast as we could, the remaining man was getting closer and closer behind us. I remember shouting to Ian, "Behind you," as we used to say at Saturday morning pictures when a villain was about to pounce on the good guy; but this time, the good guy was behind the villain. Ian laughed even more and now couldn't run because of it. As we reached a corner, we split up, and Ian went straight ahead down Boston Road, a stupid move; while I turned the corner and ran off down another side street and into an alleyway that ran behind the houses.

I heard Ian get caught, and he shouted, "It wasn't me. It was all Tony's idea." What's new? He was collared by the house owner and was frog-marched back to the house, being dragged along by the man holding Ian by his coat collar. As for me, I collapsed laughing and had to catch my breath before checking out what had happened to Ian.

Talk about something embarrassing! Ian was dragged back to the house, by his collar, and had to face the music. He had to clear the whole lot up, which took him at least an hour. They made him clear up their whole front garden as well as place all the leaves into big bags. I waited before creeping back to see if he was OK. As I got close, I peeked out from around the corner at Ian having to shovel all the leaves up. I watched him, making sure there were no other people from the house around, but I couldn't stop laughing at his bad luck.

I called out to him, "Psst," from my "safe distance," but he ignored me and pretended he couldn't hear. I called again, "Psst, Ian, you missed some over there behind you." He, needless to say, was not impressed at all. "I'd like to help," I half shouted, half whispered, "but I'm so tired from all that running and actually getting away," to which he gave me the evil eye. I stayed though till he finished and knocked on the front door to let them inspect his cleaning up, and we walked home together.

I told him that if he hadn't run straight ahead, he may have gotten away; but some of my wisdom falls on deaf ears. Ian was tired from all that leaf clearing and having to shovel them all up into bags. "You know," I said, "if we had played our cards right, and if you hadn't laughed so much, we could have charged them two and six for cleaning up that mess."

But unfortunately, he didn't see the funny side!

A plan made on the spur of the moment often leads to unplanned results!

CAROL SINGING

Making the most of my skills was rewarding...financially

SINCE IAN AND I were both in the St. Thomas's church choir, we could both sing all the words and harmonies for all of the Christmas carols that we learned in church, so we decided on the way back from choir practice one cold evening in mid-December to try our hand at carol singing to make some extra cash. At that time, in many of the streets in London, there were lots of carol singers; and though some were really bad some, I have to admit (like us) they were really good, as we should be since we were part of the church choir.

So we got the carol book from church and tried it. At first, we couldn't sing for laughing so much and had to run for it. As time went on, though, we got better and went from door to door singing some terrific harmonies, or so we thought; and as the doors opened, we would carry on singing and even asked for requests.

We made loads of money and promptly went to the off license at the side of the Royal Hotel to buy as many sweets and pop as we could carry. Though it was freezing, we would sit down and scoff as much as we could eat. We even made up our own words to some of the carols and pretended we were singing in Latin, and we had a blast.

Ian and I were as close as brothers, and we were also quite competitive, so while carol singing we would always try to out-sing each other, getting louder and louder. Ian's mom and my dad always thought we were at a late choir practice for Christmas, and we had to make sure we didn't sing too close to our own houses or that Richard didn't get to know; otherwise, he would have wanted some of my money for keeping quiet.

Christmas was always amazing. We were so busy at Scout and at choir practice twice a week and at weekends in December we would sing around the local old peoples and children's hospitals with a small group from the choir. I loved doing that as the faces of the patients were always so happy to see us, and anyway there were the nurses. We would compare notes as to which nurse was the prettiest; and if there was a really pretty nurse, we would sing our very best, drowning out all of the others in the choir.

On Christmas Eve, there were always two services, one at 7:00 p.m. and one at midnight, and we were both required to be there. At one of the side chapels in the church, there was a nativity scene with stars and desert looking just like the real thing and had the manger and the three kings, some animals, a field of sheep with the shepherds, and a small town of Bethlehem. It was quite beautiful. All was well at the church until several months later the vicar decided to have an affair with a local builder's wife, who was always coming to church on Sundays and who was very attractive. He was quickly moved on, and we got a new vicar.

For the most part, we were so busy all the time we practically never watched TV. We did watch *Fireball XL 5* and *Four Feather Falls* or *Thunderbirds*. On Saturday nights, we watched *Doctor Who* or *Dixon of Dock Green*

I always seemed to be able to find ways to make a living and I had fun doing it

SAINT PAUL'S CATHEDEREL CHOIR

Even in the most prestigious of places in England there's still room for some fun, even if it is a serious occasion!!

IAN AND I were picked from our choir to sing Handel's "Messiah" at St. Paul's Cathedral as a Christmas Special, which was to be broadcasted over BBC radio live that Christmas. We were picked because we could reach "Top C," which for us was a breeze. We both traveled together on the tube from Boston Manor to St. Paul's and walked the remainder to the cathedral.

We practiced from October to December in 1962, and the final recital was over three nights the week before Christmas. We were part of a large London Choir that joined the St. Paul's choir for the event, which we sang together with a bunch of apparently famous sopranos, altos, tenors, and bass singers who each had the solos. In front of us was a large orchestra that accompanied our singing, and we were all conducted by a famous conductor, though I can't remember his name now; but it was doctor something or other!

We rehearsed every Tuesday, and as the time to our performance came closer, it became Tuesdays and Thursdays. We robed in one of the crypts under the huge cathedral, and next to where we got changed into our choir clothes was a huge iron funeral carriage. The carriage was made to be drawn by six huge Clydesdales and had four large spoked wheels and was all made of black cast iron. The top that held a coffin was very ornate, but we thought it must have been very, very heavy to pull along. We sometimes laid on the platform, pretending to be dead while trying to imagine what it must have been like to actually be in it, but hopefully we would never ever find that out.

It had one great use for Ian and I, though, as somewhere to put our sandwiches on for the break. There we were both sitting on the driver's seat, munching away when the dean of the cathedral came over and really told us off for desecrating the carriage. We couldn't understand it; it was old and was not in use at the moment, so what was the big deal?

As we were to find out, the funeral carriage was made for Queen Victoria and her husband Prince Albert, though little did we care about that except that it was great for keeping our sandwiches on while we were practicing and for sitting in the driver's bench seat while eating them during the one break or when the conductor was going through stuff with the orchestra. Sometimes try as you might, you just can't do the right thing!

As the time drew near, we were ready for our performance, and although we were both placed in the front row, right in front of us was the orchestra, and we were next to the cellists.

On the opening night, Ian and I agreed to out-sing all of the rest of the choir, which was some fifty people, and pretended that we had a volume control in front of us when we sang the "Hallelujah" chorus. We could both reach "top C" with ease and decided that on that refrain we would gradually get louder and louder as we reached the crescendo, building up to the highest note of the whole performance.

The cellists in front of us all watched as we began the "Hallelujah" chorus refrain, "King of Kings and Lord of Lords"; and although we both sang it "normally" on our rehearsal nights, we really turned up the volume on the actual performance night to see if we could be heard on the radio during the recording of the performance.

We sang the chorus so loud and with so much gusto as we both turned our fingers as if we were turning our volume control up each trying to outdo the other. We were mouthing the words perfectly with real exaggerated syllables like true professional singers. We were grinning from ear to ear as the cellists in front of us were glancing at us out of the corner of their eyes at our outstanding and perfect pitched high notes, or so we preferred to think.

At the end of the performance, we all went down to the crypt, and the conductor told us that was one of the best he had conducted, especially the "Hallelujah" chorus, which was in no small part down to Ian and I. To sing in Saint Paul's Cathedral and to sing Handel's "Messiah" there as choir boys was, even for Ian and I, a huge honor; and we were so glad that had been given the opportunity. The special sandwich cart, placed there just for us, was the icing on the cake; and ever since that one Christmas, I have always loved Handel's "Messiah." And when I hear the "Hallelujah" chorus, I go right back to that one moment in time.

I learned that though my own part in an event may be quite small; the sum is often greater than the parts. Each performer had practiced for hours and hours on their specific parts. The finished product was absolutely incredible. I took this into my work environment and always sought the help from others in my company.

THE LONDON FOG

Even the smallest memories as a child are treasures to the adult!

THE LONDON FOG was very real in the fifties and early sixties and came down so thick you couldn't see anything three feet in front of you. This was no ordinary fog; this was "smog." Still, there was no getting off school, and we had to walk there anyway. Internet hadn't been invented, so there was no banner at the bottom of the screen telling us that school was out because of the fog.

What some of us did was to walk along the edge of the pavement with one foot on the road and one foot on the pavement, counting the side roads along the way and having to get right up to the street signs, which were always located on a wall on the corner of each street. It was very unusual being out in that thick "pea-souper." There was absolutely no sound as the fog or, as it was really called "the smog," was so dense it deadened all sounds. I quite liked it as I could see if I knew the way to school as if I was "blindfolded."

There were no cars on the roads as none could drive through it; so all was very, very still. As I walked through the smog, I used to sing at the top of my voice any song I wanted on the way to and from school and pretended to be a pop singer. I knew all of the words, for what I was singing, and I was certain that I was an impressive singer; but if I wasn't, I didn't care anyway.

It was not for several years later, in 1961, that all the London houses had to change their fires over to clean burning coal, so London would be rid of the smog. This was called the "clean air act," and all of our fireplaces had to be converted so they could burn the clean burning coke instead of the hard and rough natural coal.

In winter, the flat bed coal truck would slowly pass by traveling down all of the streets, and the coal men would deliver huge heavy black sacks of coal into our coal shed at the back of the house. The men were always covered from head to toe in black coal dust, and they wore a leather hat with a neck and shoulder cover that would come down from their head at the back to protect their neck from the sharp pieces of coal coming out of the bags. They would heft the bag that weighed one hundredweight, onto their shoulders from the flat bed of the truck, and sometimes even one on each shoulder and tip them into our coal shed.

One winter, in 1963, the snow came down so thick it was three feet high and stacked up all over the streets in drifts. I loved it—no school. I did, however, have my paper round and turned up to do it walking the first footprint in the brand-new snow at 6:00 a.m. Richard didn't bother to do his, and the paper shop manager was so surprised to see me he gave me double the money for each bag I delivered. I made out like a bandit, and off I went to deliver the morning papers. It took me all day; and after each round, I went back for more, getting two and six for each full bag I delivered door to door.

I loved the fresh new snow and loved being the first and only footprints along the now completely quiet roads. Normally, I made ten shillings for the week; but on that day, I made two pounds, which was amazing to me. I bought a new Dinky toy, which I had been looking at for months. It was a black and silver Bentley Continental complete with very real-looking jeweled headlights and suspension that steered if you pressed on one side while rolling the car forward. It was my best toy and was very real-looking I kept it for years.

When the snow came down like that, I loved all of the white trees and covered streetlamps. The lamps cast a bright glow in the night, and all the world was quiet and still. I even remember the lamp lighter who would come 'round our street to check on the streetlights in case any did not light. He always had a ladder with him, and I watched as he placed the ladder on one of the arms that went out from the lamp and climb up to check on the lamp or repair it if it didn't light properly.

Sometimes I would just go out of the house when I saw him coming and walk with the lamp lighter, chatting as we walked together down my street. There was never any danger at night, and London for me was perfect. The lamp lighter told me stories of the things he had seen when lighting the lamps, and I was fascinated to listen to what he told me. Though he was old, he managed to climb up every lamp he needed to without ever getting tired. He wore a flat hat, a scarf around his neck, a coat over his overalls, and a pair of leather boots; and his name was Tom.

Once every month, we would hear the rag and bone man calling as he came slowly down all of the streets. "rag 'n bone," he would shout, which he repeated as he rode slowly while sitting behind his horse on an old cart full of old broken bicycles, washing wringers, and any bits of metal you wanted to give or sell him if he wanted to buy. If not, he would take it anyway for free.

Also, there was a gypsy knife sharpener who would slowly go down the streets, on a gypsy caravan pulled along by a cart horse. The milkman would also deliver milk and groceries, billing us every week from a book where we had our own page. Our milkman, whose name was Ron, would arrive early in the morning and deliver bottles of gold top, silver top, or blue top milk from Job's Dairy along with any other dairy items we asked for. The service was a little more expensive, but after all, it was delivered door to door; and Mom would leave a note in one of the empty bottles that were left outside the front door.

If we missed or needed anything, I would cycle all around the streets to find where the Job's Milk's electric van was located to get butter, eggs, or anything we had forgotten to leave on the note. I knew his rounds by heart and where to find him at any time of the day. If he was heading back toward my house, I would wait until he set off and hang on to the back of his van while riding my bike for a free lift; he knew I was there but didn't mind at all.

Everything had its own special smell—the night, the snow, the early morning, our church, the coal, autumn, and the London fog. I could close my eyes and know where I was by the scent of it.

As time drifted on and because of Mrs. Osborne, my case worker from the Middlesex County Council, I had been allowed to go back to Lowestoft for my holidays, which gave Dad a break and gave me some of my roots back again. I loved visiting Auntie; and now that I was older, and with Beatrice and William living there, we found plenty to do all summer long. The nurses were becoming more and more interesting to me now that I was a young teen as well. There was one nurse in particular called Maureen, who was eighteen and seemed very interested in me. We went out a few nights together and walked along the beach at night.

I also had my best "other friend," Beatrice; and we did everything together like brother and sister. We would go to the beach, spending all day as often as we could there. Auntie would sometimes take us out in her little car "Arabella," which was a 1937 black Austin Seven convertible, down the coast road for afternoon tea.

Auntie even taught me to drive Arabella when I was just eleven years old, and I have a photo that Beatrice took of me driving the car around our driveway, that is until I accidentally left the lights on a caused a flat battery. The car was difficult for me to drive as it had a crash gearbox requiring that I double declutch to change gear up and down, and I could only just see over the bonnet.

I learned never to take anything for granted as everything can change in a heartbeat which it did for me many times over.

ANOTHER MOM

A new broom sweeps clean!

AROUND TWO YEARS after Mom had died Dad told us both that he had found a new girlfriend. Rich and I were enthralled at this news and immediately bombarded him with questions about her.
"What's her name? How old is she? Is she pretty? Are you going to marry her? When will we meet her?" Well, after several months, we finally got to meet Jill, Dad's new fiancée, one Sunday afternoon in April. We both got up to the bay window at the front of our house to see if we could see her walking with him down our street.

Dad was forty-two, and Jill was only twenty-one. Richard was fourteen and I was now twelve, so things were going to be very interesting. Jill had red hair and was quite attractive; Richard was mixed in his feelings for her as he was seeing her as replacing his real mom. For me, she was my third mother so it was OK by me. But for Richard, it was just two short years since his mom had died. I think he was both excited at having another mom live with us and upset at the short time since she passed away.

Jill came round more and more often and eventually got to stay whole weekends, arriving on Friday after work with Dad and leaving with him for work on Monday morning. Jill introduced us to her younger sister, Avril, who was a blonde and very different from Jill. She also introduced us to her mother and father whom we called Nan and Pop. I liked both of them, especially Pop. He was very much like a grandfather I had never had; in fact, I didn't know what having a grandfather was really like, but I knew I liked him.

Dad and Jill got married on May 23, and Jill moved in with us permanently from then on. All was well for a while at least. Jill was quite intelligent and did crosswords and read the *Manchester Guardian* and the *Telegraph*.

Jill was quite a strong and dominant personality and soon began to rule the house. Dad was just happy to have a partner to help him and to be a companion to him. They would sit together and do the crossword.

I loved my Dad; he was very kind and did all he could to stop Richard and I from fighting. I too was very strong. Actually, on reflection, I was stubborn and would never give in; and we often got into fights after school.

Looking back, it is obvious now that we were both reacting to the events of Mom's death and her replacement by Jill.

Jill and Auntie Sis didn't get along at all, and Jill was always complaining about her to Dad when he got home from work. Jill began a campaign to get rid of Aunt Sis, even though she had looked after Richard and I for so long after Mom died and had looked after Dad in his very needy times.

Auntie Sis had cooked, cleaned, and did all our washing; and we never even thought about it. She used to ask me to get odd items of shopping and to cycle down to Hanwell to get groceries. Sis had been a real surrogate mom during these years when I was nine to twelve years old, until she came up against Jill. Sis had left her home and her life in Manchester to come down to London to look after us all.

Shortly after Jill had come to live with us, Richard and I heard sobbing from Aunt Sis's room. We knocked and entered and saw Aunt Sis in tears. We wanted to find out what was wrong. "I am moving back to Manchester," she told us and continued sobbing. "She (Jill) doesn't want me here anymore, and I thought this was my home. She gave Bert an ultimatum, her or me." I didn't know what to do for her. I was so sad, but I could do nothing about this. One didn't question Jill about these things as it would lead to a screaming and shouting fit.

Finally, only a few weeks after that tearful day, the day came when Aunt Sis moved out. She kissed us both goodbye and walked off down the street in her coat and "Ena Sharples" hat, without looking back and never to return. Dad called Richard and I into the front room only six months afterward and told us that Aunt Sis, his sister, had died. Rich and I knew she had died from a broken heart. I never forgave Jill as I knew what she had done to orchestrate minor issues that she had created to make Aunt Sis look like a troublemaker. I often thought of Aunt Sis and hoped she was in a better place up there with the angels. Jill didn't bat an eyelid; and life went on, another small door to close.

I soon realized that actually life just keeps moving on, and there's nothing we can do will stop it. For me, as I have said before, it was all normal that people around me either died or went away; and I was after all quite used to it by now, and these constant changes were after all part of my life.

Life at home settled down, once again; but living with Jill in the house was very difficult as she didn't get on with either Richard or me.

I couldn't help feeling that Dad had been conned into getting married and spoke of this to Rich. He thought the same but also said, "She's here to stay, and as long as Dad is happy, that's all we can hope for." I, of course, thought about what he had said and agreed with him, which I didn't do very often.

For two years, life moved on with Jill, Rich, and I battling over every little thing. Life got difficult with Richard and I fighting almost every night when we got home from school before Jill or Dad got home from work.

In winter 1963, I was now thirteen, and Dad became very ill with bronchitis. London had had a bad winter with heavy snow and fog. Dad was too ill to go to work and was taken to hospital five miles away. He stayed there for what seemed like weeks and weeks. I cycled over to see him every Saturday afternoon after I had reluctantly done my mammoth number of chores and saw him steadily getting worse.

He was let out of hospital in December 1963 to spend Christmas at home with us. Little did Rich or I know that this was to be the last Christmas we would ever have together as a family with Dad.

I thought that all would be OK again at home, not realizing God's plan for me had changed yet again. Immediately after Christmas, Dad was admitted back into hospital but this time into something called an intensive care unit in Acton Hospital. Again, I went to see him, but now he was in an oxygen tent and looked so very weak he couldn't recognize me. His breathing was very ragged and seemed to get worse and worse.

His condition changed into something called double pneumonia, and that had gotten into both of his lungs, making his condition worse.

We went back to school after New Year's, and then on January 7, I was called into the headmaster's, Mr. O'Brian, office, which was normally to get the cane; but this was different. "You have to go home immediately, Tony. Your father is gravely ill," he told me, and I left school immediately to walk home. When I got home at around 10:00 a.m., Jill, Rich and I went immediately to see Dad, leaving by taxi as we had no car at that time.

When we arrived at Acton Hospital, the atmosphere was all wrong for me; the nurses and hospital staff were calm and spoke softly to us. I was told I could go in and see Dad, this time though he was gasping for every breath he took and could not focus at all but was staring and gasping. It was awful; my lovely dad, who had looked after me and had kept us together, was so ill. He didn't know I was even there. Jill and Rich came in, a few minutes later, to join me; but Dad died at 11:00 a.m. while we were there with him. I felt absolutely desolate once again, so sad at losing Dad. I remember putting my arm around Rich and said, "It's just you and me now." We both disliked Jill, and we did not look forward to spending time with her without dad.

Once again, I had no one to talk to about how utterly desolate I now felt at losing another parent. I loved Dad, and he was everything to me. I loved him for keeping us together and being able to keep me in his family. So once again, I kept my feelings to myself; and once again, I was completely alone and had to find a way to close another door and to move on. I couldn't allow myself to show how I felt. I didn't know how to as I was becoming used to having to move on from people I loved.

Life to me seemed like a series of turbulence, just learning to trust people who were then yanked out of my life. I didn't understand what I may have done wrong, so I just kept going and had to put these bad things behind me.

Jill took us home and told me to go back to school "immediately" as I was not needed at home. I couldn't grasp that on leaving from school to go to see Dad, I was now returning without a Dad. I walked slowly back to school in a daze and arrived just after lunch. I was numb with shock and found it difficult to focus on anything. I sat there quietly keeping to myself, thinking about Dad not being with me anymore, not wanting to show any emotion in front of my class, even if I knew what emotion I should feel. I was deeply sad but was afraid that if I showed emotion I would show everyone my true feelings, and I couldn't do that as I had to be strong, always!

During that afternoon break, on Monday, 7 January, I was walking with one of my friends, Tommy Costello, and told him that my Dad had just died "this morning at 11:00 a.m." (always the details).

He stopped and looked at me, in shock, saying, "Tony, you're kidding. Your dad just died, and you're here at school." And I said, "Yes, that's what I had to leave school for. I went to see him in hospital one last time, and he just died right while I was there."

Tommy said he was so sorry and said, "Why are you back here at school, Tony? If my dad had died, I would be at home." It's funny how you remember some things as clearly as if they had happened just today, but I remembered this one thing in that way and even exactly where we were when I told him. I appreciated his concern but asked that he please keep it to himself as I didn't want to appear needy or weak. I kept up the brave front, while feeling sick and empty inside. I blamed Jill for this feeling and could never, ever forgive her for not letting me be at home that morning with Rich to help us both get through this very sad time.

I didn't want to go home from school that day, as it was sad and the atmosphere was dreadful. Rich was crying his eyes out and was sobbing the whole time. The curtains were pulled close in our house for the second time now. Jill seemed to cope just fine and took complete control of all matters. Rich and I didn't know who to talk to or what to think.

We did have each other and spent hours in our bedroom over the next few weeks, just sitting there saying nothing, just alone and putting a wall around us of quiet thoughts and our memories. That was one of our really close times together. I closed the door in my mind, as I had done each other time someone I loved had died, or when I was in that awful place with my stepdad in Acton, and had to move on with my life once again; though I was scared that I would be moved into another children's home.

Sometimes fixing one problem creates another!

LIFE WITHOUT DAD

Resilience was a tool I didn't ask for but one I learned to use early on.

L IFE ONCE AGAIN slowly settled down for me. I began to go out at night and skipped going to Scouts. Just what I need, I remember thinking—a little fun in my life. And I made new friends at Bordeston Secondary Modern School for Boys."

Jill went to work in the mornings, leaving home at 7:00 a.m., and locked me and Rich out of the house to wait for school time, which wasn't until eight thirty. The neighbors didn't like that and let me wait inside their house as soon as she turned the corner if it was raining.

I, though, had other plans and took the front door key out of Mom's handbag and had another one cut, which I kept hidden in the front garden well hidden from Jill. Rich and I would sit on our small front wall, wait till she went to work, and wave goodbye, like good little boys; then as soon as she went 'round the corner at the bottom of our road, we would get the key from under a stone in the front garden and let ourselves back in to the house. Many good and interesting things were to be found under a stone in a front garden.

One of my new friends, Wally (his real name was Alan Walsh), became great friends with me; and we would go out and climb into people's backyards, go scrumping for apples, often getting chased out of people's gardens by dogs or house owners (I was always being chased).

Generally, we did as much as we could to have fun. Wally only had only a mom and no father. I didn't know why and didn't ask.

I was, however, going down the wrong road; and I lost interest in many things I had loved before. Ian had been moved out of Bordeston by his mom and started going to Hounslow College, so he wasn't around at school anymore; and before he left, he was having math lessons by our teacher, Mr. Cardiff.

Next thing I knew was that I had to start going to the Ealing Child Guidance Center in Ealing Broadway. That was a hoot. I had to look at all these stupid cards with smudges and blobs of black on them and tell a counselor what they reminded me of. "A dog crapping," or "Just a blob," or anything I could think of that was not what I thought they wanted me to say. I don't know where this led to; but I was aware that Mrs. Osborne, my child care officer, came 'round to see me more and more often.

Finally, one Saturday morning, Jill told me I had to leave the house and was going to boarding school in Cheltenham and would be leaving after the summer holidays. I spent months begging her not to go and offering to be a better person and to do everything I could not to go.

Nothing made any difference; I was going, and that was that. "So how often will I be home?" I asked. "Summer holidays, Easter and Christmas, and that's all and only if I decide that I want you back," she told me.

Shortly before I was to leave for school, Pop, Jill's father, died. I was once again sad that another person that I loved being with had died. Actually, Pop committed suicide and I never knew why. He was a printer and had very bad eczema, maybe that was it, but I thought close the door and move on Tony. I spoke to Rich and said to him that he would have to be alone now in the house with Jill. He didn't like it, but there was nothing he could do. I realize now that Rich must have been scared of what was to happen to him, though I didn't realize it at the time.

When circumstances are out of our own control, we have to 'go with the flow' and do our best to make good of the things that life throws at us in order to get by and move on with life.

BATTLEDOWN MANOR

I had no idea how I was going to handle this, so I trusted my instincts.

AUTUMN 1963, I was being shipped off to boarding school. Jill said goodbye at the front door and told me how to get to the coach stop along the Uxbridge Road, and off I went. I struggled off with my suitcase, which had all my clothes in, and made it to the coach stop, having to frequently stop along the way to put my case down for a rest.   I wish they had invented wheels for cases at that time. The black-and-white coach finally arrived, and off I went to boarding school. The journey was around four hours with a stop halfway at Stokenchurch in the Cotswold's.

When I arrived at Cheltenham's main terminal, I was met by a very military-looking man with a handlebar moustache, Mr. Ward, who asked me who I was, ticked off my name, and then informed me who he was and told me to "go and wait by the car."   The car, a beautiful black Jaguar Mark 9, looked like a Bentley. The Jag, as we called it, had red leather seats and had a unique smell of leather and petrol; and I loved it. It also had walnut trays that came out of the back of the front seats for having drinks. Two other boys were on the black-and-white coach with me, but I didn't know them yet.

So three of us were taken to "Battledown Manor" in Charlton Kings, just outside Cheltenham, and arrived late afternoon on a Sunday in September 1963—me, Bobby Galvin, and Seamus Noon.

 The boarding school was a four-hundred-year-old manor house in acres of wooded and hilly grounds. Battledown Manor sat atop a hill and looked very imposing as it stood alone looking out over the Cotswold Hills. It was huge and had lots of leaded widows all 'round on every window, gray flag stoned walls, and a large oak front door with big square studs all over it, set back into a large gray stone porch. It got its name from a battle that had taken place on the hill behind the school six hundred years before.

My first impression once inside was of a very severe difference from what I was used to at home. I suppose this move was because Jill Wanted me out of the house. Well, whatever. I was here now and had to get on with it. One of my gifts—to be able to deal with sudden changes and new places to live in and to call "home"—helped me once again; and so here I was, and I had to deal with it.

As I entered the main hall, I saw it was paneled all the way up the great staircase and all the way onto the first floor. There were old paintings on the walls, and the image was exactly as one would have imagined a boarding school to be. I thought as I looked around, *This will be home for me now, so I might as well make the best of it.* Outside the main house, at the back, were stables, outhouses, and a paved backyard next to the stables, which overlooked the kitchen and "ward room."

The yard was paved in gray flagstones, and opposite the main house was a set of inner stables with a large apartment above. The roof of the stables was covered in moss. The chimneys went up very high, and there were a number of them. At the back was the entrance that we were to use and the "wardroom" where all our shoes, coats, and hats were kept and where we were expected to change before entering the school. The "wardroom" led through into a large kitchen with an Aga cooking stove. The kitchen was always warm and inviting, and I liked it in there.

I was immediately shown my dorm, sharing it with ten other boys, on the first floor, for the younger boys, and was told which was my bed and to go down stairs when the gong sounded, for dinner. Dinner comprised two slices of toast, a cup of tea, and a poached egg! I was starving, having traveled from Ealing on a three-and-a-half-hour coach trip. We had to stand up and be introduced to all the other boys.

I sat next to a black boy called Bobby Galvin, who had also arrived earlier that day with me but who had been at the school for six months and knew the ropes. Bobby and I quickly became friends, and I learned that he was from inner city London and was there because he had no real home anymore, as his dad and mom couldn't look after him anymore.

I decided not to ask any questions. Two of the older boys I met there were Shaunty, who came from Hanwell, and Dadsie, who didn't like me on sight. Bobby warned me to stay clear of these two older boys as they were trouble. Like I cared!

Well, life settled down for the next period in my life. Some of the lessons were in a local school in the lower part of Cheltenham, where I was quite different from the local boys. Many of my new friends from day school didn't even have socks and often came to school wearing jeans and no school uniform at all. I wasn't used to that since it was an absolute necessity at Bordeston.

I cycled to my day school from Charlton Kings, which was a ride six miles downhill, right across the other end of town, all the way there, and of course six miles up hill all the way back.

I was placed in a class where the local boys were really dim or seemed to be to me. I was classed as eighteen months advanced for my age—big deal; it didn't help me any. It made schoolwork boring as I knew all of the stuff, having done it eighteen months before!

So anyway, Dadsie and Shaunty picked on me most of the time; and I always gave back as hard as I got it from them.

After all, I had been used to an older brother who had taught me how to look after myself.

Dadsie would often lie in wait for me while I was walking through the school and would pounce when I was unaware. It would always lead to a fight, and we would both be in trouble. Apart from that, things settled down quickly for me, and I got used to being thrust into a completely different lifestyle of a boarding school.

To get to the school from the road meant walking up a long tree-lined lane called Greenway Lane, and it was unlit at night. I went to night school activities for art and other stuff, which I didn't mind at all as it got me out of the school and meant I could be alone all the way to and from Elmfield School where my evening classes were; and I cycled back to Battledown Manor.

I loved cycling to and from school at night and would walk up Greenway Lane, listening to the wind in the trees and watching fascinated at the way the nighttime clouds moved silently across the sky, lit by the moonlight. Sometimes I would just sit quietly at the side of the road and smell the scent in the air and listen to the small night sounds all around me. I often shone my cycle lamp out across the fields to see the many pairs of eyes caught in my beam. I would then switch the torch off and switch it back on to see which eyes had moved, only to freeze again and stare at my light beam.

I was only scared of the dark at first, then I realized I could "tune in" to the night and my surroundings and I wasn't afraid at all. I became at one with the night sounds, and if I moved quietly, I became part of everything around me.

At my new school, they were fascinated with my very proper and excellent English, thanks to Auntie, and would listen intently as I talked noting the difference between my accent and their west-country accents. There was a gang of around seven rough kids, led by a boy named Robinson. Well, Robinson never led any trouble directly but always steered the others to cause trouble, especially for me as I was definitely different.

One day, in January that first winter after I had arrived when it had been snowing, we were all walking back from football, even though the fields were frozen. I was smashed in the side of my head by a piece of ice thrown at me full force by a little red-haired loudmouth called Ginger. Though it hurt like mad and made my ear bleed, I turned toward him and slowed down, as he threw it from behind me, letting him and his buddies catch up. As he got alongside me, I said very quietly, "If you do that one more time, I'm going to knock you out."

"Oh yeah?" he said. "You and whose army?" At which point, my two friends, Dave Soule and Nigel Rich, began to distance themselves from me. I remembered someone, maybe my brother Rich, saying to me to always go for the loudest and take him out first.

He looked at his "buddies" who were daring him to do it again and picked up another piece of ice and threw it as hard as he could. It caught me in the side of my head again, so I turned toward him, not showing any sign of what I was going to do, and walked right up to him slowly and deliberately, and punched him as hard as I could, catching him full in the face. He went down like a sack of spuds, with his nose broken and with blood all over the place. He laid there in the snow, out cold.

I turned to the others that were with him that had been egging him on, and squared up to all of them and as cool as I could, though I didn't feel cool at all and looked Robinson right in the eye. I pointed right at his face and said, "What about you? Do you want the same too?" And as I said it, I moved right in his face, daring him to do or say anything. God, I was at the point of not caring now as I had committed. As Rich once said to me, "Tony, once you commit, you can't back down . . . ever!"

No one had ever squared up to these kids, and they were absolutely unsure of "the new boy." Fortunately, they backed down. I didn't think I could take them all, but I knew one thing: if they decided to start, I would take Robinson right out in the first second. Images of my time being beaten up in Acton flashed before me, and I knew "that's not happening to me again."

After that though we became good friends, and Ginger treated me with respect. He told me later that he didn't know what hit him, saying that I was so fast that he wouldn't ever do that again. But I was not out to prove myself and told him of what had happened to me when I was eight, and I told him I would never let that happen to me again. I didn't like that feeling afterward though as I never have liked hurting anyone, but sometimes in life you have to make a stand.

I got in with another bad crowd in Cheltenham, who I used go out with on "wanders." My new friends were John Brown and Dave (I never knew

Dave's second name or even if he had one). They came from very poor families and never had money, socks, or sometimes even a shirt, only wearing old worn-out jackets. John was a scruff with dark curly hair, while Dave was a blonde scruff with a mop of wavy hair.

During these "wanders," they would case out a block of flats with a view to breaking into them to steal things. They could be in and out of the flats in what seemed like a few seconds. They would come running out to where I was standing, and we would leg it down the road as fast as we could. Though I never ever broke into anyone's house, I loved the excitement of being with these two. We had such fun doing everything and anything we wanted. I took a change of clothes and keep my uniform in my duffel bag so no one would recognize my school. I had to change again on the way home before I got back to Battledown Manor.

After that first year, I was awarded a holiday to Austria for getting excellent results at school. It was to be a three-week vacation, leaving by train with a load of other children who had also won the trip. It was brilliant as I had never been abroad before, and we stayed in a mountain hotel high up in the Alps in a town called Innermanzing. The trip was because of Mr. Ward who had put a good word in for me with the Ealing County Council after seeing my excellent report. The ultra-cool part was that there was a local Gasthoff (bar), and we could order beer, at fourteen years old! Smooth! Once again, I found myself loving the food; and at breakfast, we had chocolate-flavored semolina, which I loved. Once again, I always managed to get seconds and thirds enough to keep me going till lunchtime. Each evening, a group of us would go to the local Gasthoff to have some beers and have a good time. We were treated like young adults for once, which was very different from how we were treated at our different schools.

I saw on reflection that to place my trust in God and my own instincts turned out to be a very good decision as a way to deal with this tough event.

RICH AT LAST

Never assume what the contents are by the print on the box

ONE SUNNY SATURDAY afternoon, as me, Bobby Galvin, and Michael Shepherd (another boy from boarding school) were walking back from the local sweet shop, we saw a van parked on the side of the lane with the back doors open. Inside there was a display box, the kind that would normally have lots of bars of Cadbury's chocolate in. The three of us looked around and saw no one inside the van or anywhere near.

As we were deciding what to do, Michael reached into the back of the van and grabbed the box, whereupon we all legged up Greenway Lane as fast as we could.

We ran right up the lane and into the woods next to our school and sat on the ground behind a low wall that surrounded an old swimming pool in the middle of the woods.

Excitedly, we all peered into the box as Michael opened it up and saw not chocolate bars but loads of money. There were bags of coins—penny pieces, half crowns, tanners, two bobs—all in separate little brown paper money bags. There were also lots of bank notes, a whole stack of them, and a pile of checks.

We couldn't believe our luck. "Let's count it all and split it three ways." We all agreed, not even thinking about the consequences of what we had just done. The total of the money we had just pinched came to three hundred and eighty-four pounds, which in 1964 and for a bunch of boarding school kids on two and six pence pocket money a week was an absolute bloody fortune.

Well, pretty soon, we realized what could happen, so we warned Michael, saying "Don't get caught, and whatever you do, don't spend any of it at the local sweet shop down the road. Otherwise, she will call the old man, and we'll all get caught."

So we hid the box, with all the money inside, behind a stone in the wall by the old swimming pool in the middle of the woods. The Cotswold walls comprise of flat Cotswold stones laid on top of one another to a height of about four feet high and were not ever cemented.

Our wall was all around the pool, in the middle of the woods, and was a perfect hiding place.

We began to pull stones out of the wall until we found one with a space behind it and placed the stone back into the wall with the box of money hidden behind it and marked our "stone" with a scratch mark.

Later the next day, which was Sunday, Bobby and I went to the wall in the woods and took several bags of coins. I don't know what Bobby did with his, but I cycled on down the hill toward Cheltenham and hid the bags of money in several front gardens, inside hedges or under stones where they would not be found. I hid around fifty pounds in all.

Well, I went to my day school and took John Brown and Dave out for a slap-up dinner at their favorite café, saying to the waitress, "The dinner's on me." I did this for two weeks, buying them things they wanted and enjoyed doing it. We bought pens, lighters, bottles of cider, cigarettes, and anything we felt we wanted. Though I didn't smoke initially, I learned very quickly. I had loads of stuff, as did Bobby, but we didn't know what Michael did, until later.

Around three weeks later, as I was coming back on Saturday afternoon from a "spending spree" with my friends from the other side of town, I walked through the front door only to hear that one sound that can freeze the blood "Tony Moore!" I heard being shouted at me, and I looked around.

There sitting at his desk in the front hall was Mr. Ward, our principal He strode over to me and grabbed me by my collar, dragging me through the hall and into his study, and shut the door behind us. There sitting on the sofa was Michael and Bobby. Michael was crying, and I knew what had happened.

The old man, Mr. Ward, as we called him, asked us what we knew about a large amount of stolen money taken from the back of a van some four weeks before while parked along Greenway Lane one Saturday afternoon.

I attempted to deny all knowledge of this heinous act and began talking as fast as I could to deny everything. "It wasn't me. I was never there. How could you think I would do something like that? I don't know what you're talking about."

Well, just as I was getting into my full stride of complete and utter denial, Bobby quietly told me that they had told the old man everything. "He's even been to our secret hiding place and has got all the remaining cash." "Great," I exclaimed. "So what happens now?" I was cool as a cucumber. "The police are on their way from Cheltenham police station and will be here in a few minutes," the old man said. He sat and stared at me for a long time. "I thought better of you, Tony. I didn't believe you could be part of this massive theft," he said. I couldn't think of anything to say, so I said nothing at all. I was, however, furiously thinking, *How can I get out of this?*

I can honestly say I wasn't really scared or intimidated by the two huge cops that arrived to interview us, but I had no idea what was going to happen.

They took us down town in a black police car and split us up into different rooms to be "interviewed." On the way downtown, I very quietly said to Bobby and Michael, "Whatever you do, don't tell them about the booze or the cigarettes. Otherwise, we'll be in even more trouble." Once at the police station, a rather drab place with opaque windows between each room, tiled floors, and old drab furniture, we were to be interviewed about what we had done.

They began to question me, and I had to make up all sorts of stuff I had never bought as I still had about eighty pounds stashed in various places. Eventually, as I couldn't tell them all of the things that I had bought with the money—the cigs and the booze—I had to admit that I had money stashed in various places along the route into town from the school.

"All right," they said, "show us." So off we went for the long walk back to Charlton Kings. A police car was following us, with me walking between the two cops on either side. As we walked along the way back to Battledown Manor, I stopped and told them, "There behind that wall in the front garden under that big stone on the left or under that hedge over there." So in they went and lifted the stone, and underneath there was a bag of cash. Then farther along, I stopped again and told them, "Under the hedge on the right." So they reached under the hedge and found another bag.

In all, I had twenty hiding places for my "stash." By the time we were finished, they were both chuckling and were truly amazed that I could remember all of the places where I had hidden the money.

Finally, when I had managed to account for most of what I had said I had spent, they took me back to the school.

When we arrived back, the old man was both furious and intrigued at the audacity of what we had done. Audacious or not, we were gated, grounded, for a month, and had to do chores. Mine were potato peeling for the whole school and shoe cleaning every day and every weekend for four weeks. I sat by myself in the kitchen, peeling whole sacks of spuds, or again out by myself in the ward room shining shoes. I manage to get covered in shoe polish—black, brown, or ox blood—over my hands on my face as I wiped the sweat from my forehead and all over my clothes.

Well, I still had around sixty pounds left, which I had accounted for in my statements to the two cops, but still had hidden away This all happened around eight weeks before we were to break up for summer hols. I knew we would be searched just in case we had stashed money for the holidays. I hid my money in two places. One was in my sock, carefully rolled around my ankle. The other was in my Brownie 127 camera, inside where the film was supposed to be. At the back of the camera was a small red window showing you how many pictures you had used. So I carefully rolled the bank notes inside the camera around the film winder and stretched a one-pound note across the red film window so that the "number 1" fitted right behind the small red window. I then very carefully closed the camera and reviewed my handiwork; it was perfect and undetectable and showed that there was picture number 1 in the frame ready to be used. Boy, would I make an excellent master criminal or even a master spy! Even Dadsie and Bobby had a new respect for me after knowing what we had done. Michael though had to go away to another school as he had a history of stealing stuff that went way back. We never saw or heard from him again.

So the last day of school finally arrived. I had my final stash well hidden in my sock and in my camera. I was sitting at breakfast, on the last day of school, with Bobby (as always) and was actually feeling very nervous. The old man was sitting at the head table and kept looking at my feet as I grew more and more nervous.

Then his voice boomed out across the breakfast room, "Tony Moore!" I froze, and he said, "Stand up, boy." So I stood trying to be cool as I could. He looked at my feet directly where some of my stash was stuffed down my sock. "Why are your shoelaces untied, boy? Tie them up and get on with your breakfast," he said loudly. I looked down and saw what he had been looking at the whole time, my as usual untied shoelaces. I bent down—relieved that it was just that and not that he had seen my stash—to retie my shoelaces and carefully checked out and flattened the money lump in my sock, pushing it further down.

We left school for the summer hols, and I was taken to the black-and-white bus station in Mr. Ward's beautiful black Jag. I was so happy and relieved I could hardly wait to get home and spend my last stash. I was going to have a summer of all summers.

Once home, Jill gave me the riot act, saying nothing good would ever come of me! Rich, however, wanted to know if I had any money left. I knew he would go through my things to find any money I had left. He never found my money, and I had the best holiday I ever had, absolutely loads of money to spend all holiday. I bought as many sweets and comics as I could and actually bought a one-foot-high stack of used Marvel comics, negotiating a deal with the shop owner, and spent the next week reading and eating sweets. Brilliant!

I learned that sometimes getting away with something is more meaningful than getting caught!

A NEW FIRE ESCAPE

Even the best inventions for safety can be, for a fourteen-year-old, perfect for other purposes.

WE WENT BACK to school for the next term, and all had calmed down, for a while! We were visited by the local fire chief who declared that we needed a fire escape. Mr. Ward argued that a huge steel staircase would ruin the four-hundred-year-old building. So a compromise was agreed; and on the third floor, windows were to be fitted something called an "inertia seat."

This was the coolest thing I ever saw. It comprised a canvas sling attached to a rope, which was then attached to an inertia reel, which was screwed into one of the huge oak beams in the ceiling above the window.

In the event of a fire, a boy would place the seat around his bottom and climb out of the window. He would then jump out of the window with the canvas sling around his bottom. The rope would then zing you down the outside wall, slowing you down until you reached the ground, a bit like abseiling. After you had climbed off the seat, it would then reel itself back up to the open window. Perfect!

Bobby and I thought this was the perfect way to take our midnight feast outside into the woods where we could smoke and eat and drink, and play music on our tranny without any risk of getting caught.

We thought why not! And I gave it a try, jumping out of the window at midnight. It was so cool whizzing down the wall at midnight when everyone else was asleep, and it worked! Down I went until I reached the ground, sending the seat back up to Bobby waiting at the open window three floors up. He then came down to join me, and we tied off the seat so it would stay at the ground.

We had the greatest time while all was quiet, sneaking into the woods, in the middle of the night, to have our midnight feast.

The way back up was more difficult as we had to climb back up the rope, and then when we were both back in our room, we let the seat back up and tied it off in our bedroom.

Fun is having a healthy outlook on life no matter what.

THE BURNING HEDGE

Smoking can be dangerous for my health!

During my last year at Battledown Manor, I had the chore of mowing the front lawn with Bobby on our motorized push mower. So we went and got the lawn mower from where it was kept in the stables at the side of the school and the five-gallon can of petrol and walked them both to the large sloping front lawn in front of the school, setting the petrol can down next to the long hedgerow that separated the front of the school from the front lawn. As the manor house had been built on a hill overlooking Charlton Kings, the view was imposing, with a clear view of some fifteen miles to the Malvern hills on the horizon.

Well, we started to mow the lawn and got partway through mowing the large lawn and decided to have a smoke break as the job was nearly finished. We got down hidden from view of the school, behind the hedge on the freshly mowed grass and sat down to smoke. As I lit up, gazing over the fine job we had done, though some of the mowing lines were in fact a little crooked, I tossed the match over my shoulder and began to enjoy the moment, after all the work was quite hard and the lawn was huge. As luck would have it, and unbeknownst to me, I threw the match right into the open can of petrol.

What a brilliant shot! What happened next was nothing short of "explosive"! All of a sudden, we heard a whoosh as the petrol can exploded into flame, and we both jumped up fast as we could not sure what to do. The fire immediately caught the whole front hedgerow alight, and the flames shot up high into the air. In fact, the flames were as high as thirty to forty feet as they ignited the very dry four-hundred-year-old hedgerow.

We both started yelling, "fire! fire!" We needn't have bothered though as the flames shot straight up to the level of the upstairs windows and could be seen from as far as the Malvern's, which must have been twenty miles away.

Everyone came rushing out, and Mr. Ward immediately started barking out orders like a real pro fire chief. "Quickly now, you boys, go and get water in anything that will hold it, make a supply chain, and fast!" The flames burned so hot and high that they began to bow all of the leaded windows outward all over the front of our school. "The damn windows are melting!" Mr. Ward shouted, and we all worked even more furiously to put out the fire. Bobby and I quickly put a story together that a spark must have ignited the petrol vapors. The fire was so hot and the flames were scary, it was like looking at a column of sheer flame thirty feet high.

Well, eventually, the flames were put out. and we surveyed the damage. The once beautiful hedgerow was now a series of smoldering stumps that separated the half-mowed lawn. Worse still, the front windows were now forever halfway between a nice leaded set of windows that rose majestically all the way up the front of the house and a series of uneven severely bowed out bay windows. Though we didn't get into trouble . . . much, we were however gated again and had to do even more chores. There was no proof of what we had done by smoking; so in fact, we got away with it.

Though Bobby was black, we were now both the same color as I was covered in soot from head to toe. I visited the school many years later with Ian, and the windows were still all bowed out; but the hedgerow had been superseded by a row of rose bushes, which I thought was a vast improvement on the original hedge, so I knew it had actually happened and it was not a figment of my imagination.

I learned also that fires are bloody scary!

A LAST VISIT FROM JILL

If the actions of someone you know don't make sense it's because what you know is probably not the entire story!

SOME WEEKS BEFORE Easter in 1965, Jill wrote me a letter saying she had decided to come to Cheltenham to see me for a weekend. She had never shown any interest in what I was doing at school, but I was OK that she would come to see me, as long as she brought me money or sweets. "I can only spend a day there as I am far too busy and must get back to Ealing," she announced.

When she came, she seemed uptight, but that was normal for her. Once she arrived, she said a brief hello to me, kissing the air between us, and promptly went into Mr. Ward's study where she stayed for several hours, leaving me standing in the hallway. When she came out, she seemed very flushed and informed me she had to go back home immediately and promptly turned on her heel and left just like that. I thought, *OK, I guess she didn't want to see me after all*. There was no love lost between us; and as long as she wasn't telling me off, or shouting at me, or demanding that I do chores, I was OK with that.

One Saturday afternoon, shortly after that whirlwind visit, when Mr. Ward was making a curry, he called me into the large kitchen and asked if I would like to help him. This was a huge honor as I loved his curry, and none of us boys had ever been asked to help him. He was preparing the most incredible chicken curry in a huge pot and was leaning over the Aga range as he started talking to me. This time, he wasn't talking at me as he usually did but was actually treating me as a grown-up.

"Tony," he began, "what would you do if you had the money to do something with?" I replied, "Depends on how much." "Well," he said, "what if you had, say, one hundred pounds? And I realize that with your past escapades, this is probably a paltry figure, but what if it was yours and it was legal?" Now one hundred pounds was a lot of money at that time, so I thought for a while and replied, "Probably I'd buy a scooter." I waited for his mood to become "normal."

"OK," he said. (what!) "But we'll have to have some rules about this if we go ahead." I couldn't believe what I'd just heard. "Sorry, Sir, did you say yes?" He ignored my response and carried on, "You must pass your driving test and learn to drive it properly, OK?" I immediately agreed! "Where is the money coming from?" I asked. "Let's say it was a gift well deserved," he said and looked at me with a long serious and thoughtful stare. He went on to explain that it was a gift from Jill and left it at that.

I couldn't think why she would ever give me money, but I was to find out pretty soon. I thought nothing of it and couldn't wait to tell Bobby my news.

I just had to wait and see the outcome for all would be revealed.

MY FIRST SET OF WHEELS

What was a token gift, out of guilt, was the world to me.

WELL THIS WAS 1965, and in England at that time, we had mods and rockers. I was definitely a mod. Mods were those that liked fashionable clothes and hairstyles and who wore long parka coats, with a hood often edged with fur, and they all drove around on done up motor scooters.

I already had a parka and used it when I was cycling into town. I was fifteen and was just old enough to drive a scooter. Mods were everywhere. The other group, the rockers, rode motorbikes and wore leather gear. Though I liked motorbikes, I liked the mod look much more.

Well, I was going to move up from being a look-alike mod, riding a push bike, with my full-length parka complete with fur on the hood, to a full-fledged, fully loaded mod and with a scooter!

I told Bobby, and the news got all over the school, and suddenly I was the coolest boy in school. Dadsie hated it, but after all he had done, I was fine with that. There was nothing he wanted more than a scooter, and I was getting one.

So I spent the next weeks poring over the Exchange and Mart making sure I did it when Dadsie was around so he would be so envious.

I was looking for a scooter that I could afford. Finally, I settled on a model LD, which was a Lambretta and a very plain one at that, painted in an insipid light blue. Though it looked like something an old man would be driving, I knew I would do it up with high-chrome exhaust pipes, crash bars, and loads of mirrors all over the front. It would be so cool, and I would be one of them, an actual mod with my own wheels.

I bought it, driving it carefully up the driveway and into one of the stables ready for its transformation into my very own mod mobile! I took it apart and began planning the transformation of my plain "Lambo," which was the name we called a Lambretta, into my mod mobile. It cost me fifty-seven pounds, and with the money I had left over, I transformed it into a dream machine. I bought the best, and noisiest, flared tube silencer I could find and fitted it to the engine. It fitted to the cylinder head and went upward at an angle from the side of the scooter sticking up in the air with a wide chrome tailpipe that was flared out toward the end and made a sound you could hear for miles, with a sweet spot that really roared.

I modified the engine a little to get more speed, by removing the cylinder head and filing out the cavity; and it could do eighty-five miles per hour, plenty fast enough for me. It was weird though, not having to cycle to move along; all I had to do was twist the throttle, and away I went.

I never felt so proud as I did when it was finally done—all my own work—and I made my first trip out from the Battledown driveway. I cruised slowly, not wanting to make any mistakes as all of the other boys were out front looking at me, or upstairs peering out of the upstairs windows. Mr. Ward came out to survey my handiwork and harrumphed when he saw all the chrome. He did say though that I had done a fine job, but that I must be careful driving it as he thought they were a little unstable. "Such tiny wheels," he remarked, looking at what I had done to improve the drab little machine.

The scooter was red white and black and had chrome everywhere; I had to be careful not to open up the throttle too much in front of Mr. Ward as he might finally flip.

I met some of my school friends in downtown Cheltenham who also had scooters, and we rode all over town in a small group, making a very loud noise.

On weekends, we would go out in a convoy of up to six scooters, all done up with mirrors, crash bars, and loud silencers. Mine was the coolest as I had spent the most time doing it up and definitely had the most chrome (that was the measure of a truly brilliant scooter). I can still feel the eyes of all those watching us as we rode through town, noisy like hell but so cool. As we rode, we leaned back, with our feet riding on the edge of the running board looking very cool.

It's often not the amount of money but what you can do with it that counts!

ANOTHER HOME

When one door closes another can slam in my face.

A FEW WEEKS LATER, it was half term, between Easter and summer hols; and I went home this time but not on the Scooter as I had too much stuff to carry home. I got off the coach in Hanwell and dragged my suitcase home, a walk of about two miles, reaching my front door at 107 Clitherow Avenue.

I knocked on the door, and a strange lady answered it. "Hi," I said, "who are you?" I promptly went to enter my house, walking past her and into the front hall. "I live here," she said. "Who are you?" I dropped my bag in the hallway and turned to her as she said, "Oh dear, I think I know who you are. You're Tony, aren't you?"
As I stood there in the hallway, she told me she had bought the house from a Mrs. Whitehead and had moved in several weeks before.

"Oh," I said, "well I guess that's that." I picked up my bag and promptly left. I didn't want to make any more of an issue, though I was acutely embarrassed and felt really stupid, but I wanted to be away from there as soon as possible. "What will you do? Where are you going?" she called out as I quickly walked off down the street, what was my street, for the last time.

So let's just hold on a mo! I'm fifteen, just got home from boarding school, and someone else has bought my house, moved in, and I have nowhere to live.

Worse still, no one had told me! I felt stupid that I didn't foresee this happening or that, that was the reason for Jill's quick visit, not to meet me but to see Mr. Ward, and she had said nothing at all to me at that visit, though she did tell me in a phone call that she had met someone else and may be living with him sometime in the future.

I did the only thing I could do. I walked 'round the corner to my friend Brian Phillips's house and stayed there for the hols. They were shocked at what had happened but readily agreed. I have been blessed with good friends who have truly loved me and have helped me at my times of most need—sorry to say there were many of those—while I was growing up, but there's nothing I could do about that.

I told them what had happened just before Easter and about the quick visit by Jill, her very sudden departure, about her not talking to me since, and they couldn't believe it. I also asked them not to say anything to the children's department, as they would send me back to school.

So another door to close—what had once been my lovely home, one that had allowed me to leave the orphanage with Me, Rich, Mom, and Dad, was, for me, once again no more. And it was time for me to move on. Well, I was used to that by now, but it didn't make it any easier only that I knew I had to move on and could never go back.

Never looking back is sometimes hard and it forced me to only look forward; but in doing so I was ready for the next step even if I didn't know what it was going to be.

A CHEF FOR J. LYONS & CO.

We always remember our first job.

I MANAGED TO GET a job when I was fifteen, during holidays, working as a chef in one of J Lyons new hamburger restaurants in West Ealing. The regional manageress who interviewed me knew Dad very well and told me what a great and kind person he was to work with, adding that they all missed him very much. Funny though, she also told me how Jill had pursued him every day when she worked in the same office as him, never letting up until she finally snagged him.

I always found it amazing how pieces of information came to me from unusual sources; and when that happened, from out completely in left field, I always knew it to be true information.

I got the job because of Dad; and I learned to cook in full view of the customers, from a chef called Hassan, who taught me how to break eggs with one hand (I was really proud of that) without breaking the yokes. Though I had to admit it cost J. Lyons dozens of eggs, and I have to say though that I hope they were not looking at the bottom line, as I managed to break the yokes of at last thirty eggs while attempting to break each with one hand.

I also learned how to manage several orders at the same time (my first multitasking job) and how to present the food I had prepared so that it looked appetizing. Ian and his mom came in for lunch some Saturdays while I was there, I looked very professional with my tall white chef's hat, my white high-collared jacket, and blue pin-striped chef's pants.

I got to eat all the food I could sneak under my large hot plate grille and take out the back to eat it when we had a quiet moment. I liked the job, and I liked seeing all of the customers come in, and I especially liked my new pay packet every week. At that time, there was only the Wimpey Bar in West Ealing that made hamburgers as it was fairly new in London at that time. J. Lyons was trying to follow the new style of "fast food." It worked well as we were always very busy, but when the holidays ended, I went back to school, saying my goodbyes to the staff, never to return to that job.

This first job led to me loving to cook throughout my life.

BACK TO BOARDING SCHOOL FOR THE LAST TIME

Sometimes someone's opinion of you can be a nice surprise!

WELL, I WAS a senior at school and had all the privileges of a senior. I could drive my scooter and could go out more or less as I wanted, and even better. Mr. Ward now treated me as a grown-up.

I asked him what had happened when Jill came to see him. He told me that she had dropped it on him only when she arrived and had told him she would not be moving until I was OK and I had found somewhere else to live once I got back to London after boarding school.

He also told me she had told him how bad I had been and how ungrateful and nasty I was to look after.

He told her that I was a very normal boy and that I was a pleasure to have around.

WHAT? He actually said that about me? And then he said, he meant it. "Yes," he said turning back to me, "of course, you got into some fine troubles but you were never a problem for us, and after what you had dealt with before you arrived here, you were fine, Tony."

He told me he that told her to leave immediately! Told her to get out of his office there and then and never call Battledown again!

Wow, good for you, Mr. Ward. I never thought you would be sticking up for me, but thanks!

I learned not to underestimate what you think people are prepared to do for you especially when you don't think you need their help.

MY FIRST REAL JOB INTERVIEW

Being truthful during my interview meant I was given the opportunity of a job that would change my life; and I saw that everything is related!

I HAD BEEN LOOKING for a job in London after I got back to school for the last time and had traveled from Cheltenham to do several interviews in and around Ealing. One interview was with a company called Taylor Woodrow, a huge building contractor that had an apprenticeship program. This meant I could go to college and get paid for being at work as well. So I wrote off to the company and got a letter back saying that I was welcome to come to London for an interview.

The interview was with a Mr. Peter Purvey, an older man who was very kind and eventually became like a grandfather to me. I think he had a soft spot for me and always treated me well. I grew to love him like a father figure as he later took a personal interest in my career.

At the interview, I was shown around the company. I saw the biggest truck-mounted cranes, tower cranes, bulldozers, and some of the biggest contracting plant machinery I had ever seen. I was hooked and couldn't wait to start. The heavy equipment really attracted me, and being paid to go to college was a godsend for someone like me who had nothing else at all, and it was another example of divine intervention at the right time and just when I needed it.

I finally left school and was so happy. I was free to live a normal life, or so I thought. That final Saturday was warm and very sunny when Brian Phillips, Ella, Albert, and his sister Lynne all came to pick me up from school, like a family of my own. I had known them ever since I was nine years old; and next to Ian, Brian was my other best friend. They arrived in their Morris Minor Traveler and all my stuff was loaded into the back. I said my goodbyes to Mr. Ward and his staff and left as fast as I could. I finally headed back to my other friends and a new life in London. I never looked back at the school as I rode off on my scooter and was really glad to have left there forever. I moved in with the Phillips's and started my first job. I had signed an apprenticeship, which was to last for five years and would finish when I was twenty-one years old.

Life with the Phillips was great; we made homemade elderberry wine, went camping for weekends, built a two-person canoe, and generally did family things that I really liked to do; and I was like a second son to them as well as being a very close friend to Brian, who was the same age as me.

They had a cleaner that came 'round twice a week, as both Ella and Albert worked full-time. Ella worked in Hanwell at the most beautiful thatched house in old Hanwell, where her company Pictorial Charts Educational Trust was located.

This was a fascinating place located in a large barn at the back of the house next to a small lake. What they did there was to produce and distribute the many colorful wall charts and educational posters that went into schools all across the country. Brian and I worked during summer with Ella there to earn some cash when I was fifteen before I took on a full-time job.

I made money in the strangest of places and always had fun earning it.

MY FIRST REAL JOB

I was finally on the treadmill, earning and paying taxes!

WHEN I CAME back from boarding school, I was sixteen, and it was April. I had my GCSEs in art, math, history, science, English Lit and English Language, and I think geography; and as I didn't need to stay on until summer, because I had already finished my GCSE exams and got all seven with good grades, I was set. I had gone for an interview with, a company called Taylor Woodrow, which was located in Greenford. I had never had an interview before and had no idea how to go about it.

The interview was with Peter Purvey, who was an older man, very tall with white hair and a white coat, which he always wore at work.

He was the manager of the apprentice shop of which there were around twenty hired each year. I was shown around the building and saw huge tractors, earth movers, a machine shop, truck-mounted cranes, huge bulldozers, and just about everything possible that was used in building large projects. I was mesmerized. The job I was going for was an engineering apprentice, which paid me and paid for a college course, whereby if I went to college I would get my standard pay for attending. It was too good to miss.

Peter Purvey, my soon-to-be manager, was really nice to me and wanted to know all about me being in care (which I didn't want to talk about)and asked me about boarding school and had talked to my counselor as he was concerned about whether I really wanted to do this job. I hated talking to people about my past as they always had the same look, which I didn't understand or want, so I kept my answers to an absolute minimum.

I got the news that I was hired a month after my visit and interview in a letter sent to Battledown Manor, but I already knew it before I left so that when I got back from Cheltenham, I already had a job. The real significance of this did not really matter to me at the time, but it was a perfect next step.

I took having a job straight from school very lightly, now though, in hindsight we are all lucky if we have a job!

THE PHILLIPS'

My friends helped me in my time of need and I never forgot that!

SOMETIME LATER AFTER I had moved in, with Brian and his family after having left school, Albert was made redundant from Cross and Blackwell, a job he had always had; and after some weeks of consideration as to what he and Ella would do next, they decided to manage a Courage pub.

I had lived with them, off and on, since I was nine years old, and had become a permanent "live in" since leaving school. I started making plans to move and grew excited at the prospect of becoming completely independent, and at sixteen, cool beans!

Together with Brian and his family, we had all gone camping at weekends, made homemade wine and beer, built a two-person canoe from scratch in their back room, and generally did a lot of really good family activities that I was very happy to have been a part of, so this seemed a perfect next step for them both. I was at that time going through my own change from a boarding school boy, to an independent, soon-to-be, working teenager and had some adjustments to make of my own.

It had hit Albert very hard to be made redundant at his age and with two children aged sixteen and eighteen to look after. It changed him. He became introspect and lost some of his confidence. He was like me though and soon got over it and decided that they should have a pub!

So they went away for training on how to run a pub and finally got their own in Islington, way over the other side of London.

As for me, life was about to take another turn. Brian and his family could no longer have me living with them and they were away on training; and as a result, I had to move out from living with them. Unfortunately, I was still under the care of the Middlesex County Council, who had nowhere else to put me other than in a hostel for disruptive teens, which I was definitely not one. Although I was not a disruptive teen, well, not completely, and had never ever been in real trouble with the law, not counting the incident in Cheltenham, Mill Hall was the only place I could go at the age of sixteen.

A friend's change in circumstance can sometimes affect ours also.

MILL HALL

When you can't change what is, or what will be and end up in a bad place, small victories can compensate.

THE HOSTEL 'Mill Hall' had a bad reputation and was located in the other side of Southall by the railway bridge, on the way through to Hayes. I hated it and really disliked the man that ran this with his insipid wife.

I suddenly found myself living back in a dormitory with seven other boys, all of whom had been placed there by various authorities; and I had to line up before breakfast, have my bed made to the satisfaction of the old man, and had to put up with the strictest rules and regulations. This was like being in Borstal or a halfway house, and I had no business being there. I was very angry. But as was explained by my new case worker, Mr. Brown, "It's the only place we have for you, Tony, so you will have to stay there until you are eighteen!" Two years! No way was I going to have any of that.

Worst of all, I had to relinquish my pride and joy, my scooter, as I was told, "It is unfair to the other boys that you should have a privilege." The scooter was placed inside a locked shed, and that was that. I had also started my five-year apprenticeship with Taylor Woodrow and so had to go on the bus to work, while my beautiful scooter was locked in a shed!

The place had the most ridiculous rules and regulations. We had to buy a suit, a pair of light blue jeans (no more bleached bell-bottoms for me) and a pair each of black and brown shoes. It was a miserable time, and I hated it, especially as I had done nothing wrong to get there.

One of my close friends was a boy called Ian Banfill, whose mother owned a large hotel on Ealing Common. He was in Mill Hall for theft and passing false checks and was, as I began to notice, very gay.

He called himself "Stephanie Shag" when out with his other gay friends. I used to go with him to Ealing Common, mainly to meet his very beautiful sister; but I was too shy to ever ask her out. I liked Ian Stephanie" a lot, and I never cared what his personal persuasion was; to me, he was just my friend. Ian Banfill always made me laugh and had the strangest singsong way of talking that I had ever heard. On weekends, we were allowed to go out; but unless we had very special permission, we had to be home by 11:00 p.m. I was even given an allowance, and it was from my own earnings!

I had to go out and buy a boring suit, light blue jeans, and white T-shirts to wear with the "light blue jeans" that I hated wearing; and generally, I had to conform to become exactly the same as all the other boys. If we went out in Southall, you could tell the Mill Hall boys by the stupid light blue jeans they all wore in town.

Sunday mornings were the worst. We all had to sit in the "communal" living room and suffer one of the old man's lectures about how to behave and what to think. He would always end up by saying, "There can never be a winner without a loser. There are always ten times as many losers as there are winners. And if you are all here listening to me, then you are all losers" Well, not for me. I bought my own clothes and stashed them in a hiding place, under a bush on the way out of the place, and got changed once I was out of the hostel. To say that I hated it there would be to underestimate how I really felt.

The rules and regulations were simply ridiculous. I just dealt with it and knew I would get out of there one way or another. As for my scooter, I found where they kept the key to the shed and got a soap image made and got a spare key made at a local hardware store. On weekends, I watched and waited till no one was around after all the boys had left for the day and take my scooter out of the shed roll it down the curved driveway, out of view, walk it down the road before getting on, and *freedom.*

They never had a clue as I never ever mentioned the scooter at any time while I was there, and the shed was never opened. It made me feel really good to put one over on their stupid rules. I rode it loud and fast through Southall and Ealing, nodding to all the other mods, and went to join Ian on his scooter; and we would go out together.

Sometime later in 1971, Ian Banfill "Stephanie" was nicked and put in Borstal for passing forged checks at a pharmacy. What an idiot! I went to see him there several times with my then girlfriend Cezara and decided that he probably was going to be a loser all his life. Ian did introduce me to cool stuff like "Oliver Goldsmith" sunglasses and designer silk shirts by Michel Axel, and I loved all that. Thanks, Ian "Stephanie." And I promise I never slept with your sister despite what you always thought, mainly because you never left us alone!

In this bad situation that I found myself in, I made it more tolerable and certainly more fun!

AN APPRENTICE

Sometimes you just know that you have made an important decision about your life and this was one for me.

I STARTED MY FIRST job at Taylor Woodrow in September 1966 as an apprentice, along with nineteen other boys. I earned a princely sum of six pounds a week for a forty-hour working week. I did all the over time I could as I hated going back to the hostel and wanted to stay out as long as I could. I planned to either run away from there or leave within one more month.

My first weekly pay packet was six pounds a week—ten dollars—and I thought I was rich. Think about it/ I could go to the pub (illegally), I was earning money, and I was *independent* at last! Well, for a short time. So I was now an employee for Taylor Woodrow and began my apprenticeship, which was to last five years; and little did I know it then, but the skills I was to learn were to take me through my whole life. I was learning skills of being able to fix things, repair engines, and make new again electrical, auto-mechanical, and all kinds of equipment.

On my first day, I was introduced to the rest of the apprentices, and we were all together in an apprentice workshop. The way it worked was that as we were given jobs to do either with other apprentices or with fully indentured engineers, while our work and time was charged out to each department. In that way, we were each able to contribute to the company in return for being able to be trained and go to college; it was a good system.

I was to work "my time" as an apprentice in each department from light engineering, engine workshop, cranes, heavy equipment, and machine shop. I got to work on Caterpillar, huge Ruston Bucyrus heavy lift cranes, Rolls-Royce diesel generators, Drott, International Harvester, Lister diesel engines, and just about everything there was to work on.

It was a fantastic job; though the pay as an apprentice wasn't that good, the experience was incredible, and I was taught by experts. My pay would increase every year, and with certain milestones, I could achieve more along the way.

The part I liked the most was when I was placed in the auto repair shop working on brand-new cars that belonged to executives. Part of my job was to convert the executive cars from dynamos to alternators, fit radios, and fix small problems. I even set the cars up onto our "in-house" dynamometer where I could set the car wheels on the huge long rollers and drive up to one hundred miles per hour on the test bed to test brake horsepower and even test the brakes.

It was the coolest thing at every opportunity I had, I would take one of the cars I was working on onto the dynamometer, finding any excuse to do so.

I loved my time at this company and despite the low pay scale it made no difference.

THE ROYAL FREE HOSPITAL — TWO HUNDRED FEET UP

Proving oneself is important when doing it in front of someone whose opinion we value.

ONE FEBRUARY, WHEN I was working in the crane section, I had to go to the new Royal Free Hospital that they were building in Hampstead to fix a tower crane that had a frozen jib end pulley, which was the pulley right at the end of that long arm you can see high above the ground on a tall tower crane. That meant climbing right up the two hundred feet to the long straight jib of the crane with a "fall-harness" on that was strapped around my waist and around my legs then fixed to a horizontal safety rail that ran along the jib to the end. I had to walk out slowly to the very end of the jib and lubricate the gears at the end, removing ice that had stopped it working. I was working with an ex-marine sergeant major called Stan, who was a fitness freak and was always telling us how we were all weak and couldn't keep up with him. So out we went—him and me—and I said to him, "So you think I couldn't handle this job then?" And he said, "No way." That was a challenge, wasn't it?

"OK, I'll go up and I'll go by myself." And he had to agree.   It sure was a long way up, and I had been shown how to place the fall protection harness on around my waist and legs and to attach it to the safety rail. I climbed up all the way with the can of lubricant and very gingerly reached the high cab where the operator was sitting in his small square windowed box. I told him that when I freed up the pulleys, he should go through the silent hand signs for a "trolley in," "trolley out," and lift a test load that we had set on the ground near to the crane.

The hand signs were clenching and unclenching my hand, for slow, then making circular motions with my fingers pointing up or down for lift or lower; and I would remain on the end of the jib. He told me I must be absolutely mad to go out onto the jib, especially on a freezing cold February morning.

I slowly went out onto the jib, holding on to the safety rail, sliding more than walking out to the end. I looked down. Fuck! It was a long way to the ground—at least two hundred feet—and there was nothing between me and the ground at all. I was wondering if birds get dizzy!

I hated heights, but if there is nothing actually connecting me to the ground, I was sort of OK. I could absolutely never stand on a tall building and look down as it always made me woozy, but I could stand on this jib and do so. Weird, huh!

I knew I was being watched by my partner, Stan, so off I went to reach the end of the one-hundred-foot-long jib. I reached the end, and the wind was gusting all the time, and I was absolutely freezing my arse off as I surveyed the job at hand. Bloody hell! What the fuck was I doing up here at all? I wanted danger money, but fat chance of that!

I had a great view of London though and looked out at all the scenery as I could see clearly over to the post office tower. I finally reached the end of the jib and greased the pulleys; and I gave the signal for trolley in and trolley out, which he did.

What I didn't know though was that the crane leans backward when at rest, because of the counterbalance weights on the other end; and when it lifts a load, the end of the jib drops at least six feet as the load is picked up and rises again when the load is released. And I got to see this first hand and from above and looking down at . . . nothing at all. When he "slewed" left or right, it felt like I was on a huge merry-go-round, spinning at the end of the jib. I had never ever and even since experienced anything like this as I was perched on the end of the tower crane.

I could see our tiny little van and all of the building site two hundred feet below. But I did it, and that shut Stan up for good! After I slid back the crane, driver thanked me and gave me some hot coffee when I got back in to the small cab, wondering what makes a person want that job sitting all alone in a cab like this way up there.

He asked me why I did this, and I said, "I should ask you the same question." We laughed, saying goodbye, and I began the long climb down. "Good job, Tone," my partner said. And we drove back to Greenford in total silence. I couldn't talk anyway as the adrenalin was still pumping high in my veins.

I also got to work on huge Rolls-Royce sixteen-cylinder diesel engines used as power generators, stripping them down and rebuilding them from scratch and placing them onto the test bed to certify them as ready to be used. Of course, I could never work on them by myself, only with an experienced engineer.

I even worked on the very first Jaguar XJ6. No one had ever seen the car, and there I was at nineteen years old, fitting a radio in it. I got to take it out onto the street and took my overalls off as soon as I left the company grounds so I could pretend that the car was mine (as if)! I drove it through Greenford and into Ealing with everyone staring at this superb new Jag.

Funny though, I loved doing my job as an apprentice; and learning for me was fun. I had no idea that all of this was to be so important for my future and would affect whatever I did after that. I was moving gradually forward in a direction that would take me onward through my life-learning skills that I would need right through everything I ever did.

There was an artist who worked there, also called John, a slight man with reddish hair, that I got to know well; and every opportunity I had,

I would sneak over to watch him at his work. John was a sign writer, and he painted by hand all of the huge signs that Taylor Woodrow had all over the world. I was fascinated to watch him making his perfect lettering on walls, signs, trucks, and anything that needed a sign. I asked him if he enjoyed it, and he told me that if he had to paint one more man pulling on a rope, he would scream! That was Taylor Woodrow's corporate signature, four men pulling on a rope that signified teamwork.

I laughed and asked him why he did the job then. He told me his first love was art, but that it would never make enough money to live on, so this was at least working with paint and brushes; so for him, it used a tiny part of his skill, and he could paint in his spare time.

For extra cash, I used to make small model figures, which I welded or soldered together out of nuts, bolts, and pieces of metal. I sold them to local gift stores, or I made them for friends.

John's Mom and Dad were having a twenty-fifth-year wedding anniversary. He liked what I created, and he asked me if I would make something special for his parents as an anniversary gift from him to them. I made two figures holding hands, walking together, and passing a twenty-five-year milestone. I made them out of metal with round ball bearing heads. For the woman, I made a large hat, and for the man a cane and a top hat with coat tails. I placed it into a box that I also made and wrapped it in a piece of blue tissue paper so they would fit properly, and I gave it to John.

He loved it and agreed to paint me a picture in return, and we swapped many items like that, and I kept all of his paintings as I thought he was a very gifted artist.

So let's see what I was doing—I was working for Taylor Woodrow, singing at night and making enough money to live on, and making small models for sale—I was by that time beginning to be an entrepreneur.

I stayed at Taylor Woodrow for the five years needed to complete my apprenticeship, got my degree, and decided that I didn't want to remain in that business. And I didn't want to become a specialist mechanic.

What was so cool to me as a schoolboy was not so interesting for me now that I had completed my five-year apprenticeship. I even learned to be an auto electrician or what we called an "auto-sparks," and the expert that taught me was none other than Jimmy Marshall's brother. Jim was the founder of Marshall Amplifiers, now seen on all of the rock concerts behind the bands from the Who to Elton John, Led Zeppelin, and many others. At that time, Jimmy Marshall had a small shop selling guitars and amps in Hanwell, near where I lived. I was introduced to him, but at that time, he only had a fledgling company. I bought my first guitar from the shop in Hanwell.

Anyway, his brother was Fred, (at least as *he* told me); and Fred had a limp, could hardly walk, and seemed to me to be at least sixty when I was apprenticed to him. He called me "Tone" and directed me to do all the work while he told me exactly what to do. I liked him a lot and really looked forward to my work days while working with Fred.

He showed me how to troubleshoot and fix almost anything electrical on many different cars and vans that belonged to Taylor Woodrow's fleet.

I got to drive many of the cars off the premises and 'round the streets to "test-drive" them; though most times, there was nothing wrong with the cars, and they definitely didn't need a "test drive." Still it was one of the perks with the job.

I moved through each of the workshops, working for two to six months in each and going to college on a one-month block and two months' work at Uxbridge College in order to take my degree (*City and Guilds*, parts 1 and 2). I had no car at that time. I couldn't afford one, as my pay was so very little, and I needed it to pay the rent at Paddy Gallagher's Mom's house.

I learned that respect is earned but it is so much easier when you enjoy earning it through doing something that you love.

OOPS!

Even a huge mistake can be offset by our past good character.

WHILE I WAS working in the crane section, I got plenty of overtime and often worked Saturday mornings for extra cash at time and a half. I was still only seventeen; and one Saturday, I was finishing off the electronic "Wiley Safety System," which was an audible and visual warning system in case the operator overloaded the cranes lift mechanism. I had just finished working on it that Saturday, and there was hardly anyone around, so I took the huge truck-mounted crane for a "spin" around the yard.

It was so cool; I had full control of this huge beastie and was determined to put it through its paces, so off I went driving it up to the back lot. They had just opened a brand-new paint spray shop that could paint complete vehicles, and mine was scheduled to be painted on Monday.

The spray shop was really professional and had been featured in the monthly *Taywood News* and had pictures and articles on the advanced technology it had adopted. So there I was, cruising around the yard, pretending to be a professional crane operator at seventeen with no heavy goods vehicle license, and honking the horn going all over the yard. I even went to the outer perimeter and parked up to extend the telescopic jib fully, looking out of the back sky roof window in the cab, while admiring my handiwork. I set a test load on the ground, locked it onto the cranes hook, set the outriggers to stabilize the truck, and lifted it up, placing it carefully back down . . . way cooler still!

Noticing the time, I retracted the jib, locked it in place, and began to drive it back to the workshop. Halfway back, I had a great idea and decided to park it in the spray shop so it wouldn't have to be done on Monday. I honked the horn to let anyone who may be inside know that I wanted the automatic doors to be opened, and they began to open.

As I drove the crane into the spray shop, I heard a huge "CRUNCH"; and bricks and bits of debris came showering all over the crane and the cab.

Little did I know that the crane was too big, and I had completely smashed into the brand-new and soon-to-be officially opened automatic doors of the equally brand-new super-duper paint spray shop.

Well, fuck it! I was in serious trouble, and what I thought was a fairly empty workshop on a Saturday morning was suddenly full of people running toward me. They came from everywhere, including the manager. I stepped down from the cab and surveyed the damage. Oh shit! Where the top of the entrance wall was, there was a huge hole.

The top of the automatic door was bent and twisted. And bricks were still falling while my jib was poking right through to the inside of the building. I was devastated at the damage I had done. Funny how quick a great day can be ruined. Ever noticed that? I did and how.

I was sent home and was told to be in the manager's office on Monday morning. I had a lousy weekend and thought I would surely be fired.

When Monday came, all of the other apprentices were laughing at me and joking about my superb driving skills, I didn't think it was funny at all and was wondering how I was going to get out of this one. I went to the manager's office, and Peter Purvey came with me. There were several of them there and a representative of the union as well. I listened to their statements as they read out the extent of the damage I had done and the approximate cost of repair.

I had never gotten into any trouble there and had a completely clean apprentice record, not even a missed day or even a late day. Peter Purvey told them I was an exceptional apprentice, and that I should be given a second chance as there were other things that needed to be considered in my case. I was certain he was referring to my background, and he was making sure that he defended me and put me in a positive light to them.

I was asked to explain myself, and I told them that I was trying to save time on Monday by parking the crane inside ready to be painted. One of the managers said I should make sure that the door is open first, and they laughed. I wasn't laughing as I didn't want to lose my job but had nothing to say in my own defense. I did apologize several times and offered to pay or to fix the damage I had done. I mentally calculated that I would probably have to work one hundred hours a week for at least two years to pay for it. I had to wait outside while they conferred about how serious my damage was.

They all agreed that it was after all an insurance claim, and that they would probably make the door higher as a result. I was however given a three-day suspension without pay and was not to be fired. I asked if this would go on my apprenticeship record. The union leader told me that if I maintained a clean record and didn't do anything else stupid, over the next twelve months, it would not go on my record. I felt lousy though as I had caused so much damage while trying to be cool.

Outside, I thanked Peter and assured him I would be more careful in future and left to begin my three-day off. I called Ian and told him what had happened. We both laughed, and he was surprised as I was that I still had a job there.

At that time, we were just starting to sing. And Ian and I learned to play guitar so that we could both earn money while we were at college; otherwise, I would honestly have had to starve at weekends.

As it was, on many of the weekends while I was starting as an apprentice, I had no food at all, so I would try to keep some food from the canteen on Friday and try to make it last right through. I managed the three days off and practiced guitar, learning some new songs so as to make use of my time.

Work was great, and I really enjoyed my apprenticeship and had even been presented with several awards from Taylor Woodrow for achievements along the way—best apprentice, best made tools, etc.

Auntie came to see me receive one of my awards, which was Christmas 1968, at Taylor Woodrow's open house. She came to all my functions, weddings, and the like. She was more than my lifelong mentor; she was my supporter and my dearest friend, a "surrogate mom." She was so pleased to see me doing well with my job.

She took me to Veeraswamy's Indian restaurant in Regent Street after my award as a reward for doing so well. I loved having Auntie with me when we went out, especially to a restaurant like Veeraswamy's.

The road to hell is paved with good intentions, but when the experience from which you make decisions is limited you seem to get there much faster!

JIMI HENDRIX LIVE

I was there, when Jimi performed live!

IN 1967, I had tickets to see Jimi Hendrix playing at the Finsbury Astoria; and I was in the fourth row from the front while watching him do something no one had ever done before. He actually set fire to his Fender Stratocaster guitar.

Unbelievable! I was so close and was right there watching him as he, completely spaced out, placed his guitar on the floor in the middle of the stage while squirting it with lighter fluid and set the thing on fire. Brilliant! I knew I would remember this night forever and hoped I would see him again live; but unfortunately, I never got to do that as he died of an overdose. *What a waste*, I thought, but then there was that moment in time for me when I did enjoy his music.

I had to find a place to live, so I looked around for a flat and found one just off Northfields Avenue; at least it wasn't a complete flat but a single room at the back of a house where a very old lady lived with her two sons. The sons were aged eleven and seventeen. I don't remember the older boy's name, but his younger brother was called Paddy Gallagher.

Now Paddy was a real street tough guy and was already going the wrong way at eleven years old. I liked Paddy though, and we got along really well. His mom was not well, and I used to do small errands for her. My room was very small, but I was independent, and it was mine. And I had all I needed there; and anyway, it took me out of that awful place—Mill Hall.

If I got too hungry while I was living at Paddy's Mom's house, which was almost every weekend, I called Brian Phillips to see if his mom and dad could use some help in their pub in Islington. It was always OK for me to go there as they were like family. Brian and I were close friends, and I could do lots of work there to earn my food. I liked that, and I would get the tube over to Islington on a Friday afternoon after work, to work at their pub to earn my free food. I loaded shelves, kept the bar clean, worked the cellar, and helped Ella out in the kitchen.

I witnessed this incredible performance live, almost everyone else only saw it in videos!

FIRST MAN ON THE MOON

When you are aware that what you are watching is an historic moment it prints an eternal image in your soul that you will never forget

IT WAS WHILE I was at the pub working for Ella and Albert in 1969, in Islington, that Brian and I watched the first lunar landing that year with Neil Armstrong, Edwin "Buzz" Aldren, and John Collins, who was the command module pilot.

We were sitting in the pub on July 20, which was a Saturday afternoon, watching TV in the now-closed bar after the morning session and before we opened up the bar for the very busy Saturday evening session. We watched as the small landing module approached the moon and began to slowly descend. We heard the distance to the surface being called out as it continued with its descent. We sat in awed silence as the black-and-white scratchy images of their lunar module slowly descended to the surface of the moon. We listened to the soundtrack indented with a "peep" after each sentence in the communication between Houston and the astronauts.

We watched the descent of Neil Armstrong as he climbed awkwardly down the steps of the landing module in his silver spacesuit, ready to step onto the surface of the moon. We watched in utter silence and with breath held as he took his first step onto the moon. I was so moved at what I was watching that I couldn't breathe, worried and praying that nothing would go wrong at the very last moment. We listened as he announced to the whole universe, "That's one small step for man, and one giant leap for mankind." We cheered at that and again watched the reruns and the commentary on TV in the bar.

Cool, huh, to have witnessed that too and live on TV actually as it was happening. I was nineteen at this time and was watching as history was being made right there on TV and right before my eyes. I had also gone to the Great West Road to watch as Yuri Gagarin, the first man in space, drove past us, waving at us as we watched him go back to Heathrow for his return to Russia in a convoy of VIP cars.

Even the scratchy image of a momentous event in living history seemed to add a touch of magic to that moment.

PIRATE RADIO

Not many understood the risk that a few took to change the future of British broadcasting.

As I WAS NOW a full-fledged MOD, possessing everything I needed to be recognized as one, I used to listen to the two pirate radio stations—"Radio Caroline" and "Radio London" (Wonderful Radio London)—and these stations were both amazing to listen to. They were completely new and played the latest rock and pop bands that the Beeb wouldn't play. They played the Kinks, Cream, the Rolling Stones, and, of course the Beatles, the Animals, Pink Floyd, and the Who. They played all new pop and rock music, all of which were seldom, if ever, played by BBC.

The BBC, the Beeb as we all called it, was so stuffy and had no passion for what it really was—*"a radio program"*—there to entertain us and to play what we, the plebs, wanted to hear. It was as if we should feel privileged to accept all of the programs the government chose to put out for us and to grin and bear it. *Wow,* lucky us!

The "BBC Light Program" was the only popular (not pop) channel that we could listen to, and they were part of the government who were definitely not interested in entertaining the public, unless of course you were being entertained at "Her Majesty's Pleasure," which was something entirely different. I use the term popular very loosely, since the only other program was Radio Luxembourg, which faded in and out the whole time and mostly couldn't be heard at all!

The two independent radio stations were playing requests, were making jokes, were conducting interviews with rock musicians, were advertising cool new stuff, and were doing live chats on the air. The stations were broadcast from two ships moored off the coast of England and were not licensed by the government who had to license all broadcasters.

Of course, both of them applied for, and reapplied for, broadcasting licenses from the government; but naturally, the government would have none of it and refused to grant them a license to broadcast their programs.

They continued regardless, while trying to appeal against the refusals, and broadcast from 1964 till 1966, perfect for a new young MOD eager to listen to all of the new music that was being played at the time. The Who were our standard bearers and sang about being a MOD. They had hairstyles like ours, short and spiked on top and longer at the back, and were often photographed in the same clothes as we chose to wear.

Everyone listened to these two pirate radio stations; if you didn't, then there was only a very faded Radio Luxemburg that often faded right out of sound. I listened to Radio Luxembourg on a small crystal radio set complete with earphones that I made from old bits and pieces in my bed at night under the covers The adverts that they played caused a major stir as the advertisers could target their audience very precisely, unlike the Independent TV that catered for a much broader audience; and sales of their products went through the roof. They advertised hair products, makeup, chewing gum, and a myriad of other previously unheard of new products that younger people wanted to buy. This single event started the radio advertising and paved the way for a new style of television ads that would be the basis of advertising for the next fifty years.

Apart from this, the music and interviews were "here and now" and not managed by a committee of government employees that knew little of, or cared for, or understood the new market for music and young people's products.

The government in its infinite wisdom, at that time, began a campaign using legalities aimed at preventing "that sort of music" and "those sorts of people" from being able to broadcast on "its airwaves."

In June or July a year or so later, the government passed "an illegal broadcasting law" under a new maritime law that made these stations illegal so that they could board the pirate radio boats and shut them down, even though they were in international waters.

But at the end of the day, what actually happened was that a revolution had just occurred. These two pirated radio stations had caused a chain of events that would enable better broadcasting standards and eventually the breakdown of BBC's stranglehold on all programming in Britain.

The BBC had to accept that its formula for radio broadcasting at that time was old and tired, and that it did not meet its own standard of being accountable and meeting the needs of its audience. Quite apart from that the pirate stations were fantastic and alive and were really doing for us what no other radio programs before had done.

They were actually asking us what we wanted and then playing it with live feedback on what people thought right there on the airwaves. The "live call-ins" were funny, and we could hear ordinary people chatting on the radio to the DJs, and the DJs were talking back at them, saying what they wanted to say and not bothering who was listening and certainly no one was criticizing them for their opinions they were being very natural.

One part I loved listening to was when they were asking people on the shoreline to flash their headlights if they were listening from the mainland. Then they would talk, on the airwaves, live and find out through a series of questions answered by the flashing of headlights on shore the names and music preferences of the listeners. It was fascinating, and we all felt truly connected through these radio stations and we were able to communicate live on the airwaves—even as far as being able to get the names of the people in the cars and actually referring to them by name—amazing!

Quite apart from this, they were part of the times we were living in—fashions from Carnaby Street and Kings Road, *New Musical Express*, Twiggy, miniskirts, new short hairstyles (club cut, Paige boy, and MOD crews), the new rock culture, discos (these were new also), and the very beginning of "flower power," which was soon to become the ultimate in nonviolent radical change. So, Mr. Gandhi, you were remembered. We listened to you. After all, we followed your lead and did the same.

Radio London was probably my favorite, and I listened with my friends in places like Hyde Park, as they were telling us they were to be shut down. We listened as Radio Caroline was telling us that they had been "boarded," and we listened as they told us they were sinking in the ocean off the coast.

We were shocked at what we were hearing in real-time news right as it was happening (forty years before CNN did the same), and we didn't know if it was real or if it was "Memorex." I listened sadly as I heard the last broadcast of "Wonderful Radio London" in its unique electronic sounding slogan, which was repeated continuously until 3:00 p.m. that day, in the middle of summer, 1967, and then faded out forever.

I knew when I heard this that history had just been created, and also that I had been part of the audience hearing what was going on at that time. They had played music by Cream, the Who, Pink Floyd and Jimi Hendrix, Long John Baldry, and Chicken Shack, all of which would never have been given airtime on the Beeb.

When governments can't handle the outcome of outdated legislation, they simply change the law to outlaw those that got it right.

A FINAL EPITAPH FOR CAROLINE AND LONDON

I saw that for change to take place a few have to make the sacrifice.

BUT THESE TWO pirate stations, as the government referred to them, did make a difference. They started a chain reaction that was to change the British and European music radio broadcasting scene forever. They had given a challenge to the government; and although the government had won the battle, they absolutely had lost the war.

Several years later, licenses were granted for other broadcasting stations like Capital Radio, which was modeled exactly like Radio Caroline and Radio London. Capital had adverts, live talk, and chats with their audience; and even some of the DJs from the "pirate" radio stations had come over to join them.

Capital Radio had begun, several years later, with Kenny Everett and Dave Cash to head up their lineup in the important morning "drive-in" program.

"Kenny and Cash," as they were known, were brilliant together, zany, up to the minute and held that spot for many years, placing Capital Radio as the most listened to radio station in England and giving it a very firm foundation that was to endure for decades as it still is some thirty-five years on.

Great going, Radio London and Radio Caroline! You really did start something very special; and like all things that are truly great, your endowment to the broadcasting scene, the music scene, fashion, and up-to-the-minute issues lasted a lot longer than your initial concept!

I learned that what is illegal in one year can so easily become legal in another. The only difference is the timing.

My Mother Rosina May as I remember her taken on her wedding day not long before she passed away

Aunties house 35 Kirkley Park Road, in Lowestoft

The back of Aunties house, with our climbing frame on the right background, and the bowling green in the foreground.
The verandah is looking over the garden.
There is another part of the garden behind the camera

Top From the left: Auntie, Auntie's sister, Zannie Nurse Rosemary (sitting) is third in front from the left. I am not sure who the other nurse is.
I am 2nd child front row from right.

The climbing frame in the garden. I am leaning out of the frame in the lower right, with black hair. Beatrice is the girl sitting with her hand in front of her face, in front of me. Mary Brooks is in the lower left inside of the frame, with her blonde hair and her hand next to her face.

Tony and Mary Brooks on the stairs I loved Mary at 3 years old

Me learning to drive in 'Arabella' Aunties 1937 Austin Seven at age 12 complete with a 'crash gearbox' as Aunty put it, "so you can learn to drive properly" Picture (blurred) as taken by 11 yr. old Beatrice

Norwell (Noz) Roberts, QPM; at his investiture of the Queens Medal for services to the Metropolitan Police after his retirement.

Norwell Roberts in the Metropolitan Police Uniform

Tony Holland, as I remember him, was very talented writer, He is the inventor of East Enders and also writer of the *Z Cars* series

Back Row: Tony Moore, Robert Jones, Kevin Cromer, Brian Parkes, Michael, Prior, Robert Mc Ghee, Ralph Herbert, Michael Bulmer, Robin Reece
Second Row: Peter Fothergill, Ian Howard, Christine Putnam, Adele Rosevere, Lesley Goring, Rosamund Want, Linda McFarland, Linda Shepherd, Christine Jaks, Madeline Arnette, Diane Rodgers, Russell Gordon, Robert Gwyther
Front Row: Roisin O'Connor, Monica Newman, Janette Andersen, ?, Margaret Hall, Mr. Hughes, Carolyn Davis, ?, Vivian King, Susan King, Iris Nunn

Aunty in 1988 in Scarborough, with her MG Midget, she often drove it down to London and always loved driving.

Jumbo Fiske, OBE (1905-1977), probably the greatest herring skipper of the twentieth century, a legendary fisherman. His two trawlers, the "Suffolk Venturer" and "The Suffolk Warrior," were part of the Lowestoft fleet. I went on his boat whenever I visited Lowestoft, if he was in port. His daughter, Rosemary, was one of the nurses that looked after me to age eight and whom I stayed in touch with all my life.

The Snow Queen 1960

The cast of 'The Snow Queen' at Fielding Junior School. I am kneeling on the right side front (looking at the photo) of the front row Ian is at the top row on the right (looking at the photo) of the Snow Queen

Ian and I playing at The Old Swan in Battersea with 'Blind Bob' playing Bass in the background. Adrian played with us here. (Low light Picture taken by Ray Chapman)

I'm the tall one standing on the right! Dee Anderson joined us later

Me with the very talented Vick Elms, formerly of the band 'Christie' famed of their 'Yellow River' hit single and number one hit, and who was married to Dee Anderson. *Picture by Ray Chapman*

'Dressed For Business As Usual'
This was the advertising image of me that went 'global'
Courtesy Tony Yates, Publitek

1.7oz Eau de Parfum Spray   3.4 oz Eau de Toilette Spray

Stardust for Men by Parfums Llewelyn

 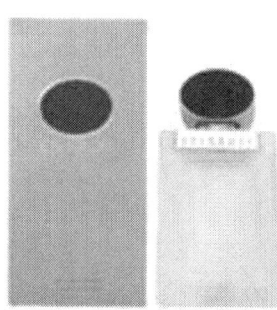 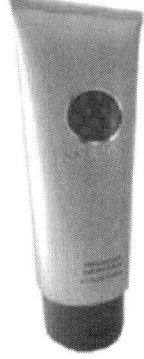

Men's After Shave Balm   Men's 1.7oz Cologne   Men's Moisturizing Body Lotion

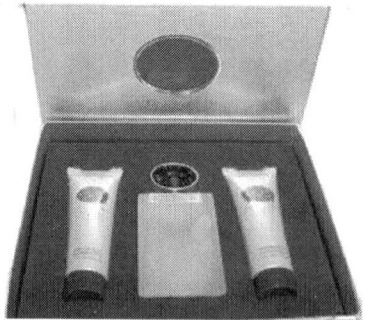 

1.7oz Gift Set   3.4oz Eau de Parfum Spray

THE UNION JACK

Our national flag became, and still is, a symbol of fashion, loved by all.

I DECIDED TO paint Ian's scooter, which was a Vesper "GS," with large "bubbles" on either side. And as you by now know, Ian and I were mods; and I painted it into a complete Union Jack. His mom, Peggy, didn't want that at all; but with persistence, she finally gave in and we began to transform Ian's bland-looking machine into a true mod mobile'

I marked out the red white and blue Union Jack with masking tape on the front panel, going from the handle bars right down to the front mudguard. I marked out a Union Jack on each of the side bubbles, and we both began to paint the scooter.

When we had finished, it looked truly amazing a complete up-to-the-minute, high-fashion "mod" scooter. We showed Peggy, and she actually had to agree that it looked really great.

This was now summer 1967, and the best music ever was out on the airwaves. The Beatles had just released their *Sergeant Pepper* album, Small Faces had released "Ichigoo Park," and Procol Harum had their huge hit "A Whiter Shade of Pale" (though I never understood the words). The music was unbelievable! Pink Floyd was all over the place, and even the Beach Boys had an amazing hit with "Good Vibrations." Now well in to the charts.

The music that summer in '67 was the best ever, with hit after hit every week, and all subsequently became classics.

Off we went, the two of us, riding through Ealing with our loud silencers making a huge racket as we drove by. We had to make sure we throttled back whenever we rode around close to home though; otherwise, Peggy would have made Ian use a "normal" silencer.

One weekend, I borrowed the "mod" machine to drive down to Selsey-Bill to meet a girlfriend, Anne Shepherd, there. She was staying with a girlfriend at her aunt's house.

Anne was the daughter of my doctor when I was living at Mill Hall in Southall and was the light in my life at that time. I was crazy about her, but because of where I was living, her father forbade her to go out with me. I never understood why that was, but it made no difference to us; we still saw each other whenever we wanted to, and she was finishing off at Notting Hill School for Girls, which was an exclusive school in Ealing.

I was so cool, at least I thought so. I had my full parka coat with a fur edging around the hood and a Union Jack on the back, a Union Jack crash helmet, a Union Jack scooter, a tent, and all I needed to be completely independent.

I camped in a field near where Anne was staying with her friend, and we all went to the beach together every day. Donovan's "Catch the Wind" was number 1 for a while, and I had to look the part. Even my jeans were bleached in rough broad stripes all the way down front and back, and I wore a pair of small "John Lennon" round sunglasses with my long hair worn down past my shoulders.

Anne wore a pair of heart-shaped rose-tinted glasses, and she looked just like Mary Quant in her tiny miniskirt, her slim figure, and with her dark hair cut in a Paige boy style. We looked great together; and I took Anne and her friend on the back of the scooter, one at a time, of course, to different places on or near the beach. I stayed for a week with them; and we had a great time there, going to the bars, beaches, and shops.

On the way back, I stopped at a petrol station where the attendant came out to fill my scooter with two-stroke petrol. At that time, you had to fill it with one gallon of petrol then have the attendant put three squirts of "two-stroke" oil put into the tank to make "two-stroke" fuel, which is a mixture of oil and petrol. You then had to swish it around in the tank by rocking the scooter side to side.

As he was doing this, he said to me, "Boy, you're patriotic, aren't you, with all this Union Jack stuff?" I replied, "I have to be patriotic because of where I live." He said, "So where do you live then?" I told him, "At Buckingham Palace. I live at Buckingham Palace, of course."

He stopped what he was doing and looked at me incredulously and said, "You're kidding, right?" I said, "No, not at all. My dad's a butler to Her Majesty the Queen, and we both live in the servant's quarters, and the only way he would let me ride this into Buckingham Palace is if it was painted in patriotic colors."

"Well, I never," he said, "I must tell my wife that I've met the son of the queen's butler." Well, I couldn't burst his bubble, could I? I let my little (or huge) white lie stand and drove away grinning from ear to ear.

Later on, I took Ian to Selsey Bill; and we both drove our scooters for weekends there, sleeping in doorways of offices along the way. One morning though, at around 5:00 a.m., we were woken up by two local policemen who stopped their Panda car and woke us asking, "What the hell are you two doing here? Move along." We had to move along and find somewhere for breakfast. So much for "life as a mod."

So what the hell is a mod? Well, I was one at sixteen. I wore bell-bottom jeans with striped bleached lines all the way down each leg (bleach poured directly onto the jeans while lying in the bath), long black hair down to my shoulders, and a parka coat with a fur-trimmed hood. And I rode a modified motor scooter all over London. I also had a striped jacket in red and black stripes. We would go to a "meet" where all of the other "mods" were hanging out. Though we never really caused trouble, we were the forerunners of "punks" as they went on to become. Most mods had short hair cropped really close, but I didn't.

My scooter had twenty mirrors on the front and sides, at least eight spot lamps, and a beautiful set of chrome crash bars with a high backrest.

I had a Union Jack crash helmet, and I was "in" with the "in crowd." I looked very cool (or at least I thought I did) and dressed exactly as I wanted. We listened to the Who, Cream, Hollies, and all of the current music. I even had a striped jacket just like the Who.

On weekends, some of the mods would go down to Brighton and fight with the "rockers" who were exactly the opposite of us. Rockers rode motorbikes and wore leathers, rode around in gangs, listened to Elvis, and, to us, generally looked old-fashioned. We bought our clothes from places like Lord John or Mr. Howard in places like Carnaby Street and Kings Road or Biba in Kensington where I used to frequent every Saturday morning. I loved the music, the styles, and the up-to-date fashion that was in at the time.

I was always interested in wearing the latest fashions and of course so were the girls I went out with at that time. Twiggy had just begun to make a name for herself in the fashion mags. She was the absolute girl version of us mods, and I loved her waiflike look and short cropped blonde hair; and she had the biggest eyes I ever saw. I thought she was the sexiest girl on the planet!

The clothes we were wearing were bell-bottoms, shoes eventually with ridiculous platform soles, wide blade ties, and shirts with "penny" rounded collars. We wore big striped shirts, flower power shirts, and even paisley patterns while listening to Mamas and Papas, Beach Boys, Edison Lighthouse, Christie's Yellow River, and songs like Ode to Billy Joe, which were my favorites at that time. While we were doing straight pop and rock style music, the Philly Sound was emerging from the United States with full strings, harmony, horns, and keyboards. The Motown bands I loved were Temptations, Four Tops, and the Isley Brothers. I thought the musical arrangements were so much more advanced than what we were doing in Britain. But still our British music seemed to be the most popular.

The Beatles and the Stones were producing hit after hit after hit, and their music was truly amazing. The Beatles occupied the top 5 slots in Britain's Top 10, which no one had ever done or has ever done since. We were so lucky that we were in our teens when all this new music hit the charts and we were part of the music revolution.

These DJ's changed an entire government's position.

LEARNING TO SING

When we have to, we learn real fast how to make money to survive.

MY FLAT AT this time, was at a young eleven-year-old Paddy Gallagher's Mom's house and cost me four pounds a week; and I had practically no money left over for food or petrol, so I had to work as much overtime as I could get. This became a real problem for me; and one weekend, Ian and I discussed that we both needed money and agreed that since we could both sing fairly well, we should learn to play for money, cash, gelt, or readies. So we practiced and practiced and learned as many songs as we could. We leaned folk songs by Peter, Paul, and Mary; Bob Dylan; Pete Seeger; the Kingston Trio; and Simon and Garfunkel.

After some six months of practicing every weekend and some evenings each week, we were finally ready to play to an audience, or so Ian's Mom thought; and we rode our scooters to Uxbridge where there was a folk club behind a pub called the Load of Hay in Uxbridge, well, actually Hillingdon. We plucked up our courage and played as a guest, our first actual gig in a folk club at the back of the pub the Load of Hay; and in fact, we became guest singers there for more than a year. I really think we actually sounded a lot like the real thing as we had always learned to sing harmonies and could play and sing like Simon and Garfunkel.

We learned all of their many hits and we built up a repertoire of more than one hundred songs. We practiced over and over again until we knew all the words by heart.

This was to become the most important part of our teenage life as we were both at college and both needed the money very much. My daytime job, as an apprentice, went well but didn't pay me enough. Ian and I began to play pubs and clubs all over London, getting better and better the more we played and gained a reputation as well with a fan club of regulars who followed us around everywhere we played.

Using my talent enabled me to be financially independent as a teen

CEZARA

Some relationships are best short term and learning this can save both from painful mistakes later on.

I MET CEZARA AFTER Andy and I had finished when I was nineteen. Cez was a stunningly beautiful Polish girl with long ash blonde hair and light gray eyes. Cez had several brothers that were a lot older than her. Zbyszek lived in Australia, Joe who lived in Kensington; and Lolek who lived in South London, , none were married, and all were very independent.

Cez had an elderly mother who was a fantastic cook and could cook any Polish dish ever created, though she could not speak English well at all. As for me, I could pronounce two things perfectly: Polish food and swear words! So I learned all about the Polish way of life, along with some really perfect phrases that I can never repeat in good company. I also loved the Polish food—*gwumpky, borscht,* and *pierogi*—and could cook some of these dishes myself, but not anywhere close to what Cez's Mom could do. By the way, if you love food as much as I do, then you have to be able to cook it to be able to have it whenever you wish. So I learned to cook fairly well—French, Italian, Polish, and Indian; and thanks to Brian Phillips's family, my boyhood friend, I even learned to cook several Scottish dishes.

In 1969, the Rolling Stones were playing at Hyde Park, and Brian Jones had recently drowned in his swimming pool. Cez had a flat in Mayfair at the time, and so we both went to Hyde Park with some of her hostess friends to see them play in the open air. It was a very hot summer's day on July 5, and we were both very close to the stage, as they let out thousands of butterflies in memory of Brian.

Cez was working as a nightclub hostess at the Crazy Horse and the 800 Club and was making more money that I ever did at the time. Despite how well Cez and I got on, as good and very close friends, I knew it wouldn't last as I had no vision of marriage with Cez; and I still had way too many things to do.

We often went to a Polish club in South Kensington's Exhibition Road called Ognisku, after I had finished performing and if she had a night off from the 800 Club.

Ognisko was a Polish drinking club that was open till the early hours and was somewhat old-fashioned inside but was a great club where the drinks were dead cheap. It was like stepping back in time though, being with all the Polish crowd. The club looked like and felt like a Second World War club that you would see in a black-and-white movie. The Polish people that I met at that time were all heavy drinkers and seemed to always be drinking vodka, getting drunk almost every night, and ending up falling about all over the place.

Cez and I were an item; we went on holidays together with Ian and his then-girlfriend Sandy. I took her to visit Auntie in Lowestoft, which was a disaster as Auntie got on Cez's case and made her very uncomfortable. To this day, I have no idea why she did that, but sometimes Auntie was a little unpredictable.

We lived in a flat right in the heart of Ealing Broadway, which was close to all the Ealing life and was within walking distance of all the pubs and clubs. I shared a flat with Mike and Colin, whom I had also shared a flat with previously. Cez shared a basement flat with her school friend Eva in the same building. We lived together there for about eighteen months, and we settled in to what for me was a boring home life. I was now singing full-time and was performing at the Penthouse, the Old Swan, working men's clubs, and many other places all over the south of England to make enough money to live on.

Cez often left for work at around 9:00 p.m. and didn't get home until around 5:00 a.m. or later, depending on how busy the club was that night.

The difference between liking someone a lot as a friend and loving someone is the difference between a girlfriend and a wife.

AN INDENTURED CRAFTSMAN

Something that takes years to achieve is well worth achieving

I HAD SPENT FIVE years at Taylor Woodrow, from sixteen to twenty-one, and had become a fully indentured professional. I could, if I wanted, work anywhere in any blue-collar or engineering job; but I didn't want that. Only six of the twenty that began the apprenticeship finished, and I was one of them.

At the final ceremony, when Frank Taylor came down himself to address us all and to award the completion certificates, I had asked Auntie to come as many of my fellow apprentices had parents and family there.

We were each asked to make something that would represent our skill at these annual awards; and all of the exhibits were placed on tables, along with a small card in front to say who had made the exhibit, to be assessed and awarded points for skill and workmanship. I made a set of Trammels (God knows why as I've never ever used them) and also made the metal box for them as well as making a green felt backing that held the trammels in place. I have to admit they looked very professional.

Trammels are used for scribing a precise circle on metal, for perhaps permanently marking or for cutting out the marked area, and could be attached end to end and locked in place together to make a circle as wide as three feet in radius. So now you know, and I won the award for the best made tool. For that, I got another certificate and £100. Cool, huh!

A really good friend of mine, John Brown, also completed his apprenticeship at the same time as me; and we often hung out with our girlfriends and went together on our scooters. John lived just 'round the corner to Taylor Woodrow in the adjoining side street. His mom and dad, girlfriend Anne, and his sister were all there to see him receive his completed indentured apprenticeship papers. Sadly John was killed at work when a steel bolt holding a 6,000psi hydraulic line gave out and shot through his head. He died instantly.

Auntie had come to watch me receive my indentured papers, and I introduced Auntie to John's family, my other friends, and managers; and she was like the Queen Mother in every way. I was happy she was there with me.

On one award ceremony race car driver Graham Hill, the Formula 1 World Champion, was to give us all our awards for excellence; but he had sadly died two weeks before in a light plane crash, which was all over the world news. I really was sad as I wanted to meet him, but it was not to be. Instead, his beautiful wife came; and when she gave me my award, I thanked her, squeezing her hand in mine.

She told me she wouldn't have missed it for the world as her late husband always talked about the importance of apprenticeships in the racing world.

She was so elegant and so beautiful, and she actually admired my work. Cool, huh! I still have a photograph of getting the award, and Auntie was there too, to see me complete what I had started out to do five years earlier, as a young school leaver and straight from school. She was so proud of me, and having her there at that time was as good as having any real mom, I imagined.

I left Taylor Woodrow later to become a professional singer with Ian and Dee and never looked back.

While working for Taylor Woodrow, I had gone from a young boarding school boy into becoming a young man, independent, with a career, a degree, and was a fully indentured master craftsman. I didn't realize it then, but I could work anywhere with that, even thirty years later in the United States I could have used my skill there to be a professional "Journeyman," as it is called in the United States, and would have been hired in preference to others not having being an indentured apprentice.

I had learned auto electrical on cars and trucks, heavy equipment hydraulics, rebuilding engines, even sixteen-cylinder Rolls-Royce engines, all sorts of cranes, tool and die making, and how to think through problems and how to solve them. I have used the skills I gained there throughout my whole life, and these skills have both saved me a fortune and made me a great living ever since. Having that apprenticeship was the sole reason I gained my green card in 1993 while living in the United States, I was considered to be a "professional" with the potential to succeed here in the United States.

Finishing something, as a man, that I started five years before, as a teen, despite all of the ups and downs proved that I could do anything I ever set my mind to do! I took this lesson into every situation I ever found myself in either at home or at work.

REGGIE PERRIN

I never took my singing too seriously but more as something I loved to do.

During a gig at a pub in North London, we were approached by a well-dressed, very slim middle-aged man. He wore an overcoat and a white silk scarf, and he introduced himself as Reggie Perrin. I guess he was around forty-five years old, and he really seemed to know the music business as he talked to us both about what we should be doing with our music. We listened while he talked of all the things he could do for us. He offered to be our manager, to promote us both, and to get us better gigs in more high-profile places, and maybe even a recording contract if we followed his management. So we both talked about it on the way home; and, of course, the real issue was the 25% that Ian wanted to negotiate down to 10 percent.

We had never negotiated with a manager before; and eventually, as Reggie explained all that he could do, we both agreed to give it a try for the 25% fee. He also told us that we should consider having a girl singer to enhance the sound as well as the look of the band.

At that time, we called ourselves "Size Two," although I wanted the band to be called **TONY** and Ian, with the emphasis on the TONY. Ian, of course, thought it should be the other way round, which I couldn't agree on. I told him that as I was the good-looking one, so I should headline the name; but, of course, Ian said he was and was also taller, so he should headline the band. Eventually, after a lot of non-serious discussions, we agreed on the Size Two name. We were told by Reggie to get some stage photos made, and he gave us the name of a good photographer. We decided to have a London look and went to downtown London very early one Sunday morning in May so there wouldn't be too many people around. I told Ian this would be best; otherwise, he might scare off our fans!

This was a period of pure fun, as neither of us ever thought we would become superstars

PROFESSIONAL PHOTOS

Photographs are a moment in time that we can never repeat.

So OFF WE WENT to have the portfolio photographed in several locations around London. We climbed up onto the tall lamp posts outside the Royal Albert Hall, then we went to the South Bank of the Thames and had pictures taken there with the river and Houses of Parliament in the background. We also had some photos taken on Battersea Bridge as well. The shots came out very well and were mainly in black and white; and as usual, we saw the funny side of what we were doing.

I told Ian that we should probably crop him out and only have me in them, and I could picture him somewhere in the background; we often dissed each other. In fact, during the whole shoot that lasted nearly all day, we both kept trying to get in front of the other to be in the foreground; or at the last second, we would quickly move in front of the other's face so he was blocked out. We both did exactly the same, and Ian even pushed me off a concrete pedestal just as the photo was being taken, so all you could see was the top of my head in the shot as I crashed down to the ground below. We never stopped laughing, and our friendship was as close or closer that any brothers could ever be.

We never went for the same types of girls. I always went for really pretty, well-dressed intelligent types (although the last attribute was often a secondary consideration); whereas Ian didn't! He went for more plain types, which I constantly reminded him that they really suited him. Ian in the end looked perfectly normal in the pictures; while I, ever the poser, tried to look famous, not knowing what famous looked like, anyway, Ian wouldn't agree so reluctantly I let him stay in most of the pictures. This was, of course, the way we were all the time we were doing anything together.

At this time, our reputation was growing; and our small but dedicated fan club was growing along with our reputation. We started to get better and bigger gigs, moving from pubs to night clubs and even as backing to some major bands.

We didn't believe we were better than we actually were, so we just had fun and made money at the same time.

US AND THE EQUALS
(OR THE OTHER WAY AROUND)

When you meet people on their way up you hope fame never changes them.

ONE GIG THAT Reggie was responsible indirectly for was as a backup band to "The Equals" who just about to launch their single "Baby Come Back," which went on to become their first big number 1 hit. We met them while both of us were sitting in a waiting area at a record label, the name of which I can't remember; but I do recall it was in Wardour Street. We were both there to meet with the A & R (Artist and Recording) manager that Reggie had set up for us.

We were sitting in the waiting room and talking to several members of the band, and we ended up talking to a great guy called Eddie (Grant). Eddie wanted to know what sort of music we played and wondered if we might like to support them in an upcoming gig just outside London.

The gig was at the Watford Top Rank, which was an absolutely huge venue, holding thousands of people, just off the M1 near Watford North of London; and we readily agreed.

At the Top Rank, the stage we were performing on was very large and wide and had a turntable set into the floor. We even had a complete set of stagehands and sound engineers to assist us. We were supposed to set up behind a large panel in the center of the rotating stage that separated one-half of the circular stage from the other, out of view of the audience.

Then when we gave the nod to the stagehands, they would start the turntable going as we started playing our opening number. Well, as luck would have it, Ian set the gear too close to the outside of the turntable (I'm sure it was Ian's fault); and as it started to turn, on the biggest gig we had ever managed to get, our amps and speakers started disappearing behind us as we came into view of the mega audience, we were both scrambling to get our gear back with us as it disappeared behind the turning stage. Well, the damn thing kept turning as we came into view of our audience. Can you imagine seeing this as part of the audience? The sound starts, and the band is facing the wrong way as they came into view.

The gig went well despite this, and lots of the audience that came up to us afterward asked for our autographs.

We learned that for a really big performance, always check it out first!

ADRIAN JOHNS

Sometimes we only get to meet a special friend for a very short time.

ONE OF OUR FRIENDS was Adrian Johns, who Ian had known for a long time as Ian had always gone on holiday to Newquay in Cornwall; and Adrian was from that area. So they would meet up in summer when Ian went there for holidays. As we were all at college at the time, Ian doing pure math at Brunel, Adrian at Imperial College taking Physics in London, and me doing Mechanical Engineering at Uxbridge Tech. Adrian needed the extra money to help him get through college, which was the same for us also. Adrian's mother was bringing him up in Cornwall, and he had a brother called Julian who looked a lot like John Lennon and even had the same round glasses as John, with similar long hair.

Adrian had quite a strong West Country accent and seldom, if ever, talked on stage and definitely didn't or maybe couldn't sing. But as he, like us, didn't have a lot of money, we asked him if he would like to play with us in the band.

Adrian was a gifted guitarist, learned the songs easily, and played with us for over a year. He also played on our demo album that we cut in a studio in the east end of London.

Adrian didn't have a car, so we had to pick him up in either Ian's old Ford Anglia Estate car, or as luck would have it, in my very small yellow Frogeye Sprite. My frogeye was very, very small; and three guys plus guitars was a real stretch in a strictly two-seater car. So I put my guitar and Ian's in the small trunk, which was basically an open space behind the two front seats and had no hatch or boot lid opening, so anything that was put in the "trunk" had to be slid in by leaning the seats forward in order to get to the "boot" or trunk space. Ian sat on the passenger seat, and the only way we could get Adrian into the car was with Adrian sitting on his lap. Now Adrian was very tall, around six feet three; and the only way we could get him into the tiny car was to have his head sticking out of the sliding passenger side window, while he was sitting slightly sideways on Ian's lap.

So there we were—the three of us—Ian and Adrian on the passenger seat and me driving with a guitar laying half across my lap with poor Adrian's head poking out of the side of the little yellow sports car. As we drove from

South Kensington, where Adrian's college was, to Battersea Bridge where the Old Swan, our current gig, was located, I began to see how funny this must have seemed. London streets are not that wide, and the oncoming traffic moved very fast, as did I when I was driving. So with Adrian's head sticking out of the car, I began to see the funny side of what we were doing and what it must have looked like to anyone else seeing us pass by; and I started to drive as close as I could to anything we overtook along the way.

It got worse; and if I overtook any double-decker bus, of which there were several along the way, I made sure I hung the car right next to it, driving at the same speed as the bus. And just as we got level with the large spinning bus wheels, I gradually moved the little car with Adrian's head sticking out the side, closer and closer till his head came along side and practically grazed the wheels. He couldn't get his head back into the car as there was no room whatsoever; and he was frantically trying to grab the steering wheel from me, without being able to see inside the car, to get the car to move away from the fast-moving and spinning bus tires.

Of course, I would never let anything bad happen; but it was so very funny. I also slowed down if the bus or truck's exhaust pipe was sticking out on Adrian's side of the car, to make sure he got blasted with the exhaust smoke, while pretending of course that I hadn't noticed. Such is life, and into every life, a little rain must fall; and for Adrian, we were his downpour.

Now taxi drivers in their black cabs were notoriously rude to other drivers as they picked up and dropped off their passengers, or cut in front of us other drivers, believing themselves to be the divine users of the London streets. So I drove right up alongside one, waiting for the lights to turn green, and started honking my horn making as much noise as I could. The driver looked around to see what the trouble was, and as he eventually looked down at the tiny yellow sports car sitting next to him at the traffic lights, he saw Adrian's head right next to his cab window staring right up at him.

The driver looked as though he was going to kill Adrian, so Adrian, pleading, shouted up at the taxi driver, "It's not me. It's the stupid driver." But I just kept honking from the safe side of the car shouting, "Get out the bloody way." The taxi driver was not amused at all and shouted at Adrian, "You better f*#k off then, mate, or I'll get out of this cab."

Adrian was desperately trying to apologize to him. Have you ever seen anyone physically "shrink"? Well, Adrian did just that as we passed too close to the lorries, (trucks), and busses. Needless to say, when we arrived at the Old Swan, Adrian's hair was a sight, blown all over the place with soot on his face from being so close to the exhaust pipes of the trucks, lorries, and busses that we had overtaken on the way.

Our drive took us around forty-five minutes from Imperial College to where we were playing in Battersea, so we had all the time in the world to have fun, unfortunately, at Adrian's expense.

Well, after the gig, Adrian absolutely refused to get back in the car ever again with me driving and said he would feel safer walking, getting a cab, or even getting a bus home. So I pleaded and pleaded with him and promised absolutely, looking him right in the eye, while promising on my mother's life, that I would not do it again under any circumstances. "I'm so sorry," I said to them both.

So very reluctantly, giving me the evil eye the whole time, Adrian got back into my car, once again sitting on Ian's lap with his head poking out the side window; and off we went back from the gig in Battersea to Imperial College. Well, once they were both back in my car, they were mine! I did exactly the same all over again and started laughing like a witch, all the way home, with Adrian cursing and yelling at us both. Ian, of course, was laughing his head off with me, with tears rolling down our cheeks; and we finally let Adrian out of the car once we arrived at his college after I made him promise not to hit me. This was, of course, all in fun; and we loved playing our music with Adrian on lead guitar.

After the three of us finished college, Adrian told us he was thinking of joining the navy, "The navy," we both said in unison, "what a complete waste of time." And though we tried to convince him otherwise, he went ahead and joined up. We wished him good luck, and we said we would keep in touch. That was the last time Ian and I saw Adrian for three decades!

In 2008, I got a call from Ian, and he said to me, "Do you remember Adrian who used to play lead guitar with us?" "Of course, I do," I replied, immediately recalling our journeys to and from our gigs, with Adrian, in my little yellow sports car. "Well, go onto Wikipedia and look him up and give me a call."

I looked up his name, and there right before me was Sir Adrian Johns, second sea lord of the Royal Navy, vice admiral of the Royal Fleet, having been knighted by Her Majesty the Queen for outstanding services to the navy and the country.

I was amazed to see Adrian's face smiling out at me on the Wikipedia page along with a complete chest full of medals, a very sharp uniform, and a biography, while recalling the gigs we had done, and the rides in my tiny Frogeye Sprite.

So I called Ian back and laughingly said, "We told him it would be a waste of time to join the navy. Now see what he's done." However, we were both so proud of what he had achieved.

What you should know, on reading this, is that the Royal Navy is one of the most traditional of the armed services; and to rise that high, coming from a single parent family, having to have a scholarship to get through college, is in itself a stunning achievement. Normally, you would have come from a naval family with a long tradition of achievement in defending the Realm from the marauding hoards on our high seas. When I looked up "Second Sea Lord," I saw a long line of sea lords going back to 1830; and the last name on the list, at the time I read the article, was marked Adrian Johns, marked 2005—with a dash next to his name and no termination date, as he was the present second sea lord.

He relinquished his position as second sea lord and vice admiral of the Royal Navy when Her Majesty the Queen appointed Adrian to become the governor of Gibraltar in 2009. He was taken there as guest of honor on board a naval vessel and presented with the Keys of Gibraltar.

I went online and found the address of the governor of Gibraltar and decided to write a letter to him.

My letter went like this:

August 29, 2010
Dear Adrian,
I doubt that you will remember me, but Ian Howard yourself and I played in a band while we were all in college. You were at Imperial College taking physics, Ian took pure math at Brunel and I took mechanical engineering at Uxbridge while completing an apprenticeship at Taylor Woodrow.
You were exceptionally good at lead guitar, as I recall, and we played at 'The Old Swan' in Battersea together where, once after a very scary drive in my very small yellow Frogeye Sprite with you sitting on Ian's lap with your head sticking outside of the small sliding window, you vowed never to get in a car with me again.

Sorry for that, Adrian, and I note your hair re grew after me driving far too close to the buses we overtook on the way to the 'gig with your hair brushing the tires of the buses and lorries along the way.

You also played on our demo album. I was so happy and so very proud when I saw your amazing progress with your career in the Royal Navy. Ian and I have kept in close contact over the years and he called me to ask me to look you up on Wikipedia.

I read with great interest your meteoric rise through the ranks and your knighthood leading to your present appointment as Governor of Gibraltar.

Congratulations, Adrian. You haven't changed though, in your picture, but undoubtedly in other ways you must have as a result of your immense responsibilities and the weight associated with your official capacity.

As for me, I moved over to Indianapolis in 1991 with Alfa Laval having managed their global customer service operations in Brussels. After leaving them I started up a fragrance company which we sold and then became General Manager and CEO of a glove company of all things. I designed and built firefighting gloves including one which is presently the most widely used in the US and Canada. I was asked to take part in the US Army's Rapid Field Initiative in 2004, after the beginning of the war in Iraq, to be part of a group of specialized manufacturers and advanced materials specialists, to help redesign the apparel for the US forces.

I designed, among other things, a glove for the US Army which, after being shown at the Pentagon, is now installed in every U.S. GI's kit bag, and me a Brit!

Life is sometimes so strange, isn't it Adrian, and very exiting with your success in the Navy, Ian's success in his music businesses and my diverse career we all scraped through. I am married to Sue for 22 years with 2 girls living in Ealing and 2 boys living here in the US.

I am writing a book, which I hope will inspire young people to reach their potential based on all the things I have been so fortunate to have done, but which pales compared to your success.

However when you consider that the three of us, you Ian and I, had somewhat difficult upbringings we have all done exceptionally well despite that, or perhaps it was because of that that we three succeeded.

I realize this may never get to you, but in case it does I would love to hear about the things you have done, and I'm really glad you didn't take Ian's and my advice not to join up but to stay in the band!
Yours Sincerely,

I received a reply from him very shortly by e-mail:

Tony,
Thank you so much for taking the trouble to write. It was great
to hear from you and I can only apologize for taking so long to reply. I had been meaning to put pen to paper but then decided to ask Ian for your e-mail address—undoubtedly a quicker means of communication to and from the colonies!
I feel very guilty that I only caught up with Ian just over a year ago, just before we moved out to Gibraltar. It was 35 years since I'd seen him (and you) and the stupid thing was that we lived in London for the last 13 years—so close yet we never met.
Anyway, we had a terrific catch up session at his place and had a

really good laugh about your old frogeye Sprite. I remember only too well tearing along the roads perilously close to the parked cars and buses with my head stuck out of the passenger window—some problem with the heater I seem to recall!

I was fascinated to hear about how life has treated you—evidently not too badly and certainly very interestingly. I would never have put you down as a glove man, but there you are—life is never predictable. You know the three of us ought to catch up with each other again and, as I keep telling Ian now, none of us can afford to wait another 35 years or whatever the interval is. I may be out in the US (Iowa) next year for a wedding; if it works out well, I'm hoping that we can spend a week or so traveling—perhaps there's an opportunity there. But in any case, a warm welcome awaits you (and Ian) in Gibraltar—maybe we ought to have a musical reunion!

Whatever happens, let's ensure we keep in touch this time.

With warm regards,

AJ

 His message back was as if no time at all had passed between us in more than thirty years.

That's the thing with friends; time doesn't matter at all, and we are all still the same people we were then as now.

 Well, congrats, Adrian. Way to go! Hope we meet up again sometime soon, but hopefully not in another thirty-five years, and maybe one day when I come over to England to see my family; but after Ian and I talked a bit, we decided, "Don't call us. We'll call you when we need you as a lead guitarist again.

I recognized in Adrian the same drive I had in myself and he, like me, stuck to what he loved and he also, like me, made it no matter what. You will know yourself by the friends you keep so take a look around you, what do your friends say about you?

THE PENTHOUSE

Bob Guccioni was one of a kind, a gentleman when I met him.

WE WERE PLAYING in a pub in Mayfair called the Red Lion, on Half Moon Street, which was next to the Penthouse Club, when Bob Guccioni came with several of his absolutely gorgeous "Penthouse Pets" and sat in the upstairs bar opposite us for a while listening to our music. From that point on, we found it difficult to remember our words and even more so to remain standing while he and these beautiful girls were sitting opposite us. Each of them wore extremely short skirts or hot pants; and during our break, Bob came over to talk to us. He told us who he was, but we knew already, as Ian had seen his face in his *Penthouse* magazines (which as I recall he was always buying). He asked us to play at his club next door and invited us in for drinks later that night, after we had finished at the Red Lion, as his guests to see where we would perform.

His house band, "The International Trio," was off playing on the QE 2 for six months.

So we got to play at the Penthouse club, in the International Room, where the best-looking girls we had ever seen now worked; and believe me, there were loads of them there every night. They were his "Penthouse Pets" and were often featured in his *Penthouse* magazine.

We were actually able to recognize some of them with their clothes on! They were very similar to *Playboy*'s "Bunny Girls" at the Playboy Club, which was just down the street and had recently opened not far from where we were playing on Half Moon Street. The Playboy Club was opposite Hyde Park. The "pets" wore very tight body-hugging costumes that started halfway down their boobs and finished at the top of their very long legs. Their tops were very low cut, and they also wore dark fishnet tights, with high heels that finished off their costumes . . . perfectly. I said to Bob one night, when he came down to hear us, that we'd do this gig for nothing; but to get paid for being in the Penthouse Club was a such a blast! Bob, looked at me and offered to let us play for nothing, if that was what we wanted, but we told him the "No! Money was fine." He laughed at that and said " I thought so too"

Our gig was from midnight till 3:00 a.m., depending on how busy the club was. One night, one of the "pets," called Julia, came up to us and stood right in front of me as we were singing or trying to. I had noticed her from the first night but also thought that the girls were probably off limits to us. Julia told me right there and then, as we were halfway through a song, that she had no lift home and wanted me to take her home after the gig! I said I'd think about it and after about one nanosecond said. "OK!"

I took her home to her flat in Fulham, which was on my way home. Julia was great fun to be with, and we went out together for around three months. I would go to the club at weekends to pick her up in my sports car, and I remember thinking, *Life Just doesn't get any better than this*, as I was driving through London in an open-top sports car with one of the most beautiful girls in the world, with a "Penthouse pet," sitting next to me with her long hair blowing in the wind!

Bob Guccioni was one hell of a guy, and I never cared what anyone else thought or said; to me he was a hero and was a very genuine person. The drive it takes to reach the top in any profession is the same drive that sometimes offends others.

LADY PENELOPE

Sometimes you can just get lucky; after all every success has a little luck!

WE WENT THROUGH the process of looking for a girl singer, and we came across a beautiful blonde "Dee Anderson." Dee was a stunningly good-looking girl; she wore the shortest hot pants we had ever seen and had very sexy legs and a very pretty face. Dee was slim, petite, and had the great voice to go with it. In short, Dee had the complete package and was absolutely perfect for us.

Dee, as we found out later, was the daughter of Sylvia and Gerry Anderson, who had created produced and directed all of the *Supermarionation* TV series: *Thunderbirds*, *Fireball XL-5*, *Supercar*, and many more children's TV shows since the late sixties, going back as far as *Four Feather Falls*, which Ian had watched while we were in junior school.

We used to practice singing with her sometimes at Ian's house and sometimes at her mother's house in Gerrards Cross just twenty-five miles west of Ealing.

At her mother's house, there were alcoves set into the walls, all the way up the sweeping staircase, with the actual puppets that were used in the TV series. I was fascinated at the detail in every model. I was looking at Mike, Virgil, Brains, and of course Lady Penelope, from the *Thunderbirds* series; and every costume had the tiniest stitching, and each was finished right down to the smallest detail. Brains even had a small pen in his top pocket along with a tiny pair of glasses. When her mom wasn't around, I used to make Parker, the chauffeur, bonk Lady Penelope, much to the disgust of Dee, who was petrified in case her mom came back into the room.

Singing with Dee brought us some class and a third part harmony, which we needed, and enabled us to do more complex three-part musical arrangements.

Dee was married to Vick Elmes, who was the lead guitarist with a band called Christie, and we even sang some of their numbers. Christie had just had a number 1 hit in England and all over Europe, a couple of years earlier, with "Yellow River" and were currently away on a South African tour.

Christie also released other songs "San Bernardino" and "Iron Horse," but these didn't do as well as "Yellow River."

Dee sang with us for a long time; and although she was a little younger than us, she was a true professional and had the most amazing "stage presence," adding a third dimension to our playing.

Together with Dee, we did some big shows backing people like Ruby Murray, who although now is no longer singing having retired a long time ago, at that time they were headliners and were still big names in the British music scene.

I decided to make our stage costumes, for our cabaret gigs, as we had no money to buy them with. We went out and looked at fabrics and finally settled on bright pink satin for the trousers, with white satin baggy shirts. I made the trousers for Ian and I; and Dee, of course, had the shortest "hot pants" ever made and looked stunning in whatever she wore, so I made her hot pants with the small offcuts leftover, not really though. I could no doubt have done it.

During one gig with Dee, we were playing in front of a large working men's club in North London that was packed with people who had come to hear us as we had been billed for several months.

We were playing one Sunday lunchtime, and at the end of one of our numbers, we all kicked our legs into the air together (God, did we actually do that stuff). Unfortunately though, as we did this on that particular day, Ian's trousers were a little too tight; and as he kicked his leg as high as he could, exactly as we had rehearsed it, his trousers split all the way from the front zipper to the back waistband right at the crotch.

Dee and I heard a ripping sound and looked 'round at a very red-faced Ian. He immediately felt "quite free." Dee and I burst out laughing but had to carry on with the song, and luckily he was wearing underwear (sometimes he didn't), so it could have been worse.

You should have seen the women's faces on the front row as they ogled the scene. Ian, of course, was bright red and tried to lower his guitar to cover his underwear in case the fly opened. Unfortunately for him though, the guitar strap wouldn't let it drop down, so there he was kind of crouched over as if he was dying to go to the toilet in order to make the guitar hang lower. In fact, it wasn't the guitar that was hanging lower at all. We quickly finished the number, and Ian had to rush back to the dressing room to change.

Together with Dee, we also got gigs in many variety shows. They were a lot of fun to do, mainly because we only had to sing four or five numbers, and were getting paid more than we usually did playing all night in clubs and pubs.

Our crowd of fans came with us everywhere to support us all the time. Christmas was the greatest time of all, and we had a number of Christmas songs that we played—Slade, John Lennon, Wizard, and many others—and we were good at getting people dancing and singing along with us. We were in high demand and had to be booked up for New Year's Eve and Christmas Eve months or even a year in advance.

Our favorite gig though was the Old Swan in Battersea, where we played overlooking the river Thames and sang there off and on for more than two years.

Ian had a girlfriend called Sandy, another blonde who, as I recall, loved animals and was obsessed with dogs. I thought Ian would marry her, but that wasn't to be. I was still with Cezara, and the four of us used to go on holiday together in Cornwall. We drove down and booked a cottage to stay in. Life for us both was so easy, and we seemed to be able to do whatever we wanted.

Dee Anderson and I have remained close and true friends and we follow the successes of our true friends with great pride.

MOIRA

When people have different needs from a relationship the strongest usually wins, though the outcome is seldom enjoyed at the time by the other.

It WAS AROUND this time after I started working at Alfa Laval and singing almost every night that I met Moira. Moira was eighteen years old with naturally beautiful long blonde hair, and she was working at Beecham's just down the Great West Road near my office at Alfa Laval. We met in a pub, one lunchtime, when I was with some work colleagues though I'm not sure which pub it was as I went to so many.

Moira was absolutely gorgeous, and I just had to go up and talk to her, though I wasn't sure if she would talk to me; but I didn't care. It was worth a try anyway. We started to talk and arranged to meet a few days later, always at lunchtime and always in the pub. I told her that there was a job going at my company as a secretary to one of the service directors if she was interested in applying for it.

Well, she was interested, and she applied for and got the job as personal assistant for a service director called Jim Henderson, who was a little scatty but a good bloke.

Moira was the most stunning-looking girl in the entire company. She came into work often in short miniskirts, which of course were very "in" at that time; and sometimes she also wore a pair of metallic maroon knee-length boots, which coupled with her naturally light honey blonde hair, worn down past her shoulders, made her devastatingly beautiful.

All of the guys working there, in the offices, wanted to go out with her; but she was quite shy and would only talk to a very few people. I of course was a lucky one that she did talk to.

Although her first name is Irish, she was very much a London girl. She dressed beautifully all the time and had a nice lilting voice with a sexy laugh that was always just under the surface. I seemed to be able to make her laugh a lot then.

Our paths crossed while I was working in the spares office, as she often came in to check on something or other for her service team. I knew she could have done it over the phone but took the fact that she came in to my office instead to mean one of two things; either she needed to get out of her boss Jim's office, or she wanted to come in to my office to see me. I of course chose to believe the latter, and we started talking, eventually meeting for lunchtime drinks; and we met almost every day getting along really well.

She was very kind, very thoughtful, and better still she paid her way, not letting me always buy the drinks but insisting on paying for them as well, unlike most other girls I knew then. She took life and her job quite seriously, which is more than I can say for myself as I was just a clown. We went out together for about nine months, during the time she worked there, but we very seldom, if ever, met at night. I was always playing and singing all over London and really had little time for a steady girlfriend at that time, which was not what Moira wanted.

Moira told me one day that she had a boyfriend, and she was considering marriage. I saw our relationship as mostly daytime friends, almost like brother and sister, and didn't think of a permanent relationship at that time, with anyone. Moira would have been the girl I would have married if I had been in a different frame of mind, but life was too busy, and there were too many fun things to do to ever consider getting married.

I knew that she wanted a permanent relationship with me, and I knew that she loved me; and that was why she was telling me this, to see what my reaction would be. I also knew though that I was not right at that time for her as I had so many things I still wanted to do and didn't want a permanent relationship. I certainly never wanted to cause any problems for, or ever hurt, Moira but knew that if I did go out with her on a more permanent basis let alone get married to her, at that time, it would have ended in disaster and it would have been caused entirely by me.

Moira wanted more from her relationship with me; and after her boss, Jim, was transferred to the States to run a service operation in Lake Geneva in the Midwest, in 1973, Moira left Alfa's, never to return. We did, however, still meet up occasionally for a lunchtime drink, to catch up on things, for a long time after she left, though by now she was happily married. We became very close as time went on long after both she and I had left Alfa Laval, and Moira became my soul mate. We have now known each other for nearly forty years, she in London and me in the States; and although we never meet in person, we have kept in touch for nearly forty years.

A break in a relationship for honest reasons can make friends forever.

JEANETTE

A femme fatale once in your life is being on a rollercoaster!

I HAD A RED MGBGT at the time and decided to change it for another one, just because I could! I started looking through Exchange and Mart and eventually found a late model automatic. I arranged to meet the seller, a French girl, outside Alfa Laval's offices in Brentford where I worked. I took the car for a test drive and asked all the right questions. The next day, I bought the blue MGBGT from Jeanette, and we became friends. We talked over the phone for several weeks before actually meeting up again and began going out together.

I went out with Jeanette for two tumultuous years and can honestly say that she was the one person that really taught me all about girls and how a boy should act when going out with a girl. Up to that point, I was only interested in one thing! One detail though, Jeannette was married and had a son called Toby, who was five years old and, at that time, which I was not certain about at all.

She told me she was divorcing her husband, Richard, a minicab driver, adding that they didn't get on at all well and that he sometimes hit her. Jeanette had a very sexy French accent that she could turn up or down at will, and the amount always depended on what she wanted from whomever she was talking to. She was very elegant, beautiful in fact, tall and slim with long brown highlighted hair. She had such a magnetic presence about her that when we went to restaurants or clubs in London, she would always turn heads as she entered.

She loved the attention she got from any males, married or not, and made sure when she moved everyone noticed her. Her family was from Toulouse in Southern France, and she had a sister called Katherine, "Kati." She was blessed with incredible looks and the charm to go with it.

I became completely infatuated with her; and Jeanette and I went out all over the place, to clubs, restaurants, parks, art galleries, and anywhere she wanted to go to. And I learned how to act cool (cooler than I thought I already was) and learned what sophistication was all about.
Yeah right!

"Tonnie," she would say in her very French accent, "ow you do dress so droll, you look like a plouk. I weel take you out and pick out some cloths that soot you more." "Wha's a plouk then?" I asked her. And she told me, "Plouk is a word for a French peasant, just like you." And we used the word a lot as I liked the sound of it. "Plouk" was a perfect word.

So we went out to buy new clothes, and I changed my "look" just like that! I was so bloody gullible. She had me wearing horizontally striped French-cut T-shirts, a black neck scarf, and flared jeans. I thought I looked like "Falconetti" from *Rich Man, Poor Man*, a current show on TV of the time. Jeanette looked a lot like Barbara Streisand—not only because she had similar features but also because she acted like her too. At least she acted like the parts Streisand played in the movies she was acting in at the time, like *The Owl and the Pussycat* with Walter Matthau, and made sure that everyone saw the similarity. She desperately and constantly sought recognition for herself and was extremely high maintenance. Me, I had enough money, was single, and could afford to deal with it, at least for a time.

Jeanette had also done some modeling for some magazine or other, and so I guessed she knew about fashionable dress sense. Once for my birthday, when I was twenty-five, she took me to the most expensive restaurant I had ever been to—"The White Elephant"—on the river and gave me my birthday present, which was a solid silver very chunky bracelet with the letters of my name *TONY* actually cast into the links of the bracelet (It's in the photo of me with Vick Elmes).

It was very ostentatious, but I loved it; it was unique, and I still have it. I had never seen anything like it; and apparently, as she continued to inform me, "Eet kem from a very expenseev and excluseev designer gallerie in Paris. So you see ow much I love you, Tonnie. I av made you into a not-so-plouky person . . . all by my leetle French self." God, how could I not fall in love with that!

Things at her house, with Richard, got progressively worse; and she convinced me to drive her home to Toulouse. "Eet will be so much fun, Tonnie. I can teach you ow to speak French like a true Frenchman, and we can live in the south of France together." Well, for me, that sounded absolutely great; and I could do with a change of scenery.

So we moved on our plan. She began to teach me French, and I was a good learner. I had a knack for languages, or so I thought, and could learn and speak the absolute worse slang phrases imaginable and come out with them just at the right time, just as I had with Polish phrases.

I was after all now a multilingual swearer. I could swear with the best of them in three languages—Polish, French, and of course English. I wonder what I could use that for.

Jeanette had a health issue though, causing her to go into a freezelike trance that she called Tetany, which was some kind of illness that caused her to collapse on the floor completely stiff. This was not a problem for me, as it happened very infrequently. When it happened, she had to take some dark brown liquid that she always kept in her purse in a sealed glass phial that had to be snapped at one end in order to get the liquid out. Weird, huh! I had met some of her friends from Toulouse when they came over to London just after Christmas in 1974, and we got on so well. There was Jean Louie and Jackotte, Eve and Michel, and Georges. When they came over to visit her, at her house in Pinner, I was introduced to them; and they looked so cool. They each wore a different style of hat and dressed very "French" in dark corduroy trousers in colors that matched their hats. For example, Michel had a pair of light brown cords and a light brown fedora, Jean Louis had a gray pair of cords and a gray beret, while Georges wore dark brown cords with a dark brown hat.

I tried out my newly learned French, which they thought was great; but because I did try to speak with them in French and tried the many slang phrases as well as conversational French I had been taught by Jeannette, I could blame my lousy French on my very bad teacher.

They all came over just after Christmas, in late December, and we took them to clubs and pubs all over London.
Jackotte and Jean Louie were quite wealthy and had their own farm. Eve was a gifted artist, and Michel was the absolute rough and ready French male chauvinist; but I liked him a lot, especially since Jeanette often called him simply "the plouk." Georges was single, and they all knew each other since school. I envied that part as they were so alike and were so much fun to be with—my "French crowd."

It's hard to tell if a relationship is infatuation or love?

THE FRENCH CONNECTION

When love is blind even a pair of glasses won't help!

I WAS BY NOW completely crazy about Jeanette and was quite prepared to do anything to help her. So in summer 1976, I met with my personnel manager and told him I had to take a temporary leave so that I could take my girlfriend back to her family in France.

Alfa Laval agreed, and Jeanette and I left London to drive down to Toulouse in my MGB-GT, initially for a vacation. The weather that year was the hottest summer we had had in Europe for decades, with eight weeks of very hot sunny days and temperatures in the nineties. We drove my car down through Paris to Rouen in perfect weather, which became hotter and hotter as we drove south toward Toulouse. Jeanette wanted to show me how beautiful her capital, Paris, was; although she constantly reminded me, "Toulouse is of course much more important than Paris."

We passed through Le Mans, so we could drive "The Strip" where the famous Le Mans Twenty-Four-Hour race is held; and having a sports car was great. We drove like a GT racer through some of the most beautiful countryside I had ever seen. We passed through the Loir Valley where it was so hot we went for a swim in the Loir River. We then went on through Clermont-Ferrand in the Massif Central Mountains that were very high up.

Clermont-Ferrand was an expensive ski resort with a casino in the middle of town.

Jeannette had her way and insisted we meet the mayor of Clermont-Ferrand, who was quite taken by her; and he made some phone calls for us so that we stayed in a beautiful hotel overlooking the town with the mountains in the background.   I loved it! That was typical of Jeanette, to make last minute arrangements at the highest level. That night, we got into the casino, compliments of the mayor, and had a blast. I knew nothing of gambling and was really quite naive, compared with Jeanette. She showed me how to play roulette, blackjack, and poker. She won at everything, while I lost! The casino was fabulous, very old money there, and the rich from all over France went there for weekends.

We then got back onto the road to Toulouse the following day, heading east through Brive-La-Gaillarde then to Limoges where we tried the local wine on our drive south. The most beautiful place we passed through was Uzerche, on our way down from Limoges, where the local wine was absolutely incredible.

The town was very pretty and had a river running right through the town. The local shops restaurants and bars were so quaint, and we had lunch while in Uzerche and I hoped one day to go back through there. Little was I to know that my wish would come true, but that's later. We lived on wine, local saucisson (French country sausage), and local cheeses that were delicious.

We finally drove through Montauban and finally into Toulouse, "The Rose City," called that because of the rose-colored roof tiles and the pink brick that the town was built from.

Although we were not actually staying in Toulouse, as her friends lived just outside in a small town called Bruguier's, just to the north of Toulouse.

I was introduced to Jeanette's parents, and I was accepted as her "friend" who had brought her home from England. Her mother was a very attractive well-dressed and elegantly "chic" lady who taught English at an "Ecole du Langue" in Downtown Toulouse. She was clearly the "in-charge" head of the family; and while her father, an Englishman, was pleasant, he said very little to me. He seemed very different from her and was from somewhere in the Midlands, judging from his accent.

I didn't want to stay with her parents, even as Jeanette insisted that I did, as I felt uncomfortable not being Jeanette's husband. Eve (pronounced Ev) and Michel insisted that I stayed with them, so that's what happened. I moved my stuff into Eve and Michel's home in Bruguier's, which was only a twenty-five-minute drive.

I grew very fond of Eve and Michel and loved their house. They had two hunting dogs that were kept outside always, whose names were "Boogie" and "Patou"; and their house had a beautiful view to the South of Andorra, a tiny country that borders on France and Spain and is located in the Andorra Mountains.

In the evenings, we could watch the thunderstorms that often occurred in the high mountains around Andorra where the warm air from Southern France met with the cooler air off the mountains.

Eve and Michel became very close friends to me, with Michel taking me with him into the local village every evening to meet his friends at the local bar. I became well known and was often asked to play guitar for them all. We had party after party, and I met lots of Eve and Michel's friends from all over the south.

Eve lived a very "country" lifestyle, and they were people who lived for the day, never making arrangements but making dinner arrangements on the spur of the moment. They had two children: Olivier, who was eight years old, and Isabelle, who was six years old. The children were a lot of fun, and I was the local superstar who played all over London and was apparently "famous" there, according to Jeanette (she always exaggerated).

One thing about life with Jeanette was that it was difficult to separate truth from fiction. She had a way of embellishing any story that made it larger than reality. She had told her friends and family that I was a famous musician and had a great musical career in London, adding that I was going to go back to a tour of gigs all over Europe.

So I sang for my supper, whenever they wanted me to, which was fine by me, and even got gigs in some of the local restaurants and in clubs in Toulouse. I didn't make a huge amount of money, but it was enough for me to get by and allowed me to buy petrol for my car and to help Eve pay for food. I was even in a local music magazine with a picture of Ian and I. Eve and Michel were not well off, and Michel was often away on sales trips all over Southern France. Michel came from a large family who lived on the same plot of land with an open-air swimming pool placed between Eve and Michel's house and his parents' house. His older brother, Bernard Nicolas, was a news announcer with "Canal Plus," a nationwide TV station. We often saw him announcing the evening news on TV where he was broadcasting the day's events.

I stayed mostly with Eve, while Michel was away. I helped her with the family and rode around on her little moped. That was a blast in itself; though it didn't go fast, it was fast enough for me, especially since the local drivers were so bloody dangerous and drove so fast that I took my life into my hands whenever I got on the thing. Often they would come right up behind me and blast their horns to let me know they were passing regardless of a bend, a narrow lane, or whatever.

They would shout out, "hey, englese, ow is the queen," so bloody funny as I was quite well known in the small village of Bruguieres; and several times I was forced off the road and into the ditch, which was a real hoot!

Needless to say, after some three weeks of vacationing in Toulouse, it was time for me to get back to work.

The drive back was fast, and the weather was still very hot, one of the hottest summers on record. We arrived back in England, and I dropped her off; it was now September, and soon the weather would change.

I went back to my job at Alfa Laval and got back into my routine of singing at night while working during the day. Life was good, and I never seemed to have time for anything else as we were playing six nights a week and working five days.

Things with Jeanette at home got steadily worse. She had moved ahead with her divorce, and she wanted me to take her back to France to live there permanently; however, she had met up with an old boyfriend who stayed at her house for a few weeks, someone she had apparently known for many years. His name was Jean Paul, and they seemed very close.

I didn't care though as I was not the jealous type and believed in our own relationship. By now, my French was really pretty good; and one afternoon while the three of us where playing cards, I heard them both talking quietly in French as we were playing, and she was saying, "Mais je'taime plus mon cher" to Jean Paul, or something very close. I knew what it meant, and she was telling him that she loved him more.

So I told her that I had understood what she had just said. She immediately began to laugh and began an elaborate explanation that it was another French expression that meant they were close friends and nothing more. Later I gave her an ultimatum, either stay with Jean Paul or stay with me. She chose me, and he promptly moved back to France.

Shortly after this incident, she decided to move over to France permanently and set up there. I discussed this with Ian, and we agreed that I would set up gigs for us to play there and he would come over and join me to sing to a French audience. We drove over in October, and I moved back in with Eve and Michel; while Jeannette and Toby moved in with her mom and dad in downtown Toulouse. We found Toby a French school, and he began to attend, with me taking him and picking him up. I had no experience with looking after a seven-year-old but gave it my best. It was a difficult time, and I began to have doubts about our relationship and whether I could make it there as I was now planning to live there permanently.

I could speak a little French, and it was improving day by day. I had to find gigs in restaurants, bars, and clubs by myself. Jeannette's mother had given me a job teaching English at her private school, but I didn't like it much. Jeannette's mother didn't like what she was doing and made it clear to me I was unwelcome. Things had changed for us both.

Jeannette was finding it very difficult to live back in France with her mother, and this was the cause of numerous and increasing problems between us. It got so bad that Michel actually banned her from the house after a blazing argument in which she broke into fast-talking French that Michel and Eve understood, and Eve explained to me that she was crazy and Michel told her to get a job and begin to stand on her own two feet and not to rely on me.

Meanwhile, as I had been living there for a while, Alfa Laval were contacting me to see if I would like come back to work; and as money was getting very tight for me, gigs I did manage to get did not pay that well and certainly not enough to support Jeannette and Toby, so after some careful thought, I decided to return back to London and to leave Jeannette to her own devices back in Toulouse with her family. I had not seen her for three months and didn't miss her, since I was very busy trying to get more work. Eve and Michel were true friends, and even after I left them, we have stayed in touch for many years.

After I left France and had finished with Jeanette for good, I sent them some money for Christmas in a letter I wrote, telling them that this money was for all of them to spend or squander on whatever they wanted for themselves and not to be used for paying bills. Eve told me years later that as she read it out to Michel and showed him the money, he cried at what I had done. I told her, "No, not that, Eve. I only wanted to repay some of the kindness you both showed me while I was living there." It was such a small thing in return for all that they had done to help me. We were and still are true soul mate.

I learned from this that if a relationship, in life or in business, becomes bad make the decision to do something sooner than later.

LIVE ON RADIO IN FRANCE

I was singing on a radio station in Toulouse, now that was cool!

I TOOK JANE TO Toulouse to see Eve and Michel in 1979, some four years after I had left to return to London, and took my guitar, as Michel had sponsored a concert with me as the headline.

Jane and I learned several songs together, and we played the gig. There was a local radio station doing a live recording as we played; and when we played "Hotel California," by request, the whole place started lighting candles and cigarette lighters and moved toward the stage. It was a magical moment, and we were well accepted by the crowd. We were interviewed live by the local radio station, and Eve had to translate for us.

Later, Eve played the radio program for us to hear our gig. We were billed as coming all the way from London to be there, and they played excerpts from several songs that we did.

My French "sojourn" was finally at a close, and I began to pick up my life again in London. My job had been left open for me, and Alfa Laval had called me several times to get me back. As I had nowhere to stay immediately I got back, I lived at Ian's house for a couple of weeks, before moving into a flat with two of Ian's friends, Fred and Mark.

Fred, who was a tall guy with a beard (looked like a hippy), was dating Annabelle, Ian's sister; and I could not see what Annabelle saw in him, but it was OK with me as long as he made her happy. Annabelle was eighteen anyway and was a stunner with her long blonde hair and her slim figure. Fred was older than Annie, as I called her. Annabelle often came round to our pad to see Fred.

It was time to return to London and I never looked back.

GOING SEPARATE WAYS

Music or business!

IT WAS AT THIS time, after I had returned from France, that Ian told me he had started a business; and that was why he wouldn't come over to France despite me getting gigs and having articles written about my playing.

Ian's business was a second-hand records and tapes business with Alan, a friend of ours. He had opened a small shop in Putney called Music Market and was planning to open more shops as his business grew.

I felt very let down as I had looked forward to moving on together in music, and I had planned for us to sing in France for as long as we could.

"Look," Ian said one day when I we were talking about his new business and I wanted to know why he hadn't told me about it, "there is a space for your name on the letterhead if you want to join us." I knew though it wouldn't work; and that if it was meant to be, we would have done it together already.

This was the point at which Ian and I stopped being such close friends and started moving in separate directions. We didn't see or contact each other much over the next thirty years, and both of us moved in different directions. More of Ian's exploits later.

It is a tough decision to make—that you are not going to make it big in the music business by performing, although many of the artist managers and agents that had heard us play had wanted to represent us and move us up in the business.

One had even started making plans that we should become the next "New Seekers," but we didn't like that idea. I was now twenty-six and decided that if we were meant to make it, we would have done so by now.

I had written several songs; and Brian Longley, who was managing Christie, Edison Lighthouse, and others at that time, wanted me to sign the songs over to him as the band "Middle of the Road" were looking for a follow up to "Chirpy Chirpy Cheep Cheep," a terrible song that had actually made it in the charts.

Brian had played them my songs, and they liked one called Penny Farthing. The deal though was for 25 percent of net, and I knew that by the time he had taken his cut, and all of his expenses were taken out I would have nothing left, so I declined. Brian certainly knew the business and was managing several other bands at the same time.

I decided that I since I had a degree in engineering, I had better start using it and start focusing on my job, which by the way was really taking off; and I was getting a good reputation in the company, not that I thought much about that as I always focused only on what I was doing and not about what others thought of me.

Knowing the difference between being a good performer and having the star quality required to make it in the entertainment business is hard. It's worse though to continue in the belief that you are better than you really are!

A CLAIRVOYANT'S WARNING

When information comes to you from out of 'left field' it is often spot on!

SEVERAL YEARS LATER, after had finished with Jeanette and was now seeing Jane, she and I went to see a clairvoyant that Jane knew, called Peggy. Peggy was a very gifted person and told me several very accurate things. One of the things Peggy had told me was that there was a dark attractive woman coming to find me (at least she's not ugly), and that she was headed into my "circle." She warned me that I must not go with her and under no circumstances must I let her know where I was or to agree to meet her under any circumstances.

She also told me that she was foreign, was very unstable, and that she was erratic and was probably psychotic. I knew exactly who it was after that last part of the description—"psychotic." It was Jeanette, and Peggy described her absolutely to the "T." Peggy also told me that I had a guardian who spoke the same foreign language as the dark woman. She said that my guardian would "block" her from seeing me and would send her away. My guardian was an older lady and had short blonde hair.

I was very happily married to Jane and had no plans at all to go back into the past. I had closed that door a few years before Jane and I met.

Well, Jeannette did come back to London four months after my meeting with Peggy; she started going into the same pubs in Ealing that I had been frequenting and eventually met up with a friend of mine Lillien. Now Lillien was a Parisian living in Ealing and had been living with a very close friend of mine, Tony Upton. Lilly, as we called her, owned her own hair dressing salon in Ealing; and the three of us—Lilly, Tony, and I—had often gone out for drinks together (seems my whole life revolved around the pub). Tony and I had worked together in a new boutique called Mr. Howard and became close friends; but how Lilly and Jeanette met is a complete mystery to me, since Lilly had never actually met Jeanette. I had described her to Tony and Lilly many times, and they knew all about her sometimes erratic behavior; but meet they did in the Bell in Ealing.

As Lilly told me several weeks later, she overheard a girl, with a strong French accent, talking to the bar staff while ordering a drink. Lilly and

Tony were in the Bell in Ealing Common, standing at the bar with their friends. So after Lilly heard her French accent probably put on very strong, Lilly went over to talk to her as they were both French.

As they talked, my name soon came up, of course; and Jeannette told Lilly she was a very close friend of mine and started asking questions about where I was and what I was doing. Lilly was no fool and knew that I had left France to get away from her!

I had already told Lilly and Tony all about my tumultuous affair with Jeannette, how I had fallen in love with her, and how she had lied to me about her situation with her husband, who was really a decent guy and not at all the wife beater she had me believe and how she had left me in France, no money, nothing except Eve and Michel with whom I was living. Jeannette was also a girl who could never have only one relationship at a time; she always needed to have other men in her life to somehow make her feel good.

So Lilly sat down and had a drink with her and told her that I had been moved to the United States with Alfa Laval (funny because many years later I would be moving over there anyway), and they hadn't seen me around for at least six months. Jeannette gave Lilly her contact information in London and Toulouse then left the bar and never came back into my life again.

As it turned out, after not finding me, she went back and lived in Pau in France, marrying Jean Paul and had two children with him. I had no regrets at all, but what I did learn though was that women like Jeanette can never accept it when someone else ends the relationship and people like her always have to have life on their own terms and only let it be on someone else's terms if those don't conflict with hers.

She had been "blocked" by Lilly, exactly as had been told to me by Peggy and I probably owe my sanity to Lilly; and she didn't even know of my meeting with Peggy, some four months earlier.

There are many inexplicable events that have happened to me and some events that were told to me before they happened, but then, what is normal anyway?

It's up to us to use information or ignore it, the choice is ours to make. After all I had seen, in my past, I decided to use this information; it proved to be a good choice.

JANE

Comes a time to settle down.

JANE AND I MET at the Queens Silver Jubilee party at "The Haven" pub in Ealing on June 6, 1977, when everyone in England had a street party to celebrate the queen's twenty-fifth anniversary. John and Mary, who ran the pub, knew us both separately as we both spent quite a lot of time there in the evenings and weekends but moved in separate circles.

We began dating soon after, and Jane had recently divorced from Lesley, her first husband. Jane had a young daughter, Amanda, from that marriage; and Amanda was only eleven months when Jane and I met. I liked Amanda immediately as she was such a quiet little girl with light blonde curly hair, and she and I became instant best friends. Jane and I had been dating for several months, during which time I often moved between my pad and her apartment, which was located in a very expensive part of Ealing.

At that time, both Jane and I had good careers, so money was never a problem. I worked during the day at Alfa and during the evenings playing at pubs and clubs all over London. I reckon I could have become a taxi driver with so many places I knew how to get to. After we had been going out for several months, she asked me if I wanted to move in with her as it would be cheaper for both of us. I was a little concerned about whether Les, her ex-husband, would make it difficult; but as he had been the sole cause of their marriage break up, Jane told me he had nothing to say in the matter. So I moved out of my very cool and trendy little bachelor pad in Acton, and moved in with Jane, in Ealing.

Life went on for the both of us, and it seemed we were always having parties, going to parties, or spending late nights at the Haven pub.

Often at weekends, and even during the week, John and Mary, the proprietors of the pub, would close the bar and allow us to drink after hours. We would play music and party like there was no tomorrow. On Sunday afternoons, we used to go to a club on the Kings Road in Chelsea, which was packed on Sunday afternoons.

My boss, Peter, lived directly opposite the Haven, our local pub, and often was really amazed at how I could be in the bar till 3:00 a.m. and still get into work at 8:00 a.m., but never be late and definitely never tired. "How on earth do you do it?" he often said, even now, in retrospect I don't know either, working all day, managing a sales operation, while managing a very busy wine bar at night.

If we didn't end up at the Haven, we would all go on to "Maddox," which was a night club in Ealing Broadway and was the place where the Rolling Stones first began to perform. At that time, though, it was called the Ealing Jazz Club.

But the club had never changed, only its name. It was a downstairs dive bar and was very busy on weekends with long lines outside as the pubs closed with people waiting to get in. We always went to the front of the line as we were well known by the owners. Maddox was open sometimes all night. The managers were also very good friends of ours and were always happy to see us, as we usually brought in a crowd. Amanda was never a problem for us, and when we worked at the bar or when we went out, Amanda was well looked after by Eve or Mimi and Alice, who were Jane's aunts, or even Rene, who was Lesley's mother and Amada's grandmother. Amanda loved staying with Meme and Alice and was never ever a problem.

We were inundated with babysitters, and since Amanda was so good to look after, it was never a problem. In fact, they would often argue over who was to look after her. Eve was the manageress of Russell and Bromley, a high-quality shoe shop in Ealing Broadway. So we got all our shoes at a discount; needless to say, I had loads of really good shoes.

After six months of living at Jane's apartment in Ealing, we decided to buy our first house and began to look all over the area. We finally decided on a small cottage in old Hanwell and obtained a mortgage for the house, which we bought for £17,500. I loved doing building work and sometimes took time off to work with a friend of ours, Brian George, who was a builder and decorator. I loved it. I loved seeing how things could be transformed from old to new and how to rebuild houses. I would often take three or four days off work, vacation time, to go and work with Brian.

I completely rebuilt our cottage in Claireville Gardens Hanwell, knocking right through the downstairs rooms and building a "hanging kitchen table" from the ceiling joists above the kitchen ceiling. It was brilliant when I finished it; though at one point, while standing on the stairs, halfway through the work, with Brian and Bill who was Jane's mother's live-in friend. I noticed some black specs on the back of my hand. I wiped them off, and they reappeared, so I looked up to see the upstairs ceiling forming a black and rapidly growing crack right above us. "Run for it," I shouted to Brian and Bill, and we legged it as fast as we could outside the open front door just as the entire ceiling collapsed right where we were standing only seconds before.

The idiot we hired to replace the water tank in the loft had cut right through a ceiling joist to get the new tank into the loft. The weight of the now-full water tank on the unsupported ceiling joist brought the whole lot crashing down. Smoke and dust from over a hundred years in our loft all came right down in an instant, and we were left coughing and spluttering as the dust cloud came billowing out of the front door.

The three of us looked like black men with white eyes; and as we stood outside our not-quite-finished first home, we burst out laughing, leaving white streaks on our faces as the tears, partly from the black soot in our eyes and partly from laughing, left their tracks down our faces.

After a near miss if we are still OK then we carry on…but with more caution.

VISION INTO REALITY

It's the planning that turns a vision into reality.

THE THREE OF us became an instant family—Jane, Amanda, and me. I was working at Alfa Laval, in the "spares department," while Jane was in the film business. Jane was an actress, an extra, a stunt double, and a hand model—all at the same time! We decided to buy a house in Hanwell, as Jane wanted to live near her mother Eve, Meme, and Alice. Meme and Alice were Amanda's aunts on her mother's side of the family, and both lived downstairs in her mother Eve's house in Drayton Bridge Road in Hanwell.

Eve had a lodger, Bill, who was a Geordie who had lived with her many years and who spent all of his time in a Catholic club in Ealing.

Meme and Alice had looked after Jane for many years and were old family friends. We bought a cottage in old Hanwell in Claireville Gardens. The house was a two up, two down, but with a large kitchen overlooking the garden. I decided to completely remodel the house and knock though the front and back rooms to make a larger open plan room with arches.

I had help from Brian, a local builder. Brian and his wife, Barb, became good friends with us both.

We knocked through the rooms, added a very gentle arch across the ceiling, then took the door out between the living room and the kitchen and built a bar under the stairs. When I had finished, it looked very modern and had a lot of character. Nothing was too difficult for me to do. I did electrical work, plumbing, floated walls, and even ceilings.

The centerpiece was the kitchen where I decided to make a suspended kitchen table, which would be hung from a four-inch-square beam dropped down through the ceiling above.

I went upstairs and measured the floor and took up the floorboards. I made an exact four-inch-square hole in the ceiling, next to the big wooden ceiling joist, and cut the same-sized square hole in the concrete floor in the kitchen below. I measured and cut a breakfast bar that would have a suspended round table with a square hole in the middle that I hoped would fit together and would enable the square pole to go through the breakfast bar from above coming through the ceiling, through the round table with the square hole cut in the middle, and on into the square hole cut into the floor.

When I finished the work, I checked once again for the umpteenth time; then I slid the beam through the ceiling and through the bar as it slid through right into the square indentation in the floor. It looked great, and the whole thing went together perfectly. In fact, it was such a perfect fit that it had to be tapped in with a hammer. The overall look was exactly as I had planned and gave the house a very unique look. The breakfast bar was suspended from the ceiling and was attached to the work surface seemingly as one entire piece. Brilliant! As luck would have it, it worked beautifully.

I learned that when we spend a lot of time planning we are more likely to succeed!

MY LITTLE BROTHER

This was to be one of the saddest friendships in my life.

OPPOSITE OUR COTTAGE, a friend of ours, Carolyn, who was a very talented artist lived together with her two children—Adrian and Sarah—and had moved in shortly after we did.

Adrian, who was eleven years old, was in the "Corona" drama school for stage and music; and whenever I got home from work, he always came over to spend time with me. I used to take him and Amanda out with me, and Adrian loved making models with me or he would help me make one of my own in my very limited free time.

Adrian would come over to our house and bring his models to get me to show him how to make them or paint them. Adrian was like a younger brother and was always interested in whatever I was doing.

Adrian was a really sweet kid, always very polite, always interested in everything; and I became very close to him like an older brother. I used to take him to the Model Shop in Harrow where we would both spend all Saturday morning looking at the possibilities of what he and I could make together. Adrian's sister, Sarah, was also a very sweet girl; but I spent more time with Ade (as we called him).

To be able to spend the time to mentor someone else's life, even for a short while, is a blessing.

ANOTHER BRICK IN THE WALL

Music! The best way to remember friends who are no longer with us.

ONE DAY WHEN Adrian came home from school, he told me he had been singing with his class on a new record by Pink Floyd for a soon-to-be-released album called *Another Brick in the Wall*. He and his class had sung the children's chorus. At that time, Pink Floyd was huge in England; and once again, we never knew how big that single would eventually become. Several weeks later, I went with a friend of mine, Lenny Lewis, who was selling studio equipment at the time, to the "Konks" recording studio at Muswell Hill, which was owned by the Kinks. We heard the fully expanded single from the album on a forty-eight-track reel to reel master tape of *Another Brick in the Wall*, before it was to be mixed down and put through a compressor and a limiter, which were two processes in the final mixed-down sound ready for broadcasting.

The music was played on the "reel to reel" tape machine in the studio's huge monitor speakers, which was exactly as it had all been recorded by the Floyd and was "raw." As we were listening our clothes were being moved by the huge bass line—boom de boom boom boom—which was moving our chests along with it, it was incredible the sound and the recording. I had never heard such a unique single before that and we knew it would become a huge hit after listening to it.

As we know now, it is a rock standard and is as good now as it was then! Sadly, several years later when I met a now much older Adrian, now in his early twenties, he had become a very changed person and very different from the great kid I knew when he came over to our house.

He now had a child of his own; and very sadly, he committed suicide because of what is sadly a very treatable mental illness, depression.

I still think of Adrian all the time, especially at Christmas and if I hear Pink Floyd's best ever single "Another Brick in the Wall"; and I always listen for his voice so in a way he is always with me. I realize how easy it is to see only the bad things, when you are in an extremely low depression, and you don't see the good things. Adrian had been in several movies and actually had great career potential in the film business. Sadly, that was not to be for him.

Carolyn Mann, his mother, who was and still is a great friend of mine, sent me this message when I contacted her after a gap of over twenty years.

Here's what she said, in an e-mail, of my little "brother" Adrian and I:

> "I remember how fond Adrian was of you and of course vice versa—you added something to his life that was essential for him—I always knew that the presence of a really good adult male figure was what he not only wanted but needed, and his relationship with you was so important—thanks so much for that—I'm really touched by the inclusion of Ade in your book and of course, your life."

I was happy that while our circles touched, I was able to be with him in his very short time on this earth. I find it hard even now to think of how sad he must have felt to take the route he took, but part of me is happy also that he is in a better place than many. In the words of Dick Lewis, a high-flying police officer at New Scotland Yard, that I also met after a twenty-five-year gap in 2011 in Brighton while there for my sister-in-law Lesley's Wedding: "Tony, some people are wired up wrong and there's nothing we can do about that.
   At some point they will do the inevitable and we can't protect them forever from themselves." Sadly, though, Dick was referring to his own daughter who took her own life while she was excelling at a university with a beautiful life before her.
   I was so very happy that Carolyn's message could be included as she is not only an old and gifted friend of mine with her art but also has had to put up with her own share of life's difficulties; and like me, my dear and very talented Carolyn is still standing!

Carolyn wrote this poem for Adrian (Ade):

Fat Black Plastic Sacks

Fat black plastic sacks surround my bed
delivered to my door by his sad and distraught friends
each bag enclosing proof of his terrestrial life
his suits, his shoes, his socks, his shirts,
his rambling crazy midnight notes are here with me
and here am I
encircled for three years within this ring of tactile memories
their secrecy and comfort colluding in my denial.
And now
as if from a chrysalis, I emerge into the light of day
and I must face these horrors
these demons clutching at my heart and lungs
so I can live and speak of him again
and speak of him as one would speak of any child
whose tiny body clings to love
to smile its pleasure into its mother's eyes.
Methodically, for many hours I move among this treasured trove of earthliness
to sort, to save, to allocate with folded tissue' d care
until I'm done
then crouched in genuflection and wet with anguished tears
I feel a sudden rush of wind blow past my face
A breeze as if from nowhere encircles me in his cool remembrance.
When Carolyn had finished going through the black plastic sacks of
Ade's life, left by his friends, after a period of three years, a cool breeze
blew through the room; though no doors or windows were open as if he
was now free as was she.

We will never forget you Adrian your charm, your humor, your too short life!

STAR WARS IN THE MAKING

Sometimes, the simplest experience, seeming to be quite normal at the time, becomes a momentous event on reflection later on in life.

W HILE WE WERE at the beginning our relationship, I would often drive up to Boreham Wood Studios, where Jane was working on a new movie called *Star Wars*, as Carrie Fisher's "stunt double." I would leave my office and drive as fast as I could to Boreham Wood, where, with my name left at the gate by Jane, I could go right on through to the film set. Jane was always very natural with her "film friends," and they were a great bunch of people.

We sat at a standard canteen table, no frills, and had a canteen lunch with Wookie, Darth Vader, C-3PO, and several of the other characters who were in that day's shoot. It was funny as Daft ADA as we called him had a strong west country accent and was, at that time, well known from his role in the Green Cross Code man wearing a silver "Superman"-type suit with a bright green (very gay) belt in the adverts, telling children to be careful crossing the road!

They were good fun to be with; and when "on set," no one did the "star" thing at all, and no one knew how big the film was going to become as it was only in the filming stage when I went to see it being made. I loved standing behind the camera and watching, in quiet fascination, the acting without any special effects, which were to be added later on.

To this day, I can still see the particular scenes that I had seen first-hand being filmed while standing with Jane behind the camera.

One day while I was standing quietly behind the camera, watching a scene where the small space craft belonging to Hans Solo had landed in what was to be a swamp, though when I was there it was just a studio floor with tape markings all over. Actors came running onto the ramp, pretending to fire prop guns at some enemy that I couldn't see. I have to say it looked very "tame." George Lucas came up and stood next to me, watching the scene, and asked me what I thought.

Now at this time, there was no *Star Wars* film released as yet; and though it was a new "sci-fi" movie, no one had any idea how it would look or how big it was to become. And I had never heard of George Lucas before that film.

So I turned to George and said in reply, "Great. I suppose, though, I have to say your imagination is probably a lot better than mine." George went on to explain some of the plot at that point in the film, and I told him I couldn't wait for it to be released so I could see what he was explaining.

As a "stunt double," Jane's role was to do all the running, jumping, and falling that Carrie Fisher or "Princess Leia" had to do; and so she was fairly busy. I was mesmerized by the way that the crew got everything together. Anyone wanting to know what "controlled chaos" really looks like should see a film crew at work. Absolutely crazy until the "recording now buzzer" goes off, after which you could hear a pin drop.

As a scene finished being filmed, the camera man or director would see that something needed changing and would make a simple statement like, "The key is off a little. Bring it round."

Then all hell would let loose as they made the correction for the next shot. My full congratulations to all of the actors as they had to repeat the same scene over and over again until they got it right to the director's satisfaction.

In one scene, George Lucas was getting quite cross at Wookie for not moving his head correctly when he made his growling sound when talking to Hans Solo in his beaten-up space cruiser. They had to do that one piece of the scene over and over again. Finally, George went over to Wookie and actually showed him what he wanted, mimicking the correct movement.

After the film had been completed, Jane and I went to the *Star Wars* premier in Leicester Square, where I was reintroduced to a lot of the crew, who greeted Jane as an old friend. The film became legendary and was absolutely unbelievably great, and we couldn't believe how the special effects had transformed what we had seen being filmed into what was now the finished movie.

I also went to meet Jane on various other film sets, if I wasn't playing somewhere, when we were courting, including the set of the first couple of *Superman* movies, where we sat with the late Christopher Reeves while we were having sandwiches. I was at the scene where he flew past a jet airliner's pilot's window and waved at the pilot and copilot, while they were flying the plane.

That scene was filmed over and over until it was acceptable to the director. Superman, Christopher Reeve, was in a big harness and was reeled back and forth in front of the cockpit windows, in front of a huge fan to give the effect of the high wind as he was flying while keeping up with the airliner and did the same wave with as many slight variations as could be managed with each successive take.

Christopher Reeves was a very ordinary man, working for a living, with no "star" image of himself; almost as if he knew at that time how privileged he was to be doing what he was doing. Jane and I often talked to him over our lunch dates while eating lunch in the canteen during the filming.

Imagination drives innovation which drives technology.

AN AMERICAN WEREWOLF IN LONDON

Don't ever lend your new car as a film prop!

ONE DAY WHILE I was working at Alfa Laval, Jane called me and asked me if she could use my car to go uptown for a "night shoot" of a new movie called *An American Werewolf in London*. I said, "OK, no problem. I'll use yours." Jane had, at that time, a very small sports car, which was an "old English white" MG Midget. So that night off she went to work and wouldn't be back until just before dawn.

When I got my brand-new company car back, after she had borrowed it for getting to the set, I noticed that there were spots of red flecks all over the windshield and bonnet.

I asked Jane if she knew what it was, as the car was only a few weeks old and was perfect when she took it to the shoot. "It's nothing," she said," just flecks of blood." "WHAT!" I said. "Has someone had an accident in my car?" I asked, as I began to inspect my one-week-old company car in more detail. Jane just looked on saying nothing.

"Well, OK, then," she finally began, "if you really want to know what happened, I was a pedestrian, running away from the werewolf, as he came out of the cinema in Piccadilly Circus. I got run over by your car, so the car was used in the shoot. It was in a staged accident where it was covered in blood all over the hood, and the windshield had cracks placed all over it, and I was laid over the bonnet, quite dead.   Your car had crashed into a bus." I immediately went outside to see if there was any damage; of course, there was none at all.

"So," I said, "let me get this right. If anyone at Alfa Laval takes a look at that scene, and they recognize you, they'll also see my present, and not to be for long if they find out, company car, covered in blood, with you dead on the bonnet." "Fraid so," she said. Now I have to say that getting information out of Jane when she didn't want to tell you something was like pulling teeth!

Anyway she added, "I had them drape my leg over the number plate so no one could see it was your car." "Well, that's OK then, I s'pose," I added, and that was that.

The funny thing is I often see Jane in small bits and pieces of British-made films; she was a red head with a mass of curls that were definitely unmistakable. Many years later in 2012, Amanda found an old film poster of a film called *The Belles of St. Tinian's* on Google and posted it on her Facebook home page. The film was a comedy about a very rough girls' boarding school; and Jane was, at eighteen, one of the so-called belles.

It was often like this with Jane, when we were dating and then when we were married: she was always either with no work for months or in work for weeks or months. Sometimes, others, my work colleagues or friends would tell me that they had seen her in this film or that. Even some of the modeling work would be in a newspaper or in a magazine.

Funny thing, when we were looking for a mortgage, from Abbey National, there was Jane on a full-page advert in the *Observer*, for none other than Abbey National looking as if she had just got engaged to whomever it was that was standing next to her in the ad! Neither of us knew it was going in the paper; but there it was, a full-page ad featuring her for the same mortgage company that we were looking to get a mortgage from!

To see a movie during filming, and afterwards as a finished product, is to see true magic happening. It is the same magic to create anything that has never been done before.

VICK ELMES BRIAN CONNOLY AND ME

The moment when talent comes together unexpectedly is a memory forever.

WHEN I GOT back from France and was getting over my stormy relation with Jeanette, I met Dee again. Her husband Vick Elmes was just finishing with his band "Christie" who had a number 1 hit with "Yellow River" and had several other hits with 'San Bernardino' and 'Iron Horse.' Vick was the lead guitarist and harmony vocals behind Jeff Christie.

Jeff Christie had quit the band to begin a solo career, and Vick was now playing gigs solo. After meeting with Vick, when he returned from a world tour, the band had split up; so Dee suggested that we should perform together, as the sound would be much better than as single musicians. So we practiced in their flat in Chiswick for several months and then began to play as a duo. Vick was a brilliant guitarist and at that time the Eagles had just released, "Hotel California" with one of the best guitar solos of all time played by Don Felder and Joe Walsh.

Vick could play that solo note perfect and with the exact same sound and not as a dual guitar solo but by himself. He was that good!

The crowds that we played to loved it and always demanded that we sing that one song. Will Chichester, who used to work with me at Alfa Laval several years earlier, was himself a pianist and also played drums for us so now on some gigs we were a trio.

Vick though had one tiny little problem, with alcohol, and was rapidly becoming a serious alcoholic, which sometimes manifested itself during gigs. Though I understood why he had this problem, as many performers do, after having to deal with the downside after the fame and fortune was over, it was to become very difficult to perform. Vick wrote and performed a score for our former singer Dee's parents, Sylvia and Gerry Anderson, for their new series, *Space 1999*; but now he was becoming more depressed.

Dee and Vick were moving toward divorce, and I hoped that the music would keep him together; but sadly, I was to be proved wrong. Dee and I spent many hours trying to get him to seek help, but he had to decide that for himself. At that time, he, like so many others in his addiction, didn't agree he had a problem.

One night we were doing a pub in Gerard's Cross when Brian Connolly of the Sweet came in to hear us play along with an entourage of friends and another band member. During the break, they came over to talk to us, and we agreed to jam together. And on a quickly made-up song list of potentials, we played a set with them both.

Vick never ever broadcast to our audiences who he was and preferred to go *incognito*, maybe because he was embarrassed at not being right up there. The pub was packed, and no one knew who was playing until we did a version of one of Brian's songs. Brian unfortunately did not have his legendary long blond hair at this time as he was going through a similar situation as Vick and was struggling with his addiction, which at that time left him looking very different from what people would remember.

However, that one night, when Brian opened up his vocals and let go with his unbelievably great voice, the packed bar began to realize who was singing; not only that, but also both Christie and the Sweet had each reached number 1 across the whole of Europe. Vick told me on the way home that it reminded him of playing like that together with Joe Cocker, which I would have loved to have seen.

I will never forget that one night when I was lucky enough to have been playing and singing with Brian and Vick. WHAT A NIGHT! We jammed for nearly a whole set!

Sadly, Brian died way before his time; but that one night for me was a life's highlight. Brian made truly great music, and I'm certain our audience that night were still talking about it long after that one magical night!

Later though, as Vick, Will, and I were playing at a club in Chiswick, Vick had a meltdown in front of a packed club where our audience, fans, had come from all over London to hear us play. He arrived thirty minutes late and was absolutely trashed. We got him onto the stage and hoped the music would sober him up, but it didn't. He was standing next to me on stage, smashing at the strings on his guitar and making such an awful noise that I turned his vocals off and his guitar right down. After only five numbers, I had had enough and looked over to Will who was shaking his head. Vick was swaying at his mic next to me and could hardly stand up so I switched it off; and we left the stage to a very bewildered audience, to which, I had to apologize for Vick.

I can say that I died a thousand deaths that night, as anyone who has had such disaster in front of an audience understands; but for Vick and I, the party was over. Dee and I were very sad to see such a waste of pure talent go out in this way. I remember him proudly telling me that when he cut the sound track for *Space 1999*, he did it in one take, to the amazement of the entire orchestra that were playing with him in the studio as they laid down the theme tune. He laughingly said that he arrived, set up to play, made sure his guitar was in tune, and when the red light came on did the whole thing in one take. As soon as the producer gave him the nod, he packed up and left, leaving a stunned orchestra in the studio.

Dee and I have kept in touch, and many times we have both wondered what happened to Vick; but we didn't ever see him again. I will choose to remember his superb lead guitar and his funny sense of humor. One last thing about the great side of my friend Vick: he used to do a whole skit on the *Muppets*, where he took on all of the voices of Kermit, Fozzy Bear, and the two old men; and it was so good that he could have been one of them.

Years later in 2001, James was dancing with a troupe from the Dance Refinery, at a national dance contest in Myrtle Beach, to the Sweet's hit "Blockbuster." I told him when I saw him dance to it that I had sung with Brian Connolly, the lead singer with Sweet, for just one night in England but I'm certain he still doesn't believe me!

It's better to remember someone at the top of their life's achievements, not at the bottom as hitting the bottom can so easily happen to any of us.

THE VILLAGE WINE BAR

Creating something new, is harder than it looks

SOME SIX MONTHS or so later, a friend of ours, Paul, who was the accountant to an electrical shop in North Ealing, told us of a business for sale in North Ealing near "The Greystoke" pub. He also told us that his brother had mentioned that the owner may be interested in selling the business, or that he may let someone take it over as he was looking to retire. I found the location, a few days later, as I was driving through North Ealing. I stopped and parked my car on Queens Drive and for no reason sat in my car and studied a parade of shops next to "The Greystoke" pub.

I was thinking that this location would make a great wine bar. I don't know why I thought that, but I did. So I went straight to the electrical shop located between a pharmacy and a flower shop. Above the parade of shops were apartments, and the "parade" had some twenty shops from "The Greystoke" to the North Circular Road; and the location was excellent.

I entered the shop, and while I waited for the owner to come out to see me, I looked around and saw that it was a perfect size with a large window looking onto the street.

It was around 3,500 square feet; and it had a wooden grid below the ceiling, upon which were hundreds of lighting fixtures were hanging.

I was imagining how I could convert it into a wine bar when the owner came out to ask me what I wanted. He was elderly man, slim tall and with white hair, obviously Jewish; and I asked him if he was interested in selling his business. "Maybe," he said, "but out of interest, what do you want it for?" "I think it would make a great wine bar," I replied.

"Hmm," he said, "a wine bar. Do you know much about them?" "Yes," I said," I do know a little, and I know this would be a great location. It's perfect, off the main road, plenty of passing traffic, and no other one anywhere close."

He seemed interested, and we talked about it some more, while standing outside his shop, which was clearly not very busy at the time we were talking. He told me his health was forcing him to think about retirement, and that he had considered selling. As we talked, he became more thoughtful and seemed to like the idea of not having to work in his shop much longer.

The day was very sunny, and I took that as a good sign. He told me he would have to speak to his wife Sally, and that he'd call me back in a few days. He did and had agreed to let us go for a change of use and to convert it into a wine bar.

I didn't wait a moment. I went home told Jane all about what I has seen and immediately started to draw out how it could look. I drew the bar, the window, the seating, and even designed wooden paneling all around the bar area. The concept took on a life of its own, and we began making up lists of what we needed to do to get it started. A friend of ours was Freddie Barrett, who owned a number of "off licenses" (retail wine liquor stores) and was often advertising on radio and TV. Freddie's son was Hugh Barrett, and he owned Barrett's Liquor Store in Ealing Broadway. I went to see him to seek his help as we had often met for drinks when we were out in Ealing, and we knew him quite well.

Hugh offered to set us up with some of his wine suppliers and even offered to help with the wine list. There was so much to be done, and we had never had a business of our own before that. There were the legal issues of getting a resale alcohol license, wine suppliers to be found, capital that we would need to start up, and many more things.

A few days later, the owner called me and said that he would be interested to allow a change of use, and that he thought it would be a great idea to convert it. He told me he would work out the contract with his accountant, Paul; and we could go in any time we wanted to see what needed to be done. Jane went in more than I did as he seemed to really like her. I took measurements and began to make my sketches into reality by adding a scaled drawing of the floor layout, to estimate the bar size, how many customers we could fit in, and what it would take to make the change of usage from a retail electrical store into a wine bar.

There was one thing we couldn't short cut, and that was the license application. This had to be dealt with through the courts, and we needed a specialist attorney who understood license applications. Once again, Hugh helped us by giving us the name of his license attorney. Hugh was a fantastic help and got us wholesale wine and beer prices, and names of good suppliers that he trusted and got us contact addresses and phone numbers.

I met with Paul, our soon-to-be accountant, and asked him what I needed to do to get finance. He gave me a shopping list of things, bank references, business references, cost estimates of equipment to buy, conversion costs, rent and utilities, wine prices, and even a sample wine list to take to the courthouse pending our license application.

We made a complete list of all that we needed to get done and began assembling all of the items.

We were so excited; and we went 'round to Roger and Jill Watson, who were very close friends of ours. We explained it all to them and asked them what they thought. Roger was very thoughtful and asked us what we thought about competition in Ealing and if we thought there was room for another wine bar.

Of course, we thought, Ealing could easily handle another wine bar, as they were the latest trend in entertainment; and pubs didn't cater for everyone especially women who wanted to go out to drink and meet friends. The pubs were fine, but women didn't go in them unless with a friend, usually a male.

We were going to do this come hell or high water; we were determined to go ahead.

Sometimes when things are meant to be, they fall into place with ease, and it was that way with this new business venture. We didn't tell many people about our venture and quietly proceeded to get all that we needed to be done, completed.

We called our new best friend, the licensing attorney, and we had to give him money up front. He told us that we needed to make a scale map of five hundred yards all around the prospective location and mark out every pub, restaurant, and off license within the marked area. Told us to make it complete and easy to read. He set up the license hearing, which was to be at Brentford County Courthouse, which was the area authority for license applications. He also told us that the other license holders would object, especially the Greystoke, as it was only fifty feet from the bar. The date was set for July 7, 1981.

I got hold of the potential wine distributors, and we began assembling a wine list of reds and whites. We needed a house red and a house white and were told that these would be our most important wines, ones that customers would measure us by and the wine that we would make most profit from.

I asked a friend of ours, Carolyn Mann, who was a talented graphic artist and who lived opposite us in Claireville Gardens, if she could help design our menu and wine list covers.

She did, and we chose one that was an ancient etching by William Blake of Saint Michael, with one hand holding his bowed head and the other on the hilt of his sword, which was resting point down. He looked to me like he had a really bad hangover it was perfect. Carolyn not only designed the menu, but we also used the same design for our house wines.

My next task was to see if we could get money to open the bar with, and I went to see my bank manager at Barclays Bank and where I had been banking since I started work at Taylor Woodrow, some fifteen years earlier.

I had prepared everything—cost schedules containing all of our work from wine costs, capital expense for tables, chairs and conversion estimates, glassware—in fact, everything we had worked on, including cash flow forecasts, with three estimations—a minimum, medium, and maximum sales revenue.

I met the manager at 10:00 a.m. and went into his office. My bank account was in good shape, and I felt confident about our numbers. He didn't even look at my folder, but instead told me that I should think about staying with my day job and decide to have stable employment and not change anything.

I couldn't believe what he was saying, so I asked him if my numbers were wrong, was there something I had missed, and did he know a reason why this would not work. He said no, my numbers looked good, but he didn't think it was a good idea to go into business for myself.

I was really pissed off with his blasé attitude and his simple denial with no explanation, I stood up and told him what I thought of his response and told him I would open my new business regardless with or without his help, and that I would be changing my bank on the day I opened my new business.

Back to square one. We met for drinks later that night with John and Mary at the "The Haven"; and after the pub was closed, we sat and talked about the bank and their refusal to lend us the money. For me, it was a minor setback. John told me of his bank manager at the Allied Irish Bank in Ealing Broadway and said that he thought they could help and gave me his number. John also told us he would have a word with the manager who was a friend of his and put in a good word for us.

A few days later, I met with the bank manager, who was a tall Irishman and was so easy to talk with. His staff were really nice and already knew why I was there.

He came out, immediately shook my hand, and took me through to his office. I sat down and showed him my folder containing all of our background information and all of my numbers. He looked through all of my calculations, estimates, wine list, and cash flow projections. He told me that the numbers looked good and asked me where I thought our true numbers would be. I said I thought it would be all three, great at weekends, quiet during the week, and would probably average at the middle numbers. He agreed and said that they still looked acceptable. I only needed £12,500 to get started, and he gave me an overdraught facility that would only be charged for the amount that we used. The whole meeting took around fifteen minutes, and we now had our funds. I told him we would be moving our accounts from Barclays but didn't tell him that they had refused. One thing though, it depended on our ability to get our license, so he said the money was there ready immediately but advised me to wait until we had the license.

We wanted to open the bar in time for Prince Charles's upcoming marriage to Diana, which was set for July 21, 1981, in London.

I learned not to accept NO from a bank and that if I decided to do something I would make it happen!

OUR DAY IN COURT

When we have done all we can do in preparation for an important event we are far more confident of the outcome.

W E NEVER MET our license attorney until the day of the hearing, which was set for July 7 at 9:30 a.m. at Brentford Courthouse. Jane and I went to the courthouse, with all that we had prepared in a thick folder, and finally met our man. He told us what to expect and that several big breweries had grouped together to oppose us, along with all of the local pubs from Ealing Broadway to the Greystoke.

I was optimistic but also annoyed that they had "ganged" up on us, and Jane was a little angry at the opposition trying to stop us opening our bar. "Why would they care?" she said. "Our business is tiny, and it cannot offer any serious competition to them." We had to sit through a load of prior items, ranging from bar brawls, license renewals, police issues related to pubs that we knew were always having fights and were opposing the renewal of the license, transfers, and all related matters. We sat there through it all and became more and more nervous as we waited for what seemed to be hours.

Our time finally came, and we had to go through and sit in the witness box; it felt like we were criminals. The judge was very good and had moved along at a fast pace, but he seemed fair. He told us right up front that he wanted to get this finished before lunch, as this had been a very busy session.

He notified the court that he was reviewing a new license application made on behalf of a Tony and Jane Moore, and asked if there was any opposition. The attorney who had introduced himself to us in the ante chamber rose and informed the court he was opposing the license application.

This was it, pass or fail at this point; everything we had done had led us to this point, and now it was out of our hands and into the famous British legal system.

I was first up, and the cross-examination began. "There are approximately twenty-five pubs already in Ealing, and at least three wine bars, plus another twenty restaurants that have been satisfying all of the local needs," he opened loudly for all in the court to hear. "What makes you think that Ealing needs yet another bar?" He demanded, he then went straight on with several rapid-fire questions that were designed to trip me up, and he didn't give me time to answer any of them, before bombarding me with more questions. He wanted to make me seem like I was fumbling, but I had put too much into this and was not going to be tripped up now, and especially by this ruse and by such a bombastic attorney as him.

I took a deep breath and prayed to God to help me get through this ordeal without screwing it up too much just this one time! I began to answer the first question and took my time talking over him as he wouldn't stop with his tirade of questions. The judge intervened and told him to allow the witness to answer the questions. "That's OK, your honor. I have a good memory, and I can answer all of his questions, but only one at a time," I told the court. "Your first question was how do we know there is a need?" I said. "Well, this past year, beer sales have grown at only 2.2 percent and spirits sales had actually declined by 4 percent. And the national sales growth has been 6.2 percent, which is actually higher than both of these numbers, which would indicate that neither are meeting the needs of the market." "And exactly how do you know this? Is it based on fact or purely conjecture on your part?" he huffed to the large assembly in the court.

"Well, actually," I began slowly, "these are published numbers from a publication that you in fact represent, the License Victualers Association's annual report."

"Prove it," he sneered. So I produced the publication, from out of my folder, and asked if the judge would like to see it.

A court bailiff came over and took the publication from me and took it directly to the judge, who began leafing through my evidence.

"And how did you come by this information?" he demanded. I replied, "I work for a company that designs breweries, supplies equipment to all manner of the wine, beer, and food industries." And that I had got the information through my company. The court found this very funny, and a murmur ensued throughout. I looked over to Jane; and she winked, happy that we had scored a big one.

The judge announced that since this was a trade publication, that the opposing attorney did indeed represent it was admissible, and asked if could we move it along while taking a slow and deliberate look at his watch while peering at our opposing attorney over the rim of his half specs with one eyebrow raised. The opposition attorney then arrogantly looked over our wine list and tried to tell the court that the local pub was able to offer all the wines that people wanted and could meet the demands with ease.

I had to explain that "Wine consumption had increased by 300 percent in annual sales," and I asked if he knew what the percentage wine sales had been in any of the pubs he represented. He ignored my question, so I asked the judge if he could please answer my questions as I had to answer his. The judge was clearly enjoying this exchange and agreed. "Do you have that information by any chance?" the judge asked him. "Actually, I do, but it's not here with me," he said. The judge was not impressed and went on, "Well, if that's all you have, let's move it along."

"I would like to bring Jane Moore to the witness stand," he said. I whispered to her, "We've got this," as she passed me and nervously entered into the witness box, adding a "good luck" as she passed by me on her way to the front of the court to sit by herself in the witness box.

He was just as nasty to Jane and started asking her about what food she was going to make. Jane answered, going through all of the things we had discussed over the many weeks of preparations.

"The Greystoke has an extensive food menu. Why would people want to eat at your bar?" he asked sarcastically. Jane was no fool and began by praising the excellent food that was available at the Greystoke, saying that she and I had often eaten there and probably would continue to do so. I had to smile at her deftness in taking the wind right out of his sails by her over pleasant demeanor.

"Nevertheless," he said, "why would they choose to eat your food?" He demanded testily as he was getting nowhere with her. Jane smiled and answered, "Because we will be cooking it fresh daily."

"And exactly what will YOU be doing in this bar of yours?" stabbing his finger at her as he asked.

"Cooking," she said, looking right at the magistrate, as if it was a stupid question. She was brilliant, and the whole court laughed with her.

The judge finally intervened and said, "I've heard enough. If that's all you have, we're finished here." He smiled at Jane, asking her politely to step down from the witness box.

"On reviewing, all that I have seen and heard here, I'm granting this license," he said, adding, "I wish you both the best of luck with your new venture and I may even drop by to try some of your, personally cooked food." He smiled. "You will be very welcome," Jane replied as we left the court room, not believing that we now had overcome our only hurdle in starting up our business.

We were jumping up and down outside and shouting, "We did it. We did it," shaking our attorney's hand. Just then, the other attorney came out and offered his had to mine "I knew you would get this," he said. "It was a predetermined win for you both." I didn't want to I shake his hand though.

"Why were you so rude?" Jane asked him. "It's just how things are done in license cases like this," he replied. "We do this to see how much you know about the business, and to see if you can argue your case. You both did very well, and if you need a good attorney, I would be happy to represent you in any future issues." I took the card and couldn't wait to get out of the place.

We went straight to "The Haven" and had a bottle of champagne with John and Mary. The news was out now and would be published in the local paper along with the name of the bar, the location's address, and our names; it was a legal requirement. A week or so later, many of the locals were asking about our new venture and when it would be open. I had only three weeks from that day until the anticipated opening day to manage the complete change-over
from an electrical shop into a new wine bar.

I called in to my office and took my three weeks' vacation (I had five weeks in all) to begin the work; it was July 1981, and we finally began to see our new business venture begin.
I pasted the drawing I had made of what I wanted it to look like on the wall, and I had two friends help me to do the work. One was in the film business with Jane; the other was just about to go into the Royal Navy. They both really worked hard, and I gave them each jobs to do, paying them by the hour. I felt like a foreman. Many of our friends came in to see the work progressing, and as I worked, lots of passersby came in to ask if this was going to be the new wine bar and when the bar would be open. I worked late into the night, often not finishing until three in the morning in order to complete the work as soon as I could.

I had never made wooden paneling before, but it seemed straightforward; and so I began at the back wall and worked my way forward, making each of the wooden wall panels and measuring for the next. It looked very professional when I had finished, and I had to cover it with a thick coating of flame retardant varnish to meet the fire code.

The ceiling was covered in a crisscross of wooden beams, two feet apart, that we used to place film props like old cameras, film lighting, clapper boards, and props. I began to transform it from the place it used to be into what we wanted it to be—a wine bar.

We painted the ceiling all black so it would effectively disappear and not show the smoke stains that would inevitably start to form when the bar became busy.

Day by day, it became more and more like the sketch and was gradually taking shape. Finally, we took delivery of the wines and put them all either in the fridge for the white's or in the large wall rack I had placed behind the bar for the reds.

We were ready for the opening day set for Saturday July 25, 1981; and we finally got clearance to open the bar complete with our license, which we proudly placed on the wall at the end of the bar.

Opening night finally came after a year of hard work, and we were absolutely packed with people out back and out on the street in front of the bar. The *Ealing Gazette* was also there, snapping away; we were too busy for an interview, so they agreed to come back during the week.

One thing though, the kitchen and the painting of the toilets were not to be finished for another three weeks and required another coat of paint and some small finishing off items. There were curved bars on the back windows in the kitchen and toilets that the previous owner had put in place to protect all his electrical stock of lights and fittings.

We realized that everything our clairvoyant friend Peggy had predicted when we saw her a year before we had embarked on this new venture, had in fact happened exactly as she had foretold it two years before, and it wasn't until we were opened that Jane and I saw the truth of her words.

I knew from my childhood that if I worked hard enough and planned it all out I could make anything work.

LONG HOURS HARD WORK

It's one thing is to plan an event it's quite another to make it happen.

WE NEVER ANTICIPATED how much work was involved. We had hired great-looking girls to work with us behind the bar so that the bar was an attractive place to be, and it worked. The girls attracted the boys, and the boys in turn attracted more girls.

There was so much to do, wine and food buying—sometimes daily—and staff issues almost daily; and Jane had most of the burden of the food menu, along with the staff that sometimes forgot to show up. I was working during the day at Alfa Laval and at night in the bar; so I took a change of clothes in my car, left my office at 5:00 p.m., and made it to the bar by five twenty, ready to open the doors by five thirty every weekday.

Jane ran the bar at lunchtimes and decided on the daily menu, making sure that our food was different every day compared with that found in the pubs.

Our food was more eclectic—Italian, Greek, French, even Indian occasionally (even if I had to remove all of the raisins one by one). We did go through a number of cooks though, and often Jane had to take care of the cooking herself. Lunchtime trade picked up, and our customers had to book ahead, as space was limited. Cool, huh! People were actually booking ahead at our wine bar.

When we opened the bar, Amanda was six years old, and she was an absolute delight to have around. On weekends, she often came in with Jane; on Saturday mornings, other times, she would go with whoever's turn it was to have her for the day. And believe me, there was no shortage of people to choose from—Meme and Alice; Rene, her grandmother; Lesley, her father plus a host of available babysitters.

Don't underestimate the amount of work it takes to build a company; especially when working in the restaurant business.

GEORGIA

The birth of a daughter! THE event of our lives.

ON OCTOBER 23, 1982, Georgia was born; and I had to rush Jane off to Queen Charlotte's hospital for the birth. The weather that morning was beautiful—dry, warm, very sunny, and all of the autumn colors were on the trees.

Georgia came with little fuss, as I guess she was eager to get started, and that was her trait all through her life.

She was born with a mop of very dark hair, and she was definitely a Moore; there's no mistaking that fact!

We took her home, and Amanda now had a younger sister to look after. Amanda was a natural and loved Georgia from that very first day. Amanda and Georgia were to be very different as is often the case with sisters. Where Amanda was quite laid-back and nonjudgmental, Georgia was a go-getter and had to have things her way most of the time. She was a perfect addition to the family, and with the help of many babysitters, we managed to work at the bar as well as look after both of them. She was a beautiful little girl, just like Amanda; and from the moment she was born, we became very, very close. She loved being in the middle of everything, and as she grew up, she was a real compliment to her older sister Amanda.

Many times as she and Amanda were going through life's difficulties as we all do, and I remember saying to them both that they should be their own closest friends. As time moved on, they were in fact and still are the closest friends. The most difficult part was not the hard work from 9:00 a.m. till midnight and often until the early hours of the morning; it was the fact that the bar had to be open on time every day regardless of staff, illness, or any other thing that happened. We opened at 11:00 a.m. until two thirty weekdays and till 11:00 p.m. weekends, and that had to happen each and every day.

We decided to have music five nights a week, and the music brought in more trade, One problem was the people living in the apartment above the bar who began complaining, nicely at first but continuously even on nights when we had no live music. Eventually, we were visited by the local authorities who took sound readings upstairs with a "noise level meter." We thought we may be closed down, as they told us that we needed to have better soundproofing to prevent the noise from getting upstairs. We tried to find someone that knew what to do and couldn't find anyone ready to take on the task.

We had friends in the film business, and Jane knew of some film crew carpenters that may be able to help. She put the word out; and some days later, one of the crews of "chippies" called her and agreed to take a look to see if they could fix the problem for us.

They were amazing. They came in, took a look at the ceiling, and told us that this was easy to fix; and they would start immediately after they had finished the film they were working on. One night at closing time, a whole bunch of them arrived, six in all, and literally put a drop ceiling in two nights. They called it a "moving mass" ceiling and placed beams around the walls, with thick rubber mounts so that the new ceiling would rest on it; and as the sound made vibrations, it would be trapped as the ceiling took up these vibrations and prevented most of the noise from going farther up to the flat upstairs. It worked, and they were really a great bunch of workers they completed the job—no mess, no fuss in and out—and we were so relieved.

Eventually, the people upstairs realized they would not get rent-free accommodation from us, as they were trying to do, so they moved out . . . problem solved.

Our sales were on target, and we were doing well. The music was always varied from soloists, duos, and even four-piece bands. We had a small stage at the front window, and when there were no bands, we placed tables there right in the window. We were rocking! We were always in the press, and we always took care of the local reporters; in fact, we had more press than any other bar in West London.

The articles were positive, and we always called the papers to let them know what we were up to in weeks to come. We advertised in the local cinema, and many people came in because of that.

Once every couple of months throughout the year, we organized a French, German, Italian, or Greek night. We decked the bar in flags and paraphernalia representing that part of the world and made a one-night-only special menu from the country we were representing.

We also brought in new wines from each country, and the idea really worked well. These nights were always booked solid, packed wall to wall with several "turnovers" of diners.

Our favorite night was the French night, when we prepared a huge pot of "moules mariniere" and made sure we left the front door open so that the aroma of wine, garlic, fresh lemons, and seafood wafted across the pavement. Slick, huh! But it worked, and it worked well; and even more people came in, having smelled the cooking all down the road.

We were quite a small operation though, and we really wanted a bigger place, but that was not possible with our location. After we opened and the first article came out in the papers, a full page and with our photo standing outside the front window of the bar, our secret was out. The following week, Bo Wirsen, my managing director at Alfa Laval, came down to my office to see me and showed me the article, asking if I was leaving the company. I told him no, and that Jane was running it during the day, and it would not affect me at all. I invited him to come and have a drink with us, and he agreed to do just that. In fact, several of my directors came in for lunch, and I always worried if our service and food was OK. I needn't have. Jane did a really great job and looked after them as she had always done.

The most rewarding things in life are those things that we work the hardest to achieve; and when we look at what we have created it is reward in itself.

FRANK SINATRA

To see "The Greatest" perform live on a stage was amazing.

LATER AFTER A year or so, Jane and I were invited by one of our customers, Ash, who was a film distributor, to go to the Frank Sinatra concert at the London Palladium. He had fabulous tickets, and we were both in the second row with all the stars. Carry Grant and his wife were sitting in front of us; Cubby Broccoli, producer of all the *James Bond* films, was next to us; Dudley Moore was two seats down; and Roger Moore was on the other side of us.

In the intermission, all of the press descended down to the front of the theater and began taking pictures of all the stars sitting around us. I said to Jane and Ash, "I bet all of the people looking at these pictures in tomorrow's morning newspapers will be asking, 'who are all those people sitting around Tony and Jane?'" We had to laugh, but we then went outside for some fresh air, during the break; and we bumped into Dudley Moore who immediately recognized Jane and asked how she was and what she was working on.

Jane and Dud chatted a while before the buzzer went off for the second act. Jane later told me she had been working with him on *The Hound of the Baskervilles*, and Dudley didn't run too much; so as Jane was the same height and build, she did his stunt doubles, so the running scenes where he was getting away from the hounds were actually Jane.

Buddy Rich was backing Frank Sinatra, playing the drums, and did an amazing act when he began playing a drum solo as Frank left the stage for a break. He started with a drum solo played on his drums then moved across the stage playing the mike stand, the floor, and then right down the stairs leading from stage right, to the front row of seats, moving right across the whole row, playing the arm rests, people's heads sitting there, the hand rails and back up the stairs stage left, across the stage floor, and finally back onto his drum set to a now standing ovation. He never missed a beat and kept the rhythm going the whole time. It was amazing to see.

I was happy to know that I had seen the greatest, and live on stage!

ASSAULT OF COURSE

Getting a group of 'twenty-year-old' girls to try an army assault course was harder than herding cats!

W E DECIDED TO have another charity fund-raiser for our chosen charity, multiple sclerosis; and we had arranged to see if we could use the army's assault training course at the military base in Aldershot. We called them and told them what we were doing; and they really liked the idea, especially the part when I mentioned that we would be having around twenty to thirty mostly eighteen—to twenty-five-year-old girls with us.

We planned it for weeks and hoped the weather would be good; we called the local papers (as always) and arranged for everyone to be picked up outside the bar on a Saturday morning in July and took them all down to Aldershot barracks in a big bus.

The day was to end with an auction for our charity, back at the bar; and we would show a video of all of us on the assault course. So off we went at 6:00 a.m. The weather was perfect, as it had been all summer—hot and dry—and we arrived right on time at seven thirty.

I had spoken to the camp commander and asked if he could make it as realistic as possible, which he happily agreed to. There were ropes, high beams, climbing nets, and terrible-smelling pools of mud that they had freshened up with more water to make them even more disgusting.

There were around forty of us altogether, and many local police that were regulars in our bar also came along as well.
Our favorite friends were Richard Lewis and Bob Lewis, both very Welsh; and John Done, whose father was an infamous Welsh poacher and who had been in jail many times for his highly effective poaching skills.

John like his dad had often been poaching ducks on Ealing Common at 3:00 a.m. using his police squad car's headlights to mesmerize the poor ducks while catching them and taking them home to the police section house to cook them. Also, we had several ex-SAS and other military regulars with us, who showed us all how easy it would be.

Everything went off well; and we had plenty of footage of the girls and the guys climbing up rope ladders, crawling under nets, shinning up logged inclines, and always falling into the muddy pools while attempting to do all the activities on the course. They were always falling into the mud; and all the while, the real-life sergeant major was yelling at them, telling them how sissy they were and they were no good and weak and not fit for the army. This caused them to start laughing even more; and, of course, they all failed the course miserably.

The more he yelled, the more they kept failing. By midafternoon, everyone was covered in mud from head to toe. Finally, we said our goodbyes to the camp and invited the soldiers back with us to the bar; many of them came.

Later that night, after we were all cleaned up, we held an auction for our charity; and the bar was completely packed, spilling right out onto the street. We raised £3,000 for the charity, just for having a lot of fun and someone had donated to us a free ticket on Concord. Another donated a bottle of Louis XIV cognac (worth hundreds) very rare bottles of wine and many restaurant free dinners for two or four. It was one of those rare events where everything fell into place, and people that we knew, from suppliers to customers to friends gave with considerable generosity. Needless to say, we were in the local papers again.

I am certain that decades later these girls that took part never ever forgot this charity event.

PLANES CHUTES AND CROSSES ON THE GROUND

I just had to chance this, just once.

WE LATER HAD another such event where we all went parachuting for charity; and although I had already done this before, we decided to see who could land closest to a one-foot-across white "X," which was placed on the ground in the middle of a field near our big crowd of onlookers that had traveled with us to see the jump.

We had spent the weekend training and learning how to jump and how to open the chute. We all suited up and got ready, and we were carefully checked over by the jump master everyone was in great spirits.

The weather was dry hot and sunny, as it had been all summer long; and after we climbed in the old twin-engine stripped-out plane, we each sat around with our backs against the fuselage.

Next to me was the open door, a big square hole in the side overlooking the back edge of the wing, which was fine when we were taking off; but when we got really high, it was a strange feeling to be looking straight down at the ground way, way down. We climbed up to altitude, and things looked very different on the ground as I gazed out of the doorway. We circled around the general area of the drop zone, and the jump master dropped some bright orange markers to check the wind direction and speed and to decide where our drop zone was to be set.

We banked round and headed across the zone at a height of around five thousand feet. Then a buzzer sounded as we all lined up next to the big square gaping hole in the side of the fuselage. It was just about now that each of us were looking at each other and thinking, *"Why the hell are we jumping out of a perfectly functioning aircraft?"* We looked out of the open door at the ground below, reality bites just about here.

One by one, they all jumped out, shouting and screaming in nervous excitement as they left the safety of the plane. I watched them as each of them stepped out of the aircraft then all fall away, rapidly shrinking as they fell, one by one; and I looked on as they descended down toward the ground. One thing is for absolute certain: once you leave the plane, there's only one thing to do, fall und keep falling until you hit the ground.

I was last out, to make sure the rest were all out OK; and as the jump master nodded, I leapt out of the plane, forming an "X" with my body to gain control of my descent and to make certain that when I pulled the rip cord, I wasn't upside down. If this happens, the chords can run between your legs; and as you can imagine, the sudden halt in speed would be very painful. I would probably be able to reach those high notes I reached when I was a soprano in the choir!

We were told that the first thing to do was to make sure your chute was opened properly with a complete circle above your head. The next was then to get our bearings, take a look around, and look up to make sure no one was above or directly below. I free fell for around five or six hours; actually, it was less than ten seconds. Then I prayed loudly,
figuring I was real close to God right at that moment, and pulled the chord to open my chute. I heard a loud rushing as the silk sped out of the backpack and was suddenly yanked up to where God was actually sitting, looking on in amusement at my utter stupidity.

My free fall came to an abrupt end as this all happened in a split second. I remembered to look up again, as I had been told repeatedly, to make sure my chute had opened fully. What if it hadn't? What if it wasn't a full circle? What if only part of it had opened or the chords were tangled? Everything rushed through my mind along with my life, which was by now flashing before me!

The feeling is amazing; the wind hits you first, and it hit me full in the face, as I left the safety of the plane, Next, the sound of rushing as I picked up speed headed in one direction . . . down, down, down.

I opened the chute at around two thousand feet, when the buildings were as big as my fingertip. As soon as my chute took my weight, I screamed at the top of my lungs, YEaaaaaaah," as my descent slowed; and I began floating gently down. Now I could look around to see the beautiful site of the ground below and more importantly the perfect shape of my chute. I looked at the sky all around me and above me and relaxed for the three-day fall to earth. I could turn the chute in any direction and began to guide the chute toward the field and the tiny "X" no bigger an X written on this piece of paper, and dangerously close to all our friends below in the field next to it. I gradually began to get closer and turned the chute around at about fifty feet to turn into the gentle wind by pulling on one side of the chords and to slow the forward momentum of the chute down, which was now about fifteen miles per hour. I saw the "X" right below but didn't see the high clump of grass right under my left foot.

As I landed, I kept my ankles together as I had been trained, but I felt my ankle crunch as my left foot landed on it and twisted as I came down. *Bugger that!* I thought, as I began to get up grabbing the chute as I arose.

Determined not to let it show, I walked slowly back with the others carrying my chute back to the barracks. We were all laughing as we all returned, and my ankle was getting worse. Many of those present had taken pictures and videos of our descent, and we couldn't wait till later to see them all at the bar. As I drove back with Jane, I decided to head for the hospital on the way back to Ealing.

Jane drove me to a local hospital to have my ankle looked at. I was still high on adrenaline, so it really didn't hurt so much. I saw the doctor who told me it was definitely broken. "I figured as much," I told him, and I explained that we had a huge charity function that night and asked if they could hold off with the cast for my ankle. They reluctantly agreed but gave me some incredibly strong painkillers, Vicodin, warning me that these were so strong that I shouldn't drink with them. *Yeah right,* I thought, *I'm running a bar.* And I left with only a bandage around my ankle. I played it down when we arrived as the bar was packed again from door to door and all out on the street, with hundreds of our customers and friends ready for the auction that we had planned to begin; and we had a very busy evening with live music and videos of our exploits of that day.

The evening was a huge success and was once again in the local papers were comments about the jump and the money we had raised for charity.

Once back at work a few days later, my managing director, Bo Wirsen, came down to see me in my plaster cast leg and asked me to promise not to continue with any more dangerous sports as they didn't want to lose me! I agreed.

Parachuting is dangerous and like most things, for a young man, dangerous things have an immense attraction.

MICROLITES IN A SUIT

Sometimes you just have to go for it!

ONE AFTERNOON, AROUND a year later as I was driving back through Oxford, on my way back home from a business trip, I noticed the little "Microlite" aircraft circling above. They were tiny and various shapes—some looked like small motorized hang gliders, some looked like motorized dragonflies, and all had brightly colored wings. I was fascinated and decided on a whim to go and get a closer look for myself.

So I drove into the small airfield and parked up at the end of the runway, sitting in my car in case someone started shouting. This was way too cool to miss, so after a while, when no one seemed to care that I was there—well, actually there seemed to be no one around—I went around to the hangars and met a couple of flyers there. Both were standing at a work bench next to a couple of Microlite aircrafts.

"Fancy coming up for a ride?" one of them asked me. Without any hesitation, I said, "Are you kidding? Yes." So he got me a form to fill in. "What's this?" I asked. "Oh, just a waiver," he said, "just in case." So there I was in a pin-striped suit, white shirt, and tie, dressed for biz "as usual," getting into the smallest aircraft in the world. It was a funny-looking thing comprised of a triangular base made of the flimsiest aluminum frame with a motor mounted on a small platform up and behind a plastic double seat, the backseat being set higher than the front seat. The motor was mounted right behind the upper seat with a large propeller at the back.

"OK," my instant new "best friend" in the world, my own personal pilot told me (his name was James, by the way, which was all it could be for someone with a handlebar moustache and a leather "Biggles"-style leather helmet on), "this is the prop just behind your head." He casually informed me, pointing to a wicked-looking eight-foot propeller. "And you will sit in this high seat right here, and I'll be sitting in the seat below and to the front of you," he went on as I climbed into the flimsy little aircraft.

Not for one moment was I afraid or did I think of the danger; it was way too cool. "Just one thing," he mentioned as I climbed in, "the takeoff may be a little dramatic, so hold on." I looked around at what to hold on to, and there was absolutely nothing—no handle, beam, or anything that remotely looked like it would do. So I grabbed the edge of my seat.

He walked around behind me, switched a few things on, and grabbing the prop with both hands turned the prop, which instantly began spinning with the loudest noise I have ever heard, like a huge angry buzz saw; and it was about one foot behind my head. Very cool!

So he climbed onto his seat, in front and just below my seat, so I could see in front of him as he began to push a small pedal down and grabbed hold of the horizontal metal bar in front of him. We actually began to move across the grass under power. It was very bumpy as we moved across the grass to the runway, and I was amazed that this one propeller was able to move us along so fast.

We reached the end of the runway, which comprised of a mowed grass strip about a quarter mile long, and he turned and asked me if I was OK. He realized I couldn't hear him, so he simply gave the thumbs-up, and I returned it.

With that, he pushed down on the pedal, more like a stirrup, and the roar became ten times louder behind me; and we began moving faster and faster along the grass runway. Bumpy was an understatement, my teeth were rattling, and the tiny craft was shaking and rattling as we continued to build up speed; and I prayed that it wouldn't break apart before we got off the ground. I was hanging on for dear life, to the edge of my "plastic" seat, thinking that it probably wouldn't do much to save me if we fell out of the sky. As he pushed forward on the "A" bar in front of him, he pushed the throttle hard down, making the tiny engine scream even louder. We immediately lifted off. I think we were doing around seventy to eighty miles per hour as we lifted off, but it felt like 150! Suddenly, all the shaking stopped as we left the ground, and all became calm and serene, except for the noise of the engine.

We climbed very fast in our little triangular craft, higher and higher, really so fast I couldn't believe how fast we climbed, circling as we climbed; and I could see the ground getting smaller and smaller behind us. The hangars looked like tiny matchbox models, and I could no longer see my car. We got to a height of around five thousand feet and throttled back to cruise. Now I have flown many, many times before that and have always had a drink, a stewardess, windows, toilets, and all those things, not to mention a tough hard fuselage all around me. Not so now; there was him (my new best friend) and me, a plastic seat molded for two people, a very loud engine, and a wicked propeller right next to my head. I loved every minute of it. As we flew in circles, diving, climbing higher and higher, turning on a dime and doing all the tricks he knew, I felt liberated, free as a bird; and it was the closest thing to actually flying by oneself.

I now knew how lucky birds are—they were by the way far below us. The pilot turned to me and shouted above the roar of the engine, which seemed only three inches behind my head and the noise of rushing wind, "So what do you think?" I said, "Amazing! Bloody amazing, and I love it!" I shouted back, and he laughed and told me that was how he saw it too and that he loved being up there high above the ground.

The sun was setting, and the sky was lit up in all colors of red and orange as we sailed across the evening sky free as a bird . . . literally.

The few clouds there were lit from behind by the setting sun, and the whole scene was unbelievably beautiful and somewhat surreal. It's times like this that I think to myself that's where God is, right there in that amazingly beautiful sky; and I've always thought that, whenever I see a very beautiful sight like this. All was calm, and I had tuned the buzz of the motor out of my mind. I was gazing around at the new sights now seen from an entirely new perspective. As he turned the little craft, the ground below spun beneath us. I had never seen this before, and the sun moved around us as we turned. Really, that was the only way I could tell how fast we turned, seeing it flash across my vision.

After around forty-five minutes of cruising, doing the bumps, turning, climbing, and diving, he began the descent; and we banked as we made our way to the runway. Funny thing though, the slow motion of the altitude suddenly becomes a ground rush as you get to around thirty feet above the ground. I gripped the seat until my knuckles were white as we touched (or rather thumped) down, and I was tingling all over.

We got back to the hangar, and I was talking my head off about the experience. He and the others there were laughing with me, remembering their first trip up in one of these, and they swapped stories as I listened. I thanked them all and invited them to the bar for a free drink any time they wanted and left driving home still tingling all over.

I met Rich St. Clair in "The Bell," one of my local haunts, later that evening; and he asked me how my day went. I proceeded to tell him what I had done earlier that day. "Funny you should ask, because on my way home, well, I stopped off in Oxford on the way back and decided to go up in a Microlite." "Bloody typical," Rich said and followed by adding as an afterthought, "as you do, I suppose, as you do. Just a day out of the office; anything else?" "Nope," I said. "I did some work, visited a few customers, drummed up some business as well, but I've forgotten what it was now." and we both laughed and continued chatting.

I was kept busy all the time, working by day at Alfa Laval running a sales department and at night in the wine bar; and I kept it up for eight years. My work at Alfa was going very well, and business was booming.

The wine bar was doing very well also; and we managed both, working as a team, in one long and continual "shift."

Amanda and Georgia were happy and came in many times on weekends or played in the wine garden while we worked. I would get up for work at 7:15 a.m. for work at the office then come back to the wine bar with a change of clothes in the back of the car. I would go into the kitchen and open the bar at 5:30 p.m., getting changed in the back with the clothes I had selected that morning, ready for my second job.

We stayed open till eleven; and if we had a good crowd, we didn't get home until 2:00 a.m. or 3:00 a.m. the following day. Sometimes I would love it, and sometimes I would find the hard work relentless. We had plenty of staff, but we still had to be there all the time. Either Jane or I were always in the bar, every night, seven days a week. This was not for the lazy or faint-hearted as the hard work was nonstop, but it was what we had wanted to do; it was foretold to us. And despite it all, we loved the bar and especially the crowd that we had come to know. I had drawn it out on paper, built it exactly as I had drawn it, and worked at it day after day to build it up into a very successful business.

The great thing about the business wasn't the furniture, the décor, or the location but the wonderful locals, Kiki, Ash, little port-drinking Jeffrey, not to mention the villains like Scottish Jack, the robbers, the fraudsters, the cops, the actors, the stunt men, the camera operators, even my work colleagues who came to see me on business from overseas.

All were a part of our rich tapestry, and we were interwoven right through it so much so that we could never get away far enough to actually see the whole thing or visualize all.

Would I do this again? Probably not, but then again, I did do it once!

BIRTH OF *EAST ENDERS*

A chance conversation can lead to a momentous event.

EARLY EVENINGS WERE the best, especially in summer when we could leave the front door open with the evening sun slanting its rays along Madely Road and along the street outside. I sometimes sat outside at one of the tables outside and listened to our music drifting out to the street, which for me was mostly new wave eighties bands like Spandau Ballet, Bronski Beat's "Small Town Boy" (we knew little Jimmy Summerville, the lead singer, who used to be a barman at Pete's Wine Bar in Pittshangar Lane), Fade To Gray, ELO, and of course Fleetwood Mac. At these early times, we had time to get things organized before the hordes came in demanding our undivided attention and wanting to know where Jane was; and if she was joining me later, of course, she would as she always did every night.

It was during these quiet times in 1983 that one of our bar staff, Chris, who had become a good friend and who was also a hair dresser in a small salon opposite the bar, introduced us to a close friend of his, Tony Holland. He was a screen playwright and had co-written *Z Cars*, a popular TV show in the early seventies.

Tony was a quiet, elegant man in his mid-forties, with an introspective air about him that made you lean forward to listen as he spoke. After a few months of coming into our bar, he began to outline his new brainchild for a brand-new TV series. Tony was tall, slim, and had a well-trimmed beard, though not a full beard, more like one an artist or jazz musician would wear.

It made him look like an artist or a college professor teaching probably English. When he spoke, we just had to listen in case we missed something; and he spoke very carefully, thinking about what he wanted to say before saying it.

Tony began coming in to see us and eventually became a regular at the Village. He sometimes came in with another lady, Julia Smith, who was a BBC TV studio producer; and as he came in more and more often, he began to tell us that he had a concept to write a TV series that was to be all about London street life, barrow boys, pubs, wheelers and dealers, and all the things that happened day to day in London, following not a single street but a whole area and would probably be set somewhere in the East End of

London. He told Jane and I that his idea was that it would be an ongoing life drama, similar to *Coronation Street*, but a London version.

As time went on, it became more and more obvious that this may actually happen. He announced to us one day that his new series would be called *East Enders*, and that he was starting production.

We often sat with him listening to the unfinished story lines and the concepts for each character and going through some of the story lines with him adding bits here and there when asked. Sometimes when he came in, he would sit, with a bottle of wine, and tell us of a problem he had with one of the characters or that the story line was stuck at a particular point. We all sat around the table and, with more and more wine, began discussing ideas for solving his script problems with the story. We thought our ideas were brilliant, though I'm not sure that Tony shared all of our solutions, maybe some ideas though.

Tony was a very perceptive person and could see things in people's characters that others missed, and he could characterize people's nuances and build them into a truly three-dimensional part. None of us at the time had any clue just how big it was to become; and thirty years on, it is still running and is as popular now as it was then, in fact probably even more popular than it was in its first season.

Well done, Tony! What a great contribution you made for all those seemingly real-life characters and all of the people's lives you made just a little bit more bearable as they looked forward to watching your epic series day by day.

The careers you created for your actors, film crews, producers, and writers. You could out do even the biggest corporation, and if that wasn't enough, every one that worked with it enjoyed it immensely. Not many people could say that about the company they work for or had built from scratch.

When I went back to London after a twenty-year absence, after living in Brussels and Greenwood, Indiana, I still caught some shows at Amanda's house in Hanwell, just to see what was happening as if it were real life and I was seeing old friends again.

To see the characters that were still in the current show from the original episodes as I had seen it then all those years ago and seeing them as they now looked, like me—older wiser, a few more lines of wisdom on their faces, and a little less hair, some aging better than others. Why is that? Watching the series occasionally now in my present day, and from thousands of miles away, takes me right back to a specific time earlier in my life and reminds me so much of the words from one of the saddest but truest songs, "Landslide" by Stevie Nicks: "Time grows bolder, children grow older I'm getting older too," and seeing all the characters again now as if in a three-dimensional "snapshot" with me looking on while looking with one eye in the mirror, seeing if I had changed that much too. Unfortunately, I had as well, so much for that!

The big "normalizer," it eventually reduces everyone to look the same in old age even as we all did when we were born. Maybe that's what it's all about, the big equalizer proving to us that as we get older we look all the same, filled with life's experiences; and it doesn't matter what we've done in the meantime. We can only pass on so much, after which we are all just somewhere in the past. Boy, it makes you want to live life to the full and not waste any time. I even saw *East Enders* when I was traveling around the United States and while I was staying in so many boring hotel rooms, which seemed to be my life's destiny while working within the United States. When that happened, it always seemed to prove to me that these things had actually taken place, in my former life. It proved to me that I was there when it did happen, and I remembered when and exactly how that series had been born, maybe even contributing to these events in a small way.

I sometimes felt like a real-life Forrest Gump, while writing this, and having to get all my thoughts and in particular my deeds in some semblance of chronological order. I seem to have been always there at the time somewhere in the background, or right in the middle of it, being part of the most incredible change in human history, viewing it and, like so many others born into this time period, adding small pieces to help it along the way. How lucky I was, and in fact as we all were, to have been born at this time, in this century, and to have seen these changes as if we had been watching our own epic series taking place.

Tony Holland sadly died on 28 November 2007, aged sixty-seven, but what plays he created! And I am so very happy that we passed by each other during his time here, like two passing ships in the night, bright lights in a dark starlit ocean. We'll all miss you, Tony, but thanks for the truly great shows and for making all our lives that much better in being able to be totally immersed in your daily saga of *East Enders*! Whoever thought it would rival *Coronation Street* and would still be one of the top TV shows in the world after thirty years.

Thanks for the good times, Tony, and I'm so very glad we spent as much time as we were able; and I still think the story about the radiation poisoning was a brilliant story line, but sad you didn't go for it!

Tony Holland's legacy would live on for a very long time

MORE CHANGES 1985

Change is a fact of life; things never remain the same so get on board for the ride.

THINGS BEGAN TO get a little tough for both Jane and I. I was working at night in the bar and for Alfa Laval by day while traveling all over the place to Europe, Middle East and everywhere in England, building up my Alfa Laval business.

The business I had started in 1980, the "customer service marketing" operation, had now really taken off; and the Swedish senior management was beginning to see some great results from what I was doing.

I was invited to go over to Sweden and to meet with the business unit heads in Tumba just outside Stockholm, where the corporate headquarters of the company are located.

Jane was invited too and came over with me to Stockholm; but it was, to say the least, a tough few days. We had been drifting apart for some time and were now looking at divorce. I hoped that maybe the offer of a new beginning would help heal things between us, but it wasn't to be. We had both made mistakes in our marriage, and Jane had no intention of ever moving away from London as her life revolved around Ealing, and she didn't ever want to relocate.

I, on the other hand, didn't want to stay living in London as I knew my destiny was somewhere else. Even when I was at school in geography lessons, at age eleven, I would open the book to the United States and imagine what it was like to live in places with names like St. Louis, Denver, Cheyenne, Los Angeles, and San Francisco. All of these places held a mystery for me, and I wanted to know what it was like there.

The names were so different from those that I knew of with names like "Scunthorpe" or "Wolverhampton" or "Rottingdean," which may have all been beautiful towns but just didn't have the same pizazz as those names I read in America I realized when Jane and I were in Stockholm that sadly we had so much of a gulf between us now that it would be difficult or impossible to rebuild our lives back together. Conversation was difficult, and Jane was distracted the whole time we were away; and since Jane had no intention of ever moving away from Ealing, any future I had with my job would be in jeopardy or at least would become too limiting if I were to remain only in the UK operation.

The night that Jane left Stockholm to return back to London was the saddest and most miserable I had ever had, but I could see no way back. So I had to shut that door too and begin to move on with no particular direction; but whatever it was going to be, it could only be forward and never backward.

I don't want to go too much into the reasons for our divorce, but suffice it to say, we both made mistakes and it was an inevitable result. We had both agreed, after that trip to Sweden, that we needed to get on with our lives; and we were both looking at separation.

When I returned to the wine bar, Noz Roberts called me and asked if we could meet for a drink; sWe met in a pub in Southall, where he was well known. And as the night wore on, he asked me, "What do 'you' want, Tony? Do you want to try to make it back with Jane or do you want a divorce?" He added, "The choice at the end of the day is down to you, mate. It's your choice, so what do you want to do?" I thought he had been talking with Jane, and I wondered what that conversation may have been like. Jane had already moved on and had a boyfriend, so my decision was an easy one.

I already knew what my answer would be, and I told him that there was no way either of us would be able to pick up the pieces. I remember telling him that marriage was like a beautiful crystal vase that held beautiful flowers that you could change as the seasons changed; but once it was broken, even if it was repaired, and repaired well, it would never look as beautiful. There would always be a crack that showed the damage every time the light shone through it. And even if it was repaired, the slightest knock could shatter it again.

While we were going through this, I still had a lot of travel in support of my job and had considerable pressure to keep up the momentum.

My problem was that I loved to work and loved what I was developing, doing whatever it took to get ahead and to "prove" myself; though for the life of me, I had no idea who I had to prove myself to.

The business, though serious, could be made fun; and we made sure we did have fun every day!

Will left Alfa to work on his family home in making it into a very upscale golf course and club. We kept in touch and still do; though on hindsight, it was more amusing to remember him coming to work in his family Rolls-Royce, the cost of which was more than his salary!

My business at Alfa Laval grew and grew, and the company had built a brand-new service facility in Brentford; and we were all moving into a very modern ten-floor office building along the Great West Road, just next door to our old offices that the company had been in since the early 1920s. We were moving into the ten-story building that used to house the now-closed Brentford Nylons. Brentford Nylons used to advertise continuously on radio and television ad nauseum. A colleague of mine who had retired, Alf Shrimpton, had shown me some photos of the old Alfa Laval building during the Second World War and others taken later on in the huge 1953 London flood that showed water as high as three feet right across the Great West Road in Brentford. In the picture was an old vintage 1935 Ford service van with "Alfa Laval Service You Can Depend On" written along the side.

I now had hired a full six-person sales operation and also had a marketing secretary. I had hired a really great and highly talented group of young salesmen: Mike Corrigan, Richard St. Clair, Mark Pacey, David Pollard, and Steve Harlow.

My boss was now Brian Divall, who was divisional director of the Customer Service Division, and was great fun to work with. I trained each of my new sales team in marketing and sales and had completed the hiring within a three-month time frame. Each person had their own marketing plan for sales and marketing activities and a car.

We unofficially called our department the Big Bucks Department. Pretentious, huh? We even had a dollar bill enlarged to nearly two feet long and pasted on the glass door of my office, much to the amusement of Bo, but to the seeming annoyance of the other managers.

Our office was on the mezzanine floor above the spares office, and we overlooked the Great West Road and the M4 motorway in a corner location that was open planned. We were doing well, and each of my team went about their jobs promoting a wide variety of newly developed service products, many of which we had "invented" and were selling well.

This service, "After Sales Marketing," was to become very important in the company as it was applicable to all of our installed equipment, whatever age, wherever they were located, and in every one of the more than thirty countries that Alfa Laval operated in. What had started in 1980 was now a fully operational business unit with a budget, sales, and marketing plans, a full sales team, and a complete range of highly profitable service products that we had developed and were still developing.

The reason that we were able to make such a success of this operation was entirely because of our managing director, Bo Wirsen.

Making work fun is when you make magic happen and when that happens everything begins to take on a life of its own and it seemed as if we could do absolutely anything we set out to do.

MIDDLE EAST

Hard work in business will always pay off.

MANY MONTHS LATER I got a call from a foreign telephone operator in Saudi Arabia, of all places; and she asked me to identify if I was Tony Moore, working for Alfa Laval in London. I said yes, and she asked me to be ready to accept a call the following Friday at 10:00 a.m. from a "field telephone" in a location called Al Jubail in Saudi Arabia; and that I was to wait for the call next to the phone I was presently using.

When I got the call, it was from two ex-British Steel Managers calling me from a "field telephone" via a satellite link (brand-new at that time).

They had both left British Steel, which was facing financial, market, and competition issues, as at that time BSC was government owned and too cumbersome. They had both left to work for a company called Saudi Iron and Steel in Al Jubail near Dhahran on the eastern side next to the Persian Gulf. They had some of the biggest plate heat exchangers we had ever made at that time and had called me in person to set up a service plan for them similar to that which I had done for them in their former UK British Steel operation.

They explained that they were now managing the maintenance and production operation for this newly formed Saudi company and wanted the same service that I had developed for them at BSC some years before because they could never ever shut the Saudi operation down. The Saudi government was being really smart and was using some of their oil wealth to divest their massive oil money into new markets in order to be more independent of imported products while building up an improved infrastructure, which would in itself become a new export market for them.

The deal was worth more than £1 million in sales over time. It was a highly profitable sale and was the biggest order my department had ever received. Bo came down and awarded me the sales prize for getting that order, but then "the shit hit the fan" . . . again. The product they bought was an invention by me and my department called a "Strat-Pack" or strategic plate pack, from which they could service any of their many units with minimal disruption to production. I got a great prize for that little gem, a watch, a beautiful Dunhill gold watch with a jet-black face and gold numbers that was only a few centimeters thick. I still wear the beautiful watch today, remembering when I received it from a very happy and smiling Bo Wirsen.

Even a small reward from someone, who's opinion you value, is a treasure forever!

TO SWEDEN AGAIN

I was on the carpet again, but this time it was a red carpet.

NEXT THING I knew was that I got summoned over to Sweden to explain how I had got the Saudi order since they were responsible for all international sales, and it was not a UK market that I should have even been involved with.

I once again discussed this with Bo, who told me to go over and explain what I had done and how I had done it, telling me, "It's always easier to seek forgiveness than it is to ask for permission." I told him, "I am not giving them the order as we won it fair and square." He simply said to me, "Go over there, Tony, and see what happens." I had no problem in going over to see what they wanted, and I certainly didn't want to give my watch back!

I had been to Sweden many, many times; but I had never been summoned at such short notice by such senior staff as the head honcho of the Thermal Division.

Anyway, after I arrived in Lund in southern Sweden, via Copenhagen, where the thermal business unit was headquartered, I was shown into a large theater with seats arranged in ascending rows in a semicircle around a raised stage with a presentation projector set on a pedestal and a huge screen behind.

In came the business head of the thermal operation, Sigge Haraldson, whom I had heard of but had never met before that point. He was followed by several others, including a design engineer called Lars Áke Johansson, who I had never heard of but who would become a key figure in my immediate future. There were six other various department heads who sat around with notepads and wrote copious notes during the long meeting. Lars was a tall, slim blond-haired Swede with a serious disposition. Lars was the opposite to me. Where I was at that time brash and somewhat irresponsible, making quick decisions and going with a hunch, Lars was serious thoughtful completive and slow to react, typical of the design engineer that he was.

I was introduced to them all and asked to tell them about my Saudi order. I took a deep breath; and instead, I told them of the services that we were now offering, all of the products that we had developed, and how my small team was winning new customer service business within the UK operation. Eric Annestrand, the Business Unit manager, told me he already knew about us as they had been measuring how the UK operation was outselling all of the other market companies.

He then put a slide up and showed me a graph of global sales for the past four years, where all of the other country operations were showing moderate sales increases. He then overlaid the UK sales, which went up at a staggering rate of increase every year and was nearly double the sales all of the other countries.

What they ended up wanting was for me to show them how to develop and market a customer service business into all of their other markets.

I was shown a potential market opportunity in all of the Middle Eastern countries, as that was what had piqued their interest, including Saudi Arabia, Kuwait, Iraq, Iran, Dubai, Abu Dhabi, and other smaller countries in the United Arab Emirates. I was amazed at this turn of events.

The outcome of this meeting was that I should work with Lars Áke Johansson and visit each of these countries together with him to develop each market as well as my UK market.

They would pay the United Kingdom for my time as a consultant, and some of the resulting sales would come back to United Kingdom so that my home country could gain from my time in the Middle East.

I came home on a cloud. I had now been given an international market to work in, and I still had my UK operation as well. Instead of being berated for taking the Saudi order, I had been promoted.

I thought I was busy before but was soon to see how busy I would be in developing the new markets in the Middle East.

I learned that a successful service in one market could be duplicated into many other markets if it adds value to our customers.

AL JUBAIL

Saudi, a tough country to work in, but when you focus it's very rewarding.

LARS AND I made many trips to the Middle East, and together we began to open up millions of dollars of sales. In Saudi alone, there was a huge industrial development comprising steel, plastics, chemical, pharmaceutical, and herbicide companies located on each lot. Each one was exactly the same sized square lot, and each lot was surrounded by a series of wide canals set out in a grid around each of the two square mile lots that were fed directly from the Persian Gulf. The complex was less than a mile away, and the canals were used as cooling Water for each of the operations.

There were several hundred pieces of our equipment, and all were critical to each operation.

We made our plans, and I got visas for some of the countries we would be visiting. After several trips that we made each year, the resulting business was estimated at more than £2.5 million or 25 million Swedish Krona, and resulted in huge "Strat Pack" sales along with some incredible servicing business for the United Kingdom and Sweden as we "shared" the service business between us. We had arranged the shipment of hundreds of containers of equipment that would be serviced in Brentford in the United Kingdom and Lund in Sweden.

I won another sales award, and business was building up continuing to be even more successful. I learned that if I did my homework properly and thought out what I wanted and planned out in advance how to go about getting it, and spent time "thinking" instead of just "doing," then winning orders was a lot easier. I constructed my proposals on a purely technical basis first and made the commercial basis second. It was easier to explain to the engineers I met that what I had outlined made perfect sense on technical as well as a commercial basis.

The business we were developing was worth millions and was a lead into other positions that the company would ask me to do, though I didn't know that at the time.

The area we were at, in Al Jubail, was later to become a staging ground for U.S. troops stationed in Saudi to mount operation Desert Storm and operation Desert Shield.

While staying in Dhahran, we often passed by the tall apartment building that was destroyed by a huge bomb killing many American nationals a decade later. We could sense that things were becoming more edgy for travelers like us as the airport controls were becoming more persistent and more visible as we went back each time.

Little did I know what was to follow in the Middle East, but I could see that all was not right and I learned to rely on my instincts. But what I did see was that my Saudi partners wanted nothing different, from life, than I did.

SUE

To make one relationship work is better than a hundred that don't.

It WAS AT this time, in 1985, after Jane and I were nearing the completion of our divorce, that I met Sue while out in Ealing with my sales team. We were out for the evening, as we often did in a restaurant in Ealing, when a friend of mine, Jan Friday (Jan), came in to the bar. She saw me with my friends having a great time, celebrating some order or other (like we needed an excuse). Jan at first didn't want to join us as she had taken a few days off without calling in to her boss. Like I cared! Jan worked for the divisional head of our marine department.

She introduced Sue to us all, and Jan asked me not to tell her boss that we had met her that evening, just in case it got her into trouble, as if I would. Anyway, Sue and I gravitated toward each other and started talking. We seemed to get on very well, and I found Sue easy to talk to, perhaps because of the fact that we had been out since leaving the office; and by the time we met, I was feeling no pain.

Anyway, I invited them both to meet up with us later at the "Maddox" night club in Ealing, and they both agreed to see us later.

Sue was a very slim and a very attractive girl with a "mane" of beautiful curls that were highlighted in streaks of blonde and light brown, and she had a great 'earthy' sense of humor. I had never seen her around, but it turned out that she knew many of my work and personal friends, although we had never moved in the same circles.

Richard and I met up with Jan and Sue in the "Maddox" club at 10:30 p.m. that night, as Maddox was open until 3:00 a.m. long after the pubs had closed. Maddox used to be "The Ealing Jazz Club," where the Rolling Stones first started playing their own and unique rhythm and blues together during the early '60s.

Now, however, the club was a popular members-only late-night hangout. I had a membership since I knew the owners who had been regulars at the Village. I usually went there in a crowd of friends after we had closed the bar but never before midnight as it usually picked up around 12:30 to 1:00 a.m. Sue, Jan, Rich, and I all met up later that night, listening to the DJ playing Hamilton Bohannon, Gloria Gaynor, Kid Creole and the Coconuts,

KC and the Sunshine Band, and all of the eighties "club" music. Sue and I were getting along great, and after that, we started seeing each other more and more. We were in fact both going through a divorce at the same time, me with Jane and Sue with her "ex," Derrick.

I eventually moved out of our house in Bruton Way Ealing, after we had sold it because of the divorce, and moved in with Sue into her ground floor flat in Acton for a short while. Jane had a boyfriend who eventually moved in with her when she moved from our home into her newly purchased cottage in Hanwell.

Sue's flat was quite small, especially after having lived in a large detached house in Ealing, but had plenty of room for just the two of us and her black-and-white cat called Pickle.

Things began to settle down for Sue and I as well as for Jane and her boyfriend, and we began to look for a house soon after. We had been looking all over from Ealing to as far as Wembley and Pinner, an area of around fifteen miles.

After several weeks of searching, we finally found one that we liked; and, of course, as usual, I was away while the negotiations were taking place.

I was also in the process of selling my own home, as well as the wine bar, and so Jane and I had to coordinate one with the other.

Jane and Sue got along fine, as our divorce has nothing to do with Sue and I. It was while these negotiations were going on that I had to make a call to our solicitor in Ealing to set up the purchase of one house and the sale of the other while I was away in Dubai . . . again.

The phone call from Dubai cost a staggering £350 ($500), during which I was agreeing the purchase of our new house. Anyway, the home that we both liked was in Oldborough Road in Wembley and was located in a large Tudor estate of similar homes. Our house was a corner house with a front and rear garden as well as a wooden garage on the side. It had diamond-shaped leaded windows with large bay windows on the ground floor as well as the upper master bedroom. There were three bedrooms large enough for Amanda and Georgia to come and stay during weekends.

The street was tree-lined with beautiful tall lime trees and was a nice quiet suburb with a park at the bottom of our road. It was perfect for us. The house was newly painted and was, of course, black and white, making it look every bit the Tudor style it had been designed to be.

We took Amanda and Georgia to see the home, and they both liked it as well, so it was decided this was to be our first home together.

Jane and I had completed our divorce, but Sue had not as her husband had not yet signed the paperwork. Sue and her ex had not seen one another for over two years and that the divorce "Decree Nisi" had been granted over a year before, so a final "decree absolute" was inevitable. So we continued with the purchase, and Jane had also found a beautiful cottage in old Hanwell in St. Andrews Road.

Jane had enough money from the divorce to be able to buy her home, almost totally for cash, but she chose only a minimum of mortgage payments. I also, at that time, had the deeds to her mother's house in Hanwell, from which I owned half together with Jane. I had agreed with her that if we could both manage an amicable divorce, I would hand over my half of Jane's mother's house back to Jane so that she could sell the downstairs apartment and keep any money from that sale, while allowing her mother to stay upstairs. I also agreed to let Jane have the Beemer (BMW 528i), which I had been mostly driving, as I now had a company car.

We both lived there at Sue's apartment for about three months while we were looking to buy our own house somewhere in the vicinity so that Georgia and Amanda could come and stay during weekends. Sue and I were a happy couple, and we grew to love each other as we learned more and more about ourselves.

Sue had a very strong, and close, family that I was introduced to a short time later. There was her mother Sylvia, her dad Maurice, her younger sister Lesley, and her brother Paul. I liked them a lot, and they became an instant family to me, accepting me even though I was not Jewish, which they all were.

We finally completed the sale of Bruton Way and the purchase of Oldborough Road; and we finally moved in, with Amanda and Georgia helping us to get the move completed as a way of getting them used to the new arrangement. Amanda was now eleven, and Georgia was four.

Soon after we had completed the move, I was off again to the Middle East for another three-week stint of travel. Jane and I had decided to sell the wine bar, as after our divorce, it would become more difficult for Jane to manage Amanda and Georgia, while running the bar. In fact, I had made this a condition of our divorce settlement just for this fact. I knew that as they became teenagers, it would be more and more important for Jane to be there for them even if I could not because of my extensive travel.

We were both concerned about Amanda and Georgia and felt that they had been somewhat neglected in our managing of the bar and my job; and they had both been looked after by a series of nannies, some of which had not been good for them at all.

I felt that our divorce was bad enough for them to deal with, without adding to it by Jane having to manage the bar as well as managing baby sitters and nannies and with me being often gone away on my many business trips overseas.

I also felt that they would need more attention from us both as times may get difficult for them. We finally sold the bar, and what we had started for very little more than a couple of months' wages when we opened the bar was now worth twelve times as much as "a going concern" with an excellent reputation and had given an income for both of us the whole time.

Financially, we were both OK; but the downside was with Amanda and Georgia who would have to now deal with a broken home, something that was now unavoidable.

This was, for us both as in any divorce with children, the worst part of it all; and we would have to manage that as best we both could. We had agreed that I would have them every weekend and even during the week if needed or if it was wanted by either Georgia or Amanda.

While Amanda quietly accepted our decision to divorce, Georgia was excited at the possibility of having two homes instead of one. She couldn't see any downside at her age. Amanda was more retrospect about the situation, and things for her became more complicated, as I'll explain later.

I told Amanda that I wanted them both to remain best friends and be closer to each other than even their mom. As I saw it, they would always be there for each other as friends and sisters. That wish came true as they are still each other's closest friends; and while they argue like cats and dogs, they are nevertheless extremely close.

Soon after we had both moved in and had begun a new life together, I had received another huge order from Saudi. One of my contacts in Saudi wanted to come over to visit and to see London and the facility in Brentford. So I made the arrangements for him to come over and asked if he would come to see our brand-new facility while dressed in his traditional robes. Imagine what that looked like when he arrived at the Brentford operation complete with his flowing white Arabian Emirati traditional robes, his red and white patterned Ghutra covering his head with his black woven traditional Saudi Igal on top of his head.

He even wore a pair of black sunglasses as well just to complete the image. I told him it would look so cool to our staff; and as he was quite young, he loved the idea, especially when I told him that he really looked like a very rich oil sheik. We both laughed, and I like him a lot. And I knew the feeling was mutual. He may have in fact been a rich sheik, but I didn't ask about that.

I took Sue to meet my Arabian visitor when he arrived as he was staying at the Hilton in Mayfair. Sue and I both picked him up at his hotel. When you are in Saudi, it is very polite to introduce business friends to your family; so in fact, I was giving my colleague, Ahmed, a real compliment in return for his hospitably extended to me while I was over there. We took him to Trader Vicks under the Hilton in Mayfair, and he had no idea that Sue was Jewish. Neither would it matter to him, but since Ahmed was an Arab, we decided that we wouldn't mention that small detail. This was another first for my small but profitable operation, and Ahmed was our first international visitor from the Middle East.

To remain friends after a divorce is always well worth the effort.

BOMBED IN KUWAIT

Bombs in movies are not the same as in real life!

LARS AND I were at the "Kuwait Oil Company" and had traveled up from Saudi to meet with our contacts while staying at the Kuwait Hilton. The reason I mention this is that just outside the Hilton's entrance were two large machine gun installations, either side of the entrance to the hotel, manned by soldiers from the Kuwaiti army.

Things had been getting worse between Iraq and Kuwait as Iraq, or rather Saddam Hussein, had decided that Kuwait still belonged to Iraq; and although Britain had made Kuwait a separate kingdom or emirate way back several decades before, Saddam believed it had no business existing as a separate entity under a separate king. So there were many skirmishes going on while we were there, and we could often hear gunshots and explosions in the distance.

The border with Iraq was only a few miles away from where we were meeting at the KOC oil terminal, and while we visited the terminal, we always had our passports taken by the security guards. We were taken inside the terminal by an armed escort in a jeep, and we also had to bring a visa with us signed by a Saudi senior manager, stating the time and date of our meeting.

The airport at Kuwait was designed to look like a large stone and glass version of the "Concord" supersonic aircraft with the entrance to the airport through what would be the huge Olympus engines if it were a real aircraft.

It was cleverly constructed so that the concourse leading to the gates was down a central aisle as it would have been on the actual aircraft, but instead of seats, there were gates for boarding planes. The main entrance to the airport was constructed with a huge wall of glass going up some thirty feet high, making the inside very bright and airy.

As Lars and I were just passing through passport control, some thirty feet inside the entrance of the airport, a deafening "thud" came from the direction of the entrance to the airport building. We were both suddenly pushed by the compressive force of that loud sound, and we were both thumped with the force. It was like being "punched" in the chest.

Immediately following the loud "thud" was the sound of the mass of glass windows at the front of the airport being shattered, and I shouted to Lars, "hit the deck." Lars, not knowing what I meant, looked at me in bewilderment as I grabbed him and dragged him to the ground.

What happened next was incredible, as millions of glass shards from the shattered main window came flying through the air toward us. After that, everything went deathly quiet; and we were ourselves partially deaf not by the loudness of the thud but by the compression that followed it.

An explosion had occurred outside the main entrance, just after we had entered the airport; and we had missed it by seconds. People started running and shouting all around us, and some were lying flat on the ground. Absolute panic ensued, and the mess and the smell were incredible. As for Lars and I, we were fine and were untouched by the bomb or its devastating effect on the airport all around us. What had just a few seconds ago been a peaceful and quietly efficient airport had now become a mass of running and shouting people milling around and chaos was everywhere. Glass and debris was all over the floor, and the airport was a complete mess.

We got up and proceeded to walk quickly toward our flight departure gate, moving away from the entrance while looking backward over our shoulders all the way.

When we reached our gate, I noticed that the flight crew was English, so I quietly asked them what had just happened; and they couldn't tell us. I got up next to one of the stewardesses and asked her again very quietly, "Was that a bomb?" She told me it was a car bomb but to keep it quiet in case the passengers got scared. Our flight, from Kuwait down to Qatar, was the first out of the airport after the car bomb went off; and as I boarded the plane, I leaned into the cockpit and asked the captain, who was also English, if he could bank the plane over the car park outside the entrance so we could see what had happened. He told me that we had to go in that direction anyway, and that he could make a tighter turn than usual so that we could see how much damage had been done as he was curious also.

We took off, and everyone was very quiet. The pilot swept a tight right turn as he told me he would immediately after we took off, and Lars and I looked down to see what the damage was.

We were still low in the air and could see all the detail of what had happened below. We saw that all of the glass was missing from the entrance to the airport except for some huge pieces still dangling dangerously in their frames very high up. There was a black stain all over the light gray of the remaining concrete outer structure.

What was most noticeable was that six or seven of the cars that were moments before parked right outside the front of the entrance had been turned upside down and were either leaning upright against the wall and doorway or were rocking upside down atop other cars that were tossed around like matchbox toys.

Funny thing was that there had been a total of seven bombs that had gone off that day, including the Hilton where we had stayed, KOC headquarters where we had spent the past few days, and the airport missing us by a mere few minutes. But despite their efforts, they missed us both, so we were fine. After the short twenty-minute flight, we began our descent into Qatar's Doha airport; and as we began to descend, the pilot came on the speaker system and asked us to do exactly as we were told by the Qatari staff and that everything would be fine.

It was like that scene out of the movie *Airplane* when the pilot told everyone on board not to panic. As soon as he said that, everyone began frantically talking and getting very excited. I was OK, but poor Lars was scared out of his mind and was clutching on to the arm rests until his knuckles were white, staring straight ahead.

"What does he mean, do whatever they tell you to do?" he whispered to me. "What is happening now?" I told him, "I don't know, but we'll soon find out, won't we? Let's just wait and see."

As the plane descended and began to touch down, there was a line of armored cars and jeeps loaded with heavily armed soldiers flanking both sides of the plane as we continued to touch down.

The pilot announced to all of us, "Nothing to be afraid of at all. Just a standard safety precaution." He said that as the aircraft was led to a remote area at the very edge of the airport.

"What a load of bollocks," I said to Lars as we were told to sit and wait further instructions. Well, by this time, Lars and some of the other passengers were freaking out; and he was still holding on to the arm rest with all his might becoming as white as a sheet.

I felt sorry for him as he was after all Swedish people, and Sweden has never ever had to deal with the IRA or any other terrorist organization as far as I knew. In fact, I very much doubt that there is even a word for "terrorist" in Swedish vocabulary.

Anyway, if there was or wasn't, I wasn't helping poor Lars, who was by now looking decidedly ill. I turned to him and said, "Look at it this way, Lars. If the terrorists who planted the bomb were any way half intelligent, they certainly wouldn't be on the first flight out going to Qatar now, would they? That would be an obvious place to look for them. And anyway, if they were, how would any authorities know what to look for as it only happened fifty minutes ago, and how would they know so soon?"

Well, not a good thing to say as I tried to make light of the situation for Lars's sake. "If they were that intelligent, they wouldn't have planted the 'f 'ing' bomb," he said. "And they would do exactly that." He replied, "They would get out of town on the first available flight." "Nah, I don't think so," I said. "They would already be gone by land headed for the Iraqi border, which is only a few miles down the road."

As we sat there surmising what neither of us knew anything about, the doors were opened and the army personnel came on board, slowly moving down the aircraft. It was funny to me. What were they hoping to see? Someone who "looked" like a terrorist?

To me, they all looked very suspicious anyway, as I told Lars, looking around at the other passengers wearing traditional robes and headdresses.

Some even had a hawk on their arm, which I have never seen on an aircraft except out there. "Personally," I announced to Lars, "I would suspect anyone traveling with one of those 'killer' birds on his shoulder. Trained to kill," repeating it in case he didn't hear. "Sshh," he said to me, "they understand English and you're talking too loud," "Oh, come off it," I said. "Like I actually look like a terrorist." But Lars was dying inside and was by now breaking out into a cold sweat.

I noticed and told him quietly, "Hey, Larsy, I wouldn't go sweating like that if I were you. It's a dead giveaway. You look nervous as hell. I even wonder now if it was in fact you." He turned and looked as if he would kill me on the spot.

"This is not funny," he said. "People may have been killed or injured." I replied, "Lars, old chap, that's the general idea. They want to do just that, but you and me, we are still here, so don't worry about it." Anyway, as we were chatting like this, the guards came past us once again; and one looked at me and said, in KwEnglish, "Wherre are you from?" rolling his R's. "I am English," I replied in my most English of English accents, "but he isn't," pointing my thumb over my shoulder at Lars, not offering to say where Lars was actually from.

He stared at poor Lars, who by now, I was sure, was going to faint or shit himself any minute; and the guard asked him, "And wherre arre you frrom?" staring right at Lars. Now at this point, it would have sufficed to say, "I am Swedish," or better still "I'm from Sveden." But no, not Lars. He had to say, "I am from Lund," like the bloody Qatari security guard at the very edge of an airport, armed to the teeth in the middle of the bloody dessert would know where the hell Lund is. I have been there loads of times, and I still

Don't know where it is!

Typical of a Swedish design engineer to go into far more detail than what was necessary. "Show me yourr parrssporrt," he said as Lars shot me a look that said "I'll kill you." I was humming along and putting my earpiece in, so I could listen to my favorite CD, *Greatest Hits* by Fleetwood Mac, while pretending to be totally cool with it all.

After looking through Lars's passport, which by the way was upside down until he saw Lars's photo, after which he sheepishly turned it the right way up so as not to look too stupid, and gave it back. Well, we were finally let off the aircraft; and by now the authorities had placed armed soldiers all around the aircraft, in a ring of steel, as if they were expecting a fight from me and my fellow travelers.

All of our luggage was taken off the plane and was placed on the tarmac, next to the aircraft, while we were told to go and identify which was ours. "What the hell are they looking for?" I mumbled to Lars. "A parcel marked bomb inside! or Bomb! Fragile. This way up?" That only made him worse. By now, he was trying to ignore me.

I on the other hand was seeing this as all rather funny. We were after all quite fine, as were all of our other fellow passengers. I decided to give it one more try and said quietly to poor Lars, "Let's see if we can guess which one of these passengers is the terrorist. Definitely that guy with the sparrow on his shoulder."

That did it! "That's not a sparrow. It's a falcon," he said, adding, "and it's a mark of extreme wealth and high standing. You think this is very funny, don't you? Do you ever take anything seriously?" he whispered as quietly "loud" as he dared. "Winning orders," I said in response. "Now that's what I call serious." But he was beyond all reason.

"Look, Lars," I said, "I come from a country that has been overrun by terrorists from all over the world, even before the word was added to our very extensive vocabulary, including, I might add, terrorists from Sweden, men wearing horned helmets on their heads," adding as I thought of it, "as well as Galls from Germany, Normans from France, Scottish and Irish, and even the bloody Italians more than once. And as for the Indians, they bloody well took over all our 'fish and chip shops' and turned them all into curry houses, whereas you and your lot have never ever been overrun by anyone ever—probably because Sweden is so bloody boring they would die of boredom as soon as they got off their boats. Even Abba had to leave as soon as they could afford it." He finally started laughing . . . at last.

Well, by now, we were all taken with our luggage back to the terminal, in the jeeps; and that was that. Nothing, no search, no passport inspection (except for Lars, but then he was after all Swedish); and we were finally allowed to go on our way.

I explained the difference between where he comes from and where I come from. "In Britain, we are very used to acts of terrorism from our history, especially from being in a conflict with the IRA who had been setting of bombs all over London, and we had been involved in an urban war for well over a decade. It didn't make it easier for us, but it did make us take life into perspective. Where Lars came from in Sweden, they haven't even been involved in a world war let alone any conflicts with neighbors or warring factions, so his reaction was quite normal.

I still had all my bits! So it wasn't as bad as it could have been!

ROME LADY IN RED

I knew she was the one for me, and Rome was the best place to see it.

I WAS TO ADDRESS a conference in Rome, and I was out again in the Middle East and had arranged to come back to London via Rome so that I could be at the meeting. I told Sue about it and invited her to meet me at the Hotel Michelangelo and bought her a ticket to meet me in Rome.

I flew from Dubai to Rome and caught a taxi from the airport making my way to meet her in the hotel lobby. Of course, we had no cell phones at that time; so once the arrangements had been made, you had to hope nothing had gone wrong.

I arrived at the hotel and waited for Sue to meet me and called up to her room to let her know that I was here.

When she came out of the elevator, she looked absolutely the most beautiful girl I had ever seen, and this one moment for me was for me was a moment in time I knew at that very moment I would never ever forget. She was wearing a brightly colored summer dress in white and red, with many brightly colored flowers on it; and her hair had highlights that seemed to match her dress. As she came out of the elevator, she took my breath away, and I was stunned. Her mane of curly hair had caught the late-afternoon sunlight as it came in dappled light across the lobby from the windows and shone, lighting her and the whole lobby up.

I told her she looked stunning, and she replied, "I suppose I do after looking at all those Middle Eastern women for the last three weeks with veils hiding their heads."

We went out on the town to several street cafes and bars, enjoying every moment. We ended up in a family-run restaurant. I would say Italian, but they all were; and we sat down outside to order in a small raised garden to order dinner and wine.

After we had ordered an appetizer, Sue got up to go to the bathroom while I ordered a bottle of Italian red wine. After the wine arrived, I sat and sipped while waiting for her to return, before ordering our main course; but after half an hour, she still hadn't shown up.

I asked the waiter if he had seen her, and he said yes she was out back, so I got up from the table to find her and to see if she was OK.

Well, I found her sitting at a huge table in the kitchen with all of the family; there must have been at least fifteen of them. They were the family of the owners of the restaurant, and Sue was eating and drinking with them, while I was sitting out front waiting to order!

"Hi, darling," she said, smiling. "I was looking for the bathroom and made a wrong turn, ending up in the kitchen when they invited me to join them and sample their food, and before I could say no thanks, they made a space at the table and sat me down." They were all laughing and talking to Sue in Italian and broken English, offering her their wine and samples of all of their food; and she was having the time of her life.

She was laughing too, even though she couldn't understand what they were saying; but then she didn't need to. She was having a blast; and I realized at that moment, seeing her there at the table, that Friday night in Rome, tilting her head back laughing and enjoying herself, with her eyes alight with happiness that I had at that moment fallen in love with her.

I loved her spontaneous laugh and her ready sense of humor and especially the way she looked that night. The song by Chris De Burg, "Lady in Red," would from that moment on and forever be my special song for Sue, reminding me of how beautiful Sue looked that night in Rome. Whenever I heard it played, it would always take me back to that one moment in time when she came out of the elevator, in the Hotel Michelangelo, with the evening sun glowing in her hair and her highlights shining out matching the color of her eyes. I knew I would remember all of the details of that night forever.

Love can smack you on the arse!

CHRISTMAS AT THE OFFICE

Not the best idea, to return to work after the pub!

THAT CHRISTMAS ON the last day of work, we all went to the pub for a Christmas drink, as we always did on the last day of work before Christmas. Rich, myself, Brian Divall, Jan Friday, and my secretary Sharon all went to a pub called the Red Lion in Brentford.

We all loaded into Brian's gold-colored Volvo estate car, which we had nicknamed the "Pimpmobile" because it made Brian look like he was a pimp. I mean, who on earth would have a gold Volvo estate as a company car unless their company was involved in "pimping"?

Anyway, we got to the pub at around 11:00 a.m. and began to celebrate in our usual manner, and met up with several others and proceeded to "take over" the pub. We really had a great time, laughing, joking, dancing on the tables, playing drinking games, and didn't leave until 3:30 p.m. By this time, all except for Brian, who was driving, were, to put it mildly, absolutely and completely drunk as skunks.

We thought, stupidly as it turned out, that we should at least go back to the office and wish everyone a very merry Christmas and then go on by cab to Ealing and finish of our celebrations.

So, we all piled into Brian's Pimpmobile, all seven of us. We drove to the office, and Brian parked his car right outside the fully automatic sliding glass doors on the curved driveway at the lobby of Alfa Laval.

Now it's fair to point out here that in order to open the sliding glass doors, all you have to do is stand outside and the sensor will open the doors for you, well, in theory anyway.

As Brian's car came to a stop, the doors flew open, and everyone literally fell out onto the pavement all on top of each other. Jan, as usual, wore a very short tight miniskirt and was unfortunately the first to fall out of the car. As soon as she fell out, everyone else fell out on top of her. So there she was, legs apart, knickers showing to all, and a heap of giggling idiots on top of her.

There were a few steps up to the automatic doors, which Jan and Sharon were climbing up on all fours.

Jan was then attempting to find her way inside the lobby by standing at what she thought was the doorway, but it wasn't. She was too far to the left and was in fact standing, demanding that the solid window at the side of the automatic doors now open to let her in. When this didn't happen, she began to try to force the window open by leaning against it, to keep her from falling over, while she was sliding her hands along the glass in a lame attempt to get the solid glass window to slide open.

In other words, Jan was trying to open an automatic door while standing at the left-hand side window and not the door.

She finally got in when one of the others got in front of the automated door, and it quite calmly slid open.

"There you are, you little bugger!" she exclaimed to the door. "You moved on me," she said and slid along the glass window before falling into the lobby.

She was being watched by the HR manager who was leaning over the mezzanine floor looking down over the banister at the front door.

The rest of us went to our offices to clear up ready for the holiday from work for Christmas. After around an hour, we were all ready to go out again except that my secretary, Sharon, was nowhere to be seen. We called each office to see where she may be, but she was nowhere to be found.

Finally, we got a call from the HR manager saying that she had found Sharon after hearing snoring while in the ladies' toilet at the rear of the lobby. She climbed up in the stall next door to the snoring sound and found Sharon, knickers around her feet, sitting on the toilet fast asleep and snoring.

Well, once again, the shit hit the fan, as Brian was summoned to the tenth floor to explain to the HR director, how a bunch of drunk employees had been seen falling out of a car onto the road, believed to be his car. As if that wasn't enough, they were then seen falling or staggering up the steps to the lobby; and after reaching the automated doors, Janette Friday was seen "attempting" to get in while standing at the side of the door instead of at the front of the door. To make matters worse, she was trying to slide the eight-foot-high solid glass pane open, a feat I might add that is almost impossible since it is designed to be an automatic door.

Then as if that wasn't enough, young eighteen-year-old Sharon, a secretary, in Tony Moore's office, had fallen asleep in a most unladylike fashion, with her underwear around her ankles, and I might add snoring, while sitting in a locked stall, atop one of the ladies' toilets. My manager, Anne, had to climb over the booth to unlock the door in order to get Sharon, who was paralytic at 4:00 p.m. on a workday, out of the toilet and into a cab home. Brian could only apologize and promise to deal with us after the holidays.

The only good thing was that it was Christmas, and many of the top managers were already away for the Christmas holidays. When we met up with Brian later, he was very worried about being caught. "I'm a bad influence," I told him over another pint of Guinness, and I added hopefully, "but as long as our results are the best in the company, I suppose they'll give us some leeway."

I love Christmas best of all seasons, after autumn; and I especially loved it when we all had had a really good year at work as I has seemed to have had for as long as I could remember.

I learned that the actions and behavior of friends is often how we ourselves are measured and guilt by association is a bitch!

TONY YATES

Even the most boring of jobs can be fun, with a highly talented team

To HELP MARKET and promote our new business, I had sought the help of a London-based and highly talented advertising firm, "Publitek." The account manager was a guy called Tony Yates, who I knew from my wine bar. Tony's company had been mainly in the pharmaceutical business and had been responsible for one of the world's most effective advertising campaigns ever. They had marketed and advertised a drug called Zantac for Glaxo Labs, and Publitek's concepts had helped to place Zantac into the *Guinness Book of World Records* as the most prescribed drug in the world. So I figured if they could do that for an ulcer drug, I wonder what they could do for us.

"Into the Guinness Book of whatever," I said to Tony when he told me of their success with Zantac. "Guinness, you say? That's good enough for me," I told him laughingly. In case I forgot to mention, Guinness was my favorite beer. Did I mention that? And we began what was to be an exceptionally good partnership to help promote my marketing operation together. We had such a laugh dreaming up ideas for brochures, adverts, and some very zany concepts. Some of the concepts we had included making replicas of the rubber gaskets used in our heat exchangers made from liquorish, with the idea being to promote "a sweet deal on regasketing."

Another idea was a dice loaded with gold-plated chocolate money to "sweeten the deal and save big bucks" and even a box of bath salts to help take away all the fatigue from managing engine room breakdowns on board the worlds shipping if they were not using our "preventive maintenance."

All of these concepts had been packaged and shipped all over the world to our marketing companies that I had been asked to set up as "duplicates" of our first operation in London. The concepts had been a huge success as no one else had ever done this kind of marketing for these types of products; and because of this and the service, we had put together became a resounding success.

After each of our successful ad campaigns, we went to "Yates Wine Bar" (no relation) in London's West End to celebrate. I was told many years later that I had become famous amongst the London advertising set because I sent several bottles of Champaign back because the bubbles were too big! Did I really do that?

To celebrate small successes often leads to more successes!

A SILENT MOVIE

When working with the best, hang on tight as it's a rollercoaster.

LATER ON, WHEN I was working in Brussels, we decided to make a movie to promote "preventive maintenance," which by any measure was a very boring product. Tony and the team at Publitek came up with a brilliant idea to make a ten-minute movie with no words using "mime" accompanied by grunts and a few noises of things "happening" as the movie moved on. We had an "infinity" studio where there was no backdrop at all, only a black background. In the foreground was a whole company made in a straight line with the opening scene showing a very pleased CEO and behind him a wall chart showing climbing sales and profits; while the CEO, complete with his handlebar moustache, was lighting a big cigar.

The camera pans to the right to a machine with white boxes going in on a mesh conveyor belt, representing production units, into a packaging machine, which then breaks down with a siren going off as the machine stopped. Meanwhile, the previously happy CEO was now in a rage with the wall chart showing sales drooping down to the floor and the company founder, his dad looking like a much older version of him, looking equally enraged.

As they call for our service, the machine starts up again, and all is well; but the production manager, who didn't use our service prior to the breakdown until it was too late, leaves to go home. But his car won't start, meaning that he should use "preventive maintenance" on that too.

Needless to say, with no words at all, the short movie could be shown all over the world in every market company; and the film was a huge success, thanks to Tony and his team.

Some thirty years later, in 2011, I decided to reach out to Tony and began to search on the Internet from the United States and found several companies in Richmond, in the advertising media specialized in pharmaceuticals that he had either owned or started up. So then I sent an e-mail to the general e-mail address of one such company called Pan Advertising, saying that "I used to work with Tony at his former company called Publitek," adding that, "they probably would not have heard of me."

But I asked if they knew how I could get back in contact with my old friend Tony Yates as I was now living in the United States.

Well, I couldn't believe it when I got an e-mail back from a guy called Ben, who was the managing director and used to work with Tony at Publitek; and, yes, he remembered me very well.

He went on to tell me in the e-mail that I had become "a legend" in the advertising world because of some of the crazy things I had done. He recalled to me that one story was that I sent four bottles of champagne back while celebrating a new campaign in "Yates Wine Bar" because the bubbles were too big. "WHAT? Are you kidding," I replied to him. And then later after I got in touch with Tony, he confirmed that and some other stories that I could not possibly repeat even in this book.

Tony had been awarded an honorary doctorate at a prestigious London University for his work in the specialized advertising world of pharmaceutical advertising.

I was so proud to learn of his achievements, and we spoke of meeting up again when I came over to London next time.

I learned that it's sometimes the life achievements of others that we have the privilege to work with or to have come into contact with that inspires us to do what we can do and to do it as good as we can possibly can.

Tony, my good friend, was one of those people that I was privileged to work with.

When I got hold of Tony, after twenty-five years, once again, I was very happy that we had managed to keep in touch. I was stunned to hear of Tony's working career and was so very happy to hear all that he had achieved. He really was the best! So on top of being bloody good fun to work with and being able to put a great team together, he was now a PhD; and I was so glad to read about his achievements. I did have a drink for you, Tone!

WHAT A TEAM WE MADE! and, WHAT FUN WE HAD working together.

Thanks, Tony!

I learned a valuable lesson in business, that if the right personalities, talent and skills can be put together and work as a team, everything is possible.

A GUNNESS WORLD RECORD

Sometimes, I really am an idiot!

WHILE I WAS traveling to the United States with Lars, we began our trip in Houston; and the date happened to be March 17, which meant nothing to me at all, being from London.

We were having lunch in a very large sports bar and restaurant with a group of ten distributors who we were there to train. A waitress with hideous bright green hair came over and proceeded to take our order for lunch; and when she got to me, on hearing my accent, she announced excitedly while chewing gum and blowing bubbles, "Oh, you're from over there, aren't you? You're from Ireland or something." "No," I said, "I am actually from London and not from Ireland at all." "Oh," she said, "London. Isn't that right next door?" And the table I was on started chuckling. "Almost," I said, "at least compared with some of the distances in America." She started giggling. "So what do you all do on Saint Patrick's day?" she asked. "Well, actually," I said, joking, "we normally shoot them." Immediately, the whole place went deadly quiet, and I thought, *OOPS! Wrong thing to say!* So I added quickly, "At least we try to before they shoot us first." And my table started laughing . . . phew. As I left, she gave me her phone number on the check, with a note saying, "I'd love you to shoot me too!"

Anyway, from there, we went on to New Orleans; and we ended up on Bourbon Street at Pat O'Brian's Pub just off the Street. Lars told me we have to try a Hurricane, which is a drink I had never heard of before.

We had one each, in a tall tulip-shaped glass with some wickedly tasting cherry drink inside. I drank mine down fairly quickly and said to Lars, "Mmmn yummy. Think I'll have another." "I'd take it easy if I were you," he said. "These are very strong drinks." Anyway, I had another and then another after that.

Finally, when the two of us left the bar and turned onto Bourbon Street, it hit me; and I started to see double and had to hang on to the lamp post in order to stand up. "Fuck," I informed anyone and no one at all, "What the hell was in that drink?" I looked over and saw that Lars was as bad as I was.

We both staggered off down the street and looked for somewhere to get something to eat so that we could feel better.

We found an open-air hamburger place farther down on the left-hand side of the street and sat down in a vague hope of actually being able to order something from the menu.

I couldn't even talk, and we started to giggle while trying to read the menu. I had to read it with one eye, as when I opened the other one, it refused to see the same menu as my other eye and kept looking somewhere else, which made us both laugh hysterically.

We finally ordered by pointing at a customer sitting at a table nearby who had a very large cheeseburger. "One of thosh," I said, not looking up with my one good eye. "Me 'swell," uttered Lars. "Sho two more of the shame." I informed her now quite drunk. She understood, and we both ordered a large pitcher of iced water as well.

We ate our food with some difficulty, tried to get up without seeming too drunk, and staggered out of the restaurant. We made it back to our hotel, and we were both violently sick.

The next day, we were heading up to New York on our way home when I received a call from British Airways who informed me that my Sunday afternoon flight had been cancelled and that they could get me back from New York on Concorde if that was OK. "Let me think for a second," I said to the girl on the other end of the phone. "I suppose that will have to do," I said, and she started laughing. She added, "I should think so. I work for British Airways, and I have never flown on it, so enjoy your flight, Mr. Moore. It's on us."

I couldn't wait to tell Lars, and he was so envious he could hardly speak to me. All the way back to New York, I kept dropping the name Concorde as we chatted on the flight from New Orleans to JFK, just throwing it in there in the middle of our conversation. "Did I mention I'm flying Concorde, by any chance, Lars?" I said, while nudging him and winking.

As we parted at JFK, I made sure to ask an official, "Where is the Concorde lounge?" right in front of Lars just to rub it in. As we parted, Lars said, "Have a great flight and don't forget to tell me what it was like." "What's what like?" I said, pretending not to know what he was talking about. "Oh, you mean flying on Concorde?"

I said, sounding innocent. "Of course, I will. I can't wait to see what it's like to travel at twice the speed of sound. Are you flying coach, Larsy? Shame . . . still, if you feel a bumpy ride, then it's probably me in Concorde passing you by at twice the speed of sound." He glared, and we waved goodbye.

I arrived at the lounge, and it was amazing; there were canapés with caviar, shrimp and lobster, as well as a drinks cart with the biggest collection of the best brandies and single malt whiskeys I had ever seen; and that was before we even boarded. Well, we finally began to board the aircraft, and I was so excited.

Once inside the doorway, there was the cockpit with two pilots and an engineer who sat behind them facing the side. In front of him was a wall of gauges and switches. He saw me looking and said, "Impressive, isn't it?" "Yes," I replied. "I have never seen anything like it." He then pointed to a long slot in the panel in front of him that went up to the low curved ceiling and told me, "See that slot? When we are at Mach 2, it opens up to nine inches wide." "Why is that?" I said. He replied, "Because the aircraft stretches that much because of the drag on the airframe." "No," I said. "Are you kidding me?" He said, "Tell you what, when we are up to speed and the seat belt signs are switched off, why don't you come up front and take a look." "Cool," I said. "I definitely will do that. Thanks." And I went on to my seat.

The seating inside the cabin was in two rows of two large gray leather seats, very luxurious and very high class.

As we began to take off, it was very bumpy, a bit like being in a very fast sports car with tightened up suspension. The speed of acceleration was incredible as the four Rolls-Royce Olympus engines throttled up faster and faster for takeoff speed.

Now in most aircraft, you get used to the rate of climb and the angle of climb. In Concorde, it is twice as steep; and it feels like you are almost vertical. As we climbed higher, there was a green digital gauge at the bulkhead of the cabin that showed all of the passengers the rate of climb, which was spinning furiously fast as we climbed so rapidly. We soon reached 38,000 feet, which is where most passenger aircraft normally flew; but we were continuing up to twice that height.

Meanwhile, the gauge began to show our speed in miles per hour and as a percentage of Mach 1, which is the speed of sound. It began reading 0.8 Mach 1, then 0.85 Mach 1, then 0.9 Mach 1. The ground speed was also showing alongside the "Mach meter." And we were now exceeding 650 miles per with our ground speed continuing to increase and on up to a staggering seven hundred miles per hour, and still accelerating past Mach 1.

I was trying to feel or listen to the sound barrier as we went through Mach 1, but sadly I could feel nothing. The speed continued upward and the digital gauge now showed our altitude as well. We were now at one thousand miles per hour and still accelerating; it was simply awesome.

Our altitude was now sixty thousand feet more than twice that of any other passenger aircraft. I was stunned at it all as I watched the Mach meter now showing 0.8 Mach 2 and so on. We finally leveled off at 65,000 feet or more than twelve miles high, and we had now reached a staggering 1,420 miles per hour; and at that altitude, we were now more than Mach 2. The gauge finally stopped spinning and settled at our speed as well as the distance flown and how far we had yet to go.

The seat belts sign finally went off, and I had to see the "stretch" panel in front of the flight engineer. But on my way, I decided to go to the bathroom, which faced sideways to the aircraft.

As I stood in the tiny bathroom, I suddenly had a brilliant idea—what if I stood facing the direction of Concorde and peed in the direction we were flying. I would in fact be peeing at more than twice the speed of sound and faster than Concorde flew. It was difficult to say the least, but I was determined to manage it and looked at my watch to begin the calculation. I peed for two minutes, and I estimated the rate of flow as fifteen miles per hour. That meant I peed for a distance of sixty-one miles and at 1,435 miles per hour, at a height of 65,000 feet and at more than twice the speed of sound! Very cool!

I was so proud of myself and couldn't wait to inform the flight engineer of my astounding new world record.

I asked the stewardess if I could go to the cockpit, adding that I had been invited by the flight engineer; and she gave me permission. At that time, passengers were allowed to enter the flight deck with the captain's permission.

I walked to the front of the aircraft and noticed that the sky color was a deeper blue than I had ever seen on my many flights in the past.

Maybe it was our altitude, which was now 65,000 feet or a staggering thirteen miles high. The flight deck, for me, was truly incredible. The panel in front of the fight engineer had opened up to a gap of at least nine inches where it had been closed before when we were on the ground. He showed me the gauges and the famous "droop snoop" at the front of the craft, which drooped at takeoff and landing in order for the pilot to see where he was going while on the ground.

He also showed me a second very hardened glass composite that had come up in front of the windshield as the air pressure was so high that it would have glowed red hot at this speed and altitude. I began to tell him what I had done in the bathroom, telling him of my rather unique calculations and estimations of time and distance. At this, all three of them looked 'round at me as if I was mad, and I said, "No, really, I think it may be a world record. What do you think?" The copilot shook his head and started laughing. "You did what?" he said, thought for a moment, and turned to me and said, "You know, you may be right. I can't think of anyone flying this high and at this speed and in this type of aircraft actually thinking of doing such a thing."

The fight engineer told me that there was no aircraft in the world capable of keeping up with Concorde. "What about some of the military fighter jets?" I asked, and he replied, "Not even those that can fly at Mach 3 or higher, as they can only sustain that speed for about twenty minutes because of the rate of fuel burn," adding "we (Concorde) could keep this speed up for three and a half hours, and no other aircraft could ever do that."

I went back to my seat and enjoyed the flight, which took us three hours and ten minutes to Heathrow from New York's JFK airport, wondering along the way, if I had in fact peed over the longest distance and the fastest time in the world. I reasoned that astronauts were after all in space and not within the earth's atmosphere. On that basis, I reasoned, I probably had a fair chance.

I would never ever forget that flight, and we were all given a double pack of "Concorde" playing cards in silver and blue, a certificate showing the date and time of the flight, which the captain signed for me (which I still have).

I wrote to Lars and told him what I had achieved, and he said, "Only you would even think of something like that." The aircraft was Concorde number 004, the fourth one to have been built. Concorde is now out of service sadly, but I am happy that I had the experience and that I did what I did; and I still wonder if I would have made the *Guinness Book of Records*, though I never contacted them with my stunt. They probably wouldn't have got it.

Although I never made it into the Guinness Book of World Records, I did the next best thing by giving the Guinness company my hard-earned money... whenever I could and I still support that company whenever I can ☺!

BLACK FRIDAY

Bad managers can destroy the careers of all who work for them.

AROUND THIS TIME, one Friday afternoon in 1987 in the Brentford office, forty-five of the food processing division's sales, engineering, and support staff were all laid off each with only a fifteen-minute warning.

The way this was done was by the HR director (name withheld to protect the guilty) placing a small red ticket on each person's desk during lunchtime. Each small red ticket had the phrase "See me at 2:00 p.m." or "See me at 2:15 p.m.," and was signed by the HR director. Each person had a fifteen-minute window set for the meeting that was to terminate their positions. Some had worked for the company for twenty-five years and were treated the same way as someone having only been there for a few months or weeks.

Prior to "Black Friday," the department comprised around 110 staff with divisional heads each responsible for food, dairy, and brewery markets, with an engineering department servicing all three of the marketing units. Each division had sales, marketing, design, and installation engineers all specializing in their respective markets.

After the layoffs, the company was in shock at how this had been done, and even our market and customers showed their distaste for the company after this "Black Friday" had been completed by refusing to place orders for impending new equipment.

Well, little did I know that this was to become a "promotion" for me as I was assigned the task of managing the remaining sales operation reporting to the newly appointed divisional director who had previously been running an engineering team and who had never ever run a complete division with sales and marketing.

The new director was a very tall, very slim, silver-haired Swede with an enigmatic manner about him.

I was informed by Bo, who had recently been promoted onto the main Swedish board in Stockholm, that in recognition for my work in setting up the "Customer Service Marketing" operation and in setting up the Middle East and French markets, I was to be promoted to a new position as general manager of Sales and Marketing for the newly formed Food Processing Division, reporting to its new divisional director. The new single division would replace the three now defunct divisions, which, since "Black Friday," had all been shut down; and their divisional directors, along with 40 percent of their staff, had all been let go.

Bo had instructed, through the same HR division, that I was to produce a market plan for the entire operation; and that I would be trained by the highly publicized and well-known "Professor Malcolm McDonald," who had written several books on marketing and strategic planning and was considered to be the country's leading expert on the subject. Malcolm had been retained by Alfa Laval for the sole purpose of changing the way we did business and to help us get into market planning rather than sales planning.

The atmosphere both in the market place and in the newly reduced division was to say the least difficult and combative, but I knew this would soon be forgotten as companies often have to make tough decisions in order to survive.

Markets continue, as does life and in the words of my nemesis, the HR director (name withheld to protect the guilty), during one of my sessions with him, "Put your hand in a bucket of water and pull out as much water as you can from the bucket in your hand. See how big the hole is in the water that you've left behind. Tony, that's the effect anyone has on a company when it's time to go, either because you resign or because you were fired. Everyone and everything simply fills in the space you left behind, and life and business moves on."

I have remembered that comment all my life, as it is really part of what I also believe in that when it's time to move on, just do it and don't look back. Of course, we all do look back at what we liked and disliked in our past; but I don't let the bad things in my past haunt me for my future. I tried many things, some with better results than others; some I succeeded at, while others didn't work out as I had planned. But then again, you have to risk failure to risk success. Failure and success are both opposite sides of the same coin.

I learned from this that we have to expect the unexpected and the anticipated outcome is often not what always happens. I also learned that hard work and dedication does pay off.

AN UNFORTUNATE MEETING WITH H.R.H PRINCE PHILLIP

Even the simplest of fixes can be disastrous!

ONE OF MY functions in my new position was to organize the various events that Alfa Laval sponsored; and one particular event was the "Royal Shire Horse Show" in Peterborough, which was one of the events that Prince Phillip attended in person.

The event was one of the nonregistered or informal events that various members of the royal family can attend without being in the public calendar.

When I say informal, there is nothing informal about the event, which is a show for, mainly, shire horses that are owned and used by the big breweries in shows around the country.

We received a formal invitation to the show; and we at Alfa Laval were to present, along with Prince Phillip, a cup for the "Pairs in Hand," which meant two horses pulling a smaller dray. Along with our invitation, we were given a "dress code" and "Royal Etiquette" explaining how we were to address the prince if we were ourselves addressed by him. We were also shown how to bow for us men, while Sue was shown how to curtsy.

As for the correct dress code, there were three apparent dress codes: formal dress for the Friday night's dinner when Prince Phillip would arrive, informal for the dress code for Saturday night's awards dinner, and very informal for the dress code while at the show itself. Informal meant a business or lounge suit, while very informal meant a shirt and tie as well as jacket and trousers; but they didn't have to be a suit.

As for the formal meeting, we were told that in the first response, should Prince Phillip address us, we were to answer his question ending with the phrase "Your Royal Highness." If he engaged us further, we were to end with "Sir." Sue and I drove up to Peterborough for the show; and I had a formal evening suit, or tuxedo, while Sue, who was seven months pregnant with the soon-to-be Nicky, had a two-piece evening suit. And when we arrived at our hotel, this was soon to be very apparent. As we were dressing for the formal introduction dinner, Sue discovered that her black velvet two-piece evening suit didn't fit her.

Unfortunately, nature had done its normal thing in preparing my darling wife's body for her upcoming event by enlarging her boobs to a size 38 double "D"! She was in fact still not showing at all, but her boobs were now quite enormous! So, no problem for me I called down to the front desk and obtained a couple of stout safety pins to fix her now gaping jacket. The fix was perfect . . . well, almost.

Off we both went to the dinner and waited for His Royal Highness to arrive, which he did shortly after we did. He was shown around the large dining room and was introduced to the entire event's sponsors, which included us. He came over to us and asked about Alfa Laval being a Swedish company, and horror of horrors! As Sue quite correctly began her perfect curtsy, the stout safety pin that I had place reverently and purposefully in her jacket to hold her boobs in let go!

Aaargh! Out popped her beauties, all of them, in their bountiful perfection and glory, wobbling and bouncing as they leapt out of their confinement right in front of Prince Phillip's face as he leaned over to take Sue's hand as she curtsied. "Oh my," he said, as he couldn't help seeing both of her 38 double D's bouncing out in front of him. "Oh no," said Sue, as she quickly tried to grab them both as well as her jacket in a hurried motion in an attempt to limit the damage. To Prince Phillip's credit, he moved on and smiled at her as he did so, while Sue was standing there clutching the front of her jacket, attempting fruitlessly to prevent them from obtaining even more freedom.

All was well, and we fixed Sue's coat and got ready for our next meeting with him the following day at the awards ceremony to present the cup to the winner of our event "The Pairs in Hand," quite aptly named as it turned out.

When we were presented to the prince again, he looked at Sue and smiled at her saying, "Oh yes, my dear, I remember you very well!" And Sue was mortified that he remembered her for her perfectly formed "'38 double D's," which, only a few months before were more reasonably sized and not nearly so outrageously bouncy as they had unfortunately become while being presented, along with my darling wife, I might add to Prince Phillip.

As for me, I didn't fare much better as I had no suitable necktie for the Saturday's events and had to buy a hideous one from a market trader at the show. The only tie available was a full-color shire horse tie that contained the most hideous, and what seemed to be, almost full-sized color pictures of the real and fully grown shire horses, yeeugh; and one of them was so big that I could only see its arse on the front of my tie as the rest of it was around the back, a fine way to present one's self to the queen's husband.

The tie was all I could find there, and I had to wear it in order to make the dress code; but I noticed that Prince Phillip had an almost identical tie as well, so I didn't mind so much. But one difference was that his horses were a lot smaller than mine and probably a lot more expensive!

So the only thing I can say is that we were in fact the proud sponsors of "The Pairs In Hand," which although was a meaningful term in the fine dictionary of the Royal Shire Horse Society, for us it meant something else entirely!

My confidence in being able to fix anything, under any circumstances, proved not to be as good in reality as what I had imagined in my head! Luckily for me my wife, by being herself, saved the day!

ANOTHER JOB

Learning from the best there is, is a valuable experience!

NOT LONG AFTER starting my new job, I went to meet Professor McDonald at his faculty at the Cranfield School of Business, just north of London.

I attended an intensive course in marketing learned how to make a three-year market plan, including a market and competitive survey; strengths, weaknesses, opportunities, and threats (SWOT) analysis; a one-year business plan; and a three-year market plan complete with a financial projection leading to a profit and loss statement on my business.

Whew, that's it? Anyway, soon after I began my new position, I realized that what Bo wanted was not what my new divisional head wanted. I hired a New Zealander, directly from Professor McDonald's faculty, who had recently achieved his MBA. His name was David Foreman, and he and I would work closely together to create a market plan for the newly formed division.

So we both began our mammoth task and hit our first road block, in getting my new sales team, to tell me all that they knew of their market.

The reason we hit this roadblock was that none of them had a clue about their market, despite having, in some cases, worked in their "specialized" markets for a decade or more.

This was to be a real problem and one that I went to my new boss to discuss.

I was amazed to see his response, which was "You were given the job. You deal with it." I could see he wasn't going to help me. We got most of the job completed except for two salesmen who refused to comply and vehemently refused to have the company, as they put it, "look over their shoulders to see what they were doing." I told each that since they were employees of the company, the company had every right to demand of them anything that they wanted in order to gain business, which after all was what they were paid to do.

I had all that I needed except for these two bits of market data and went again to my new boss to let him know that unless I was to threaten them with being fired, there was nothing I could do to force the information from them. I also told him that it really didn't matter since I could effectively leave out their particular information with a footnote saying that these two were unable to produce the necessary information and that their area was to be left blank!

He saw what I was telling him in that these two had no idea of what their market structure really was they were order takers not order getters.

I was aware that something was going on, but I didn't know what except that our main competitor, "APV," had an advertising campaign showing that they were "lean and mean" and were a slimmer fitter organization and were capitalizing on the "Black Friday" that UK operation had just come through.

When your boss is not supporting you, it's time to move or be moved on.

DRESSED FOR BUSINESS AS USUAL

How a simple ad campaign uncovered hidden agendas!

APV WAS OUR biggest competitor and had a series of adverts that were being placed all over the world and were causing a lot of controversy in our markets and with our mutual customers who were telling us they either liked or hated the ads, which, either way meant they were very effective.

In the Middle East, the ads were very unfavorably viewed as each advert in the series of around six or seven in the campaign showed a naked man or woman, viewed from the side, crouched while "getting set" at a starting line just ready for a race around an athletic track. I knew that in Middle Eastern countries, nudity was unacceptable in any form, especially advertising like this.

I called Tony Yates and told him I had a great idea for a response campaign called "Dressed for Business as Usual," with a picture of a very well-dressed senior manager on the phone calmly taking an order or talking to a customer.

Tony discussed it with his creative team, took a look at the APV adverts, and called me back, saying it was a great idea and could he and his team come to our offices in Brentford to discuss it.

A meeting was set up, and he came to meet myself and my boss to show us the new advertising campaign. During the run-through of the new campaign, they explained that the so-called Black Friday was our way of emerging stronger and more than ever ready for new business. He then opened an art board showing an artist's impression of a manager extremely well dressed in a suit and tie while sitting at a desk, with a pen in hand, taking an order over the phone. In other words, a direct hit at the nudity of our competitor APV.

My boss loved it until the next statement came out. "This should be a real manager, not a hired model," Tony added, and my boss agreed. "So, who better than your own general sales manager . . . Tony Moore." at that, my boss said that he didn't agree and that we should use a generic, which would have a longer ad life in that if anything was to change, then the ad would have to be pulled. I have to admit I missed that little "cue" as to what was being planned.

Tony argued that it would be a false statement if it wasn't a "real" manager, adding, that our competitors would soon respond once they found out that it was a "hired" model, and that would be even more embarrassing for us and could leave the door open for them to respond negatively toward us.

I listened and wondered what it was all about as something was not right. Tony finally had his way, as he usually did; and I was to be in the one page advert, shown in beautiful high definition through a black-and-white photo, taken with a large format Hasselblad and was to be placed in every one of the many food, dairy, business, and major news media as well.

I went to the studio in London, and we took the photo in only two takes. I wore a light gray faintly checked suit with a striped tie and a white shirt; actually, it was my Armani shirt that I had bought for my wedding with Sue.

The photo we had taken was now plastered in magazines and printed news media all over the country and was headed "Dressed for Business as Usual," with the Alfa Laval logo clearly visible underneath.

As if that wasn't bad enough, I got a call from our Swedish Head Office's Marketing Department who wanted to know who our advertising company was and if I minded them using this campaign all over the world. I put them onto Tony, and he readily agreed "for a fee" to let them use the campaign.

So there I was all over the world in magazines in just about every language; and in every country where APV had advertised with their "nude" campaign, there was I right there on a full page!

As I was to find out shortly afterward, the reason that my boss didn't want my picture to be used was that he was trying to get me out of his department. To this day, I don't know why and I didn't then, nor do I now care as what transpired next was truly remarkable.

The HR director (HRD, as I shall call him, who now, shall remain nameless) called me into his office for a series of meetings to discuss how I was doing in my department. I had two meetings a week for around three weeks, during which he probed as to whether I was still in touch with Bo or not and I smelled a rat.

During one such meeting, he showed me a resume that he had just received from a headhunter and read it out to see what I thought of the candidate.

As he read more and more, I commented, "Wow, that's someone that we could use," adding, "He seems to have really great credentials. Maybe we should we hire him?"

HRD looked at me and replied, "We already have, Tony. Why don't you take a look at this front page? It's yours!" I snatched the resume front page, which was missing from the document he first gave me, out of his hand and saw that it was in fact my own! FUCK! It was the resume that I had sent to a headhunter in London, who had then stupidly sent it to my own "f 'ing" company. "You really have no idea what this is all about, have you?" he asked.

Of course, I knew what it was about, which was why I had made up my resume; but I certainly wasn't going to show my hand to him and chose instead to reply, "I have no idea what you are talking about, but I have to get back to my office, as I have a ton of stuff to get done." And I left without waiting for his response. Outside, I was braving it; but inside, I was furious at being caught looking for another job.

I had nothing really to say to HRD on my way out but told him of the management style of my boss, and that he had consistently failed to support me since I was given the position. "And by the way," I pointed out, "I never asked or applied for that position. I was given it by Bo!" On my way out, HRD said, "Tony, you realize that this is a serious situation, and you'll have to leave it with me to decide how best we handle this matter." My response was, "Fuck you! Do what you want." I didn't tell Sue about all of this as I didn't know yet what would happen, though I had a good idea; so I thought I should wait to tell her when a decision had been made.

I went out that night with Dave Foreman to a pub in Ealing; and we talked about the probable outcome, which for me was "stay or go"! I told Dave not to worry, and that I would make sure he was OK and that he would be fine; but I suggested that he should begin to distance himself from me from this point on "just in case." Dave, bless him, didn't want to do that and instead told me that he had plenty of other positions available to him and could go to any other company with his MBA.

The following day at lunch in our canteen, I noticed that one of the HR managers, a very attractive woman whom I liked, called Anne, who had always been very straight with me and my department, was staring at me across the large canteen. It was one of those pieces of info that doesn't seem to fit in at the time but which "registers" with you at a deeper level, for a later confirmation of what it meant. In other words, an "aha moment." But I now knew, or had a damn good idea of, what was about to happen to me was to be let go. I carried on with my lunch, with my mind racing, and was now listening to what Dave was talking about with only half an ear as the rest of my mind was both sad and exited at the prospect of a new beginning. Typical of my mental agility, resulting from all the stuff I had had to deal with, I began to imagine myself in another and far more exciting career in a yet to be named new company.

I felt better at that and even imagined myself being interviewed for a new 'dream' job. I was also thinking of all the successes I had achieved—After Sales Marketing, Middle East business, the French business with Sandrine, setting up a new department, and of the huge orders I had won and the ground-breaking business concepts I had started. I thought of all of the things I had done for the company and knew it made no difference in the end, what was to be would be, and there was nothing I could or was interested in doing about it.

I had "crossed the bridge," which was to say that I had switched off from this company and was now looking to my next job, whatever that would be. That afternoon, I was called up to the HR director's office and was told that my position was being changed, and that I was being made redundant; that they had decided not to have a GM but instead have a series of territory managers instead. I was not shocked at the news and felt elated at the chance of having a whole new career in an entirely new business and began mentally to make plans as to what I wanted to do, not listening to the boring comments that were being made by he who shall remain nameless . . ."Another door to close."

I left immediately and went straight home to let Sue know what had happened. She was shocked and was asking me about the mortgage payments and all of the other things that needed to be paid. I told her I had a severance pay, and we would be fine for a short while, and I really didn't care at all as I was very excited at what may happen for me next.

The only part I would miss was my old work friends, as I had known them now for fifteen years, but I had to only think about my new opportunity.

A few days later, as I was having a leisurely coffee and mulling through the newspapers looking for headhunters and job opportunities, received a call from none other than Fred Grubb, the company chauffer!

"Is that you, mate?" he asked me, and I told him it was, recognizing his strong east end accent and wondering how in hell he got my number. Now Fred always sold me boxes of cigars or malt whiskey as well as bottles of excellent brandy, which he "obtained" from his many visitors while picking them up and taking them around London; while they were visiting Bo and the UK head office while Bo was managing director. Fred and I were close friends (friends in low places), and he often told me all the gossip when I went to see him downstairs in his tiny office while he was waiting to pick someone up some visiting VIP or drop them off. I never ever discriminated as to what someone's job was and always took time to talk to everyone from shipping workshop floor to filing and on up to my peers and above.

"Fred," I said, "why are you calling me? You know I was made redundant a few days ago?" "Yes," he said, "but you're not going to believe what has happened since you left."

He went on to tell me that Bo had heard what had happened, while he was in a board meeting with the main board in Sweden; and that he immediately left the board meeting, called Fred to find out my home phone number, and wanted to call me later that afternoon. Fred told me, "Boy, have you got friends in high places, Tone." And he told me that Bo had arranged to fly over from Sweden immediately to find out what the bloody hell had happened in his former UK operation.

I got the call from Bo while he was in Sweden, and he asked me to tell him exactly what had happened, so I told him. What I told him was that I had been spending 80 percent of my time in management meetings, and that I had not been supported and in fact had been left to deal with major issues and had no support in attempting to deal with two sales staff that believed their positions to be gold-plated and all without the support of my boss. I also told him that because of the many meetings, I had completed the market plan under great difficulty, having to do most of it in my own time. "As a result," I said, "I had my resume out and had been actively looking for another job when it suddenly appeared on HRD's desk." Bo listened and didn't comment at all until I had finished. "That," said Bo, "was very unfortunate, but what he should have done was to get to the bottom of the issue, and as HR director, he should have resolved it." He added finally, "Tony, you don't go from all you have done for this company to becoming seemingly incompetent in only four months.

That's simply ridiculous." He then got very serious and asked me to promise that I would not take another position until I received a call from him directly as he needed to find out what had been going on as soon as his back was turned.

I promised but added that I would not have a problem finding another job. "That is what I and this company do not want," he said finally. Later when Sue got home from work, I told her of the conversations with Dick Grubb and with Bo.

A few days after that, I got another call from Bo telling me that he had arranged for one of his senior managers to come over to my home and to discuss an exciting opportunity for me within the company, adding that I was to keep this confidential. I had prepared to move on though and was not sure that I even wanted to stay any longer in that company, as I was certain that there were other jobs I could get that would not have as much politics as this one seemed now to have.

Sure enough, a few days after that phone call, Fred arrived in the company limo with a very tall Swedish man, another Lars, who came into my home to discuss a new position for me. Funny thing, he was so tall he had to stoop to get into the front room.

I invited Fred inside as well, but he winked and declined, saying he should wait outside while we talked things over.

The new position outlined to me was to head up a new project for developing the market planning for the entire company and would involve me working directly with Professor McDonald and his team for a period of two years or however long it took in order to complete the process.

He told me that they had taken my UK plan for the food operation and found it to be very complete and well thought out. He also said that Professor McDonald had remembered me from his tutorials and thought I would be the "champion" for getting this project off the ground.

"Your title will be international marketing manager, and we have set aside a travel budget for you, which will be more than enough to complete the task. You should begin as soon as possible and plan to have visas and whatnot for visiting the company's major markets." I asked him which ones. He replied, "All of them. There are around thirty major market countries from Australia to Japan, most of Europe, and across Canada, and North and South America."

So let me get this straight. I went from being laid off to having a promotion. I said I would have to think about it, and he invited me over to Sweden to meet his staff and to go through in more detail what would be required and what my responsibilities would be in more detail before making a final decision.

So I had a first-class ticket sent to my home and was to meet none other than my nemesis, the "HRD who shall remain nameless," at Heathrow on the way. He met me at the airport, and once we were on the way over, he started telling me how there were two types of powerful people in a company or even in the running of a country or government.

There were those with "formal" power and those with "informal" power, he explained. While some people had a position and title with all the power that went with that position and title, others had a reputation and a following based on achievement and success. And in these instances, their "informal" power was more powerful than their leaders'.

I had a good idea of what he was saying, but I was more interested in what I was to hear in Sweden. I didn't trust him and never would, after what he had done; and I had no interest in being "buddy, buddy" with him now. I spent the rest of the trip pretending to read the airline magazines and, for the most part, ignored him from then on for the duration of the trip.

We arrived in Stockholm and were taken by the company limo to the offices in Tumba, a town just outside of Stockholm, where the head offices were located. David was making small talk, and I was just gazing out the window and thinking if I should accept the job offer or carry on with my plans to leave the company and start a new career.

We finally arrived and were ushered into a large meeting room, where I was sat at an elegant long table while he who shall be nameless chose to sit on one of the chairs placed around the room, away from the table.

Several business unit heads I knew came in, and I was told that Bo would be in on a conference call later on.

The position was outlined, and I was to visit some thirty countries plus in all and was to go and train each operation on market planning, leading to a summary plan containing the direction for the company's global business for the next three years.

This was a huge undertaking, and I asked if I could have some help to get this task done. Lars, who headed the meeting (yes, another Lars), told me I would be working with two MBAs from Professor McDonald's faculty, and they would assist me with the task.

This sounded unbelievable and very exciting. I had traveled, but not like this. They were all explaining what they wanted for their respective business units, and I took loads of notes. After a few hours, Lars let his secretary know that we were ready for Bo's call, and he came on the speaker phone. Suddenly, everyone sat up to listen, not saying a word, as Bo told me that this was a very important project and one that would change the direction of the company. He also told me that I had a direct line to him should I require his assistance on anything at all and that I should give him regular updates. This, I knew, was to let the business unit heads know that I was being supported from the very top.

So I agreed to take the job, and Bo thanked everyone for taking time out of their busy day to take part in the meeting. He added that he and I would be speaking later.

We left the offices for our return flight, and when we were seated on the plane, he who shall remain nameless said to me, "You know, Tony, I had no idea that you had such support in Sweden." I replied that I had no idea either, which was no lie.

He then went on to tell me that if I hadn't taken the job, he would have been automatically fired as soon as he touched down at Heathrow.

I looked at him in amazement at his honesty . . . finally. He looked at me and said, "Tony, you knew all along what it was about, didn't you?" I said, "If you're referring to me being fired, of course, I knew what was going on. That was why I was getting my resume updated and sent out, and by the way, I already had interviews lined up. That headhunter who sent you my resume, by mistake, was going gangbusters to make amends for what he had done and didn't want to be sued by me for unprofessional conduct."

I had no more to say to him. He was a political player and had just scraped through keeping his job. We sat in silence all the rest of the way back. He had no more influence over me and could never ever affect me in any way in the foreseeable future. We had both learned a lesson from this: mine was that hard work can sometimes pay off. I have no idea if he even thought more about this, and I didn't care. He would have learned not to listen to one side only but to ensure he got the whole story before acting.

I doubted if he ever realized how lucky he was, and I had no hard feelings at all except to say that I never trusted HR departments after that.

Help can come when you least expect it and I saw firsthand the difference between formal and informal power.

A NEW HORIZON

This one meeting, with the best there is, was to help me forever! All I had to do was to listen and learn.

I WENT TO CRANFIELD to meet Professor Malcolm McDonald; and on arrival, he met me and took me to his office and he sat next to me in front of his desk. He said to me that it had been the most stupid thing he had ever seen in a Fortune 500 company: that someone who had been promoted for a job well done, given the task of preparing a market plan for his new operation, and then fired for doing it, with no help in between. I was surprised at how much he knew, so I asked him how he knew this.

He said that he and Bo shared many ideas for the company, and that he admired Bo's management style, and that they had outlined this new job, adding that I was a "shoe in" fit for the position.

I then met my two new partners, Ian and Yvette, both of who were graduate MBAs; and both had been in consulting and teaching marketing for several years. Ian was a tall slim man of around thirty-five with dark hair and a well-trimmed short beard; while Yvette was a very sharp, slim very attractive blonde in her late twenties. We were going to get along just fine, and we swapped contact information ready for our new assignment. Together with Malcolm, we outlined the plan for the mammoth task of making a three-year market plan covering thirty countries. Malcolm outlined to us some ideas for how to get the job done and how Yvette and Ian would interface with me. We split the globe into east and west. Ian would take the west, including all of the Americas and Canada; while Yvette would take Europe, Australia, New Zealand, and up to China and Russia.

Initially, I used an office in the Alfa Laval building and hired an assistant who had two young daughters, Kate and Mauve, who were the same age as Amanda and Georgia.

She and I worked together very well, and she was very efficient; but as for me, I didn't want to be in the Brentford building, so I moved to work from home and hired Sue as my assistant. It worked out very well. I was traveling all the time yet could call Sue from anywhere in the world, part private and part work.

Malcolm McDonald was so easy to understand and I finally got it!

AN INTERESTING DINNER PARTY

Even the best laid plans can go spectacularly wrong.

ONE NIGHT, SUE and I decided that since we had recently decorated our house and had just finished installing a brand-new all-black dining room suite, we should have a dinner party for our close friends.

It was to be the following Saturday; and we invited Tony Yates and his fiancée, Rich St. Clair and his girlfriend, Dave Forman who was to accompany Lesley, Sue's sister, and the two of us. The dinner would christen our beautiful dining room, which was decorated in gray walls, gray velvet curtains, and a black dining room suite.

I had this amazing idea that we should all do it properly and have the men wearing tuxedos and the women wearing evening gowns. Sue and I worked at the menu, which included individual champagne cocktails, hors d'oeuvres comprising Danish aquavit and Russian canapés with salmon, caviar, and cream cheese on black Russian rondelles of bread. We also planned a main course of spiced chicken fillets with fresh steamed vegetables and a desert of truffles and cream-filled crepes that Sue would make and finally vintage Port with blue cheese on light wheat crackers.

Now my brilliant idea included the aquavit that I had been given during a trip to Aalborg in Denmark. This was the famous and very expensive 'Linje Aquavit' (pronounced linni) Aquavit that had been matured in old sherry barrels while traveling in a ship's hold, during which it had to pass over the equator twice. On the back of the label was the date of the voyage, the name of the ship, and the place the ship sailed from and where it sailed to, very cool and very expensive. However, "the road to hell is paved with good intentions," and the dinner started off extremely well, with everyone arriving by cab to our house and being offered a champagne cocktail on arrival. Sue, bless her, had been slaving over the stove the whole afternoon and had together with me prepared a fantastic gourmet dinner.

After we had finished the cocktails, in our front room, we then all moved into the dining room; and all were seated around our brand-new shiny black table.

"OK," I announced, "here's how we do this," holding up my special bottle of aquavit, which had been freezing all day in the freezer along with the shot glasses. "I'll pour out a shot for each of us, and you knock it back in one, followed by eating one of these canapés." We all loved the idea, and I proceeded to pour out a shot for everyone, adding, "To make it more interesting, each time we raise our glasses, the next person on your left will announce the next toast, which will be starting with 1987 and moving backward until we either fall over or can't remember what the next date is." Everyone laughed, and we began.

There were plenty of canapés and plenty of aquavit; however, prior to this, we had each had a number of brightly colored champagne cocktails, compliments of our newly purchased and very colorful cocktail recipe book; and, I forgot to add, that the aquavit was extremely strong. Sue left the table to quickly finish off preparing the main course; meanwhile, we were all knocking back the very easy to drink second bottle of fine Danish high-quality aquavit. Tony Yates's fiancée, Liz, was sitting opposite me wearing a very low-cut black dress, not easily concealing her ample boobs. Each time we told a joke—and I, Tony, and Rich were wickedly on form—she would laugh, which made her boobs jiggle inside her low-cut evening gown.

Suddenly, it dawned on me as to what she reminded me of; and I immediately, without forethought, which was by now impossible as we had already reached somewhere in the seventies in our backward toasts of each year, announced my stunning revelation. "I know what you remind me of," I said looking at Liz's boobs, "your boobs remind me of a road worker, working with a pneumatic road drill with his pants half off his arse." I was laughing. "His arse cheeks look just like your boobs jiggling." And we collapsed in fits of laughter. She, however, didn't see it that way, saying, "Ha, bloody, ha, very funny." And she proceeded to stab me in the back of my hand with her fork repeatedly.

Tony, though nearly crying with laughter, tried to grab her hand to stop her, as I was laughing and howling at the same time, while moving backward on my chair to get out of the way of her murderous fork-wielding hand as my chair collapsed under me with a very loud "crack." I ended up on the floor on my now completely smashed chair, while clutching on to the tablecloth as I went down. As Tony reached over to grab her hand, she pulled away backward; and they in turn both went back on their chairs, which also made a very loud cracking sound, and they both broke their chairs also.

As Tony tried to help her in a somewhat badly aimed "grab," he managed to grab her left breast, which immediately freed itself from her totally inadequate fine black fabric, low-cut gown, revealing itself to all. She went backward, with Tony who by now was falling on top of her, with her legs up in the air on either side of his torso.

Rich then said through laughter, "Hey, both of you, save that stuff for upstairs, not at the dinner table." And we laughed even more. My sides were now hurting. That did it! We were by now all nearly crying with laughter, no doubt helped along by the malicious mix of champagne and aquavit. She then tried to get up, but the drink had its way; and she fell forward onto the table, unable to move any more.

So Tony and I helped Liz upstairs and put her onto our bed, quickly returning to the dinner table.

Sue bravely returned with the main course, glaring daggers at me; and we attempted to finish the dinner, though without any luck. We had to bring in two more chairs for Tony and I to sit on as Liz was flat on her back, now passed out in our upstairs bedroom.

We actually never made the main course, and Sue was furious with me for that, blaming me for the events of the evening. We were still at the table at 1:00 a.m.; and we made a valiant attempt to eat the chicken, for several hours. But try as we did, we couldn't finish it. Dave and Lesley stayed the night, and we had ordered a cab for Tony and Liz.

When the cab finally arrived, Tony and I helped Liz down the stairs to the waiting cab driven by an Indian with a turban. As we came down the stairs, both getting in our own way as we stumbled down, with her between us, once again, her dress gave up the task of trying to contain her ample breasts. As she leaned forward, her boobs fell out of her dress, as Tony and I got her out of the house toward the waiting minicab.

The driver looked over and saw two very large creamy white breasts coming toward him, seemingly suspended in midair, as the black dress beneath them blended with the night's darkness, and the boobs were gleaming in the clear moonlight. "Oh gor blimey," he said, in his strong Indian accent, both shaking and nodding his head at the same time, while Tony and I were busy trying to stuff them back into the dress. It was like trying to get two melons into a shoe bag, almost impossible.

Tony was still trying as I helped shove them both into the cab and said, "G'night, mate. Hope you had enough to eat." He was concentrating on the job at hand, with her like a rag doll completely unaware of the events of the evening.

I went up to bed and collapsed thinking, *"I'll deal with everything tomorrow."* I awoke the next day feeling terribly hungover and went downstairs flabbergasted at the now very evident damage done the night before. I really did feel bad, and Sue came down some time later as I was attempting to clear up. "G'morning, darling," I said, trying to look much more cheerful than I really felt. "I thought our dinner party went really well, if you ignore the actual food." Sue wasn't impressed though and looked daggers at me, saying, "I spent hours cooking that dinner, and it was ruined," looking at all of the wasted food and dished piled up on the worktop.

"We never even made the main course," she said. "Well, there was that," I said adding, "Still, it really was a good evening." I was still hopeful that I could get her in a good mood, while hiding my damaged hand with the prong marks on the back. I had tried putting all the dishes in the dishwasher to clear up but had not succeeded, as I was feeling really bad seeing all of the half-eaten food.

"Why don't you go back to bed," Sue told me like the Trojan she was, "since you are useless here, and I can get this done faster without you than with you." I was feeling really hung-over, so I had to go upstairs. The following day, which was Sunday, we went to the large furniture store where we had, only a week before, bought the dining room suite from a very happy salesman, only this time it was to return the broken chairs.

As we entered the large store, Sue opened the doors for me, and I followed her in with the three broken chairs lying on my outstretched arms like a sad black shiny pet.

No sooner than we had entered the store, all of the previously very eager and willing sales staff disappeared, melting behind all of the brand-new furniture. We made our way to the back of the store, with Sue leading the way and the chairs and me following, to explain to the manager that we had simply had a nice quiet dinner party with a few close friends when the chairs collapsed under us. I got the chairs replaced and couldn't mention the true reason they had failed. So much for that! It was a long time before I was allowed to have another dinner party after that, but I was still forbidden by "she who must be obeyed" from ever making cocktails or drinking aquavit before any future dinner party. Oh well, into every life, a little rain must fall!

To keep the peace, I agreed not to have another party at least for a while but added the caveat that as long as we didn't mix the drinks that should be OK. Sue said nothing but was still furious with all of us.

All I can say about this is sorry Sue!

A SECOND MARRIAGE

A simple question can lead to a life altering answer.

When Sue told me she was pregnant, I was not certain how to react, as I had always believed that a child should be born in marriage. We were out for an evening walk to the park at the bottom of our street when she told me, and I knew I would have to decide to get married. I just hadn't thought about marriage up to that point.

This was no reflection on our relationship, but we were so busy with everything day to day that we hadn't got 'round to it yet. There was only one choice to be made, and that was that we should get married; we loved each other, so that was that. We decided to get married in April with a registry office marriage, as we had both had big church weddings; and we wanted a smaller affair with family and friends.

I invited Auntie, of course; and she brought John and his young lady, Jane, who was several decades younger than him with him. Although the weather was dreary on our wedding day, we were very happy as all of Sue's family came too.

The funny part was when Auntie met Sue's Aunt Sally, who was quite stuck-up and always had been. Auntie was introduced to Sally and as if right on cue said, what was to Auntie a total stranger, "Isn't your Sue lucky to be getting married to my dahling Tony?" To which Aunt Sally who was completely taken aback said, "I'm sure it's a mutual thing." At which Sue immediately took Auntie's elbow and steered her away to introduce her to our friends in order to avoid a crisis. After the ceremony, we all went back to our house where we had catered a reception, and it had finally stopped raining.

Auntie came to join me in our garden and said to me, "Tony deah, what is it that you really want? What is it that you will have that will tell you that you have finally arrived or finally have made it? Is it a Rolls, is it a big yacht, or a huge mansion, or maybe to be a millionaire? Look at what you've done—a wine bar, a great career, traveled all over the world—so what's next for you Tony?" I had no idea at that point what my answer would be as I had never thought that far ahead, so I replied, "I don't really know yet, Auntie, as

I've never really thought about it. But I will now, and I'll write and let you know." "And then you can tell me when you get it," she said with absolute certainty.

Around a month after our wedding, I thought of some measure of success while I was mowing the lawn outside in our back garden.

I thought, *"What if I had a house with a garden big enough that I had to have a riding lawn mower to cut my grass?"* My perspective at that point was from living in London where all of the back gardens are made to basically the same width of your house, which is around thirty to forty feet wide and anywhere in length from around ten feet in a small garden, to one hundred feet in a more expensive London home.

Our garden, being a corner house, was wedge-shaped and was around ninety feet long. So, my perspective of life and success was from that viewpoint and experience.

I wrote to Auntie and told her of my revelation in being able to answer her question, and she replied simply, "That's nice, Tony deah. If that's what you want, let me know when you get it then." I laughed at that, thinking, *Yeah right, like that'll ever happen.*

I realized that, in setting a goal that seemed impossible when I set it; that it could be achieved in ways that I never expected. And, I also saw that when we achieve one goal it's time to set the next one without fear of failure.

NICKY IS BORN

Nothing remains the same after your child is born.

NICHOLAS ANDREW WAS born on August 29, 1988, at Wembley Hospital after Sue had an eighteen-hour labor. Seems he was quite comfortable where he was. I had been out the night before with a friend of ours, Caroline, at the huge Michael Jackson concert at Wembley that Caroline had booked tickets for months earlier, not realizing that Sue couldn't go so she invite me instead. The concert was the one with his spectacular white sequined glove and the now globally famous "moon walk." With his white sequined socks, he was fantastic, and the concert was packed that night.

Sylvia and Maurice had come over to stay to look after Georgia, while I went to stay with Sue for the birth of Nicholas. The labor lasted eighteen hours, which was a very long time; but Nicky was born at 9:10 in the morning of August the following day, we brought Nicholas back home into his well-prepared room and to a very expectant pair of grandparents and with Amanda and Georgia close at hand.

Sue didn't know how to prepare formula or any of the other things that were now a very central part of our lives, so I showed her how. I taught her how to mix, heat, and test the mix. Sue was a fast learner and did just fine. Georgia and Amanda were both very excited at our new addition as were Sylvia and Maurice who were very happy that their oldest daughter had born a son. Nicky's birth really changed everything for us both as we now had a complete handful at home, no more freewheeling at nights and no more unplanned nights out. We did enjoy taking Nicky to the park and spent time teaching Georgia to ride a two-wheeler at the same time.

Sue decided that she now wanted a dog, not just a silly lap dog but a bearded collie of all things. So we all went to a kennel in Chertsey to pick one out. The kennel had six or seven young black-and-white puppies; and as we were standing there with Georgia and Amanda and with a very littler Nicky in tow, one of the puppies came over to me and nuzzled my leg as I stood there watching all of their antics. "It seems he has picked us,'" I said and picked him up. "He's beautiful," Sue said, and we bought him there and then, taking him home with us. We loved Ben as all families should, and he grew up right alongside Nicky, becoming Nicky's buddy all through school. We took him from London to Brussels and then on to Indianapolis so he was a true globe-trotting "Beardy."

My children would have what I never had, a family of their own, of that I was certain and no matter what I would keep my family together.

A NEW JOB

Hard work will always pay off!

Soon after Nicky was born, I began to plan my travel arrangements, literally going around the globe from North America, South America, Canada, around Northern and Southern Europe, India, Australia, New Zealand, and up to Japan and back via Russia. All in all, I would be actually traveling to thirty-three countries in the space of one to two years.

I would visit each of the more than thirty countries at least twice. I would go once to carry out a market audit and to train the local management on the development of a three-year market plan. The second was to review what they had done and to summarize with them all that they had to undertake, as a "sounding board," and to advise if they needed it. The project was a "doozie" for me, and I was learning from two of the very best in marketing that there were in England. In addition, I had a direct help line to the "Prof," Professor Malcolm McDonald, for any help I might need along the way.

The amazing thing was that as we progressed through our meetings with the senior management of each market company, we began to become really good at assessing what was in need of improvement within each market company.

I always thought that really big companies, with assets in the billions, like ours, and spanning almost all countries around the globe, managed their sales with a high level of skill and aplomb! Not so! The issue was that our products were so damn good, were extremely well designed by the Swedes, and had a very high level of technical know-how and difficulty in the manufacture that they almost sold themselves. So as a result, the company grew because of this fact and despite the sales efforts that in many instances seemed to do their utmost to lose business.

Bo wanted a more systematic approach where each market company had to analyze their markets, showing a SWOT analysis as well as a market size and a competitor analysis. They had never done this before, and so our job was to train them in the MBA techniques for doing it. This was to be immense fun for the three of us, and we learned about the markets for our global operations very quickly. In some market countries, the staff had absolutely no idea of any of the critical information that they really needed to make an effective strategy for sales, let alone increasing market share.

We did encounter some interesting customs though; for example, in India, Yvette had arrived a day earlier and had attempted to begin the audit process before I had arrived. Unfortunately, in India, the protocol is such that they would not allow her—a female, English, and a visitor—to begin until I had arrived the day later. Poor Yvette wanted to leave India immediately and to let them "stew," but I had to talk her out of it; though I did sympathize with her. We had to start the next day, and she had to remain very professional and put her emotions behind her in order to get the job done.

India had our only female managing director, Leila Poonawalla, who was a very effective and a very competent leader. I got on very well with Leila as we had been introduced several years before, when she had just joined the company after graduating from university. Our first meeting was in Brentford, when I was just starting with my new marketing department and she came to meet me.

I liked Leila a lot and thought she would have made a great country leader for India, if politics allowed it; she was that good. She ran a complete manufacturing facility, making centrifugal separators, and had more sales managers in more sales regions that any other country operation we had; and she did it very well, indeed. I found after that meeting that Indian people are both perceptive and very intelligent, with incredible memories for data, names, and detail. In Australia, we arrived after some eighteen hours in air travel from London, got there for a normal and preplanned start at 8:30 a.m., and then had to wait until 10:30 a.m. before the managing director and his staff ambled in to begin work, which they did over the next two hours.

Yvette and I sat there with a pot of coffee, in the board room, drumming our fingers while waiting for the senior managers and sales staff to show up. Needless to say, that was the reason that they were underperforming. Big changes were made one month after we left that first meeting.

In Brazil, they had a strike for the factory workers; but the strike, Brazilian style, was to samba music being played out loud on a truck with the biggest bloody boom box I had ever seen. Everyone was dancing, just at the entrance to the factory, while they were on strike; it was very funny, and you had to love their style. Brazil was in the throes of massive inflation rated in the thousands of percent, which meant that wages agreed on Monday were not enough to live on by   Friday Japan was very interesting too, and we got to travel on the bullet train from Tokyo up to Nagoya, which traveled at an astounding 215 kilometers per hour. We had lunch on the train with a beautiful backdrop of Mt. Fujiyama in the background. The train was as smooth as silk, and the scenery was very beautiful. The mountain looked like a painting of what a "perfectly symmetrical" mountain should look like and as seen through the train's very large picture windows made the whole experience rather surreal. We visited the Sapporo Brewery.

The president of Sapporo personally took us around and explained that he or anyone else saw something wrong had to stay and fix it, and not to leave the problem until it was fixed. That year, I traveled to all of northern and southern European countries to New Zealand, Australia, India, Japan, Brazil, Argentina, Venezuela, Panama, Chile, Mexico, the United States, and Canada and to each country twice. It was around the world trip that most people would have loved. The work was good fun and was a great change from being stuck in one office.

Change can be good and an apparent disaster in my career led me to make a positive and profound difference to my company. I learned from the best there is, and I got to see the world, gaining a global perspective on life, something that few ever get to experience!

BRUSSELS

Belgium! A strange country with two languages and very high taxes!

AFTER I HAD finished the marketing project, finalizing on a very detailed summary to the board, during which Yvette helped me make the final presentation, I was offered a new position working with another of my friends, Christer Kraftling. Christer and I had worked together in Brentford way back when I was only twenty-three; and he was married to Annette, who also worked for Alfa Laval for a while. Christer and Annett got married in Acton when I was going out with Jeanette, and we were both witnesses to their wedding. I still have the photo of the four of us. Christer, Annett, and I were so close that they named their first son Tony, after me. Cool, huh!

Christer, on our way over to Sweden after my big presentation to the board, offered me a new position in his newly formed marketing department based in Brussels. As my dream project had now concluded eighteen months after I started, I now had to get a new position within the company; and this was a perfect next step.

Sue and I decided to leave for Brussels and began to settle our affairs in London. We had decided that we should rent out our house in Wembley and place it through an agency in order to keep it occupied while we were away. The house was in excellent condition, so we knew we could rent it out easily. I went over to Brussels to check it out and to see our new office, which was located in a large brand-new house around twenty miles to the south of Brussels. Sue came over with me to take a look at rental homes, of which there were hundreds since Brussels was a major center for NATO, SHAPE (Strategic Headquarters Allied Powers Europe), as well as the headquarters for the European Parliament or EEC as it was called then.

The town that we chose, Overijse, was a few miles just west of Brussels and north of Waterloo, where Napoleon made his last stand, and was a Flemish town. Interesting thing about Belgium is that there are two distinctly different people living there: there are the French and the Flemish. People speak both languages as well as English, and they learn it at school; however, neither, want to, or try to, speak the other's language; and all documents are in both Flemish, and French, as well as English.

For the life of me, I cannot fathom why anyone would choose Brussels as a European headquarters for anything with all that going on. Added to this, neither the French townspeople nor the Flemish townspeople get along with each other very well. This manifests itself in the fact that each town and street name throughout Belgium has to have both the Flemish and the French name written; and if the town is Flemish, that version of the name of the street or town goes on top with the other underneath and vice versa if it is a French town. Talk about stupid! So every day people go around and paint out the alternative language version of the name, leaving only their version of the street or town's name on the sign.

The house we chose was a three-bedroom with an L-shaped living room, which turned a corner into the dining room. The main reason we liked the place was the tidy garden and the L-shaped living room. We planned the move for September 1989 when Nicky was thirteen months old and had found a Chinese couple to rent our house, so all seemed well. Everything was moved into our new home with ease, and I made sure that Amanda and Georgia came over for their half term in order to be with us. Jane needed the break, and I loved having them with me. They flew in from Heathrow and were escorted on and off the aircraft by an airline chaperone. We picked them up from Brussels airport and took them both to the new house. Needless to say, they were both very excited, and we took them into Brussels and to the "Grand Place," which was a very beautiful part in the very center of the city. The Grand Place has old cobblestoned square surrounded by very old and beautiful buildings.

Sylvia and Maurice also came over for holidays and loved being there with us, especially with the children Amanda and Georgia; we had a house full of life. In the garden was a strawberry patch fitted over a small kidney-shaped pond that had been covered over to support the strawberries The location of our house was perfect and even had a pub right at the bottom of our street, which served several hundred different beers as well as Guinness on draft that was the one for me. This was perfect. We had all that we needed; and very near us were all sorts of other "expats" from England, Scotland, the United States, and many other countries, which was to be very important for Sue as I was going to be traveling all over the globe with my new position.

After we had been living there for around a year, we cleared out the strawberry patch in the back garden, and I worked on a pond that was under it, resealing it until it was leak proof, then filled it up with water. It held, and the water didn't leak out; so Georgia and I, while she was over for the summer holidays, chose seven various colored small fish to place in the pond. Georgia was so excited as she had never had a pond before. I asked her to name the fish, which took her several hours; and finally, she came up with names like "colors" and "silver," very imaginative! I bought a jukebox for the house as Sue and I had several hundred singles from across the sixties, seventies, and even some from the eighties.

The juke box worked really well and was located in our dining room, and we used it every time we had a party at the house.

Fortunately, with so many new friends, Sue had plenty to do and had arranged for little Nicky to attend a day school where he was actually learning to speak in Flemish! He used to come home and say something to us both, waiting for a response; but she could not understand what the hell he had said. "English in the house, Nicky, please," she told him.

And Nicky, now only two years old, was doing well at learning both languages Flemish and English.

After a year of living in Brussels, I made arrangements for Sue to come with me to meet Eve, Michel, Jean Louis, and Jackotte in Toulouse for a long weekend as the flight from Brussels was very cheap; and the flight to Toulouse was only just over hour. I hadn't seen Eve and Michel for nearly ten years, and I had called them in advance to see if they would have us there as guests. I needn't have worried; they were over the moon and were very excited that I was coming back with my new wife Sue.

They all came to meet us at the airport and greeted both Sue and I like long lost family; it was as I hoped it would be. And we stayed there for several days. It gave them a chance to get to know Sue, and Michel and Eve had arranged a gourmet dinner for us at a local bar and restaurant in the town center of Bruguier's where they still lived.

The dinner was absolutely incredible and told me how much I meant to them both, with or without Jeanette; and in their book, anyone who was a friend of mine was also a friend of theirs They asked about Jane, as they had met her many years before when I took her and a very young five-year-old Amanda with me to meet them. We told them that Jane and I were still very good friends, and they sent her their love.

We met up with all of my old friends who came over to see us at Eve and Michel's house, and we were made to feel like celebrities. We ate and drank outside on their patio just like we had before, all of us together laughing and talking and eating till the early hours catching up on all that we each had done in the twenty years since Jeanette and me, then later Jane, and now Sue had been up to.

Though we only stayed in Brussels for two years, it was a turning point for us both, as we now had left England, our home country, to begin a lifetime of living abroad.

Amanda and Georgia came over to stay for every holiday, and I had plenty of reasons to go back to London to see them both often. Many other friends from London came over to see us for long weekends, so we never felt really away from home. The drive was only three hours plus the channel crossing.

True friends are friends forever!

UFO's OVER BRUSSELS

UFO's they do exist as I have seen them first hand!

ONE NIGHT, GEORGIA and I were walking Ben, our lovely bearded collie—something we did every night, sometimes with Sue and sometimes by ourselves. This was my special time with Georgia who loved hearing about all my travels and which countries I had been to since last we met.

The night was cool and very clear in April 1990 when Georgia and I were taking the dog out for a walk. Georgia was looking up at the night sky stars, which were much easier to see from our new location than in London because there was much less ambient light that made them much more visible from Overijse.

She cried out, "Dad, look at that," pointing up at a series of lights moving in formation very fast across the clear night sky and they were making absolutely no noise at all. There were several lights, and they were changing direction in the air as if they were on rails while moving at what seemed like incredibly high speeds and at least ten times the speed of normal jetliners, as they moved over the forest just to the south of our house.

We both stood and watched them in wonder as they went careening all over the sky. Next thing we heard was the roar of jet engines somewhere off to our west toward the moving lights.

The following day in the news, we heard that NATO had scrambled a flight of F-16s to chase the unidentified aircraft that were seen on their radar screens. The unidentified aircraft was moving at speeds in excess of 15,000 miles per hour and was able to change direction, seemingly, on a dime without changing speed. Although the F-16s were following them, they moved away and simply disappeared from all radars, both in the air force jets and from all the array of ground based radar.

We didn't know what they were, but we did see them along with hundreds more people all over Belgium; so, they probably did actually exist.

We saw what we saw with absolutely no mistake and there is no 'spinning of this truth.

PREGNANT AT SEA

A calm sea can change in a heartbeat.

WHEN SUE WAS seven months pregnant with Nick, we went on holiday to Greece, as she was still not showing at all. One very hot day there, we decided to rent a small boat with two friends of ours and have a picnic in a quiet cove somewhere along the coast. We sailed in our small four-seater converted rowing boat with a hopelessly inadequate outboard motor attached to the back, for around forty to fifty minutes when we spotted a perfect cove that could only be reached from the sea.

We pulled in and got the boat out of the water and up onto the beach. The weather was perfect—blue skies and a warm breeze. After we had been there for several hours—swimming, snorkeling, and sunbathing—we decided to leave for home.

By now the weather had changed quite abruptly, and a strong wind had blown up. The sea that was only hours before, very calm and blue, was now black with very high waves.

We headed out from our small cove and out into the bay to head south for home, but as we reached out from our somewhat protected cove, we saw just how bad the sea really was. As we continued south, the waves by now were getting steadily worse and worse; and our little motor couldn't get us over the crest of each wave.

I told the other three to don their life jackets only to find that there were only three anyway, so I didn't have one. Sue being her normal self said jokingly, "Ay, ay, Cap'n," as if she didn't care and was not really worried.

I, on the other hand, was beginning to get really concerned at our predicament as the sea was getting rougher by the minute; and the waves were now well over eight feet high.

We had been traveling for about three quarters of an hour, and I guessed we were somewhere close to our bay "St. Georgios." The waves had become so high that we couldn't now see which direction was land, and I had to go by the wind direction and the direction of the waves coming over us as I was scalloping our tiny boat over the waves. Water was beginning to come into our open boat, and we were getting into serious trouble.

We rounded another bay, and I looked ahead to gauge if we could make it across this bay and around the point ahead of us to where I thought our own bay was just the other side. I estimated this on the length of time we had been sailing, but I didn't know I was in for a big surprise.

That little, small voice told me to heave to into the small cove that was to our right and not to risk going across the extremely rough bay. The sea was now completely black, and we were in the middle of a squall with huge waves crashing onto, and into, our boat. Our outboard motor was hopelessly inadequate and was unable to get us up and over each wave as I tried in vain to head the boat bow first into each huge wave. If I didn't, we would have been capsized; and though I didn't know much about sailing or boating, I knew that we had to face into the waves and not let them broadside us.

I listened to that small voice and told them all that I was heaving the boat to, whereupon Sue laughed and said, "What the hell are you talking about?" I said nothing but knew that I had to get us out of this mess as soon as possible as the open boat was taking in water from the huge waves that were crashing across our bow.

I pointed the bow directly toward the small sandy cove, and we made it there, in a now waterlogged boat, where, looking like four drowned rats, we all got out of the boat to wait out the storm.

A little while later, a brightly colored water taxi arrived to take three people that had been nude bathing behind us, off the cove and home. I shouted across the water at "Adonis," the blond, curly-haired, and cocky taxi driver dressed in shorts and a leather open fronted vest, and asked if he could take us too.

I will pick you up in a little while he told me as he gunned the huge double inboard engines to leave with his three passengers. We watched him as he went crashing over the waves and disappeared around the point into the ocean.

Some two hours later, he returned to pick us up. "£70," he said before we could get on, and we had to agree. We all got into his boat, which had a ski pole set in the floor at the stern end. Sue and the other girl that was with us grabbed the ski pole to hold on as we took off at full speed across the bay.

Now Adonis to begin with was showing off to the girls that he was in complete control of the powerful ski boat, but pretty soon it became clear to us all that this was not going to be a picnic as he had to grip the wheel with all his force to steer the boat. We went across bay after bay, and we were a lot farther out than we thought. When we left that morning, the breeze and the current were with us, and we had covered a lot of ocean. As he was driving the boat up and over each of the relentless waves, the boat, and all of us in it, came crashing down as he too was scalloping the boat over the waves. We were going up with each swell then crashing down the other side, as each of the wave crests passed under our keel.

By now, Adonis's hands were knuckle white, and I'm certain he was thinking, *I hope we can make it OK.* For over an hour of crashing through the stormy sea, we were being pounded into our seats by the rough weather. As our boat went up over crest, we were pinned to the floor; but when it came crashing down, we were smashed into our seats, every time. We finally made it back to our bay, and we all very shakily got off the boat, thankful to still be alive and all of us had no feeling at all in our bottoms as a result of the extreme crossing.

Once on land, Sue was out for blood, and we went striding over to the renter boy to have it out with him. I thought I would let Sue handle this and stood back to enjoy the fireworks. "How could you rent a boat out to us with only three fucking life jackets?" she told him. "There were only three of the fuckers, and there were four of us, and why didn't you fucking well tell us there was a fucking storm headed our way, huh?"

He was taken aback by her anger and apologized to her profusely and told us he thought we would be OK. "I'm fucking seven months pregnant!" she shouted at him, pointing to her completely flat tummy, and I hoped he wouldn't say what I thought he would say next, 'cause if he did, she would hit him. Well, he gave us half of our money back and was annoyed at having to go to pick up his boat; but we took the money straight to the beach bar and had a stiff brandy there.

The funny thing was that his girlfriend knew me from the Village Wine bar and had been in many times; and here we all were in Greece, arguing over a very near and potentially fatal mishap. Still, we were all OK, though shaken up a bit, and were none the worse for wear. The storm had passed; and now, at seven in the evening, it was as if nothing had ever happened. And I knew that had I not listened to that very small voice, we probably wouldn't be sitting in the evening sun enjoying a brandy. We felt lucky to be alive and to look at the beautiful evening sun you would never have guessed. Life's like that: one moment, all's well; the next moment, everything can change and sometimes forever.

I learned to respect the sea and to never underestimate its power I also learned that sometimes we have to play it safe, as indeed I did, in order to survive.

HELP FROM NOZZER THE COZZER THE HIGH FLYING ROZZER

Big help from a big man

WHILE WE WERE still living in Brussels, I received a phone call one day from Wembley police, asking if I owned a house in Wembley; and they went on to give me the address of my house. I said yes but added that we had rented it out to three elderly people.

They asked me if I was planning to come over to Wembley, and if I did, would I call in to talk with them. The drive over was only four hours, including a hovercraft trip across the English Channel; and that Friday, I went to the police station at Wembley.

That Friday after I arrived, I went over to Wembley Nick and met with several detectives who began to ask me about the house—how long I had been away, were they paying rent, etc. After a while, I became very uncomfortable with the general direction that they were going with their questions and asked them, "What's all this about?" They began telling me that I had rented the house out to three known criminals who were involved with a scheme of major credit card fraud!

"WHAT!" I said in disbelief, telling the investigators that they must be mistaken. "They are all around sixty years old plus," I said, but they confirmed what they knew and went on to explain how they worked their scheme.

They rent a house then make sure they get onto the electoral register at the town hall. This is one of the checks that are made by credit card companies before issuing a new credit card. They then get electricity and gas bills in their own name with their address the same as the home they have rented.

After being accepted for one credit card, normally Visa, they make small purchases from it immediately. They then pay off the card in full within the first month as this apparently makes their automated credit rating with the card very high. Next, they apply for all of the other cards—Amex, Diners Club, and others—and repeat this activity, paying off the small purchases opening balance immediately. Then comes the scam; they max-out each of the cards with purchases and have around three to six months before anyone notices that they are scamming the card issuers.

I got it, but it didn't get me out of the uncomfortable feeling that I was being questioned in case I knew of this, which of course I didn't, though I have to admit it was a great scam. I told the detectives that I had met my renters only three times, and each time I had to tell them the exact time of the day I would come by to check on the house. I added that once I had noticed a huge pile of dog food and other stuff stacked high in the dining room, though I thought it was strange, I thought it may have been something to do with their line of business. That part at least was true as it was in fact part of their business illegal or not.

I asked them at this point, if they knew Noz. They stopped at my question. "Noz who?" one of them asked. "There is only one Noz Roberts," I replied. "You know Noz Roberts?" one of them asked, and I replied that we were old friends. "OK," said the lead detective, "let's see how well you know him then!" And they made the call to "Nozzer the cozzer the artful dodger!" as we called him (among other things).

I watched their faces in amusement as they got hold of Noz, who by the way was at a secret meeting at his Freemason's lodge. They all looked over to me as they were answering his questions about me, which I found highly amusing. "Yes, he does. Yes, he is. OK then, that's fine.

Then we'll put him on." They were answering him over the phone. "He wants to talk to you," one of them said sheepishly, and they now looked at me in a completely different way. I took the phone, and we both started laughing at the fact that these detectives were questioning me.

I agreed to meet with Noz the next day, making sure they heard our arrangement as I now had a real problem, which was how to get rid of them. We parted with them asking me about the famous wine bar that Noz used to frequent when he was at Acton. I left the police station at around 7:00 p.m. after some three hours of grilling, amid profuse apologies and thanks for my help and for coming back from Brussels to meet with them and comments on the fact that I had been right I did know Noz and very well indeed.

I wondered if the Queen had anyone she wanted removed from the Palace either through an upstairs window or through the front door, after all she did give Noz a QPM!

TWO WAYS TO LEAVE

Sometimes a choice with two options is really only one choice to make.

I TOLD NOZ OF my problem in getting these thieves and scam artists out of my house. If I did it the correct way, it could take a year or more with a loss of any rent, during which time they could absolutely trash my house; and my cost would be very high.

Noz said to me, "Leave that to me, Tone. Tell me where your house is, and we'll deal with it!" And he arranged for me to meet him the following day in the evening at 6:30 p.m. when I told him that they were usually home that time.

I waited over the road at six fifteen to watch the house, my house, while waiting for Noz to arrive. Now one thing I should mention is that Noz was built like a "linebacker," black as the ace of spades and huge at six feet six inches tall and arm muscles the same as an average man's thighs.

Noz was the very last person you would think of as a cop; if you were to see him, he was well into rap and had a car tricked out with two huge boom boxes on his back shelf. I heard him approach when he was at least a mile away from the thumping boom, boom, boom of his music as it was being played out over the incredible stereo in his car. I knew where he was exactly as he approached and could hear his wheels screeching as he rounded the curve at the far end of my street. He came into view with one very large arm hanging on to the roof outside his car window as he was nodding his head in tune with some rapper piece or other. I smiled at his arrival, at the sight and sound of my friend, when he jumped out of the car. "Hey, Tone," he said as he gripped my hand in his huge bear paw of a hand. "So which one's yours?" he said, and I pointed to my house on the corner.

"OK," he said, "here's what we'll do. You ring the bell, and when they answer the door, you step aside and leave the rest to me." "OK," I said, "this is your show." We both went over the road, and I rang my doorbell. I could hear them coming down the stairs inside and could also see them through the glass of the front door window. "Who is it?" one of them asked. "It's only me, your landlord." I shouted through the still closed door. "Is everything all right?" one of them said. And I replied that all was OK, but I had left something in the house (them).

As they opened the front door, Noz quickly stood in the doorway, immediately blocking out all of the light with his huge six-foot-six frame, looking like a huge "bouncer" and said, "I am a friend of the owners, and they know what you've been up to and they want you out of their house, so I'm here to let you know that there are two ways you can leave this house. The first is through the front door with all of your shit, right now, and the second is through the upstairs window! So what's it to be?"

I had to stop myself from laughing as these three weedy old fraudsters looked at each other in total shock at what had just been said on this nice sunny Saturday evening in a very warm April. "We w-w-will leave through the f-f-f-front door if, if it's OK with you," one of them said, and they scrambled upstairs to get their stuff. "Give me your keys," Noz told them in a stern voice that if I didn't know him better would have had me quaking in my boots.

They were out of my house in less than twenty-five minutes with all their stuff, and Noz made a note of their car registration number for further use. I had brought with me a new set of locks and changed them immediately. After they had gone, we both burst out laughing, recalling their dismay and shock as they began to get it! We both had a drink at one of Noz's local haunts and caught up on all that had happened since we had closed our wine bar. He told me how he really missed it, and I agreed as I did also; but things changed, and so did people.

Noz and I have kept in touch for thirty years, although it is years since we have met in person. We both have remained close friends. Noz is one in a million, literally, and was awarded the Queen's Medal for services to the London police force on his retirement several years ago. He spends all his time doing charity work for underprivileged kids all over London. He sent me pictures of his investiture when he was awarded his QPM in his bright yellow waistcoat and tailed tuxedo, looking on top of the world; and he deserved to feel like it.

I am very proud to know such a truly wonderful person as Noz, especially knowing the many trials he had to go through in his career that would have surely made a lesser man quit and choose another career. He like me was never a quitter, and I still laugh at how he dealt with things. When Noz was awarded his Queen's Police Medal in 1996, Prince Charles told him, "We need more people like you." And he was right. Noz is now Norwell Roberts QPM (Queens Police Medal).

A quick solution is sometimes the only way to go.

A NEW MEMBER OF THE FAMILY

Brussels was a stepping stone to the USA

After living in Brussels for two short years, my marketing job was completed; and Alfa Laval had acquired a competing company based in Indianapolis called Equipment Engineering. This small company had been reverse engineering our spare parts and was busy selling them to our customers at half of our prices.

I was offered a position as vice president of the new company, which would mean moving to the States; and after discussing it with Sue, we were once again on the move. As we were busy preparing for our move to the United States, Sue, who was finally beginning to show at eight months, was busy getting all the things she needed for the new family addition.

I redecorated the bedroom for our soon-to-be new arrival, and we had decided to have the baby in a big hospital in the ancient town of Leuven just twenty minutes away from Overijse. Sue had had a miscarriage while we were in Brussels and was nervous about the upcoming birth in case anything went wrong. Leuven was a really beautiful town with a large hospital and a world-renowned university. All over the town were tall buildings built in the eleventh century, and each of the buildings had sculptures of saints and important figures from ancient history as well as other historic figures and all were exquisitely carved all over the front of each building.

The town center had cobblestoned roads, which made for very bumpy driving, and I commented to Sue that if she had any difficulty giving birth I would driver her at speed over these cobblestones, just to help. What I loved about the town, apart from all that though, was that it was the home of Stella Artois, which was another of my favorite beers.

Once when we had gone there to see the town with Nicky, I made sure we drove past the brewery just so I could say that I had been there.

David Forman who had worked with me in Brentford and who had come over to work with me again in a new marketing role in Brussels had become a close family friend. He often came over to stay for weekends at our house, and we often went to the local pub at the end of my street after work even if it was only on the days when I was not traveling.

One Monday night, we had decided to have a beer on the way home from the office as Sue had invited Dave to have dinner with us that night. We drove from our office to arrive at the pub, which after all was on our way and was only at the bottom of my road, when as we swung into the car park we nearly drove right into a barricade that had been placed over the entrance. WHAT! They had closed my local pub . . . just like that.

What a bummer! Dave and I got out of the car and walked around, but sure enough, there was a sign written in Flemish and French, saying it had closed down for good and our pub had been sold. Fortunately, a short time later, it reopened as the Mexican Grille, which was an all-you-could-eat buffet where you chose all that you wanted and cooked it yourself on one of several very large open charcoal grills.

This at least compensated for the loss of my "local"; and whenever we went there, usually in a small crowd with our friends, us men offered to do the cooking while loading ourselves up with numerous jugs of beer that were included in the cost of the meal, for a small additional fee.

We went up to the bar and ordered as many jugs of beer as we each could hold, usually around four or five each, as each jug only held just around one liter. We placed them on the shelf over the grill ready to drink as we cooked dinner. We were nearly always tipsy before we sat down to eat, so dinner was a lot of fun whenever we went there I should mention that in Belgium there are reported to be over six hundred different beers available, and each one has its own unique glass.

So every time you order a beer, you get the special glass with it, which I thought was really good marketing, and decided that when we left Belgium we would take as many beer glasses over to the United States as we could pack.

That last Christmas, in Brussels, was spent with Lesley, her current boyfriend and Georgia who both came over for the holidays. Amanda who was now a teen sometimes didn't want to come but instead chose to stay with her friends, which was fine by me, as long as she was happy. In 1990, I had to go over to Indianapolis with Sue to meet the new company and all the staff at their Christmas party, which was in downtown Indianapolis in the Grand Union Station. Though Sue was seven months pregnant, she didn't show at all; and despite being tired from our long trip from London, we were ready to meet my new company.

We arrived late afternoon, on Friday, December 15; and Sue had a chance to rest for only an hour before we were to leave to meet the party and to be introduced to all my new staff. Sue wore a long evening dress in deep green, which was stunning; and she looked a million dollars, making me proud that she was my wife. When we arrived at Grand Union Station, where the company party was being held and which was a short distance from where we were staying at the Embassy Suites Hotel, we were amazed at all of the beautiful decorations inside the grand ticketing hall. There were two huge, twenty-feet-high Christmas trees; each was decorated in silver with what must have been a million lights. All of the station had been decorated with garlands and lights, and the whole effect was beautiful. There were crowds of people in the old station, and the décor was old world with gas lamps and restaurants in the main hall it all looked very festive. One thing I was to learn about the United States was that they did everything on a huge scale . . . no half measures there!

As we went up the stairs and entered the upstairs party, all heads turned to see Sue; I had met them all previously, but they were all intrigued to meet her. We were shown to our table where the previous owner, Bob Behrens; my new secretary, Linda; and Urban Swensson, the new CEO; and their respective partners were all seated there to greet us.

After we all made the introductions, we sat down and had a chance to relax. Sue was overwhelmed at the company that were present but was very used to me and company Christmas parties, though here I had to be on my best behavior as I had an important role as the new general manager. We met Charlie, a realtor, the following day to look at houses; and we couldn't believe what we were looking at. Compared with our house in London and Brussels, which were three-bedroom houses and very nice ones at that, what we were looking at were mansions for the same cost as ours cost only three years before.

All were decorated with thousands of Christmas lights outlining the windows. We had never seen this before; and certainly, at that time, there were none of the Christmas decorations that we were seeing in Greenwood, Indiana.

When we had returned back to Brussels, the time came for our new baby boy to arrive; and it was March 7 when I got the frantic call that Sue had broken water while in a restaurant with several girls on a girls' night out. They brought her quickly home and wished us both good luck as we sped off to the hospital as fast as we could. On the way though, with each contraction that Sue had, she grabbed the steering wheel with all her might. I nearly crashed the car several times in trying to prize her vicelike grip off the wheel while attempting to negotiate the winding twisting roads on the way.

When we arrived, the nurses began babbling in Flemish to us, refusing to speak English; and we couldn't understand a word they were saying. This really pissed Sue off as she was dealing with a rapidly approaching childbirth, and she let them know in very loud, very fine swear words, which they pretended not to understand, while all the time their faces were getting redder and redder. The birth, this time, was very fast; and our son, James Alexander Moore, was born, without any mishap. Although we still couldn't understand anything of what they were saying, at that moment, we didn't care. All was well with the now-growing Moore clan.

Sue stayed in hospital for a day longer, and I picked her and our newborn son and took them home. Over the next few weeks, we were inundated with visitors while I was preparing to make our move to our next adventure in the United States.

James was born in Leuven, where Stella Artois is brewed; a fitting conclusion to our time there!

BIG HATS IN BRUSSELS

Aunty, her mere presence seems to get things done.

NOT LONG AFTER James was born after I told Auntie about our new addition to the family, she announced that she would come over for a week, with Nurse Rosemary, to give Sue a break. I was very happy at that as we had a spare bedroom with two beds that they could both use, and there was plenty of room for my two oldest friends.

I went to the airport to meet them with Sue, Nicky and our new baby James, and there they were right on time. Auntie came through customs, sporting a bright blue hat and a matching outfit. Rosemary was wearing pink and another hat, making them stand out from all of the other "gray" passengers. I heard her calling across the entrance, "Tony deah, there's my darling boy." And she came rushing over to give me a huge hug with Rosemary in tow, and I was so very happy to see them both after such a long time.

When we all arrived home, Auntie did what Auntie did best: she completely took over all of the cooking, all the cleaning, and all of the preparations for our two very young boys. Sue was very happy at that and was told in no uncertain terms that she was to rest completely for the whole time that Auntie was staying with us. We took Auntie in to Brussels for afternoon tea, and the weather was very bright and sunny. She once again sported her very large brimmed hat as did Rosemary, and we sat outside in the afternoon sun with Nicky and James around a table at a café in the "Grand Place." The waiter came over and was soon put to task as Auntie quickly informed him exactly what we were all to eat and drink, and I watched in amusement as he quickly got the message that she was entirely in charge.

I loved it, and I loved her. I went over to her at that moment and put my arms around her and told her, "Never ever change, dear Auntie. I love you just as you are." I went over to Rosemary and told her the same as we were both so happy that they were here with us.

The whole time they stayed, Sue had a very much needed break and loved every minute of it. When they left, wishing us good luck in America, we were left once again as a small family ready to move once again for our next big adventure; but Sue had some renewed strength and was back on form.

We left Brussels finally on April 26, 1991, for London where we were going to spend two weeks there before moving on to Indianapolis for our new life in the new world.

This was the end of one chapter, in my life, and the beginning of another!

THE NEW WORLD

My life's goal was soon to be realized.

WE MOVED OVER to the United States on May 5, 1991, and spent the first night in a hotel as our most needed personal items had been flown in a half container. I had shown Sue videos of various homes I had seen as she had been too pregnant to fly. The home we had both settled on was a palace and was only a couple of years old having a three-car garage, five bedrooms, and a huge living area.

While we were waiting for our things to arrive the day after we had arrived in Greenwood, I showed Sue the garage door opener and asked if she would like to have a look 'round while we were waiting for our things to arrive from the airport. She pressed the button as the door began to open, and there sitting in the middle of the huge double garage was a Sears brand rider lawn mower! I couldn't believe it. I had apparently made it at last! "It's here," I said out loud. "The rider mower is here" Sue looked at me as if I was crazy. "What on earth are you talking about?" she asked me. "Of course, it's there. It's a mower." And I reminded her of my conversation with Auntie several years before when she told me to let her know when I "arrived." And that would be when I had my own rider lawn mower to cut the grass around my house.

I knew at that very moment that she had been right; and that although it didn't feel any different right now, I had something I never knew was possible from my perspective of a future success while living in London.

I wrote to Auntie and told her my news, to which she said simply, "So what's your next goal, Tony deah?" And once again, I had no idea, well, maybe to be a millionaire . . . maybe if cows learn to fly! Sue had her hands full with our two young boys, Nicky and James, while I was immersed in my new job.

Urban and I got along very well and made a great team. We decided to move the company from its ramshackle and leaking building in South Indianapolis into a brand-new multimillion dollar facility in Greenwood, Indiana, some twelve miles south of Indianapolis.

We both worked at the design; and the new building was built, with seventy thousand square feet of floor space, forty thousand of which was for the workshop and thirty thousand for the offices. For the next few years, we were busy the whole time with work and home. Amanda and Georgia both came over as did Lesley and Sue's Mom and Dad, for summer, for Christmas, and any time they wanted.

We had plenty of room for visitors, and they had a complete suite on the upstairs of our "ranch-style" home.

Urban and I turned that little company "Equipment Engineering" around from a $7.3 million company into three times that and all in the space of a few years. We were rocking and in a subsequent survey by an outside consulting company showed that we had now moved from being last in "perceived value" by our customers into becoming the number 1 service provider. It didn't just happen, but Urban and I worked well together; and we each got on with our work and knew what we had to do. In my case, that result was where I intended to take the company; and I took it right there, exactly as I had planned to do. I had laid it out, planned it, and made the plan happen pretty much as I had trained all of the other market companies to do.

We can achieve anything; turn a company around, run a company and succeed in a new country, if we just focus on the task at hand using our skills and training.

THE INDY 500

Living now in the most famous racing city in the world, how could I not be part of it?

Soon AFTER WE had moved to our new premises, we got involved with the Indy 500 race, as a race team sponsor, since we were in Indianapolis. Every year in the month of May, we took as many as one hundred customers to the track for the prerace time trials. These took place two weeks before the actual Indy 500 race and were the time trials that all the race cars that were considering to enter had to complete before being able to enter the race. Each team had to bring their cars up to perfection and could use the track for two weeks before the race in order to do this. So they set up their cars for the qualification time trial in which each team had to submit their car for examination, and then the track was closed for a "fastest four laps" of each car separately. Then the fastest times were entered, and their position on the starting grid was set according to their average times for the four solo time trial laps or qualifying laps.

It was a lot of fun, and I got to know our team and many of the technical settings that our team "McCormack Racing" were using; and on race day, we met our customers or VIPs in Greenwood then took them in a convoy of five large fifteen-seater vans with a police escort all the way to the track.

On race day, we were allowed to go right through red traffic lights and cruise at high speed over sixty miles per hour past all of the thousands of race fans along the twenty-mile distance from Greenwood in the south to the Indianapolis Speedway on the east side of Indy. We traveled in a convoy of five, fifteen-seater vans; and I always drove one of the vans to the race track.

We had arranged breakfast at the track and then a group seating for fifty right at the start-finish line. The atmosphere was electric with a packed stadium and a show that only America could ever put on. There were marching bands, thousands of balloons released, and even a flyby of the U.S. Air Force, which was always very moving.

The race was a five-hundred-mile race of tough endurance for both the cars and the drivers and normally lasted around four hours depending on how many yellow lights or pile-ups there were. I was at that time, in 1992, one of the first to have a cell, or mobile phone; it cost a staggering $1,100 and was a flip phone made by Motorola.

Not many people had a cell phone at that time mainly because of the cost, no wonder; and when I first took it with me to the track in a clip mounted on my belt, there were three girls standing the other side of the fence, by pit row, and they each lifted up their T-shirts and flashed their boobs at me while asking me if they could call their friends on my phone. I declined but did take a peek.

I used it to call Georgia in London, during one of the many days at the track during the time trials and told her where I was. "That is so cool, Dad," she said. "Can I talk to a racing driver then, Dad?" She was ten years old at the time; and just as she said that, our driver, Jeff Woods, came walking back from turn 1 of the track. Our car had broken down on turn one, so he got out and walked back to our pit area. I told Georgia to hold on, and as he approached me, he stopped to tell me what had gone wrong with the car. I asked him if he wouldn't mind talking to my daughter in London, and he looked at the phone and said, "Sure, I will. What's her name?" "Georgia," I said and passed the phone over to him.

"Well, hi, Georgia," Jeff said to her and listened for her reply. "Hello, Georgia, are you there?" he asked again and still no reply. After trying a third time, he passed the phone back to me and said, "I think she's gone." "I doubt it," I said and took the phone from him. "Georgia, are you there?" I asked, and she said, "Dad, was that a real race car driver?"

I told her it was, but she was speechless and couldn't think of a thing to say to him! We both walked back to our pits together while I was talking to Georgia, but she never did talk to a real live Indy 500 race car driver! Sue loved it at the track as the atmosphere was electric, hundreds of thousands of people all fanatical about the Indy 500, and the whole city was decorated in black and white checkered patterns support of the world's most famous race.

Georgia, when the moment came she was speechless!

AN UNFORTUNATE MERGER

Huge egos can make huge mistakes!

IN 1993 WHEN everything was really going well on all fronts, Alfa Laval had merged with another company Tetra Pak, also a Swedish privately held corporation, which was of equal size as Alfa Laval at around seven billion dollars in sales and was similar in structure except that Tetra Pak was owned by the Rousing brothers and focused on high-speed packaging for drinks and liquids for human consumption. As time went on, both companies were to meet one another to see how the other half lived and worked; and as we met each other, it became very clear that the cultures of two companies were vastly different.

Alfa Laval was an engineering-led company with managers that had been in the business and learned the company's style and products. Tetra Pak had mainly young MBAs, fresh out of college, as managers and recruited in the United States, around two hundred each time they wanted managers, of which less than five would stay.

If two Swedish companies in similar markets could be more different, these two were it. Alfa Laval had a culture of careful management and a very standardized budgeting process, making sure we flew coach and rented average or appropriate cars. Tetra Pak staff, on the other hand, flew first class and often hired limos to visit their customers. Another difference was our customer base; we had 2,500 customers within the United States, providing the same sales volume as only a few dozen high-speed packaging customers of Tetra Pak. As we were all figuring out how to merge the two huge companies, Bo came over to meet us in Greenwood with senior members of the Tetra Pak corporate staff and wanted me on his "Tetra Pak" team. Urban didn't want to join Tetra Pak and instead moved over to the Alfa Laval marine division. We gradually split up; and he took over the U.S. Marine Department, moving to Philadelphia while I stayed with the Tetra Pak organization based out of Chicago. When Urban didn't get the president position of Alfa Laval US, he resigned from the company to start up his own consulting company. I never saw my friend Urban again, though we often traded Christmas cards together. I have to say that I didn't like the way Tetra Pak did business and the extravagance they lavished on their market, but it was what it was; and that was that.

Soon after the merger, in a phone call from my new CEO, I was informed that I was promoted and was to take over five of their technical service divisions as well as running my own. I went from managing one division to managing six divisions with 110 staff on top of my own.

I got an immediate pay rise and was moved from a vice president to a General Manager, which accordingly was a much bigger position. Next thing I knew was that Tetra wanted to shut down Greenwood after it had only been opened for a few years. I was shocked and wanted to know why. The reason was that they didn't want a separate organization in Indiana and instead wanted it all under one roof in Chicago.

A mismatched merger of two companies; what a waste of good talent that left both as a result. Tetra Pak later engaged Professor Malcolm Mc. Donald to change its corporate culture, now that was finally a good decision!

A PROPHETIC DREAM

Sometimes advice comes from the strangest of places

Around this time, I had a very strange dream; and it was so very clear to me after I awoke and every scene in my dream was so crystal clear, that I knew while I was dreaming that I was being told something very important; but I didn't know what it was at the time.

In my dream, I was camped between two tall buildings, not skyscraper, tall but older four- or five-story houses with steps leading up to the front door as in the style of a Chicago town house. Between these two tall houses was a space where possibly a third house could have been, but instead there was only a grassy space between them, both on which was my tent.

Looking up, I noticed, standing on the street, a work colleague of mine, Frank Schmitt, who was standing looking at me, not saying a word. I called out to him to say hi, but he said nothing at all to me and instead turned his back on me and walked away. I couldn't understand why he did this, but the dream was in dark colors and the atmosphere was remote and heavy for me. When I awoke, though, I had no idea what the dream was about. I knew I could remember it all in perfect clarity. Little did I know that this was one of several such dreams where I was being shown something very important, and I was either being warned or advised of what was happening around me and that I would know when the time came that the dream was forewarning me of events that I didn't yet know what they were to be. It was not until several months later that the events of that dream became very clear to me.

I didn't always understand the information I was being given at the time, but it became clear later and I knew what to do.

AN ENGLISHMANS PITCH TO SWEDES IN CHICAGO

Fighting for what we know is right is seldom easy; fighting for the jobs of others is a fight that is worth taking on.

I TALKED ABOUT THE impending decision to close Greenwood with Linda, my secretary; and we agreed that I had to try to stop it if I could. I had to stop this madness because if we shut down Greenwood, at least sixty-five of my staff would lose their jobs; and I knew all of them on a personal level. So I had to do something about it.

I began by gathering all of the state info and city info I could on housing costs, factory overhead costs, wage comparisons, and even flight delay costs of Indianapolis compared with Chicago. I got information on taxes, property rates, and average wages in both places and even how much of the time the roads were congested in Indianapolis compared with Chicago.

I went to a very senior meeting in Chicago to present my case. Only my secretary Linda knew of my visit and the reason why as I didn't want anyone from Greenwood to know in case I failed to keep their jobs for them and in case the facility was to be closed down.

I made my case with information from the FAA, the governor's office, the local town hall, and even several trades unions based out of Indy. In fact, I went with reams of statistical data all aimed at keeping the Greenwood facility open and keeping the jobs of our staff.

I presented a careful set of arguments one by one as indeed an attorney would in managing his closing arguments. I won the case hands down, and the senior board decided to keep the Greenwood operation, eventually making it an America's Center of Excellence where it remains to this day; and they grew it into a major production facility building complex and very high-tech aseptic modules that were shipped all over North and South America. No one to this day knows how close they all came to losing their jobs, and Tetra Pak didn't care at all about that, and neither did they know the work I had put into trying to keep that facility open. Urban had been moved on so that fight was mine alone to undertake. We won though, and for me, that was the important thing.

Preparation had saved the day, and believe me, I had prepared long and hard.

Though I won the battle, I lost the war which, for me, meant moving my family to the company's location in Wisconsin.

For the next two years, I had to travel up to a place called Pleasant Prairie in Kenosha Wisconsin, which was the location of our head office. We called the place 'Kenowhere' as that was what we thought about it at that time as Kenosha or rather, where our office was located on Lakeview Parkway, had nothing close except a large power station with plumes of steam coming out of the huge cooling towers. I told Sue that we were expected to move to Wisconsin; and she said, "If you think I'm going to eat cheese and brats while wearing lace hats surrounded by Amish people, you can forget it!" I tried several times to broach the subject with her, but it always ended in an argument, so there was little I could do.

To win the battle and lose the war is sometimes better than to never take on the fight at all. We can look at ourselves in the mirror and know, on reflection and with our family intact, that we did the right thing.

A KEY DECISION

After we have made a big but carefully considered decision; don't second guess it.

ONE EVENING AS I was watching Nicky play football at a rare time when I was at home and not in the office at Kenosha on a Wednesday night, I thought to myself I really want to be able to bring my children up right here and not keep moving them all over the States as soon as the company makes another nonsensical decision, seemingly at the drop of a hat. With the merger of Alfa Laval and Tetra Pak, it was clear that things would change, and that meant any of us could be moved anywhere and at a moment's notice.

I made the choice not to move; and come what may, I decided then and there that if this cost me my job, then so be it. Maybe it was time to move on from the company. I wanted to be able to spend time with my family and more than that to let Nicky and James have life-long school friends without being moved from location to location at the whim of my company. I also wanted to take more control of my own future more than I could do while working for such a mercurial company that, under the Tetra Pak umbrella, seemed to bounce people and families all over the place with absolutely no care as to their families' happiness of stress.

Each time I tried to discuss this move with Sue she refused to even consider a move, especially to Wisconsin; even though she had never been and knew nothing about life in other places in the States. I told Sue of my decision, made at the side of the soccer field, while watching Nicky play with his team mates. The decision not to move was mainly because she simply refused to move anywhere else; but for me, it was to allow Nicky and James to remain and have life-long school friends that I never had apart from Ian. So really I had decided that I would be looking for another job. After that point, I "crossed the bridge"; and everything inside the company, from that moment on, looked different to me.

I knew it would lead to a confrontation between me and the company, but that couldn't be helped. I had made my decision and that was that!

Being prepared the consequences of our actions makes them easier to accept.

AN UNBELIEVABLE COINCIDENCE

There are sometimes less than six degrees of separation

DURING THE TIME that I was working from Kenosha, during the week, where our head office was during the week and traveling up and back Mondays and Fridays, I rented a house and shared it with two of my colleagues who also had to be relocated to the head office, George and Blair. I had hired both of them, and we made a fine trio.

I was once again traveling the whole time but found that one very cool part about Wisconsin life was that there were loads of pubs there seemingly on every corner. This at least meant that we had places to got to in the evenings, a small ray of sunshine in a bad time for me. I found a local dive bar called the Coffin, aptly named for its décor, which was dark to say the least. The bar was only down the road from our rental house, and I went there frequently midweek.

Once they got to know me, and being English certainly helped, they told me that there was another local who talked just like me. They told me they would introduce us both when he next came in. I thought that to most Americans I had met so far, I may as well be Irish, Welsh, Australian, or a New Zealander, and thought nothing of it. Some three months later, I was in fact introduced to my new friend; and it turned out that he did in fact come from London. As we began to talk, and of course drink, I asked him where in London he had come from. He replied that he had lived in West London, so I asked where in West London, and he said Ealing. I was now interested to see if he knew the same places or people that I knew. "OK," I said, "what school did you go to?" And he replied, "Fielding." I told him over another drink, "So did I." And I asked him, "So what teachers do you remember there?" And he told me his favorite was his music teacher, Mr. Woodcraft! I couldn't believe it as we both said, "Woody Woodcraft" in unison. He went on to tell me that Ms. Hunt was still the headmistress, and many of the same teachers were still there that I remembered. Unbelievable! Here I am in the middle of nowhere—Kenosha, Wisconsin—and I meet someone who went to the same school as I did.

I asked him if he recalled seeing the many black-and-white photos all along the wall outside Ms. Hunt's office on the entrance wall to the main hall. He told me there were loads of pictures there, so I asked him if he had seen some pictures of a school play called *The Snow Queen*, and he had. When I told him that I was in that picture and another next to it, he even recalled seeing the photos. I told him of the very happy times at Fielding, and he had the same experience. I asked him what he was doing in bloody Kenosha, Wisconsin; and he told me he was forming another band.

He was in a famous punk band called UK Subs, which were around at the same time as the Stranglers. We shared stories about the various music and bands that we had played with, and the evening was so surreal for us both. He told me that Fielding had a really good reputation still and was a highly sought-after school, and although he was probably ten to fifteen years younger than me, he had enjoyed the same things I had. Mr. Woodcraft had made a big difference to many children and was a very gifted teacher. He taught us what music was really about and we got it.

To this day, many of us old alumni still have an excellent understanding of music because of his teaching. The best I can do for him is to remember him in this book; and by saying, "Woody, you really did make a difference, and thanks for that." During my final few months, I had been part of a corporate decision to be part of a study where the company had brought in a consulting company based in Canada to evaluate each of the five main sales and marketing divisions to see how they were being managed and to see what changes may need to be made for more success within Tetra Pak USA.

After the team of consultants had been to each of the other divisions, they came to my department and asked me how I ran it and what key information I had to manage my operation. At that point, I had a very large organization of sales, order handling, spares, and field service.

I asked that they first meet with my sales staff and ask them those questions then come back to me, as I had trained them all and they should be able to answer any questions about their markets.

After a few days of meeting my sales staff, the consultants came to me and told me how impressed they were with the knowledge each of my sales team had about their market their goals and key accounts. They asked for a copy of our market plan and took the documents to show our CEO. They told us all that ours was the best run division in the company and was a model of how a marketing and sales operation should be run. I had to laugh as I knew that the company would be making a move on my position, and now there was no way they could say my operation was in trouble. In addition to this, I had managed to turn a huge loss-making operation into a very profitable one.

It was George who told me he had been shown an organization chart that my name was not on. I knew that I was being moved out and decided to wait to see it through.

Well, after a year of living in Kenosha, during the week while still living in Greenwood, I was eventually called to the head office and was given an ultimatum, shortly after George had talked to me. I went there with Blair as we had both been summoned, and we were called in to the board room. I was told to either move or leave. I had already decided not to move, so I was fired. The strange part of it was that as I came out of the board room and walked down the corridor, I passed Frank's office, which was between the board room and my own office, and thought I would say my goodbye to Frank. I had known him for nearly fifteen years, but as I approached his office, he shut his door to me. Though I was surprised that he should do this, I didn't care as I had made the decision to move on and had "crossed the bridge" many months before.

It was on the way back to Greenwood that I understood the meaning of my dream. The two tall buildings were my offices in Greenwood and Chicago; and because I was not moving, I was camped temporarily between the two places—one building was representing my Greenwood office, while
the other was my Chicago office. In my dream, Frank, who I had never had crossed words with ever, turned away just as he did on May 5, 1997, when I left Tetra Pak.

It was an immense relief not to have to work there anymore, like a load being lifted off me; and I threw a huge leaving party at our house for all my staff. The corporate attorney, John Felzan, called me a few days later and asked me not to make any rash decisions as to my future. John and I had spent a lot of time together trying to stem possible law suits against the company over the non-supply of spare parts to competitors, and we had managed to stave off a potential major law suit. John told me I had a potential law suit for age discrimination, and I had already seen an attorney of my own to check out my legal status.

I knew that if I told John this, he would be alerted to the direction I was considering, and so I told him that I already had an attorney. He asked me to give him time to put a really good package together and asked me to think about what I wanted. My attorney told me that I could go for loss of wages for the remaining time I would have had a career at Tetra Pak, and the key item was the consulting group study that found my department the best run in the group; meaning they had no other reason to let me go as my refusal to move did not in any way impair my ability to do my job as I traveled around the country 60 percent of my time. John came back with a staggering package totaling two and a half year's full pay with all benefits and averaged out bonuses, plus unlimited time with a very expensive outplacement agency. He said that Tetra Pak had ignored the fact that I had been in the company for twenty-five years, and this had become a major issue. I discussed this with my attorney, and he asked if I could survive with a two- to three-year lawsuit, and I had to agree that I couldn't.

I signed the non-compete contract in order to get the severance pay. John told me he had really enjoyed working with me and told me they were really scared that I could start up my own company and compete with them, as I had set up the marketing operations all over the globe.

I laughed at that and told him I would never consider competing against the company as I wanted to get into a completely different type of business and never ever wanted to be involved with the equipment industry again.

Sue and I took a much-needed vacation before I began to consider my next move. As the saying goes, "The world was now my oyster."

When it's time to move on from you job, do it gracefully and without anger. The decision to move on was mine and I have never regretted that family based decision. Many of my friends stayed on at this company and were later unceremoniously let go which is the way of corporations. It's better, if we can, to choose for ourselves than for that choice to be made for us without warning.

STARDUST

I was to learn that investing in a startup requires more than passion and hard work.

AFTER A BREAK of six months when I was attending an outplacement agency, I was shown how to make excellent resumes, and I started going to several meetings downtown to network with both entrepreneurs and investors. It was at one of these that I met a very tall black lady called Cynthia Prime. Cynthia asked me to visit her at her company on the north side of town where she was a headhunter.

I met with her a few days later, and she began asking me about what I wanted to do next. I explained that I wanted to either start up my own company or buy one.

It was then that she told me about her husband, Phillip Prime, who used to be the "nose" for Elizabeth Arden; and he had developed several very well-known fragrances—Chloe, Red Door Lagerfeld for Men, and Burberry.

I used to wear Lagerfeld for Men and really liked it. She asked if I would like to meet her husband to discuss a new fragrance company under the name Stardust, named after the famous Hoagy Carmichael song of the same name. We met a few days later; and Phillip was a tall retired scientist, as he called himself, who was looking to start up his own company. After a few more meetings, they made a pitch for me to invest in their company and help them to get it off the ground. I told them both that what I wanted was a job, something long-lasting and something interesting, but completely different from what I had been doing.

I asked them for some samples of the fragrance, and Phillip gave me ten small phials or small testers to show friends so that I could get their feedback. I told Sue about it, and she was as excited as I was about launching a fragrance company. Now Phillip and Cynthia made it very clear to me that they were both very religious; and in fact at each meeting we had they ended up praying. I thought this was a little over the top, but nevertheless, it was fine by me. Sue passed out the fragrances to her friends, and they loved it; not one person had a bad thing to say about the fragrance.

I called them and set up a meeting in order to discuss how much was needed to launch Stardust and what the next steps would be. Most important to me was my role in this company and what my level of investment would be.

During the next meeting, I asked them about their company and that if they had anything, I should know about before I invested. They both told me about a prior company called My Choice that they still had, which was a design company involved with the design of the first Stardust bottle. Cynthia showed me the bottle, which was a glass orb with a woman sitting on the top wearing a long flowing robe and her hands running through her long flowing hair. It looked a little "retro," and I told them that I thought the detail of her face and hands would be difficult to replicate in a full production mode.

Phillip smiled at that and said that he thought so as well. Obviously, I had struck a nerve as Cynthia began to defend her design. I explained that although I knew nothing of fragrances, I did know about manufacturing; and as they had spent six years trying to get this company off the ground, in all probability, the bottle design may be part of the problem.

I had to be honest with them both; and I told them that this being Indianapolis, the middle of a very conservative Midwest, meant that to get a large investment behind two black people may be another issue and that while I was fully OK with the investment and had every belief in them both, others may not be, so we needed to find a management company to head up the investment drive.

We met with an investment company in downtown Indianapolis and met John Bernard and company who seemed very interested in taking up the project. He passed us on to a young partner in the company MBA called Tim, who was to be our assistant in getting the company off the ground.

I asked how much was required to make a new design of bottle as I wasn't prepared to invest in that particular concept. Phillip thought $25,000 would be enough for Marc Rosen in New York to come up with a great design as I wasn't going to invest in their old bottle design.

With any investment, there comes a time to decide to do or not to do it!

DUE DILIGENCE

I decided to go ahead with this start up to see if I could do it!

BEFORE PLACING ANY cash into this fledgling company, I asked Phillip and Cynthia again if there was anything else I should know about their past company My Choice and asked them for a financial statement from that company. Phillip gave me the name of his accountant who was somewhere out in Greensburg, I called and set a meeting for the following day and drove out to meet him. When I got there, the office was closed, so I called again and got the answer phone. I waited for over an hour, and no one showed up, so I left and came back. I thought at the time that this was strange.

I asked Phillip what had happened to My Choice, and he told me it was simply a design company to get the fragrance and the original bottle design, and that was all. I told Tim about the aborted visit to find out what had happened, and we agreed that once the company was funded we would have a proper board; and that both he and John would be there to help us build it up, so I thought nothing more about it.

After signing an agreement, overseen by Bernard and Associates giving me shares in the company, I gave them part of my severance from Tetra Pak in order to get a new bottle design made. We went to New York to meet Marc Rosen in his Manhattan offices. He showed us all of the designs he had made for other fragrances, and I was really impressed by his knowledge and his very well-known designs. He had made the "Red Door" bottle, "Catalyst for Men," the "Perry Ellis" collection, "Fable," "Heaven Scent," "Lelong," and many others. He was a unique and gifted designer and in fact was probably one of the best in the world. We were very lucky to get him to come on board and come up with our new bottle design. Mark agreed that Cynthia's bottle design did not go with his interpretation of the name. He explained that he saw it as a modern fragrance with a starlit bottle that would be bright and would be exciting, unique, and not so much in the "retro" mode. We left it up to Marc to come up with our new design and left for Indianapolis later that day. We named our new company "Parfums Llewellyn."

When we commit, there's no going back!

BAD ADVICE

Bad advice is only bad if we rely solely on it.

I HAD $100,000, which I intended to invest in the fledgling company in order to get us off the ground. The money was from a pension fund that Tetra Pak had insisted I take into the United States before the end of 1997. They had invested it for me in Switzerland, and I had to give them a bank address before December 31, 1997, as that was the end of their fiscal year. I spoke to Phillip, and he put me onto an attorney that he knew downtown to advise me on how to make this a payment into the company as another IRA rollover to legally avoid tax on it as an income.

I was advised to set up a separate account and move the money through this account and into Parfums Llewellyn and mark the check IRA rollover. So I did what was suggested and invested the money, the second investment the company had. This was partly to get us moving and partly to attract other investors.

The money came through from Switzerland at the end of 1997, and I did what I had to so passing the money through into the company for preferred shares.

I had my hands full as we needed to make financial projections of sales and costs along with the estimated timeline and how much capital investment we needed to get Stardust off the ground. Financially, Sue and I were fine as I still had a year of salary from Tetra Pak left before my money ran out.

A few weeks later, a very excited Marc called us to say he had found the perfect bottle design for Stardust. It was unique easy to make and was exactly what he had envisioned.

We went again to New York to see what he had come up with and were absolutely stunned at the bottle he had created.

It was a prism with a triangular base that leaned back slightly, having a flat glass face that reflected light, throwing off "starlight" prisms of light. The cap would have midnight blue oval center, which was the shape of the universe with tiny stars set in surrounded by a brushed silver oval surround.

We loved it! It was perfect and had come from a concept from Tiffany's in New York where Marc was passing by and noticed in the window a beautiful crystal paperweight that sent out sparkling light as he passed. He told us that as soon as he saw it he knew that it should be our Stardust bottle and bought it there and then.

Next came all of the costing for the bottle, the cap and the packaging, which I took on and placed the details onto a large spread sheet that would form the basis of our bid for startup capital. The cost of the molds was staggering at over $120,000 for the bottle the cap and the perfume bottle. But it was a necessity, and so we moved on as these would become assets of the company.

Phillip was busy working with Fermenich, pronounced "femanich" in Switzerland, who were going to make the bulk fragrance essence and ship it to wherever we were going to get the filling done. I was busy like hell but loved it. I was working many times all night, getting everything ready for the capital investment drive. I had to prepare a PowerPoint presentation, which would contain all that an investor would need to see, images of the bottle, the price points where we would be selling into, and what the cost of operations and production would be. I prepared everything and made the presentation time fifteen minutes, leaving time for discussion.

I now had enough detail to estimate the costs of the bottle and fragrance with shipping costs and now needed the packaging costs. I found several packaging companies and sent out the package designs to get that moving while I was searching for contract filling companies.

I had made the commitment so there was no going back especially when others were going to become committed along with me.

FINDING INVESTORS

When getting others to invest, you have to believe totally in your product

I HAD FINISHED THE investment presentation; and after several meetings with Tim and Phillip, we made the changes, while Cynthia prepared a bunch of investment packages.

Tim, myself, John, and Phillip came up with a stunning list of potential investors who may be interested in our start up. Our list included basketball stars, attorneys, TV celebrities, and a previous owner of the National City Bank, Nick Frenzel. Phillip and Cynthia had decided on the price points; and that we were to only target the top tier stores like Bergdorf Goodman in New York, Saks Fifth Avenue, Niemen Marcus, and Jacobson's. Tim and I were concerned that there were only 350 of these "top tier" stores, whereas the second tier had 3,500 stores. Phillip insisted that with the high price point of $95 for a 1.7-ounce, $135 for a 3.4 ounce, and $300 for the 50-milliliter perfume these were the only stores we should focus on.

The prices were very high, but I used them in my financial projections, as I had no idea if this was a good or a bad price point. I did know however that Phillip had been in the fragrance business for over thirty years, so we bowed to his knowledge. I now had everything ready for our next step, which was to find $2.5 million for the launch.

I ran through my final projections and all was correct, at least as far as a financial projection could be. I designed a spreadsheet so that we could work with any number of stores and simply plug in new cost numbers at any month after the launch as any potential investor may need to see our break-even point. I wanted to be able to provide financial arguments right there and then during any presentation. Every time I sent the information back to Cynthia, she spent hours trying to correct the grammar so in the end, I finished it myself and paid for thirty sets of Stardust folders made in brushed silver and blue with the logo, which incidentally I had drawn up at home. We had our list of investors and practiced our presentation in front of John Bernard and Tim Tichenor. After a critique, we were finally ready to go.

When something appears to be wrong, it usually is, we just have to find out what it is.

TOM BINFORD

Good advice from a reliable source is always worth listening to.

I HAD BEEN introduced to Tom Binford, who was very famous in Indianapolis and was one of Indianapolis's most influential men; Tom was a civil rights leader and had been involved in many civic, philanthropic, cultural, and political aspects of the city and state. He was highly respected and was well thought of person who was valued for wise counsel, personal and financial support, and sincerity. He led a group to buy the Pacers basketball team in 1975 and served as its president and general manager for one year from 1974 to 1975. He was instrumental in getting the Colts to Indianapolis and also served as the chief steward of the Indianapolis 500, presiding over its transition into the Indy Racing League or IRL as it is still known today.

Tom headed his own investment company and was an investor himself. His offices were high up in the Bank One building, which was the tallest landmark in the state.

I met him with Phillip and Cynthia who told me how close they were to Tom, and we arranged to make our pitch to them. Tom said he would think about it and asked me for my contact information, which I gave him.

Several days later, Tom called me and asked me meet him for lunch, which surprised me. I went to meet him and another colleague Tony who was part of Tom's company. During lunch, Tom began to explain that he knew "The Primes" as friends but not more than that and had never had any business dealings with them. He went on to warn me not to make an investment because of his name being used by the Primes. I asked if he would be investing, and he said probably not! This was the first time I had seen a crack in the Primes' information but saw it more as Tom telling me to be careful in dealing with them. I asked Tom and Tony if they trusted John Bernard and Tim, and he said, "Absolutely.

They will never steer you wrong, and you should listen to John he knows what he's doing." I didn't ever talk of this to Cynthia and Phillip but did have a talk with Tim about it. Tim said that all investments had elements of risk, and that we would have a serious company behind us to carry us through.

Phillip and Cynthia were name-droppers for sure, but Tim said, "Let's just get on with this and find the money elsewhere." But I was stunned at Tom's honesty and thought that I should be more wary in future.

Over the next eight weeks, we met dozens of investors and gradually got commitments for $1.3 million, which was enough to get us off the ground.

As Tim advised us, "It's easier to get more money when you have a finished product than a mere concept." I liked working with John and Tim as they were both very straight shooters, and I knew I could trust their judgment, so we prepared for the launch of our new company, "Stardust."

Setting up a new company takes a lot of talent but also a lot of good advice.

LAUNCH OF STARDUST

Having made it this far it was time for the real work to begin.

WE NOW HAD SOME cash, though not all that we really needed, but enough to get our first production run made. We had bottles being made by Bross in France, caps being made in Georgia, fragrance made in Switzerland, and packaging from a company out of New York. We were already an 'International company.'

I found a small contract packaging company in upstate New York, while poring over the trade mags, with capacity to fill enough sets for us to launch the product. The company was Sicilian-owned, and I went there to meet them.

They agreed to package our fragrance. "The only thing is Tony," one of the owners told me in a broad Sicilian accent more like the Mafia, "is that when we do it . . . you pay for it, capische?" Yes, I got it loud and clear, fearing that if I didn't I probably would never be found again.

I purchased all the components we needed for the upcoming launch with the help of Tim, and we had decided to take on a cosmetics marketing and sales expert. After some weeks, we found Don Hilgeman, who had a great resume with many well-known cosmetics and fragrance companies as well as having excellent knowledge of the buyers at the biggest high end store chains where we intended to sell in to.

Don and I got on very well, and we split the work up between us, with Don taking all of the front-end sales and me the production. We began to really get the company up and running with everything on purchase to be delivered to our offices in downtown Indianapolis where I would do the assembly of the two layer cartons for the two sizes of bottles. The perfume was to be placed inside a very beautiful box to make it worth the $300 price tag. Our offices were on the eighth floor of the Guaranty Building, where we had an office suite a warehouse space and a board room, right on the circle in the very center of Indianapolis; and we got our launch into Bergdorf Goodman in New York planned as well as Jacobson's on the north side of Indianapolis.

My task was to get all the filling and packaging finished, Don's was to get the in store displays ready, and Cynthia's was to get some handouts ready for our launch. The date was set in November 1998 in New York, then, Sunday December 6, in Indianapolis, which was my birthday.

How cool was that? We all went to New York, and Bergdorf's staff met us at the entrance and led us to the made-up counters all decorated in blue and silver. They took us outside and showed us the store window featuring Stardust as the centerpiece of their most important window. What a display! and on New York's Fifth Avenue, of all places. We were not only in the most famous of all stores for our launch but in the most prestigious address in the entire United States and featuring our very own Stardust.

It was an unbelievable sight to see our conception realized into a finished product. I was very proud of all that I had done. Marc Rosen came to the launch with his wife Arlene Dahl, who graciously greeted us and talked up the fragrance, doing what film stars do in public which was to act the part.

The next step was the launch at Jacobson's on Eighty-Sixth Street, right at the entrance to the mall. I had a limousine to take Sue and several friends from our house to the store on the evening of 6 December 1998.

There were eight of us in the limo; and when we arrived at the store, I couldn't believe it—the whole front of the mall entrance was lit up with stars moving across the mall entrance, the car park, and even the sky! It was an awesome birthday present. We all went in to the store on a red carpet that stretched from the car park where we parked right into the store.

As we entered Jacobson's, the CEO came out to greet us; Tim, John Barnard, Phillip, Cynthia, and Don were all there. There was a stage set up in the middle of the store with a mic, and local TV crews were there to video the event for the news. During the evening, Phillip got up and was introduced by Jacobson's CEO; and he and Cynthia thanked everyone. The evening was a tremendous success, and we were so happy with all that we had done, so far.

Both Phillip and Cynthia practically ignored me the whole time of the launch, and it was Don who came up to me and said, "These two are fucking incredible. They behave as if this whole thing is about the two of them and not about all of us who have helped to get Stardust launched!"

I agreed with Don but didn't think too much about it. Sometimes people do things without thinking! We gave Marc a sample of each of the finished product, and he agreed to get us several Factice bottles for the stores. The Factice was a supersized bottle a foot in height that was for display purposes and was filled with an alcohol colored to match the fragrance.

We had plenty of products for the limited number of stores that we had initially, and Don's job was to get us into the remaining stores on our list. As time moved on, we began to get into more stores; but we couldn't get into Nordstrom, which was a key store. We all went up to Seattle for a meeting with the "Guru" of the fragrance world, Dale Crighton, who was the fragrance buyer for Nordstrom. We had a ten-minute window to present our fragrance to Dale and a team of around twenty-five others.

We were given a room with around thirty chairs facing a long table where we were to place our fragrance and make a presentation of how it would be launched, what gifts we would be giving customers, the price points, and everything that Dale and her staff would need to know.

At the presentation, there were a total of ten other new fragrances to be launched at the same time as ours. We had carefully prepared our ten-minute presentation, and each of us knew our part well. We had one chance to get in, and we had left sample phials, placed inside a small "Stardust" card, on each of the chairs. At the allotted time, all twenty-five of them breezed in and sat down to listen. Cynthia was first up, at her insistence, and wasted five whole minutes on cause-related marketing, talking about women's causes. I could see we were losing the crowd and hoped Phillip would have the balls to cut her off and get on with the concept. He had little time left to present the steak, after Cynthia had delivered all of the sizzle.

Dale was gracious, and it was clear that she knew the fragrance business and had insight, when she asked that we reconsider our cause-related items, as these were secondary to the fragrance itself. She quizzed us on the high price points, and I left that up to Phillip. She thought the fragrance was good but rather sweet and a little heady.

Her last comments were for us to focus on what the fragrance was all about and the "spiffs" and marketing tools like advertising and in store giveaways. We weren't ready for Nordstrom yet and needed to get more publicity and some sales before we would be ready for them.

We headed back to Indy for a regroup, and Cynthia had arranged for the *Indianapolis Business Journal* to do an article on Stardust; but the article did not mention anything about the team that had put the company together, although I was in the office the day the writer came in with the photographer. This was about Cynthia and no one else, and Don was there but not one of any of the rest of us. This was the second issue that caught me off guard, and I thought back to Tom Binford's discussion and warning to me.

The product was perfect but I was now beginning to see that talking the talk didn't match walking the walk.

HELPING MY DAUGHTERS

Family comes first and always will!

JANE, IN 1998, during my weekly call to talk to Amanda and Georgia, told me that Georgia was not going to school and in fact had been absent for most of the term. I felt I had to try to help when she told me that she would not be allowed to finish her GCSE exams as she had missed so much time off school through truancy. The GCSE exams were the same as a graduation exam in United States, with the difference being that in England you could take several exams covering all of the subjects. Some of your final score was based on course work during the year, and some was based on the final exam results.

Just around this time, I had a conversation over the phone with Amanda; it was one of those phone calls that I knew I was being led to have.

Jane also told me that Amanda had anorexia, and that she had hidden it well for several years. In Amanda's last years at school, she had suffered from anxiety attacks; and sometimes I had to drop everything and go to pick her up from school. So I was aware that she did have some issues to deal with, but I thought this was all behind her.

During one of my weekly telephone calls to Amanda, I was asking her, as I normally did, how she was doing with her health. I made a joke to her that her behavior was as if she had been abused as a child, but I was certain that this wasn't the case as she had been with me as her father all the time. At that comment, she suddenly broke down on the phone with me on the line, as soon as I had said that it couldn't have happened!

I could have bitten my tongue off and wished that I hadn't said that. Nevertheless, I had hit the nail on the head, and she was sobbing on the phone. I didn't know what to do, and no words I said could comfort her as she was sobbing on the phone. I was absolutely devastated at the implication of what I had just found out and was in shock myself.

Sue could hear the change in the conversation and asked me what was wrong. I covered the phone and asked Sue to take the phone from me and talk to her, which she did as she too had similar experiences when she was younger.

Despite being so busy at work with the start-up company, I decided to leave immediately for London to help Georgia and Amanda. I flew over to London immediately and met both of them as I knew Jane needed my help right then and there.

As soon as I arrived in London, I went with Georgia to her school and met with the headmaster together with her. When we met him, I told him I had flown over six thousand miles for that meeting and thanked him for seeing me. Jane had said it won't help. He won't do anything; but me being me, I had to at least try!

I asked the principal to please allow my daughter Georgia to sit her exams, and she had promised to go to school every day until the exams. He agreed to let her sit them, provided that she attended every single day; and I spoke to her afterward to try to get her to see that this was important and that she absolutely had no chance in life if she didn't bother. Well, she did bother; she took the GCSE exams and got good grades in six subjects, which showed she really was able to do it almost with ease.

Next, I had to go to see Amanda's clinic in Acton with her. She was nervous about me being there, but I told her I loved her and I would move heaven and earth to help her. That was why I was there and why I had flown over to help.

We went to her meeting and went into a room with opaque glass windows, a vinyl floor, and a row of seven metal seats set in a semicircle. Amanda was to sit in the one chair facing the other seven. She begged me not to say anything but to listen, and I told her I would do my best.

A group of doctors, counselors, and whoever filed into the room for Amanda's meeting; there were seven in all, and they sat opposite her on their appointed seats.

"So good afternoon Amanda and how are you today?" one of them wearing a white coat asked her while making notes on a clip board. "Fine, thanks" was all Amanda said. I said nothing. "So how are you doing with your eating, Amanda?" another asked. "I'm doing fine, thanks," she replied again. "Good, good," he said to her. The meeting went on like that for around twenty minutes, achieving absolutely nothing. I could see that my darling Amanda was nervous at the meeting, and clearly it was not helping her at all. "Good, good," one of them said, "So that's all for now. We'll see you in a month, OK?"

After remaining quiet, I could stand it no more and said to the group, "I'm sorry," at which Amanda shrank in her seat, not knowing what I was going to say but I held her hand in mine and said quietly, "don't worry, darling." "And who are you?" one of them said. And I replied, "I am her father, and I have flown thousands of miles to be here to see what help you are giving her. And from what I have seen here so far, it is as I suspected, not much help at all!" They asked me where I lived, and I told them, after which one of the group told me that I should take her with me to the United States as their help for these illnesses were far better than what she could get from the NHS.

I told them I couldn't accept that logic as if they were happy with the status quo and were therefore helping to make these kinds of situations worse. I asked them who among them was in charge of this kind of therapy and how on earth did they justify this to themselves as professionals?

They told me they do the best they can. "That's not good enough," I said. "Simply asking her how she is doing isn't helping my daughter. There are no milestones, no weekly guidelines, so how will she ever measure her success or failure with this?" They wanted to move on and were obviously uncomfortable with my comments about rather poor performance as doctors and counselors.

I could see that we were getting nowhere, so I took Amanda's hand and we left there. I told her that she shouldn't bother to go there and stress herself out any more as it clearly was not something that would benefit her.

Amanda told me several years later that me flying over to help her made her realize that she had to beat this herself as I had shown her that I would do anything to help her, but she also knew I couldn't really do more than be a source of strength. What she did do was to learn to become a Reiki healer, so that she could help others; and by doing that, I think it helped her a lot and she made it through. She is fine now and doing well, Eliza Jane's (Ellie's) birth also helped her as she now had to be there for her baby daughter, and she knew she couldn't let Ellie down ever. This is one of those things that although never goes completely away can, as in Amanda's case, be managed to a "normal" or almost normal situation.

No matter what I was doing at the time I was prepared to support my daughters immediately; as aunty had always supported me, and decades later they too could see what they meant to me.

PARFUMS LLEWELLYN TROUBLE ON THE HORIZON

Stubbornness at the top can ruin an entire company

ON MY RETURN to the States to carry on with our start-up, Cynthia had got us into a televised women's league, conference, of some sort, downtown at the conference center in Indianapolis and had asked that we take Stardust there and sell what we could but also get our name better known among the delegates. Though we had placed a full-page advert in *Vogue* magazine for a couple of months, each placement had cost us $50,000 for one insertion, and we couldn't do many of those as sales couldn't support it yet. Don and I got more than three hundred boxes of the EDP and perfume ready and took it to the conference center. Phillip and Cynthia had tickets to go and were on one of the top tables, partly to spread the word and partly to get better known within the group that she wanted as Stardust buyers.

We lugged tables and fragrance up to the mezzanine floor where the conference was being held and set up the tables with hundreds of cartons stacked up in pyramids outside the main doors, so everyone could see the display; and when we were satisfied with our display, we waited until the conference had finished.

At around half past ten, they began to leave the conference, so Don and I prepared to start selling the fragrance having waited from six thirty for four hours, until the conference was over.

As they all began to file past us, several came up to ask about Stardust; we sold some of the fragrance, though not as much as we would have liked, when we spotted Phillip and Cynthia coming out with a group of people. Both of them walked straight past us and didn't even acknowledge us or the set up that we had carefully made and instead continued walking right past us, saw us, and walked straight on!

Don and I were dumbfounded and were speechless at what had just happened. "Did you see what I saw, Don?" I said, and he looked on at them both, shaking his head.

I was angry, but my controlled anger was nothing compared with Don's. As we prepared to dismantle our display, Don told me, "That's it for me. I am done with these two bozos. Who do they think they are?"

I got worried at what he was saying and asked him if he was serious. He replied that we needed a "come to Jesus" meeting with John Bernard and Tim to discuss what had happened and what was going wrong with the company. Don and I were doing all the work; while Phillip and Cynthia were not following any protocol, seemed uninterested in the fact that we had other people's money invested, and were not even bothering to come in during the week before lunchtime then leaving around 3:00 p.m. having done nothing for the company.

Don began to get us into more stores, and sales began to climb; and for that first year, we were hitting our targets. Cynthia wanted to get more expensive giveaways; but our cash flow was insufficient for what she wanted, which was a very expensive box wrapped in silver with a blue base, which she had priced at over $5 per box. I researched it and found another version that I could get made up for less than $1.50 each and refused to get the more expensive version as it was a freebie and we shouldn't pay that much for it. Cynthia was going around Don and I to get what she wanted and costing the company all of the meager profit we were making at that point. Our costs were still higher than our sales, so we had to be very careful until we became more profitable.

As for me, I was just happy that I had managed to do all that I could to get this company off the ground, and a little hard work was no problem for me as I had been doing this all my life.

Sadly, some people are destined to screw up their chance of a lifetime when their dream is within their grasp!

AUNTIE ONE LAST TIME

To pay our respects to someone who is worthy is never a chore it's a blessing

I TOOK TIME OFF in order to go to see Amanda and Georgia in London as I hadn't seen them for quite a while, and to go to Auntie's ninety-second birthday at Scarborough as I had missed her ninetieth as I was looking for work at that time. They had both learned Reiki and Amanda and Georgia now had a business together and were both Reiki masters.

I didn't understand Reiki. I knew that it was something to do with "grounding" the psyche of people, and that they could heal people suffering from many psychosomatic illnesses. The time at Glastonbury was amazing, just the three of us like old times. I could be their Dad again, their hero, although I didn't feel like that very much. We went for breakfast, lunch, and dinner together and spent all the time we could in each other's company. I love them both as much as is humanly possible, but I am still living far away from them both.

They took me to their small shop, called "Enchanted," in Northfields, West London; and their little shop was thriving. Apart from the Reiki, they were also selling paintings by local artists, angel greeting cards, and many other crystals and "healing" stones to their customers who believed in these things.

Georgia and I went up to Scarborough to meet Auntie for what I knew to be the last time I would ever see my angel. Amanda couldn't come as someone had to run the business, but she was fine with not coming. We met all of the people that had looked after me as a very little boy—Nurse Rosemary, Iris, John, and of course William. Auntie's other relatives were there, and they actually remembered me from my time at Lowestoft.

Georgia loved it with Auntie as she knew what she meant to me, and Auntie really took to Georgia as if she was a granddaughter of her own.

The party was a great success, and John had found an old diary that the nurses had to fill out every night while working for Auntie. He opened up a page dated April 1958 when I was eight years old. He read it our loud to the amusement of all that were there. "Tony was up again all night, talking and singing at the top of his voice. God, I could kill him! Why doesn't he ever sleep like the other children? Thank goodness it is nearly morning at last, and my shift will finish!" I couldn't believe it! There was proof that I did exist somewhere after all. Georgia and I loved our time together as it was precious time, and we treasured every moment.

I left to go back to Sue, Nicky, James, and Ben, and back to the fragrance business, hoping I would see her again but in my heart knowing I probably would not see Auntie ever again.

I wanted to see aunty to say my goodbye and to thank her, by making this trip all the way from Indianapolis, Indiana to Scarborough, and to thank her for all that she had done. I knew this would be the last time we would ever meet.

MOTHERS DAY

Commitment is to 'stay with it' no matter what!

WE HAD OUR first in store deadline to meet for spring the following year—Mother's Day, which in the fragrance world was second in sales to Christmas. We began planning in November for a March shipping deadline, plenty of time; and Phillip, Cynthia, Don, and I with Tim sitting in set up a plan for a new product line of gift sets, comprising a body lotion, bath gel, and moisturizing lotion spray. This would involve having some of our fifty thousand bottles "frosted" to differentiate the body spray from our EDPs.

Don headed up the meeting, and we delegated the tasks to be completed. Phillip was to complete the formulations; Cynthia had to complete the verbiage for the side of the tubes and small pamphlet inserts for the packaging. The inserts were to explain the basis of each product and the fragrances, etc., and would be inserted into each Mother's Day gift box.

My task was to get all the components sourced, designed, purchased, and manufactured and the packaging of the gift boxes that were to hold the three-item gift set containing a body lotion, a bath lotion in new silver and blue tubes, and a body mist spray in an opaque version of our EDP completed and shipped by early February.

Don would take care of the "sell into" our stores, which now totaled around fifty doors. We were still short of our goal of 200 of the 350 top tier stores.

My part went smoothly, and we met several times over the next few months to follow up on the progress and to ensure that all was moving ahead on schedule and according to plan. For Don and I, this was exciting; Cynthia, however, had done nothing on her written piece as yet, but we still had two months yet before we would need them.

I found a great company for the new tubes in Barcelona, Spain; and Phillip wanted to agree the "Pan Tone" of the silver that the tubes would be colored. I was working with an English guy in Barcelona, so business discussions between the two of us were easy.

Phillip had finally agreed a color and signed off on the sample in late November, but now we needed more cash to manage the up-front costs of the purchasing. I got together with Don to put together an estimated sell though and cost/profit summary, which if all went well would show good profit for this, our first, Mother's Day gift set. The first sample tubes came in during December with an eight-week delivery and were made to Phillip's color requirements.

Philip decided to change the color to a darker shade of silver as he had changed his mind. I really thought that he was being belligerent as the color didn't make a difference to the product or the display inside the boxes and was exactly as he had signed off.

We were getting tired of the silly and unnecessarily finicky behavior of the Primes who now the hard work was on in actually running our company still didn't bother to come in to the office before eleven thirty or much before lunchtime, if at all, and did nothing constructive for us when they did show up. Phillip insisted that the color of the tubes be changed, so we incurred costs associated with the change and our supplier although trying to help was confused as to why we made the change as production had begun.

In the meantime, Cynthia had insisted that we purchase two hundred and fifty gift boxes, which were to house a small phial of fragrance set in a card as well as a small booklet of poems. Our problem was the cost that for her version was to be nearly $6 per box, which Don, myself, and Tim warned her was far too expensive and would take us into the red.

I refused to sign the purchase order and instead had another made, which looked identical and was an in-stock item, so was very cheap to buy. It was a three-inch square box with a silver top with our dark blue logo on it with a blue bottom.

Don, Tim, and I agreed to purchase the low-cost boxes at less than a dollar each as they were already manufactured and were a standard stocked item box. We added our logo on the front for a few cents each from a local printer; and, "pronto," we were ready to go. In the meantime, Cynthia had gone around our necessary but tight purchasing system and had ordered her boxes directly with no money to pay for them, no permission, and we were heading for a nightmare. She actually got Phillip to sign the purchase order without us knowing.

Despite the fact that things were going south for my dream company, I had to give it all I could since I was fully committed when we made our investments.

A TURNING POINT IN PARFUMS LLEWELLYN

Stubbornness makes little sense!

It was now January, and we had four weeks left to get everything together for the ship date of the end of February in order to make the in-store deadline of third week in March.

We had another planning meeting with Don, Phillip, Cynthia and me and we used our production timeline on the whiteboard to check that each of us had completed our tasks. The timeline had been placed on the board back in November when we took the decision to have a new product line ready for Mother's Day on May 11.

My part had been delayed because Phillip had changed his mind about the tube color, but the formulations had been completed. I couldn't get the tubes finished because we were still awaiting Cynthia's verbiage to be written, which by now because of the tightness of the timeline was too late. I had gone ahead and sent off some spin to go onto the tubes, so we wouldn't miss this deadline, even though hers was the simplest of all the tasks.

Don asked Cynthia to let us see her wording for the new packaging, and she told us that hadn't written a single word as she didn't have the time. We sat there in stunned silence, but Don was having none of it. Don turned to Cynthia and said to her, "Cynthia, you knew the timeline. It's been on that board since November. We all agreed it together, and I have now placed my reputation on the line by promising that we would have the gift sets completed by the end of February, and it is now February.

Why haven't you even written a single thing?" We waited for her reply, so he asked her again, while Phillip just sat there saying nothing. Instead of answering him, she just ignored the question and started humming a hymn and closed her eyes and began rocking to her tune back and forth with her head bowed.

I was absolutely furious and could see all my hard work and investment money going down the drain at this moment in time. I looked at Don, and we both sat there in stunned silence.

I asked her, "Cynthia, did you go ahead and purchase those expensive boxes that we agreed not to buy because of our limited finances?" I got no reply, but she carried on humming and rocking back and forth on the seat like a child would when it knows it's done wrong. The boxes had all arrived along with the boxes we did in fact agree to purchase.

Don and I left the office and went over the road for a drink as it was now gone 5:00 p.m. "I think we are fucked, Don. And if we are, it's my money not any of theirs that will be gone, and I'm not going down without a fight." I told him of being dissed at the opening and being left out of the news article when I had all the hard work in getting the company off the ground, making the financial projections, and setting up the investor presentations before Don had come on board. He told me then that he had been very aware of Phillip and Cynthia's selfishness regarding the company and had seen much of this but couldn't understand why. "Did you ever fall out with them?" he asked. And I replied, "No never, not once, in fact it was me who got the company the first funding!"

I told him that Phillip was blaming him for the lack of sales, and Don told me that one of the main reasons we did not have more doors than we did was because the price points were way too high. "I knew it!" I said. "I went to Nordstrom and Von Maur to look at the price points for all of their fragrances, and they were all in the mid seventy-dollar range." I asked Don to get me the sales statistics of a leading fragrance, which was the number 1 selling line; and if he could do that, I would analyze the data for an upcoming board meeting scheduled for three weeks' time.

We were in a precarious position now and had limited funds to get things moving forward. He agreed to get me the data. "They are going to cause us to fail," he said, and I agreed with him. Later that evening, Tim came in to join us in Nicky Blaine's, which was our "early doors" venue for an end-of-work drink. We told Tim of the issues that were going wrong. He asked us both, "Would either of you like to run the company?" I answered absolutely not but added that Phillip and Cynthia were a liability to us in their total lack of responsiveness, fiduciary responsibility, and leadership. I felt sick to my stomach at what I was seeing and kept thinking back to what Tom Binford had told me and for the first time could see the end of Parfums Llewellyn.

A week later, Don gave me a large computer readout of the sales data I had asked for. I grabbed it and began immediately analyzing the data.

I worked once again right through the night and made up a spreadsheet of all the data, preparing it into a chart to be presented to the board the following week. I was amazed at what I saw. Out of thirty-seven products or Sku's, only four made up more than 85 percent of their sales; all four were refillables, and all were priced at below $72.

I e-mailed the data to Don, and he asked that I present this data to the board the following week as he felt his days were numbered because of the lack of sales.

During our first financial year, we had made it to second place in national sales as the second most purchased fragrance in the United States, but that was short-lived as we were now struggling with repeat business because of the high price that Phillip and Cynthia had set for the EDP and perfume line.

The problem was that we had relied on Phillip and Cynthia for both the price points of our line as well as the type of bottle. Phillip had ordered all "crimp-top" bottles that could not be refilled. In other words, when a bottle was finished with, it had to be thrown away; and I knew from Sue that many women like to get either something off the next purchase or to be able to refill their fragrance bottles.

The purpose of the board meeting was to get enough money for the completion of the launch of our new product line and for our salaries. All of our investors were there, and Don began the overall presentation ending with the fact that our price points were wrong. He asked me to come up to present my analysis, which I did and ended with two conclusions. The first conclusion was that we were far too high priced to get a second buy through of existing customers, and second that we did not have refillable bottles. This meant that every customer had to pay a second far too high price for our product.

They all looked to Phillip; and he said that for our fragrance, the prices were good, telling them that it was Don's job to get us into more doors. We were at a stale mate, but we got the additional funds for the completion of the Mother's Day gift sets.

It was during that board meeting that Tim and John revealed that they had got the final financial statements of the Primes' former company, My Choice, and that there had been moneys owed to suppliers as well as the IRS who had filed an injunction and now had a lien on their property. So much for honesty!

The tubes arrived very late because of the color change, and I had to scramble to get all of the hundreds of empty tubes and the lotions hand-carried to a contract filling company in New Jersey to begin the job of filling. I had to work through the night alongside their production staff, mostly Mexican, to help the get the job completed on time. Midday following the job was complete, and all of the tubes were filled. I now had to take ten huge boxes back to Indianapolis.

I came back to Indy with ten huge cartons of filled tubes that I had to lug to the airport in New Jersey and then from Indianapolis airport to our eighth floor warehouse to begin assembling the 1,100 gift boxes, which had to be completed.

I asked Phillip and Cynthia for help but got none! I was at the warehouse packing the 1,100 boxes by myself as I wanted to make sure that all went out on time. It was funny though; the whole warehouse was filled on every surface of all of the long tables we had with 1,100 empty gift boxes, which I had to place two tubes and a frosted bottle of body mist and a small "PL" logo sticker to seal each box. I started work after I arrived back from New Jersey and worked all night to get the task done on time. I was dog tired but felt I had to get this job done if we were to succeed with the launch.

By Monday, everything was ready to ship to all of the doors we now had, and I began to work on a small conversion to our "crimp-top" bottles to make them into screw-top versions.

I made a design for a small brushed silver top that would crimp onto our bottles with a small rubber seal that wouldn't leak. I then researched all of our suppliers to find a cheap clear glass bottle that would hold 50-milliliter or 1.7-ounce of refillable fragrance. I found one; and it was perfect and would cost us only $5.25 for each complete bottle with packaging, which we could sell for around $50 to $65, not too shabby profit.

I had a design and engineering company on the north side of town to make up and test my design, and they said it would work without leaking. I also designed a small cartridge based 10-milliliter purse spray that we could present with a beautiful perfume spray plus two extra push in refills. It was fantastic idea and had never been done before. This would be a low cost spray option and would enable our market to have the EDP in a purse spray.

In effect, I had developed a very acceptable solution to our problem that we could work with that would be at the right price and highly profitable for us.

I told Don, and he asked that I show Phillip the concept so when Phillip came in a few days later, as he now seldom came in at all. I told him I had something to show him.

As I showed Phillip the concept and explained what it could do for us, in converting the crimp-top bottles into simple screw-top version, he got up from the chair and left the office with me in midsentence, throwing out over his shoulder as he reached the door, "it won't work, and I don't like it." I watched him leave, knowing that this company could never ever succeed with him in it.

Don came in the following week, and we found that we didn't have enough cash to pay our wages! I was sitting behind Don when he asked Tim where his wages were and was told there was no more cash. I saw his neck, as I sat behind him, get bright red as he got so furious at not being paid. "That's it for me," he said, "I'm suing them for everything." And he walked out never to return.

As for me, I had given the company eighteen months without pay in getting the company launched and invested more than $100,000; and now we were broke, having spent all of the invested money for the most part in fifty thousand of the wrong bottles!. I felt empty inside.

My dream had gone up in perfumed smoke, and my hopes dashed to the ground; but I felt that I had to work on to help the investors and to do what I could for my company as they had invested in the company partly because of me.

After another two months, I stopped coming in at all and told Tim and John that in my opinion Phillip and Cynthia were the root cause of our demise, and that neither of them had the experience stamina or mental capacity or ability to actually work in the company that they had convinced us all to help them get started up.

I left some three months later and had to begin legal action to get my three months back pay as there was no way I was giving them that as well. I saw an attorney, and we filed the lawsuit against the company two weeks later.

Tim came to see me after a few months and told me the board had looked at my numbers again and had checked for themselves and agreed that I was "right on the money." They asked me through Tim if I would come back to run the company as president and COO; and if I did, that they would all support me financially to finish the job. The down side was that they could only pay me half of what I needed to keep my house and pay my bills. I had already used up my severance pay, giving them my unpaid time. It would mean selling our house and moving into a flat; and I now had a tough decision to make. I considered everything—how I had been treated by the Primes; how Phillip would still be the majority owner and therefore in a position to still ruin the company as he had done with his limited knowledge of the industry; how he had led us into having a great product but in the wrong price and with the wrong bottles, which was the most significant problem we now faced.

I had given it all I had and had even had the insult of having to pay out another $37,500 in taxes because the recommendation of a tax attorney, that Phillip had told me to see, which had also proven to be a complete waste of time; and though I followed his advice to the letter, I had to pay tax on my investment. To that point, I had put in more than any of the other investors and had done the most to get this company started, which at the beginning I was happy to do. I gave in total eighteen months unpaid work and had worked the hardest, and had remained fully committed throughout to get it going plus start-up cash.

I told Tim I couldn't do it financially, and that I couldn't work with the Primes. And as long as they were involved in any capacity, the company would unfortunately fail.

Tim asked that I take time to reconsider and eventually reluctantly I agreed, and we parted ways. I kept in touch with Tim when I needed references, and he was very happy to do so.

Some nine months later, Tim called me to tell me that he had set up a key meeting with a sales agency that wanted to promote Stardust into thousands of stores at the midlevel market, which was what Don and I had wanted to do; and he had arranged for Phillip to go with him for the meeting.

They met at the downtown office; and Phillip, true to form, left his car on the circle with the engine running and his keys in the car. Needless to say, after the police had been called to get into Phillip's car, they missed the flight, the meeting, and the important deal was off. Tim told me that that was the final straw. Phillip was banned from having any more function in the company, banned from the offices, and was no longer a president or anything within Parfums Llewellyn.

I had to laugh at that as Tim, like me, had done so much and had been let down same as me! The company was sold on to another fragrance house, so at least the name Stardust continued on. And as for the rest of us, we all moved on. I got my money back, well, most of what I had invested; so really, I lost nothing at all, just some time and a lot of effort.

I did everything to make this company succeed but the line between prejudice and truth in decisions involving people of different religions, race, creed or culture is thin, but when I made my final decision it was based purely on performance and I was fine with this.

LESSONS LEARNED

Hindsight is 20/20 but it's what we learn looking through our rear-view mirror that is sometimes more important

I LEARNED A VALUABLE lesson in that hard work alone doesn't cut it; that in a start-up business, everyone must work their hardest and not leave it up to only a few. The most important lesson was not to be blind-sided by someone's apparent and highly visible "faith" with open prayers and little else in the form of, "doing instead of saying." In other words, I will only trust people who "walk the walk, don't just talk the talk," especially when faith was used for the purpose of getting what they wanted, which they both had been guilty of whether they intended it or not. And I really think they may have meant well.

I was so concerned at my deep feeling of dislike for both Phillip and Cynthia, still believing that they were both basically good people though misguided in their beliefs that I went to see my pastor Greg Ponchot to ask him if my feelings were wrong against the Primes.

I sat with Greg a few weeks later and told him of the whole thing from start to finish and especially my feeling of being deceived by them both as I am certain that all of the other investors had felt. His reaction was very clear. "No," he said, "you are not wrong to feel angry. What is the basis of your anger? Was it that you had not succeeded with the company or was it that you had been deceived?"

I took no time in responding, "I was deceived" I said. "Completely taken in by their apparent religious beliefs, their prayers at work and at meetings and I believed them to be a good investment mainly because of that."

Greg told me that he had been brought up in a family of missionaries in Africa, and that both his parents were missionaries that had planted churches and started building schools. He went on to explain that many of the local "so-called" preachers drank heavily and were notorious womanizers on Saturday nights yet breathed fire and brimstone of bigoted righteousness from the pulpit on Sundays while adorned with the trappings of being a religious leader. He told me that these were often traits of such people that wanted to demonstrate their fervor to others as a way of becoming accepted.

The company was sold, and I got my investment back over time in the form of tax deductions each year for my lost investment. So philosophically, I didn't lose that much; and I did learn that one business I am not interested in was the fragrance business. Time to close the door and move on, I was not feeling good about the lost chance, but I knew that I had done all that I could do.

Determination and skill sometimes isn't enough but when it comes time to make the decision to move on, do it and don't look back. I also learned from this that when I was offered the chance to turn my company around, which I knew, I could easily do, I knew that I would be facing the same stubborn attitude at some point in the future from the same people that had brought us to this point! If they were still 51% owners, so, the deal was definitely no go.

JAMES THE DANCER

James is very much like me; determined to make it.

SINCE HIS EARLY days at school, James had since age five years old decided that he wanted to dance; and dance he did, right through school and on to college. When James was only eight years old, in 1999, he was dancing for the Ballet International, a professional dance troupe based in Indianapolis. The role he got was as a party boy in the story, to dance on stage at Indianapolis's Murat theater downtown in their production *The Nutcracker*, which they performed every Christmas.

He did that for two years before landing the principal role as the lead boy part of Fritz. This was a fantastic achievement for him as he auditioned for it against over fifty other boys. Each Christmas, we took many of his friends from school to see him perform; and when we went to the opening night that first year, we were so proud of what he had achieved.

The rehearsals started in October and involved either Sue or myself or both of us taking him downtown to the rehearsal studios every Saturday morning. Although he had been in many, many competitions while learning, what was to be his trade, at the Dance Refinery in Greenwood, this was a professional validation of all his hard work.

I should mention that James was a kind quiet boy at school and had to put up with the "jocks" teasing and bullying him all through his primary and middle school; but instead of complaining to us, he dealt with it for years by himself and stood up to these ridiculous bullies. We eventually found out about it when he came home one day after putting up with it for many semesters. He was angry and certainly not allowing himself to continue to be victimized. We took him to school and made a formal complaint to the headmistress of the school. She reacted immediately by summoning the boys' parents to the school and informing them that the school was considering legal action against them. Needless to say, the school, Center Grove, had a very strong choir and performing arts program in place and had in fact won the state championships for seven years in a row; this kind of intolerance could never be accepted.

We were very proud that James had managed to deal with this for such a long time and had not wanted us to interfere. However, that is what we are here for, and we could not and would not let him deal with this any longer without our help.

James was very talented and had every intention of going on to college to become a professional dancer and had never swayed from his dream. So it was up to Sue and I to make sure that we supported him in his desire to be a professional dancer.

The school made it clear that the behavior would never be tolerated; and if they did one more thing or stepped out of line one more time, they would be taking legal action against the parents. Wow, that was positive action. James was very well liked by all but these few stupid jocks of redneck parents that knew no other way but to be completely intolerant of anything or anyone that was different than them. Every summer, we went to Myrtle Beach for a national dance contest in which contestants from all over the United States and Canada took place in four days of dance contests.

All of this plus the many other contests and recitals, that he regularly took part in, made him very confident indeed; and he loved being on stage in any performance.

If 10% of all the words that we say to our children takes hold in their character then they should be OK, no matter what, as we will have given them some of the tools they need for their own success.

JAMES AND THE PRIMA DONNAS

Being comfortable with who we are gives us confidence for all to see.

It WAS AT THE opening night's performance party after his first lead role, at nine years old, in *The Nutcracker*, that Sue and I were standing at the bar talking to the show's director when we watched a young James kneeling at a large coffee table while all of the cast, including the two stars, the prima donna ballerina, who was Russian, and the lead man who was also Russian, all were sitting next to James who was completely at ease talking to them; and they were listening to him. As we were watching him, he began to show them card tricks, and they were all together laughing with James.

It was one of those moments when I knew that this was where James belonged, and I turned to Sue and told her, "Look at that. James fits in perfectly with all the cast, and they are treating him as an equal."

Sue looked and agreed. "He's always been happy when he is in the stage surroundings and in a show." We both realized that this is probably what he would do when he left school; he would become a dancer! Many of his friends came to watch him, and I found it amusing to see their faces as they all watched him perform at that theater. They had never ever seen a live performance; and for them, entertainment was through the TV and was never live. They were mesmerized at his performance, and I was mesmerized at their expressions of intent focus taking it all in. The stage show of *The Nutcracker* was brilliant for them as it had the right mix of special effects and dance, and the costumes were amazing to see.

After the show, James came out, and he was surrounded like a rock star. He loved it but didn't act the big star. I told him to never act out being a star as that would eventually lead to disaster. He remained as the lead boy for three years with the Ballet International, which was a great accomplishment and also was great stagecraft practice. He also went to Los Angeles with the Ballet International on tour, where he called Sue from the Prada store while pretending to be Nicole Kidman putting on a very plausible Australian accent, which Sue completely believed. Clever little bugger!

We supported James by taking him to all of the dance recitals and shows all over the country. He had decided long ago that he was going to be a dancer and had never ever changed his plans. He would dance until he was too old, probably around thirty! Then he would have his own studio and teach other children all that he learned in a lifetime of dance.

If our children have a plan to succeed, then to a parent it doesn't matter if the stated plan or another plan succeeds; as long as they have a vision to succeed in whatever they want to do.
Vision drives ability!

SEPTEMBER ELEVENTH 2001

The moment that changed the world was to change mine also!

There were several students, in the training center, of the company I was now running called MasterPro. The company specialized in high level IT training. We had recently opened a second office in Cleveland and we had one on the north side of Indianapolis.

The students were using the computers, as usual during the day, and all of the sales staff were in the front sales office each doing their fifty calls a day tele sales.

Several of the thirty computers in the training room were on CNN and other news channels that morning and were showing a burning building in New York. The students gradually began to stop what they were doing and began to watch the events unfolding in New York as we switched several of the other training computers over to various news channels.

CNN had the most up-to-date information; and as we turned up the sound, the building was one of the Twin World Trade Towers. They were saying that an airliner had crashed into the building, and at that point, we all thought it had been a terrible accident. As we were watching, unsure of what we were seeing; the building up around two-thirds of the way up the very tall skyscraper. I had been up the World Trade Center with Lars on one of our trips to New York, and it had 127 floors. We continued to watch the news unfold as an unbelievable event happened right before our eyes, as a second passenger jet flew straight into the second tower right in front of the news cameras. We watched in stunned silence as the plane disappeared completely into the tower and burst into flames.

We all looked at each other, not knowing how to react, what to think, or even if what we were watching was real. It became obvious as we continued to watch that the events were very real as we saw people running and screaming at the scene. Each of us had our own horror as we were watching the flames continue to burn in both of the buildings.

The camera was on the ground looking up, and the flames grew bigger, and the smoke coming from the buildings was billowing out across New York. We could see people running in the street and could hear the hundreds of sirens from fire and police emergency responders. We continued watching as the news began to unfold that these were terrorist actions and were deliberately aimed at the Twin Towers in the height of daytime work when the buildings were full of office workers.

We then heard that a second plane had been flown into the Pentagon, and we were now all talking about how many more there would be. One of my colleagues said that this was another Pearl Harbor right in the middle of New York. I knew as I was watching that this would change everything in our world from that moment onward.

Things were getting worse and worse as the cameras rolled on at the scene, which was complete chaos. The flame and smoke was getting worse and worse, and now we could only look on in horror as there were desperate people jumping out of the upper floor windows with now no way down below the flames that were below them. It was a scene out of hell as people on the ground were all looking up to the growing smoke coming from both buildings.

Then as we continued to watch, I called Sue to see if she had seen the news, so she turned it on at work as well. Next, there was a huge rumbling sound as one of the towers began
to slide down itself as smoke billowed up like a huge explosion. The first tower had collapsed in a massive cloud of smoke; and as we watched in abject horror, the second tower began to collapse as well. People were running screaming and crying at what was happening. A camera over
the other side of the Hudson River showed the huge plume of smoke drifting over to the east across the now partially hidden New York's skyline; and it looked like a third world war had begun.

The plume of black and dark gray smoke hung low, below the high-rise skyscrapers, making the surreal scene look like a movie; but it was very and all too real. The news media had shown the whole thing over and over again, and we were mesmerized at the constant streaming of data and supposition about who may have done it and all the while we still didn't know how to react as we continued to see the events. Much of the original camera work had been edited not to show the poor people jumping out of the windows, which I was very happy never to see again . . . ever.

That afternoon people were calling in to tell us that they wouldn't be in for the training sessions. I called the office in Cleveland and got no answer as they had all gone home in shock. We carried on that day, but no one felt like calling their sales leads; and when they did make calls, no one answered. I checked as to how things were at the Cleveland office; but that late in the day, around 3:00 p.m., no one answered as they too had all gone home early like so many others early in shock to be with their families. I felt like we were the last ones left in a nightmarish dream where the world had stopped, and we were left to carry on when everyone else had gone. I personally was not as shocked as my American friends as my background in London had always been for the past twenty years listening to the terrorist bombings with the IRA with attacks both in England and Ireland. The shock all over the United States was palpable, in the streets, in the shops, in the gas stations, everywhere.

Later on, we were told that not only had another plane been flown right into the Pentagon, but yet another had crashed into a field out east. That flight we were told had crashed as a result of some very brave passengers who took the plane back from the terrorists who had hijacked it and who had the apparent intent on flying into the White House. It kept getting worse and worse!

This one attack on the USA was to change everything throughout the world.

PRICE GOUGING AT THE GAS STATIONS

I saw firsthand of the greed inherent in the culture of the oil industry.

ONE OF MY sales staff, Tom, who lived in Greenwood, was so shocked that he told me he couldn't drive home in case any bombs dropped on Indianapolis or Greenwood. I told him that it was highly unlikely, but there was no calming him. I wasn't bothered about anything locally as who the hell would bomb Greenwood!

Outside our office, there was a gas station; and we were watching as the price of a gallon went up every ten minutes until it went from $1.25 a gallon to over $6.75 a gallon, for absolutely no reason except that people were lined up at the gas pumps "topping off" as they were scared stiff that gas would suddenly stop flowing from the pumps. All of these were ordinary people's reactions out of shock at what they had seen on the news.

Gas stations had long lines of cars desperate to fill up for no reason at all except that they had reacted and were making irrational decisions. I agreed to take Tom, the Greenwood-based salesman, home and to pick him up the following day if he felt like coming in. Poor Tom really believed that there would be bombs going off all over the country and was too shocked to drive.

As I took him home, we could see hardly any cars on the road by 5:00 p.m., and that the lines at the pumps were still long. I dropped him off at his house and told him to call me if he wasn't coming in to the office the following day. I looked at all of the gas stations all the way home; and they had all put up their prices, gouging people while they were in shock. It was disgusting! I couldn't believe the callousness of the oil companies doing this on a day like 9/11.

The following day and many days after 9/11 was extremely quiet in sales, and I hoped that it would pass. Many of the students that we had recently signed on had rescinded and cancelled their courses, wanting money back, and we were hemorrhaging as we needed a constant stream of new students to cover the weekly payroll and other costs. As the weeks went on, sales still didn't pick up, and we were getting very short on cash; but with the new store in Cleveland and the loans for all of the computers and furniture, which had to be paid as well as the exorbitant fees for the software license that we had to pay each month, we were now getting into financial trouble.

I had no idea, when I was watching the horrific events on 9/11, that the potential students upon which our company was based would dry up to such a level that we would not be able to survive. As the weeks drew on, we were only getting 10 percent of the required base sales amount we needed to make the business break even, let alone profitable.

I realized that there were probably hundreds if not thousands of companies that would be negatively affected by 9/11 as we were, but the stories in the news were only about the immediate damage, the hunt for Al-Qaeda, and the ongoing reparation and cleanup of the now called Ground Zero.

I saw that catastrophic events affect everyone. Some go into shock and do nothing at all, while others try to ignore it, as a way of personal survival, pretending that all is still ok. But, this 'corporate greed' manifesting itself at a time like this at the gas pumps was the most despicable and shameful event alongside of the 911 disaster.

ANOTHER CHANGE

Losing everything we have worked for is tough but it's also a time to make life altering adjustments.

I KNEW THAT WITHOUT work, after I had finished with Parfums Llewellyn, we would be forced into bankruptcy; but compared with the horrific events in New York, my problems were nothing at all.

For me though and my family, it was everything. I had no job and had to start looking all over again, once again online from predawn to late at night. I spent another twelve hours or more each day sending out resumes, hundreds and hundreds of them. After seven months of no work, I took a job selling cars on a car sales lot and in February when it was freezing. That year, I had seven jobs while trying to make ends meet. I sold Living Trusts to old people, having to drive all over Indiana using what little income we had on gasoline. I worked with Sue selling mortgages, or trying to, and eventually got an idea for a new company of my own.

My new company was in the optical business. We were building small desktop computer systems with a high-resolution camera mounted on top and a software system for taking pictures of a person wearing a new pair of glasses that they may want to buy. The system allowed them to take six pictures with five new frames and one showing their existing frame for a comparison.

My system allowed each person to wear their own glasses while trying on new ones and the five high-resolution images captured on the flat high-res screen showed them what they looked like wearing the different new frames. The system worked excellently; and with the help of a friend who was well known in the optical and eyewear field, I began to sell my software system into opticians businesses all over Indiana. For me, however, and my family, although my fledgling company was climbing in sales, the income was not enough to keep from filing for bankruptcy.

9/11 had happened on September 11, 2001; and by June 2002, we filed chapter 13 as an effort to keep from losing our home. I called the mortgage company to ask them if I could make interest payments only until I found another job. The woman I talked to said she would talk to her supervisor, and I had a conference call with her and her supervisor. I repeated to him what had happened, after I had explained our position and offered to pay interest payments in the interim until I found a new job. He told me, "You pay the mortgage or you lose your house." I kept trying and told him that this had been our home for ten years, and my job loss was as a direct result of the 9/11 attacks. I also offered again that if the house stayed in foreclosure, then his mortgage company would get far less than it was worth selling at a sheriff's auction.

What I was offering made complete sense to anyone, but he was completely unmoved and he simply repeated his message that I either pay the mortgage and the months owing immediately or lose my house.

The lady that I originally spoke to stayed on the line after he had gone and told me that maybe my church could help as she had seen this many times over the past months since 9/11.She at least wished me luck, and I knew I would lose the house as we simply couldn't pay the mortgage in full.

It was probably the worst feeling I had ever experienced, to lose everything I had built up for my family, my house, my beautiful dream fulfilling house, and the company I was trying and succeeding to build up. The events of 9/11 had affected my family financially in a very, very bad way; though I knew that at least no one in my family had died as they had at ground zero, I felt that we were at least far better off than those poor families.

Once again, the open greed that was prevalent within the banking and mortgage industries, even after 911 that I personally witnessed here, was to affect the entire global banking and financial industries less than a decade later. As one man said, "All that evil needs to succeed is for good men to do nothing." This was just the very tip of the iceberg of disaster, that was to follow, motivated again by greed.

Idiots can't be negotiated with.

AUNTY PASSES AWAY

Some people we are lucky to have met leave a lasting legacy way beyond their life, and we who are left behind are better people for having known them.

ONE SUNDAY AFTERNOON, in 2002, John Bleby called, telling us that Auntie had died of a brain aneurism. I was very sad, of course; but Auntie had been preparing me for this day for many years. I was happy for her and happy that she had done so much good for so many orphaned and terminally ill children. She had adopted William and Beatrice as well, providing the both with a home of their own when they had nothing at all except a life in and out of foster homes. She had also taken in terminally ill children to nurse them and to make their so short time with us here in earth as happy as possible, knowing that they would pass away before their time. These were the children at the bottom of the pile that no one wanted or really cared about, that is, except for Auntie.

As for me, she had asked that I not be sad at all as she had done all that she intended to do with her life and was ready.

I didn't cry at the sad news but celebrated her amazing life and quietly thought about all that she had given me, her trips to be with me for my weddings, to both Jane and Sue, and her visit to see me when I got my apprenticeship papers at Taylor Woodrow. I thought of her visit to help Sue in Brussels when James was born, and I thought of the hundreds of phone conversations I had with her from the States just to let her know that I cared about her and that she was never far from my thoughts.

She told me over and over again not to be sad when she "goes to the fairies" as she put it, and I wasn't. She was after all, in the words of Churchill, "The stuff that Britain was made of." Auntie is buried in a small church, in Scorby, just outside Scarborough; and I have a photograph of her sitting among her flowers in a blaze of colors in her garden, smiling at me in the picture It makes me happy to know that she is just fine! It made me happy to write this about her and in this way to thank her for all she had done. After all, as I said, Auntie is, and always will be, just fine.

I was happy for my aunt in that she was able to improve so many young lives

A DIVINE INTERVENTION

When you seek divine intervention and sincerely ask for help, you will receive it, that's for certain.

WE WERE NOW left in the position of filing for chapter 13 as I had lost my job, again; and we now had no means to pay back the mortgage. So, although we struggled to keep payments up, we had to then file chapter 7, which was to lose everything. We now had to find somewhere else to live, and I was still building my new little business Optasia; but we had no funds at all for any down payment on an apartment. I started to look for new places to live, and we found a great house not far from our home, which had recently become available for rent.

It was now that it finally hit me while driving back from making an Optasia sales call to an optometrist thirty miles south of Greenwood. Sue had told me a shadow had appeared on her breast after having a mammogram, a week before; and as if that wasn't bad enough, we had no money even for a rental property down payment, and I was struggling with the upcoming move from our home. As I was driving back, I stopped the car after Sue told me her news; and everything hit me at once—Sue, the bankruptcy, losing everything, and no money to find somewhere else to live. I began to shout at the top of my voice, angry at God, blaming God for allowing everything to happen that had happened to me all throughout my life. I looked up and shouted, "What have I ever done to you? I've believed in you all my life. I've defended my faith in you to friends that don't believe in you. I've been the best I can be, and this is what you throw at me.

Throw some more at me. Let me have all you can throw 'cause I can handle all that and far more than even you can ever throw at me. You don't give a damn about us here on earth. You're too high up to ever care." I was very angry at all that had happened, and I knew that I had to show a brave face in front of my family and friends in order that they would see a positive me, not a negative me.

I got out of the car to calm down and get ready for whatever God could throw my way next; and believe me, I was giving God the worst evil eye I could muster up, glaring up at the clouds. The gray stormy clouds matched how I felt, but I would deal with it as I had dealt with everything else before this by keeping on moving forward. The owner of the house that we wanted to rent, Rick, had called Sue and asked her to speak to me that night to see if we were going to take his house or not.

I remembered a line from what the mortgage representative had said before she put me onto her unfeeling boss when she said, "The church can help you." So I decided to call Greg Ponchot to see if the church could help us, and I explained everything to him. That's an easy fix for us. He said, "We will pay the deposit and the first month's rental payment for you if it means keeping your family under one roof. As for Sue, I'll hold a prayer meeting for her tonight, and she will be fine." "Who is the owner of the house?" he asked, and I told him it was Rick who was a former pastor in Greenwood. "Rick"! he said. "I know him well. He was a pastor same as me. Then that's fine. We'll take care of everything for you. Go 'round as he asked and meet with him tonight at 7:00 p.m. and tell him to call us."

I told Sue the great news and all that Greg had told me. She called Rick back, and we agreed to go 'round to the house half an hour later. Rick had called Greg Ponchot in the meantime, and Greg had confirmed that everything was fixed.

When we arrived at the house, we all went into the kitchen, and Rick was very happy to confirm that my church had intervened. "I spoke to Greg," he said, "and he said to me he is known to us." It's strange that I knew for definite that on hearing that one phrase, "he is known to us," that it was a message for me to understand that a far bigger force was at work for me. I believed that a normal line would have been. We know Tony, and we can help; but the phrase used was "he is known to us," as if I was known to others as well. Yet in the church, I really only knew Greg. I was being given a message loud and clear, "All you had to do was ask!"

We had agreed on the moving date, which was a week later, I spoke to Sue on the way home. "Sue, do you see what just happened? Until I called the church, we were in a real mess. Now in one phone call, everything is fixed. We have a house, that has all the space we need, as well as the fact that all of our furniture will match the décor. It's as if we have just seen a miracle." I told her also that Greg had offered a prayer for her results to be negative and that he was certain that she would be fine. I asked her point-blank, "If the result is negative tomorrow and we have the house, will you believe that a miracle has just happened for us?" She said, "Yes, I will believe that."

I then told her, "Sue, never ever forget what happened today and how easily it was fixed because of my faith and the help that the church gave us.

Don't forget this." The following morning, Sue had a call from her doctor that the results of the biopsy were negative and that the sample tested had proved to be nonmalignant. She now had to believe in the truth there is a God and that God had intervened very directly to help us in our hour of need.

Some who read this may not yet believe that God exists, but for me there is no other truth.

A "BLUSTERY" DAY FOR MOVING

Nature can change things in minutes and a tornado is just the tool.

WE HAD TWO very close friends who lived on the same edition as us, Ros and Tim who were both English and had moved over around nine years after us, but had bought a home just down the road from us. We got along great; and they became very close friends, having two children, Ollie and Amber, who went to the same school as Nicky and James. On the morning that we were moving into our rental home, there was a wind brewing up, not that we really noticed it as Ros and I were too busy moving some of our things into the new home that day.

I had hired a big box van, large enough to get our belongings in, and we began to load up our most important things out of the house and into the large van. By midmorning, the wind had really blown up, and the van was beginning to sway, but we were far too busy to really notice. I did look up at the sky and noticed that the clouds were moving in different directions, not a real good sign, but as I said no worries at all since we were still too busy to stop packing. After another hour of loading up, the warning siren went off at the fire station just a mile away, and I said to Ros, "What a stupid time to be testing the tornado siren. I thought they tested it at 11:00 a.m. normally." And she agreed, but as I said, we had more important things to do.

Well, as luck would have it, after we had got in as much as we could, we closed up the van and drove out of our edition and on to Morgantown Road. As we turned out from the front entrance and onto Morgantown Road, we noticed that all the trees were blown over everywhere. We drove slowly along to see damage everywhere we looked.

Apparently, we had just missed a tornado that had, just a few minutes ago, touched down just outside our edition, and the siren was for real!

I began to drive, carefully maneuvering around the many fallen trees now strewn across the road and said to Ros as I looked in my rearview mirror, "I bet all those cars and people following behind me actually think I know what I'm doing." And as I looked in my rearview mirror again, there was a long line of cars following slowly behind me. I told her, "I don't know what I'm doing at all, like an Englishman has any experience with tornados." And we laughed.

The thing is that it was very real, and it had torn roofs off and blown over some huge trees. As I drove on up and over the hill, the damage there was even worse as several houses that came into view were destroyed.

People were standing around, looking at all of the debris of branches and pieces of houses strewn around. We slowly drove on through, looking at the utter devastation all around us and hoped that it had missed our new home just a few hundred yards on. Fortunately, it had missed our new home and had in fact skipped across the edition where our new street was to be. The day was a Friday, and the following day we had around ten friends to help us move in so we could get it done by Sunday night.

The new rental house was perfect, and all of our belongings fitted in just fine and even went well with the décor as we slowly dragged everything through and into the house. This was to be our next home until we had got ourselves back on track with our credit restored and maybe a job that would enable me to buy another house, but right now, I could only think about the present, not the future.

It was around this time that Ian got back in touch with me, after nearly thirty years, and we caught up on what each of us had been doing. Last I had seen of Ian he had a group of shops called Music Market which sold second-hand record and tapes which he then sold for a small fortune to W. H. Smith—the very large retail giant with shops and music stores all over the country.

Ian had then opened up a restaurant in Covent Garden called 'Break for the Border', which was a Tex-Mex restaurant which at that time in the early eighties did not exist in England. He had live bands playing cover versions of Beatles, Stones, Bowie, and others because as he explained to me, "People don't go to a restaurant to hear original music," and I agreed. Around three months after he opened, he was sitting at the end of the bar watching and listening, and the band suddenly stopped singing right in the middle of a Beatles' medley of songs. The lead singer said to a very packed restaurant, "I don't think we can sing these songs all that well tonight, so let's see if there is someone in the restaurant who can help us out." And the people looked around as the band stopped playing. He went over to a table of around twelve people and said, "Paul, can you come up and help us out?"

Paul McCartney, who was sitting in his restaurant at the time, went up on stage and sang a set for about an hour. UNBELIEVABLE! And, as Ian told me when he looked out onto the street, there was a crowd of hundreds of people outside his restaurant listening to Paul McCartney singing inside, not believing their ears or what they were hearing and seeing.

A while later, Jon Bon Jovi went up to Ian's office and asked if he could sing with the band, and so it went on making his restaurant a huge success. He even got to meet Heather Locklear; well that would have been my life's dream come true, as I think she is one of the most beautiful women alive.

"Well, after that we were made, and the restaurant really took off." "Good for you," I told him. "So what else did you get up to?" "Well, I then opened up a series of live music venues called 'The Academy,' and we had them all over England. There was the Brixton Academy, the Liverpool Academy, and many more which were refurbished cinemas converted into live music venues." "So who did you have performing?" I asked him. He told me that he had the Rolling Stones, David Bowie, and the Who, and just about anyone who wanted to perform there.

When I went over to England, we met up and I even met his mom, Peggy Evans, again. I hadn't seen her for decades, and she still looked great. I took Georgia and Amanda with me as well as my sister-in-law, Lesley, to meet him at his home in Marlow.

We went through old photos and sang to his family, and my own children were amazed at what we had gotten up to all those years ago.

I saw Ian once again at a huge party he had thrown in his house, and we had a really great time. It was so good to see Peggy again, and she and I even danced together. Peggy was eighty-nine years old and still looked great and was every bit as alive as she was when she was filming *The Blue Lamp* with Dirk Bogarde!

Ian had married, a second time, to a very nice girl called Mary, who was good for him and had been happily married with four children, pretty much like me.

Our true character never changes we just get wiser with life's experiences!

A DIVINE MOMENT

One experience in less than a second can change everything we know.

PART OF THE THEME of my book and my life explained in it is based on my unshakable belief in a divine presence. This is by no means a simple blind faith though there is nothing wrong with that. For me it is based on reality and being open to things that happened to me and around me, most of which affected my life and some that affected others but that I could see happening.

Not long after the move, I went to my local church almost every month, after an absence of decades where I was simply too busy with life and survival to even bother. Anyway, as I explained rather lamely to myself, I went three times a week as a boy, while singing in a choir, so I figured I had earned a leave of absence.

One Sunday morning as I was standing on the upper balcony of my absolutely packed church, during a hymn which I didn't really want to sing, as I was not "feeling it" at the time, I was looking around at all of the congregation standing and singing their hearts out while I was standing not singing but miming the words while thinking or daydreaming.

The thoughts I had in my head were very clear to me, and I was saying to myself, "I don't belong here with all of these really good people"; and I was gazing around the packed church as I thought, *I really don't belong here with these good people. I'm certain that they are all far better people*
than me.

All of a sudden, as I was lost in my thoughts, a tingling feeling washed down over me slowly from the top of my head moving slowly down my body; and as it happened a voice—very, very clear and very loud in my head—said to me, "You do belong here, Tony. You belong here."

To say that I was stunned would be an understatement; I was shocked and stood very still looking around at all of the people, though I thought I would fall over at that moment, almost expecting a light to go on above my head. I became very calm and knew at that very moment that whatever happened to me in the future and whatever had happened in the past, God was aware of me, little me, of no significance whatsoever and had spoken to me very directly; and I heard his voice and knew then that my belief in a divine presence was based on truth.

I was in shock at the depth of that one moment. Was what I heard true? And the more I thought about that very simple sentence and the feeling I had at that instance, the more I thought that it was true and it was real.

That one simple but profound moment would validate all that I believed to be true, and I didn't care what anyone else believed at all. I now knew the whole truth, and that was enough.

I went home after church and told Sue, looking carefully at her reaction. She believed that I believed it, and I knew that she was one person who, if she did have a belief, never discussed it, sadly.

In my whole of life this one experience may never ever be experienced by you, my reader, but nevertheless, it proves to me that there really is a God and whether it's cool or not cool to admit it to others, (not cool for the most part these days) but for me it is an undeniable fact.

BACK TO WORK AGAIN

When we are suddenly out of work. All religion, fun and enjoying life goes out of the window until you find another job!

I had been out of consistent work for a year by the time I received an e-mail from a head hunter in Florida, asking if I was interested in joining a company making specialized racing apparel and gloves in October 2002. I was intrigued and responded that maybe I was. I received several more e-mails concerning a company looking to hire someone with my skills as general manager to run the company on behalf of the owners who were all quite old and all in retirement.

I checked out the Web site for the company called the Glove Corporation to find out what the company profile was like and saw it made firefighting and industrial gloves. I was told that there would be a series of interviews with the family members that owned the company, that the interviews would be by phone and that if I was successful this would end with a face-to-face interview in Alexandria where their head office was located in Indiana.

The phone interviews were arranged, with three of the family members making up the board of directors. There was Joe Sturm, a gruff man, formerly a radiologist and now retired, Rob, their nephew who was younger and a full-time cop, and finally Allen, the other nephew who was some sort of consultant. These interviews went on over a period of two months as they were apparently hard to get to, which as I would find out later was a common trait.

I found out during these telephone interviews that the company had been around for some eighty years and had been a family-run business ever since. The current president, Frank Sturm, Joe's brother, who was now seventy-five years old and who had run the company for thirty years and was, in their opinion, incapable of managing it presently.

Sue was in London, visiting her parents and sister, at the time of my interview; and we were now living in a rented house, after our bankruptcy. I called her while she was over there and promised her that I would get this job no matter what. So, the interview was set up, and I drove to Alexandria which was seventy-five miles and one and a half hours drive to the north of Indianapolis. The town was a dump with many now closed and rusted old General Motor factories, a bunch of poorly maintained houses and a high street of mostly closed-down shops. Still I didn't care as I was out for the kill, and I was absolutely determined to get this job.

I arrived at the building, for my face-to-face interview, which was located in the very center of Alexandria in Indiana, at the crossroads in the middle of town, in a large old partially dilapidated building.

The Glove Corp headquarters was a large square three-story red brick building with its top floor comprising of mostly partially boarded-up windows and looked quite sinister. The entrance was an unmarked black door, under a squeaking, swinging rusting old sign, straight off the high street, if you could call a bunch of closed-down shops a high street, and was located between two shops on either side of the Glove Corp's entrance door. To the left was a small rather sad computer repair business, and to the right was a fire equipment sales dealership.

I entered the door, a little late I might add, and went up the squeaky, uncarpeted, plain dusty wooden staircase that creaked with every step and entered the office on my right through a tall door at the top of the staircase.

Once inside, the office was not too bad, but there were only three people in the whole "head office." I was shown into the boardroom where seated around a long plain wooden boardroom table were several people that I would eventually get to know "very" well.

There was Rob, the thirtyish tall, slim police officer and part owner; Frank, seated at the end of the table who was an elderly man and was the president and chairman of the board; Allen, same age as Rob but heavy-set with dark circles around his eyes giving him somewhat of a piggy appearance; another elderly man called Mr. Rae, though I didn't know why they were so formal, who was the accountant; Sharon Summers, who was the office manager; and me.

During the interview, I gave it everything I had and made sure I answered all of their questions properly even asking them if I had answered their questions satisfactorily, something I had learned from poring over the many job search sites while learning how to handle interviews.

As the interview got under way, I gained momentum and realizing that this was it, I gave it all I could to give the best impression of myself. During the interview, I showed them a box of "Stardust" perfume, and I told them that in a way this was exactly the same as gloves, (yeah right) in that it had a number of components that came from several suppliers and all went together to make a finished product. They understood what I was saying though, and I think that small demonstration was key to getting me over the finish line and to being offered the job.

The interview lasted around two hours and was interesting. They all told me that the company had great future under the right leadership but also that they were not certain of the future as the company had been losing money for several years. Allen Town said nothing during the interview, and I understood by that that he had probably wanted the job, just a feeling.

After the interview, I felt certain that I had the best chance possible and called Sue, telling her that the interview had gone really well. The next day I called the head hunter, who turned out to be the wife of Joe, who owned 25 percent of the company.

She asked me how I thought it went and I told her; she then said that subject to a background check, I had the job. I couldn't believe it; I would be back in a proper job after several years of trying anything and everything to make ends meet so that we didn't starve.

Talk about a tough time, that in year 2002 I had seven jobs in order to make ends meet: a car salesman, a living trust salesman, and a certified computer training company general manager. I had even managed a start-up digital imaging company, worked as a salesman for a UK imaging company, and had worked with Sue for a few months as a mortgage broker as well as a consultant for a plastic company. Despite all this, I had managed to keep our heads above water, and we seemed to be able to just about make ends meet throughout. I called Sue, still in England and told her my good news; she gasped in relief as I told her "I nailed it, I got the job."

"When do you start, and how much is the pay?" she asked. I told her that I would be starting on my birthday and would be paid weekly. The money was less than half of what I had earned at Alfa Laval before I left, but that's better than nothing. I had agreed to a low start in salary, as a gesture to the company, but agreed also that if I exceeded their expectations and succeeded in turning the company around, they had to increase my pay as a result, and they agreed.

I then got a call from the head hunter who had found me the position, now just two days before I was to start my new job, telling me there was a problem as I had filed for bankruptcy. My heart fell; maybe I wouldn't get the job after all, but I wasn't about to lose it for something that wasn't my fault.

I told her that "If the company sees this as an issue, after the events of 9/11, then maybe I wasn't right for the company and then neither was the company right for me." I remember saying that I didn't want to have bankruptcy as baggage in starting a new position running a small company like this especially when it was out of my control.

She was OK after that and told me that it would be all right for me to take the job and that she would not mention this to the others. Anyway my background check was fine as I had never ever been in any trouble ever.

I started my new job, as general manager of the Glove Corporation, just around my birthday, on Monday December 2, 2002, driving from Greenwood to Alexandria, earning half of what I had earned some ten years before and having to drive seventy-five miles each way to and from my new office, a total of three hours' drive time every day.

I was nevertheless elated to have a new job, at last, and didn't care about the money or the drive. I was going to make my mark in this new industry! Gloves! Are you kidding? What the hell did I know about gloves? Oh well, I was certain I would make my mark and also that I would give this my absolute best shot.

We were so broke I had to buy a car, a light blue Ford Taurus from a "buy here pay here" dealer in the seedy part of town. The "buy here pay here" was a no-down payment pay as you drive business that if you failed to make your payments, they would come around and repossess the car even if you had paid 95 percent of the total cost. The car though was fine and drove well; I even named her "Blue Bessie," and she never let me down once although she did overheat in summer, and I had to drive her with the heater full on in order not to overheat the engine.

The first issue I was to face was that the board wanted me to fire Frank Sturm as my first action only a week after I arrived, and I refused to do this for them, telling them that they should have done this as a board action and that having read the articles of incorporation I did not have that power. I liked Frank and understood that he had run the company under the direction of the board, for more than thirty years, and had done exactly what they had asked him to do; that is all except being able to make profit for them mainly because they had never allowed him to make any investment in the company. I worked with Frank, giving him a chance to help me as much as I could although he did nothing at all to help me during the first months of my leadership in his family company.

Rob had decided to work with me in order to make sure that Frank didn't try to stop me doing, what was prior to my hire, his job.

The company was around $4 million in mainly firefighting gloves but also industrial and special protection gloves used for welding, firefighting, driver, rope rescue, industrial work gloves, and many more.

The company sold its products to a wide range of more than three hundred privately owned fire and industrial distributorships throughout the United States and Canada with sales going as far as Australia and South America.

They had seven sales management companies managing the distributors and who took 5 percent of the sales value in their respective territories to do this. After I had begun to gain market knowledge, I could see that the industrial glove business was dying because of very low-cost imports from China and Asia. I estimated that we would lose this business within two to three years unless we could do something about it. The industrial sales were a quarter of their total sales and were in very low-priced gloves that each sold for around $15 a pair. The fire glove market had a higher price point, and we had some eight models that were each required to be annually certified in order to meet the NFPA certification requirements for the firefighting industry. The annual certification was very expensive and took around four to six months to complete each year. After completion, the gloves were allowed to contain an NFPA certification label inside.

This was very expensive and was a necessary part of being in the firefighting market and something that we had to comply with annually. In order to pass the annual certification, we had to send out hundreds of pairs of gloves in different sizes, swatches of materials, and numerous carefully filled-out pages of paperwork for every style of glove we made. Sharon and Keith had been used to this as they had both been doing this before I joined the company.

We already have all the tools we need so instead of simply praying for a solution, do that while you working your arse off 15 hours a day to find a job and you will find work!

BEHIND THE OFFICE

Hoarding stuff is an unhealthy anchor that ties us to the past.

BEHIND MY OFFICE, on the second floor in the old dilapidated building, was a pale green double door leading to a now closed-down factory where the once busy shipping department was located with long tables for shipping goods. The large wooden floored room housed among other things old disused and broken computers and printers, hundreds of files in dusty cabinets, old brochures that could or should have been tossed away years earlier probably going back as to just after the earth cooled. There were boxes and boxes of the worst-made gloves I had ever seen, and I hoped that these were not what was being shipped out to customers now.

Everything was "hoarded"—all the old stuff all being kept for no good reason, and it was so negative to the forward movement that I was going to bring to the company.

There were welders' gloves, electrical linemen's gloves, freezer gloves, firefighting gloves, work gloves, leather aprons, leather spats for welders to protect their feet, and many, many different kinds of gloves that I had no idea what they were all for.

Though it was fascinating to see, to me the building and the boxes of old badly made products was all like an anchor, tethering the company to the past, old stuff now totally irrelevant in today's business environment, yet none of it had been let go by Sharon; and she was an anchor not a foundation.

In the office were old desks, scattered around, faded black-and-white maps on the wall, old posters from previous advertising campaigns. It was awful, and I was determined that no customer or supplier of mine would ever come to Alexandria to see this mess.

Holding on to old files and badly made products was backward looking. In order to look forward get rid of the past and focus on the future.

BATS AND "GUANO"

Looking at the company as it was now showed me all I needed to know about its past!

THE UPPER FLOORS of our building were infested with bats so bad that they had called in a team of specialists to get rid of the hundreds of bats living there. It was so bad up there that their droppings corroded the large old freight elevator wiring, causing it to frequently break down. It was absolutely disgusting, and on some days bats would be seen in our offices, and the girls would freak out asking me to get rid of them.

Farther back, in the now-disused shipping office behind the double doors, was a very narrow creaky wooden staircase leading to an upper floor which was all but completely dilapidated. It comprised of mostly boarded-up windows and a ceiling that had at some time mostly collapsed and was now partly held up by wooden batons nailed roughly and haphazardly to the ceiling beams seemingly by an amateur to hold up what was left of the ceiling. There were large dilapidated areas that showed the wooden laths where the ceiling and wall plaster had fallen off. There also was black mold around the walls, missing plaster, and heaps of pigeon and bat droppings which were all over the floor and on the old sewing equipment.

There were many old sewing machines and folds of old material left as if they had been quite suddenly abandoned like on the "Marie Celeste," left exactly as if the workers had vanished into thin air.

It was creepy in the closed factory, behind my office, and there was the added junk that the Sturm family had seen fit to use as a dumping ground for their old disused furniture which had absolutely no value at all; rusty, filthy old hair dryers and old torn settees faded and filthy with stains all over, broken tools old rusty chairs a rusted-up drum kit that was probably crappy when it was new. I hated all this junk, it was for me indicative for how the family saw their business, nothing important just for use as and when they wanted it as a dumping ground for their old stuff.

Despite what I had been told in my interview, reality was very different.

THE GLOVE FACTORY

The worse the condition a company is for a new CEO, the harder it is to transform it.

FRANK TOOK ME by car to the factory which was just as bad as the head office and was located at Heber Springs in Arkansas. I met Pat and Keith along with the eighty-five sewing staff, all sitting in straight lines facing the blank gray walls with opaque windows, and all of whom seemed at that time fairly disdainful of my position.

The factory is comprised of a low building set in a grass field with no outside lights at night and only some badly laid stones as a way of allowing cars to park at the facility. It had heaps of old moldy leather of all kinds and all colors; some of which, as I was to find out, had been there for more than ten or fifteen years, showing evidence of either rats of mice with droppings on the floor by the leather. What was it about this company that they had to have creature droppings all over their operation? There was not even a staff canteen, only a set of old plain tables located near a rusted window that had not been cleaned for a decade. The steel beams on the ceiling were all covered with at least six inches deep of dust, knap from old leather sewing, and dirt that had accumulated over the past fifty years that the factory had been in that location.

I asked Pat if the building had ever been cleaned, and she said not that she knew of but added that this was clean compared to when they first arrived there some five years before.

As I sat looking around having a coffee, while meeting with Pat and Keith at the "open plan" dining area, bits of dust and dirt were falling off the ceiling beams onto the table and us. The mood was bad, and no one seemed happy to be there. There was no air-conditioning, only some old "chicken" hatchery coolers comprising of four, four-foot-wide, square "down shafts" which came down through the roof and when utilized would blast out hot air that had been slightly cooled by water pipes running across the air flow coming in from the roof. These blast coolers made no difference to the heat inside the building in summer which got as high as 110 degrees and with humidity of 95 percent, making it even worse. It got so hot in the Arkansas summer that the factory had to close at noon because of the heat from June right through to September, and those that sat at their sewing machines within a ten-foot radius from each "cooler" had to have a cardboard wall set in front of their workstation in order to stop their work from blowing away.

When it rained hard, there was a torrent of water that flooded through the front office where Keith's desk was as the land grading outside the factory was so poor that the drainage was right through the office and foundations. When it rained, which it did with a vengeance, the roof leaked all over the factory and had to have buckets placed on the sewing tables and floors.

When I discussed this with Pat and Keith, they told me that the company owners had never let them put in air conditioning or a canteen or especially re-grading the outside saying "What do they need all that for, open the doors and let the fresh air in, and why do they need a break room anyway? They are there to work not to rest." Or they were told to use buckets as it only rains sometimes, and the cost was too much to pay out of slim profits.

Unbelievable! What a mess I had got myself into. Still, I also knew it couldn't get worse than that, so it had to get better. This factory had been neglected for more than thirty years, with no investment; and all of the meager profit, if any, had been taken out in the form of monthly dividends by the owners leaving only a slim operating capital enough to last for two months, not more.

The sewing machines were mainly old Singer chain stitch machines that were new in the 1930s, and there was not much that was newer than that. Some even had mechanical operating systems that were at least seventy years old. What a compliment to the Singer Sewing Machine company that these were still in operation. There were some Juki and Mitsubishi's dotted around as well.

There were two lines of leather cutters totaling thirteen in all, and all were men who stood in front of mechanical "clickers" that "clacked" loudly as the large mechanical arm was swung into position by the cutters and snapped down onto the glove pattern dies. These were placed onto a steel table with a plastic cutting board onto which the large pieces of leather, some as big as half a cow, were placed to be cut into glove components.

The factory produced around five hundred to one thousand pairs of gloves each week and only half that in summer, partly because of the early closing because of the summer heat inside the factory and partly because of the sales of fire gloves being slow in the summer.

All factory purchases had to run through Sharon who had only ever been in the factory a couple of times in her more than forty years of service with the company.

She believed that when the factory ran out of leather, which they did nearly every month, they should make something else instead even if they had no other orders to be made. She also believed they were "saving" money when the factory staff was laid off, and she knew nothing of the cost of shutting down the factory with all of the operational costs remaining and with no production from which to cover these costs.

It made no sense having a large factory in Arkansas, with eighty-six staff, and a head office in Indiana with only three people, especially as their work could easily have been managed in the factory.

What a great business to run; it certainly couldn't get any worse. According to the customers I spoke to, we had less than one year before we would shut the doors forever because of diminishing sales.

> *A bad company is bad from the very top and the only reason it remains in business is that there are people working there that are desperate to have work; This company had survived because of this.*

A MIC IN THE LIGHT

Stupid people do stupid things!

ONE DAY NINE months after I had started work in Alexandria, I came back from getting a sandwich to eat while continuing to work over lunch, when Sharon told me that Frank had been "fixing" the light over my desk. I told her that the light didn't need fixing as it worked fine but said I would take a look. What on earth was he up to? I climbed onto my desk, and above it was a strip light with a plastic cover. I flipped open the cover and let it swing down, as it did so I noticed a very small black object attached to a wire hidden inside the light fixture.

I started to gently pull the object down and saw to my amazement and utter disbelief that it was a tiny microphone that had been hidden up there at some point by Frank or one of his family members, as I doubted that he would have been able to do this himself. I stared at it in disbelief, what the hell! I was stunned and stood there looking at it for several minutes.

I called Rob who was on duty that afternoon and asked him to come to the office immediately. He told me he was in his police uniform but would be off duty later. I told him he probably needed to be in uniform and needed to be here as soon as possible, and yes he should probably be in uniform.

Rob arrived fifteen minutes later and came rushing up the steps, three at a time, and into my office. "What the!" he started to say, but I put my finger to my lips telling him not to say anything and pointed up to the light fitting.

Rob being over six feet tall reached up and swung the cover down at which point the tiny microphone now dropped out and onto his head as I had pulled some of the wire through which made it drop lower this time.

Rob was furious. "What the fuck!" he shouted and began pulling all the wire out of the false ceiling in my office. Imagine what it looked like, both of us standing looking up pulling yards and yards of wire down, with ceiling tiles flying in all directions as we followed the long wire out of my office, pulling the wire down from where it was hidden above the ceiling tiles, straight across the board room ceiling, across the hallway with the wire bundle I was holding getting so big it was becoming difficult to hold.

The wire continued straight into Frank's office going across his ceiling down the side wall, where it had been carefully hidden in with a load of other computer wires running down his wall until it finally descended under his carpet and ran straight into his desk drawer! Unbelievable!

Rob got more and more angry as Frank, his uncle, watched the now-enormous bundle of wire that I was holding in both of my outstretched arms while Rob was now in his office pulling up the carpet to expose the wire hidden underneath.

All the while Frank was standing in his office, arms crossed, with his hand stroking his chin while he looked on bemused at what was rapidly unfolding, looking on as if all this was nothing to do with him. "What the fuck have you done, Uncle Frank? What is this? A mic running into your office from Tony's office?" Rob shouted at him, continuing on, not waiting for a reply. "I can have you arrested for this, it's illegal to record someone's conversations and phone calls, and I'm going to arrest you right now!" Rob shouted.

I asked Frank how long this had been there. "Oh, that's nothing to worry about," he said to both of us. "It's been there for ages, and I just never bothered about it," he said rather lamely in an "aw shucks" kind of voice.

I left Frank's office, and Rob followed me back into my office where I told him point-blank, "I'm not working with Frank anymore, and I refuse to have him in my office, and president or not, I cannot trust him anymore."

I turned to Rob and told him that he had better deal with this and fast, as legally I cannot since I am not an owner, and this was absolutely an unacceptable behavior and from someone that I was supposed to fire immediately after joining. I reminded him that I was the reason Frank was still there, saying that he was useless to the running of the operation and had done not one single task I had given him.

The next morning, I had a conference call with Rob and Joe, who both wanted Frank, fired immediately. "Fire his damn ass!" Joe growled into the phone, and I told them that if they did this it would lead to a serious lawsuit that the company would lose as a result of illegal dismissal of a board member. I had read their articles of incorporation, and a chairman or president could only be removed following a decision of the board. Also I told them that they have to get an extraordinary board meeting set up giving Frank forty-eight-hour minimum notice.

I explained to them both that we had to do this by the letter, and we needed to accomplish very strict guidelines with an offer of removal, the reasons why, a timeline during which he could disagree with the offer, a vote, and a severance agreement.

I immediately sought the advice of a local corporate attorney and began the preparation of the severance agreement. Rob wanted to use the opportunity to buy Frank out of the business an opportunity that showed me another side of the "family." As for me, I was only interested in getting Frank out with the minimum of fuss.

It took several weeks to get a draught severance agreement; the content of which gave Frank twenty-one days to disagree with the offer, after which time the offer, if not taken up, would be withdrawn.

I cautioned Rob that he needed to call a board meeting, take a vote, and make sure that Frank understood what was being said. I also told him to repeat everything three times, give Frank the agreement, and to encourage him to seek advice of an attorney. The offer was extremely good, and I saw to it that it was fair, though I knew Frank would ignore it as that was a family trait.

The board meeting was called, and Rob followed my instructions to the letter. Because of this there were no legal ramifications, and when it had been done correctly, Frank had no legal possibility to sue the company—something I wanted to avoid at all costs.

Frank, of course, ignored the offer to pay him for his shares according to a fair market value along with an offer of full pay for eighteen months. He was stupid; he left it until the twenty-second day after being told he had twenty-one days and called Rob to discuss the agreement. Rob told him it was too late; the offer was now off the table, and he was out. I knew from past experience with this that when done correctly, it was like nothing had happened; everything went smoothly, and I also knew that the family had just learned a valuable lesson.

I learned that no matter what; when it's time to let an important employee go, do it with dignity and with legal help. It will save a fortune in legal costs in correcting the mistake later.

A NEW DIRECTION

The buck stopped here with me now....no going back.

WITH FRANK NOW gone, I had the full reins in the running of the company, and I began by analyzing the revenue stream and by looking at the sales by region, product, and customer. I also looked hard at the production costs and saw that the factory costs were high, prices were low, and profit was very, very slim.

I loved the analysis, having made this a skill that I had fine-tuned having been taught by the best there was and knew this was the key to understanding how the company performed, which would lead to how to fix it.

The office staff, of three women, was somewhat negative to work with, but I would deal with that later, not now. The company had lost a third of their distributors without even knowing it and had two business segments: one was firefighting gloves and the other was industrial gloves—both of which were unprofitable.

After several days of analysis, I created a market plan from which I would develop the "big fix" for this small company. It was clear that we would lose the industrial market to low-cost importers that could sell gloves at less than our leather cost alone.

My impression so far was of a rather dusty old company that had seen better days and was living in the past. Sharon repeatedly told of better days in the past when the company had many sewing operations in that head office building, on the second and third floors in Alexandria, but something told me this was not entirely true as I could see no sign of any wealth, only old and dilapidated furniture and equipment that even when new was probably the cheapest they could get.

I started by trying on the many gloves we made and found them to be of poor quality, wide seams, differing in fit between right hand and the left hand of the same pair of gloves mainly because the final inspection comprised a bunch of old women whose hands were too small for the larger sizes we mostly made and therefore could not possibly see how the large and extra-large gloves fitted.

The company though had an ISO 9001 quality system, but this did not reflect the poor quality of the final end product. The firefighting gloves had to be certified each year by a third-party testing facility, and they frequently failed repeatedly to pass the rigorous NFPA annual tests because of the poor leather quality, since there were no technical staff able to remedy this, and the company often used the cheapest leather they could get.

The good thing though was that the company had been well known in the industry, and I believed I could turn this around, but it would take a lot of very hard work to succeed.

I met with the independent sales rep agencies to see if I had their support, and I did have their promise of support provided I started improving our products and position in the market.

I focused on the market plan, as I had been trained to do, to gauge if all of the work involved in turning this company around was going to be worth it.

THE TURN AROUND

When eating the elephant, we do it one bite at a time.

I BEGAN BY RE-ENGINEERING the gloves, as that would immediately improve sales, after realizing that many of the components in our gloves did not fit together and that the finish of the cuffs and seams in our firefighting products needed improving significantly as there were loose threads all over the finished product.

I reengineered the firefighting glove patterns and by "walking" around each of the patterns to see if the seams were matched up to each other. I also modified the glove design by lowering the position of the little finger crotch in order to make it fit the hand better than it did.

The results were astounding; the sewing staff found that they didn't have to "work" the leather, which was their term for making the pattern fit when the pattern was incorrect and was extremely tiring to the operator to get the sewn components to fit together while completing each glove. When they did this, the gloves became twisted and didn't look good.

The staff was beginning to understand that my methods may be different from my six predecessors, and they could see that the gloves seemed to be easier for them to sew.

We had a fifty percent annual staff turnover through new hires not wanting to stay in the company as it was a "sweat shop," and I had to turn that around as well as all the other things that had to be done.

I also designed several new gloves, showing the market that Glove Corp was getting its act together at last.

My days were absolutely filled up, working as hard as I could to improve the company, leaving home in the morning at 6:00 a.m. and arriving home at 7:30 p.m. while driving 150 miles a day to the office in Alexandria and back. Still I didn't mind at all as I was happy doing what I do, and I was even more happy to have a job that paid me.

In 2004, just as things were at last really turning around and our business began to improve, we began to get our biggest-selling glove made from elk skin being returned from firefighters all over the country saying that they had simply fallen apart. What had happened was that the leather was "tender" and was simply becoming full of holes having no strength, yet we didn't know why.

The problem got steadily worse and affected all of our firefighting gloves. Fifty percent of our sales, gloves which were made of elk skin which was imported from Finland, were showing problems. We were getting gloves back by the dozens, and I called our competitors to see if they had the same problem. They told me they didn't though I was later to find out they were not telling the truth. What a surprise! A competitor not admitting they had a problem!

We contacted our leather importer who told us that we were the only ones having this problem, so I decided to fly to Finland to meet our tannery in a place called Kokkola up in the northeast coast of Finland toward the Lapland border right on the edge of the Arctic Circle. I flew via Helsinki and then took a small plane to Kokkola where I met Ekki whose family had owned the tannery for four generations. I wanted to meet them face-to-face to see what could be the problem.

Ekki picked me up from the hotel, and I was shown around the tannery. They told me the problem may be the freezing of the hides while they were left outside in the months of the freezing weather in the Finnish winter. That night, I took Ekki out to dinner in a local restaurant. Ekki's idea of a nice evening out was to get absolutely blind drunk until he fell over bursting into song while lying on the floor. Funny thing was no one seemed to notice as all of them were doing the same thing; it was like being in Sweden all over again. But unlike Sweden who only had two domestic beers when I was there, Pripps number 1 and Pripps number 2, Finland had some great beers!

I left Finland, hoping that my visit would spur them to improve their quality of leather to us. But it was up to me in the end to develop a new glove that would look different in order to win the confidence of our customers again.

Don't trust what your suppliers are telling you if the likely outcome of your problem is going to be very expensive to them to fix!

AMANDA AND ANOREXIA

No matter how important my work was it took no precedence over my daughter's immediate needs.

ON MY RETURN from Finland, I came back to the States via London where I met my darling daughters, Amanda and Georgia, as I hadn't seen them for several years since I had left Parfums Llewellyn. I stayed over for several days, and the break was very welcome. They took me to their favorite place in the world, the ancient city of Glastonbury. I could see why they loved it there as it had a great atmosphere of England in an older day. There were small shops selling what to me were "alternative medicine" items like herbs, spices, prayer bowls, and mixtures of all cultures of religious and homeopathic medicines.

I was surprised though that when I took them both to a local Italian restaurant, Amanda did well, but after eating only half of her food she had to place her plate on the floor and out of her view. I could say nothing, and she knew that I knew she was still fighting her anorexia. I had no intention of putting her on the spot with this and wanted her to feel my support in not saying anything. Sometimes less is far more; I held her hand and gave her a kiss to which there were tears in her eyes. But we both managed just fine. I said a silent prayer for her that she would win her fight with this awful mental illness, and I remembered going over to England while at Parfums Llewellyn to help by supporting her in joining her at the meeting she had with her doctors and councilors. Still I had to admit she looked much stronger now than she had then.

Later when she gave birth to Ellie, Eliza Jane, she had more to focus on, as baby Ellie had been born with a problem with her feet, and that involved her having to undertake a series of arduous operations all through her young years in order for her to walk. This gave Amanda something else to focus on and caused her to leave her anorexia behind her. Thank goodness for that.

Sometimes a willing dad can do what a willing mom alone cannot do.

STARTING AGAIN

When I set my mind to the future, not the past, it was amazing how quickly I could gain everything that I lost, back again.

AFTER WORKING FOR the Glove Corp. for only eighteen months after we had filed bankruptcy, we were able to buy a new home, and so we began to look for another. Sue hated living in rented accommodation although I didn't mind it; I was in no real hurry to get into another mortgage as I didn't trust the owners.

After looking for several weeks, we found a perfect house close to the school where James and Nicky were attending. The house was a two-story Tudor-style home on a hill in an older edition surrounded by a golf course. The house had a basement and a kidney-shaped swimming pool in the garden. What I liked was the bay window in the kitchen that overlooked the garden. It had a large stone fireplace and was exactly what we had been looking for.

Looking for a new home after bankruptcy is therapeutic as it gave us both something to look forward to rather than living in a beautiful but "rented" home.

The garden had been modeled for a TV program called HGTV and had been completely landscaped including the pool. The kidney-shaped pool had fiber optic lighting that could change color around and in the pool at night moving from pink to green to blue and to white and it even had two fountains on the side which housed flowers in the summer. The control for the pool was in the kitchen on the wall where the computerized system could remotely work the pump, the cover, and the automatic heater cleaner and all else. We both loved it and decided to buy it, as the price was at that time far less than it was worth only two years before because of the housing market slowing down. Sue managed the paperwork and got us a mortgage after only a few months, and we happily moved in. I would never again mind mowing our lawn or keeping the house in full repair!

I learned not to waste my energy focusing on what was, but on what will be. Very soon we had everything back that we lost but now we valued it all much more.

NICK AND STEVENS JOHNSONS DESEASE

When a son is critically ill nothing else matters except to help him get well at all costs.

THINGS WERE GOING very well indeed at home and at work, and we were finally getting everything back in place. It was Christmas that year, when Nicky, now fifteen, who was on some mild medication for acne that was sulfur based, when I noticed that he had come out in spots and his eyes were itching.

I took him to Dr. Jeff on New Year's Eve, and Jeff thought he had "pink eye" prescribing him with sulphacetamide which was another sulfur-based medication.

Later that evening, Sue and I could hear Nick struggling to breathe, and we rushed in to see him. He was covered in spots and was wheezing and couldn't breathe. We took him directly to the hospital, and he was immediately admitted overnight. He got steadily worse and worse, and by the early hours he had come up in blisters all over his body. One of the doctors told us she thought he had a disease called Stevens-Johnson, and he was getting worse by the minute.

He was taken by ambulance to Riley Children's Hospital downtown with us driving behind him, very, very scared of what could happen to our poor son, Nicky.

Sue and I were beside ourselves with this and had never ever seen anything like it.

As he lay there in the intensive care assessment unit, lying on a gurney in the middle of the emergency room; we could see that Riley were moving into an emergency mode and before less than five minutes he was surrounded by all of the specialists including eyes, ear nose and throat, dermatologists, internal medicine specialists. All were deadly serious, and all were consulting with the head administrator whose job it was to accumulate the incoming information and between them all to arrive at a direction of treatment. Meanwhile poor Nicky was getting worse, and where one of the nurses had touched him to get a pulse on the side of his neck using two fingers, he had now right before our eyes a blister the size of a very large grapefruit forming.

He was looking terrible as his body was reacting to the intake of sulfur, which he had a violent reaction to. Sue was by now sobbing while we were both looking at our son who was dying right in front of our eyes. His face was bright red and swollen, and he now had blisters all over his body, on his face, his body, his eyes, under his fingernails in his ears, and all over his mouth and digestive tract.

It was decided to treat him as a severe burn patient, and they took him immediately to the intensive care where we were told he would get far worse before he got better. We were very scared and prayed for him as we sincerely believed he may die from this. We were also told that there was no medication to treat this disease, but that it had to run its course.

The most important thing, we were told, was to make sure that he did not get any infection on his body as that would result in scarring. I sent a message that day to the church; in a note I wrote to our pastor Greg Ponchot for them to pray for him to survive this horrific illness.

Over the next four weeks, both Sue and I spent as much time as we could with him in the ICU, and although I had to run the company, I made sure I went to see him directly from work every single day. Sue went to see him during the days also and spent almost all of her time there including sleeping in his room every night for the first two weeks.

We had to wear a mask, a hat, plastic overalls, and plastic shoes to see him in his intensive care unit as the risk of airborne infection was very high.

Nicky now had blisters over 97 percent of his entire body and was having difficulty seeing as they were on his eyes and under his eyelids.

He had to have a food line inserted though his nose and a drip into his chest with medication for pain control.

He was placed on a specially constructed air bed with covers that were changed several times a day, as if this wasn't bad enough, he also had the risk of losing his sight. Every day, five times a day, the ophthalmologists came in to scrape under his eyelids to prevent any scar tissue forming. He also lost the sclerotic coating on his eyes   He lost his fingernails, toe nails, and the blisters were all in his mouth and down his throat.

We had never ever experienced anything like this, and for the first two weeks he didn't know we were even there.

Gradually though he managed to show his strength of willpower and could talk to us about overcoming his disease. The road to recovery was long though, and at fifteen years old, he was strong enough to make it through. When our friends, Ros and Tim, came to see him, Tim broke down and cried at seeing our poor Nicky lying in the intensive care unit in such a bad way, his face swollen up and covered in blisters, his skin coming off all over his body.

That Sunday, I knew I needed more help than what Sue and I could manage, and there were prayers for him at our church; when they heard about how he was, there was a gasp as many of the congregation knew Nicky from being a little and mischievous schoolboy.

Greg Ponchot, my pastor at New Hope, came to see him in hospital, and I know that it made a very big difference; it also made Nick very happy to see him as it gave him some help from above in his struggle to beat this. One Sunday afternoon, our close friends, Jerry and Jacque, came to see us and just turned up at the hospital, we were very pleased to see them both, and they said that many people were asking about Nicky at the church and at school.

Other friends brought round food for us as neither Sue nor myself felt like cooking, and by the time we got home from the hospital, we were both absolutely tired out. It was these little things that helped us get through this extreme situation.

Nick was in the ICU for four weeks and slowly, because of the excellent care he received at Riley, he began to get better. During the last week, he was allowed to take a bath to help him slough off the dead skin all over his body. The bath had a hydraulic chair to help him in and out as he was far too weak to stand, let alone get in and out of the bath.

When we were there, we saw as he was being taken to the bathroom, in a wheelchair, but when they helped him out of it and into the bath chair he was like a little old man. He could do nothing by himself at all. The bath was very special and had purified warm air jets all over it, under the water, to help him in with oxygenating his body to help it heal as it also sloughed off his skin. He had to keep ejecting the layer of skin inside his mouth. As big chunks of it came off we knew though that he was gradually getting better.

We brought him home, but he was very weak and would have to recuperate for another three months at home in order to become well again. The result was that he stopped caring for himself when he was told that he may never be able to wear contact lenses again, because of his eyes not, at that time, having a strong enough sclera over them.

The whole illness changed him, and he didn't care about himself, but over time we knew he would get over it. He blamed our doctor for not diagnosing his condition correctly and for giving him the additional sulphacetamide eye drops. That most definitely took him over the edge and caused his dramatic and horrific reaction.

He then had to have tubes inserted into the corners of his eyes as his tear ducts had closed over because of scarring of the thin tissue around his eyes. They were removed, but he still had a little redness in the corner of one eye. We explained to him that we were happy that he had recovered so well after the terrible illness. After two years though, we found out that he could wear contacts again, and so there was, in the end, very little outwardly visible from his bout with Stevens-Johnson syndrome.

This was the hardest thing we had ever experienced but, as a family, we got through it

FIXING PROBLEMS

Necessity is the mother of invention!

SOON AFTER MY return to the United States, we received a letter from Underwriters Laboratories, or UL as they were better known, telling us that three major firefighting glove companies had had a serious elk-skin problem that needed to be fixed. So my competitors, as well as my tannery, were lying, they did have the same problems as we had but of course had been telling the market that it was a Glove Corp issue in order to lose us our business.

We were losing business fast, and it was time to do something about it. It was clear as to what had happened: the "firefighter" glove that we began to market had become a huge success, and as a result, our competitors had also decided to make and sell their own version of elk-skin firefighting gloves.

If I was to change this I had to find a way to reduce our dependency on elk skin or to change from a "suede" to a top grain leather back on the glove where the problem would be eliminated as it was impossible for God to make an elk with holes in his skin and our problem was only with the suede. The suede is the split from under the outer or top grain leather and depending on the thickness of the hide it allows you to have a split grain or suede cut from the hide. You can only ever have one split for each hide and tanners know that you cannot take a second cut of suede from a single hide as the middle split often has vast weak spots where the grain becomes vertical for some reason leaving the leather very soft and weak.

I got to work to develop a new "top grain" leather for our gloves, which would fix the problem and give the glove a completely new look hopefully letting our customers know we had not only fixed the problem but had improved the glove at the same time.

The total loss for Glove Corp was around three quarters of a million dollars that year not to mention a loss of many customers right at the point where we were gaining market share after years of decline. All the positive work I had done in reengineering the gloves was now at risk. The problem with the elk skin was caused by nothing more than greed from the tannery.

Glove Corp had developed an all-elk-skin glove that was softer than any other on the fire glove market which had then become the biggest-selling firefighting glove. As a result, the competitors had copied the idea by introducing their own elk leather glove.

The problem was that there were only a limited number of elks "culled" each year in Scandinavia, and the increased need for elk suede had resulted in the only supplier making double splits instead of a single split from each hide. This resulted in a middle split which always contained weak leather that fell apart. The strength of leather is through the crisscross pattern of the fibers in the hide. A middle split has areas where this doesn't happen and instead the leather fibers are straight and have, as a result, no strength.

I introduced a new glove with a "top grain" outer leather shell after rushing to get it certified, and it began to reduce the damage that had been done. I stood behind our market and replaced all gloves that were damaged, and even many that were not, but had been supplied together with some that were bad.

I replaced six times the number of failed gloves returned in order to keep hard-won customers from leaving us. If they bought thirty-six pairs and had a problem with only one glove I replaced all thirty-six pairs in order to keep their confidence in the company.

This leather problem affected our profitability, and we were lucky that it didn't close the company down. Because of the immediate action taken in reengineering a new product, we were still in business though barely.

The board was not impressed at the loss of profit and didn't bother to understand that we were very lucky that we still had a company at all as this had affected all companies selling elk-skin gloves. All the board cared about was the monthly profit that they could take out. "You'd better get this fixed and damn fast!" growled Joe in the board meeting following my redesign of a replacement glove.

I knew what had to be done, so I simply did what my instincts told me was correct and went ahead and did it.

LEAN

The tools already exist to help reduce costs; all we have to know is where to look.

I KNEW I had to reduce manufacturing costs significantly if we were going to be able to stay in business as the company was barely breaking even every month in summer from June till September because of the low demand in summer for fire gloves, there was nothing I could do about that. It was a seasonal factor in the fire industry. I contacted the Arkansas Department of Economic Development to see if they could help us, and after coming to the factory they told us that we needed to introduce LEAN manufacturing, which was a very advanced form of production started by the auto industry, in order to increase production without increasing costs.

After going to several seminars on the LEAN process, I decided to introduce this into the company as fast as possible. We began the process in April 2004 and had it completed by July 2004, which was in itself a small miracle. Together with all the staff we cleaned the factory, painted all the machines, threw out all of the old leather while working weekends in order to complete the daunting task.

We moved everyone into production teams, and the new LEAN process was a huge success for us. When we had finished the process, we had successfully reduced costs by 30 percent, while at the same time making the same number of gloves. We reduced the production staff levels from eighty-six to sixty-two. I also had to move the operation away from "piece work" which only a few of the staff were able to do well but most could not.

Piece work forces staff to work flat out as fast as possible all day long with a very low base pay, each having to rely on a bonus based on how many units they made. The problem was that since most of the female sewing staff could not work fast enough to get their high-based "piece" rate bonus pay, they were instead on base pay only which Sharon and Frank had kept to $6.30 per hour, which was not enough to even keep any family in food and clothing.

The only way they could make money was through sewing at high speed, for eight hours per day. Many could not even feed their families on what Glove Corp paid them, but what did Sharon or Frank or any of the owners care about that! They were the ones that had kept their staff down and below a livable wage. I hated what this had done to the hardworking staff they had in their factory, my factory.

I changed this archaic system, leftover from the last century, and instead got all my staff onto a production bonus while increasing their base pay significantly then I added a bonus on top of that. The new bonus was based on all those in each team working together to reach a common production and quality goal that was definitely achievable. We measured each of the standard sewing times it took to sew every glove component and made that the "standard time" based on an average speed that they agreed they could manage all day long. If they were able to sew to the standard time, they would make a really good bonus and at least 20 percent more than they were getting before. I also set up a new wage scale which gave them increased base pay for time served in the company.

The factory now looked good, had a good atmosphere, and was turning around very well; people were finally smiling, and the atmosphere was becoming much more positive.

There are always ways to improve the bottom line; some are harder work than others so I started with what gave us early gains get people motivated.

HOME TRUTHS

Stubborn attitudes are hard to change.

IN SUMMER 2004, after we had installed LEAN, I invited the Heber Springs town council and elders, the mayor, bank managers, other business owners, Dept. of Economic Development staff who had helped us improve our operation, and the Heber Springs Chamber of Commerce, in order to reach out to them to show the new and positive direction we were now moving toward. There were seventeen in all, in our newly built training room and the room was packed. I had also put in air-conditioning to keep my staff in a more comfortable temperature rather than the sultry summer heat that was often over 100 degrees with as much as 95 percent humidity during the hot summer months.

We gave our distinguished guests lunch in our new training room that we had built next to the brand-new staff canteen which we had also put in so that they all had a quiet place to eat lunch that was not directly inside the noisy factory.

During the meeting I was told, by the mayor and another man who was an idiot appropriately named "Dick" claiming to speak for the community that as far as the town was concerned, they really didn't care if Glove Corp left the community and never returned as they didn't like the owners and didn't want a "sweat shop." I listened to all of the negative comments, not saying much, and tried to tell them of the positive actions I had taken in improving the factory and conditions. I asked them if any other company had put more than a million dollars into the Heber Springs community, as we had, since 1953 (it was now 2004), but they were not listening. I told them of the improvements in pay and conditions, but they were stubborn and didn't seem to listen.

Sitting at the back of the meeting was one of the state leaders, a smartly dressed man in his early thirties in a black suit and white shirt, sitting and listening as I tried to bring the others around to a more positive perspective.

I was stunned at the negativity I had heard and told them at the end of the meeting how sad I was that Glove Corp, who was the oldest company in the town of only 6,500 people and who had placed $1.3 million in wages and taxes into the community over a fifty-three-year period, something no one else had done, was so poorly thought of and left it at that.

One of the most vocal had been the newly elected mayor who reiterated all that had been said, after staying on to talk to me, Pat, and Keith one-on-one; and I told him that as far as I was concerned his was an elected position that could, and probably would, change at any time and instead of decrying what we had done, he should be encouraging others to do the same which would increase his tax base. I looked at him and thought how perfectly he fitted in to this, one of the most ill-informed of all communities in Arkansas.

After they had all gone, the young man at the back came up to me and introduced himself as Spencer Sessions who was working in the governor's office and told me how very embarrassed he was at what he had heard from the mayor and the Chamber of Commerce visitors that had been invited to our factory.

As far as his office was concerned, we had done what other companies in and around Arkansas needed to do; we had made significant improvements to our company and now had the best chance of survival which was something they were trying to get all Arkansas companies to do. He disagreed with all of their comments and promised to help us in any way he could.

At Christmas that year, I got a call from Spencer saying that he had discussed our case with the Department of Economic Development, and they had unanimously decided to help us.

Spencer told me he had sent a check for $30,000 as a gift or Christmas present of encouragement in recognition for all the hard work we had done in getting the first glove factory in the United States, and maybe even the world, into the advanced LEAN manufacturing techniques. The money was to be used specifically for a new tarmac covered car park at the front of the factory to pave over the uneven grassy, often muddy, parking area outside the building. Not only that, but they had sent the check to the mayor himself, with express directions to be passed on to Glove Corp to be used for paving our new car park.

I called Spencer to thank him and the team for their kindness and help. Spencer and I laughed at the fact that their mayor "would bloody well fall of his seat when he got that big check." Spencer laughed as well and told me that they were sending him a loud and clear message in that he should be supporting factories and business improvements, not criticizing them.

We got the new parking lot, and it transformed the look of the factory from a low flat building appearing to be sitting in a field to looking like a professional business. I told the owners in the next board meeting about the gift, and they were unimpressed making no positive comments at all . . .

amazing, but not surprising. "Will it improve the output" was all that Joe growled into the meeting. So much for that!

I didn't care at all as I was going to continue to improve the business all I could as that was what I had been hired to do.

I knew that we couldn't survive on fire gloves alone and that the industrial gloves would all be lost to importers from China and Asia in only a matter of time, so I had to find a new business to get us into, and I had to do it quickly if we were to survive.

Vision is the absolute, required to be a leader. I learned here that many companies have such a short-sighted vision and only copy what everyone else has done rather than innovate for themselves.

SOME TECHNICAL PROBLEMS

When your back is up against the wall, focus only on the solutions to the problems.

ANOTHER PROBLEM TO be resolved, and now I had to develop a new breathable barrier for the inside of our firefighting gloves and began work immediately. Our barrier was not breathable, and Crosstech® had done such a stellar job at marketing that we were either to be forced out of the market, or we had to find an alternative barrier that was both breathable and non-Gore marketed.

I found a UK company and asked them to come over to meet me and to talk about making a flame retardant blood-borne pathogen barrier to go inside our firefighting gloves. We met in Kings Lynne in Norfolk in the United States, and the company had a breathable barrier that was far superior to our existing barrier. After months of trial and error, we finally had a barrier, but their quality was inconsistent and this made their barrier often pull out of the glove, a problem that had dogged Glove Corp for years. Added to this, our barriers were pulling out of the gloves; there was to be a new NFPA standard which included a "liner pull out test" which might prevent us from passing the annual NFPA certification tests.

I needed a new adhesive system, and I needed it fast. I called some manufacturing friends in UK and asked if they knew of any system that could be used. At that time there was a huge manufacturing show in Germany, and one of my contacts called me and gave me details of a system that he had seen there that could be used to get a better adhesion for the barrier and lining inside the gloves.

After months and months of development work, I had finally designed a system that would work and work extremely well and that would allow us to get a thinner, more flexible barrier inside our gloves with a unique adhesive system that would in turn allow us to make firefighting gloves with better dexterity that any on the market. More importantly it offered a superior end product than any that used Gore's liners currently.

The system I developed was state of art and would never allow the lining to pull out of the glove. We nailed it! We had a superior product to the mighty gorilla Crosstech® brand, and we had a far superior glove system that would revolutionize the firefighting glove market; at least that was my hope.

It was very advanced and had a high-tech method of keeping the barrier inside the glove barrier and which under no circumstances could ever be removed or pulled out of the glove. It was perfect! We had fixed all problems in one go; we had a new breathable barrier, a new adhesive system.

I presented the new system to the board to get agreement to purchase the adhesive system The board were reluctant to spend the money, but I explained to their almost deaf ears that if not, then we would lose our glove business as our gloves had a bad reputation for liners pulling out.

They let us go ahead and get the system which we set up and after some fine tuning and several more weeks of work finally got it to work consistently well.

I called the new system "Glove Bond" and began to market the system to all of our customers, making cutaways of the glove so that they could see how the new high-tech design worked and to explain to the firefighters the new improvements.

Our market share began to climb significantly, and we were beginning to do very well, however staff issues were always a problem in Heber Springs, since the new hires did not want to work and despite the pay and health benefits we offered, they were always quitting.

This became such a problem that we were replacing 50 percent of our staff annually which meant we were always training new hires. I think that it was a problem of the area we were in, an Arkansas problem, and something I couldn't change without moving the factory to another location.

Our new glove system was winning more and more business, and I had innovated another new concept which was a high temperature labeling system where instead of having a huge NFPA label sewn into each glove that got in the way of getting the fire gloves on and off, as used by all of our competitors. Our new label used a flat flexible label that was bonded onto the glove and couldn't be removed—another first for us.

Hard work does pay off but only when coupled with focus, vision and a determination to succeed no matter what!

MILITARY OPPORTUNITY

My market plan was being put into operation exactly as I had envisioned.

EARLIER ON, I was asked to take part in a new military program called a Rapid Field Initiative or RFI in order to improve the hand wear and apparel for our soldiers now fighting in Iraq. I was asked, by a military contracting group in Natick, if I would like to take part in a technical committee which included W L Gore, DuPont, and many other advanced materials manufacturers; and we were all charged with designing and producing better apparel for our military. During the first meeting, we were asked to place our cell phones on the table in front of each of us. When we did this the meeting leader showed us a mobile phone used at the beginning of 'Desert Shield' and 'Desert Storm' wars only ten years before. It was a large bag phone, and we all laughed. The point as he explained to us is that weapons and warfare has changed as much as these phones have changed. We all got the message loud and clear!

I was one of a very few glove makers in that technical group and I liked the challenge. During these meetings, I met with many manufacturers who made various military clothing from boots to Kevlar bullet proof vests and body armor.

Glove Corp was the first and only LEAN manufacturer in the United States, making gloves, and some of the military R & D staff wanted to come down to meet us and to see our factory. We began to start making, under contract, combat, and other military gloves which were very advanced, high dexterity multi-material gloves are required a far better sewing technique than that which we had been used to while making gloves in the industrial and firefighting market.

I had meetings with the entire factory staff, early in the mornings to win the staff over and to explain that if we were to survive in glove making in the United States, and if they were all to keep their jobs, we had to learn new skills and widen our knowledge.

We began to make these new gloves for companies like Camelbak and Wiley X, and we were advancing our methods into becoming one of the best in the United States. The Camelbak glove was very difficult, and they sent someone to get us started who had no idea how to sew at all. Still we learned a lot and moved forward into the very high-end products. I was then asked to design a new "light duty utility glove" that would eventually go into every kit bag for every GI in the U.S. Army, if I designed it well and was given several samples from which to design a new glove.

I made my designs on Microsoft Word as we did not have the money for a CAD system which could do the designs and produce workable drawings. I learned how to make new glove patterns, as I had already done this in reengineering our other firefighting gloves, so I applied this knowledge to these new gloves.

I started the new military glove in 2005 and finished it in 2006 sending samples to the R & D headquarters, to Valerie Banville, who was the handwear engineer responsible for engineering the new glove products for the army. Though quite young, in her late twenties, Valerie was brilliant and easy to work with; and she had visited our factory several times. She told us that we had the most advanced operation and one of the cleanest. I liked working with her as she was always so positive and very good at her job. She was easy to work with and knew what she wanted.

I completed a new design, and after testing the new glove in their labs at Natick they ordered three thousand pairs to be sent all over the world for field testing by the military personnel who would be wearing the gloves. I told the board during one of the bimonthly meetings about the new opportunity, but all they wanted to know was how many and what would be the profit. This was all they wanted to know about any of the things we were doing in their company and for the next three years during any board meeting they would continuously ask me "So where's the military order?" One owner, Tom, another family member and a complete idiot, even accused me of possibly taking the design somewhere else! We were steadily rebuilding the operation, and we were getting better and better in our production methods, but still having problems with staff losses every week. Pat and Keith had grown in their knowledge of production but still needed all the help they could get.

Keith had managed operations in Jamaica with nine hundred staff making shirts as well as in Mexico with five hundred staff. Pat, his wife, had been in manufacturing and had been in the front office when I took over the company.

As time went on, I had promoted Pat into the factory to assist Keith where she had been key in implementing LEAN and had come into her own steadily growing as a manager as I gave her more responsibility.

Keith was a very good manager. Keith though wanted to retire and didn't need the job or the money, whereas Pat wanted to continue to grow and to learn more about advanced production methods. Neither the head office nor the board and owners had any idea how hard Pat and Keith worked, every day to keep the factory running, and nor neither did they even care!

Pat and Keith both distrusted the head office staff and with good cause as after so many years of working with her, Sharon had never allowed them to purchase new equipment that they needed nor to allow them to increase the pay of the production staff, or put in air-conditioning. They both knew also that Sharon, after forty years in Glove Corp's business, had little idea of what went into any of the gloves or how they were made. Sharon was not interested in learning more.

In an effort to fix this disconnect, I instructed the head office staff to come to the factory to see all the improvements that had been made there. I gave them three months' notice, but as the time approached, they grew more and more negative about the visit. I knew that they had given the factory such a hard time over the years, through ignorance, that they had painted themselves into a corner. I cared nothing of the situation caused by, none other than, themselves and told them that if they backed out they would be looking for another job.

They finally went and I drove them by car as none of them wanted to fly. We arrived at the factory at around four in the afternoon, and as soon as we went through the entrance Sharon made a comment to Pat and Keith who had spent hours upon hours in cleaning, painting, reorganizing, and in completely transforming the operation and to all those that were within earshot that she could "see nothing different" and that it looked the same as she had seen several years earlier!

That was a stupid thing to say especially after all of the staff had worked tirelessly to improve their working environment. Our customers had seen the turn around, so had the Arkansas Manufacturing Systems staff who had been instrumental in getting us into LEAN and so had the Arkansas Department of Economic Development but apparently not Sharon!

I had had enough and asked the board to allow me to replace the three head office staff and to relocate it to Heber Springs. I showed them that it would save us nine thousand dollars a month in unnecessary costs and that none of the head office staff had any knowledge that was worth keeping as they offered nothing that would help improve the company. The board flatly refused to allow me to make the very necessary changes, which was strange in that these costs savings would go to them, and I thought there must be another reason. We kept "apparently" losing money despite all the cost savings that we had made in decreasing factory costs by 30 percent while increasing the profitability of the gloves we were now making.

We ran out of materials on a regular basis, and I made some advanced spreadsheets to enable them to better manage the inventory, what materials were needed, how much we had on stock, and exactly what needed to be ordered. Sharon couldn't use the spread sheet and kept running us out of material; the board was uninterested in taking action to make any change.

I was for the most time fighting the continued negativity coming from the head office staff. They didn't communicate with each other despite sitting no more than ten feet apart for decades. Still this was a battle for another day. I had too much to do to keep this company moving forward.

It was to say the least an uphill struggle working to improve that company, but I wanted to do what I set out to do, despite the board and owners, to make it the biggest glove operation in the United States—that was my personal goal.

There are some things that are almost impossible to change inside a company; so, either leave or carry on with your vision and whatever you do don't become side tracked.

A VACATION WITH GEOGIA

One week with my daughter would bring decades of memories

GEORGIA CALLED ME, while I was in the middle of everything, to see if we could have a holiday together and wanted it to be in the States. We discussed it, and I thought what a great idea! She and I could spend some great time together, and as I had customers on the northeast coast that I had planned to visit I could certainly take her with me. I arranged to fly her over to Boston where I would pick her up, and we would mix business with pleasure in a trip to Maine.

She told me she was three months pregnant, and this would be the last time for a very long time that she could be a single girl and able to do this. I asked her about her boyfriend, Lee, and she told me she hoped it was going to work out with him as she wanted a family including a father for her soon-to-be child.

I began to plan the trip, and I looked for hotels finding one that was, according to the online brochure, right on the beach. I called and asked the owner, who was Australian, "Are you saying that the hotel is in fact right on the beach?" And he said, "Yea, mate, right on the beach." "So it's right there with no other building that you're not mentioning in front between your hotel and the beach?" "No, mate nothing." "So if I book it, there's sand coming into the room like it seems in the brochure?" "Yes, yes, and yes." He said, "Now either book it or not, but let me know either way." So I booked it and hoped he was telling the truth. I next had to book a car, so I rented a convertible and hoped that the weather would hold; it was after all the middle of summer.

Georgia finally made it over, and I couldn't wait to see her, as it had been some two years since we had seen each other; and I was very, very happy to be spending a whole week, just her and me. As she came through Boston Airport, I met her at the passenger exit from the international terminal.

We hugged for at least an hour and just stood there letting the world go by as we both said nothing just to let that one moment linger. I wished Amanda could have come too, but unfortunately that wasn't to be. We picked up the convertible, a white Sebring, which was going to be perfect for our week together and headed north from Boston and up the coast toward Maine. We decided to meet up with Annabelle, Ian's sister who lived in Newhaven which was about an hour north of Boston.

Annabelle and her family, lived in an artsy house just back from the coast, and we all went to walk along the beach; Annabelle her husband, Forest, Georgia, and myself. Georgia wanted to know all about my childhood and Annabelle talked about Ian herself and me filling in details as we walked.

Forest taught dramatic art at Yale and had a good musical talent, so I played one of his guitars and sang some songs for them and their two children, Rye and Keele. We stayed the night and left the next day to get to the hotel I had booked near Oyster Bay on Old Orchard Beach, which I hoped would be perfect.

We left the following morning and drove up the coast road listening to the radio; the weather was absolutely perfect, hot, dry, and sunny; and I knew Georgia was making a memory of us both together as father and daughter which would last forever!

We arrived at the beach and found our hotel which was right on the sand as promised. The hotel was a two-story building and faced the ocean, with the beach actually at the doorway of our room. The owner hadn't lied at all, and the whole place was perfect, meant to be. Old Orchard Beach was a stretch of miles and miles of golden sandy beach that arced around the sea forming a very long wide bay. All Georgia wanted to do was to walk along the sand with me and talk about our past together going over her memories and filling in the missing details, I loved it and I love her very much. At night we got changed and drove into Portland to find some restaurants and pubs which were very prevalent in Portland. I told Georgia that I had always wanted to spend some quality time with her, just the two of us, exactly like this.

We stayed at that beach hotel for four days, walking, talking, and swimming; and I took some beautiful pictures of Georgia by Oyster Bay in the sunset just when the sky was a deep reddish purple reflecting on the still water of the bay. There were fishing boats in the background, and as I took the shot I noticed just behind Georgia a fisherman casting out, perfect. We took a leisurely drive back to Boston and stopped off at Kennebunk and Kennebunkport an area known for its beautiful homes and the mass of flowers in the town center.

I sat Georgia on a seat in front of a huge flower display of every color ever made, with thousands of flowers growing in a floral monument right in the middle of town. In the photo she is sitting in the middle of the flowers and is completely surrounded by all the colors in perfect bloom. We went on to Boston, talking and singing along the way completely oblivious of anyone else and just before we reached Boston International Airport, Georgia asked what Boston was famous for, and I told her that present day it was lobsters. "Let's get some and take them home to eat," she said on the spur of the moment, when we were only ten minutes from the airport and, as luck would have it, just at the moment she said that we came across a low white building on the side of the road advertising "Live Lobsters Hundreds to Choose From," and I swung immediately into its small car park. They advertised fresh live lobsters ready to ship to anywhere in the world! I hoped that Included Indianapolis, so in we both went and saw six huge tanks teeming with live lobsters of all sizes.

I knew nothing of picking out a lobster and asked the owner if he could pick out two for us which he did. Georgia was fascinated to see the writhing creature as it was picked out of the huge tank and placed carefully into a box of dry ice. We picked two of them which should be enough for Sue, Georgia, and me as they were huge. I placed a picture of them on my Facebook page. We were both going back to Greenwood before I went back with Georgia on business to England where I could spend time with Amanda.

We arrived home in Greenwood complete with our two huge lobsters and prepared to have a feast sitting outside by our pool in the back garden. I must say that I was not happy to be cooking the live lobsters as I don't like to kill anything, but I managed it after borrowing a huge cooking pot made for these creatures.

The dinner was perfect, and Georgia got to spend some quality time with James and Nicky, as she hadn't seen them both for several years. After two days at home, we left for London where I stayed at Amanda's house for a week.

That time was the best time I ever spent with my daughter Georgia; it was meant to be, and it was perfect. We had driven up the coast, went to restaurants and pubs, and walked along the beach in the hot sun. We also went to Kennebunkport where I took a beautiful picture of Georgia sitting in the midst of a towering array of flowers in the middle of town and spent the week catching up on everything. We both knew that may be the only time together for a long time.

I learned more about my now grown up daughter in one week than in a thousand conversations over the phone.

COMPETITION FROM OVERSEAS 1997

A threat is only a threat until you have analyzed it and found that it is really an opportunity (Malcolm McDonald).

BACK AT THE GLOVE Company, just as things were really looking up and sales were steadily growing, a new glove came into the fire glove market which had been made in Pakistan of all places. The glove had apparently passed the comprehensive NFPA testing which none of us other glove makers could understand how, since it seemed so flimsy and had only a very thin leather covering on the palm which in itself should not have been able to pass the rigorous wear test.

When all similar products in a given market have to pass the same rigorous testing procedures, it is reasonable that they would all take on similar characteristics in design and feel. This was not so with the new glove which took 20 percent of our sales within three months and had very quickly rendered Glove Corp. as a loss making operation. I knew that this would be our undoing unless I could do something about it. My competitors called me within days of each other to take action with them to try to stop this glove from entering the glove market.

One of my competitors had even produced many pamphlets full of really negative information about how bad the new glove was including photos, descriptions, and technical data all explaining why no one should buy this new glove. Their tone was venomous and stopped at nothing to warn all of the customers in no uncertain terms that the new glove was a sham, something to be avoided. They published *Dealer Advisories* full of test data attempting to prove that this glove was a dangerous product. I decided to test the imported glove, against rumors that I had heard, to see if it was in fact flammable. I cut the glove in half and asked Sharon for a lighter. When I held the flame to the glove, the liner went up in a 'whoosh' of flame. What was even more hilarious was that the CEO of the company importing this glove was actually on the phone to me asking that I stop my sales reps from making derogatory statements about his products. He didn't believe that his product was flammable so I told him "good luck with this"

'See for yourself' if a rumor is true to become armed with fact not fiction.

MORE HURDLES

Many companies try to force their customers to buy their products that are sometimes inferior to their competitor's instead of making better products.

I KNEW WITH ABSOLUTE certainty that if we were going to keep the company going, we should design something far better and make it in the United States as competition to the imported gloves instead of the other way around. I didn't believe that we should "buy American" simply because it is made here, but only because it is as good or better than what is being imported. Well, that was my decision—to make a better product and to do it in our factory, which would make it a U.S. product.

I began to design a new glove from scratch, not one, but a family of gloves—something that none of my competitors had done yet. I never bothered about my competition or what they were doing, but instead focused entirely on what I needed to do and in doing that left them to worry about me and not the other way round.

In this case though, it was a problem of survival—if I did nothing, we would lose the company within one year, so I had to take action, and fast.

To begin with, I got all of the gloves in our market from all of our competitors and placed them on a table in the factory. I then asked my staff to put each pair on and compare them with ours. I asked them what the difference was, and they could find little difference between ours and our competition. In fact, every one of them looked the same! No wonder competition was now filtering into the biggest firefighting apparel market in the world.

I then brought out the glove from Pakistan and asked them to now compare all of the gloves with this new one, passing it around from person to person.

The factory staff only ever saw their own products, never the competition's. They saw the difference in quality and sewing, and I then called the whole factory out and showed them what I was seeing and asked them what they thought. They told me that although the glove had better dexterity, it couldn't compete with ours as, as they saw it; we had such a history in the firefighting market. I explained to them all that it already had and that it had taken a chunk out of our sales and that if it continued, they would not have jobs anymore.

I told them that we were going to design a new range of gloves to beat the competition and that I would need their help to do this. They unanimously agreed, and I laid out to them all what we had to do. I told them it had to have no seams on the fingertips, no seams between the fingers, had to be very soft with excellent dexterity, yet with exceptional protection, and finally it had to have a thumb that would feel like you were wearing almost nothing.

I learned that to share my vision, of survival and the possibility of future success, with my employees made it easier to get it done with their help than without it.

LONG DISTANCE COMMUTE

Sometimes you just have to do what it takes no matter what.

I HAD TO DESIGN a new glove to compete with the imported products and started by dismantling a ski glove that we had in the front office. I have to say that I was needed more and more in the factory to help Pat and Keith to manage the operation as nothing could be done from the head office; it was simply a useless piece of real estate.

I had to keep my costs low by driving down to the factory from Indianapolis to Arkansas, a drive of some ten hours for the 560 miles each way. I had to leave my house on Sunday night at 11:30 p.m., drive through the night to arrive on Monday at around 8:00 a.m., ready to work the whole day until we closed the factory at 4:30 p.m.

I left the factory at closing time each Thursday afternoon arriving home very late and more often not until midnight on Friday or in the early hours. On Fridays, I worked from home doing my sales work contacting all of my reps and more than four hundred distributors I had all over the United States and Canada. I did this for more than three years in order to make it work. After some three months of doing this, I got challenged by Joe in a board meeting, of course, demanding why I wasn't in the office on Fridays asking me if I was part-time now, and if so, why did they need to pay me full-time!

I had to explain to him that I had driven twenty hours already to and from the factory and preferred not to drive to the office another three hours on Fridays. It was better and more effective to work from home.

Sharon had been up to not good but we carried on working together because she was immune from being fired, but after that board meeting, I moved some of her work to the factory office to reduce her influence and potential for damage.

To undermine the CEO is a one-way street often resulting in failure later.

THREATS FROM THE FAMILY

When you receive, a threat left on an answering machine always record it!

Not long after that, I got to the factory, one Monday morning to be greeted by my ashen-faced young front office manager, who was very upset at something. She told me I needed to hear the messages that had been sent into the company overnight and were on the answering machine. The messages, twelve in all, were swearing and calling me insulting names shouting down the phone calling me a son of a bitch, a lousy manager, incompetent, spending company money like water, and some other words and indiscernible phrases I will not put into this book. Needless to say, from what I could now see Tom was drunk when he made these threatening calls to the factory. There were many threats made to me in that set of twelve phone messages, which incidentally became more and more indecipherable the more drunk Tom became throughout the tirade of what was now becoming an almost incoherent string of verbal abuse.
He rambled on and on even slamming the phone down on himself,. At this point I went out to Radio Shack and got a small recorder and recorded all twelve of these abusive messages, and I still have them, for prosperity, and as a reminder of the stupidity of people.

The reason we had been losing money, as was the case at this time, was through diminished sales as a direct result of competition from imported products that I was now trying to deal with. I lived on crummy hotel breakfasts, McDonald's or more often Subways for dinner each night.

I had kept costs down as much as possible in order to keep the company going until we had better more competitive products. I brought up the abusive messages I had received from Tom Walsh to the board, during the next board meeting, but was told not to worry about it as this was not unusual for Tom. I told Rob that he had damn well better make sure Tom got the message as I was doing everything possible to keep their business going. Something would have to give, that I knew for certain, but for now I was far too busy to be bothered by it.

I don't suffer fools; I let other people do that!

INNOVATION THAT WORKED

When I focused my vision of what was required for the company to succeed, nothing could stop me from making it happen.

I CONTINUED TO DEVELOP the new glove which I was going to call "Blaze Fighter" often doing a lot of the work at home on weekends as I was too busy helping run the factory which was getting harder and harder as we tried in vain to keep a more stable staff level.

The town of Heber Springs did little to nothing at all to attract more workforce into the area as they were only interested in the Greer's Ferry Lake, which incidentally you could not see from the town. The lake was huge and did attract vacationers, but the only way to see the lake was when you were on it as there was nowhere to see it from the town.

I finally had the glove design I wanted, and it looked very cool; the design was nothing like any other product on the market. The glove was a totally new concept, and no other product on the U.S. market was even close to my radical design. The back was made of black military grade Kevlar, with several layers underneath to make the thermal protection to the firefighters as high as possible. There were roll over fingertips requiring no seams at all, no seams between the fingers, a three-dimensional pre-curved design that fitted perfectly to the hand and was probably the most advanced design on the U.S. market. The dexterity was unbelievable, and the whole process had taken me some seven hundred hours, most of which was done at home to get the job done.

The next hurdle was I had to get the glove tested and certified which was extremely hard to do and was outside of my control.

After several additional modifications and another two months of work on the design, we finally had a new certified firefighting glove. I had planned to do exactly this. I had laid out a set of design criteria onto a clean empty piece of paper and had created something that was U.S. made and so different from anything else in the market that firefighters, hopefully, would not want to buy gloves made overseas especially from Pakistan where we believed that Osama bin Laden was in hiding. Unbelievably, I had told many, many people at the time that that was where he was, and it was obvious as he couldn't be in Saudi or in Iraq, and that was the closest country. Anyway I was not content with one glove only; I also made a second glove which was even more advanced and was a dual purpose firefighting and extrication glove to be used with extracting victims from vehicles involved in road accidents. I succeeded in making two glove designs and getting them both certified within three months which was a miracle since the certification process especially for a brand-new product was usually a real problem. I had done it though, to my utter amazement, and had designed not one but two brand-new products. I had gotten both through the extremely hard to pass "liquid integrity" test that left me pulling my hair out!

We finally got the news that our new Blaze Fighter gloves had finally passed the NFPA testing process, and I let everyone know in the factory that we were now ready to go to market with our new gloves.

I took the final version of the gloves around the factory to each of my employees. The final glove was black on the back and palm with bright yellow leather between the fingers and a yellow knuckle patch on the black Kevlar back. It was like nothing else in the market, and I let all my staff try on the new gloves, thanking all those that had been involved in the development and reminding those that told me how much they loved the new gloves, that although they loved it now, they would hate it later when they were making more than a thousand pairs a day! I always involved my factory staff in both the successes and the failures of our products and our market, letting them know, in early meetings usually at 5:50 a.m. with all the staff present, what the issues facing our company were.

I thought that in this way they could be given the opportunity to help resolve the problems as well as helping find solutions.

I also had to ensure that my new breathable glove moisture barrier was fixed in a much more effective method than the old low tech method that our competitors used. W L Gore had refused to supply us with barriers and tried very hard to force us out of the firefighting glove market. They had no idea of the power of 'One' and that was me!

It's not easy to invent a brand-new product while your company is losing money; but one thing is for certain, you can't give up just because it's a difficult task!

NO COMMENT

When working with stubborn people who can't be fired, keep focused on what you are doing and don't worry about them.

I SENT SAMPLES OF the new "Blaze Fighter" and "Blaze Fighter EXT" glove to the head office and asked them to give me feedback. They didn't bother to respond but I wasn't letting them off the hook though, I called them after a week and asked if they had received the glove samples. They had and told me it was "OK" and as Missy said, "It's just another glove," and that was all. However at the factory the staff were very proud of what they had helped to create, and they truly hoped it would win us orders so they could all keep their jobs. One of my older factory employees told me that she had prayed daily that we would make it through these tough times, and I let her know how much I appreciated her thoughts and asked her not to stop. I said to her be careful what you ask for because you may actually get exactly that, and we both laughed trying to imagine what that could be!

I sent the board members samples and got the same result, as I had got with Sharon and Missy, they only wanted to know how much profit it would make. Again they just didn't get it; this was shit or bust! If it didn't "take off" in the market, they would lose their company within a few months, and that would be the end of it for all of us. I could get another job, but many of my sewing staff could never get another job. I got very little positive response from my head office or the family owners, which showed me again that they really didn't have a clue as to how their business worked.

I wanted to see the market reaction and had at this point no idea if the market would like or dislike our new Blaze Fighter gloves as I had only sent out around two dozen pairs to gauge a reaction and to test them in the market, and the results were good. I had worked my ass off to get this done, and I had succeeded despite the people around me, and I knew what the downside would be if I didn't succeed.

They say that necessity is the mother of invention, and it's true. I prayed for guidance in this difficult time, not for myself, out for the jobs of my staff. They were the important ones, and they were the people that had no ability to control their destiny, as far as their work was concerned, but if they did what I asked them to do, and I was convinced of what was required, their jobs would be safe; of that I was certain.

I remained focused on developing our new product, now it's up to the market to decide if it is any good!

THE LAUNCH

There's more than one way to get a job done.

I LAUNCHED THE GLOVES at the biggest fire equipment trade show in the United States, the FDIC, in Indianapolis in May 2008. I asked the board to let me have some advertising money from our disused line of credit that we had for more than ten years, and they flatly refused, as it would reduce their monthly dividend.

So I found another way to get the job done. I made eighty pairs and sent each pair to our top eighty distributors and waited to see what would happen. During the launch at the FDIC in Indianapolis in 2008, the glove was a resounding success, and I had asked Pat and Keith to travel to Indianapolis from Arkansas, to be present at the show to talk about the work that had gone into the development as PR. I was disappointed though that the two people who did the least for the company to keep the company going, and whom I could not remove, quite apart from being so negative, while having the easiest time of all my staff, who seldom if ever worked a single minute past 5:00 p.m. had not shown any interest in the new gloves or their potential success for their company.

In December 2008, I called Sharon and asked her what our sales were like for the two Blaze Fighter gloves, although she probably knew, she said she needed to check and call me back. When I got no call back I e-mailed her and asked her for the numbers. She finally told me we had sold $1 million and in only in six months. I was elated and made sure that I told all the factory staff of our success. The other point is that before we had launched the new glove the company had been making losses each month as a result of the impact from overseas competition into our U.S. market. However, by the end of 2009, only eighteen months after the initial launch, we had turned the significant losses in 2008 into a 'significant' profit and all because of the Blaze Fighter designs.

Up to this point, I had designed a total of twelve new products for the company, installed a new and advanced LEAN manufacturing process, designed and built a high-tech adhesive system like nothing that had ever existed in the U.S. glove manufacturing, and had done it all to ensure that each problem we had encountered had been dealt with effectively. My belief was that if ever I encountered a problem, I would fix it to a better level than it was before the problem existed. In short, we were now "kicking ass," and before the board meeting in January 2009, I had asked Rob for a raise. I had not had a raise since 2005 and gas prices, food prices, mortgages, and everything else had gone up significantly. Rob promised to do something as I had managed to turn the company around.

However my issue was never brought up, despite an outstanding year end result and despite a near fatal position in our marketplace. Sue was furious with me as she could see that in her view I had done more than enough for the company with all of the travel, being away every week, living "cheap," developing new products, and being insulted by owners in the process etc., etc.—it was tough for us, but I would save that battle for later.

What had passed them by was the fact that we had managed to save the company from imminent closure again and again and had instead placed ourselves in a position of potentially becoming the biggest glove manufacturing company within the United States, still read on! Worse was yet to happen!

I managed to pull the company out of potential failure again and it didn't matter to me if the board recognized it or not because the jobs I saved for my factory and staff were reward enough for me!

PINE BLUFF!

Though I hate to use a cliché sometimes we have to think outside the box.

WE STILL HAD A serious problem in finding staff at the Heber Springs operation, and since the town of Heber Springs was unwilling to offer any help, or even bother to come to see all of the improvements we had made, I had to find another solution as our glove sales were increasing; and we had an even worse problem with staffing the production lines. That was easier said than done, so I called for help to the one single organization that had helped us in the past. I called the Arkansas Department of Economic Development (ADED) and they came immediately to meet me once again at the factory.

I explained what our problem was, in not being able to keep our staff, despite having great and high selling products and asked for their help. I should say here that again we are given all of the tools we will ever need to succeed, but it's up to us to make sure we use them. I knew that ADED had a vested interest in seeing our company succeed and would help us find a solution. The town of Heber Springs was uninterested in Glove Corp as too much damage had been done by Frank and the board long before I had ever taken the company over.

"Have you thought of using correctional facility workers, you know! Using prison inmates," they suggested. I thought about this and asked how much we would have to pay them. I was told that we had to pay the inmates a required minimum wage which in Arkansas was $7.15 per hour since all of their upkeep and medical costs were covered by the State. I thought this to be a brilliant suggestion and agreed to look into it as soon as they could set up a meeting with the Arkansas Department of Corrections.

We met them two weeks later and were invited to go to a correctional facility (prison) in Pine Bluff which was two and a half hours south of Heber Springs to see what was involved. I had never been inside a prison, and this was a real experience. All of the inmates were dressed in white prison uniforms and walked around the compound to and from their jobs in small groups behind an armed guard.

I took Pat with me as Keith had to stay to manage the now very busy factory. We got through the security guards and finally after a lot of information about the prison dos and don'ts and the federal laws of what we could do and couldn't do while we were inside the facility. The room that they had set aside for us was around five thousand square feet and was completely empty but had air-conditioning, an office, a bathroom, and our own prison guard who would sit behind a desk every production day. The whole prison facility was a large sprawling operation located in a wooded area interspersed with tall trees, sprawling buildings, and of course numerous high barbed wire fences everywhere.

It looked like a camp with dusty roads, grassy areas, sprawling buildings, and each area separated by ten feet high razor wire fence. While working outside, the inmates were always covered by guards with heavy carbines on horseback, always watching over the many inmates of which there were upward of over one thousand at Pine Bluff.

Just outside our building was a guard post comprising a tall round gray-colored concrete tower, some forty feet high, with a windowed office that had 360 degree visibility. The part I thought that was funny was the fact that once they started their daily watch, they were not allowed down under any circumstances. So each tower guard had to pee in a bucket which was hoisted up and down, yuck, on a rope at regular intervals, as well as the prison food that they were given during the day. The doorway was locked and was not opened until their watch had finished when they were replaced by another armed guard.

I asked the warden who accompanied us to our potential facility, "What if they have diarrhea, what do they do then?"

He looked at me coolly and said, "They order more buckets." It was funny though, and I thought if I wanted to escape I would give them some heavy dose of laxative and watch the fun.

In order to get to our building, we had to go through the metal screening process, leave our cell phones and all other objects at the front office. We then had to wait for each of the five locked gates to be unlocked by a guard in order to get to the factory.

Our room had several security cameras covering 100 percent of the room with a small army of guards watching us the whole time. We even had our own prison officer to remain with us while we were setting things up.

I could imagine that any staff we had here would always show up for work, never ever have a day off, never be "ill" with a Monday morning blues that devastated our Heber operation but would become well again on Tuesday as our Heber Springs staff were often prone to do.

We could have a steady work flow and could plan on good production numbers—that is if we could train them to and if they could manage to sew. I wanted to do this, partly because it fixed a problem that Heber Springs had in staff actually bothering to show up, and partly because it offered us a "win-win" alternative.

Each inmate was paid minimum wage at $7.15 per hour of which some of their earnings went to the victim's fund, some went to their upkeep, and the remainder was banked for them unless they had a judgment in which they had to pay some reparation or support to their family. They could spend some of their money in the concessionary store on Thursdays and had to line up early on these days in order to go over on their weekly visit to buy things using the money they had earned. We agreed to give it a try, and I wanted to begin small with fifteen inmates only to see if it would work.

We set up some pre-screening criteria in which we would only accept inmates who had been nonviolent while doing time and who had not had any serious infractions while inside. We also insisted that each potential hire had at least a General Education Diploma (GED).

There are many options to get a job done if you are open to new ideas.

NICK JOINS THE COMPANY

Family comes first every time!

WE NEEDED MORE help, and I managed to convince Nick, who had been struggling with drugs, to work with me at the factory. I had decided that he needed to be shown some responsibility and to feel that he was needed and was earning his own money. I convinced him to at least come with me to the factory and see if he could do the work. Fortunately, his school friend, a very pretty girl called Brooke, also convinced him to give it a try as well. He came with me and began to work with Pat. Pat had a soft spot for Nicky as she had the same issues with her daughter some years earlier. Nick responded well to Pat's guidance and was given some responsibilities after a few weeks.

We had at that time won a contract for a high dexterity military combat glove which was nothing like anything we had made before. The glove was in camouflage green leather and had a very hard polycarbonate contoured molded knuckle piece on the back.

Nicky helped with the design of an adhesive process for the knuckle which required an infrared heating system, and Nicky managed and operated a small production line of workers to make the hundreds of knuckle pieces every day. He did this with no effort and the staff he was responsible for liked working with him. I took him with me every Sunday night and got home late Thursday or early Friday with Nicky sleeping most of the time along the way. He responded very well to the responsibility we had given him and began to get off drugs which was a monumental effort for him. I thanked God for the opportunity to turn him around and hoped daily that he would stick with it. We started the process of designing a hiring process with an aptitude test for the first fifteen inmates, in the newly formed prison operation. We were going to hire based on a "test" program to see if the prison worker program would work for us.

Pat took Nicky to Pine Bluff with her, and after Nicky was given his "Prison Pass" he designed an aptitude test whereby each inmate had to control the operation of the sewing machine to make the foot follow several bold black lines drawn on a piece of cream-colored material, using the sewing machine properly.

There were no sewing needles in these test machines, but Nick explained to each potential hire how to operate the machine and how to lift, turn, and sew with the foot while following the drawn lines on the fabric as exactly as possible. Nick would time them for fifteen minutes and see how they followed his instruction and if their speeds increased.

He also observed them during each interview process and gave Pat some very insightful observations while watching each interviewee's behavior during the interview.

Pat told me that he was very observant and possessed a good understanding of people, noticing a lot in body language that Pat missed. She relied on his input, and if Nicky didn't think an inmate would work out she didn't hire that person. She and Nick got along really well, and Nick was responding positively to the experience.

I got grilled by the board after three months following Nick's employment as to why I had hired Nick and what his job was and how much I was paying him, thanks but not surprisingly to Sharon, again. I told Sharon in front of the board that if she had any problems with any of my hires she was welcome to go each week to Heber Springs and do the hiring and training herself. I also told the board that if they didn't trust my judgment, then they should find someone else to do the things I did, and I would gladly leave and find an easier job with a more responsive board. There can only be one leader." I told them that Nick had become a valuable employee and that if Pat or Keith didn't think he was pulling his weight, they would not let him work as a supervisor. I said nothing of this to Nick, but it infuriated me nonetheless, and we kept him in the facility until Christmas 2008 when he decided that he wanted to find a job closer to home, which was fine by me, at least he was back in the mainstream of the working community.

The work had given him responsibilities, and he had risen to the task. This experience was a key item now on his resume, and his brief spell working in my environment has taught him what real responsibility was all about.

The decision to give Nick some responsibilities was the right one as he did very well, and he contributed to the company at a time when we needed help. My managers trusted my judgment as I trusted theirs, and it paid off!

IN PRISON!

You have to risk failure to risk success!

WE STARTED WITH the prison operation at Pine Bluff Arkansas but rapidly outgrew that facility and had to move our operation to Newport in Arkansas during 2009. We had begun with only fifteen inmates as a trial operation and now had fifty-five in total.
It was awesome seeing fifty-five inmates all dressed in white, sitting at sewing machines and doing real well at it. They had to operate at full production capacity for four ten-hour days with Fridays off.

In January 2010, one of the inmates spoke to me as he was working sewing palms to backs. "Can I talk to you, Mr. Tony?" he asked, as that was how they all addressed me. "Yes," I replied, "but keep on sewing as we are under constant surveillance." He went on, "I've done some pretty bad things in my life." And I knew that to be true, now this inmate was a murderer and was doing well in one of my production lines. "But one thing I truly regret," he said, "was that my sister had given me $1,500 for college fifteen years ago, and she has never had much money but I got caught doing some bad things and ended up here," he told me.

"Is this going somewhere?" I asked him. And he replied, "Yes, it is." So he continued to talk quietly to me so as not to draw attention to his conversation. He went on to tell me that he asked the warden how much money he had in his prison bank account just before Christmas and was told that he had $2,500 accumulated as he never spent any money at the concession shop.

"I have never had that much money ever in my life," he told me. "And I knew what I had to do. I asked the warden if he could find my sister in Alabama and find a way to give it all to her," he said. "Well, that's good," I said, but he went on and told me that just after Christmas he got his first visitor in fifteen years, and it was his sister coming to see him.

"I saw her for the first time in fifteen years," he said, and she told me that both her and her husband had been laid off at the Tyson chicken processing factory and had absolutely no money at all. She told him they were about to lose their house and even maybe their children may have to go into care until they could get themselves straightened out. "Then suddenly, $2,500 came to me out of the blue, from you!" she said. "And after all this time it came just when we needed it most. Thank you so much!" she told him. "You saved our family, and you did it while you were inside prison."

I'm not an idealist, but, I could see that the load of guilt that he had carried had now been paid off in full, though there was the reason he was inside still to deal with. "So that's a good thing then," I said to him adding, "so please just keep doing exactly what you are doing and keep focused on this." I said to him. "Oh I will, and I am sending her every penny I make here each month. Thank you, Mr. Tony, for giving me this chance!"

Cool huh! Some good coming from our work there while making gloves at the prison. Just as an afterthought though, despite this, whenever I had to do a "time out" for the fifty-five inmates, I always made sure that the exit door was right behind me and that it was wedged open with an armed guard standing next to me . . . Just in case!

Some risks are worth taking and if the only downside is a little difficulty to get it done, then it's still definitely worth it. In this case we increased our workforce cost effectively at a critical time.

JAMES COMES OUT

We don't control the conditions under which we are born.

JUST AFTER JAMES had graduated from Center Grove Senior school, he texted me asking that I stop what I am doing and take the time to read an important message from him. I texted back and told him to go ahead, though I had no idea what was so important. The text arrived shortly after saying that James was gay, and that we could take it or leave it, but it was nevertheless a fact that despite trying to go out with girls, that was not for him!

I read the message and called Sue, "Well?" she asked. "What do you think?" I laughed and told her that we had both known that since he was five years old when he went shopping with her and helped to pick out her shoes!

I texted James back telling him that both I and his mother had both known this for years and that it was absolutely fine with us both. I told him I loved him very much, and he would always have my love, affection, and support in whatever he wanted to do with his life, and no matter what he was our son and nothing would ever change that. I thanked him for feeling that he had to tell me but DUH! We both already knew.

He texted me back breathing a sigh of relief in his message and seemed deeply relieved that all was still well and that he knew we both understood him very well and that we were both fine with his "coming out." I replied that he should have known us both much better than to have even thought that it would be an issue as it certainly would never ever be. After that, and with being away from school, he was finally able to be James, the James he wanted to be, spiked up hair with red flashes, or completely blonde looking like Billy Idol, I didn't care, after all I was a "mod" when I was younger, so what the hell!

I was happy that James felt confident in telling us he was gay, though we already knew; he was in fact born gay. So, if we are born gay how can that be wrong!

NEW YORK NEW YORK!

FDNY was my target when designing my new glove now was the moment of truth.

As SALES WERE now climbing in 2009, from the Blaze Fighter, samples had been given to FDNY which was the biggest fire department in the world with around eight thousand firefighters and every equipment company making firefighting products would love to have FDNY as a key account. This was not only the biggest department but also the busiest the most prestigious in the world.

I was to present my glove and to explain how the design was different from any other in the market. Now Gore with their Crossetech® brand had been marketing their product to FDNY for over a decade and had spent millions of dollars in promotions to ensure that they "had" New York's finest as their exclusive account selling breathable blood-borne pathogen barriers inside gloves, boots, and turn-out gear. FDNY was also the toughest for any company to get their products into. One strange thing though was that around this time, I noticed that all of my Blaze Fighter patterns had been removed from my computer over one weekend. A whole file left on the desktop of mine, and Pat's computer had gone. I mentioned it to Pat and Keith but got no response.

It didn't matter much though as I had all the knowledge in my head and didn't need hard copies at all.

I knew that my glove didn't have a "Gore" barrier inside and instead had a completely different one not made by Gore as they still refused to sell Glove Corp their vapor barrier. If I was to have even a slim chance of winning FDNY I had to explain to them how my barrier worked and why I had used it instead of using a Gore's Crosstech® barrier. The management of Crosstech® within the fire glove market had threatened my competitor Shelby that if he continued to make gloves with another barrier they would "divorce him," so he buckled and stopped using any other barrier. Glove Corp was the only U.S. glove manufacturer that did not have their Crosstech® barrier which they had refused us.

I took some samples with me and had a meeting set up with five of the heads of the FDNY's research and development group, through which any and every product that FDNY wanted to use had to go through to be thoroughly tested before a decision was made. The head of the glove project and I worked very closely together.

I made a presentation at FDNY's head office in New York, at their Randall's Island research facility with my local representative, Frank Mc. Ardle, sitting next to me.

That first meeting took me one and a half hours to complete. During that time, I managed to convince them that our manufacturing system was far more advanced than what was being offered by any of the other glove companies using Gore's Crosstech® barrier. I succeeded, and they liked my design. "Why don't you use the Crosstech® barrier?" one of them asked me, and I told them that we were the only glove company in the entire United States that Gore had refused to sell their barrier to, and I didn't know why. I also explained that Gore's senior staff that worked with fire and military and even sat in the same glove military committee meetings and had told me that "they make fillet mignons, while Glove Corp makes McDonald's." That gave them all in that important meeting a real laugh. I also told them of the design work I was doing for the U.S. Army for several gloves for combat, light duty, and razor wire handling and that did it.

They told me this was a very important part of what we had to offer and that when the time came I had to make sure I mentioned this to the fire chiefs I would meet after they had completed their internal testing of the glove.

When you've never had the business in the first place you don't lose anything in trying your hardest to win it. However, losing business that you've already had is another thing entirely!

FIVE REAL SUPERHEROS

Some people we meet, although for a fleeting time, leave a lasting impression

THE TESTING WENT very well and the glove had proven itself to be all that I had said it would be. I was called back to New York to the research and development department again to meet with five of the busiest fire chiefs in the world, located at various fire stations in New York City in order to present the glove to them. There would be three other companies who had also become the finalists in the ability to supply a new style firefighting glove. These were the "on-scene chiefs" that had managed to deal with the terrorist attacks on 9/11 and who had lost many of their firefighters. To me these were the true heroes in life, and I felt privileged to be meeting them in person and to show them what I had created. At that point I realized that I really hoped FDNY would take my glove design.

I was introduced to the five of them as they entered the room, all were dressed in crisp white shirts, and they each shook hands with me, looking me straight in the eye as they did so. I felt in awe of the five of them, as they sat there in front of me in their white uniform shirts with their medals, from 9/11, and the fire captain's badge on their chests. It was a humbling experience to be discussing the design and concept of my glove with them, for it was their choice as to which glove they would decide to wear. This meeting was a highlight in my present career, and I didn't want my glove to fail.

I said a quiet prayer and hoped that I wouldn't screw this up. "Please, God, don't let me fuck this up," I prayed. The five chiefs sat quietly around the large square table in that research and development headquarters by the entrance to New York City on Randall's Island and let me present the glove. The room went quiet as I took a deep breath and began to present the design, how long it took me to complete why I felt compelled to make a new glove, where it was made, testing, and the final product samples of which I had brought for them to see at the meeting. I mentioned in passing that imported gloves from Pakistan were probably helping our enemies as everyone knew that Osama bin Laden was hiding in Pakistan. When I had finished my presentation, they asked many questions but seemed happy with what they had learned during our meeting. I left them with 250 pairs of gloves as requested to be used as a field test of the glove and could do nothing more than wait to see the results.

A week later I was called by one of the R&D chiefs who told me that they unanimously agreed that the presentation I had done was the best of the four. That feedback was great news, but now it was up to the glove to perform well which I hoped it would. Well, so far so good, the rest is now out of my hands ('scuse the pun)!

All the work had been completed so we now had to wait for the goal that we had been working towards. Second guessing at this point was not an option.

U.S. ARMY

Just when you least expect it everything comes together all at once!

JUST AT THE same time as we were getting into FDNY the army glove I had designed three years earlier was finally being decided upon by the army. Everything was coming together; all of the hard work was finally showing fruition.

In the three years since I had completed the design for the new Light Duty army glove the Glove Corp board, whenever we met, had constantly asked where the army order was and why we had not received it yet. Tom Walsh was asking if I had non-compete and if I was looking to steal it from the company. All this while at the same time he insisted on calling me Roger all through the board meeting. I should point out that Roger Rue was one of my predecessors who had been fired some fifteen years earlier and had in fact been replaced at least three times over!

In December 2008, Valerie, from Natick headquarters, called me to let me know that my glove had gone to the Pentagon and had been well accepted as a new "kit bag" item which would lead to hundreds of thousands of pairs per year being bought from whoever won the contract to supply the glove. This was a final part in the acceptance of that glove, and it was now ready for purchasing which would now happen very quickly. I was asked by the contracting department to let them have all of my size patterns so that they could be digitally reproduced.

During the next board meeting I told the board that the army glove was going ahead and I had until January 20 to complete all of the documentation. Of course, the board members were only interested in knowing how much we would make on each pair and how many we could sell. I told them that we had not won the contract yet and had to bid for the glove and that if we were awarded the contract we would have to invest in new machines and material to get it ramped up into full production.

I decided that since this Light Duty Utility glove was my design, I would do everything I could to win the contract, and I asked Pat and Keith to "imagine" us winning it and making the gloves because if they did that, it was going to happen. This was after all the vision I had for this little company, back in 2003, to make it the biggest glove production company in the United States, and we were now finally on that path. I completed the documentation and sent our bid proposal out, along with an absolutely perfect sample glove, making sure it got there well before the deadline.

Pat came up to me in the factory a few days later and told me of a dream she had several months before in which she saw me standing in the factory surrounded by hundreds of machines and the factory was completely full of people making thousands of gloves daily. The way she described it I knew when she told me that that we would win the order and that we would have more business than we could handle.

We were next visited by a factory inspector from the army who went through our numbers and agreed that we could make the glove in our facility. I had to make a layout drawing showing where all of the glove production lines would go. We actually won the army glove bid in May 2009! And we were overjoyed at that accomplishment. The board were, for some reason, getting cold feet after three years of design and very hard work to make it happen. They had been hounding me as to where the order was for the three years since we started the project, and now we had it they realized that we would have to spend money! When we knew we had won the contract, I called a board meeting to let them know we needed investment capital in order to buy new machines, and we would need to hire around forty-nine new staff and machines to make the glove. There was no vote of thanks, no well done, no remotely positive statement about all the work it had taken to do this and to finally win the contract.

Where I should have felt great I felt lousy and at the very point in time when I should have been happy with what I had done. We knew it would take around twelve weeks to ramp up, and we had prepared a ramp-up plan to show the board. We could only bid for 60 percent of the contract as we were a small business but that would still be ten thousand to fifteen thousand pairs a month. I showed the spreadsheet on Saturday, to Rob and Allen, but Allen refused to even see it and chose to walk off from the meeting at a Starbucks on the north side of Indianapolis.

After we had won the contract though, I was told that our preparation was so well prepared that the army contracting office wanted us to make 100 percent of the contract which was minimum over twenty thousand pairs a month, on top of what we were already doing very cool.

The board agreed to let me use our line of credit in order to get the army glove line up to speed. In the factory, we were hiring staff getting leather in and buying more sewing machines and leather in order to make the vast quantity of army gloves that we now had orders for. I have never been so busy as I was now, but that was fine I knew this would happen. The board though were becoming aggressive while we were ramping up, demanding to know where the profit was, Duh!

We were near the end of ramping up for the new army glove and completely on time with all we had planned but in December 2009, we naturally showed a loss since we were training forty-nine new staff members for three months along with purchasing leather to make the new glove. I was now spending 100% of my time on the new military glove line. The board however got cold feet, and before we were fully up to speed, they pulled the plug on the ramp-up costs just as we were a few weeks from full production! They did this because they did not want to continue with the investment and due to our staffing issues, we were, not surprisingly, over on our cost estimates.

Anyway they had stopped us using the line of credit, just when we were almost at the end of the ramp up phase and had almost reached the point of profitable operation and at our most vulnerable point.

Strange that sometimes when you get what you ask for, you actually do get exactly that, which in this case was the biggest army glove contract that was possible. Now that they had the contract and had to invest, they were not prepared to see this through.

As a side point, I contacted the mayor and Elders of Heber Springs to see if we could get a small grant to buy sewing machines. I told them that we would be hiring forty-nine new staff, at a time when the country was in the deepest recession since 1927, and this would double our weekly payroll that would pay back the grant in the form of spending money and payroll tax in the town and county in only a few months.

They refused and instead offered me a paltry payroll tax reduction of around 2 percent which would amount to around $30 per week after promising us that they would help us. This refund would not come until after a year of increasing staff. Also this payroll tax reduction would only be on the increased payroll of the forty-nine staff that we had hired and would be in the form of a tax credit payable some two years later. I thanked them but declined their "generous" offer.

Funny thing is that this insightful decision of the local Heber Springs town council was another of the key elements in starting the downfall of the Glove Corporation who as I said earlier had been there since 1952!

The Blaze Fighter glove continued to become the single biggest-selling glove in the United States and was now requiring more staff and more sewing and leather cutting machines in order to make them. The correctional facility operation now had fifty-five staff and was humming along. We had moved all the inmates from Pine Bluff to Newport which was a lot closer and easier to get to. FDNY told us that in the end it may be a political decision and that despite the excellence of the glove we may or may not get the contract.

All that Pat had seen in her dream had come true, as we now had 126 staff all making gloves, a factory completely full of staff, and thirteen leather cutters cutting more leather than the company had ever cut in its entire history.

January 2010, the results of 2009 sales and profits were in, and we made a very small loss. The Blaze Fighter had sold millions of dollars that year, but we had invested in a large new glove line comprising forty-nine new staff and forty-nine new sewing machines. That plus the new materials and the hiring and training of the new staff had cost the company in investment in the new glove line. However, we had a four-year profitable contract to produce thousands of gloves each week from that point forward and the start-up costs has all been concentrated in a three-month period from July to September and was exactly to plan.

The board though had got cold feet and had pulled the plug just as we were entering the final phase of the start-up, with maximum costs and with profitability just weeks away, and in doing so had severely damaged the company.

As a result of their sudden decision in the fall of 2009 not to let us use more from the line of credit, despite having decided to allow us to do so before we began the production, they had created a situation where we were limping along with insufficient funds to buy leather right at the final stage of ramp up.

It made the already difficult job of hiring and training the new staff, while making a quota of gloves that we had agreed to for the army, almost impossible now. The board meeting was a fiasco, with Joe shouting down the phone as per usual and the meeting became intolerable. Allen was the most insulting and vocal, and he was the one who had attended the least number of board meetings since I had run the company.

A week later I was told that their nephew, who had no experience in ever running a company like this and knew little of this business, would now be running the company, but I was to help him. I thought that he was probably giving a month's notice at his present job, and that would be all I had in time before the other shoe dropped.

This was now an intolerable position for both me and the company and would inevitably lead to the company's demise as I would not put up with this situation. I doubted that there was anyone who knew enough to run this unique operation.

Anyway, despite being told that all would be OK for me as long as I let him make all the decisions, I ignored it and carried on making decisions and letting him know what I had done after I had done so with the full knowledge that this would absolutely cost me my job. I was past caring! I would never accept to work for someone far less competent than me especially a family member who had no experience. I warned Pat and Keith that I was going to be leaving on Monday, and they would have to carry on with the nephew, Allen Town, as their new boss.

On Friday evening on the February 12, I received a phone call from our webmaster who had designed our Web site and who hosted our e-mail system. He said, "Tony, I don't know how to tell you this but you are going to be let go on Monday morning at 8:00 a.m.!" He told me that he had received a phone call from someone at Glove Corp telling him that he was now running the company and that he had to switch off my e-mails at 8:00 a.m. on Monday. He underestimated the number of friends I had around the business.

I was not surprised at all as I knew that this would in all probability happen very soon, and I was already "across the bridge" and looking to my next job as I had been for several months.

When we know what the likely outcome of a difficult situation is going to be, we are already prepared for it good or bad. I chose to proceed on regardless and do the best I could while preparing for my next challenge.

UNDOING OF GLOVE CORP.

What I had predicted came true, sadly!

NEXT I RECEIVED an Email from Rob, that weekend telling me that my presence was required at a special board meeting on Monday morning. I knew that he was following the same protocol that I had set for Frank when he was fired and told him that I had no intention to ever see or hear from him or them again.

So after eight years of fighting with increased competition, improving the factory, installing LEAN, trying to win over Heber Springs City council, I had succeeded in my vision of making Glove Corp the biggest glove making operation in the entire United States with lucrative military contracts as well as a successful firefighting glove operation. I had saved it from disaster, many, times over and now had to close that door and move on. I was very happy that I had done all I said I would do and also that I never had to travel to the town of Heber Springs at eleven thirty each Sunday night, not getting back until late Thursday night.

I called Pat and told her the news; she was shocked, but I reminded her that I had been warning her that this would happen over and over again.

For me, to close that door was easy and now I was ready to move on! I now had to look for another job which I was going to do with as much energy as I had put into running Glove Corp.

The following weeks I got calls from just about everyone from competitors who were shocked, from suppliers, our many distributors not to mention FDNY and from the army contracting office. FDNY wanted to know if Glove Corp could fulfill a contract that they were considering to give them, if I was not there to run the company, after their extensive testing. I told them that they had to call Pat or Keith, and if they said they could do it, FDNY could take that to the bank!

Needless to say, Glove Corp won the FDNY contract for $855,000 in April 2010, after all my hard work, to become the sole supplier of gloves to FDNY making them the supplier of choice to the biggest fire department in the world. This alone would secure new business worth millions of dollars as many fire departments followed FDNY in their choice of protective apparel. They had won the contract based on all that I had done.

Glove Corp lost the military contract, soon after I left, and in doing so had lost the second part of their manufacturing base that could have guaranteed them survival as a preferred supplier to the U.S. Army. They didn't know that in not wanting to invest sufficient funds for the contract, they were preparing their own demise. This was another nail in their coffin. The first was from Heber Springs city council in not wanting to help the company with a grant, the second was passing the company on to a family member who had little experience, and the third was losing the military contract, which would have given them a second market to the fire market. The company now had all their eggs in one basket and with no technical or knowledgeable leader and they were now heading for a fall.

I took a week off but had phone calls from all over the country asking me what the hell had happened and what would I do now. I even had a call from my competitors wanting to know what my plans were. I wasn't surprised at all because I had taken market share from all of them and had severely limited their sales. I was now looking to a new career and had to start the work all over again making a new resume, getting back on the Internet, and looking to a new career.

I was very happy at not having to make the ten-hour drive every Sunday night to Arkansas returning late Thursday or in the early hours on Friday mornings and also at never having to deal with the family members that owned the company, but part of me was sad for the employees, as I knew with certainty that the company would fail before too long.

We can sometimes make things happen that are perhaps not meant to be, if we have the spirit, the drive and determination; but it only lasts as long as we ourselves, who made it so, are prepared to keep driving it on.

A HELPING HAND FROM THE FIREFIGHTING COMMUNITY

The sum of good work, a good reputation and total commitment, will win you friends even with our competitors!

OVER THE NEXT few weeks many customers, suppliers, and fire departments called me telling me that they were shocked I had been let go, apparently I had made my mark. They were genuinely concerned and wanted to keep me in the fire business. In March that year, I took the family on a vacation knowing that I still had no job as yet; but they, like me, needed a break from the hard work of building the company up and having to deal with the owners.

We were in difficult financial trouble now as we had just remortgaged the house and had just recently paid for James's college fees while he went to Columbia College in Chicago. Nevertheless, I had to take a break, after all the hard work I had done, so we went to Boca Raton in Florida—Sue, Nick, James Chase, James's friend from dance college, and me. Lesley, Sue's sister, and her new fiancé, Steve, came to join us from England; so the family was all together.

One of my suppliers had a holiday home there and had kindly offered it to us free as I had given him so much business. One of my good friends, Jeff Stull, who sat on the NFPA committee had called me to see if he could help me find me a job in the industry, telling me that a friend of his had recently become CEO of a very large competitor, Honeywell. Jeff sent me the contact details of the new CEO of Honeywell, and I sent him an e-mail telling him who I was and that I was the designer and developer of the Blaze Fighter glove adding that it had sold over three million in sales. I congratulated him on being the new CEO and asked how his competing "Superglove" had been selling.

Only twenty minutes later, I received a call from the Jeff Morris, CEO of Honeywell First Responder and the company Jeff Stull had suggested me to contact. He introduced himself to me by saying that he was in New York and was about to get on a flight to Chicago when he received my message.

He told me that he almost fell off his seat when he saw who it was e-mailing him. "Did you really sell that much with the Blaze Fighter glove?" he asked, and I confirmed that we had. He told me that he was about to get on a flight and would call me when he arrived in Chicago. We arranged to meet at a three-year planning meeting in three weeks' time in Bolingbrook, a suburb of Chicago. It would be a chance to meet his team and to see where we went from there. I agreed on condition that since I was formerly a strong competitor, he would guarantee my safety and make sure I didn't get lynched.

I drove up to Chicago despite the fact that we hardly had enough money for the gas to get there. Jeff came out to meet me and to take me into the meeting. When we went into the large meeting room, there were around twenty vice presidents and other senior staff there sitting around a large "U-shaped" table with a large projector screen at the front of the room.

At the end of my meeting, Jeff and a consultant both took me to a small meeting room to offer me a job. Jeff explained Honeywell's market position adding that within two years they would be over a $2 billion company and focused on the global first responder market. He told me that he wanted me in his organization. I met Jeff four times over the next three months, and we had traded numerous e-mails. The stumbling block though was my non-compete agreement with Glove Corp which was apparently binding.

We had a final meeting in April saying that he had never ever had so many interfaces with his legal team, and they could find no possible way that I could be hired without a serious risk of the mean-spirited Glove Corp suing both them and me for something called "tortuous interference" with their business. Funny isn't it that Glove Corp had let me go for no reason given, yet could prevent me from gaining another job in the same or even remotely similar businesses. But after three months of communication back and forth between Jeff and I, the deal could not be done to hire me, and he told me over lunch just after the FDIC show in Indianapolis, that he was immersed in a huge acquisition and had to focus on that. Needless to say, all of my hard work had paid off, at least for my former company; they had won the order from FDNY in April, in my absence for a newly certified glove, and this news would spread like wildfire across the firefighting community that they had the won the biggest firefighting glove contract in the world!

Still I had to get a job regardless, and while I was away on a very much-needed vacation, I got a phone call from one of my now former customers, Ron Myers, who owned a company called Fireforce 1 in Ohio, while I was on the beach. He was away on spring break with his family and they were also on the beach when he had decided to call me. He told me, like many others, that he was shocked at the news and wanted to help as he recalled that I had helped him in the past.

Ron asked that I send him my resume, and he would help if he could. I sent him my resume and left it at that as I was still disappointed that the deal with Honeywell had not worked out for me as I knew that I could have done very well for that company.

When fate plays a hand, in your future, you hope that fate is on your side!

A NEW JOB

A new job is like a breath of fresh air!

ONLY A WEEK later, after I had sent my resume out, I got an e-mail from the COO of a company called FireDex which was a company that I had come across many times. They were in the same business of firefighting apparel, but I knew very little about them, and I had discounted them as competitors because they had not ever shown up as a named competitor in any of my glove sales meetings with my distributors. Although they did make gloves, I had no relationship with Bill Burke, the owner. However, the one resume I sent to Joe from Fire Force 1 had been immediately forwarded to Bill's company, "FireDex."

By now, true to form, I had sent out hundreds of e-mails and resumes, and we were getting further and further behind in the mortgage payments and other bills. My cell phone had been switched off, and that was the worst thing to deal with, since all of my contacts knew my cell phone number. I called Verizon and after getting many dead ends, I finally got through to a financial controller that I could talk to. I explained that I was out of work and really needed my cell phone otherwise it would be impossible to respond to any calls. Finally I got through to someone in the accounting department, and he agreed to place me on a payment plan and to switch my phone back on.

Now at least I had a connection to my network of friends and colleagues. Thanks to Sean, who understood and let me continue with my cell phone.

Soon after my phone was switched back on, I was contacted by FireDex and asked to go to Medina in Ohio, where the factory was located. I drove up to Medina and met the COO, for the first of a series of interviews.

I was shown into the boardroom where I was to be interviewed over several hours including an aptitude and thinking style test. The whole way through the interview process as well as the written communications between me and FireDex, there was agreement that as soon as my non-compete was finished with Glove Corp, I would help them with a new glove program to compete.

The interesting fact was that no other glove company, United States or overseas, had yet been able to copy what we had done, at the cost we had managed, and there was no other glove like the Blaze Fighter currently in the market.

I started my new job with FireDex in May 2010, so now I had a job and this company unlike my previous one, everyone in the head office, and especially the factory, were positive and had common goals and were happy to be there. I wasn't used to that as in the last company, the head office staff were extremely negative, making it difficult to keep that company going, let alone have some fun doing it.

I learned that the most valuable lesson in business was to stay focused regardless of all distractions. When you have a vision of what is necessary to take your company forward into success, involve the entire company in the analysis of the problem and the solution; then go forward to make it happen without fear!

NICK 2010

Drugs are a cancer in our society but even this can be overcome with faith.

IN AUGUST 2010, while I was once again getting on with my new career with FireDex, Nick, now twenty-one years old, had been on drugs to one degree or another since he was fifteen years old. We don't know what started it, but we both knew that the lovely boy we used to see as a laughing, happy, sometimes mischievous boy with light, blond hair had long gone.

The drugs had slowly removed our son and replaced him with a gaunt, pale, thin, angry, and very unhappy person we called our son. I prayed for him, alone, or in my car going to someplace or other or in a hotel room or whenever I thought of him, which was all the time.

I knew also that's our way as parents, when faced with a problem of this nature, drugs, often is to hit out in anger and frustration at what we could not see or do anything about except to see the devastating effects on our sweet boy. Nick was somewhere in the background, trying to come forward, but his dependency on drugs wouldn't let him.

He lost job after job, and I could see that his spirits were getting lower and lower with each rejection. These were of course his own fault—he had been showing up late or was too tired or as in one case earlier on he had blacked out while at work, all because of drug use. We even had to pay to avoid getting him arrested for money missing from the cash register at one of his jobs. In this case, he was adamant that the missing money was not him but a girl who worked with him. In any case we paid the missing money to avoid charges being leveled at him.

All of his friends that had known him since primary school had gradually stopped seeing him, fading away into his and our past and had been replaced by a new set that we didn't know, like, or recognize. The last we saw of his school friends was when we held a twenty-first birthday party for him and around twenty of his old-school friends came over to see him. Now however these good friends were replaced, and these new friends didn't bother to say hello when they came in to our house, ignored us while here, and things were getting steadily worse for Nick. I could see that his new "friends" had no interest in anything else other than keeping themselves in friendships with others who had the same needs so that they could be with others that justified their own pathetic way of life.

Nicky though used to be a happy, funny, always up to something little boy, though now a young man at twenty-one, with little visible will to try to get away from drugs; he was a very different person. His speech became slow and lethargic as did his demeanor, which was getting worse and worse. I kept trying to talk to him but each time, he got angry and embarrassed, and that led to arguments, which I wanted to avoid at all costs, as I didn't want him to turn away from the only two people that loved him and cared for him without condition. I prayed for him every day, on the road traveling, on the way home at night, in the mornings, and in bed at night.

I am not one that believes God is only in church. I believe God is with you every day—in the store, sitting in my car with me, in fact everywhere—so it didn't matter where I asked for help. One night, he told me he had stolen a little money from our bank account; in fact, he had been doing this for some time and had drained our cash over a long period of time. He had been using both James's and Sue's bank card either at an ATM at night while we were asleep or by passing forged checks at the grocery store and had been helping himself to our hard-earned money, to support his habit, as he had no money of his own and no possibility of a job to earn it.

Nick drifted from one job to another being fired from almost every job. He admitted to me that he had stolen $150 by using James's and Sue's ATM card and had decided to tell me before Mom did, adding that he was sorry and he needed to stop taking drugs! That was only partially true, as I was about to find out. The truth was that he had in fact taken checks as well, forged them with Sue's signature, and when they bounced we had not only the check amount but the added overdraught and representation fees at $33 per representation.

This alone cost us hundreds of dollars and just when we were already flat broke and trying to get our finances back in order. This was Nick kicking us while we were already down and just as we were trying to recover from my being out of work for four months, while we were trying to make ends meet to pay off our debts incurred through being jobless.

We got very angry with him, though Sue had known about this for some time and had decided not to tell me, using this as a threat to Nick in exchange for "good" behavior while getting us financially lower and lower.

Once we had decided to help with Nick's drug problem we had to see it through. And, with God's help we would prevail!

CHANGE IN THE WIND

A loved one on drugs is the very toughest problem to deal with.

THIS THOUGH, BEGAN to bring the matter to a head which was rapidly approaching. Nick promised to try to get off drugs and told us how much he hated who he now was and hated what he had done to us. I wasn't convinced; words are easy to say, and it's actions that count, not words.

I encouraged him by telling him he could have a better life but never while on drugs. I told him to look at all of the movies, how many had ever shown the users winning while using. They never did, and that was his heading right now. He had moved from the age of fifteen when he had started smoking weed, to seventeen being on crack cocaine, and now at twenty-one had moved on to heroin. Each was more powerful than the last, and each took him deeper and deeper, moving further and further from all who loved him. Nick had gone, and we were talking to his drugs not to him.

One night, it was August 18 when I was coming back from Springfield Missouri; I got a text from James telling me to get home soon as there was trouble at home with Nick. Great! What can I do—drive faster, maybe go 150 miles an hour or even teleport myself there?

I arrived home and rushed into the house not knowing what to expect and into the middle of a blazing row with Sue and James both shouting at Nicky, and Nicky looking thoroughly pissed off while shouting back. They were all shouting at one another, and no one was listening.

Nick was trying to defend himself verbally but not succeeding while they were both so angry with him that he resorted to swearing at them both, and it was steadily getting worse. I took a step back from what I was seeing—all the noise, the red faces, the anger—and instead of joining the fray became very calm inside as I tried to decide the next course of action.

I was very worried, on watching Nick's demeanor that this would lead to something uncontrollable happening very soon, and immediately tried to calm everything down by telling them all to stop shouting. I could see their pain, the same as mine, all three of them, their anger and high emotion, getting louder and angrier.

Nick shouted at us, telling me that he wanted to end his life and would do it whatever we said as he had no hope at all left for him. This again was the drugs talking. He shouted that we all hated him, every one hated him, and so did he; and that this was the only way out. That stopped me, dead cut me like a knife through my heart, as he stomped into the kitchen and grabbed a razor from the kitchen drawer to start cutting his wrist.

I ran and grabbed the razor from him, and I found it hard to talk for the grief and sheer desperation that I felt for him right then and there and told him, "If you do that, Nicky, I'll die with you. You are so very precious to us all, and no matter what you think about us, you always will be our son whom we love no matter what, despite what you think."

I found it hard to speak to him but felt compelled to tell him how much we loved him. "We love you more than you will ever, ever know, and despite what you think, we all want you to be happy and be in a better place than where you are right now." I'll never forget that moment maybe because it was a breaking point, or maybe because I felt his pain because it was our pain too. I have an empathic nature, and I could feel his absolute and abject loneliness; but he had to decide to want to do something for himself as a first step then take action to change his life.

I told Nick that we were all very angry at not being able to help him as he had continually rejected us again and again and also that when we feel so helpless to help him it makes us even more angry and that in turn makes him angry and when that happens we shout, then he shouts back, and so we go off again and again into the same circle, spiraling around and round getting nowhere.

I tried to calm him, feeling his utter dejection going right through him; and my heart went to him, feeling so completely unable to fend off all of us, his family, as well as the drugs in his system. It had affected his speech and thinking, but that aside it was time for action.

Even as I am writing this, the pain of that moment makes me stop and pray for him and for all of us that together we can get him through this as that's what families are for and was what I had given up my own dreams for, to help take care of my family no matter what. I know that he had to make the first move, but we had to let him know that we were here for him no matter what.

These are the times when I am not sure where God is. We ask, even shout at God to help us help Nick, and nothing changes. Sometimes it's very hard to see the big picture. He went back into the living room and lay down on the floor, physically and emotionally exhausted, and after a while asked me to massage his back which I did while trying to sooth my son's pain. At that moment, it didn't matter that this was the result of his decisions only that we had to get him into a better place and fast.

As I stayed there with him, I spoke quietly and told him again and again how much he meant to us all and how much we all wanted to help him. I told him that all of us shouting only made it worse, and there was to be no more shouting; we had to deal with this but not with anger and accusation. I told him I would never ever stop loving and helping him, but he had to do his part too, and that every step was up to him now. He lay there, gradually calming down after the very high emotional outburst; I saw tears in his eyes at my words of love and support and told him that we would never ever give up on him ever, that we were his family, and we would all be with him to get him through this.

I continued to massage his pain, and I noticed that he was so thin and had no muscle tone in his shoulders, probably because of his drug use. He was very thin and seemed utterly exhausted and drained as he lay there on the floor "coming down" from the raw emotion of moments before.

The following day I had to leave again but called New Hope Church and left a message for Greg Ponchot who was my pastor there. Greg called me back, later on that day, and I had to pull over in my car to speak to him. I told him what we were dealing with and how much pain this had caused us all and that Nicky had no insurance so he couldn't get help through the medical field.

Greg listened and told me he would call a friend of his who had a facility in Bloomington, some twenty miles south of Greenwood that he would call his friend, Eric, who was the contact; and I needed to talk to him. Later that day on my way home from Missouri, I got a call from Eric who apparently went to our church and wanted to know all about Nick's situation. Sometimes, as I have said, things come into my mind to be said that I can't explain at the time but just say words becoming surprised at what comes out. I think these times are some kind of "divine interference," and I told Eric right out of the blue, that I kept with me, always, a picture of our friend Corky McCormick who had died of an overdose several years before. Corky was only eighteen when this happened on his graduation night from Center Grove School.

Eric stopped dead from his sentence and said, "Wow, that's a blast from my past. I was with Corky that night, and I had supplied him with drugs as I used to be a dealer." He also said that he, Eric, had gotten really down low in his life until God had intervened and saved him from what would have been certain death had he carried on doing what he was doing.

Greg told me that after he got clean, he realized that he wanted to help others and had started a facility which now had fifty-seven people going through his program of hard work and "personal change-based" rehabilitation. He said that he had helped ruin so many lives, so now he wanted to rebuild as many as he could.

He explained that Nicky's problem was one of selfishness, and that he had only ever done what suited him and not what pleased others . . .ever and had never put others' needs before his personal needs.

This was news to me but when I thought about what Eric was telling me, it made sense, and I agreed with him totally as I had never thought of this as Nick's root problem; but now it had been said, I could see the truth in those words like a blindingly obvious truth heard from a total stranger. Eric went on to explain, "He does a good job, but only when he feels like it, then either doesn't show up or can't be bothered. He does things that you as parents tell him to do sometimes and then only when it suits him or not at all, often leaving it to the last minute, and after you have told him again and again. He sees you as his problem and not himself and has become so selfish that no one and nothing else is important to him other than what he wants for himself." "That's why he has stolen from you, because he sees this as your fault, and he feels he deserves the money as it's your fault he is as he is," Eric went on to say.

Eric told me that his facility was a one-year program and that once admitted Nick could not communicate with anyone for three months at all, no drugs, no alcohol, and no tobacco. He would work during the day at: homeless shelters, cooking food for the shelters and soup kitchens, and generally earning his keep. He would learn to do things as and when he was told, and he would learn to put himself last and that he would keep his room spotless. He would learn to do more than what was asked of him, as and when he was told to do it and would have Bible studies and homework to keep him busy day and night. He would have no TV, no books, no media of any sort for the first three months. After this time, he would be allowed to see us once a month, then once a week.

I told Eric that the only thing that Nicky had ever expressed as possibly wanting to do was to become a counselor helping people in need.

Eric told me that if Nick really wanted to do this, then they could teach him and help him get a degree in counseling, and he could then have a well-paid career, and this training would be free of charge for him.

A degree! "Nick has to make that call himself, you can't do it for him" were Eric's last words to me.

I couldn't believe it! Here was help of the best kind available and help that would allow us, Sue, James, and myself, to get our own lives back on track and to do something for ourselves while Nick was in a safe place. I called Sue and she told me that "although it's what he needs right now, Nick won't go for that, and you know it."

We talked some more, and Sue had agreed to call our doctor, Dr. Jeff, the following day. She did, and he had made arrangements for Nick to see Dr. Jeff the following day at 5:30 p.m. Things were at last starting to move, hopefully, in the right direction, and I knew Nick would learn a lot from Jeff. That night, which was Thursday, we got a call from Dr. Jeff. It was now 9:30 p.m., and Nick had been with him for over four hours.

I put my phone on speaker on the kitchen table so Sue and James could listen too. Jeff told us that he had had a very honest and fruitful talk with Nick, and a lot had come out of it saying that he had heard a lot of promising things that he hadn't heard from Nick for a long time.

Jeff had done a considerable amount of research into male testosterone and its importance in helping the body to heal properly. Jeff had told us that when people start taking drugs, the side effect is that they significantly reduce the testosterone level in men and in turn they begin to become laid-back and unmotivated.

This is a common trait among drug users especially with weed. Weed is one that causes this to happen, and it is this that causes us to say "He's a very laid-back kind of guy, seldom gets upset with anything." Bollocks to that! It's the drugs that have done that resulting in slow speech, a slow thought process, lack of memory, lack of willpower, and lack of drive and all because of low testosterone caused by drug use.

Jeff explained to us that in Nick's case the drugs had probably lowered his testosterone to practically nothing, that in turn that reduction had prevented his "fight" in trying to overcome his drug use. Also that his back pains were probably caused by inflammation along his spinal muscles which couldn't heal because it was being blocked by lack of sleep, lack of testosterone, and drugs that were all preventing his body's normal immune system from functioning.

Added to this the drugs were in turn preventing his immune system from functioning to heal as they were sending false signals to his brain which was not able to make corrections as the signals were not matching up to his normal functionality, and therefore he wasn't healing properly.

I was so happy to hear this and knew that this could be a real breakthrough for Nick, who was sitting next to Jeff as he was explaining this to us, and we hoped it would help get him back, on form, and fighting fit ready to stop taking drugs.

I told Jeff that Nick had told me that he didn't take drugs to get high; he said he took them to get by the pain he always felt all over his body. Jeff confirmed again that that was because of the lack of sleep and lack of testosterone which was making him worse.

Dr. Jeff prescribed a sleeping pill and an anti-inflammatory drug that would reduce the back pain. He also said there would be no charge to us for this, and he would do a complete blood work up, the following morning, to see what else was happening with Nick.

Dr. Jeff had also told us that Nick had spoken of our love and how much he needed this now to offer hope for his future. Nick arrived home more hopeful than we had seen him in a long time, and I was now cautiously optimistic of his chances for healing. The following day, I sat with Nick, and we discussed a pact together (he was in a better mood that morning). Our pact was very clear; Nick had to be honest with us if he "used" again, telling us what he had done and we, in turn, would not shout or get angry if he told us the truth; and we would help him all we could to become clean. We would, however, from this point on and after he was physically well again, because of Dr. Jeff's help, make him call Eric to be admitted into the church-run rehab if he continued to use after all of our help and assistance. He agreed! Nick had the chance to get free of his debilitating drug habit with all of our intervention and will need all the help he can get. Eliminating excuses like "pain management" as a "cause" for his drug use will identify this to him leaving only the actual fact of his drug use plainly visible if he should fail.

Nick must have been draining our accounts for a very long time as his habit continued, since I am now earning far less than I was, and we seemed to be broke when we should have had enough money to be financially OK. Every day I found a reason to tell Nick that I loved him, and I don't care if he ignores it; he's going to understand that we are here for him no matter what; we offer unconditional love and support; we are in his corner as all families are.

It's a long road with many miles to go, but one that we can take and reach the end of, by taking one step in front of another and by helping each other as a very strong family unit. From all of our discussions with doctors, counselors, psychiatrists, the pastor at my church, other families, ex-users, and even police along the way was that this drug use depends on an individual's personality and certain people have naturally occurring triggers that enable them to become more easily addicted to drugs, cigarettes, alcohol, gambling, and any other forms of more passive kinds of addiction. Eventually these "triggers" will be identified and will be able to be treated in a new and more complete ways, but until then we use all the tools we can to get the job done.

Part of me felt that Nick's drug use was as a result of his Stevens-Johnson disease as it all started around that time, but it made no difference now as to the reason why he began except he had and it had affected or infected all of his family. For now though Nick was moving in the right direction and with Jeff's help was beginning to put on weight as a result of the testosterone he was now taking. We allowed him to stay at home for six weeks in order to fight his drug use, but it was a struggle as he was constantly up one minute and down the next.

Sue wanted him out of the house because she had borne the brunt of all of his mood swings and all of his bad behavior, his anger and shouting because he wanted to stay in bed when she had tried to get him up for work, but he was so far gone he couldn't even get up in the mornings to go to work.

I felt the same in wanting him out of the house and was torn between whether we were enabling him or helping him, but either way he was our son; we loved him, and we had to support him because if we didn't bad things would happen to him, and maybe he wouldn't survive. This was what we both thought, but then at a deeper level, maybe that was what he needed in order to reach his bottom level from which he would finally "get it" and begin to get out of his predicament.

In November that year, Nick found a clinic in Indianapolis that specialized in alternative treatments for drug abuse that were additional to simple counseling which had been an abysmal failure. The clinic was on Forty-Sixth Street, and they agreed to take Nick on for treatment.

The treatment was to substitute the illegal drug heroin, which he had been using, with methadone which was an alternative drug which would gradually reduce his dependence and more especially his craving for heroin which was now his drug of choice. We had been told several years before, while Nick was in rehab when he was fifteen, that most addicts move on from one drug to another often ending on the really hard stuff like heroin or meth.

Once they come out of rehab and if they get back onto drugs, they are likely to continue from the point they left. In other words, if they start up again, they will continue where they left off.

He had to go to the treatment center every day, and we had to pay for each daily treatment. He had begun hairdressing at Paul Mitchel school, and things seemed to be getting better for him but . . . one day at a time.

I was ever hopeful but not convinced yet. He got up, with difficulty, at 5:30 a.m. each day, and I tried to make sure that he attended each and every day since I was always up at 5:00 a.m. He went to the clinic then went on to school for an 8:30 a.m. start. We had to get him his money each day and only gave him the amount for that day's treatment to avoid any possibility of him "storing" money for more drug use.

Around Christmas that year, we had to change our bank account, as Nick had compromised our account and had stolen a lot of money from our accounts.

Not surprisingly, it caused yet another serious problem for us at home and a quiet Christmas for the family. Nick's habit had to be stopped, but the only one to stop it was him.

When we pray for divine help or intervention, it will come; but not always in the way we expect it.

OUT OF OUR HANDS... AT LAST

It's the hardest thing placing the outcome of something we can't handle ourselves into God's hands and to then let go.

IN MARCH, LATER that year, Nick got stopped by the police while sitting in his car and found drugs in his possession. He was wheeled away to jail without passing go!

We were relieved because at least he would be clean, and when he came out he was remorseful for a full two days, then it was more of the same. The damage Nick had done to us in stealing money from our accounts, stealing and selling my tools and other things from the house as well as selling Christmas and birthday presents had all mounted up, along with the enormous rehab bill, to well over $40,000. But that was nothing compared to the anguish and worry that had been draining us since he was fifteen.

Nick, after being stopped one night by the police again, was finally sent to jail for five months and is now finally getting on with his life and now has to take "each day one at a time." But at least he is now trying, and we, as every family should, are supporting him to keep clean. If he can continue to stay clean, then it will all have been worthwhile, as in the words of Dr. Jeff, "Heroes are made from coming through adversity, never from having a blessed life where everything is normal and uneventful."

After Nick came out of jail that July he remained clean, got back into the Paul Mitchel School, found a part time job and began to get his life back on track. He was promoted, in his second job, and is now a key holder and an assistant manager.

He has been clean now for nearly 2 years, looks great, is fit healthy and 'on his game' at last! He now has his act together showing no sign of getting back into his old life and, as ever, we are there for him!

Way to go Nick! Keep moving forward. Sue and I met the police officer, who put him in jail, at a local charity event that we were both involved in, and we both thanked him for saving our son's life.

Seeking divine intervention was the right thing and we recognized it when it came to help us.

A PREDICTION CAME TRUE

The owners were about to find out what it took to run their company.

IN JANUARY 2011, I was at a trade show in Iowa when one of my former sales reps came to see me and asked if I had heard the news about Glove Corp. He showed me, on his Blackberry, an article saying that Glove Corp had lost their certification for the Blaze Fighter glove! There had been several firefighters in New York that were burned while wearing the glove. Although the burns were not serious, the result of an investigation had later shown that they had not certified the glove with the components they were now using. Glove Corp had a different liner than that which they had certified in the glove, and as a result, the glove they were selling was not the same as the glove they had certified.

Sharon, who made up the certification paperwork from the head office in Indiana, was, seemingly but not surprisingly, unaware as to what the factory was sending out and testing in the form of samples that were to represent the Blaze Fighter glove. The result of this was that when she sent the paperwork out to accompany the samples for testing it was the same paperwork that she had sent the previous year, whereas the factory was now using a different liner in the FDNY glove and had not placed that new liner material into the testing samples. Since she was doing the purchasing it was surprising that she didn't see the difference in what was being purchased against what had been certified.

Their NFPA certification was rejected on the last Friday in January 2011, and on the following Monday, January 31st. The board had decided that they had no funds to replace the gloves purchased by FDNY in the contract, so they closed the factory down. In August 2009, they had the biggest sales in one month they had ever had, where did the money go?

The final insult to the factory workers, by the board together with Sharon, was the way in which the notice had been delivered to the factory. The notice of closure was sent by e-mail at 4:00 p.m. that Monday telling Pat and Keith to inform all the staff that as of 4:30 p.m. that Monday saying that everyone was laid off permanently and the factory would be shut down!

I was right in that Sharon was the downfall of the Glove Corp! This was the end of that company, after more than ninety years in operation and almost one year to the week since I had left them, with around thirty minutes' notice emailed to their factory staff.

So where are we right now? James spent a year at Columbia College in Chicago and won a scholarship because of his "Artistic Achievement" after graduating from Center Grove in 2009. He then got accepted by Point Park University, with another scholarship for Artistic Achievement which was exceptional. He is now doing great. Point Park University is second only to the one and only "Julliard" in New York and for him to get to point Park from Greenwood, Indiana, was an exceptional feat of endurance skill, dedication, and drive. His dream is to have his own dance studio and maybe to back Lady Gaga, and I hope he gets his dream. You go, Jamesie!

Sue twice won an award for "Excellence in Customer Service"—a five-star award issued by an Indianapolis Monthly magazine as the result of a blind survey carried out over several months and which she had no idea they were even doing.

Nicky is free from drugs at last, and has been for over 2 years, he has a girlfriend and is looking physically very good and is also doing really great. He is at the Paul Mitchel School for hair and cosmetology he has a part time job; is completing his training and one day he will have a string of hair salons and his own cosmetics line, which I can help him with if he wants me to! So, in the end it was all worth it.

As for me I have a great job and finished this book which took two and a half years and three broken laptops, to complete; but now it's done.

I wrote this after realizing that I was in fact telling many of the people I came in contact with, friends, family, and business colleagues, some of the things I had managed to do. My life is "One of a Kind" although not one of my friends or family ever knew my whole story until now, it's all here!

The outcome of failure was a certainty, as I knew what it had taken to keep this company going.

LESSONS LEARNED... SO FAR

When we take a look in the rear-view mirror we see what we couldn't see beforehand.

WHAT I LEARNED from everything "so far" was first finish what you start and don't ever give up. It was extremely difficult at first, after leaving school, as I had so little money, not even enough to pay my rent or to live on when I left school; but the dividends later were paid in ways I could not ever have imagined.

I finished my apprenticeship, even though I was not a very serious person at that time like most teenagers. I stayed with it though, not knowing just how much it would help me during my entire life, and even in getting into the States through the hard work I had done as an apprentice all those years before.

My green card was easy because of my five-year apprenticeship and the education I had earned twenty-five years earlier. I never thought at aged sixteen that what I was about to do was to take me right through life and to enable doors not only to be opened but also to remain open. I used the skills I learned as a young man and even as a general manager running an entire company. I learned also that when talking with my workforce in my factory role, that I could talk their language and at their level, and indeed I could communicate to all of the people I met along the way about doing things that needed to be done and showing them how to do what was required.

Even when I ran that glove company, I asked my managers there, "If you were to describe me to others after I have left here, what would you say?" Pat, my senior manageress, said, "I would say that you are the most energetic person I have ever worked with and also that when Tony decides to do something, you better get on board or get out of the way, because one thing is absolutely certain. Tony will do what he says he will do and will finish what he started." That was fine by me and I did in fact make the Glove Corp the biggest glove manufacturing company in the entire USA. That question I asked of my managers is something we all should ask of people we work with as it is through their eyes that we learn who we are. I also won a huge military glove contract and designed the biggest selling firefighting glove in the world I learned as I have already said that I truly believe that each of us are given divine tools —"talents"— to use throughout our life; talents that are there for us and will enable us to do things we want to do. If we use these tools, it is a natural thing; and when we use them it's as if nothing has happened, a "natural talent" with each of us often taking them for granted. This is part of who we each are and what we do with each of our lives.

Many of my friends along the way never used their gifts and chose instead to cruise through life reaching a point later on as they got older to think about what they might have been; dwelling instead on past failures and mishaps instead of the positive lessons they could have learned from these experiences. Many never learned from mistakes that we all make, and boy, did I make huge mistakes along the way, as I have attempted to show in this book.

In a recent survey of over 1,500 retirees, they were asked, "What would you change about your life if you could and with your knowledge now?" Most answered quite honestly that they wish they had taken more risks with their lives. How sad it must be to think that thought and at a time when you are now too old to do so. Taking a chance sometimes can be a bad thing, but that's a risk you take. But if you do take that risk, chances are that it will change something in your life, and at least you can look back and laugh at yourself for trying or congratulate yourself for succeeding!

I never asked people to do anything that I wouldn't or couldn't do. My family has both suffered and gained from all that I managed to accomplish and because of my constant traveling. They became strong and despite my travelling I was nevertheless very, very, close to them all. I also came to realize that my children, of whom there are four, and grandchildren, of whom at this moment in time there are five, have to have their own experiences; and those will be for them to try, fail, and try again all throughout their lives. My daughters have their own business and I smile when I hear them discussing ideas with me, their energy and positive attitude is a legacy I was happy to give.

Life is a rich experience and it's not where you end up, it's the journey along the way—that is the real life so enjoy the ride.

I also believe that there is a divine presence—God—and this has been shown to me with undeniable truth, throughout my life so far, that God can and will help if you want his help, but you may have to change as well. Without that belief, life for me and for everyone else, as I see it, is a meaningless experience that can give you pain and suffering or happiness and success, perhaps in random order; but in the end, if that is your belief, life leads nowhere at all as we all die. It is clear to me that evil also does exist, and it is present more and more in our everyday life as we learn more and move gradually away from God. The weaponry that we have developed is ten times more powerful enough to wipe out life on the entire planet, why have we done this?

My "uncle" John Bleby once told me, and this was while he was head of the Royal Veterinary College, "You know, Tony, we scientists don't believe in God because when you get right down to it on a microbiological level, which is where we are at, you realize that everything is measurable and interrelated, a series of chemicals!" I answered him that I believed he was missing the point, that God in my view is in the spaces between, that stuff that holds everything together, and you can't measure that.

So, here I am, and who would have thought that in today's world, we would be having religious wars; or that seemingly good people, leaders of men, voted into their office by reasonable people just like me, right here, in the USA, in a country that was based on sound Christian values would want to relegate the word of God away from our founding fathers' ideals and to remove it completely from our daily life.

The people that propagate this belief have no idea that in their fervor and entirely logical and almost believable explanations of truth and half-truth as they see it, they are helping us to move away from God and the good values that have led us this far. Everyone I have ever met along the way agrees that there is an evil force moving against us all, and as we get further along, we need to keep our feet firmly on the ground.

I will not allow myself to be swayed away from my faith. I had one more dream that I had experienced back in the mid-nineties, when Sue and I were going through a very rough patch in our relationship and were both drifting apart, possibly to divorce. I had a clear dream in which I was walking toward a long straight path ahead of me, in Hanwell, London, of all places; and the sky above me was filled with gray billowing clouds, full of an imminent storm, and there were houses on both sides of me that ended at a barrier just a few feet ahead of where I stood.

Ahead of me, the sky was very dark with heavy storm clouds above. There was a path ahead of me that was blocked by a red-and-white barrier across the road, where the houses abruptly ended, with an old friend of mine standing next to it with one hand, ready to lift the bar to let me pass.

As I approached, he said, "Hi, Tony, you have to go that way." As he lifted the barrier, he pointed down the very long dark path ahead. I entered the path as he had shown me; and I walked down the path, which I now saw was elevated with a slope on either side of it like a levee. On either side were dark stormy waters thrashing against the path I was now walking on. On my left was the ocean, with huge waves broiling and black crashing into the levee, while on my right was a huge lake with equally violent waters being blown by a very strong wind. The ocean side on my left was thrashing, with huge waves crashing continuously into my levee; while on the right the black lake water was chopping, forming high peaks and troughs of the storm that it was in and the waters were smashing into the other side of my leveed path. The clouds above grew even more menacing and stormier as I continued on.

I knew that I had to stay on that path and not move in any other direction than straight ahead. In front of me, miles ahead, was a faint glimmering light somewhere where I couldn't see it clearly; but I knew it was there and was directly at the end of the path I was on. I knew that whatever happened and however bad things may get, I had to keep moving forward and not be led off to one side or the other.

It has been the hardest struggle for me to keep my family together throughout a very turbulent life with the normal ups and downs of living. All the way, it would have been easier to simply let go and do my own thing leaving all else behind me. What would that say of me and anyone else who allowed that to happen? My own childhood was a little rough at times but certainly nothing that I couldn't handle nothing at all, yet in today's life, there are more things to make separation at every level a very easy thing to do—from marriage, from work, from beliefs, and even from family, all is getting harder to remain on track. My divorce from Jane taught me that divorce is far reaching for my children, so I made certain that we remained as friends and in very close touch so that we were there for each other. Most divorces are angry, nasty events with self-centered emotions that tear a family apart. I learned that it doesn't have to be this way and if at all possible spend your energy trying to make your marriage work, as I assume it was based on love at some point when you made the decision to get married. If that is not possible then at all costs try to make it a friendly and graceful parting so that the children don't have to experience their parents hating each other.

Throughout my life, right at the moment I needed help, I got it through the people I passed along the way; though sometimes at the time I didn't realize, I was being helped along, but I very clearly was. The role Auntie played in my early life was profound, and I know she was placed into my life just when I needed her help the most.

Shakespeare said, "Give me a child to seven years old, and he is mine for life." I get that, Billy boy! What he clearly meant was that those early days are the formative years and are so critically important for each child's development into adulthood.

The question I ask myself is this: "If I could change anything, what would I change?" Probably not much at all, but if there are things that you would change, then go ahead and change them; and if it doesn't work out, then so what? Learn from that and try again but never stop trying.

I learned to never ever give up. Even if the future at that point looks bad, I knew not to worry about the past, but to learn from it and move on; and if I got it wrong, I tried again. "I closed the door and moved on." My hero was Colonel Sanders of the KFC fame; he didn't make it until he was over seventy years old, and he made it hugely successfully! If he can do it, anyone can!

Ian, Adrian, and I had all come through difficult times in our childhood; and despite this, each of us had made a success of our lives. Ian is now a multimillionaire and if that was his goal then he succeeded. Adrian was appointed governor of Gibraltar by Her Majesty, the Queen.

And me? Well, I made my mark in the United States with one of my glove designs now inside every GI's kit bag, a fragrance company that reached number 2 in sales, my third book, and, for a short while, I made the biggest-selling firefighting glove in the world, not bad for three Brits coming from very humble backgrounds.

As for me, I still work like a Trojan, I have just completed my third book called "**He's A Funny Cat Ms. High- My 32 Years Singing with James Brown**" a biography of singer and performer Martha High.

I managed to keep my family together, through thick and thin, with a mom and a dad stronger than ever and I am happy, though my next dream is to be living somewhere near the coast, and to be able to visit my daughters and grandchildren as many times a year as I want to be closer to them.

Me? I am still "a work in progress, I'm busier now than ever before and loving it!"

Wiser but I'm still going to keep succeeding!

My New-Old Family

Never underestimate what life can bring

It's Christmas 2017 and my son James, bought me an Ancestry.com DNA kit as a Christmas Present. I told him thanks but don't expect anything to come from this as I have no other family in England.

Wow, was I wrong about that! In February 2017, I received the results from Ancestry.com that I had a 1st Cousin with a 99.9% accuracy that this was correct.

I wrote to my new first cousin and yesterday, March 22nd I received an email that would explode my life. I not only had a first cousin in England, called Francis Smith, but I also had many additional cousins there. It turned out that my beautiful mother Rosina, had seven sisters and five brothers!

Francis, my "new" First cousin, also told me that shortly after my mother married my step father, Mr. Willats, he told the family he would bring me up as his son and they were never to have any contact with me from that point forward.

It was aunty who contacted the authorities, after coming to see me, and who forced Wilatts to release me into the care of the London County Council. I was placed into an orphanage and he simply walked away. Both my daughter Georgia and I, tried to find out from him if I had any other family but he told us he knew nothing of any other relatives from my mother's family. Of course, he was lying.

In the end, due to new technology with DNA testing and the internet I eventually found my lost family, and what a very large family I now have. Francis Smith, my first cousin told me I had many, many first cousins.

They tried to find me many times but once I was under the care of the London County Council, finding me was extremely difficult and in my case impossible. Only one person, my awful step father, knew the link between me and my mother's family and he was saying nothing at all.

At the end of the day, as a result of everything, and despite all that happened to me, I now have friends all over the world, who's lives intertwined with mine. I became successful across continents; however, this is measured, and I am happy, even happier now that I know I have a huge family, that I never knew existed. I have many cousins, actually forty-five First Cousins, I have grandparents and everything a "normal" family has …. love! Maybe another book is in the works!

      God definitely has a sense of humor!

We can all make it through life with or without a family but having one often makes life all the richer!

THE EXPERIENCE FACTOR IN LIFE AND BUSINESS

I learned from childhood that you can't ever change the past, but you can use these experiences for future decisions and apply these towards the best result in work and at home. I tried this and it though it didn't always work out, as I expected, it didn't deter me from trying.

I have tried to show in 'One of A Kind' that life is such a very rich experience if we allow it to become so, and, even the bad times make us wiser and more capable of giving help to others who we pass along the way and we all should do this anytime we can. I do this whenever possible.

Losing one's job these days is a very, very, serious and sometimes a life altering event. But getting a new position is not hard once you set your mind on succeeding. Most people know beforehand that something is wrong with their current employment and should be prepared for the outcome.

I learned also a most valuable lesson; there are none so blind as those that will not see, so when we come across stubbornness its best to keep focused on what we are doing; as we are responsible for our own success or failure. My experience came from lessons learned from four years old and I have never stopped learning what success really is in business as at home.

I hope that in reading this you, my reader can see that what I have experienced from the very earliest age has provided me with a pathway for my own future success as it can for you; Never, never, never, give up.

Change in life, in business and at home is guaranteed, even as our children change and grow up. In accepting this, embrace the changes and be part of them. It is when we become a willing part of change that we can most influence how it will affect us.

Finally, if nothing else, I learned that we should never blame past failures, at home, in our work or with our friends, as something that is preventing us from achieving a brilliant future, as it will with certainty do just that, if we allow it to so!

I dedicate this book to my children and to my many, many, friends, and family now living all over the world, in USA, Canada, France, Sweden, South Africa, New Zealand and Australia who upon reading this may decide to risk failure in order to risk success. Success after all is whatever we chose to make it and measure ourselves by.

So, go do it! Live life, and make it through regardless as I have done and you too will become *one of a kind*.

For my children:

>Amanda Jane, living in Ealing, West London
>
>Georgia Mercedes, also living in Ealing, West London
>
>Nicholas Andrew, today living in Greenwood, Indiana
>
>James Alexander, today living in Greenwood, Indiana

>And for my grandchildren in London:

>Jesse, age twenty
>
>Eliza Jane, age sixteen
>
>Ruby Rose, age ten
>
>Mason, age seven
>
>Ziggy, age six

To each of you all, I hope one day you will read this book and enjoy it as much as I did in living and writing it. In passing it on to each of you, I ask that you write your book too, the good, and the not-so-good, experiences of your lives and be truthful. Add your story to mine, and, when the time is right, pass it on to your children as I have done for you. In this way, we can all learn from our successes and failures, and we can all laugh at ourselves along the way! I certainly did!

>With love to all of you,
>
>Tony Moore

Made in the USA
Lexington, KY
30 March 2017